2026
중등영어 교사임용

권영주 임용 전공
영어 교육론

임용 기출문제 해설서

PREFACE

 **단순한 개념정리에서부터 복잡한 사고를 요구하는 적용문제까지**

'중등교사 신규임용후보자 선정경쟁시험'은 지난 30년간 다음의 형식으로 변화를 겪어왔습니다.

1992년 ~ 1996년	객관식 시험
1997년 ~ 2008년	서술형 시험
2009년 ~ 2013년	객관식 시험과 2차 논술시험
2014년 ~ 2019년	기입형·서술형·논술형 시험
2020년 ~ 현재	기입형·서술형 시험

이번 2026년 대비 영어교육론 기출해설서를 내면서 그동안 출제되었던 모든 영어교육론 문제에 대한 모범답안과 해설과 함께 채점기준을 추가하였습니다. 새롭게 강화된 내용은 다음과 같습니다.

- ✓ 각 문항에 출제기준을 표시하여 답안을 쓰는 이해도를 높였습니다
- ✓ 필수 개념정리와 원서읽기를 포함하여 심층적인 추가학습을 할 수 있습니다.
- ✓ 유사 내용의 문제들을 묶어서 분류하여 읽기 쉽게 구성하였습니다.

1990년대 문제에서부터 논술문제까지 모두 수록하여 이 한 권으로 영어교육론 기출문제에 대한 정리는 완벽하게 마칠 수 있게 하였습니다. 답안을 작성할 때 출제자의 의도를 파악하고 모범답안에 가까운 답을 쓰는 것이 가장 중요하다고 할 수 있습니다. 이 책은 영어교육론의 기출문제를 제대로 공부할 수 있도록 다음과 같은 사항에 중점을 두어 해설을 작성하였습니다.

✓ 철저히 수험생의 입장에서 해설을 작성하였습니다. 처음 기출문제를 풀어보는 수험생부터 시험을 앞두고 마지막 마무리로 기출문제를 풀어보고자 하는 수험생까지 요구를 충족시키기 위하여 한 문제 한 문제 상세히 풀이하였습니다. 각 문제마다 난이도를 표시하여 자신의 실력을 스스로 가늠할 수 있도록 하였습니다.

✓ 미래의 시험에 적용할 수 있는 방법에 중점을 두었습니다. 기출을 풀어본다는 의미에서 한 단계 더 나아가 새롭게 나올 시험에 대비할 수 있는 변형문제를 이용하여 효율적으로 문제를 풀 수 있는 방법을 제시하고자 하였습니다.

✓ 기출문제를 보아야 하는 본질을 놓치지 않으려 노력하였습니다. 기출문제를 토대로 새롭게 읽어나가야 할 핵심 개념과 ELT ARTICLE을 첨부하여 문제에 따른 심화학습을 할 수 있도록 하였습니다. 그것이 바로 답안이 나오게 되는 근거가 되기 때문입니다.

합격자 선생님들에게 합격의 비법을 물어보면 각자가 다 다른 공부법을 이야기합니다. 모두 자신의 공부법으로 공부하고 또 합격을 하였다고 볼 수 있습니다. 그러나 모두 공통적으로 강조하는 점이 있습니다. 바로 기출문제를 확실하게 분석하고 공부하는 것입니다. 임용시험에서 기출문제는 이제까지의 출제방향을 알려주는 척도이자 부족한 점을 알려주고 앞으로의 공부법을 제시하는 역할을 합니다. 영어교육론은 단시간에 암기하거나 이론만을 가지고 풀 수 있는 문제가 아니고 기본이론과 주요개념을 중심으로 하여 각기 다른 교실상황에 적용시킬 수 있어야 합니다. 교실 안 수업을 위한 실제 해결책을 제시할 수 있다는 마음으로 풀어나가면 내년에 영어 선생님이 되시는 좋은 결과 나올 것이라 기대합니다.

노량진 연구실에서
권영주 드림

기출문제 분석표

2002년-2025년 영어교육론 기출문제 분석표

▌2025학년도 ▌ 영어교육론 기출문제 내용분석표 (36점)

	기입형	
A3	(교재론) 자료를 학생들의 동기를 높이기 위하여 modifying하여 개정한다.	
A4	(영어 평가) 평가원리에서 interrater reliability의 중요성을 이해한다.	
	서술형	
A8	(중간언어) semantic deviation & number of arguments 오류를 서술한다.	
A9	(말하기평가) clarity & authenticity를 말하기 평가 항목을 위해 서술한다.	
A11	(수업목표) reception & production의 수업목표를 서술한다.	
A12	(읽기전략) 문제점을 파악하고 그에 대한 읽기전략을 제시하여 서술한다.	
B6	(PBL) 프로젝트교수법 과정에서 잘 못 수행한 목표 & 평가에 대하여 서술한다.	
B7	(듣기지도) 듣기활동에서 intensive듣기와 창조적활동에 대하여 서술한다.	
B10	(문화지도) reflecting, comparing, interacting과정을 선택하여 서술한다.	
B11	(ICT지도) 디지털 도구를 사용하는 원리에 어긋나는 내용을 서술한다.	

▌2024학년도 ▌ 영어교육론 기출문제 내용분석표 (38점)

	기입형	
A1	(영어평가) 평가원리에서 시간과 경제성을 중시하는 practicality를 이해한다.	
A2	(2언어습득) 언어의 빈도나 특정언어의 salience을 높여서 언어습득에 도움을 준다.	
B1	(말하기지도) 의사소통에서 함축된 의미인 illocutionary acts를 이해한다.	
	서술형	
A8	(듣기지도) 듣기의 macro와 micro전략을 구별하여 서술한다.	
A9	(말하기지도) 의사소통을 위한 활동을 구별하고 서술한다.	
A11	(교수요목) 다양한 항목을 위한 교수요목과 교사의 수업방식을 비교·서술한다.	
A12	(교수도구) 학습자들의 요구에 따라 맞는 디지털 도구를 서술한다.	
B6	(영어평가) item analysis를 위한 구체적 항목을 서술한다.	
B7	(과업수행) 언어의 난이도와 수행조건을 변화시키는 과업수행을 서술한다.	
B10	(문화지도) 유형의 문화산물을 위한 문화교수원리를 서술한다.	
B11	(문법지도) 귀납법과 연역법을 통한 교수방법을 서술한다.	

▎2023학년도 ▎ 영어교육론 기출문제 내용분석표 (38점)

	기입형
A1	(2언어 습득) 언어습득과정에서 backsliding되는 과정을 이해한다.
A4	(평가) computer adaptive test의 특성을 이해한다.
B1	(연구) action research를 통한 교사의 연구 활동을 이해한다.

	서술형
A8	(교수법) 실제 삶과 연관된 수업과 cognitive skill을 높이는 수업을 서술한다.
A9	(읽기지도) word master와 graphic organizer를 활용한 읽기 수업을 서술한다.
A10	(언어습득과정) 언어습득과정의 실제 사례를 서술한다.
A12	(문화지도) culture를 지도하기 위한 다양한 방법을 서술한다.
B6	(말하기지도) speaking 활동의 문제점과 해결 방법을 서술한다.
B7	(쓰기지도) content와 organization을 향상시킨 방법을 서술한다.
B10	(어휘지도) collocation과 grammar 향상을 위한 방법을 서술한다.
B11	(평가) multiple choice평가를 만드는 guideline을 이해하고 서술한다.

▎2022학년도 ▎ 영어교육론 기출문제 내용분석표 (36점)

	기입형
A1	(평가) 평가 유형과 평가 원리에서 washback이 미치는 영향을 이해한다.
A2	(교수법) 두 교사의 대화를 통해 효과적인 integrated approach을 이해한다.

	서술형
A8	(듣기지도) comprehension-based 학습을 위한 processing 방법을 서술한다.
A9	(개별전략) 개별적인 언어학습 전략에 대하여 추천하고 특성을 서술한다.
A10	(실용언어) 학습자 언어의 pragmatic 측면을 구체적으로 서술한다.
A12	(교재론) online 교재에 근거하여 speaking과 발음연습의 방법을 서술한다.
B6	(언어지도) lexical cohesive devices의 쓰임과 내용을 서술한다.
B7	(쓰기지도) genre를 가르치기 위한 쓰기지도의 방법을 구체적으로 서술한다.
B10	(평가) 교사가 목표로 하는 쓰기의 평가방법을 찾아 서술한다.
B11	(문법지도) focus on form으로 목표 언어를 가르치는 방식을 서술한다.

기출문제 분석표

▌2021학년도 ▌ 영어교육론 기출문제 내용분석표 (36점)

기입형
A1	(교재론) 실제 교실활동에서 사용되는 realia를 찾아 쓴다.
B1	(평가) 쓰기평가에서 intrarater reliability를 이해한다.

서술형
A8	(말하기지도) 말하기지도에서 fluency와 complexity중심으로 진행되는 방법을 서술한다.
A9	(통합지도) 통합교육의 성취기준을 이해하고 활동과 연결하여 서술한다.
A10	(2언어습득) foreigner talk에서 나타나는 언어의 수정과정을 서술한다.
A12	(어휘지도) collocation과 context의 사용을 사전에 대비하여 서술한다.
B6	(쓰기지도) 글쓰기의 grammar, mechanics, organization을 이해하고 지도방법을 서술한다.
B7	(2언어습득) 언어의 발달단계, fronting & inversion를 서술한다.
B8	(문화활동) culture capsule과 culture island 활동의 특성을 서술한다.
B9	(통합활동) information transfer와 partial dictation의 특성을 서술한다.

▌2020학년도 ▌ 영어교육론 기출문제 내용분석표 (28점)

기입형
A1	(어휘학습) 어휘를 익힐 때 depth의 중요성을 서술한다.
A2	(curriculum) 교육과정 작성시에 가장 시작이 되는 needs analysis를 이해한다.
A3	(언어지도) 언어의 적절성을 맞추기 위해서 formality의 필요성을 이해한다.
B2	(교재론) 교재작성의 필수요소에서 authenticity의 중요성을 이해한다.

서술형
A5	(담화론) 대화에서 사용되는 전략중에서 cataphoric words와 hedges의 쓰임에 대하여 예시와 함께 서술한다.
A10	(학습전략) outlining 방법에 대하여 이해하고 본문의 내용을 요약하여 서술한다.
B4	(2언어습득) 의사협상을 하는 과정인 trigger, indicator, response, reaction을 이해하고 각 과정의 예시를 찾아 방법을 서술한다.
B6	(영어평가) 평가에서 이론과 다르게 시행된 두 단계, internal consistency, item discrimination과 concurrent validity를 찾아 그 이유를 서술한다.
B10	(수업활동) 수업활동에서 language와 delivery가 잘 시행되지 않은 이유를 찾아 서술한다.

▎2019학년도 ▎ 영어교육론 기출문제 내용분석표 (32점)

	기입형
A1	(2언어습득) 학습자의 유형분류: auditory, visual, kinesthetic
A2	(영어평가) 통합기술을 위한 c-test, rational/ random deletion: cloze
A3	(2언어습득) 의사소통을 위한 피드백의 종류: elicitation
	서술형
A11	(2언어습득) 오류의 기원 interference와 overgeneralization을 분류하고 특히 한국어 학습자에게서 나타나는 특성을 interlingually 설명할 수 있다.
A12	(task 활동) purpose, time allocation, scoring의 교사 수업 방법을 설명한다.
A14	(writing 지도) process-based수업에서 recursive vs linear와 meaning vs form focused feedback의 비교를 통해 서술한다.
B4	(2언어습득) 의사소통 전략을 쓸 때 구체적인 예시를 통해 avoidance, appeal to authority, word coinage를 설명한다.
	논술형
B8	(수업과정) 두 교사의 수업을 비교하여 curriculum, objectives, formative assessment 에서 일치하는 것과 그렇지 않은 것을 선택하여 설명할 수 있다.

▎2018학년도 ▎ 영어교육론 기출문제 내용분석표

	기입형
A1	(영어교수법) 학습의 차이 이해: incidental & intentional
A3	(CALL) 기존의 수업과 반대방향의 새로운 학습법의 시도: flipped learning
A7	(영어교수법) sociocultural theory에서 zone of proximal development안에서 scaffolding 을 통해 학습이 나아가는 방향을 이해한다.
	서술형
A10	(영어교수법) TBLT를 syllabus차원에서의 문제점을 쓰는 것이므로 synthetic/ analytic의 비교로 언어를 separate하지 않고 whole로 가르친다는 내용을 서술한다.
A13	(영어평가) diagnostic 평가의 특성으로 before the class, 학습자의 장단점을 확인할 수 있으며 나아갈 방향에 대한 guide를 제시할 수 있다는 것을 서술한다.
B5	(2언어습득) 실제상황에서 학습자의 own ideas를 이용하여 target form을 사용하고 meaning negotiation으로 interaction을 하는 활동을 서술한다.
	논술형
B8	(영어교수법) 선임교사의 조언에 따라 잘 수행되는 활동과 그렇지 못한 활동을 구별하여 설명할 수 있다. objective request라는 function에 대한 활동과 strategies, approximation과 body language와 local error, explicit correction feedback의 설명이 포함된다.

기출문제 분석표

▌2017학년도 ▌ 영어교육론 기출문제 내용분석표

기입형	
A1	(통합수업) Ss 스스로 탐구하고 수행하는 활동: portfolio(s)
A6	(읽기지도) reading skills: skimming과 scanning

서술형	
A9	(영어평가) criterion-related validation에서 predictive validity를 알아내고 입학점수 CEE와 학업성적 GPA와의 positive association을 서술한다.
A13	(읽기지도) phonics approach에 나타난 문제점을 이해하고, sound value 중심읽기 에서의 이해도의 부족을 context로 보충해야 한다고 서술한다.
B1	(문법지도) form-focused instruction의 두 종류, formS와 form를 이해하고 그 특성을 서술한다.
B2	(교재분석) material adaptation을 하는 이유, personalize를 찾고 adding과 reordering의 기법을 서술한다.
B4	(2언어습득) meaning negotiation strategies를 두 학생의 대화 속에서 찾아 clarification requests와 comprehension checks를 각각 서술한다.

논술형 B	
B8	(영어교수법) 두 교실을 비교하여 각 교사의 다른 roles와 seating arrangement에서 나타난 class management차이를 비교 서술한다.

▌2016학년도 ▌ 영어교육론 기출문제 내용분석표

기입형	
A1	(2언어습득) 학습 방법: strategies
A3	(말하기활동) 활동 기법: jigsaw
A7	(화용론) 다양한 영어의 발전: world Englishes
A8	(화용론) communicative competence를 기르기 위해 social context안에서 습득되는 요소: sociolinguistic competence & speech act

서술형	
A12	(2언어습득) feedback 종류에 대한 설명과 효과적인 방법 분석한다.
A13	(영어평가) 효과적인 평가원리와 부족한 원리를 분석한다.
B1	(영어평가) 수업에서 summative test의 문제점과 formative test 개선점을 서술한다.
B3	(쓰기지도) schema활성화와 writing방법에 대한 서술한다.
B5	(문법수업) deductive와 inductive learning에 대하여 서술한다.

논술형 B	
B8	(영어교수법) mechanical/ meaningful drills활동에서 communicative competence를 기를 수 있는 활동에 대하여 설명할 수 있다.

▎2015학년도 ▎ 영어교육론 기출문제 내용분석표

기입형

A2	(2언어습득) output modification: lexical & syntactic
A3	(영어평가) item analysis: facility, discrimination & distractor
A4	(말하기지도) speaking function의 두 가지 종류: interpersonal & transactional
A5	(읽기지도) pleasure, within the level, own choice를 위한 방법: extensive reading

서술형

A1	(통합수업) culture-integrated수업의 objectives 서술한다.
A2	(2언어습득) feedback에 따른 학생의 uptake와 그를 위한 strategy 관계를 서술한다.
B1	(교재론) 가장 적합한 CMC자료를 선정하여 그 이유를 서술한다.

논술형

B2	(영어교수법) 수업 observation에서 나타난 문제점과 해결책을 제시할 수 있다.

▎2014학년도 ▎ 영어교육론 기출문제 내용분석표

기입형

A7	(영어평가) 평가의 유형과 신뢰도의 종류: interrater & intrarater reliability
A8	(2언어습득) 학습자 오류의 근원: overgeneralization
A9	(쓰기수업) 과정중심에서 revising 단계: time expression와 peer-feedback
A10	(읽기지도) 전략의 종류: inferencing

서술형

B2	(화용론) request에 대한 interactional moves에서 discourse의 문제점과 전략을 서술한다.
B3	(교재론) 수업 활동과 과업을 위한 교과서의 특성을 분석한다.
B6	(문법지도) meaning과 form 수업을 위한 input processing을 설명한다.

논술형

B2	(영어교수법) 수업의 강점과 약점을 이해하고 그룹안에서 낮은 레벨의 학생을 위한 해결방법을 제시한다.

기출문제 분석표

▎2013학년도 ▎ 영어교육론 기출문제 내용분석표

객관식 문항	
15	학습자 중심의 문법 교수법
16	어휘의 collocation을 가르치는 수업절차 이해
17	2언어 습득 및 학습에 대한 이론을 이해
18	두 가지 다른 syllabus에 대해 비교 분석
19	듣기 수업 절차를 읽고 각 단계 특징들을 이해
20	교재 분석 및 평가를 분석
21	online blog를 활용한 수업을 이해
22	각 수업활동의 역할과 기능을 이해
23	교사의 쓰기지도 능력을 평가
24	쓰기지도를 위한 피드백의 유형을 이해
25	multiple-choice items 제작시 유의점을 이해
26	과거시제를 익히기 위한 form-focused 수업절차
27	문항분석표를 보고 문항난이도와 변별도를 올바르게 해석
28	process-writing의 진행단계와 문제해결을 위한 협동과업

▎2012학년도 ▎ 영어교육론 기출문제 내용분석표

객관식 문항	
15	교사의 교수방법과 학생의 학습전략의 차이에서 오는 문제점
16	structure-based & experiential-based Syllabus
17	교사의 다양한 피드백
18	교재분석에 따른 평가표 이해
19	평가의 기본적 원리와 특징
20	듣기의 topdown processing을 통한 교실활동적용
22	말하기평가 유형분석으로 방법이해
23	deductive teaching 방법
24	suprasegmental (prominence)강세발음 지도
25	product-oriented Writing유형
26	읽기수업의 교수접근방법
27	통합수업의 수업계획표 분석
28	TPR과 communicative language teaching 수업 비교분석
29	collocation 수업 과정 분석

▌2011학년도 ▌ 영어교육론 기출문제 내용분석표

객관식 문항

15	수업에서의 교재론의 활용성
16	대조분석학과 상황중심교수법에서의 언어습득
17	읽기의 pre-, while, post-활동의 절차
18	Focus on FormS와 Focus on Form의 차이 이해
19	교사의 Teaching Log를 통한 교수방법
20	수업활동의 행동주의, Input, Output Hypothesis
21	Multiple choice시험에서 항목분석표 이해
22	듣기수업의 과정이해
23	Task based Language Teaching 절차이해
24	교수요목의 차이점 이해
25	semantic mapping 어휘 활동의 이해
27	ICT Web Quest활동을 통한 쓰기수업
28	교실활동의 다양한 Feedback 분석
29	발음지도의 활동방법

▌2010학년도 ▌ 영어교육론 기출문제 내용분석표

객관식 문항

15	learning log를 통한 학습전략 이해
16	Conferencing을 통한 쓰기 평가
17	최근 영어 교수법 ESP 활용방법
18	Task based Language Teaching 과업 종류
19	문법 Garden Path Strategy 지도의 원리
20	말하기 활동 Jigsaw activity 이해
21	Cloze Test와 C-Test에 대한 원리이해
22	쓰기 활동 Dicto-comp
23	Content based Instruction의 종류
24	Input enhancement 활동의 특징이해
25	읽기수업에서 자기 평가표 분석하기
26	쓰기지도를 위한 수업설계와 절차
27	말하기활동에 대한 교수학습법 이론 적용
29	교재분석의 다양한 영역 이해

기출문제 분석표

▌ 2009학년도 ▐

(1) 영어교육론 기출문제 내용분석표

	객관식 문항
14	쓰기 활동에서의 Feedback
15	Post-reading 그룹 활동
16	Integrated Teaching의 수업 방안
17	ALM 활동의 원리이해
18	Multiple choice시험에서 항목분석표 이해
19	semantic network를 활용한 어휘지도 수업
20	학습을 위한 학습자전략과 동기 원리
21	Form vs Meaning의 교수법
22	수업의 담화 방법
23	교재의 구성방법
24	Pushed output - Interaction Hypothesis
25	reading의 다양한 활동이해
26	ICT를 활용한 Process Writing
28	글의 register를 이해하는 듣기 지도

(2) 평가원모의고사 내용분석표

	객관식 문항
11	쓰기 활동을 통한 정의적인 학습자 전략
12	중간언어발달 - Interaction Hypothesis
17	meaning negotiation에 따른 학습 효과
18	듣기와 문법학습 통합지도
19	Internet Conferencing을 통한 쓰기활동
20	타당도의 종류 이해
21	중간언어발달 - Negotiation of Meaning
22	성격유형을 통한 학습전략
23	Bottomup과 topdown을 활용하는 읽기전략
26	교수학습 활동의 종류
27	교재에서 각 활동별로 의미와 언어형식의 방법
28	어휘중심과 과업중심교수법의 교수요목 이해
29	어휘 학습방식의 이해 (어원분석과 word family)
32	교수요목(Competency-based)의 특징이해
33	말하기 연습방법이해 (기계적방법 vs 인지적방법)

2008학년도

(1) (서울, 인천) 영어교육론 기출문제 내용분석표

서술형 문항	
8 (4점)	synthetic & analytic syllabus의 차이와 특성을 이해하여 차이를 세단어 구문으로 서술한다.
9 (3점)	constructivist가 주장하는 scaffolding의 개념을 이해하고 지문에 나타나는 dialogue에서 보이는 내용을 참조하여 본문의 내용을 채워 넣는다.
10 (3점)	authentic한 글의 특성을 이해하기 위하여 두 가지의 text을 비교분석하여 authentic text가 가지고 있는 특성의 기제를 설명하고 예를 찾는다.
11 (4점)	authentic material이 가져야 하는 특성을 서술한다. 내용의 단순화보다는 학생들이 하는 과업을 단순화시키는 것이 더 효과적이다.
12 (3점)	CAI 활동의 종류와 특성을 연결한다.
13 (4점)	어휘지식에 포함되어야 하는 내용들을 상세하게 이해한다.
15 (4점)	cloze test의 실제 평가하는 내용항목들을 파악하여 그 예들을 이론에 맞게 연결한다.
16 (3점)	process-writing의 과정을 수업활동에 맞추어 나열한다.

(2) (전국) 영어교육론 기출문제 내용분석표

서술형 문항	
6 (4점)	computer-adaptive test의 특성을 이해하고 본문을 완성한다.
7 (3점)	문법요소를 평가하기 위한 평가지의 필수요소에 대한 내용을 채워넣는다.
8 (3점)	글의 style에 대한 설명을 읽고 그를 잘 표현하는 내용정리를 연결한다.
9 (4점)	interaction hypothesis에서 negative evidence와 modified output의 예를 dialogue에서 찾는다.
10 (3점)	쓰기활동에서 introduction을 미루지 말아야하는 이유에 대하여 요약한다.
11 (3점)	structured word net에서 배울 수 있는 내용을 지문을 통해 파악하고 요약한다.
12 (4점)	교실상황에 맞는 수업 활동과 적절치 못한 수업활동을 파악하고 이유를 설명한다.
13 (4점)	문법지식의 declarative & procedural knowledge에 대한 차이를 이해한다.

기출문제 분석표

▍2007학년도 ▍

(1) (서울, 인천) 영어교육론 기출문제 내용분석표

서술형 문항	
6 (3점)	읽기에서 interactive compensatory model의 특성을 이해하고 두 단어로 요약정리한다.
7 (4점)	학생의 발화에 대한 교사의 적절한 피드백을 연결한다.
8 (4점)	interaction hypothesis에서 학생의 발화와 언어습득의 관계를 이해한다.
9 (4점)	input processing instruction에서 나타나는 특성을 전통식 문법수업과 비교하여 이해한다.
10 (3점)	학교 project를 통한 활동내용의 본문을 읽고 글의 제목을 7자로 표현한다.
11 (3점)	self-report 자료에 대한 본문을 읽고 그 특성을 8자로 표현한다.
15 (4점)	수업활동과 teaching principles에 대한 연결을 요구하는 내용으로 각 하나의 단어로 표현한다.
21 (9점)	교실에서 학습능력에 따라 나누어지는 ability grouping에 대한 본인이 생각하는 장점이나 단점을 두 가지 이유로 설명한다. 100 단어로 서술한다.

(2) (전국) 영어교육론 기출문제 내용분석표

서술형 문항	
2 (4점)	authentic material & media 사용의 장단점을 본문에서 찾아 우리말로 서술한다.
5 (3점)	문법지도활동 4가지를 놓고 가장 accuracy에서 fluency oriented 된 활동을 순서대로 배열한다.
7 (3점)	form-focused approach의 효과적인 교수 방법을 본문내용에 맞게 요약 서술한다.
9 (4점)	언어학습에서 문학교육의 의의와 전통적 수업에서 문학작품을 대하는 태도를 읽고 이해하여 우리말로 서술한다. (20자와 50자)
10 (3점)	Suggestopedia 영어교수법의 수업현장과 수업원리를 읽고 명칭을 작성한다.
11 (3점)	영어 교재론에 대한 문제로서 독해지문의 성격을 파악하고 각 문항에서 요구하는 이해도의 수준을 연결한다.
14 (3점)	communication strategy를 이해하고 대화상에 나타난 실제의 예와 전략을 연결한다.
15 (4점)	읽기교수방법에서 쓰이는 활동들의 이름과 활동내용을 연결한다.
18 (3점)	performance objectives의 구성요소와 구체적인 예를 연결한다.
19 (4점)	interaction hypothesis를 이해하고 본문의 내용에 맞는 단어를 채워넣고 30자 단어의 요약문을 작성한다.

2006학년도

(1) (전국) 영어교육론 기출문제 내용분석표

서술형 문항	
3 (3점)	comprehensible output hypothesis의 개념을 토대로 본문의 내용을 요약한다.
5 (2점)	adjacency pairs의 개념을 이해하고 적절한 발화의 예를 본문에서 요구하는 발화와 매칭 시킨다.
8 (2점)	syllabus의 변천을 이해하고 alternative syllabus를 찾아 서술한다.
13 (4점)	concordance 프로그램의 특징을 이해하고 이 프로그램을 통해서 얻을 수 있는 어휘정보와 어휘지도 활동을 고른다.
14 (5점)	task의 특성과 유형을 파악하고 각 class activity에 해당하는 task유형을 본문에서 찾아서 작성한다.
15 (2점)	Sapir-whorf hypothesis의 개념을 정확히 이해하고 이 이론을 비판하는 입장의 글을 찾는다.
16 (3점)	materials, classroom methods, lessons를 만들기까지의 과정을 본문을 통해 파악하고 빈칸을 채워넣는다.
17 (4점)	본문에서 설명하는 수업상황을 파악하고 그에 해당하는 수업목표를 찾는다.
18 (4점)	두 가지 drill 유형을 보고 audio-lingual method와 communicative language teaching중 어디에 속하는지 구분하고 각각의 특징을 파악하라.
20 (3점)	컴퓨터를 활용한 쓰기수업이 예를 보고 각 수업에서 적용된 쓰기 활동 유형을 찾는다.
21 (2점)	신뢰도 추정방법의 두 가지 설명이 intrarater reliability인지 interrater reliability인지 선택한다.

(2) (서울) 영어교육론 기출문제 내용분석표

서술형 문항	
2 (4점)	cohesion과 coherence의 차이와 특성을 참조하여 본문의 내용을 채워 넣는다.
7 (4점)	heterogeneous class가 가지고 있는 장점과 단점을 본문에 근거하여 서술한다.
8 (4점)	두 명의 교사가 어디에 초점을 맞추고 수업을 진행하는지 accuracy, substitution, meaningful한 이 세 가지 측면에서 25자 내외로 서술하시오.
10 (3점)	multiple-choice question을 만들 때의 주의사항을 본문의 내용을 통해 숙지하고 빈칸을 채운다.
15 (3점)	Ss의 level을 고려한 pre-reading / pre-listening activity의 특성을 이해하고 본문에서 보이는 내용을 참조하여 빈칸을 채워넣는다.
16 (3점)	explicit correction, recasts, clarification requests를 본문의 내용을 통해 숙지하고 예를 찾아 매칭 시킨다.

기출문제 분석표

▌ 2005학년도 ▐

(1) (서울) 영어교육론 기출문제 내용분석표

	서술형 문항
2 (3점)	motherese와 foreigner talk의 차이점을 본문을 통해 이해하고, 특징단어를 채워 넣는다.
3 (2점)	vocabulary learning에서 explicit/ incidental learning의 중요성을 요약한다.
4 (4점)	explicit vocabulary learning의 약점 2가지를 본문에서 찾아 각각 25자 이내로 서술한다.
8 (2점)	예시를 통해 발화의 modification의 개념을 이해한다: negotiation of meaning & comprehensible input
9 (2점)	교사의 modified input의 특징을 두 단어로 쓴다.
12 (2점)	본문에서 설명된 material adaptation의 특성을 이해하고 빈칸을 채워 넣는다.
16,7 (4점)	sociolinguistic competence를 예를 통해 특성을 이해하고 빈칸을 채워 넣는다.
18 (3점)	online learning의 특성을 이해하고 장점과 단점을 각각 서술한다.
19 (2점)	Ss의 composition을 읽고 teacher's written feedback의 빈칸을 완성한다.
20 (2점)	Ss의 composition에서 function words사용의 mistake를 고르고 correction을 제공한다.
22 (2점)	교실 상황에서 결여된 validity type: content validity
24 (2점)	본문을 통해 authentic materials 사용의 잠재적 문제점을 7단어로 쓴다.
25 (3점)	authentic materials 사용에 관한 교사의 충고를 15자로 쓴다.

(2) (전국) 기출문제 내용분석표

	서술형 문항
6 (3점)	교실 수업상황을 보고 lesson plan의 빈칸에 적절한 활동과 목차를 작성한다.
7 (3점)	unplaned and unrehearsed spoken language에서 사용된 발화의 유형을 보기에서 연결한다.
8 (4점)	지문에서의 교실 영어의 예를 보고 선생님이 사용하는 수업 활동의 이름을 작성한다.
9 (3점)	concordancing, MUDs & MOOs, and voice recognition & production을 이해하고 그 특성을 보기에서 찾아 쓴다.
10 (2점)	문항내용을 이해하고 주어진 데이터의 IF(difficulty)와 ID(discrimination)를 계산한다.
12 (4점)	collocation과 lexical chunk를 이해하고 관련된 approach와 특성을 작성한다.
13 (3점)	평가에 중요한 6가지 개념 (reliability, construct validity, interactiveness, authenticity, practicality)를 이해하고 그 개념들을 요약된 그림에 연결한다.
14 (3점)	Chomsky가 주장하는 LAD의 개념과 second language acquisition의 관계에 관한 글을 요약하고 adult와 children의 차이를 이해한다.
17 (4점)	item analysis에서의 주의해야 할 상황들과 특히 context의 중요성을 이해하고 주어진 본문을 요약한다.
20 (2점)	ESL/EFL class에서 문학을 사용하는 이유를 이해하고 관련된 세부내용을 연결한다.
22 (4점)	measure of speech rate에 관한 본문을 통해 2~4단어를 사용하여 table의 제목을 쓰고 발화속도를 단어 단위로 측정하는 방법과 음절 단위로 측정하는 방법의 장·단점에 대하여 4줄이내의 우리말로 쓴다.

2004학년도

(1) (서울) 기출문제 내용분석표

서술형 문항	
2 (4점)	지문을 읽고 학생들에게 동기부여를 할 수 있는 multimedia tools를 작성한다.
6 (5점)	교사와 학생간의 interaction을 분석한 다음 교사와 학생간의 교실현상으로 빈칸을 채워 넣는다.
7 (4점)	Gestalt Approach에 대해 이해하고 그에 파생하는 2가지 method와 key word를 찾는다.
9 (5점)	주어진 teaching material과 procedure을 분석하여 빈칸 채워 넣는다.

(2) (전국) 기출문제 내용분석표

서술형 문항	
4 (3점)	self-talk의 특성에 대해 이해하고 빈칸을 채워 넣는다.
6 (4점)	읽기에서 connotation의 의도를 알고 이해하여 짧은 phrase로 서술한다.
10 (2점)	errors에 대한 글을 읽고 오류의 근원에 대하여 짧은 phrase로 서술한다.
11 (4점)	implied meaning에 대한 대화를 읽고 분석하여 채워 넣는다.
13 (4점)	class instruction procedure를 분석하여 이 수업의 장점과 예상되는 문제점을 쓴다.
14 (3점)	immersion 수업에 쓰인 teaching strategy를 분석하여 채워넣는다.
15 (3점)	pre-reading activities의 종류에 대해 이해하고 적용하여 구별 짓는다.
17 (3점)	giving feedback in writing class에 대해 이해하고 주요개념을 채워 넣는다.

기출문제 분석표

▌2003학년도 ▌

(1) (서울) 기출문제 내용분석표

	서술형 문항
2 (3점)	implied meaning의 개념을 이해하고 본문에서 밑줄 그어진 부분의 implied meaning을 분석한다.
3 (5점)	time creating, facilitation, and compensation devices를 분류하고 3가지 장치들의 공통된 기능을 서술한다.
6 (4점)	cohesion과 coherence를 이해하고 주어진 문장을 conjunction, pronouns & article을 사용하여 수정한다.
8 (3점)	recast를 사용하여 지문 속의 학생에게 줄 feedback을 서술한다.
9 (6점)	on-line non-interactive & on-line interactive technologies의 관점에서 문화지도 방법을 각각 설명한다.
10 (4점)	주어진 발화에 적용된 foreigner talk의 4가지 특성을 서술한다.
12 (5점)	본문에서 설명하는 alternative test method (dialogue journal)을 적고 학생들의 journal에 대한 response를 할 때 무엇을 해야 하는지 서술한다.
13 (4점)	norm-referenced measurement와 criterion-referenced measurement의 특성을 서술한다.

(2) (전국) 기출문제 내용분석표

	서술형 문항
8 (4점)	본문에서 input hypothesis를 이해하고 comprehensible input과 silent period 명칭을 작성한다.
9 (2점)	지문의 어휘력 평가의 distractors가 적절치 못한 이유를 서술한다.
10 (3점)	지문의 설명과 교수법에 사용된 integrated approach의 한 교수법의 명칭을 작성한다.
11 (2점)	지문의 학생들이 사용하는 communication strategies를 보기에서 연결한다.
12 (2점)	영어 청취 수업에서 느린 속도보다 보통 속도로 된 자료의 활용을 권장하는 이유를 우리말로 2가지 서술한다.
13 (4점)	지문을 잘 이해하기 위해 필요한 담화능력 요소를 찾고, 그 예를 지문에서 찾는다.
14 (4점)	교사의 feedback을 보기의 feedback유형과 연결하고 그 유형의 특성을 서술한다.

2002학년도

(1) (전국) 기출문제 내용분석표

	서술형 문항
8 (4점)	empathic listening의 특성과 방법을 알고 예시문을 서술한다.
9 (3점)	문화가 언어에 미치는 영향을 이해하고 key word 찾는다.
10 (4점)	'dicto-comp' 수업의 특징을 이해하고 그 process를 서술한다.
11 (5점)	total physical response의 일종인 audio-motor unit과 draw the picture 기법의 공통점과 차이점을 작성한다.
12 (4점)	constructive view of language testing에 관해 이해하고 빈칸 넣는다.
13 (4점)	CALL을 사용한 지문의 수업계획안을 분석하고 이 수업의 긍정적 효과를 4가지 측면 (교재활용, 교수법, 학습자, 쓰기학습)에서 기술한다.
14 (4점)	두 대화지문을 분석하고 더 authentic한 대화를 찾고 근거를 서술한다.

(2) (서울) 기출문제 내용분석표

	서술형 문항
2 (4점)	sociocultural competence의 오류를 파악하고 적절한 표현으로 수정한다.
3 (4점)	curriculum의 차이를 파악하여 그 차이점을 요약 서술한다.
6 (4점)	학생의 작문에 나타난 의미와 문법의 오류를 찾아 바르게 수정한다.
7 (5점)	syllabus의 종류와 문제점을 알고 근거 두가지를 서술한다.
8 (4점)	한국 환경에서 instrumental과 intrinsic/ extrinsic motivation의 실례를 서술 한다.
9 (4점)	어휘 수업의 implicit/ explicit 방법을 읽고 요약 정리한다.
10 (4점)	TPR의 방법에 대한 본문을 읽고 그를 위한 실제 교실활동의 예를 서술한다.
11 (5점)	multimedia 사용의 종류와 장점을 각각 3개씩 서술한다.
13 (5점)	듣기수업에서 topdown과 bottomup 방식특징을 서술하고 활동의 종류를 구별한다.
14 (3점)	읽기전략에서 사용되는 topdown 방식의 한 예를 읽고 맞는 방법을 찾아낸다.
15 (3점)	portfolio 평가를 수행하는데 필요한 기준을 두 가지 서술한다.

CONTENTS

		Part 01 기출문제와 모범답안	Part 02 해설편
chapter 01	2언어습득 및 학습이론	23	442
chapter 02	영어교재론 및 교육과정	82	477
chapter 03	영어평가	130	505
chapter 04	영어교수법	189	528
chapter 05	문화 지도	254	570
chapter 06	이해 능력 지도	278	582
chapter 07	표현 능력 지도	323	606
chapter 08	문법 지도	392	637
chapter 09	어휘 지도	418	653

PART

01

기출문제와 모범답안

CHAPTER 01   2언어습득 및 학습이론
CHAPTER 02   영어교재론 및 교육과정
CHAPTER 03   영어평가
CHAPTER 04   영어교수법
CHAPTER 05   문화 지도
CHAPTER 06   이해 능력 지도
CHAPTER 07   표현 능력 지도
CHAPTER 08   문법 지도
CHAPTER 09   어휘 지도

CHAPTER 01 2언어습득 및 학습이론

01 Read the conversation and follow the directions. 【2 points】

2024년 A2번

T1: Hi, Mr. Lee. What are you reading?
T2: Oh, hello. It's a book about the role of input in language acquisition. It's quite fascinating.
T1: What does it say?
T2: Well, it introduces some empirical studies on the effects of _____ in language development.
T1: Oh, I think I heard that term before. Can you remind me?
T2: The term is defined as how prominent or easy a certain input is to hear or read compared to other features around it.
T1: I see. So, it means the ability of a stimulus to stand out from the rest of the input.
T2: Exactly. Some features that are more prominent or easier may be more noticeable and will attract attention from learners.
T1: During classroom interaction, I always try to highlight the keywords or phrases in various ways, and it means that I've been doing things correctly.
T2: Yeah, you're doing great. This book also says teachers need to increase the frequency of exposure because when students encounter certain words and phrases more often, they tend to notice them more effectively.
T1: I understand. I guess it's also because of the functions of salience.
T2: You're right. The more frequently specific vocabulary and grammatical patterns appear, the more likely they facilitate noticing and detection. So, it's not just about teaching a wide range of vocabulary and complex grammar rules but also ensuring students encounter them regularly.
T1: Sounds good to me.

Note: T = teacher

Fill in the blank with the ONE most appropriate word from the conversation.

모범답안   salience

02 Read the conversation and follow the directions. [2 points]

2023년 A1번

(Ms. Kim, a new teacher, and Mr. Song, a head teacher, are discussing Ms. Kim's concerns about her students' writing performance.)

T1: Ms. Kim, did the process-oriented evaluation in your writing class go well this semester?
T2: I'm still making comments to students, but there is something I'm worried about.
T1: What is it?
T2: I'm afraid that one of my students is making more errors now than he was at the beginning of the semester.
T1: He got worse as the semester went on?
T2: Yes. He turned in the writing assignment. However, there were so many errors in his writing.
T1: What kinds of errors?
T2: Unlike the beginning of the semester, now he has problems with irregular verbs.
T1: Can you give me an example?
T2: When the semester began, he wrote words like "drank," "wore," and "heard" without errors. Now I am seeing errors like "drinked," "weared," and "heared." He is suddenly treating irregular verbs like regular verbs.
T1: Hmm. Now that I think about it, he is probably progressing!
T2: What are you talking about?
T1: Well, according to U-shaped course of development, he is starting to understand the rules of the past tense.
T2: Oh, I see.

Note: T1 = Mr. Song, T2 = Ms. Kim

Fill in the blank with the ONE most appropriate word.

In the above conversation, Ms. Kim's student seems to regress, making errors with irregular verbs that he used to use correctly, due to overgeneralization. This phenomenon is commonly called _____, in which the learner seems to have grasped a rule or principle but then moves from a correct form to an incorrect form.

모범답안 backsliding

03 Read the interaction between a teacher and a student, and follow the directions. 【2 points】

2014년 A8번

(The teacher asks her student, Dongho, what he did over the weekend.)

T: Hi, Dongho, how was your weekend?
S: Hello, uh, have, had fun.
T: You had fun, oh, good. Did you go anywhere?
S: Yeah, uh, I go, go, went to uncle, uncle's home.
T: What did you do there? Did you do something interesting?
S: I play, played with childs. Uncle have childs, three childs.
T: Your uncle has three children?
S: Yeah, uh, one boy and two girls. So three childs.
T: Do you like them?
S: Yeah. They're fun. They're good to me.

Note: T = teacher, S = student

Complete the comments on the interaction by filling in the blank with ONE word.

Language errors may occur as a result of discrepancies between the learner's interlanguage and the target language. One main source of such errors is called _____, one example of which is seen in the student's use of *childs* in the given interaction.

모범답안   overgeneralization

04 Read the passages and follow the directions. 【4 points】

⟨A⟩

Below are observations and principles for the English classroom.

Observations	Principles
Among the posters hanging around the room are several containing grammatical information.	Students can learn from what is present in the environment, even if their attention is not directed to it.
The students choose new names and identities.	Assuming a new identity enhances students' feeling of security and allows them to be more open. They feel less inhibited since their performance is really that of a different person.
The teacher distributes a lengthy handout to the class. The title of the dialogue is 'To want to is to be able to.'	The teacher should integrate positive suggestions into the learning situation.
In the left column is the dialogue in the target language. In the right column is the native language translation.	One way that meaning is made clear is through native language translation.
The teacher reads the dialogue with a musical accompaniment. She matches her voice to the rhythm and intonation of the music.	Communication takes place on 'two planes.' On the conscious plane, the learner attends to the language; on the subconscious plane, the music suggests that learning is easy and pleasant.

―〈B〉―

　The teaching approach has several features. When students adopt new names and identities to reduce anxiety and inhibition, they are encouraged to engage more confidently in language practice. If teachers use indirect positive reinforcement, for example, "There is no limit to what you can do," the messages make students boost self-confidence and motivation. Lessons are often implemented in both ways, conscious and subconscious learning. So, while students focus on the language structures, the music and environment lowers anxiety and enhances absorption. Since the teacher aims for relaxed learning environment, students can absorb information from their surroundings, even without direct _____.

Fill in the blank in 〈B〉 with the ONE most appropriate word in 〈A〉.

문제분석	구분	교과 교육
난이도 ★☆☆	평가목표	Suggestopedia로 나타난 교수법의 수업활동과 원리를 잘 분석하는가?
	채점기준	• 수업활동은 학습자가 편안한 환경에서 자신의 능력을 최대화할 수 있도록 한다. • 잠재의식적 학습안에서 직접적 attention없이도 학습이 이루어지도록 한다.

모범답안	attention

05 Read the passage in ⟨A⟩ and the teacher's log in ⟨B⟩, and follow the directions. 【4 points】

2019년 A11번

⟨A⟩

Language transfer refers to the effects of the learners' previous language knowledge or performance on subsequent language learning. Transfer can be categorized into positive and negative transfer. Negative transfer can be further divided into two types—overgeneralization and interference.

⟨B⟩

(Following is a teacher's log of reflection on a task for her Korean students.)

　I conducted a task that required students in pairs to ask and answer questions in class yesterday. At the beginning of the task, I heard a student asking, "Don't you like bananas?" His partner answered, "No, I eat them everyday. They are good for my health." And another student said, "Yes, I never eat them. But I like mangos," when responding to "Don't you like oranges?" I noticed many other students make such errors later in the course of the task. So I decided to tap into the errors and explained them to students after the task. I gave them further question-and-answer exercises to provide opportunities to practice what I explained before the class was over.

Identify the type of negative transfer in ⟨B⟩ based on ⟨A⟩. Then, provide TWO examples of the identified type from ⟨B⟩ and explain why they exemplify the identified type in terms of whether transfer occurs intralingually or interlingually.

문제분석

구분	교과 교육
평가목표	언어습득에 대한 다른 유형의 교수학습 접근방법을 구체적으로 서술하는가?
채점기준	1점: 방해요소인 interference가 일어남을 정의내린다. 2점: 예시로 부정어 'no'와 긍정문이, 'yes'와 부정문이 사용됨을 제시한다. 1점: interlingual 오류임을 정의내린다.

난이도 ★★☆

모범답안

Interference occurs in ⟨B⟩. Students incorrectly answer with negative response, 'No' and positive meaning, 'I eat them everyday', and 'Yes' and negative meaning, 'I never eat them'. These errors come from negative transfer, which is the influence of students' native language interlingually. (45 words)

06 Read two teachers' perspectives on their English classes and answer the question.

2011년 16번

Teacher A: My students tend to transfer the forms and meanings of their native language to English both productively and receptively. I believe that where the two languages differ, negative transfer will result. That is, the students make errors due to L1 interference. So, I decide on what to teach in my English class after identifying the similarities and differences of grammatical points between their native language and English. Also, I prepare teaching materials based on the scientific description of English, carefully compared with a parallel description of their native language.

Teacher B: I think rote learning of isolated units of grammar is not very helpful for communicative language use. So, I usually work with units of language above the sentence level when collecting the grammar structures to be taught in class. For instance, I provide student centered learning materials in which my students can learn to comprehend and produce grammatical points in context. I am sure it will be helpful for them to develop their ability to use the forms appropriately for particular situations.

Which of the following is a correct statement about the teachers' perspectives?

① According to Teacher A's perspective, it is easier for a native English speaker to learn Korean than German as a foreign language.
② Teacher A thinks learners follow the same route of second language acquisition regardless of their first languages.
③ Teacher A thinks most of her students' grammatical errors are intralingual errors.
④ Teacher B believes learners' acquisition of grammar depends on formal instruction and controlled practice.
⑤ Teacher B believes contextualized language use facilitates grammar acquisition.

문제분석	구분	교과 교육
난이도 ★★☆	평가목표	두 교사의 언어습득에 대한 다른 유형의 교수학습 접근방법을 이해하는가?
	평가기준	• 교사A는 L1과 L2의 차이를 근거로 대조분석학으로 언어습득을 설명한다. • 교사B는 언어는 의미있는 context를 통해 습득된다고 설명한다.

기출문제답안 ⑤

07 Read the passage in ⟨A⟩ and conversation in ⟨B⟩, and follow the directions. 【4 points】

2025년 A8번

─── ⟨A⟩ ───

Understanding second language (L2) learners' interlanguage is an important step for teaching L2 learners. In analyzing interlanguage, it has been found that deviations from characteristics of the target language exist in learners' utterances. For example, deviations in early L2 learners' utterances can be categorized into several types.

⟨Deviations in Early L2 Learners' Utterances⟩

Type	Description	Example (The intended meaning is in parentheses.)
Mismatched lexical class	The lexical class does not match.	It's a pink. (It's pink.)
Semantic deviation	Utterances are semantically ill-formed.	What's the spaghetti? (Do you like spaghetti?)
Number of arguments	Utterances contain more or fewer arguments than required.	I wore. (I wore a shirt.)
Word order	Word order is violated.	I this book read. (I read this book.)
...	...	...

─── ⟨B⟩ ───

(Two students are carrying out a two-way spot-the-difference task in their English class.)

S1: Now, let's get started. In your picture, are there chairs?
S2: Yes.
S1: How many chairs are there?
S2: Two chairs.
S1: There are also two chairs in my picture. Now, please ask me about my picture.
S2: What's the pen?
S1: I'm sorry? Do you mean, "Do you have a pen?"
S2: Yes.
S1: Okay. Then, yes, I do. Do you have a pen?
S2: No, I do not have a pen.
S1: Okay. Then we've found one difference. Next, your turn.
S2: Is there a girl?
S1: Yes, there is. What is she doing?

S2: She is giving Mary.

S1: Um, what is she giving Mary?

S2: Ah, she is giving Mary a book.

S1: Oh, in my picture, she is giving Mary an eraser.

S2: Yeah! Finally, we got them all.

Note: S = student

Based on ⟨A⟩, identify the TWO types of deviations found in the students' utterances in ⟨B⟩. Then, explain your answers, respectively, with evidence from ⟨B⟩.

문제분석	구분	교과 교육
난이도 ★★★	평가목표	학습자의 언어의 발전단계를 구체적으로 서술하는가?
	채점기준	1점: Semantic deviation 1점: 'What's the pen?' → 'Do you have a pen?' 1점: Number of arguments 1점: 'She is giving Mary' → direct object, 'what' or 'a book.'
모범답안		Semantic deviation and Number of arguments are deviated. For semantic deviation, S2's utterance, 'What's the pen?' indicates ill-formed meaning that intends to imply 'Do you have a pen?' For number of arguments, S2's utterance, 'She is giving Mary' does not have a direct object, 'what' or 'a book.' (48 words)

08
Read the passage in ⟨A⟩ and the interaction in ⟨B⟩, and follow the directions. 【4 points】

2020년 B4번

⟨A⟩

When problems in conveying meaning occur in conversational interactions, interlocutors need to interrupt the flow and negotiate meaning in order to overcome communication breakdowns and to understand what the conversation is about. A negotiation routine may have a sequence of four components:

- A trigger is an utterance that causes communication difficulty.
- An indicator alerts the speaker of the trigger that a problem exists.
- A response is the component through which the speaker of the trigger attempts to resolve the communication difficulty.
- A reaction to response can tell the speaker of the trigger whether or not the problem has been resolved.

⟨B⟩

(The following is a student-student talk occurring in the morning.)

S1: You didn't come to the baseball practice yesterday. What happened?
S2: Nothing serious. I had to study for an exam.
S1: I am sorry you missed the practice. Have you taken the exam yet?
S2: Yes. I took it a little while ago.
S1: How did you do?
S2: Hopefully I did OK. I didn't get any sleep last night.
S1: I guess you must be drained.
S2: Drained? What do you mean?
S1: It's similar to 'tired.'
S2: Oh, I see. Yeah, I am very tired.
S1: You need to take a break.
S2: I sure do, but I think I am going to eat something first.

Note: S = student

Identify an utterance from ⟨B⟩ that is a response mentioned in ⟨A⟩, and explain how the speaker attempts to resolve the communication difficulty with the identified utterance. Then, identify an utterance from ⟨B⟩ that is a reaction to response mentioned in ⟨A⟩, and explain whether the communication difficulty is resolved with the identified utterance.

문제분석	구분	교과 교육
난이도 ★★☆	평가목표	의사소통을 위한 협상 과정과 예시를 함께 구체적으로 서술하는가?
	채점기준	1점: (Response) 'It's similar to tired' 1점: 문제가 생겼을 때 유사어로 설명한다. 1점: (Reaction to response) 'Oh, I see I am tired' 1점: 자신의 예시로 의사소통을 성공한다.

모범답안 Response is 'It's similar to tired', S1 explained with easier synonym word for the trigger word, 'drained'. Reaction to response is 'Oh, I see I am tired' after understanding the target word. So communication is successfully achieved with making his own example. (41 words)

09 Read the following and answer the question.

2008년 21번 | 2009년 24번

⟨Text⟩

The first stage in the negotiation of meaning is a 'trigger' that begins the sequence. This is followed by a 'signal' that draws attention to a communication breakdown. Stage 3 is a 'response,' in which the speaker attempts to repair the miscommunication. Finally, the 'follow-up' marks the closing of the sequence.

John: Did you get high marks last semester?
Yuhe: High marks?
John: Good grades. A's and B's. Did you get an A in English last semester?
Yuhe: Oh no in English yes um B.

Explain the process of meaning negotiation between John and Yuhe in the dialogue with supporting evidence.

Match each sentence below with its corresponding stage negotiation.

ⓐ Sorry?
ⓑ Yeah, but I saw her at a party yesterday.
ⓒ She's a loner.
ⓓ She stays away from others.

Trigger (　)　　Signal (　)　　Response (　)　　Follow-up (　)

모범답안　The John's initial question becomes a trigger to cause a communication breakdown. Yuhe sends a signal that indicates a communication difficulty with a question form 'high marks'? As for John's response, the trouble source is reformulated and rephrased to 'good grades'. As for Yuhe's follow-up, she comprehends John's question to make a further response. (53 words)

기출문제답안　ⓒ-ⓐ-ⓓ-ⓑ

10 Read the dialogue and follow the directions.

2011년 28번

(In a class, Ms. Yu and students are talking about what makes them unhappy.)
S1: When it rain I am unhappy.
T: Why does rain make you unhappy?
S1: When I walk to school, I wet.
T: Oh, I see. Do you live close to school?
S1: Yeah. 10 minute. (S2 raises a hand.)
S2: When mosquitoes … eat me.
T: Oh, mosquitoes bite me. Bite me!
S2: Oh, OK. When mosquitoes bite me. They bite me everyday's evening. (S3 interrupts the conversation.)
S3: Yeah, me, too. Everyday's evening, mosquitoes bite me, too.
T: That's terrible. I think mosquitoes make many people unhappy.
Note: T=teacher, S=student

Identify the question type of the teacher and describe how uptake is made through the interactional process with supporting evidence.

Choose all and only the correct statements about the classroom.
ⓐ Display questions are used by the teacher.
ⓑ An uptake occurs after the teacher's corrective feedback.
ⓒ Students are exposed to the interlanguage of other students.
ⓓ A clarification request is used by the teacher for meaning negotiation.

모범답안   Referential questions are used to lead to meaningful conversation. The student makes a grammatical error of missing 'be verb', but she manages meaningful interaction to respond to his reply. Students are exposed to the interlanguage of other students with some language error. A student's uptake with repair occurs after the teacher's implicit corrective feedback '~ Bite me'. (55 words)

기출문제답안   ⓑ, ⓒ

11. Read the passage in ⟨A⟩ and the interaction in ⟨B⟩, and follow the directions. 【4 points】

2021년 B7번

⟨A⟩

Some studies claim that there is a predictable language development. For instance, the following is one way of understanding developmental stages for question formation, which posits six stages, each with some prominent features.

Stage	Key Feature	Example
1	• Rising intonation on word or phrase	*Airplane?*
2	• Rising intonation with a declarative word order	*You like this?*
3	• Fronting (e.g., do-fronting, wh-fronting, other fronting)	*Where the train is going?* *Is the boy has a dog?*
4	• Inversion in wh-questions with a copula be • No inversion in wh-questions with auxiliaries • Yes/no questions with auxiliaries such as can and will	*Where is the book?* *Where I can draw them?* *Can he catch the ball?*
5	• Inversion in wh-questions with both an auxiliary and a copula be	*How can she solve it?*
6	• Complex questions (e.g., tag questions, embedded questions)	*She's pretty, isn't she?* *Can you tell me where he is?*

The information about the sequences in English language acquisition like the above is mostly from child native speakers. Familiarity with them can help EFL teachers estimate their students' level of development, which in turn can help determine realistic goals for language instruction.

⟨B⟩

(*Two students are doing an information-gap activity where they are supposed to spot the differences between two pictures.*)

S1: I see a dog in the middle.
S2: Me, too.
S1: Is the girl kicks a ball?
S2: The boy kicks a ball in my picture. Where you can see the duck?
S1: In the pond.
S2: I can see the duck in the pond, too.
S1: Is the boy flies kite?
S2: No, the girl flies kite. Where are the birds?
S1: In the trees.

```
S2:    I find birds on the tree, too.
```
Note: S = student

Based on ⟨A⟩, identify the developmental stages where S1 and S2 are, respectively, with evidence from ⟨B⟩.

문제분석	구분	교과 교육
난이도 ★★★	평가목표	학습자들의 언어 발달 단계를 구체적으로 서술하는가?
	채점기준	1점: S1, stage 3 1점: fronting: 'is the girl kicks a ball.' 1점: S2, stage 4 1점: inversion/ no inversion in wh-questions
모범답안		For S1, stage 3 fronting is shown, as in 'is the girl kicks a ball.' For S2, stage 4, inversion can be used, as in 'where are the birds', but no inversion in wh-questions with auxiliaries is shown, as in 'where you can see the duck.' (46 words)

12 Considering the ⟨A⟩ and ⟨B⟩, match the example with the stage.

2008년 전국 20번

⟨A⟩

To a large extent, the acquisition of negative sentences by second language learners follows a path that looks nearly identical to the stages for first language acquisition. What is different, however, is that second language learners from different first language backgrounds behave somewhat differently within those stages. In the first stage, the negative element (usually 'no' or 'not') is typically placed before the verb or the element being negated. Often, it occurs as the first word in the utterance because the subject of the sentence is not there. For example, No bicycle. No have any sand. I not like it. 'No' is preferred by most learners in this early stage, perhaps because it is the negative form that is easiest to hear and recognize in the speech they are exposed to. In the next stage, 'no' and 'not' may alternate with 'don't'. However, 'don't' is not marked for person, number, or tense and it may even be used before modals like 'can' and 'should'. For example, (1). Next, learners begin to place the negative element after auxiliary verbs like 'are', 'is', and 'can'. But at this stage, the 'don't' form is still not fully analyzed, as shown in the example, (2). Finally, 'do' is marked for tense, person, and number, and most interlanguage sentences appear to be just like those of the target language, for instance, (3). For some time, however, learners may continue to mark tense, person, and number on both the auxiliary and the verb, as in the example, (4). This sequence of stages is descriptive of the second language development of most second language learners.

⟨B⟩

a. I didn't went there. She doesn't wants to go.
b. It doesn't work. We didn't have supper.
c. You can not go there. He was not happy. She don't like rice.
d. He don't like it. I don't can sing.

모범답안   (1) d   (2) c   (3) b   (4) a

13. Read the passage in ⟨A⟩ and the conversation in ⟨B⟩, and follow the directions. 【4 points】

2015년 A2번

⟨A⟩

In negotiation of meaning, "uptake" refers to an interlocutor's immediate response to his or her partner's signal of noncomprehension. In uptake, the interlocutor often uses a variety of communication strategies such as message abandonment, topic change, circumlocution, word coinage, foreignizing, and code switching.

⟨B⟩

The following is part of a teacher-student interaction that contains negotiation of meaning.

T: Hi, Sangjee. How was your weekend?
S: Hello. Well, I had a busy weekend.
T: Did you go anywhere?
S: No, I stayed home all weekend.
T: Why were you busy, then?
S: I had to fly ten chickens.
T: Uh, what? What did you do?
S: Uh, you know, put chickens in oil, very hot oil, kind of bake them.
T: Oh, you FRIED them!
S: Yeah, I fried them with my mother.
T: Why did you have to fry that many chickens?
S: We had a big party on Sunday. My grandfather's birthday. Many people came.
T: Oh, so that's why you fried so many. The party must have been a lot of fun.

Identify where the uptake takes place by writing the specific utterance from ⟨B⟩, and select the strategy used in the uptake from those in ⟨A⟩. Then explain how the utterance in the uptake shows the selected strategy.

모범답안   Uptake takes place when the student makes an immediate response, 'Uh, you know… bake them', after the teacher's corrective feedback, clarification request. The strategy, circumlocution is used when the student notices his pronunciation error, fly. The student describes the target word with a definition instead of correcting his mispronunciation. (48 words)

14. Read the passages and follow the directions. [4 points]

2017년 B4번

⟨A⟩

Meaning-negotiation strategies such as comprehension checks, clarification requests, and confirmation checks may aid comprehension during conversational interaction. First, comprehension checks are defined as the moves by which one interlocutor seeks to make sure that the other has understood correctly. Second, clarification requests are the moves by which one interlocutor requests assistance in understanding the other's preceding utterance. Finally, confirmation checks refer to the moves used by one interlocutor to confirm whether he or she correctly has understood what the other has said.

⟨B⟩

Ms. Jeong has been instructing her students to actively utilize meaning-negotiation strategies stated in ⟨A⟩ during speaking activities. One day, she interviewed two of her students, Mijin and Haerim, about the strategies that they had used during previous speaking activities. The following are excerpts from the interview:

Mijin: When I didn't understand what my friends said during speaking activities, I usually said, "Could you repeat what you said?" or "I am sorry?" Sometimes I tried to check whether my friends clearly understood what I said by saying, "You know what I mean?"

Haerim: Well, during speaking activities, when I had difficulties comprehending what my friends said, I didn't say anything and pretended to understand what they said. I felt it embarrassing to show my lack of understanding to my friends. However, when I talked about something during speaking activities, I often said, "Do you understand?" in order to see if my utterances were understood well by my friends.

Based on ⟨A⟩, write down all the meaning negotiation strategies that Mijin and Haerim used respectively, along with their corresponding utterances from each student in ⟨B⟩.

모범답안 Mijin used clarification request, 'Could you repeat what you said' and comprehension check, 'You know what I mean?'. Hyerim used comprehension check, 'Do you understand?' to negotiate meaning during conversational interaction. (35 words)

15 Read the dialogue and answer the question.

2012년 17번

In the middle of a class, the teacher provides feedback when talking to Minho and Sujin.

[1]
Mr. Park : Minho, I hear you went to Jeju last month. Did you buy anything?
Minho : Yes. Uh, I have brother. I bought chocolate for brother.
Mr. Park : You bought chocolate for your brother.
Minho : Right. Chocolate for brother. I bought small pretty doll, too. It's for sister.
Mr. Park : I'm sure your sister liked it.
[2]
Mr. Lee : Sujin, why don't you read page 24?
Sujin : I have no book today. Jinho borrowed book yesterday. He lost book.
Mr. Lee : Pardon? I'm confused. Lost whose book?
Sujin : U-uh, umm, my book. He lost my book.
Mr. Lee : Sorry to hear that.

Choose all the correct statements about the interactions.

ⓐ Positive evidence is provided through the teacher's feedback in [1].
ⓑ The teacher attempts to resolve a communication breakdown in [1].
ⓒ The student is provided with an opportunity for pushed output in [2].
ⓓ The teacher offers assistance beyond the student's zone of proximal development in [2].
ⓔ The students make self-repair following the teacher's feedback in [1] and [2].

문제분석	구분	교과 교육
난이도 ★★★	평가목표	학습자의 오류에 대한 교사의 피드백을 이해하는가?
	채점기준	[1] 박교사는 긍정적 증거로 학습자의 오류에 대해 맞는 답을 제공한다. [2] 학습자는 교사의 clarification request피드백으로 pushed output을 만든다.

기출문제답안 ⓐ, ⓒ

16 Read the following and answer the questions.

2008년 17번

⟨Dialogue 1⟩
S: The windows are crozed.
T: The windows are what... Sumi?
S: crossed
T: crossed? I'm not sure what you're saying there.
S: Windows are closed.
T: Oh, the windows are closed. OK.

⟨Dialogue 2⟩
T: I went to see a great movie.
S: You are going?
T: Yesterday, I went to see a great movie.
S: OK. Was it fun?

Note: T = teacher, S = student

Match each dialogue <1> and <2> with its underlying assumptions.

ⓐ Meaning negotiation helps L2 learners to obtain comprehensible input.
ⓑ Meaning negotiation facilitates L2 learners' comprehension.
ⓒ Meaning negotiation provides learners with feedback on their own use of L2.
ⓓ Meaning negotiation prompts L2 learners to adjust and modify their own output.

문제분석	구분	교과 교육
난이도 ★★☆	평가목표	의미협상의 목적을 input과 output으로 분석하여 구체적으로 서술하는가?
	채점기준	⟨Dialogue 1⟩ 의미협상을 통해 학습자가 스스로 오류를 수정한다. ⟨Dialogue 2⟩ 의미협상에서 학습자에게 이해할 수 있는 입력을 제공하여 이해도를 높인다.

기출문제답안 [1] ⓒ, ⓓ, [2] ⓐ, ⓑ

17 Read the dialogue and follow the directions. 【2 points】

2018년 A7번

(A teacher and a student are talking after seeing a video-clip of a baseball game.)

T: What was happening in the video?
S: A ball, uh, a ball.
T: A ball was thrown.
S: Thrown?
T: Yes, thrown. A ball was thrown.
S: A ball thrown.
T: And who threw the ball?
S: Pitcher. Thrown pitcher.
T: Thrown by the pitcher.
S: By pitcher.
T: Yes, by the pitcher. A ball was thrown by the pitcher.
S: Ball thrown by pitcher.

Note: T= teacher, S= student

Fill in the blank with the FOUR most appropriate words.

From a socio-cultural perspective, effective learning takes place when what a student attempts to learn is within his or her _____. This is the distance between what a student can do alone and what he or she can do with scaffolded help from more knowledgeable others like teachers or more capable peers. For learning to be effective, such help should be provided to a student through interaction like the teacher's utterances offered to aid the student in the above dialogue.

모범답안   zone of proximal development

18 Read the teaching theory below and fill in the blank with the ONE most appropriate word from the passage.

2008년 전국 16번

> An optimal scenario for development, and hence internalization, is the zone of proximal development (ZPD). In other words, an essential feature of learning is that it creates the zone of proximal development; that is, learning awakens a variety of internal developmental processes that are able to operate only when the child is interacting with people in his or her environment and in cooperation with peers. Once these processes are internalized, they become part of the child's developmental achievement.
>
> One way of conceptualizing movement within the ZPD is the stages of regulation, or control over intellectual actions. It has been proposed that, in the transition from interpsychological to intrapsychological activity, the learner moves from other-regulation to complete self-regulation. When other-regulated, the learner can perform with assistance from others. The learner achieves self-regulation when, in the course of ZPD interactional processes, he or she can take control of external actions and is capable of independent problem solving. In the absence of other-regulation, the learner may be at a stage of object-regulation, a stage in which the learner is easily regulated by objects in the environment. Because assistance in the ZPD is extended as long as other regulation persists but is removed once the learner can function independently, it has been metaphorically conceived as a form of _____. Traditionally, the concept of scaffolding has referred to the supportive behaviors by which an expert can help a novice learner achieve higher levels of regulation.

모범답안   scaffolding

19 Read the passage and follow the directions. [2 points]

2008년 22번

> Miyoung learns best by movement, action, and talk. Group discussions help her understand some things better and give her sureness about her ideas. Somehow her brain only takes in so much and the rest disappears again without specific direction. However, she feels much better writing an essay about something that is important to her, where she has a strong opinion. Furthermore, she likes to write fast because she doesn't have the patience to write when she spends more than four hours writing an essay. So her first drafts tend to be short and underdeveloped.
>
> Myers-Briggs Character Types
>
> **Extroversion (E) vs. Introversion (I)**
> Extroverts generate ideas best by talking about the topic, interviewing people, or actively experiencing the topic, while introverts plan before writing and want most of their ideas clarified before they put words to paper.
>
> **Sensing (S) vs. Intuition (N)**
> Sensing types prefer explicit, detailed, and specific directions, while intuitive types tend to write best when given general directions that allow their imagination to work.
>
> **Thinking (T) vs. Feeling (F)**
> Thinking types tend to select topics that can be written about with emotional distance rather than self-involvement, while feeling types prefer topics that they can care about. When writing, feeling types tend to draw upon personal experiences.
>
> **Judging (J) vs. Perceiving (P)**
> Judging types tend to set limits on their topics quickly and set goals that are manageable. They also tend to limit their research so that they can begin writing more quickly and complete the project. Perceiving types tend to select broad topics and dive into research without setting limits.

Write the Miyoung's learning style according to Myers-Briggs Character Types.

모범답안   ESFJ

20 Read the questionnaire in ⟨A⟩ and the teacher's note in ⟨B⟩, and follow the directions. 【2 points】

2019년 A1번

⟨A⟩

This questionnaire is designed to identify students' learning styles. Each category (A, B, C, D) has 10 items. Students are asked to read each item and check their preferences.

	Learning Style Questionnaire	4	3	2	1
A	1. I understand better when I hear instructions.				
	2. I remember information better when I listen to lectures than when I read books.				
	3. I like to listen to radio shows and discussions more than reading the newspaper.				
	⋮				
B	1. I like to look at graphs, images, and pictures when I study.				
	2. I follow directions better when the teacher writes them on the board.				
	3. I can easily understand information on a map.				
	⋮				
C	1. I enjoy working with my hands or making things.				
	2. I remember things better when I build models or do projects.				
	3. I like to 'finger spell' when I learn words.				
	⋮				
D	1. I like activities that involve moving around.				
	2. I prefer to learn by doing something active.				
	3. I learn the best when I go on field trips.				
	⋮				

Note: 4=strongly agree, 3=agree, 2=disagree, 1=strongly disagree

─── ⟨B⟩ ───

Based on the findings of the questionnaire conducted in my class, I have noticed that four students each have a major learning style.

Scores of the four students			
Youngmi	Minsu	Taeho	Suji
A=38	A=18	A=15	A=13
B=11	B=36	B=12	B=14
C=10	C=10	C=40	C=12
D=12	D=12	D=11	D=36

This week, I am going to teach names of wild animals, like 'ostrich' and 'rhinoceros,' by trying different activities to address these students' different learning styles. Youngmi scored the highest in category A, showing that she is an auditory learner. So I will let her listen to a recording and say the names of animals out loud. Minsu's high score in category B shows that he is a visual learner. I will let him look at images of animals and read the corresponding names. The person who had the highest score in C was Taeho, who is a tactile learner. I am going to use origami so he can use his hands to fold papers into animal shapes. This will help him learn their names better. Lastly, Suji's score in category D shows that she is a(n) _____ learner. For her, I am planning to do an animal charade activity where she acts like different animals and others guess the names of them. I think she will enjoy moving around the classroom. In these ways, I want to maximize students' learning outcomes in my class.

Based on the information in ⟨A⟩ and ⟨B⟩, fill in the blank in ⟨B⟩ with the ONE most appropriate word.

모범답안　　kinesthetic

21 Read the passages and follow the directions. 【4 points】

2019년 B4번

⟨A⟩

(Below is a student's writing and a conversation with his teacher about the writing.)

> Someone first showed the bicycle to the public in the late 18th century. People first thought it was not safe or comfortable. But many creative people improved it. So, many people use the bicycle widely as a form of transportation or for exercise today. Bicycle makers manufacture lighter, faster and stronger bicycles now than before. Because of that, more people ride the bicycle around the world these days than any time in the past. But they used some unique types of cycles in the old days like the four-cycle.

Teacher-student one-on-one conference

T: What is this writing about?
S: It's about the bicycle. Do you ride a bicycle?
T: Yes, I sometimes do. So your writing is not about people who produce or use the bicycle.
S: That's right.
T: OK, the main theme is the bicycle. But none of the sentences has the bicycle as its subject.
S: I know. But if the bicycle becomes the subject, then I have to use many passives. They are complicated and difficult. So I tried not to use them.
T: But it would be better to use the bicycle as the subject in most sentences. That way, it will become clear that the main focus of your writing is the bicycle.
S: Well, okay. I'll try.
T: You used the word "manufacture." Did you know this word?
S: No, I didn't. At first, I wanted to use "make" but then the sentence looked a bit awkward because the subject is "makers." It would go like "Bicycle makers make."
T: I see.
S: So I looked up a different word in a dictionary that has the same meaning as "make."
T: That works. What about this word "four-cycle?" What do you mean? Are you trying to describe a bicycle but with four wheels?
S: Yes, I am. I added "four" to "cycle" just like "bi" is put before "cycle" in bicycle.
T: Oh, it is called "quadricycle." "Quadri" means four just as "bi" means two.

Note: T=teacher, S=student

─────── ⟨B⟩ ───────

When writing as well as speaking in a second language, learners who have limited command of the second language may have to use a variety of strategies that can compensate for their lack of knowledge of the target language grammar and vocabulary in order to effectively get their intended meaning or message across to a reader or listener. Strategies employed for this purpose include avoidance, code switching, word coinage, appeal to authority, and using prefabricated patterns. As these strategies constitute a significant part of strategic competence, advances in the learners' ability to effectively use them play a considerable role in promoting their communicative competence.

Based upon the student's writing and his dialogue with the teacher in ⟨A⟩, identify THREE strategies the student used from those mentioned in ⟨B⟩. Then, provide corresponding evidence for each identified strategy from ⟨A⟩.

문제분석

난이도 ★★★

구분	교과 교육
평가목표	의사소통의 어려움이 있을 때 사용하는 전략의 방법을 서술한다.
채점기준	1.5점: (avoidance) 어려운 형태, 수동태를 사용하지 않는다. 1.5점: (appeal to authority) 사전의 도움을 받아 manufacture를 사용한다. 1점: (word coinage) 새로운 단어인 four cycle을 만들어 사용한다.

모범답안 Three strategies are avoidance, appeal to authority, and word coinage. The student avoids passive forms since they are too complicated and difficult. The student appeals to authority, dictionary to use a different word, 'manufacture'. The student uses word coinage when he doesn't know the word by making a new word, 'four-cycle' for 'quadricycle'. (52 words)

22 Read the passage in ⟨A⟩ and the dialogues in ⟨B⟩, and follow the directions. 【4 points】

2022년 A9번

⟨A⟩

While styles are preferred ways of processing information, strategies are conscious mental and behavioural procedures that people engage in with the aim to gain control over their learning process. Although the definitions and boundaries of learning strategies can be varied, there are several categories of strategies that have generally been agreed upon, as shown below.

Strategy	Definition	Examples
Metacognitive	Learners being consciously aware of their thought processes and cognition	• Planning • Monitoring • Evaluating
Cognitive	Learners using their brains to manipulate or transform L2 input in order to retain it	• Keyword technique • Repetition • Inferencing • Visualization
Social	Learners involving others in their L2 learning processes	• Having conversations in L2 with other speakers • Practicing L2 with other classmates
Affective	Learners engaging their own emotions to facilitate L2 learning	• Rewarding oneself for studying • Intentionally reducing anxiety

⟨B⟩

Mina : Hi, Junho. Is everything going well?
Junho : Hey, Mina! Good to see you here. Can I ask you something?
Mina : Sure. What's up?
Junho : I know you are a good English learner and I'd like to get some tips.
Mina : Sure. Will you tell me how you study?
Junho : I try to set schedules for learning. For example, I decide what I should study first and what I can study at a later time.
Mina : That's a good way. Anything else you do?
Junho : While studying, I sometimes stop to check my comprehension.
Mina : Okay. In my case, I usually create pictures in my mind to remember the things I've studied.
Junho : Oh, you do? I've never tried to create mental images when I study.

Mina	:	Actually, it helps me remember things a lot longer.
Junho	:	That makes sense. I think I need to try it.
Mina	:	And, whenever I find some difficult English expressions I'm not familiar with, I talk in English with native speakers to find out exactly what those expressions mean.
Junho	:	I usually use my online dictionary. But I often find the dictionary explanation is rather difficult for me.
Mina	:	That happens a lot. I think asking questions to others is one of the best ways to clarify the meaning.
Junho	:	I quite agree. I'll apply your advice to my English learning immediately. Thanks for your tips!

Identify TWO strategies in 〈A〉 that Mina recommended to Junho in 〈B〉. Then, support your answers with evidence from 〈B〉.

문제분석	구분	교과 교육
난이도 ★★☆	평가목표	개별적인 언어학습 전략에 대하여 추천하고 특성을 서술하는가?
	채점기준	1점: Cognitive strategies 1점: 기억을 오래가기 위하여 영상화 전략이 추천된다. 1점: Social strategies 1점: 원어민이나 다른 사람과 대화하여 의미를 명확하게 한다.

모범답안   Cognitive and social strategies were recommended. For cognitive strategy, visualization was recommended as mental images to remember things longer. For social strategy, talking with native speakers or others can be the best way to clarify the meaning. (38 words)

23. Match each dialogue in (1) and (2) with its appropriate name.

2003년 전국 11번

Minsu: Miriam, can I borrow your…?
Miriam: My what?
Minsu: (1) <u>A counting-machine</u>.
Miriam: I see. You mean the calculator, don't you?

Mina: Steve, I need your … uh…
Steve: What do you need?
Mina: (2) <u>Something you use when you want to clean things</u>.
Steve: I got it. You need a vacuum cleaner.

Write down the appropriate communication strategy for underlined statement.

모범답안 (1) literal translation (2) circumlocution

24. Read the teacher's note in 〈A〉 and the lesson plan in 〈B〉, and follow the directions.

2002년 8번

A situational change in the value of one of the variables that define a domain may result in _____. For example, two people conducting business in English in Tanzania might suddenly switch to Swahili or, if they are fellow-members of the same ethnic and linguistic subgroup, to a local vernacular, when the topic of conversation changes from business proper to more personal matters. The same kind of _____ has been noted in many bilingual communities: in India, between English and Hindi or one of the many other local language; in the Puerto-Rican community in New York, between English and Spanish.

모범답안 code switching

25 Read the lesson procedure and follow the directions. 【2 points】

2016년 A1번

Lesson Procedure
1. Ss listen to a recorded conversation about the topic of the lesson.
2. T asks Ss to make associations among key words and to guess the meaning of the words from context. Then T teaches new vocabulary.
3. Ss read passages and find semantic clues to get the main idea.
4. Ss reread the passages and scan for specific information.
5. Ss, in groups, do categorizing activities.
6. Ss discuss the topic and write a short comment on it.
7. T hands out the checklist and has Ss keep a daily log after school for one week.

A Daily Learning Log

Name: Jihae Park
※ Respond to each of the following statements with a checkmark (✓).

	Day 1			Day 2			Day 3			Day 4			Day 5		
	1	2	3	1	2	3	1	2	3	1	2	3	1	2	3
1. I make guesses to understand unfamiliar words.															
2. I first read over passages quickly, and then go back and reread them.															
3. I make summaries of the text that I read in English.															
19. I ask a friend questions about schoolwork.															
20. I write down my feelings in a language learning diary.															

Note: 1=Never, 2=Sometimes, 3=Always

Complete the comments by filling in the blanks with the SAME word.

> The lesson procedure shows that the students are instructed to practice various kinds of _____ during the class. Also, they are encouraged to be aware of their use of _____ by keeping a daily learning log.

모범답안   strategies

26 Read the following dialogue and answer the question.

2007년 전국 14번

> Tom: What is your favorite dish?
> Jisu: Well, I like (1) **pig meat**.
> Tom: Pig meat? You mean pork?
> Jisu: That's right. I mean pork. What about you?
> Tom: Well, I don't like meat. In fact, I never eat meat.
> Jisu: Are you a (2) **vegetarianist**?
> Tom: Not quite. I eat fish burgers. Do you like burgers, too?
> Jisu: Yes, and I love (3) **the potatoes that you eat with them**.
> Tom: Do you mean French fries?
> Jisu: That's right, French fries. Why do I keep forgetting that word?
> Tom: Don't worry. I could understand what you meant.

Identify an appropriate communication strategy for each example (1), (2) and (3).

모범답안 (1) literal translation (2) word coinage (3) circumlocution

---

27 Read the dialogues and answer the question.

2003년 전국 14번

> (1) T: Do you exercise?
> S: Yes, I do. I swim.
> T: How often do you swim?
> S: Forty.
> T: **Excuse me**?
> S: Fourteen times.
>
> (2) T: And what do you think?
> S: He is coming lately.
> T: **He's coming …**?
> S: Later?
> T: Uh-hum.
> S: He is coming later.

Identify a type of feedback (1) and (2) and describe ONE feature of each feedback.

모범답안 (1) clarification request: an utterance that asks for clarification of the preceding utterance
(2) elicitation: a question aimed at eliciting the correct form

28 Read the dialogue and follow the directions. 【2 points】

T: What are you going to do this weekend?
S: I will go to a market with my mom.
T: Is there anything you want to buy?
S: Eggs. Many eggs.
T: Is that all you want?
S: No. I will buy many bread and cheese, too.
T: (1) <u>Well, you said you will buy… buy…</u>
S: Buy bread and cheese. Ah, buy a lot of bread. I will buy a lot of bread and cheese.
T: Why will you buy them?
S: I like to make sandwiches. I will make many sandwiches.
T: Do you have any other plans?
S: I have many homework so I will study for many hours.
T: (2) <u>Well, what word do we use with homework</u>?
S: Many homeworks? No, a lot of? Yes, a lot of homework.

Note: T = teacher, S = student

Fill in the blank with the ONE most appropriate word.

> _____ refers to a type of the teacher's corrective feedback that directly induces the correct form of an error from the learner. One technique of this is to induce the correct form of an error by prompting the learner to reformulate the error and complete his or her own utterances, which is seen in the teacher's first corrective feedback, (1), in the dialogue. Another technique is to use questions to lead the learner to produce correct forms as shown in the teacher's second corrective feedback, (2), in the dialogue.

모범답안   elicitation

29 The following is a conversation extract from a communication-oriented middle school English classroom. Examine the extract and follow the directions below.

2010년 논술 3번

Teacher:	What happened to the birth rate in Korea over the last few years?
Student A:	It was │ fallen by 2.4%.
Student B:	│ It was dropped.
Teacher:	Okay. Then, what about the birth rate in Singapore?
Student A:	The rate was also dropped.
Teacher:	_____

(1) Write example utterances of two different types of feedback that you think are appropriate as your responses to Student A's utterance, *The rate was also dropped*.
(2) Identify each feedback type and explain it with evidence in this dialogue.

모범답안 (1) Recast and elicitation could be the appropriate types of feedback for the students' errors in communication-based classroom. Teacher could respond with an implicit feedback or recast, "Yes, the rate also dropped" or elicitation "The rate also ...". (38 words)

(2) Recast is an implicit feedback. Teacher reformulates a student's ungrammatical utterance in an unobtrusive way. He does not interfere the flow of communication but sustain with meaning negotiation. As for elicitation feedback, teacher asks the student to complete the sentence by self repairing their error. So, students have chances to reformulate with their own answer. (56 words)

30. Read the conversation between a teacher and a student and follow the directions. 【4 points】

2016년 A12번

<A>

There are various types of teacher corrective feedback on learners' grammatical errors, including clarification request, elicitation, metalinguistic feedback and recast. I believe that corrective feedback may not have an immediate impact but it should meet certain requirements in order to facilitate language learning. I think corrective feedback should not explicitly indicate that an error has occurred so that it does not embarrass the learner inadvertently and disrupt the flow of ongoing communication. I also find it important that corrective feedback should contain a targetlike alternative to the learner's ill-formed output. Such an alternative form enables the learner to make a comparison of his or her problematic form and its correct form, which constitutes a cognitive process facilitative of language learning.

<B>

S: I am very worried.
T: Really? What are you worried about, Minjae?
S: Math exam for tomorrow. I don't studied yesterday.
T: You didn't study yesterday?
S: No, I didn't studied.
T: Please tell me why. What happened?
S: I did volunteering all day long. So I don't had time to study.
T: Well, Minjae, "don't had" is not the right past tense form.
S: Uh, I didn't had time, time to study.

Identify the teacher's TWO corrective feedback utterances in <B> and select their respective type from those mentioned in <A>. Then explain how only ONE of the utterances meets what Mr. Jeon believes is required for effective corrective feedback in <A>.

모범답안 First, Mr. Jeon uses recast by reformulating the student's incorrect utterance, 'I don't studied..' Second, he uses metalinguistic feedback with indicating '... past tense form'. But he believed that implicit feedback, recast is more effective as it provides target expression and does not interrupt the communication flow of interaction. (49 words)

31 Read the following and answer the question.

2010년 15번

In today's English class, Minji and her partner were asked to read a newspaper article and retell the story to each other. Their performance was video-recorded. Minji wrote the following in her learning log after watching the video.

Minji's Learning Log

<u>Mistakes and difficulties I had during the task</u>: The newspaper article had a lot of new words that I've never seen before. I was worried if I could accurately retell the story.

<u>Strategies I used to complete the task</u>: Since I didn't have time to look up words in the dictionary, I had to guess their meanings based on the context. I thought I understood the story. When I didn't have enough words to describe it, I simply used Korean words.

<u>Overall assessment of my performance on today's task</u>: I paused a lot without speaking while I was telling the story because I didn't know what to say in English. When I was listening, I didn't understand my partner's story clearly. But I didn't ask her to repeat it because I wasn't sure if it was okay.

<u>Strategies I will practice</u>: In the past, I wrote down new words at least ten times to memorize them. It didn't work very well, but I don't know how else I can remember the words. I will try to read more so I can learn more new words.

Identify the THREE communicative/ learning strategies that Minji used to study English in class with its rationales and evidence.

Which of the following is correct about Minji's strategy use?

① She did not use code-switching during speaking.
② She used memory strategies effectively to learn the vocabulary.
③ She appealed for help to overcome her limited speaking ability.
④ She used metacognitive strategies in evaluating her learning process.
⑤ She used social strategies to make herself understood during the pair-work.

문제분석	구분	교과 교육
난이도 ★★☆	평가목표	학습자의 학습전략방법을 구체적으로 서술하는가?
	채점기준	1점: code-switching으로 한국어를 사용한다. 1점: metacognitive 전략으로 평가한다. 1점: 암기전략은 효과를 보지 못한다. 1점: 의미 중심으로 더 많이 읽는 방법을 사용한다.

모범답안 Minji used code-switching by simply using Korean words. She used metacognitive strategies to evaluate her learning process, while analyzing her strategies to compensate for communication difficulty. She used memory strategies to learn the vocabulary to little avail, and instead, planned to read more in meaning-based approach. (47 words)

기출문제답안 ④

32 Read the following and follow the directions.

Mr. Goh is talking about his beliefs and teaching practices in English classes and his student, Insun, is reflecting on her experience.

Mr. Goh: I think it's important to expose students to as much English as possible. And it's also important to create situations where they use English. And so I design classroom activities to have students work with understandable English both receptively and productively. I require students to use English in class. I don't allow them to talk to other students in Korean or to look words up in a dictionary. I believe interactive activities maximize student-student talk time. During these activities, I prefer to let students sort out their own problems when they don't understand each other. I rarely interrupt or stop to correct their grammar.

Insun: I really enjoy learning English, but I sometimes feel frustrated in class. I don't always understand what the teacher is saying and sometimes I wish I could get help in Korean, but the teacher is so strict about using English in class. He doesn't even let us use a dictionary. Because of that, I often feel nervous and anxious. I do like the activities where we talk to other students though. But even then, I get embarrassed especially when he doesn't give us time to prepare. I want to recall some expressions that I know. And he doesn't really help us when we're having problems talking. I don't even know if what I'm saying is correct. I just wish he'd give us more help instead of just letting us work on our own.

Describe ONE problem that Insun has in class and suggest TWO solutions to improve language acquisition with evidences.

기출문제

Choose the correct statements about the beliefs and opinions.

ⓐ The teacher believes that interactions with others are essential in second language learning.
ⓑ The teacher tries to improve students' fluency by providing scaffolding and feedback on their language use.
ⓒ The student may filter out comprehensible input because her affective filter is up in the class.
ⓓ The teacher considers the hypothesis that form focused instruction can help the students improve their L2.
ⓔ The student wants planning time to activate her language knowledge before doing interactive activities.

문제분석	구분	교과 교육
난이도 ★★☆	평가목표	교사의 교수방법과 학생의 학습전략 사이의 차이점을 구체적으로 서술하는가?
	채점기준	1점: (문제점) 학생의 affective filter를 높이는 수업이다. 1.5점: (해결책) 교사의 피드백을 제공한다. 1.5점: (해결책) 학생에게 준비시간을 제공한다.

모범답안 Insun may filter out comprehensible input because her affective filter is up in the class since the teacher forces the students' English use. The teacher's corrective feedback helps to improve student's language skills. The students want some planning time to review the previous vocabulary and learn some unfamiliar expressions before doing interactive activities. (50 words)

기출문제답안 ⓐ, ⓒ, ⓔ

33 Read the text and follow the directions.

2009년 20번

(1)
Jinsoo is a high school student learning English in Korea. For him, studying and learning English does not feel like a burden. He likes to receive and produce English whenever he can. In addition, he feels that learning English is important because it will allow him to converse and be with various international speakers of English.

(2)
Hyeri is a university student who is learning English in Korea. She is taking a course in English literature taught by a Canadian professor. Even though she sometimes does not understand everything that the professor says in the lectures, it does not bother her. During her group study meetings with her classmates, she feels nervous when she speaks in English but tries to speak whenever she can. She wants to do well in English because it is important for her to show her ability to her family and friends.

(3)
Mijin is an office worker and she is presently studying English in Australia for a period of six months. She is taking an English class at a language institute there. For Mi-jin, learning English is important because she thinks that it will add to her social status back in Korea. In relation to classroom activities at the institute, she enjoys participating in small group speaking activities, particularly jigsaw tasks. The high level of challenge presented by the tasks makes her feel nervous, but this tension pushes her to do well in them. Concerning the reading activities, she doesn't like reading something in English because she feels that she should always look up unfamiliar words in a dictionary.

Identify each motivation type of THREE students and explain it with their rationales.

Which of the following is NOT correct according to the passage?

① Jinsoo is both intrinsically and integratively motivated.
② Hyeri is extrinsically motivated and engages in risk-taking behavior.
③ Hyeri has a high tolerance of ambiguity and experiences debilitative anxiety.
④ Mijin is extrinsically motivated and has a high willingness to communicate.
⑤ Mijin experiences facilitative anxiety, and she has a low tolerance of ambiguity when reading.

문제분석 난이도 ★★☆	구분	교과 교육
	평가목표	학습자들의 언어학습에 영향을 미치는 동기를 구체적으로 서술하는가?
	채점기준	2점: (Jin-soo) 내적 동기와 통합적 동기로 그 사회에 통합되고자 한다. 1점: (Hye-ri) 외적 동기로 가족과 친구에게 능력을 과시한다. 1점: (Mi-jin) 도구적 동기로 사회적 지위를 올리고자 한다.

모범답안   Jinsoo is both intrinsically and integratively motivated as he wants to integrate into the community to communicate with the speakers of other countries. Hyeri is extrinsically motivated because she wants to show her ability to her family and friends. Mijin is instrumentally motivated as she studies for the purpose of social status. (53 words)

기출문제답안 ③

34. Read ⟨A⟩ and ⟨B⟩ and follow the directions.

⟨A⟩

Types of Teacher Feedback

(1) Explicit correction: The teacher explicitly provides the correct form.
(2) Recasts: The teacher repeats a student's utterance, using correct forms where the student has made an error, but does not draw attention to the error.
(3) Clarification requests: The teacher indicates to the learner that an utterance has been misunderstood or that there is an error in it.
(4) Metalinguistic feedback: The teacher points to the nature of the error by commenting on or providing information about the well-formedness of a student's utterance.

⟨B⟩

T: What did you do last Sunday?
S: Movie.
T: (a) <u>Excuse me</u>?
S: I see a movie.
T: (b) <u>You saw a movie</u>?
S: Yes, I see a movie.
T: (c) <u>But last Sunday is in the past, right</u>?
S: Oh, yes. Right.
T: (d) <u>So, you have to say SAW, not SEE</u>.

(T: teacher, S: student)

Match the feedback type (a)~(d) with the sentence example. The same letter should be used only once.

모범답안 (1) (d) (2) (b) (3) (a) (4) (c)

35 Read the dialogue and answer the question.

2003년 서울 8번

⟨In the classroom⟩

Teacher: Now let's talk about the movie, JSA. Sumi, did you see it?
Sumi: Yes.
Teacher: Did you like it?
Sumi: Yes. I thought the movie will be very sad.
Teacher: I thought the movie will be very sad? (rising intonation)
Sumi: (No response)
Teacher: You thought the movie would be very sad. (falling intonation)
Sumi: I thought the movie would be very sad. But it was not sad.
Teacher: Really? I think it was very sad.

Describe the TWO types of feedback the teacher has implemented on Sumi's error and the effects on them.

모범답안   The teacher uses echoing or repetition feedback but the student did not show any response. After that, he uses recast feedback to reformulate into the correct form with a central focus on meaning and the student repaired the error to continue the communication. (45 words)

36. Read the review of a book on language learning and answer the question.

2013년 17번

I found the author's points all interesting and agree with him in every aspect. The author views language, communication, and cognition as mutually inextricable. According to him, language has come to represent the world as we know it; it is grounded in our perceptual experience. He further argues that language learning is not dissimilar to learning about all other aspects of the world, and that it is important to note that learning language involves building knowledge of structures, meanings, and functions based on actual instances of language use. A crucial factor in language learning is the reinforcing of features that recur across a sufficient number of usage events. The author also emphasizes the role of learner attention. Simply put, what is attended to is learned, so attention controls the acquisition of language itself. I think the viewpoints of the author may have many meaningful implications for organizing my English lessons.

Which of the following is LEAST likely to be the author's suggestion?

① It is important for students to explicitly learn abstract linguistic categories from the start.
② The use of actual data from language users is important for language lessons.
③ Teachers should help learners attend to second language input better by making it easily noticeable.
④ It is necessary to increase input frequency, which will affect the level of achievement.
⑤ Students should be provided with many opportunities to practice various form-meaning mappings in context.

기출문제답안 ①

37 Here is an e-mail which is taken from an English textbook. Read it and follow the directions.

2007년 서울 7번

The teacher read this e-mail with the class in the previous lesson. He is now asking questions to review the lesson. He asks: 'What does Min-hee do? What's her hobby?' The student's answer:

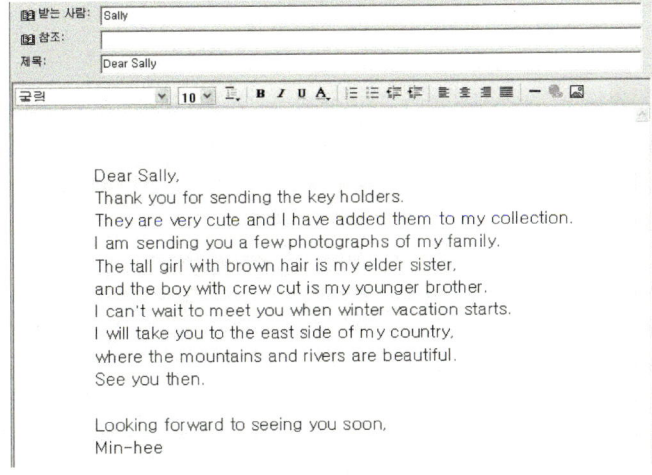

(1) A student answers, 'Key holders collect.'
(2) A student answers, 'She collects photographs.'
(3) A student answers, 'She collecting key holders.'
(4) A student answers, 'She writes an e-mail.'

The following is the teacher's possible feedback. Match the teacher's appropriate feedback with the student's response. The same letter should be used only once.

a. Say, 'Photographs? Key holders, she collects …'
b. Accept the answer, then say, 'But in English we say "collect key holders." Now, who collects the key holders?'
c. Help the student to correct himself or herself by saying 'Well, nearly – "collecting" or "collects"?'
d. Accept the answer. Then rephrase the question to make it clearer by saying 'Well, yes, she's written an e-mail. But what does she do in her free time? What's her hobby?'

모범답안 (1) b (2) a (3) c (4) d

38 Considering the dialogue between NNS (non-native speaker) and NS (native speaker), fill in each blank with one word from the passage.

2007년 서울 8번

NNS : I go cinema.
NS : Uh?
NNS : I go cinema last night.
NS : Oh, last night.

The Interaction Hypothesis suggests a number of ways in which interaction can contribute to language acquisition. More specifically, it suggests that (a) when interactional modifications lead to comprehensible input via the decomposition and segmenting of input, acquisition is facilitated; that (b) when learners receive feedback, acquisition is facilitated; and that (c) when learners are pushed to reformulate their own utterances, acquisition is promoted. The above dialogue shows that the interaction has led to successful communication, but that it does not contribute to ①_____ of the past tense, a morphological feature. Thus, successful communication takes place without the learner needing to modify his or her output by incorporating the past tense marker, showing that not all ②_____ output is in fact modified.

모범답안   ① acquisition   ② pushed

39 Read the passage and follow the directions.

2007년 전국 19번

We understand that language input may "go in one ear and out the other," and it contributes to _____ only if it is "let in" to the mind for processing. According to claims made in the Interaction Hypothesis, the modifications and collaborative efforts that take place in social interaction facilitate second language acquisition. It is because they contribute to the accessibility of input for mental processing: negotiation for meaning, and especially negotiation work that triggers interactional adjustments by the more competent interlocutor, facilitates acquisition because it connects input, internal learner capacities, particularly selective attention, and output in productive ways.

Fill in the blank with the ONE most appropriate word in the passage. Describe how the students acquire their second language according to Interaction Hypothesis.

모범답안 acquisition. According to the Interaction Hypothesis, second language acquisition occurs when students involve social interaction which makes input accessible for mental processing through negotiation of meaning that triggers interactional adjustments by interlocutors, selective attention and more output. (36 words)

40 Read the passage in ⟨A⟩ and the interaction in ⟨B⟩, and follow the directions.

2021년 A10번

⟨A⟩

In language directed toward linguistically nonproficient second language speakers, native speakers tend to show foreigner-talk adjustments in the flow of conversation. These include slow speech rate, loud speech, long pauses, simple vocabulary (e.g., few idioms, high-frequency words), and paucity of slang. They also tend to make adjustments to their speech in the area of grammar. They often move topics to the front of the sentence, put new information at the end of the sentence, use fewer contractions and pronouns, grammatically repeat non-native speakers' incorrect utterances, and fill in the blank for their incomplete utterances.

⟨B⟩

NS: So what did you have for lunch today?
NNS: I was busy. I eated cookies.
NS: Oh, did you? I see.
NNS: You want cookies?
NS: No, thanks.
NNS: You don't like cookies?
NS: Well... these days I'm on a diet and I rarely eat them.
NNS: Sorry... I don't understand.
NS: These days I am on a diet and I rarely eat cookies.
NNS: Oh, I see. You diet. You don't eat cookies.
NS: Well, I do. But only sometimes.
NNS: Mm.... Sometime. You eat cookies only sometimes.
NS: Right, because they have too much sugar.

Note: NS = native speaker, NNS = non-native speaker

Based on ⟨A⟩, locate ONE utterance in ⟨B⟩ that reflects NS's grammatical adjustment to his speech and identify its adjustment type. Then, explain how it functions in the given dialogue.

문제분석	구분	교과 교육
난이도 ★★☆	평가목표	foreigner talk의 특성을 찾아 구체적으로 서술하는가?
	채점기준	1점: 'I am on a diet and I rarely eat cookies' 1.5점: 축약과 대명사를 적게 사용한다. 1.5점: 문장의 의미를 쉽고 명확하게 이해할 수 있게 한다.

모범답안 The statement, 'I am on a diet and I rarely eat cookies' shows native speaker's grammatical adjustment. It includes no contractions and pronouns. With a full sentence, students can understand the meaning of sentence more easily and clearly to solve the communication difficulty. (43 words)

41 Read the following and answer the question.

2003년 서울 10번

In the following conversation, a non-native speaker with beginning level proficiency is seeking help from a native speaker at the information desk.

NNS : Excuse me, where toilet, please?
NS : Unfortunately, the entire plumbing system is being repaired. Perhaps you could use the public toilets which are about five blocks from here.
NNS : I'm sorry. I don't … I don't understand.
NS : <u>There is one down there. Five … blocks … from here. Five blocks</u>.
NNS : Oh, I see. Thank you.

Describe FOUR characteristics of the underlined utterances for "foreigner talk".

모범답안
- It is slower than normal speech.
- It uses grammatically simple utterances.
- It uses clearer articulations.
- It shows some repetitions to help understand.

42 Read the following and answer the directions.

When mothers speak to their children, they typically simplify their speech and make efforts to sustain communication. The formal and interactional characteristics of this kind of speech are referred to as "motherese." They may help the child to learn the language. When native speakers address learners, they adjust their normal speech in order to facilitate understanding. These (1)_____, which involve both language form and language function, constitute "foreigner talk." Foreigner talk may aid acquisition by ensuring that the learner understands what he or she hears. Foreigner talk closely resembles motherese, but there are notable differences in both input and interactional features. Generally, ungrammatical adjustments are very rare in motherese, but they can occur under certain conditions in foreigner talk. Whereas motherese displays a high proportion of instructions and questions, foreigner talk has a higher proportion of statements. The main functional intent of motherese is to direct the child's behavior; however, in foreigner talk the intent is to exchange (2)_____.

Fill in the blank with one appropriate word for each number from the list.

⟨Word list⟩

| interaction | output | instructions |
| information | adjustments | transfer |

모범답안   (1) adjustments   (2) information

43 Read the dialogue in a classroom situation and follow the directions.

2005년 서울 8~9번

T: What other advantages do you think you may have, if you were the only child in the family?
S: <u>I'm sorry. I beg your pardon</u>?
T: Er, if you were the only child in your family, then what other advantages, er, <u>what points, what other good points do you think you may have</u>?
S: It's quieter for my study.
T: Yes? It's quieter for you to study. Yes? Any other?
S: No more.
T: OK. Fine.
(T: native English-speaking teacher, S: non-native English-speaking student)

Describe the features of interaction of NS and NNS starting with the following statement regarding the underlined sentences in the dialogue in terms of negotiation strategy.

When the input is incomprehensible, _____.

모범답안 When the input is incomprehensible, NS and NNS enter into a negotiation of meaning. NNS asks for clarification requests resulting in a modification of the structure of interaction. The strategy the teacher made in the underlined utterance is a type of paraphrase to make the question easier. This type of negotiation of meaning facilitates second language development. (52 words)

44 Read the passage and complete the blanks with ONE appropriate word each.

(*Two colleagues are talking during a coffee break at work.*)
Tony   : I have two tickets for the theater tonight.
Susan : Good for you. What are you going to see?
Tony   : *Minari*.
Susan : Interesting movie. Hope you enjoy it.
Tony   : Oh, so you're busy tonight.

In this conversation, Susan, deliberately or otherwise, takes Tony's utterance as a statement of fact, rather than a request. The interlocutors are either native speakers of English or competent users of the language. It is clear from this example that interpreting dialogue, and thus establishing coherence, is a matter of readers and listeners using their linguistic knowledge to relate the discourse world to entities, events, and states of affairs beyond the text itself. It is not at the level of grammar or vocabulary that they are not able to achieve their intention or purpose of communication, but at the (1)_____ level. Susan misunderstood the (2)_____ force of the utterance within the context.

모범답안   (1) discourse (2) illocutionary

45 Read the passage and answer the questions.

Motivation is a frequently used term for explaining the success or failure of second language learning. It is assumed that learning a second language because of its value in helping to integrate with speakers of that language is different in one's purpose from learning a second language because of its value as a tool or instrument for doing something else successful, such as studying a subject in English. In the field of research on motivation in second language learning, a distinction has been made between integrative and instrumental orientations rather than integrativeness and instrumentality as types of motivation. Here, orientation means a context or purpose for learning; motivation refers to the intensity of one's impetus to learn. The intrinsic or extrinsic motivation designates a continuum of possibilities of intensity of feeling or drive, which range from deeply internal to strong, externally administered rewards that are beyond oneself. In this sense, integrative and instrumental orientations are not confused with intrinsic or extrinsic motivation. This intrinsic-extrinsic continuum in motivation is also applicable to foreign language classrooms in Korea.

Fill in the blank with the correct example from ⓐ ~ ⓓ below.

	Intrinsic Motivation	Extrinsic Motivation
Integrative	L2 learner wishes to integrate with the L2 culture. ① _____	Someone else wishes the L2 learner to know the L2 for integrative reasons. ② _____
Instrumental	L2 learner wishes to achieve goals utilizing L2. ③ _____	External power wants L2 learner to learn L2. ④ _____

a. Learning English for promotion at work
b. Korean parents send their kids to English language school in Canada.
c. Samsung corporation sends their businessmen to America for English training.
d. Learning English for immigration or a marriage to an English speaking country

모범답안 ① d ② b ③ a ④ c

46 Choose any or all the number(s) related to language learning.

Gagne's 8 types of learning
- ㉠ Signal learning
- ㉡ Stimulus-response learning
- ㉢ Chaining
- ㉣ Verbal association
- ㉤ Multiple discrimination
- ㉥ Concept learning
- ㉦ Principle learning
- ㉧ Problem solving

모범답안
- ㉠ Signal learning
- ㉡ Stimulus-response learning
- ㉢ Chaining
- ㉣ Verbal association
- ㉤ Multiple discrimination
- ㉥ Concept learning
- ㉦ Principle learning
- ㉧ Problem solving

47 Fill out the blanks with the ONE most appropriate word.

_____ occurs when the same information is presented in multiple ways within the language itself. For example, using both words and gestures to convey a message or repeating key vocabulary in different contexts. In language use, _____ helps listeners piece together the message even if they miss parts of it or do not pay full attention to every word. Even in communication in our native language we do not hear clearly everything that is said to us, nor do we pay full attention to every element of each utterance.

모범답안   redundancy

48 Fill out the blank with one appropriate word.

Transfer is a general term describing the carryover of previous performance or knowledge to subsequent learning. Positive transfer occurs when the prior knowledge benefits the learning task, that is, when a previous item is correctly applied to present subject matter. Negative transfer occurs when the previous performance disrupts the performance on a second task. The latter can be referred to as _____.

모범답안   interference

49 Fill out the blank with one appropriate word.

Language learners in both first and second language acquisition have been observed to produce errors like 'comed' which can be explained as extensions of some general rule to items not covered by this rule in the target language. This process is referred to as _____.

모범답안   overgeneralization

50 Identify the type of error as following.

- He can sings.
- It is occurs that ……
- I goed to school yesterday.

모범답안   overgeneralization

51 Fill out the blank with one appropriate word.

It is common experience to witness in a learner's language various erroneous features which persist despite what is otherwise a fluent command of the language. This phenomenon is ordinarily manifested phonologically in "foreign accents" in the speech of many of those who have learned a second language after adolescence. We also commonly observe syntactic and lexical errors persisting in the speech of those who have otherwise learned the language quite well. The relatively permanent incorporation of incorrect linguistic forms into a person's second language competence has been referred to as _____.

모범답안   fossilization

52 Identify the hypothesis principle of the following.

First, the fact that there is no demand for early speech production reduces the anxiety of the students considerably, since it allows for concentration on one skill at a time. Second, students are allowed to make the decision, individually, when they wish to begin speaking the target language. Finally, errors of any form are not corrected directly.

모범답안   affective filter hypothesis

53 Fill out the blank with two appropriate words.

Learners with low motivation, little self-confidence, and high anxiety have _____ and so receive little input and allow even less in.

모범답안   high filters

54 Fill out the blanks (㉠), (㉡) with appropriate words for cognitive variations.

There can be two different kinds of language learning. One kind of learning implies natural, face to face communication, the kind of communication that occurs too rarely in the average language classroom. The second kind of learning involves the familiar classroom activities: drills, exercises, tests, and so forth. It could well be that natural language learning, beyond the constraints of the classroom, requires a(n) (㉠) style and the classroom type of learning requires, conversely, a(n) (㉡) style.

모범답안
㉠ field-dependent (field-sensitive)
㉡ field-independent (field-insensitive)

55 Identify the communication strategy to match with the appropriate description.

(1) _____ : The learner describes the characteristics of the object or action instead of using the appropriate target language.
(2) _____ : The learner uses memorized forms of language in his competence.
(3) _____ : The learner tries not to talk about complicated structures for which target language is not known.
(4) _____ : The learner uses the native language term without bothering to translate.

모범답안 (1) circumlocution (2) prefabricated patterns (3) syntactic avoidance (4) code switch

memo

CHAPTER 02 영어교재론 및 교육과정

01 Read the passages and follow the directions. 【4 points】

2024년 A12번

⟨A⟩

Below are the posts made by two English teachers on an online teacher community where teachers can share their ideas and provide each other with help regarding the use of digital technology.

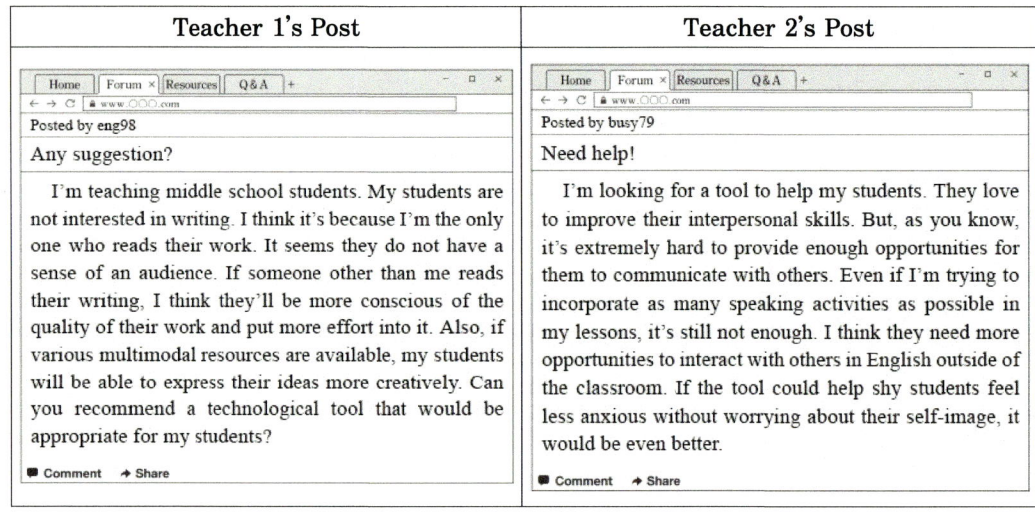

⟨B⟩

Tool 1: This is a cloud-based quiz platform. Teachers can create quizzes to help learners to practice what they have learned. Various question formats are available including true or false, matching, multiple choice, etc. It generates a report of student performance after the quizzes are completed.

Tool 2: When teachers use this virtual reality simulation app, they can invite their students into the virtual space they have created. Students can communicate with others in English in simulated real-life situations taking place in airports, markets, and cinemas. Here students can create an avatar and converse with each other.

Tool 3: Students can use this voice recognition software in order to bridge the gap between oral and written language. They can read a text on screen and then record their voice. The tool also lets students know what errors they have made by highlighting them on the screen.

Tool 4: This is an online platform where students are encouraged to write and post their written work. The platform allows them to incorporate photos and graphics or embed videos into their work. Other students can then reply to the posts. The original writer can reply back as well.

Tool 5: Using this app, teachers can create a mind map for teaching English vocabulary. It shows groupings or relationships between words visually. Moreover, there is a link to an online dictionary. QR codes can also be created to share the mind map with students.

Based on ⟨A⟩, for each teacher, respectively, suggest the ONE most appropriate tool in ⟨B⟩ that satisfies their needs. Then explain your answers with evidence from ⟨B⟩. Do NOT copy more than FOUR consecutive words from the passages.

문제분석	구분	교과 교육
난이도 ★★☆	평가목표	교사가 활용하기를 원하는 디지털 교수자료를 찾아 구체적으로 서술하는가?
	채점기준	1점: (Teacher 1) Tool 4 1점: 온라인을 활용하여 글을 서로 교환하고, 사진, 그래픽등을 활용한다. 1점: (Teacher 2) Tool 2 1점: 학생들이 실제와 같은 상황에서 가상세계에서 의사소통을 한다.
모범답안		Tool 4 is appropriate for Teacher 1. Through an online platform, students post their written work and reply to others, with the help of photos, graphic or videos. Tool 2 is appropriate for Teacher 2. In the tool, students can communicate with others in virtual space by creating avatar like real-life situations. (52 words)

02 Read the passages and follow the directions. [2 points]

Materials can be adapted by using different techniques such as *adding*, *deleting*, *modifying*, and *reordering*. For example, we can add materials when a language item is not covered sufficiently in the original materials. Materials that are too easy or difficult for learners can be deleted. Modifying can be used to make them more relevant to students' interests and backgrounds and to restructure classroom management. Reordering the sequence of activities is another technique, which includes separating items and regrouping them.

Consider the original material extracted from a grammar exercise book and its adapted version below. In the adapted version, the original exercise has been adapted by using the ①  technique.

Original Material

❶ [Individual Work] Describe the man's routine in four sentences.

❷ [Individual Work] Answer the following questions.
What time do you wake up?
What do you usually wear to work?
What do you usually cook for dinner?

Adapted Material

❶ [Individual Work] Describe the student's routine in four sentences.

❷ [Pair Work] Work in pairs and ask each other the following questions.
What time do you wake up?
What do you usually wear on school days?
What do you usually eat for dinner?

Fill in the blank ① with the ONE most appropriate word from the passage.

모범답안   modifying

03 Read the passage and follow the directions.

2005년 서울 12번

Conventional wisdom in language teaching suggests that there is no such thing as a perfect textbook. This is likely to be true whether the materials in question were commercially produced or locally created within a given program. Moreover, the task of completely reinventing the materials for all the courses in a program on a continuous basis is a staggering undertaking. One viable solution to both these problems is to use what is of value in an existing set of materials, while adapting it to the needs or changing needs of the program. The first stage in adapting the textbook is to find out whether it serves the students' needs and helps meet the course objectives. In so doing, it is important to identify the gaps that cannot be filled by the textbook. Filling the gaps is adapting the textbook. What should the gaps be filled with? Certainly, teachers in the program may know from their own experience existing materials that may help to fill the gaps, which means that materials creation may be necessary for some of the missing elements.

Complete the summary with THREE words each from the passage. (Forms can be changed.)

Materials adaptation is regarded as a teacher's attempt to ①_____ in the textbook by means of commercially available materials or materials creation. It is usually done because it is extremely difficult to find a perfect textbook or to ②_____ regularly.

모범답안   ① fill the gaps   ② reinvent the materials

04 Read the passages and follow the directions. 【4 points】

2023년 A8번

⟨A⟩

There are always sound reasons for adapting materials in order to make them as accessible and useful to learners as possible. When adapting materials, having clear objectives is a necessary starting point. The objectives a teacher may hope to achieve by adapting classroom materials can be listed as follows:

- To cater to learners' language proficiency levels: The teacher can modify the difficulty of language features such as grammar and vocabulary in the materials.
- To reinforce learner autonomy: Through materials adaptation, the teacher can give students opportunities to focus on their own learning processes to become more independent learners.
- To enhance higher-level cognitive skills: The teacher can adapt materials in such a way as to require students to hypothesize, predict, or infer.
- To encourage learners to tap into their own lives: Through materials adaptation, the teacher can increase the relevance of the contents or activities in relation to the students' experiences.

⟨B⟩

Ms. Lee is teaching first-year high school students, and she is preparing for her English reading class next semester. Based on the results of a needs analysis, she has decided to adapt two chapters of the textbook materials to meet her students' needs. For Lesson 2, which is about career paths, she will use magazine pictures of various jobs like engineer, baker, and fashion designer, along with some pictures related to jobs in the textbook. She will use these pictures as a springboard to get students in groups to share their dream jobs. She thinks this adaptation will help students think about more varied jobs in the real world. For Lesson 5, there is a reading passage about Simon's adventure in Kenya in the textbook. However, she worries that there are only simple activities to check students' understanding of the story. So, she will edit the story, intentionally deleting a few sentences at the end. This will challenge the students to think about the story's structure and look ahead to possible endings, using the storyline.

Based on ⟨A⟩, identify the ONE objective that Ms. Lee wants to achieve through adaptation in Lesson 2 and the ONE objective in Lesson 5. Then, explain your answers with evidence from ⟨A⟩ and ⟨B⟩.

문제분석	구분	교과 교육
난이도 ★☆☆	평가목표	교재를 학습의 목표에 맞추어 개정하는 방법을 구체적으로 서술하는가?
	채점기준	1점: (Lesson 2) 직업을 자신의 생활과 연관시킬 수 있다. 1점: 그림을 이용하여 자신의 꿈을 나눌 수 있다. 1점: (Lesson 5) 높은 수준의 인지 기술을 강화할 수 있다. 1점: 이야기의 끝을 삭제하여 예상하게 한다.

모범답안 In Lesson 2, students can relate the jobs to their own lives. With using the pictures of various jobs in magazines, they share their own dream jobs. In Lesson 5, students can enhance higher-level cognitive skills. By deleting the ending part of the story, they think about the story's structure and predict possible endings. (52 words)

05 Read the passage and answer the question.

2017년 B2번

⟨A⟩

Materials can be adapted for many reasons, for example, to localize, to modernize, or to personalize. We can localize materials to make them more applicable to our local context. We can modernize materials when they are outdated in terms of English usage or content. We can also personalize materials by making them more relevant to learner needs and interests. Materials adaptation can be carried out by using a number of different techniques, as shown in the figure.

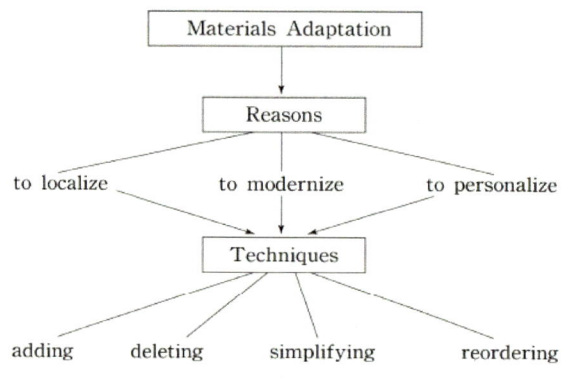

⟨B⟩

Mr. Lee is teaching first-year middle school students whose proficiency levels are very low. After conducting a needs analysis, he has learned that the students find the writing sections of the textbook difficult and that they are interested in sports. While he is planning a writing lesson for next week, he realizes that there is only one pre-writing activity in Unit 1 of the textbook. He thinks that one activity is not enough for his students to develop ideas for writing. Thus, he is going to increase the number of the pre-writing activities from one to THREE. In addition, thinking that the reading passage on sports in Unit 3 will better suit learner interests than the reading text in Unit 1, he decides to switch the two reading texts. He believes that this change will help his students become better prepared for writing and more engaged in English language learning.

Referring to the terms in ⟨A⟩, explain the reason why Mr. Lee wants to adapt the materials, and identify which techniques he is going to use for materials adaptation. Do NOT copy more than FOUR consecutive words from the passage.

문제분석	구분	교과 교육
난이도 ★☆☆	평가목표	학습자들에게 적합한 교재를 위해 개정하는 방법을 구체적으로 서술하는가?
	채점기준	1점: 낮은 레벨 학생과 흥미도를 위해 개별화한다. 1점: 방법은 추가하고 재배치한다. 1점: 쓰기 전 활동을 추가한다. 1점: 내용을 재배치하여 내적 동기부여를 한다.

모범답안 The material is adapted to personalize to learners' low proficiency levels and their interests in sports. The techniques are adding and reordering. By increasing the prewriting activities, students can have more opportunities to generate their own ideas. By reordering the reading texts, students are more intrinsically motivated in reading and writing activity. (52 words)

06 Read the following and answer the question.

Materials evaluation is conducted on a candidate textbook by a high school teacher.

Rating scale:
1 = Totally lacking   2 = Weak   3 = Adequate
4 = Good   5 = Excellent

Evaluation Criteria	1	2	3	4	5
Content and Presentation					
Do the activities exploit language in a communicative or 'real-world' way?		✓			
Do the activities support level-differentiated learning?				✓	
Do the materials provide opportunities for self-study?		✓			
Are communicative functions recycled in subsequent units?		✓			
Is vocabulary selected according to how often it is used in everyday English conversation?	✓				
Are grammar items presented progressively in terms of learnability?				✓	
Teacher's Manual and Supplementary Materials					
Are there suggestions on how to supplement the textbook or to present lessons in different ways?					✓
Does the manual provide materials for on-going evaluation and ready-made achievement tests?			✓		

Fill in the blank about the evaluation criteria with the ONE most appropriate word from the passage above.

The teacher's manual provides ideas on materials adaptation. The textbook caters to teaching multiple proficiency groups but provides little material for self-directed study. Language _____ are presented insufficiently for spiral learning but grammar is well suited to students' proficiency level. Vocabulary is rarely related to the real-world information from authentic language corpora.

Which of the following is NOT correct about the textbook according to the teacher's evaluation?

① The teacher's manual provides ideas on materials adaptation.
② The textbook caters to teaching multiple proficiency groups.
③ The textbook provides little material for self-directed study.
④ Language functions are presented insufficiently for spiral learning.
⑤ Vocabulary is selected based on information from spoken language corpora.

문제분석	구분	교과 교육
난이도 ★★★	평가목표	교재에 대한 평가를 잘 이해하는가?
	채점기준	① 교사지도서는 교재 개정에 대한 생각을 제공한다. ② 교재는 다양한 능력의 학생들에 맞춰서 제작된다. ③ 교재는 스스로 학습 자료가 거의 제공되지 않는다. ④ 의사소통 기능은 나선형학습으로 재활용이 잘 제시되지 않는다.

모범답안 functions

 ⑤

07
Read the passage in ⟨A⟩ and a teacher's note in ⟨B⟩, and follow the directions. 【2 points】

2020년 A2번

⟨A⟩

Curriculum design is a series of systematic efforts to develop a curriculum that satisfies the target learners as well as teachers. Researchers suggest that there are five main stages in the process of designing a curriculum.

```
      _____
           ⇓
    Goal Specifications
           ⇓
    Materials Development
           ⇓
  Language Teaching & Learning
           ⇓
    Curriculum Evaluation
```

⟨B⟩

Teacher's Note

I am planning to develop a new English course for winter session, so I wanted to establish the basis for developing the curriculum. The first step of this process requires me to systematically collect and analyze areas of necessity for my students in order to satisfy their language learning requirements. So, I created a survey which asked students questions about their English deficiencies and the difficulties they face in performing certain language tasks in their current classes. It also asked them about the methods they enjoy learning through as well as the types of English skills that they want to improve. For the second step of this process, I wanted to get more information about the students' preferred learning styles and interests, so I referred to my classroom observation notes to learn about them. I then asked my school's principal to show me the results of their placement tests to gain an understanding of their levels of linguistic proficiency and background experience. I interviewed students both in groups and individually to get more detailed information. In short, I conducted _____ by collecting all these data.

Based on the information in ⟨A⟩ and ⟨B⟩, fill in the blanks in ⟨A⟩ and ⟨B⟩ with the TWO most appropriate words. Use the SAME words in both blanks.

모범답안   needs analysis

08 Based on the following text, fill in the mapping picture with the ONE most appropriate word from the passage.

2006년 전국 16번

> Teaching materials and methods are embedded within a broad professional context. Whether goals are stated in terms of a national language policy, or in a more restricted environment, they will be directly related both to the learners themselves and to the whole educational setting in which the teaching is to take place. Obviously goals need to be realistic for specific circumstances. There is little use, for example, in planning for a multimedia course if appropriate equipment is unavailable or unreliable, or in making too many general assumptions about classroom methodology. The statement of goals, then, related to the learners and conditioned by the setting, leads to the selection of an appropriate type of syllabus content and specification. The broad syllabus outline will in turn have direct implications for the more detailed design and selection of materials and tests, the planning of individual lessons, and the management of the classroom itself.

⟨Picture⟩

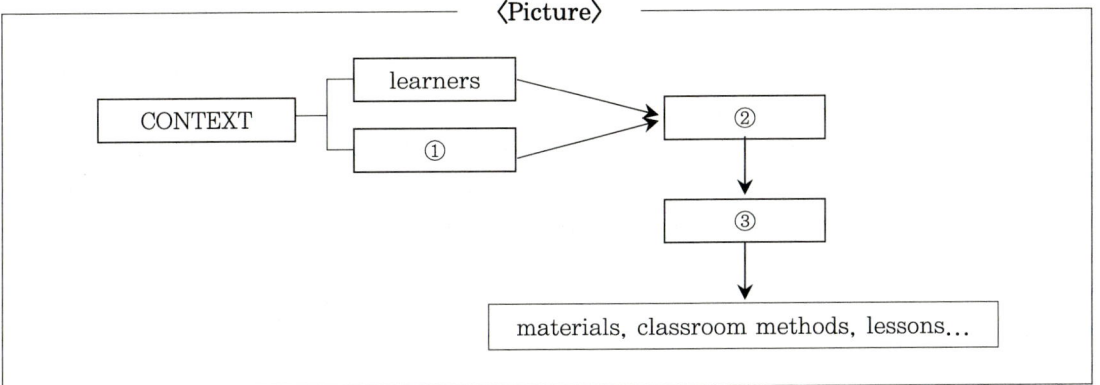

모범답안 ① setting ② goals ③ syllabus

09
Read the passage in ⟨A⟩ and the teaching procedure in ⟨B⟩, and follow the directions. 【4 points】

2021년 A9번

⟨A⟩

Mr. Yang, a middle school English teacher, believes that his lessons should help students meet the achievement standards which are specified in the school curriculum. He selects a group of standards for each semester and tries to incorporate them into his lessons. The following are the achievement standards for this semester.

[Achievement Standards]

[Oral Language Skills]
Students can
- use strategies to open and close conversations.
- explain their likes and dislikes.
- describe their dreams and future jobs.
- talk about their worries and problems.

[Written Language Skills]
Students can
- read a book or watch a film and write their feelings and impressions.
- read a short text about a familiar topic and write a conclusion.
- read a short text about a familiar topic and organize the content.
- view an object or picture and write their thoughts or feelings about it.

⟨B⟩

Teaching Procedure

Mr. Yang designed a reading lesson for his 2nd year students based on two of the achievement standards that he set out to accomplish this semester.

⟨Reading text⟩   **What Should I Do?**

Everyone has worries. When you have things you worry about, what do you do?

Sumi's Worries

Sumi thought Kate was her best friend, but now, she feels that Kate has changed and that she is avoiding her. A few days ago, Sumi met Kate in the hallway at school, but Kate turned around and walked away from her. Sumi tried to find the reason, but she couldn't think of anything wrong she had done to Kate. So, Sumi asked for her older sister's advice. Sumi's sister suggested that she simply ask Kate what's wrong.

Step 1	T tells Ss about today's topic and has Ss predict the content of the reading text based on the titles and pictures.
Step 2	T introduces new words from the text.
Step 3	T asks Ss to skim the text and tell what the text is about.
Step 4	T has Ss reread the text and complete a problem-solution chart based on what they read.
Step 5	T has Ss tell their worries and suggest solutions in groups.
Step 6	T has Ss write the key words and sentences in their learning log.

Note: T = teacher, S = student

Identify ONE oral language achievement standard and ONE written language achievement standard from ⟨A⟩ that the teaching procedure in ⟨B⟩ targets. Then, explain how each achievement standard is addressed with evidence from ⟨B⟩.

문제분석

난이도 ★★★

구분	교과 교육
평가목표	개정 교육과정에 나타난 성취기준에 따라 구체적인 교실 활동을 서술하는가?
채점기준	1점: (oral language achievement standard) step 5 1점: 걱정에 대해 말하고 해결책을 제시한다. 1점: (written language achievement standard) step 4 1점: 책을 읽고 챠트를 완성한다.

모범답안 For oral language achievement standard, students talk about their worries and problems. In step 5, students tell their worries and suggest solutions. For written language standard, students read a short text and organize the content. In step 4, students read a text and complete a chart. (45 words)

10 Read the evaluation sheet and follow the directions.

2011년 15번

Below is part of the coursebook evaluation by two teachers. They are supposed to use the same coursebook next semester. So, they want to prepare extra teaching materials for only those categories that they both marked as "poor."

Categories of Evaluation	Teacher A			Teacher B		
Language Content	3	2	1	3	2	1
(1) Are vocabulary exercises presented which exploit words that frequently occur next to each other?			✓			✓
(2) Are new grammar items introduced in context?			✓			✓
(3) Is appropriate attention given to pronunciation?	✓				✓	
(4) Are there enough models of discourse in which language is used for effective communication?		✓				✓
(5) Is there any attempt to match language styles to social situations?		✓				✓
(6) Is more than one variety of English used to meet the demand for international English?			✓		✓	

Note: 3=Excellent, 2=Good, 1=Poor

Identify THREE language contents that are not up to the standards. Explain the contents or activities to compensate for the each lack of the language contents.

Choose all and only the materials that the teachers will prepare for their classes from the list: <Potential Extra Teaching Materials>

ⓐ sets of a formal speech and a conversation between friends that show appropriate language use
ⓑ worksheets to facilitate word memorization using mnemonic devices
ⓒ vocabulary activities that prompt the use of appropriate words in context through collocations
ⓓ listening materials in which people interact in different varieties of English
ⓔ authentic stories in which the target grammatical forms are used

문제분석	구분	교과 교육
난이도 ★★☆	평가목표	교재의 평가표를 보고 개선할 방법에 대한 활동을 제시한다.
	채점기준	(1) vocabulary activities: 연어법을 사용한 어휘활동을 한다. (2) authentic stories: 문법형태를 실제 이야기안에서 활용한다. (5) formal speech: 상황에 적절한 형식의 언어를 사용한다.

모범답안 (1) Vocabulary activities need to prompt the use of appropriate words in context through collocations. (2) Authentic stories in which the target grammatical forms can be used (5) Appropriate formality between friends can be practiced to show appropriate language use for the language styles with social situation. (47 words)

기출문제답안 ⓐ, ⓒ, ⓔ

11 Read the passages and follow the directions. 【4 points】

〈A〉

Digital technology provides students with a new battery of tools with which language can be learned effectively. Below are some apps that students can use for their English learning.

• App 1

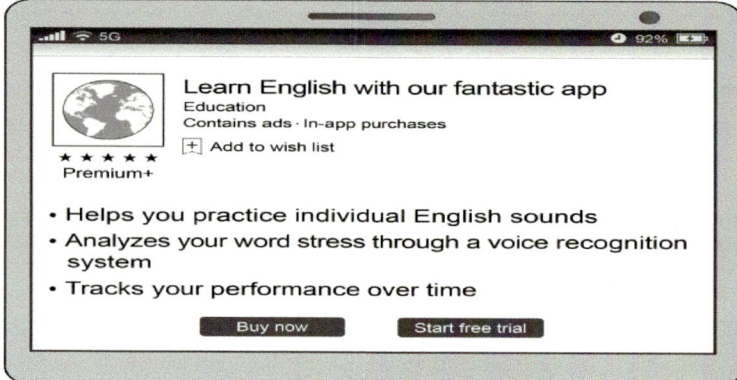

• App 2

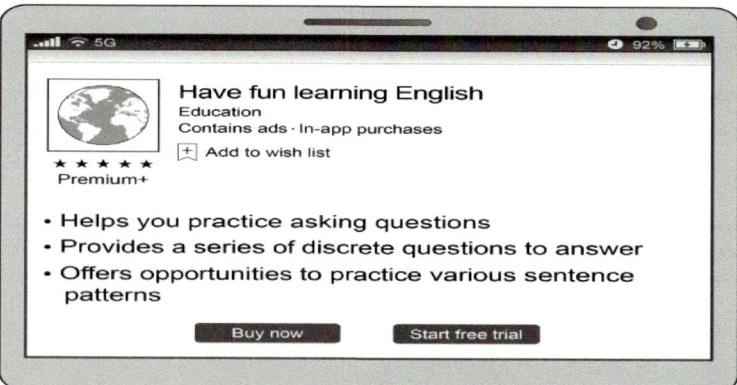

• App 3

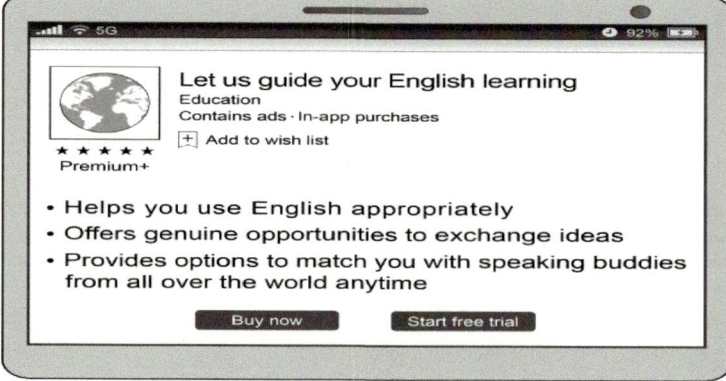

⟨B⟩

Minsu's Case

Minsu is very active in English classes and always looks for opportunities to speak English with other people. Since he lives in Korea, where English is not usually used outside the classroom, it is difficult to find English conversation partners. He once tried a conversation program where he spoke with native speakers on the phone. However, the program seemed too rigid in that he could only practice at designated times and with predetermined contents. Now, he wants to find an app where he can talk with partners whenever he wants and apply what he learns in the English class while speaking in a more natural context.

Jieun's Case

Jieun is afraid of speaking in English. But she was not like that before. She used to be outgoing and willing to communicate with people in English whenever she could. However, sometimes people didn't understand her and kept asking her to repeat the words she had just said. When she consulted her English teacher about the issue, the teacher advised her to focus on practicing pronunciation of words. Now, she is looking for an app which could help her practice pronouncing English words accurately.

Based on ⟨A⟩, identify the ONE most appropriate English learning app for Minsu and Jieun, respectively. Then, explain your answers with evidence from ⟨B⟩.

문제분석	구분	교과 교육
난이도 ★★☆	평가목표	학생들에게 적절한 앱 활동을 선택하여 구체적으로 서술하는가?
	채점기준	1점: (Minsu) App 3 1점: 실제 언어를 배울 수 있는 기회를 제공한다. 1점: (Jieun) App 1 1점: 정확한 발음을 연습할 수 있게 한다.

모범답안 App 3 is used for Minsu. App 3 gives him the opportunity to learn authentic English outside classroom, since the program can be used more flexible in a natural context. App 1 is used for Jieun. App 1 lets her practice more accurate pronunciation on her own. (47 words)

12. Read the passage in 〈A〉 and the table in 〈B〉, and follow the directions. 【4 points】

2015년 B1번

〈A〉

As part of an effort to maximize opportunities for her students to interact with others in English, Ms. Park, a high school English teacher, plans to design her lessons from a blended learning perspective. She is considering having the students interact with each other and her both online and offline. She designs lessons as follows: Online activities are based on a synchronous computer-mediated communication (CMC) interaction, and the transcripts of the online interaction are used a couple of days later for offline discussion. Realizing that many of her students seem shy, frustrated, and uncomfortable with face-to-face discussion, she would like to use a CMC tool to help students get ready for an offline discussion. By examining their online production with peers and the teacher, she believes that CMC activities will guarantee more equalized opportunities for participation and make students' errors more salient and thus open to feedback and correction.

〈B〉

Evaluation of Three CMC Tools

Criteria/Tools	Tool A	Tool B	Tool C
Easy to Use	Y	Y	Y
Saving and Archiving	N	Y	Y
Real-Time Interaction	Y	N	Y
Video Chatting	N	Y	N
Online Dictionary	Y	N	N

Note: Y = Yes, N = No

Based on the information in 〈A〉 and 〈B〉, identify the tool you would recommend for Ms. Park, and provide TWO reasons for your recommendation.

모범답안 The Tool C can be recommended for Ms. Park. The students can do online real-time interactive activities as a synchronous communication. Tool C also has a function of saving so that the students discuss their communication offline later. (39 words)

13 Read Mr. Park's comments in 〈A〉 and examine the results of a textbook evaluation in 〈B〉. Follow the directions. 【4 points】

2014년 A3번

〈A〉

Mr. Park: The goal of my class is to help students use the language to communicate and perform authentic tasks. So I want to spend most of my class time letting students rehearse tasks they need to perform outside the classroom. I also want my students to have a lot of opportunities to work together so that they can use their linguistic knowledge to convey meaning rather than just practice form.

〈B〉

Evaluation Criteria	Textbook A			Textbook B			Textbook C		
	1	2	3	1	2	3	1	2	3
pattern drill activities		✓		✓					✓
role-play based on real-life situations		✓				✓		✓	
pronunciation tips			✓		✓				✓
regular grammar review			✓		✓		✓		
group projects	✓					✓		✓	

* 1=poor, 2=average, 3=good

Considering the information in 〈A〉 and 〈B〉, identify the textbook you would recommend for Mr. Park and provide TWO reasons for recommending it based on its characteristics.

모범답안 Textbook B is recommended with role-play and group projects. Through role-play, the students can achieve the goal of performing authentic task in real life. In group project, the students work together to use target language to convey meaning to achieve the project. (48 words)

14. Read textbook evaluation and answer the question.

2013년 20번

Prerequisites			Textbook A		Textbook B	
Do the aims of the textbook correspond with the aims of the teaching program and the needs of the learners?			Yes		Yes	
Is a teachers' guide available?			Yes		Yes	
Initial Status			Accepted		Accepted	
Criteria	WT* (1–3)	SC* (1–5)	WT x SC	SC (1–5)	WT x SC	
Are design and layout attractive to learners?	2	5	10	3	6	
Does the textbook include appropriate materials for pronunciation work?	1	5	5	2	2	
Does the textbook contain enough skill integrated activities?	2	3	6	3	6	
Are topics interesting for learners?	3	2	6	3	9	
Does the textbook include materials for strategy training?	3	2	6	5	15	
Total			17	33	16	38
Final Status			Rejected		Selected	

*WT=weight (1=not very important; 2=important; 3=very important)
*SC=score (1=very poor; … 5=excellent)

Complete the result of the characteristics of textbooks with either A or B.

──────────── ⟨Result⟩ ────────────
Above are the results of a high school textbook evaluation. Both textbooks satisfy the prerequisites for acceptance. Textbook ___①___ is poorer in design, layout, and pronunciation. Topic interest is a more important criterion than skill-integration in this context. Textbook ___②___ scores higher in the criteria with the highest weight.

Choose all and only the correct statements about the evaluation results.

ⓐ Both textbooks satisfy the prerequisites for acceptance.
ⓑ Textbook A is poorer than Textbook B in design and layout, and pronunciation activities.
ⓒ Skill-integration is a more important criterion than topic interest in this context.
ⓓ Textbook B scores higher than Textbook A in the criteria with the highest weight.

문제분석	구분	교과 교육
난이도 ★★★	평가목표	교재 분석과 평가방법을 구체적으로 서술하는가?
	채점기준	• 교재B는 디자인과 발음에서 낮은 점수를 받고 있다. • 교재B는 비중이 높은 항목에서 고득점을 받고 있다.

모범답안   ① B   ② B

기출문제답안   ⓐ, ⓓ

15 Read the checklist and follow the directions.

Checklist 1 (C1)

Categories	Y/N
Is it attractive?	
Does it have a clear layout?	
Is it about the right length given the period of learning?	

Checklist 2 (C2)

Categories	Weight	Rating				
		4	3	2	1	0
Speech						
Suggests ways of demonstrating and practicing speech items						
Includes speech situations relevant to the learners' background						
Grammar						
Stresses communicative competence in teaching structural items						
Provides adequate models featuring the structures to be taught						

Checklist 3 (C3)

Factors	Comments
Rationale	
Layout / Physical Characteristics	
Publisher(s)	

Checklist 4 (C4)

Categories	Rating		
	3	2	1
Skills			
Are all four skills adequately covered given the course aims and syllabus requirements?			
Are reading passages and activities suitable for integrated skills work?			
Tasks			
Does it include a sufficient number of task-oriented activities?			
Are tasks clearly differentiated to cover students' different proficiency?			

Describe the features of each checklist for the textbook. Some list items can be explained together.

Choose all and only the correct statements about the checklists from the list.

ⓐ C1 is used to investigate the syllabus differences between textbooks.
ⓑ C1, C2 and C3 are systematic and easily quantifiable.
ⓒ In C2, some criteria can be more highly valued than the others.
ⓓ C2 and C4 allow for a more in-depth evaluation than the other checklists.
ⓔ C3 is used for external evaluation by glancing through the textbook.

문제분석	구분	교과 교육
난이도 ★★★	평가목표	교재선정을 하기 위해서 사용하는 평가표를 분석하는 방법을 이해하는가?
	채점기준	1점: C1: 전체구성과 디자인의 차이를 구별한다. 1점: C2 & C4: 점수를 이용하여 깊이있는 평가가 가능하다. 1점: C2: 항목의 비중의 차이가 있는 평가가 가능하다. 1점: C3: 외적 요소를 평가한다.
모범답안		C1 is used to investigate the differences of layout and design between textbooks. C2 and C4 are systematic and easily quantifiable with rating scores with more in-depth evaluation. In C2, some criteria can be more highly valued than the others with giving different weight measures. C3 is used for external evaluation by glancing through the textbook. (58 words)

기출문제답안 ⓒ, ⓓ, ⓔ

16 Read the conversation in ⟨A⟩ and the draft of the syllabus in ⟨B⟩, and follow the directions. 【4 points】

2024년 A11번

⟨A⟩

T1: Mr. Choi, can we talk about a syllabus for the Business English course next semester? We need to develop one as soon as possible.
T2: Sure. What type of syllabus do you have in mind?
T1: Well, I think a multi-layered syllabus would be most appropriate.
T2: I agree. I'd like to cover various aspects of Business English, such as topics, functions, skills, activities, grammar, and vocabulary.
T1: Sounds good to me. First of all, I believe all the topics should be business-related. But what about the functions? Do you have anything in mind?
T2: I think we should teach functions that are often used in business situations.
T1: Yes. By doing so, we'll prepare the students to perform well when they get a job.
T2: We also have to make sure that both receptive and productive skills are included.
T1: Definitely. We should provide activities where students can practice both skills.
T2: Okay. How about grammar? I think our students are not good at making connections between ideas, so we need to incorporate connective devices in the syllabus as well.
T1: Good. We also need to make sure there is a vocabulary component, right?
T2: Of course. You know, English courses in our school tend to focus on single words but not multi-word units like collocations, idioms, and fixed expressions.
T1: You're right. If we teach those multi-word units during the course, students will be able to speak more fluently.
T2: Great! Based on what we've discussed so far, I'll write a draft. Can you check it later?
T1: Sure. I look forward to seeing it completed.

Note: T = teacher

⟨B⟩

This is the draft of the syllabus T2 wrote.

Components	Unit 1	Unit 2	Unit 3
Topics	• Business Relations	• Business Negotiation	• Business Meetings
Functions	• Greeting and introducing in work places • Receiving buyers	• Making business contracts • Dealing with orders	• Planning business meetings • Attending business meetings
Skills	• Listening to business dialogues	• Reading business contracts	• Reading tables • Listening to meeting schedules

Activities	• Interviewing • Role-plays	• Information gap • Simulations	• Opinion gap • Group decision making
Grammar	• Relative pronouns to be used to describe people, places, companies • Coordinating conjunctions: *and, so, or, but*	• Modal auxiliaries to be used to express opinions on buying and selling products • Subordinating conjunctions: *after, when, since, unless*	• Wh-questions to be used at business meetings • Conjunctive adverbs: *additionally, consequently, however, likewise*
Vocabulary	• employer • employee • executive • manager • administrator	• sales • purchase • proposal • supplier • customer	• appointment • postpone • schedule • portfolio • presentation

Based on ⟨A⟩, choose the TWO components in ⟨B⟩ that do NOT correspond to the teachers' ideas about their syllabus. Then explain your answers with evidence from ⟨A⟩ and ⟨B⟩.

문제분석

난이도 ★★☆

구분	교과 교육
평가목표	두 교사가 추구하는 교수요목의 내용들을 작성된 교수요목 초안과 비교하여 맞지 않는 내용을 구체적으로 서술하는가?
채점기준	1점: Skills 1점: 이해와 표현 기술 모두를 원하는데 초안은 이해기술만을 포함한다. 1점: Vocabulary 1점: 다중어휘를 가르치려고 하는데 초안에는 개별어휘만을 포함한다.

모범답안 Skills and Vocabulary are not corresponded. Teachers need to teach both receptive and productive skills but in the draft syllabus, only receptive skills, listening and reading are included. Teachers want to teach multi-word units, but in the draft, only single word parts, 'employer', 'employee' are included. (46 words)

17 Read the passages and follow the directions. 【4 points】

⟨A⟩

Task-based language teaching (TBLT) holds a central place in current second language acquisition research and also in language pedagogy. Some suggest there are six main steps in designing, implementing, and evaluating a TBLT program.

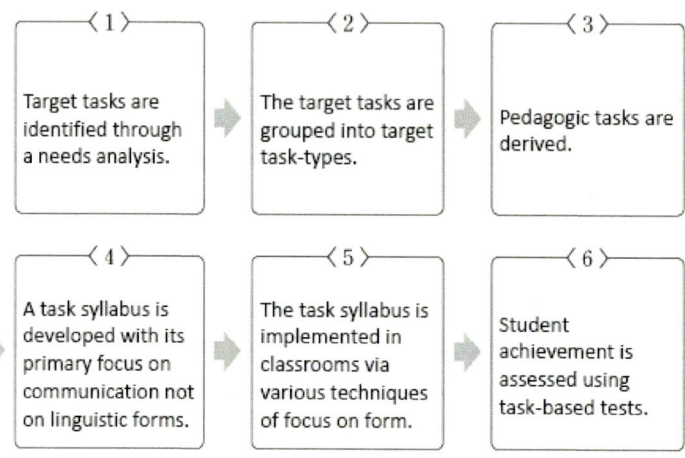

⟨1⟩ Target tasks are identified through a needs analysis. → ⟨2⟩ The target tasks are grouped into target task-types. → ⟨3⟩ Pedagogic tasks are derived.

→ ⟨4⟩ A task syllabus is developed with its primary focus on communication not on linguistic forms. → ⟨5⟩ The task syllabus is implemented in classrooms via various techniques of focus on form. → ⟨6⟩ Student achievement is assessed using task-based tests.

⟨B⟩

Mr. Kim designed and implemented a TBLT based on the six steps described in ⟨A⟩.
- Step 1. He did some questionnaire surveys with his students and interviewed fellow teachers to identify what his students would really want to do in everyday life.
- Step 2. He grouped the identified real-world tasks (e.g., purchasing a train ticket, booking a room, renting a car) into more general categories (e.g., planning a trip).
- Step 3. He developed tasks that his students would perform in the classroom. Those tasks were expected to elicit communicative language use in the classroom.
- Step 4. He designed a syllabus with a central aim of presenting different grammatical items one at a time and teaching them separately.
- Step 5. He drew student attention to linguistic forms when needed, while the primary focus of the lessons was still on communication during task performance.
- Step 6. He assessed the student outcomes, focusing on whether and how much they accomplished each given task.

Identify the step in ⟨B⟩ that does not match with its corresponding suggestion in ⟨A⟩. Then, explain how that identified step deviates from its suggestion in ⟨A⟩. Do NOT copy more than FOUR consecutive words from the passage.

문제분석	구분	교과 교육
난이도 ★★☆	평가목표	TBLT를 synthetic과 analytic의 syllabus에 대한 비교로 서술할 수 있다.
	채점기준	1점: Step 4가 맞지 않는다. 1점: 교사는 분리된 언어를 가르치는 실러버스를 사용한다. 1점: TBLT는 언어를 의사소통에 근거하여 가르친다. 1점: 학습자의 수행에 근거하여 언어가 분석되고 연습되어야 한다.

모범답안 Step 4 is not matched with the suggestion. TBLT suggests that syllabus should focus on communication rather than isolated structure but teacher designed a syllabus to teach discrete point items separately. Based on the students' performance of target tasks, the language should be analyzed and practiced. (46 words)

18 Read the conversation and follow the directions. 【2 points】

2021년 A1번

> T: Today, we are going to read a text about cooking. Are you interested in cooking?
> Ss: Yeah.
> T: Great. Let's study today's key words first. (The teacher brings out kitchen utensils from a box.) I brought some cooking utensils.
> S1: Wow! Are those yours?
> T: Yes, they are. I use them when I cook. (showing a saucepan) You've seen this before, right?
> S2: Yes. My mom uses that when she makes jam.
> T: Good. Do you know what it's called in English?
> S3: It's a saucepan.
> T: Excellent, it's a saucepan. Everyone, repeat after me. Saucepan.
> Ss: Saucepan.
> T: And, (showing a cutting board) what's this in English?
> S4: A board?
> T: Right, it's a cutting board. Good job. I also brought a couple of things from my refrigerator. This is one of my favorite vegetables. (The teacher holds up an eggplant.)
> S5: Umm.... It's an egg...
> T: Nice try! It's an eggplant.

Fill in the blank with the ONE most appropriate word.

> In this lesson, the teacher is using a type of supplementary materials called _____ to teach key vocabulary. Along with other visuals, these materials are expected to attract students' attention and to aid understanding and retention of vocabulary.

모범답안   realia

19 Fill in the blanks with the ONE most appropriate word from the text. Use the SAME word for the both blanks.

2008년 서울 8번

―――― ⟨Text⟩ ――――

The popular position has long been that the teacher's or syllabus designer's first task is to analyze the target language, that is, what is termed the synthetic approach. In the synthetic syllabus, the learner's role is to synthesize the pieces for use in communication. Synthetic syllabi, together with the corresponding materials, methodology, and classroom pedagogy, lead to lessons with a focus on formS. A growing sense that traditional synthetic syllabi and teaching procedures were not working as they were supposed to, and familiarity with the findings of studies of instructed interlanguage development have led to abandonment of a focus on formS in the L2 classroom in favor of an equally single-minded focus on meaning. The essential claim is that people of all ages learn languages best, inside or outside a classroom, not by treating the languages as an object of study, but by experiencing them as a medium of communication. Language teaching syllabi of this second kind are what is termed analytic. A third approach, which attempts to capture the strengths of an analytic approach while dealing with its limitations, is focus on form. This approach is motivated by the so-called Interaction Hypothesis. Focus on form refers to how focal attentional resources are allocated. Although there are degrees of attention, and although attention to forms and attention to meaning are not always mutually exclusive, during an otherwise meaning-focused classroom lesson, focus on form often consists of an occasional shift of attention to linguistic code features — by the teacher.

―――― ⟨Summary⟩ ――――

Focus on formS isolates linguistic forms to teach one at a time as when language teaching is based on structural syllabus with preselected and sequenced linguistic items. Analytic syllabus aims to improve learners' communicative competence based on _____ in natural environment as in the acquisition of mother tongue. Focus on form concerns how attentional resources are allocated and involves briefly drawing students' attention to linguistic elements in context as they arise incidentally whose overriding focus is on _____ or communication.

모범답안   meaning

20 Read the following and answer the question.

Syllabus A and Syllabus B are the candidates for teaching English to first year middle school students.

Syllabus A

Situations	Structures	Activities
At the park	I am ~ing… He/She is ~ing… They are ~ing…	Repetition drill Dialog memorization Role play

Syllabus B

Topics	Tasks	Strategies
Family	Survey Project Work Information Gap	Metacognitive Cognitive Social/Affective

Identify one syllabus for communication-oriented class and explain two features of the syllabus compared to the other one.

Which of the following is NOT correct about syllabuses <A> and <B>?

① Syllabus A is a type of product-oriented syllabus.
② Syllabus A focuses on predetermined language items.
③ Syllabus A uses communicative activities as the organizing principle.
④ Syllabus B is designed to promote experiential learning.
⑤ Syllabus B focuses on how language is learned rather than what is learned.

문제분석	구분	교과 교육
난이도 ★★☆	평가목표	두 가지 다른 실러버스를 의사소통중심 교실 활동으로 구체적으로 서술하는가?
	채점기준	1점: (Syllabus B) communication-oriented class 1점: 의사소통을 위한 실러버스이다. 1점: 과업을 중심으로 문제해결 활동을 한다. 1점: (Syllabus A) situation syllabus는 미리 정해진 언어 항목을 학습한다.

모범답안 Syllabus B is for communication-oriented class. It promotes communicative and experiential learning, focusing on how language is learned rather than what is learned. It promotes students' discovery work or problem solving with tasks. In contrast, Syllabus A, situation syllabus focuses on predetermined language items. (45 words)

기출문제답안 ③

21 Read the following and answer the question.

2011년 24번

Below are excerpts from two English teachers' syllabuses intended for first-year middle school students.

Teacher (A)

1st lesson	There is…
	There are… (box, blackboard, pen, watch)
2nd lesson	There is not…
	There are not… (basket, button, doll, cap)
3rd lesson	Is there…? / Isn't there…?
	Are there…? / Aren't there…? (dragon, rooster, monster)

Teacher (B)

1st lesson	Greeting
	A: How's it going?
	B: Pretty good.
2nd lesson	Asking about and giving personal information
	A: What's your email address?
	B: It's jane204@koreamail.com.
3rd lesson	Asking for and giving directions
	A: Excuse me, where's the elevator?
	B: It's behind the reception desk.

Identify one syllabus for communication oriented class and explain it with the two purposes of the syllabus. Compare it with the other syllabus with supporting evidence.

Which of the following is a correct statement about the above syllabuses?

① Both syllabuses specify what types of grammatical structures to teach.
② Both syllabuses are sequenced according to frequencies of notions and functions in authentic English.
③ Teacher A's syllabus is based on the belief that grammar points should be taught in a fixed order.
④ Teacher B's syllabus is a combination of lexical and situational syllabuses.
⑤ Teacher B's syllabus is designed to teach grammar and vocabulary explicitly.

문제분석	구분	교과 교육
난이도 ★★☆	평가목표	두 교사가 사용하는 다른 syllabus의 차이점을 이해하고 서술하는가?
	채점기준	1점: (Syllabus A) 문법구조를 명시한다. 1점: 분리된 언어들로 일련의 순서로 연습된다. 1점: (Syllabus B) 의사소통기능을 제시한다. 1점: 어휘와 문법은 묵시적으로 학습된다.

모범답안 Syllabus A specifies the types of grammatical structures. The class aims to practice grammatical forms in a decontextualized pattern with unconnected words in a fixed order. Syllabus B presents communicative functions in real-life. The main objective is the functional, authentic language while grammar and vocabulary are implicitly taught. (48 words)

 ③

22 Read the syllabus and answer the question.

2013년 18번

Syllabus [1]

Topics	Functions	Skills and activities
Friends	Asking about and giving personal information	Listening & Speaking: listen and talk about friends Reading & Writing: read and write about friendship
School	Expressing likes and dislikes; asking about and describing school subjects	Listening & Speaking: listen and talk about school subjects Reading & Writing: read and write about school life

Syllabus [2]

Situations	Grammar	Vocabulary
In the classroom	*Be*: present affirmative *Be*: present interrogative *Be*: negative interrogative	People around you: *friend, stranger, classmate, teacher, student*
At a restaurant	Simple present *Be*: past Regular simple past	Food: *menu, fish, meat, fruit, vegetable*

Choose all and only the correct statements about the syllabus.

ⓐ Syllabus [1] emphasizes performing functions in communicative interactions.
ⓑ In Syllabus [1], skills and activities are aligned with topics.
ⓒ In Syllabus [2], prefabricated phrases are given precedence over individual words.
ⓓ Syllabus [2] is a type of process-oriented syllabus.

문제분석	구분	교과 교육
난이도 ★★☆	평가목표	functional vs situational syllabus의 특성을 잘 비교하는가?
	채점기준	(1) 의사소통안에서 기능수행을 강조하고 주제와 활동이 함께한다. (2) product중심 교수요목으로 상황에서 문법과 어휘를 수업한다.

기출문제답안 ⓐ, ⓑ

23. Read the description of a syllabus and answer the direction.

〈A〉

This syllabus is outcome-based and is adaptive to the changing needs of students, teachers and the community. The focus on outputs rather than on inputs is central to the perspective. It refers to an educational movement that advocates defining educational goals in terms of precise measurable descriptions of the knowledge, skills, and behaviors students should possess at the end of a course of study. It is concerned with the attainment of specified standards rather than with an individual's achievement in relation to a group.

〈B〉

a. Language is functionally analyzed into appropriate parts and subparts.
b. The emphasis in the classroom is placed on listening and reading.
c. Continuous norm-referenced assessment procedures are used.
d. The language skills learners need are accurately predicted or determined.
e. Language learning is broken down into manageable chunks.
f. Outcomes are specified a posteriori based on the learners' knowledge.

Choose all the correct statements about the syllabus of 〈A〉 from the list 〈B〉.

문제분석

구분	교과 교육
평가목표	competency-based syllabus의 특성을 이해하는가?
채점기준	a. 언어를 형태가 아니라 기능중심으로 분석한다. d. 학습자들이 배우는 언어는 미리 정해져있다. e. 언어 학습은 운영 가능한 모음으로 이루어진다.

기출문제답안 a, d, e

24. Read the following three teaching methods and answer the question.

2008년 평가원 28번

(1) In this method, language is viewed as a system of structurally related elements for the encoding of meaning, the elements being phonemes, morphemes, words, structures, and sentence patterns. It is these elements that constitute the learner's task.

(2) This method assumes that the building blocks of language learning and communication are not grammar, functions, or notions, but lexis. It reflects a belief in the centrality of the lexicon to language structure, second language learning, and language use, and in particular to multiword units that are learned and used as single items.

(3) This type of instruction puts tasks at the center of its methodological focus. Language learning is believed to depend on immersing students in tasks that require them to negotiate meaning and engage in naturalistic and meaningful communication.

Identify each teaching syllabus and describe the teaching purposes of each syllabus in terms of language focus in each instruction.

Which of the following is correct?

① (1) places meaning at the center of a task.
② (2) views vocabulary as fillers to the structure of language.
③ (2) promotes students' language learning by using a variety of lexical phrases in context.
④ (3) encourages students to analyze language structure to perform a task.
⑤ (3) stresses the individualistic approach rather than the cooperative one to language learning.

문제분석

난이도 ★★☆

구분	교과 교육
평가목표	각 교실에 사용되는 다양한 교수요목의 종류와 특성을 이해하는가?
채점기준	(1) Structural syllabus: 언어적 항목으로 학습된다. (2) Lexical syllabus: lexical phrase로 학습된다. (3) Task-based syllabus: 협동학습으로 과업을 수행한다.

모범답안

Structural syllabus (1) is to place the linguistic items at the center of a task. Lexical syllabus (2) concentrates on developing lexis to promote language learning by using a variety of lexical phrases in context. Task-based syllabus (3) encourages students to use language to perform a task in cooperative approach rather than individualistic one. (53 words)

25. Read the text and answer the question.

2006년 전국 8번

In the late 1970s, it was widely accepted that the syllabus should focus upon linguistic knowledge and the skills of listening, reading, speaking, and writing, usually in that order. However, research in the social and conversational use of language, coupled with growing dissatisfaction with learners' apparent failure to use the linguistic knowledge outside the classroom which they had gained within it, initiated a major change in syllabus design. Applied linguists advocated a focus upon language use rather than the formal aspects of language. The initial phase of this transition was exemplified in the development of **alternative syllabuses** focusing upon particular purposes of language and how these would be expressed linguistically.

Write down two probable content items in the <u>alternative syllabus</u> above.

모범답안 giving advice, making requests

26. Read the conversation and follow the directions. 【2 points】

2020년 B2번

(*Two teachers are evaluating two textbooks, Textbook A and Textbook B, in order to select the one that their students are going to use next year. This is part of their conversation.*)

T1: So, why don't we start with the first criterion? I went with Textbook A.
T2: May I ask you why?
T1: I think that the illustrations and graphics in Textbook A portray people in the target culture more realistically.
T2: Yeah! Textbook A contains very realistic visuals that can provide our students with cultural information more accurately.
T1: Good! Then, what about the second criterion?
T2: Well, I think Textbook B is the better of the two. I couldn't give Textbook A a good score, because it appears to aim at explicit learning with many contrived examples of the language.
T1: Hmm… could you clarify your point a bit more?
T2: Well, I mean the texts and dialogues in Textbook A are oversimplified.
T1: I had the same impression, but don't you think that they may help our students by focusing their attention on the target features?
T2: You may be right, but I think that such texts might deprive them of the opportunities for acquisition provided by rich texts.
T1: Oh, I see. That's a pretty good point.
T2: So, in my opinion, Textbook B can provide more exposure to language as it is actually used in the real world outside the classroom.
T1: Yeah! From that point of view, Textbook B will be intrinsically more interesting and motivating to our students.
T2: I agree. Okay, then, I think we are ready to move on to the next evaluation criterion.

Note: T = teacher

Fill in the blank with the ONE most appropriate word.

There are many criteria that can be used in textbook evaluation. The teachers, T1 and T2, are mainly focusing on, first, the criterion of reality of visuals and then, the other criterion of _____. In the dialogue, the latter is specifically related to language use shown in the textbooks.

문제분석	구분	교과 교육
난이도 ★★☆	평가목표	교재사용에서 주요한 요소인 authenticity의 중요성을 이해하는가?
	채점기준	교재를 선택하는데 교실밖에서 사용될 수 있는 언어사용을 습득하는 것이 중요하며, 흥미롭고 내적으로 동기부여 될 수 있는 authenticity가 필요하다.

모범답안   authenticity

27 Fill in the blank with TWO words from the passage. 【2 points】

2016년 A7번

Hyun: As an international language, English has many varieties used and taught around the world. Have you ever thought about English varieties?

like it 28 | recommend it 15

Sarah: Yes! There are many varieties of English. Americans, Australians, Brits and Canadians have many variations in how they use English. Naturally, this exists between non-native speakers, too. I think we should be aware of this reality. Many English teachers in the world today are non-native speakers of English. We need to consider this issue for teacher training and language instruction.

Bill: I agree. Although I am a native English teacher, like many of you, we need to recognize the validity of a variety of Englishes, or better known as, _____. These include established outer-circle varieties such as Indian English, Singaporean English and Nigerian English.

Min: Perhaps, but what about standardization? Shouldn't we focus on the clearly understood form of the language for consistency and intelligibility?

Jun: I don't think that is applicable in all cases, Min. The needs and attitudes of students, teachers, and administrators have an influence on the norm or standard adopted for instruction; it is thus best that local norms be respected whenever possible.

모범답안   world Englishes

28 Read the following and answer the questions.

2012년 27번

Below is a reading activity in a high school English class.

1) Mr. Jang introduces the topic of the lesson by showing the class two photos, one with students wearing school uniforms, and the other with students wearing everyday clothes. After that, he asks students if they like wearing uniforms or not.
2) He distributes to each student a school newspaper article on school uniforms and a worksheet.
3) He asks students to form pairs, read it, and take notes. One student from each pair finds and writes down the advantages of uniform from the article and the other student does the same for disadvantages.
4) Students can look up unknown words in the dictionary, or ask their partners or the teacher.
5) Students tell their partners their findings and the partners fill in the information they do not have on the worksheet.
6) Mr. Jang asks students to add their own opinions about the advantages or disadvantages of school uniforms.

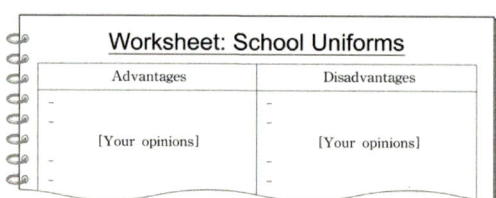

7) Finally, he asks students to debate their opinions with their partners.
8) After the debate, students individually write a paragraph on whether or not they agree with their school policy on uniforms.

Describe how authentic materials are used in language classroom for reading skills and integrated skills with supporting evidence of the activity.

Which of the following is NOT correct about the activity described above?

① Authentic materials are used in the activity.
② Students are encouraged to use integrated skills.
③ Students' previous knowledge is activated in the activity.
④ Argumentative discourse structures are explicitly taught in this activity.
⑤ Personalized writing is included to consolidate what students have learned.

문제분석	구분	교과 교육
난이도 ★★☆	평가목표	읽기수업에서 authentic 자료를 통한 수업 계획표를 분석하고 서술하는가?
	채점기준	1점: 실제자료는 학생들이 활동에 참여할 수 있도록 한다. 1점: 과거 경험을 활용한다. 1점: 4기능이 통합된다. 1점: 개별 글 쓰기로 강화된다.

모범답안   Authentic materials of school newspaper and photos help to get students to be involved. Their previous knowledge is activated by telling their experiences of wearing school uniforms. They develop integrated skills of speaking, reading the material, and taking notes. Argumentative discourse structures are implicitly taught to complete the worksheet. Personalized writing on school policy is to consolidate their learning. (53 words)

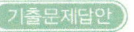 ④

29 Read the passage and follow the directions.

2013년 논술 1번

⟨News Script A⟩

Newscaster: Good evening. Tonight we will report a special story of hope about a teenage boy. He survived a very cold night in a cold store in a butcher shop. The shop is located on 4th Street. The teenage boy was very determined. Tom Hawkins is our reporter. He is now at the butcher shop. Let's talk to him.

Tom: I am inside the cold store at Kwik Butcher Shop. It is very cold inside here. This is Peter Buckle. He is 16 years old. Yesterday he was trapped inside the cold store for ten hours. Peter, how did you feel when you got locked in here?

Peter: At first, I thought it was a joke.

Tom: Oh, I see.

Peter: And then I became very scared. I did not know what to do.

Tom: Were you wearing warm clothes?

Peter: No, I was not wearing warm clothes. So I was very cold.

Tom: Did you sleep while you were locked inside?

Peter: No, I did not sleep. Instead, I ran in place to keep warm.

Newscaster: Wow, Tom. That sounds scary. Now we will go to….

⟨News Script B⟩

Newscaster: Good evening. Tonight we've got a special story of hope about a teenage boy who survived a terribly cold night in a cold store in Kwik Butcher Shop on 4th Street. He survived through sheer will and determination to stay alive. Our reporter on the scene, Tom Hawkins, brings us this story.

Tom: This is what it looks like inside the cold store. As you can see, I'm already shivering, and I've only been inside for three minutes. Joining me now is Peter Buckle, a 16-year-old who was accidentally trapped inside the cold store for over ten long hours when everyone had gone home. Peter, can you tell me how you felt when you first realized you got locked in the cold store?

Peter: Like I'd been had.

Tom: I'm sorry. What?

Peter: You know… I mean, at first I just thought someone's joshing around. So I'm freezing cold but laughing, wondering which guy pulled this.

Tom: And when you realized it wasn't a joke?

Peter: Oh, scared! You kidding me? No any idea what to do… totally panicked and tried to escape…but no windows and no key, so what can I do?

Tom: Were you warmly dressed?

Peter: No, that's the thing. If I had a coat, maybe I could've curled up and been okay. But I wasn't decked out for winter! So I had to think fast.

Tom: So you didn't get any sleep?

> Peter: No, man. No time for sleep. Well, just had to run in place... knew if I dozed off I never gonna wake up. Ran so much my legs burning like fire, but that's what I needed... that kind of warmth.
> Newscaster: Thank you for that, Tom. What an amazing story of perseverance! By the way, Tom....

(1) Identify which script is more authentic and provide TWO reasons for your choice with specific examples from the materials provided.
(2) Discuss TWO criteria for selecting authentic materials to use in a listening class and give your rationale.

문제분석

난이도 ★★★

구분	교과 교육	
평가목표	authentic material를 찾아 그 특징을 서술하고 자료의 기준을 설명하는가?	
채점기준	(1) 실제 자료	(2) 자료 선택의 기준
	1점: Script B가 실제 자료이다. 1점: (어휘적요소) colloquial language and idioms 1점: (문법적요소) ungrammatical with ellipsis	2점: 내용의 적절성이 필요하다. 2점: 수업의 목표에 맞아야 한다.

모범답안

(1) The script B follows the features of an authentic material. First, on the lexical level, more colloquial language and idioms are used, such as 'joshing around', 'doze off' and etc. For another syntactic level, some sentences are ungrammatical with ellipsis of subject or verb, such as 'You kidding me', 'Ran so much...', and etc. (53 words)

(2) As for the criteria, it should satisfy the suitability. The content should be related to the students' needs and interests with their language proficiency. The material should meet with the requirement of course objective. As authentic material aims to improve communicative competence to interact in real life, it should help students use communicative and authentic language. (56 words)

30 Read Mr. Han's materials for his level-differentiated classes, and follow the directions. 【2 points】

2015년 A2번

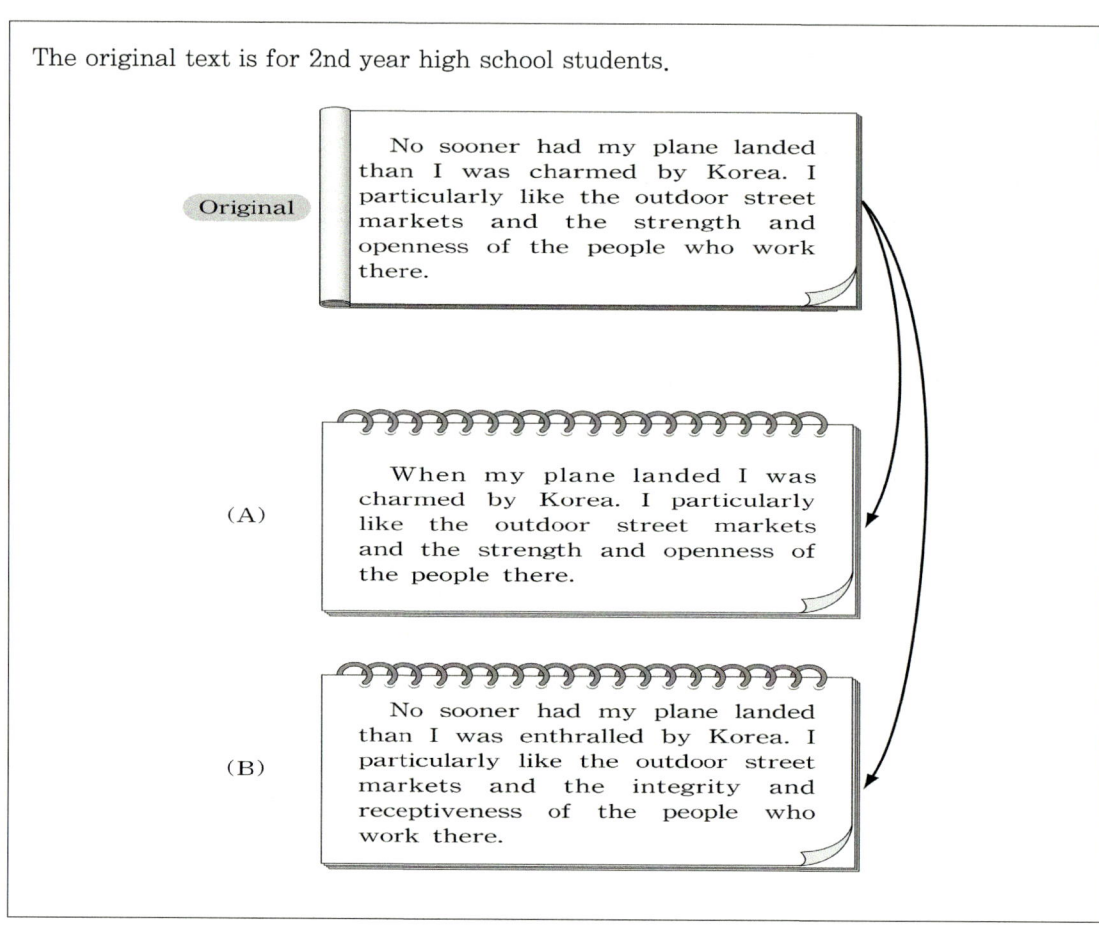

Complete the comments by filling in each blank with ONE word. Write your answers in the correct order.

The original text has been adapted to suit the students' English proficiency levels. (A) shows how input is simplified through ①_____ modification to make the original text easier for the lower level students. (B) shows how input is adapted through ②_____ modification to make the original text more challenging for the upper level students.

모범답안   ① syntactic   ② lexical

31 Read the teacher's log and answer the question.

Mr. Hwang's Teaching Log

I wanted to increase the amount of English in the classroom. To do this, I first investigated how much I used Korean during my teaching. I listened to three tapes recorded at different times over a two-week period just to determine the proportion of English to Korean I was using. It was about 50% English, 50% Korean. I then listened to the tapes again to find out the purposes for which I was using Korean. I found I was using Korean for two main purposes: classroom management and giving feedback. I drew up a plan to reduce the amount of Korean I was using for these two purposes. I first made a list of English expressions commonly used for classroom management and feedback, and familiarized myself with them. I wrote out the expressions on cards, and put them in a conspicuous place on my table. This served to help me remember the expressions I wanted to use. I then continued recording my lessons and after a few weeks checked my tapes. My use of English had increased considerably.

Choose all and only the correct statements about the teaching log.

ⓐ He tried to balance teacher talk and student talk in class.
ⓑ He carried out critical self-examination for professional development.
ⓒ He performed teacher-initiated classroom investigation based on the principles of reflective teaching.
ⓓ He attempted to address the affective dimension of the teaching situation.

기출문제답안 ⓑ, ⓒ

32 Identify the teaching approach of the following.

ⓐ The teacher distributes a handout that has a copy of a sports column from a recent newspaper.
ⓑ The teacher tells the students to underline the report's predictions and to say which ones they think the reporter feels most certain of and which he feels least certain of.
ⓒ The teacher gives the students the directions for the activity in the target language, and the students try to state the report's predictions in different words.
ⓓ The students unscramble the sentences of the newspaper article, and they play a language game. The students are asked how they feel about the predictions.
ⓔ A student makes an error. The teacher and other students ignore it. The teacher gives each group of students a strip story and a task to perform.

모범답안   Communicative Language Teaching

33 Identify the teaching approach of the following.

ⓐ The introduction of authentic texts into the learning situation.
ⓑ The provision of opportunities for learners to focus, not only on language but also on the learning process itself.
ⓒ An enhancement of the learner's own personal experiences as important contributing elements to classroom learning.
ⓓ An attempt to link classroom language learning with language activation outside the classroom.

모범답안   Communicative Language Teaching

memo

CHAPTER 03 영어평가

01 Read the conversation and the passage, and follow the directions. [2 points]
2025년 A4번

⟨A⟩

(Two teachers, Mr. Lee and Ms. Kim, recently scored students' speaking assessments. They later discussed the scoring process and Mr. Lee reflected on his scoring experiences in his journals.)

Mr. Lee: As I was reviewing my ratings, I noticed that they were staying consistent throughout the scoring process.

Ms. Kim: Good, it's actually hard to keep the same perspective when grading multiple students. But you mean you found actual similarities in your scores for the same students over time?

Mr. Lee: Yes, exactly. I think I might have benefitted from reviewing my previous scores before re-evaluating anyone's performance to see if I'm staying consistent.

Ms. Kim: That makes sense. You know, I've noticed that we have some scoring differences between us on certain criteria.

Mr. Lee: Right. I normally give a score of 10 if students have natural flow even though they may demonstrate some errors in grammar or vocabulary. How about you?

Ms. Kim: Oh, I've constantly made efforts to adhere to our scoring criteria, and I give a perfect score only when they speak without any errors or hesitation.

Mr. Lee: All right. Now I can see why we have different scoring results and it makes me think—these different results could send mixed messages to students.

Ms. Kim: I agree. Let's review our criteria and stick to following our rubric.

Mr. Lee: Sure. That would be fairer for the students.

― ⟨B⟩ ―

Mr. Lee's Reflective Journal

After today's grading session, I reviewed my scores and luckily noticed consistency in my ratings for the same students across different sessions. However, after talking with Ms. Kim, I realized that we provided different scores for the same students. I'm concerned this could lead to some confusion if they receive different scores based on which teacher assesses them. I think it would be helpful if Ms. Kim and I could go over the rubric together to ensure a more unified scoring approach.

Fill in the blank with the TWO most appropriate words.

Based on ⟨A⟩ and ⟨B⟩, Mr. Lee is concerned about the lack of _____ _____ in the scoring process. His concern is not about the consistency of rating by a single rater but about the consistency of rating by different raters.

문제분석	구분	교과 교육
난이도 ★☆☆	평가목표	수업의 개선영역과 부족한 영역을 구체적으로 잘 이해하는가?
	채점기준	두 교사의 점수를 주는 방법에 대한 논의과정을 통해 수행평가를 실시할 때 두 채점자의 일관성있는 점수가 나오기 위해서는 inter-rater reliability가 필요함을 이해할 수 있다.
모범답안	inter-rater reliability	

02 Read the conversation and follow the directions. 【2 points】

(T1 is the head teacher, and T2 is teaching English writing this semester at the school.)

T1: Good morning, Mr. Lee. How are your writing classes going?
T2: Good morning, Ms. Park. They're going well, but I find scoring students' writing quite challenging.
T1: What makes you say that?
T2: I rated my students' writing assignments last night. But when I look at them today, I feel I would give different scores.
T1: Why do you think that happened?
T2: Well, I'm pretty sure it was because I was doing it late at night. I think I was too tired.
T1: Mmm.... I don't grade my students' writing assignments when I'm tired. That way, I can avoid being inconsistent. I just put them away until the next day.
T2: I bet that would be very helpful with keeping scoring reliable.
T1: Yeah, it helps.
T2: Another issue is that over time, I tend to stray from the rating criteria. I need to find a way to stick to it for consistency in scoring.
T1: Well, why don't you go back every once in a while and check the last few essays you've marked to see that you're still following the rating criteria?
T2: That's a good idea. It'll help keep me on track.
T1: Exactly.
T2: Thanks for your advice.

Note: T = teacher

Fill in the blank with the ONE most appropriate word.

Teacher 1, the head teacher, is giving advice on the issue of _____ reliability that Teacher 2 is facing when scoring students' writing.

모범답안   intrarater (intra-rater)

03 Read the passage and follow the directions. [2 points]

2014년 A7번

At a high school English writing contest, contestants were given the instructions in the box and completed their compositions.

> Listen to a taped radio interview of Barbara Carrel, a famous writer, about her adventure to Africa. While listening, take notes. Then using the notes, write a story about her adventure. You will be given 30 minutes to complete the story.

Each contestant's composition was evaluated by two English teachers using the same rating scale. Below is part of the two teachers' scoring results.

Ratings of Contestants' Compositions

Students	Criteria	Teacher A	Teacher B
Giho Lim	Content	2	5
	Organization	1	4
	Vocabulary	3	4
	Grammar	2	5
Bomi Cho	Content	3	1
	Organization	5	2
	Vocabulary	4	2

Note: 1 = lowest ↔ 5 = highest

Complete the comments on the situation above by filling in each blank with ONE word. Write your answers in the correct order.

> The procedure used in the contest exemplifies ___①___ testing in terms of the number of skills assessed. One potential problem with the scoring process is low ___②___ reliability, which is most likely due to the subjectivity of the raters.

모범답안   ① integrative   ② interrater

04 Read the passage in ⟨A⟩ and the teacher's reflection log in ⟨B⟩, and follow the directions. 【4 points】

2025년 A9번

⟨A⟩

Mr. Jeong, an English teacher, was tasked with evaluating speaking assessment items in his students' final exam. Reviewing key principles of speaking assessment, he noted the following:

- ✓ Clarity: Prompts should be straightforward to avoid confusion.
- ✓ Authenticity: Speaking tasks should mirror real-life communication, enabling students to demonstrate natural language use.
- ✓ Integrated Skills Assessment: Tasks should assess speaking alongside other skills, such as listening comprehension, to reflect communicative performance.
- ✓ Practicality: Test items should be feasible and manageable in terms of the time spent in assessment.

⟨B⟩

Teacher's Reflection Log

After reviewing the items, I felt that the two items had some good and bad points. Item 1 asked students to describe a memorable experience that they had with a friend, including details such as when it happened, what they did, and why it was memorable. After observing students' responses, I realized that this item resembled a conversation topic in real-life contexts. However, I regret that I didn't set time limits for the item and it took too much time to score it, which made the assessment difficult to manage. For Item 2, after looking at a picture of a busy street, students were asked to describe what they saw. Most of the students did very well on this task because the item clearly described what sort of response was desired. I think this item was effective in assessing pronunciation, one of the criteria for assessing speaking skills. However, next time I want to add some more items such as asking students to listen to a short audio and discuss their opinions. It might be more challenging but I believe I can assess multiple skills in the test.

Based on ⟨A⟩, identify the speaking assessment principles applied in Item 1 and Item 2 in ⟨B⟩, respectively. Then, explain how each principle was applied in each item with evidence from ⟨B⟩.

문제분석 난이도 ★★★	구분	교과 교육
	평가목표	말하기 평가 항목에서 활용하는 항목을 구체적으로 서술하는가?
	채점기준	1점: Authenticity 1점: 학생의 반응이 실제 경험으로 서술한다. 1점: Clarity 1점: task의 설명이 명확하여 어떤 응답이 나와야 할지 명확하다.

모범답안 Authenticity was applied to Item 1. The students' responses were related to their experience with a friend in real-life context. Clarity was applied to Item 2. The description of task item was so clear that students understood what response types that they were expected to make. (46 words)

05 Read the following and answer the question.

2012년 26번

Below is part of an interview of Mr. Yu, a high school English teacher in charge of a special program for teaching on-and off-line English writing.

I: What do you think is the most important role of a teacher?
T: Well, I think the main job of a teacher is to get students to be able to work on their own. I try to step back and let my students take more responsibility for their learning.
I: But what if students are having difficulties, say, in writing?
T: Well, when they're unsure of something, they can run it through a concordancer so that they can look up authentic examples of language patterns. They can also use some of the examples in their writing.
I: Do students ever complain that you don't interact enough with them?
T: But I do interact with them in other ways. For example, I interact online through discussion forums. Students upload their writings onto the forum on a regular basis, then I look over their writings and comment on the forum. I also give feedback via email.
I: What if students want immediate feedback from you?
T: Normally I use chat rooms. Also, I give feedback during regular class time.
I: Do you ever use technology for assessment?
T: Yes, but it's pretty basic. We're hoping to get some computer testing software that adjusts the questions depending on students' performance on previous test items.
I: Thank you for the interview.

Note: I = interviewer, T = teacher

Identify the type of writing approach that is implemented. Identify the type of test that the teacher wants to implement. Explain the reasons with evidence related to computer technology.

Which of the following is NOT true according to the interview above?
① Students can check the use of language with corpus data.
② Computer adaptive writing testing is not available at the school.
③ The teacher promotes blended learning to teach English writing.
④ Students engage in behaviorisitc activities to learn language patterns.
⑤ Students learn to write through synchronous and asynchronous communication.

문제분석 난이도 ★★★	구분	교과 교육
	평가목표	ICT를 활용한 읽기 수업에 대한 다양한 접근방식을 구체적으로 서술하는가?
	채점기준	1점: Blended learning이다. 1점: 토론이나 이메일로 쓰기를 배운다. 1점: CAT시험이 시행되어야 한다. 1점: 학습자레벨에 맞추어 조정되는 시험어어야 한다.

모범답안   Blended learning is used to teach English writing by combining writing with computer technology. Students learn to write through discussion forums or emails. The teacher wants to implement computer adaptive writing testing. The test could be adjusted to students' levels to fit their own proficiency. (45 words)

 ④

06 Read the passages and follow the directions. 【4 points】

2023년 B11번

─────────── 〈A〉 ───────────

A high school English teacher, Mr. Choi, wanted to learn how to write selected-response items (e.g., multiple-choice items) more efficiently. He wrote several items before the workshop began, and found some of them were flawed according to the guidelines he learned during the workshop. The following are some of the guidelines along with examples of flawed items.

General Guidelines for Writing Selected-response Items
① Make certain that there is only one, clearly correct answer.
② State both the stem and the options as simply and directly as possible.
③ Present a single clearly formulated problem to avoid mixed content.
④ Avoid negative wording whenever possible. If it is absolutely necessary to use a negative stem, highlight the negative word.

Item 1
My forehead itches every day during the summer. Using sunscreen hasn't helped much. I think I'd better go to the _____ to get my skin checked.
a. dentist
b. optometrist
c. pediatrician
→ d. dermatologist

Item 2
Where did Henry go after the party last night?
a. Yes, he did.
b. Because he was tired.
→ c. To Kate's place for another party.
? d. He went home around eleven o'clock.

Item 3
I never knew where _____.
a. had the boys gone
→ b. the boys had gone
c. the boys have gone
d. have the boys gone

Item 4
According to the passage, which of the following is not true?
a. My sister likes outdoor sports.
b. My brother is busy with his plans.
→ c. My sister and I often do everything together.
d. My brother is more energetic and outgoing than I.

Note: '→' indicates the key; '?' indicates a possible answer.

⟨B⟩

After the workshop, to improve the quality of the items, the teacher revised some items according to the guidelines. The following are the revised items.

Item 1
I think I'd better go to the _____ to get my skin checked.
a. dentist
b. optometrist
c. pediatrician
→ d. dermatologist

Item 2
Where did Henry go after the party last night?
a. Yes, he did.
b. Because he was tired.
c. It was about eleven o'clock.
→ d. To Kate's place for another party.

Item 3
I never knew _____.
a. where had the boys gone
→ b. where the boys had gone
c. the boys where had gone
d. the boys had gone where

Item 4
According to the passage, which of the following is NOT true?
a. My sister likes outdoor sports.
b. My brother is busy with his plans.
→ c. My sister and I often do everything together.
d. My brother is more energetic and outgoing than I.

Based on ⟨A⟩, identify the ONE most appropriately revised item in ⟨B⟩ according to guideline ②, and the ONE most appropriately revised item according to guideline ③. Then, explain each of the items with evidence from ⟨A⟩ and ⟨B⟩.

문제분석	구분	교과 교육
난이도 ★★☆	평가목표	다지선다형의 항목의 타당도를 구체적으로 서술하는가?
	채점기준	(Guideline 2) Item 1: 질문을 명확하게 하기 위해서 본 문제를 간략하게 한다. (Guideline 3) Item 3: 평가하고자 하는 요소 'where'가 명확하게 나타난다.
모범답안		For guideline 2, Item 1 is revised. The teacher revises the stem as simple and direct to make the question clear. For Guideline 3, Item 3 is revised, one clear problem about what to evaluate is formulated by putting 'where' in the options. (43 words)

07 Read ⟨A⟩ and ⟨B⟩ and answer the question. 【4 points】

2013년 25번

⟨A⟩

The following are guidelines for constructing multiple choice items to assess knowledge of word meanings:

1. Make sure there is only one correct answer for each item.
2. Make sure the distractors are the same grammatical class as the key.
3. Do not provide inadvertent clues to the key which allow students to answer an item correctly without knowledge of word meanings.
4. Make sure the key cannot be selected based on students' world knowledge.

⟨B⟩

Below are some examples of multiple-choice items that are intended to measure students' knowledge of word meanings.

Choose the one that best fits in each blank.

a. I want to be a poet. I have had an _____ in writing poems, since I was a child.
   ① interest   ② doubt   ③ concern   ④ worry

b. I was hungry, so I went home _____ to eat dinner.
   ① run   ② rate   ③ quickly   ④ rapid

c. I usually go to the dentist to have my teeth _____ once a year.
   ① examined   ② checked   ③ seen   ④ fixed

d. Inventors are always coming up with new ideas because they are very _____.
   ① creative   ② sad   ③ lazy   ④ guilty

e. When tourists from Seoul go to Jeju on vacation, they travel _____.
   ① north   ② west   ③ east   ④ south

Choose all the items in ⟨B⟩ that do NOT fit with the guidelines. ⟨A⟩ and explain the rationale why they are not appropriate to construct multiple choice items.

문제분석 난이도 ★★☆	구분	교과 교육
	평가목표	multiple-choice items 제작시 유의해야 할 점을 이해하는가?
	채점기준	1점: Item a는 guideline 3와 맞지 않는다. 예상치 않은 단서가 제공된다. 1점: Item b는 guideline 2와 맞지 않는다. 품사가 일정하지 않다. 1점: Item c는 guideline 1와 맞지 않는다. 정답이 하나 이상 존재한다. 1점: Item e는 guideline 4와 맞지 않는다. 제주의 위치는 영어능력이 아니다.

모범답안   Item a. does not fit with guideline 3, as the given clue 'an' is an advertent clue. Item b. does not fit with guideline 2, as quickly is an adverb and the other distractors are all verb. Item c. does not fit with guideline 1, as there are more than one correct answer. Item e. does not fit with guideline 4, as the location of Jeju is world knowledge. (55 words)

08 Read the passage and follow the directions.

2006년 서울 10번

> Multiple-choice questions are often constructed in a way that makes it difficult to have valid score interpretation. In other words, it is not clear whether the questions indeed measure skills or knowledge the item writer intended to measure. Consider the item below.
>
> > *Choose the one word that best completes the sentence.*
> >
> > Charlie is always late for school, so his mother is going to buy an ………… clock for him.
> >
> > a. ring b. alarm c. morning d. bell
>
> In the example above, the item writer intended to find out whether the test taker knows the meaning of *alarm* and whether he or she knows this word best fits the context semantically. However, a clue to the correct answer is provided by the indefinite article *an* in the stem; *an* is always followed by a word that begins with a vowel, and *alarm* is the only alternative that begins with a vowel.

Fill in the blanks with the ONE most appropriate word from the passage.

> In constructing multiple-choice questions, item writers should avoid a(n) ………… that provides an unintended clue to the right answer if they want to make score interpretation valid.

모범답안 stem

09 Read the passage and follow the directions.

2005년 전국 17번

(1) Item Type Ⅰ

* 다음 문장의 밑줄 친 단어와 의미가 비슷한 단어를 고르시오.
Jack was <u>dismayed</u> when he heard about the new plans.
① interested   ② happy   ③ disappointed   ④ optimistic

(2) Item Type Ⅱ

* 다음 문장의 빈칸에 들어갈 알맞은 단어를 고르시오.
Jack was ……………… when he heard about the new plans.
① interested   ② happy   ③ disappointed   ④ optimistic

(3) Item Type Ⅲ

* 다음 대화문의 빈칸에 들어갈 알맞은 단어를 고르시오.
A: Jack was ……………… when he heard about the new plans.
B: Really? His proposal must have been turned down.
① interested   ② happy   ③ disappointed   ④ optimistic

Fill out the blanks in summary from ⟨word list⟩.

⟨Summary⟩

Item Ⅰ has been a conventional method to measure vocabulary knowledge. However, replacing the underlined word (Item Ⅰ) with the blank (Item Ⅱ) shows that all choices can be correct answers. There is the inherent problem with Item Ⅰ that the test taker can get the item correctly (1)_____. Item Ⅱ requires the test taker (2)_____ to answer the question. Item Ⅲ demonstrates that the problem of all choices being correct answers can be easily solved (3)_____ through the task.

⟨word list⟩

- to refer to the context
- without the context
- by providing more meaningful context

모범답안
(1) without the context
(2) to refer to the context
(3) by providing more meaningful context

10 Read the passage and follow the directions. 【2 points】

2023년 A4번

A test taker is sitting in front of a computer, examining some sample items, and quickly learns how to take computer-based tests. Meanwhile, a computer program begins to 'guess' his ability level, and keeps trying to 'match' the test with his current language ability. This is how this technique works. The computer program usually begins by showing an item of moderate difficulty, for example, an item that the test taker has a fifty percent chance of getting right. If he gets this item right, the computer program reestimates his ability level in real time and shows either an item of equal difficulty or a slightly more challenging item. If the test taker gets his first item wrong, however, the computer program will show either an item of equal or slightly lesser difficulty. The test taker keeps taking the test until, for instance, he gets several items wrong in a row. To put it another way, the computer program repeats its matching work until it collects enough information to determine the test taker's current English ability level.

Fill in the blank with the THREE most appropriate words.

The testing procedure described above enables us to make more individualized and educationally useful tests. It can also provide test takers with a better test-taking experience with fewer items, and with increased precision. This testing procedure is commonly referred to as _____.

문제분석	구분	교과 교육
난이도 ★★☆	평가목표	컴퓨터를 이용한 평가의 종류를 파악하고 이해하는가?
	채점기준	CAT는 학생의 언어 능력을 정확하게 평가하고 개별적인 학습 경험을 제공하는 유용한 도구로 활용되어, 효과적인 언어 교육과 평가를 지원할 수 있다.
모범답안	computer adaptive testing	

11 Read the conversation and follow the directions. 【2 points】

2024년 A1번

> T1: Ms. Park, I hear that the provincial office of education is going to implement an Internet-based interactive English speaking test next year. What do you think?
> T2: I think they're going in the right direction.
> T1: But, you know, I'm not sure if we have enough human and material resources at the moment.
> T2: Right. In order to develop such a large-scale test, we need to have test writers, raters, and item banks.
> T1: Well, how would the office of education prepare for this in the short time available?
> T2: The good news is that they're going to roll out pilot testing next month, starting with a small number of voluntary schools.
> T1: Oh, I see. But I'm still wondering how they'll secure the resources necessary for full implementation.
> T2: It seems they're going to recruit staff and technicians for the test centers while completing several preliminaries.
> T1: Good. I guess in the mean time they can train teachers to write test items in order to construct the item banks.
> T2: Right. I also heard the office of education has already laid out solid plans for that.
> T1: That's good to know. Then we'll be able to measure students' English speaking ability more effectively from next year.
> T2: For sure. It's a step forward for all of us working in English education.
>
> *Note*: T = teacher

Fill in the blank with the ONE most appropriate word.

> In the above conversation, the two teachers talk about feasibility in the process of developing a large-scale test. The issues they discuss are related to one of the principles of language assessment or test usefulness, which is technically called _____.

모범답안   practicality

12. Read a teacher's and a student's journal entries and follow the directions. 【2 points】

2022년 A1번

Ms. Ahn's Journal

I think I need to change my approach to teaching speaking skills. In my conversation class, I usually have my students listen to dialogues and then practice the main expressions using pattern drills, which I thought would help them speak with both accuracy and fluency. However, when I assessed their speaking performance last week, most students had difficulties speaking fluently. They frequently had long pauses in their speech, but were quite accurate. In order to address this issue, I'm going to add more fluency activities such as discussion, role-plays, and information-gap activities.

Nayun's Journal

Today, I got my final exam results. Compared to the mid-term exam, my score has improved a lot. I'm very proud of myself because I studied a lot for the test. My English teacher usually includes lots of reading comprehension questions on exams, so this time I read all the reading texts in the textbook multiple times and took many practice tests. However, I'm a bit disappointed with the test in a way. I really want to improve my English writing skills, but I just don't have time to practice them. Well… I don't know…. I want to change how I'm studying, but I can't give up on getting good English test scores.

Fill in the blank with the ONE most appropriate word.

The above two journal entries demonstrate _____ effect in that the teacher and the student each write about what they do for their teaching and studying with regard to tests.

모범답안 washback

13 Fill out the underlined blank with assessment principle.

There are many different steps a teacher can take to create effective classroom tests, so many that a whole course in language testing is strongly urged, especially for novice teachers. In the meantime, just one among many considerations that you, as a teacher, might make in the design of classroom tests is to think of a test as a form of _____. In other words, your tests are not just a necessary evil in classroom bureaucracy but, rather are important means for building the competence, autonomy, and self-evaluation among your students.

모범답안   washback

14 Read the students' complaints about three different tests and answer the question.

(1) Minju: My teacher included too many questions about material that she had not dealt with in class. When she made the exam, I think she used other textbooks that she did not teach from.

(2) Guri: We are middle school students, but the exam looked like one that high school students normally take. The printing was too small, and we had to read five pages in one hour. I really hated it.

(3) Hyuna: Let me talk about our listening test. Most of the questions were dictation questions. We even had to write a full paragraph for one question. The teacher said it was for measuring our listening skills. But it seemed like a writing test rather than a listening test.

Write down the type of validity applied for each student's complaint.

모범답안   (1) content validity   (2) face validity   (3) construct validity

15 Read the passage and follow the directions. 【4 points】

A high school teacher wanted to develop a test in order to assess his students' English reading ability. He developed the test based on the following procedures:

• Step 1: Construct Definition
He started by clarifying what his test was intended to measure. He defined the construct of his English test as the ability to infer meanings from a given reading passage.

• Step 2: Designing Test Specifications
According to the construct definition in Step 1, he specified the test as consisting of a total of 20 multiple-choice items: 1) 10 items asking test-takers to infer meanings and fill in the blank with the most appropriate words or phrases (i.e., Fill-in-the-Blank), and 2) 10 items for finding the best order of scrambled sentences (i.e., Unscrambling).

• Step 3: Developing Test Items & Piloting
He finished item development. He piloted the test to examine whether the items had satisfactory test qualities.

• Step 4: Analyzing Item Facility & Item Discrimination
He analyzed item difficulty. To increase internal consistency, he removed the items with a high value of item discrimination.

• Step 5: Analyzing Reliability & Validity
Reliability was assessed by Cronbach's coefficient alpha. To investigate the concurrent validity of the test, he asked his colleagues to review the test items based on the test specifications.

• Step 6: Administering the Test
After making the necessary revisions, he administered the test to his students.

Based on the passage above, identify TWO steps out of the six that have a problem in the process of test development. Then, support your answers with evidence from the passage. Do NOT copy more than FOUR consecutive words from the passage.

문제분석	구분	교과 교육
난이도 ★★☆	평가목표	평가의 기본원리와 item analysis를 통해 평가의 문제점을 서술하는가?
	채점기준	1점: (Step 4) 1점: 높은 수치의 ID는 내적 일관성에 좋은 수치이므로 유지되어야 한다. 1점: (Step 5) 1점: 동시간 타당도는 다른 종류의 시험간에 일어나는 타당도이다.

모범답안 Step 4 has a problem. High figure of item discrimination represents a high level of internal consistency, so the items should not be removed. Step 5 has a problem. Concurrent validity can be measured against other similar tests at the same time rather than based on the specifications. (49 words)

16 Examine part of a test evaluation checklist about the test, and follow the directions. 【4 points】

2016년 A13번

Mr. Kim, a head teacher of high school English, wanted to evaluate the achievement test of English reading in order to find to what extent the five major principles of language assessment (practicality, reliability, validity, authenticity, and washback) were applied to the test.

TEST EVALUATION CHECKLIST

Test-takers: 2nd year high school students

Content	Scale 1	Scale 2	Scale 3
Subjectivity does not enter into the scoring process.	☐	☐	■
Classroom conditions for the test are equal for all students.	☐	☐	■
Test measures exactly what it is supposed to measure.	■	☐	☐
Items focus on previously practiced in-class reading skills.	■	☐	☐
Topics and situations are interesting.	☐	☐	■
Tasks replicate, or closely approximate, real-world tasks.	☐	☐	■

Note: 1=poor, 2=average, 3=good

Post-Exam Reflection

I studied really hard for the test because I wanted to move to a higher level class. But I got 76 and I was so disappointed. Since there were no errors in scoring, my score was dependable, I think. The topics were very relevant to my real life. But what was the problem? Did I use the wrong study skills? Actually I was very surprised when I first saw the test. Lots of tasks were very unfamiliar and I believe I've never done those kinds of tasks in class. Furthermore, after the test I actually expected the teacher to go over the test and give advice on what I should focus on in the future. It never happened. No feedback or comments from the teacher were given. I was not sure which items I got wrong. I will have the same type of test next semester and I'm not sure how I can improve my reading skills and get a better grade.

Identify TWO well-applied principles and TWO poorly-applied principles among the five principles of language assessment stated above based on all the data. Then support each of your choices with details from the post-exam reflection ONLY.

문제분석	구분	교과 교육
난이도 ★★☆	평가목표	영어평가원리에서 잘 이루어지는 것과 원리를 구별하여 구체적으로 서술하는가?
	채점기준	1점: (reliability) 오류없이 지속적이다. 1점: (authenticity) 실제 생활과 관련이 있다. 1점: (validity) 수업시간의 과제와 관련이 없다. 1점: (washback) 조언이나 피드백이 없어 다음 수업에 활용하기 어렵다.

모범답안 Two well-applied principles are reliability and authenticity. The scoring process is dependable without errors and topics are related to real-world. Two poorly-applied principles are validity and washback. The test tasks are unfamiliar that they practiced in class. Students have difficulty improving their further study since no advice or feedback is provided. (51 words)

17 Read the following and answer the question.

> The six essential components of the test usefulness include reliability, construct validity, authenticity, interactiveness, impact, and practicality. The following is the four essential components focusing on the test and the test taker's language ability.
>
> The first component, reliability, is defined as consistency of measurement. It can be considered to be a function of the consistency of test scores. The second one, construct validity, is related to the meaningfulness and appropriateness of the interpretations that we make on the basis of test scores. In interpreting scores from language tests as indicators of the test taker's language ability, we need to demonstrate or justify the validity of the interpretations or inferences we make of test scores.
>
> The third one, authenticity, is related to the conventional concept of content validity in that it can be defined as the degree of correspondence of the characteristics of a given language test task to the features of a target language use task. It is a critical quality of language tests as it enables language test developers to demonstrate that performance on language tests corresponds to language use in specific domains other than the language test itself.
>
> The fourth one, interactiveness, is defined as the extent and type of involvement of the test taker's individual characteristics (i.e., language ability, topical knowledge, and affective schemata) in accomplishing a test task. The interactiveness of a given language test task represents the ways in which the test taker's areas of language ability are engaged by the test task.

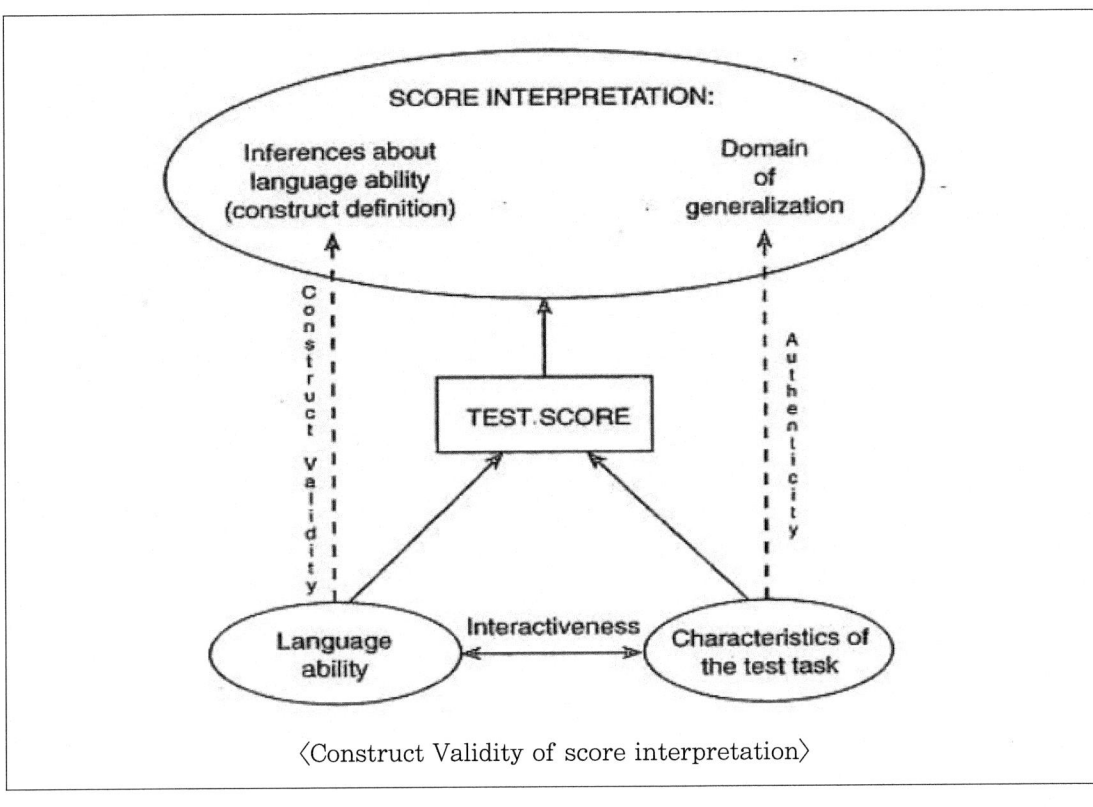

⟨Construct Validity of score interpretation⟩

Put the most appropriate term of test principle to fit in each blank from the passage.

모범답안 　(1) construct validity 　(2) interactiveness 　(3) authenticity

18 Read the passage and follow the directions. 【4 points】

2017년 A9번

Mr. Lee wants to determine how well the scores from the College Entrance Exam (CEE) predict academic success in college. The scatter plot below includes high school seniors' CEE scores from 2014 and their college Grade Point Averages (GPAs) in the fall of 2016. Their CEE scores are placed on the horizontal axis and their college GPAs on the vertical axis.

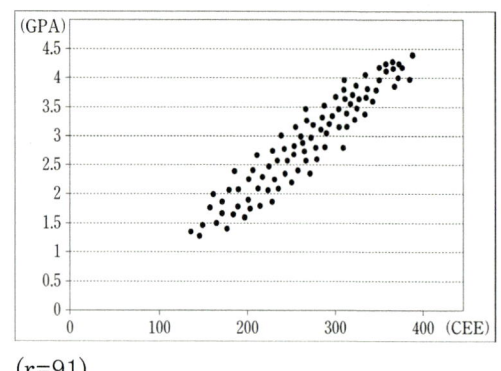

Students	CEE (Fall 2014)	GPA (Fall 2016)
A	389	4.43
B	246	2.58
C	304	3.15
D	322	3.27
E	211	2.10
F	328	3.62
G	314	3.18
H	288	2.83
I	372	4.00
J	368	3.85
⋮	⋮	⋮

(r=91)

Note: r = correlation coefficient

Based on the information in the passage, identify the type of validity within the context of criterion-related validation and explain it with evidence.

문제분석	구분	교과 교육
난이도 ★★★	평가목표	타당도의 종류를 선택하여 표의 내용을 구체적으로 서술하는가?
	채점기준	1점: predictive validity를 의미한다. 1점: 이전의 시험과 미래의 수행도를 예측한다. 1점: CEE와 GPA 점수가 밀접하게 관련되어 있다. 1점: 입학시험이 미래의 수행도를 긍정적으로 반영한다.

모범답안 The information indicates predictive validity because the result of the previous exam predicts the students' future performance. The students' CEE scores are closely related to GPA scores in the college. It means that the entrance exam positively reflects the students' future performance scores in the college. (46 words)

19 Read the passage and follow the directions.

2006년 전국 21번 | 2005년 서울 22번

(1) A middle school teacher gave an open-ended essay test as part of performance assessment for a formative purpose. Concerned that he might not have given marks to all the essays in a consistent manner, he decided to ask a colleague to mark the essays and compare the scores with his.

(2) In a listening and speaking class, a teacher covered a unit on greetings and exchanges that includes discourse for asking for personal information with some form-focus on the verb 'to be', personal pronouns, and question formation. The following week the teacher gave a test to find out how much her students had learned over the last week. It turned out, however, that most of the test items focused on how to use modals to make a polite request.

Choose a correct type of testing situation from the list.

⟨Word list⟩

| inter-rater reliability | construct validity | intra-rater reliability |
| content validity | split-half reliability | concurrent validity |

모범답안   (1) inter-rater reliability   (2) content validity

20 Read the passage and follow the directions.

A third-grade high school English teacher, Ms. Park, wanted to diagnose students' speaking ability and decided to use picture description as a performance assessment in her class. Ms. Park developed a scoring rubric and rating scales to evaluate students' performances. Then students were given a series of pictures and asked to describe them for three minutes as fully as possible. However, her head teacher, Ms. Yoon, commented on the initial scoring rubric and Ms. Park revised it. The following are pictures, transcripts of two students' picture descriptions, and Ms. Park's initial and revised scoring rubrics in tables.

〈Pictures〉

〈Speech Transcripts〉

〈Jitae〉

A family of three, uh, playing badminton.. erm.. on beautiful sunny day. It also look like, uh, they have set up, set up a tent and picnic in mountains. Wh.. Whi.. While they are away playing badminton, a e:r the:: dog, maybe a st.. st.. stray:: dog find their picnic and steal some food. The dog, dog runs away with a (0.8) sandwich in mouth. As soon as they come back to the camp site::, the family shocked to see the picnic, well, you know, ruined. He is:: hmm.. they obviously had, hmm, no idea what is going on. Then, after (1.2) packing up, I think, they head home? or motel, I mean, a place to stay. You can see people have, like, depressing:: erm depressed faces. To make things:: worse, it is getting dark. Th.. The.. Their car is still in the mountains.

〈Mina〉

I, er, I see happy family. hmm.. Father? Son? Some people:: people are playing (3.1) outside, at ground. Two e:r children:: playing with something like b.. ball. Big guy look at a boy and girl:: He is sitting on the chair. Oh, there is animal, one animal (2.4) a (2.0) dog or? (3.8) A big tent is open. It come in the mountain, oh from:: the mountain? and run to the home. And dog try, tries to get some food and e:r eating that later. They are very (3.2) su.. sur.. surprised. Girl is angry. They? are angry. They have nothing to eat (2.9) no sandwiches or kimbab for the camping? He want to go home soon. It is dark e:r outside. (0.5) They take the.. the.. their car and are:: going back.

* Transcription Convention:
(0.8) – Interval between utterances (in seconds); e:r, the:: – Lengthening of the preceding sound

◉ Table 1 : Ms. Park's <u>Initial</u> Scoring Rubric

	Jitae			Mina		
	Excellent	Good to Fair	Needs Work	Excellent	Good to Fair	Needs Work
Pronunciation	○			○		
Grammatical Accuracy		○			○	

◉ Table 2 : Ms. Park's <u>Revised</u> Scoring Rubric

	Jitae			Mina		
	Excellent	Good to Fair	Needs Work	Excellent	Good to Fair	Needs Work
Pronunciation	○			○		
Grammatical Accuracy		○			○	
Fluency					○	
Cohesion	○					
Vocabulary	○				○	

(1) ⟨Table 1⟩ has a problem regarding the principle of validity. Among content, construct, criterion, and face validity, select the one that is under the greatest threat; explain why it has a problem. (2) Two ratings are missing in ⟨Table 2⟩. Write your ratings of their performances based on the transcripts along with a specific example.

모범답안

(1) The test result in ⟨Table 1⟩ has a problem in construct validity. The test cannot demonstrate an association between the test result and overall English language proficiency in communication. The test criteria includes only 'pronunciation' and 'grammatical accuracy', which does not reflect the students' communicative competence. (47 words)

(2) For the missing ratings, 'Excellent' for 'Fluency' and 'Good to fair' for 'Cohesion'. Jitae is a fluent speaker with less hesitations and more facilitating devices of 'I mean', and 'well'. He self-corrects and uses appropriate cohesion markers. Mina displays low discourse competence without any cohesion markers to connect the sentences in time order. She uses incorrect reference words, 'they' or 'he'. (61 words)

21. Read the passage in ⟨A⟩ and the tests in ⟨B⟩, and follow the directions. 【4 points】

2022년 B10번

⟨A⟩

Mr. Lee and Ms. Min are both middle school English teachers for 1st graders, but their students' English writing proficiency is quite different from each other. The two teachers have developed tests to assess their students' abilities to write using comparatives and superlatives as the target forms.

Mr. Lee's Assessment Note
- I taught my students to write simple sentences using comparatives and superlatives and provided sentence drill activities to practice them in previous lessons. After that, I designed a writing test to assess my students' abilities to make a simple sentence using one of the target forms.

Ms. Min's Assessment Note
- My students learned how to use comparatives and superlatives in sentences. After they were able to write sentences using the target forms accurately, I offered a story-writing activity in class. Then, I made a test to assess how well the students put sentences together to write a story using the target forms.

⟨B⟩

Test 1

Directions: Based on the pictures, fill in each blank with an appropriate comparative or superlative.

   1. tall → _____

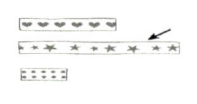   2. long → _____

   3. big → _____

Test 2

Directions: Describe the two people circled in the picture by using one of the words listed below.

1. taller
2. younger
3. older

Test 3

Directions: Choose the correct answer.

My friends and I loved watching soccer on television, but we couldn't play it. We didn't have a team. Eventually, we made a soccer team and we were happy. Last Wednesday, we had a game, but it rained a lot.

Our shoes got wet and heavy. The other team's players ran faster than us. So we took off our shoes.

Q. How was the weather last Wednesday?
a. sunny b. rainy c. cloudy d. snowy

Test 4

Directions: Describe the sequenced pictures using comparatives and/or superlatives. You should write more than THREE sentences with appropriate connectors.

Based on ⟨A⟩, identify ONE test in ⟨B⟩ that each teacher developed, respectively. Then, explain your answers with evidence from ⟨B⟩.

문제분석	구분	교과 교육
난이도 ★★☆	평가목표	교사가 목표로 하는 쓰기의 평가방법을 찾아 구체적으로 서술하는가?
	채점기준	1점: (Test 2) Mr. Lee 1점: 그림을 이용하여 비교급으로 분리된 문장을 작성한다. 1점: (Test 4) Ms. Min 1점: 그림 안에서 비교급과 최상급으로 연결어를 이용하여 이야기를 작성한다.

모범답안 In test 2, Mr. Lee asked students to write the separated sentences with the target comparatives to describe two people in the picture. In test 4, Ms. Min let students describe a story with sequenced pictures by connecting the sentences with connectors and target comparatives and superlatives. (47 words)

22. Read the passage in ⟨A⟩ and the sample items in ⟨B⟩, and follow the directions. 【4 points】

2021년 B9번

⟨A⟩

Ms. Kang, a new high school English teacher, was assigned to create questions for the listening section of the semester's final exam. In order to make the most effective test items, she goes over her notes from her college assessment class and finds the following:

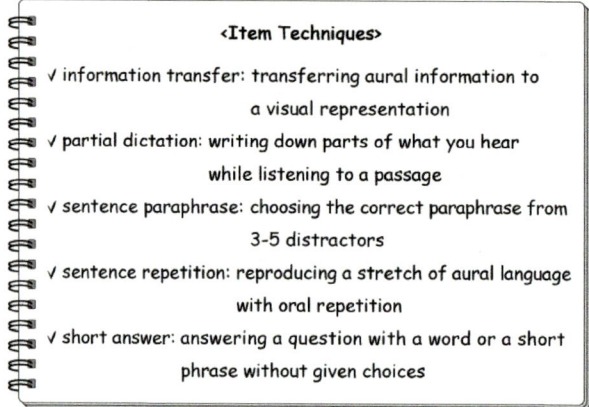

<Item Techniques>
√ information transfer: transferring aural information to a visual representation
√ partial dictation: writing down parts of what you hear while listening to a passage
√ sentence paraphrase: choosing the correct paraphrase from 3-5 distractors
√ sentence repetition: reproducing a stretch of aural language with oral repetition
√ short answer: answering a question with a word or a short phrase without given choices

Looking at her notes, she remembers that each of these techniques has its own strengths. For example, the sentence paraphrase technique has high practicality because it is easy to grade. Other techniques, such as information transfer, partial dictation, and sentence repetition, work well for assessing students' listening ability in a more integrative way.

Ms. Kang thinks that she will utilize some of these techniques because she wants to test her students' listening and other language skills simultaneously. Ms. Kang also thinks her students should be able to understand specific details, which is one of her main goals for the class this semester. So, she wants to test this particular ability in the final exam. While all the techniques in her notes are good for assessing the ability to find specific information, Ms. Kang thinks the sentence repetition technique may not be appropriate since it may only require students to simply repeat what they hear.

⟨B⟩

■ **Sample Item 1:** Listen to the information about Minsu's daily schedule and fill in his schedule with the correct information. The information will be given twice.

Minsu's Schedule

	Monday	Tuesday	Wednesday	Thursday	Friday
9-10 am					
10-11 am					
11-12 pm					
12-1 pm			Lunch		
1-2 pm					
2-3 pm					
3-4 pm					

> *Audio Script*
> Minsu's classes start at nine in the morning and he eats lunch at noon every day. He has math on Monday, Tuesday, and Friday at nine o'clock. English is scheduled on

Sample Item 2

- Fill in the blanks with the words you hear. You will hear the passage three times.
We can find many geographic regions in Korea. The _____ and _____ parts of the country have huge plains. The main rivers flow westward because the mountainous region is mostly on the _____ part of the country.

> *Audio Script*
> We can find many geographic regions in Korea. The southern and western parts of the country have huge plains. The main rivers flow westward because the mountainous region is mostly on the eastern part of the country.

Based on 〈A〉, identify the item technique used in Sample Item 1 and Sample Item 2 in 〈B〉, respectively. Then, explain why the teacher used both item techniques with evidence from 〈A〉. Do NOT copy more than FOUR consecutive words from the passage.

문제분석

난이도 ★★★

구분	교과 교육
평가목표	각각의 평가 활동의 특성과 공통점을 구체적으로 서술하는가?
채점기준	1점: Item 1, information transfer 1점: Item 2, partial dictation 1점: 통합기술을 평가한다. 1점: 특정한 정보를 이해하고 산출하는 능력을 평가한다.

모범답안 For item 1, information transfer is used and for item 2, partial dictation is used. The both techniques can assess students' integrated language skills of using listening, reading and writing simultaneously. They can also assess the students' understanding and production of specific information. (43 words)

23 Read the comments and follow the directions.

2009년 논술 1번

> Minsu: The teacher makes us memorize and practice all of the dialogs in our textbook. But I'm not sure that memorizing dialogs will guarantee any improvement in my speaking ability. When will I ever have a chance to talk about the things I want?
>
> Homin: I'm very worried about my mistakes. I'm sure that I often make mistakes, but my teacher doesn't correct me at all. I don't expect to be corrected all the time, but I'd like to get some feedback, at least, on the more serious mistakes I make.
>
> Sujin: Why does our teacher always want us to speak English in class? No matter how often I use English, it won't have any real impact on my grade because speaking in class only accounts for a small percentage of our score. Besides, he only tests how well we memorize dialogs.

(1) Based on the comments above, explain what problems each student has. (2) Design a speaking task and explain why it will help solve Minsu's and Homin's problems. (3) Suggest a solution which will address Sujin's problems in terms of the washback effect.

모범답안

(1) Minsu has no chance to make real communication. Teacher asks him to memorize and practice all the dialogues mechanically. Homin wants to learn English in an accurate and structured way but teacher does not provide corrective feedback on language errors. Sujin complains that the test is not related to their speaking class but just memorization of some dialogs. (57 words)

(2) An information gap activity can be suggested for a speaking task. The students can communicate with each other to fill the information gap to complete the missing part rather than just drill the patterns. During the procedure, they can develop accuracy by using a certain structure in a communicative context. (45 words)

(3) Washback effect is directly related to the course objectives and motivation to study. To solve the Sujin's problem, the objectives of communicative competence should be assessed as criteria items rather than simple dialog memorization. When formative assessment is used for this speaking performance, motivation to participate in speaking will be increased. (50 words)

24 Read the following and answer the question.

2008년 서울 15번

In cloze tests, it turns out that the actual score a student gets depends on the particular words that are deleted, rather than on any general English knowledge. Some are more difficult to supply than others, and in some cases there are several possible answers. Even in the cloze test below, some are less predictable than others. Item (①) is predictable, for example, because the preceding verb is required to take a particular preposition, while item (②) must agree with the following verb and keep in line with the topic of the passage. However, item ⓓ is less predictable because there are no such cues.

> They sat on a bench attached ⓐ____ a picnic table. Below them they ⓑ____ see the river gurgling between overgrown ⓒ____. The sky was diamond blue, with ⓓ____ white clouds dancing in the freshening ⓔ____. They could hear the singing of ⓕ____ and the buzzing of countless insects. ⓖ____ were completely alone.

Despite such problems of reliability, cloze is too useful a technique to abandon altogether because it is clear that supplying the correct word for a blank does imply an understanding of context and a knowledge of that word and how it operates.

(1) Fill in blanks ① and ② with the most appropriate item letter in the given cloze test.
(2) Suggest an alternative way of testing and the rationale to make up for the weakness of the test.

모범답안 (1) ① ⓐ ② ⓖ
(2) It would be better to use 'rational' or 'modified' cloze procedures where the test designer can be sure that the deleted words are recoverable from the context, rather than that just every −nth word is deleted. (36 words)

25 Read ⟨A⟩ and ⟨B⟩ and answer the question.

2010년 21번

⟨A⟩

Tumbu Fly

In Africa south of the Sahara, another _____ the traveller may _____ is the tumbu or mango fly, which lays its _____ on clothing laid out on the _____ to dry. The larvae and _____ burrow their _____ into the skin, causing boil-like _____. These can be avoided by _____ that clothes, bedding, etc., are not _____ on the ground to dry.
(Scoring method: Words that make sense in the context are marked correct.)

⟨B⟩

Tumbu Fly

In Africa south of the Sahara, another prob___ the trav___ may encou___ is tumbu o___ mango fl___, which la___ its eg___ on cloth laid o___ on t___ ground t___ dry. T___ larvae hat and bur___ their w___ into t___ skin, causing boil-like swel___. These c___ be avoi___ by ensu___ that clot___, bedding, et___, are not spread on the gro___ to dr___.
(Scoring method: Only one exact answer is marked correct for each blank.)

Compare and contrast the features and differences of ⟨A⟩ and ⟨B⟩ in terms of test type and scoring.

Which of the following is correct about <A> and <B>?

① Both tests are samples of a discrete-point test.
② Test ⟨B⟩ is a sample of a rational-deletion cloze.
③ Scoring is more difficult in Test ⟨B⟩ than in Test ⟨A⟩.
④ Test ⟨A⟩ has a higher scoring reliability than multiple-choice tests.
⑤ In Test ⟨A⟩, specific content words are chosen to be deleted.

문제분석	구분	교과 교육
난이도 ★☆☆	평가목표	Cloze test & C-test의 차이점과 특징을 구체적으로 서술하는가?
	채점기준	1점: 통합평가이다. 1.5점: ⟨A⟩ 논리적 삭제 cloze평가로 내용어휘를 선택한다. 1.5점: ⟨B⟩ 높은 신뢰도로 스펠링이 주어져서 정확한 답이 가능하다.
모범답안		Both tests are integrative test. Test ⟨A⟩ is a rational-deletion cloze test with specific linguistic purpose. In the test, specific content words are chosen to be deleted. Scoring is more difficult with alternative answers. Test ⟨B⟩ has as high scoring reliability, as there is only one answer possible with given spellings. (51 words)

memo

26 Read the conversation between two teachers and follow the directions.
【2 points】

2019년 A2번

T1: My students are having trouble with plural nouns. I'm thinking of trying a new task.
T2: What's your idea?
T1: I'm planning to give a short text where every seventh word is blanked out. Students have to guess the correct word for each blank to make a complete sentence.
T2: Well, that might be a bit difficult for beginning level students. I did a similar activity last semester. I gave a text where I blanked out only plural nouns so that students could focus on them.
T1: Oh, I see.
T2: You can also give students only parts of words in the blanks and ask them to restore each word in the text.
T1: Hmm, that seems interesting. Well, then, for my students, I'll try to use only plural nouns in the written text and ask my students to fill in the blanks. Thanks for the suggestion.

Note: T = teacher

Complete the comments by filling in the blank with the ONE most appropriate word.

In the above dialogue, the two teachers are talking about teaching plural nouns through three types of gap-filling tasks which require students to read the texts and fill in the blanks. The gap-filling described by the teachers here is _____, which can be readily adapted for pedagogical tasks in classrooms.

모범답안   cloze

27 Fill out ㉠, ㉡ regarding language assessment.

The (㉠) is constructed by omitting every nth word in a continuous passage of discourse. This may be every 5th, 6th, or 7th word. The first sentence of the passage is usually given in its entirety to provide some background for what follows. The test has been shown to (㉡) highly with tests of reading comprehension, listening comprehension, dictation, and with the TOEFL test. Therefore, the test appears to be a convenient measure of overall proficiency or achievement.

모범답안　㉠ cloze test　㉡ correlate

28 Fill out the blanks of ㉠, ㉡ with an appropriate word to explain the test.

Dictation along with (㉠), is said to be a potentially appropriate (㉡) test. The argument is that it, too, taps into certain grammatical and discourse competences and that dictation test results tend to correlate strongly with other tests of proficiency. Success on a dictation requires careful listening, reproduction in writing of what is heard, efficient short term memory, and, to an extent, some expectancy rules to aid the short term memory.

모범답안　㉠ cloze　㉡ integrative

29. Read the dialogue and follow the directions. [4 points]

2018년 A13번

T: Come here, Sumin. How was your vacation?
S: Pretty good. Thank you, Ms. Kim. Actually, I'm so happy to be taking English classes from you this year.
T: Good! You're really welcome in my class. Okay, then, let's talk about the test you had.
S: You mean the reading test you gave us in the first class? Actually, I was wondering why you gave us a test instead of going directly into the textbook.
T: Right, your class hasn't had a lesson yet. It was mainly to see how much you are ready for this semester and give you individual attention for any strong and weak points you have.
S: I see. So, how were the results?
T: Hmm…. Overall, you did quite well. Especially, you did well on the grammar questions. But it appears you had a bit of trouble with some words in the reading texts.
S: You're right. Some words are really hard to memorize although I keep trying.
T: I understand. Well, why don't you try to learn them through a context particularly relevant to you? That will be helpful, I believe.
S: Thank you for your advice, Ms. Kim.

Note: T = teacher, S = student

Fill in the blank with the ONE most appropriate word. Then, support your answer with evidence from the dialogue.

Tests can be categorized according to the purposes for which they are carried out. In this respect, the test that Ms. Kim and Sumin are talking about is an example of a(n) _____ test.

문제분석	구분	교과 교육
난이도 ★★☆	평가목표	diagnostic test의 특성을 이해하고 활용도를 구체적으로 서술할 수 있는가?
	채점기준	1점: diagnostic 평가방법이다. 1점: 학습자의 준비도와 장단점을 수업전에 평가한다. 1점: 개별적인 접근이 가능하다. 1점: 어휘암기의 문제점을 도와줄 수 있는 기회가 있다.

모범답안   diagnostic, The test was administered to check the student's readiness and strengths and weaknesses before the class. The teacher has a chance to provide more personal and clear guide to improve the student's specific difficulty of vocabulary memorization before the class. (41 words)

30   Fill out the blank with an appropriate test type.

_____ test is conceived as a prognostic measure that indicates whether a student is likely to learn a second language readily. It is generally given before the student begins language study, and may be used to select students for a language course or to place students in sections appropriate to their ability.

모범답안   Aptitude

31 Read the dialogue and follow the directions. 【2 points】

Student–teacher Meeting

T: Well, looking back over the last twelve weeks, I can see that you have written many drafts for the three essay writing assignments.
S: Yes, I have. I have a lot of things here.
T: Of all your essays, which one do you think is the best?
S: I think the persuasive essay I wrote is the best.
T: What makes you think so? Maybe you can tell me how you wrote it.
S: Well … I think the topic I chose was quite engaging. I enjoyed the writing process throughout. And it feels good being able to see the progress I've made.
T: Yes, that's the benefit of this kind of project. I can see some improvement in your use of transitions. Your ideas are nicely connected and organized now.
S: Thanks. What else should I include?
T: Well, did you work on the self-assessment form and the editing checklist?
S: Yes, I did. I completed them and included them with all of my drafts right here.
T: Perfect! I'll be able to finish grading all of your work by the end of next week.

Note: T = teacher, S = student

Complete the following by filling in both blanks with ONE word. (Use the SAME word.)

_____ can include essays, reports, journals, video or audio-recorded learner language data, students' self-assessment, teachers' written feedback, homework, conference forms, etc. As collections of these items, _____ can be useful for assessing student performance in that they can lead students to have ownership over their process of learning and allow teachers to pay attention to students' progress as well as achievement.

모범답안   portfolios

32 Read the following passage and answer the question.

2003년 서울 13번

⟨A⟩

Two approaches are particularly relevant within language testing: norm-referenced and criterion-referenced measurement. Norm-referenced measurement adopts a framework of comparison between individuals for understanding the significance of any single score. Each score is seen in the light of other scores, particularly in terms of its frequency. An alternative approach which does not use a comparison between individuals as its frame of reference is known as criterion-referenced measurement.

⟨B⟩

a. This allows for distinctions to be made between individual performances.
b. The procedures for investigating the reliability and validity of scores are well established.
c. A series of performance goals can be set for individual learners and they can reach these at their own rate.
d. Dependence on comparison across a population has been seen as being inappropriately competitive.
e. Intrinsic motivation is maintained, and the striving is for a personal best rather than against other learner.

Choose all the characteristics in ⟨B⟩ for each assessment in ⟨A⟩.

(1) Norm-referenced measurement
(2) Criterion-referenced measurement

모범답안   (1) a, b, d   (2) c, e

33. Examine the survey results in ⟨A⟩ and the interview in ⟨B⟩, and follow the directions. 【4 points】

2016년 B1번

⟨A⟩

A school administrator conducted a survey with 60 students from two classes of Ms. Lee's Practical English II in order to improve the course in the future.

Evaluation of Practical English II

Content	Number of respondents per category			
	1	2	3	4
(1) I feel I achieved my learning objectives as a result of taking this course.	4	9	25	22
(2) I feel more confident in my self-expression in English as a result of taking this course.	5	9	24	22
(3) I feel the supplementary material used in this course was helpful.	5	6	25	24
(4) I feel my speaking performance was assessed effectively based on the tests and assignments given.	29	22	8	1

Note: 1=strongly disagree, 2=disagree, 3=agree, 4=strongly agree

⟨B⟩

A: Your Practical English II was very satisfying for students. What do you think made it so successful?

T: Well, I thought it was necessary to make decisions about what would be taught and how it would be taught before designing a course, so I did a survey and interviews.

A: You mean you chose the teaching materials, contents, and activities based on what your students wanted to learn?

T: That's right. The results also provided me with a lot of information about what my students needed to learn or change, their learning styles, interests, proficiency levels, etc. Based on that information, I decided on the course objectives, contents, and activities.

A: You must have been very busy working on designing the course before it started. What about assessment?

T: Students just took one major test at the end of the semester. I regret that I evaluated only their learning product.

A: You mean just once over the semester?

T: Yes, I thought it was impossible to assess their speaking performance regularly by myself and I gave one major test to the students. So I was actually unable to gather information on the developmental process of their speaking abilities.

A: Okay. Thank you for your time.

Note: T = teacher, A = Administrator

Describe ONE strong point with evidence of what the teacher did for the success of the Practical English II course. Then describe ONE weak point of what the teacher did in the course, and suggest ONE possible solution from the teacher's standpoint.

문제분석	구분	교과 교육
난이도 ★★★	평가목표	수업진행의 잘된 점인 needs analysis와 문제점이 되는 summative와 해결책 formative 평가를 구체적으로 서술하는가?
	채점기준	1점: (needs analysis) 학습자의 요구에 따라 수업을 계획한다. 1점: (summative test) 단지 한번의 평가로 끝내는 문제점이 있다. 2점: (formative test) 형성평가로 지속인 발전을 위한 평가가 필요하다.

모범답안 One strong point is that the teacher designs the course after surveying the students' needs and wants. One weak point is to take only one summative test for the students' learning product. The teacher needs to apply formative tests during the course so that she can improve the students' ongoing development in language learning. (54 words)

34 Read the following and answer the question.

Mr. Kim has been working with first year high school students and decides to test their speaking ability using an oral task. His students who get over 10 out of 16 will pass the conversation course.

Procedure
- The students are divided into five groups and each group writes a script for an English drama.
- Each group hands in a copy of the script and rehearses.
- On the evaluation day, each group takes turns performing in front of the class.
- Mr. Kim observes the performance and scores each student according to the following criteria:
- Mr. Kim reports the grades as 'PASS' or 'FAIL' and gives comments to each student.

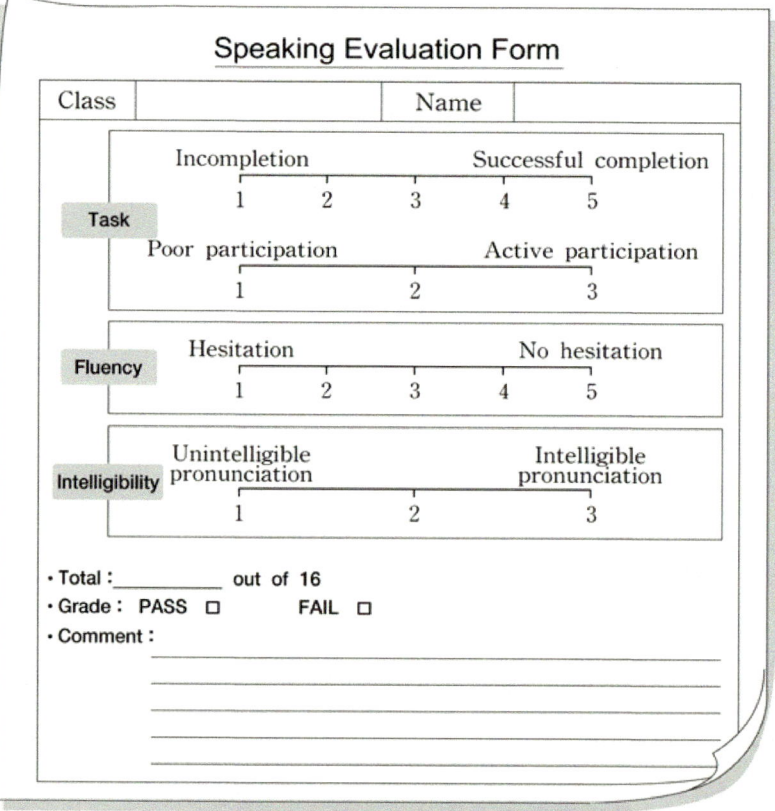

Based on the speaking evaluation form, identify the type of scoring method. Describe the THREE features of the evaluation in terms of language skills and task type and evaluation.

기출문제

Choose all and only the correct statements about the test.

ⓐ The teacher uses analytical rating scales.
ⓑ The task calls for the integration of language skills.
ⓒ The teacher focuses on the correct answer when scoring.
ⓓ The teacher provides norm-referenced reporting to students.
ⓔ The task is evaluated through direct observation by the teacher.

문제분석	구분	교과 교육
난이도 ★★☆	평가목표	speaking의 평가 유형을 분석하는 평가 방법을 이해하고 서술하는가?
	채점기준	1점: analytical rating scales을 사용한다. 1점: 절대점수로 평가하는 criterion-referenced를 이용한다. 1점: 쓰고 말하는 언어통합 평가를 실행한다. 1점: 교사의 관찰법으로 평가된다.

모범답안 Mr. Kim uses analytical rating scales to assess each item for speaking. He provides criterion-referenced reporting to students with comments. The task calls for the integration of language skills of writing a script and speaking in drama performance. The task is evaluated to check the degree of participation through direct observation by the teacher. (54 words)

기출문제답안 ⓐ, ⓑ, ⓔ

35 Read the following and answer the question.

2012년 19번

English teachers are looking for a standardized test. They will use the test results to award scholarships to the top 10%. With this in mind, they are looking over the test manual of a standardized test. The following is an excerpt from the manual:

Reading Section: This section measures the students' ability to understand written English. It is not linked to any particular textbook or specific course of study. The reading section assesses the comprehension of main ideas and factual information and the ability to infer. This section consists of (1) traditional multiple-choice questions, (2) true/false questions, and (3) questions that require students to click on a word or phrase to answer.

Students will receive a total score for the reading section and a percentile rank.

Identify the type of the test and the purpose with rationale. Explain TWO features how the scoring method is used for the test.

Choose all and only the correct statements about the test.
ⓐ The reading section of the test is a proficiency test.
ⓑ Expert judgements are not required in the scoring of the items.
ⓒ The reading section of the test is criterion-referenced.
ⓓ The reading section of the test includes constructed-response items.
ⓔ The students will receive summative feedback.

문제분석	구분	교과 교육
난이도 ★☆☆	평가목표	영어평가의 기본적인 원리와 그 특징을 구체적으로 서술하는가?
	채점기준	1점: 일반적 언어능력을 평가하는 proficiency 평가이다. 1점: 전문가의 판단이 필요없는 객관식 평가이다. 1점: 이해도를 측정하는 선택 항목 평가이다. 1점: 학생들의 순위를 매기는 상대평가를 이용한다.

모범답안 The test is a proficiency test to assess general language skills. Objective test is used since expert judgements are not required. The test consists of selected response items with comprehension-based questions. The test is norm-referenced as it needs to put students rank in order to award scholarship. (48 words)

기출문제답안 ⓐ, ⓑ, ⓔ

36 Read the passage and complete the statement which describes the problem of self-report below the word list. Use only EIGHT words from the word list.

2007년 서울 11번

Numerous insights about learners' learning processes or language use have been obtained as they provide verbal report data before, during, and after performing language learning or language using tasks. Verbal reports include data that reflect (a) self-report, (b) self-observation, and (c) self-revelation. Self-report data tend to appear frequently on questionnaires which ask learners to describe the way they usually learn and use language. Self-observation implies reference to some actual instances of language learning or language use. For example, entries in journals or diaries which retrospectively describe some language learning or language use event involving the subjunctive would count as retrospective self-observation. Self-revelation or think-aloud data are only available at the time that the language learning or language use events are taking place. Among these three measurements, self-report data have been widely used for some practical reasons. Since the self-report has been shown to be somewhat removed from the cognitive events being described, however, this approach may produce data which are of somewhat questionable validity. Efforts are often made by investigators to increase the extent to which respondents provide self-observational and self-revelational data to obtain data that describe the language learning or language use event at or near the moment it occurs. In effect, self-revelation and self-observation are intended to complement self-report data to produce convergent assessment of learning processes.

⟨Word list⟩

practicality	reveal	learners'	reliability	learning
cognitive	process	beliefs	alternative	than
actual	validity	rather	process	

Self-report may _____

모범답안 reveal learners' beliefs rather than actual learning process

37. Read the passages and follow the directions. [4 points]

2024년 B6번

⟨A⟩

At a classroom assessment workshop, a teacher trainer taught how to interpret the results of an item analysis along with basic concepts of assessment using the data from an English reading test consisting of 25 multiple choice items. Table 1 shows the results.

Table 1. Results of Analysis

Item	IF	Item-Total Correlation	Alpha	Correlation with ERAT
1	0.48	0.57		
2	0.54	0.61		
3	0.39	−0.21	0.86	0.75
4	0.43	0.51		
5	0.33	0.55		

IF = Item Facility, ERAT = English Reading Achievement Test

The trainer explained the components of Table 1.

- Item difficulty (i.e., item facility) was measured by calculating the proportion of test takers who got the item correct.
- Item discrimination was assessed by item-total correlation which is a measure of correlation between an item and the total test score (a value of 0.3 or above indicating satisfactory discrimination).
- Internal consistency was measured by Cronbach's alpha (a value of 0.8 or above indicating satisfactory internal consistency).
- Evidence about the degree to which test scores agree with those provided by a test of similar construct administered at the same time was examined by correlation with the scores of the ERAT developed and validated by a well-known testing agency.

⟨B⟩

The trainer asked six teachers to interpret the results. The following are their interpretations.

- Teacher 1: Of the five items, Item 2 shows the highest power of discrimination and Item 5 is the most difficult.
- Teacher 2: Item 3 should be carefully investigated in terms of the probability of miskeying and the construction of item response options.
- Teacher 3: There is a close relationship between the test takers' performance on Item 4 and the total test score.
- Teacher 4: The extent to which test takers' performances on this test are consistent is acceptable.
- Teacher 5: In order to increase the internal consistency of the test, Item 1 and Item 3 should be deleted.
- Teacher 6: The correlation between this test and the ERAT displays the evidence of predictive validity.

Identify the TWO teachers in 〈B〉 whose interpretation is NOT correct. Then support your answers with evidence from 〈A〉 and 〈B〉.

문제분석	구분	교과 교육
난이도 ★☆☆	평가목표	평가 원리 internal consistency와 concurrent validity 의 문제점을 구체적으로 서술하는가?
	채점기준	1점: Teacher 5 해석이 맞지 않다. 1점: 1번항목은 변별도가 0.3이상이므로 유지하고, 3번항목은 −0.21으로 내적 일관성에 문제가 있으므로 삭제한다. 1점: Teacher 6 해석이 맞지 않다. 1점: ERAT와의 상관도는 동시에 이루어지는 시험으로 concurrent validity 이다.

모범답안 Interpretations of Teacher 5 and Teacher 6 are not correct. To increase the internal consistency of the test, only Item 3 should be deleted since the item does not correlate with the total test score. The correlation between the test and ERAT shows the concurrent validity to be taken at the same time. (53 words)

38 Read the following and answer the question.

A high school teacher constructed a 20-item multiple choice English test. She wanted to find out about the test qualities. She examined the reliability of the test and obtained Cronbach's alpha of 0.45. She also performed item analysis, and part of the results is presented below.

Item Number	Item Facility*	
	High Ability Group (N=20)	Low Ability Group (N=20)
16	0.4	0.5
17	0.6	0.3
18	0.2	0.7
19	0.8	0.2
20	0.7	0.5

* Item Facility: Proportion Passing

Describe what the test means from each item number of the test results, comparing the two students' groups, high ability and low ability.

Which of the following is a correct statement about the item analysis results?
① Item 16 was more difficult for the low ability group.
② More than half of the total examinees got Item 17 correct.
③ Item 18 deteriorates the internal consistency of the test.
④ Item 20 shows the highest discrimination among the five items.
⑤ The data above shows the relative standing of each test-taker in terms of performance.

모범답안 Item 16 was more difficult for the high ability group to indicate low item discrimination. Item 17 was a difficult one, with less than half of the examinees got the answer correct. Item 18 deteriorated the internal consistency of the test with low reliability. Item 19 showed the highest discrimination among the five items. (55 words)

기출문제답안 ③

39 Read the passage and follow the directions. 【2 points】

2015년 A3번

Mr. Lee's English listening test consisted exclusively of four-option, multiple-choice items. After scoring the test, he calculated the response frequency for each item. Part of the results is presented below.

Item \ Option	Upper Group (N=100)				Lower Group (N=100)			
	A	B	C	D	A	B	C	D
1	50%*	27%	13%	10%	10%*	45%	25%	20%
2	13%	10%	70%*	7%	25%	27%	28%*	20%
3	20%	25%	18%	37%*	21%	26%	16%	37%*
...								
17	4%	0%	61%	35%*	66%	0%	29%	5%*
...								

Note: * indicates the correct response.

Complete the comments on item analysis by filling in each blank with ONE word. Write your answers in the correct order.

Items 1 and 2 seem to be fulfilling their function. Item 3 has the problem of item ①_____. Therefore, option D of item 3 needs to be revised or item 3 needs to be discarded. Item 17 has a problem with its ②_____: No one from the upper group and lower group chose option B, and many upper group students incorrectly chose option C.

모범답안   ① discrimination   ② distractors

40 Read the following and answer the question.

2013년 27번

Below are the results from a 10-item test that Mr. Park gave to his 11 students to compare their English abilities. Based on the test results, Mr. Park divided the students into three groups—upper, middle, and lower. He wanted to determine the effectiveness of the test by examining item facility (IF) and item discrimination (ID). To calculate IF, Mr. Park divided the number of students who correctly answered a particular item by the total number of students who took the test. ID indicates the degree to which an item separates the students who performed well from those who did poorly on the test as a whole. Mr. Park used the following formula to calculate the ID for each item: ID = IF upper − IF lower.

Test Results

Groups	Students	Items										Total
		1	2	3	4	5	6	7	8	9	10	
Upper	A	1	1	1	1	1	1	1	1	1	1	10
	B	1	0	1	1	1	1	1	1	1	1	9
	C	1	0	1	0	1	1	1	1	1	1	8
	D	1	1	0	1	1	1	1	0	1	1	8
Middle	E	0	1	0	1	1	1	1	1	0	0	6
	F	1	0	1	1	1	0	1	0	1	0	6
	G	1	1	0	0	1	0	1	0	1	1	6
Lower	H	1	1	0	0	1	0	1	0	0	0	4
	I	0	0	0	0	1	1	0	0	1	1	4
	J	0	1	1	0	0	0	0	0	1	1	4
	K	1	0	0	1	1	1	0	0	0	0	4
Total		8	6	5	6	10	7	8	4	8	7	

1 = a correct response; 0 = an incorrect response

Complete the summary with ONE word each from the passage.

──── ⟨Summary⟩ ────

The test is norm-referenced, ranking students in order with grades. Item 2 does not distinguish the upper level students from the lower level students. The ①_____ values for Item 3 and Item 10 turned out to be the same. All 10 items have ②_____ values which are greater than 0.3.

Choose all and only the correct statements about the test.

ⓐ The test is criterion-referenced, assessing the extent to which the students achieved the goals of the class.
ⓑ Item 2 does not distinguish the upper level students from the lower level students.
ⓒ The ID values for Item 3 and Item 10 turned out to be the same.
ⓓ All 10 items have IF values which are greater than 0.4.

문제분석	구분	교과 교육
난이도 ★★★	평가목표	문항분석표를 보고 문항난이도와 변별도를 올바르게 해석할 수 있다.
	채점기준	순위가 있는 norm-referenced평가이다. 2번 항목은 ID점수가 같아서 변별력이 없다. 3번과 10번 ID점수가 0.5로 같다. 8번의 IF점수가 0.3으로 가장 낮다.

모범답안 (1) ID (2) IF

기출문제답안 ⓑ, ⓒ

41 Read the following and answer the question.

2009년 18번

Here is one example of 'item response distribution' about an item on a test. The English teacher wanted to analyze whether the alternatives in this item had been appropriately made.

Interpretations:
- A certain wrong alternative was chosen by a greater number of high group students than low group students.
- A certain wrong alternative is suspected of having problems in the wording because more students chose the wrong alternative than those who chose the correct answer.
- A certain wrong alternative did not work at all as a distracter.

* ⓑ was the answer to the item.

Which of the following reflects all of the interpretations in the passage?

	Item No. 5	ⓐ	*ⓑ	ⓒ	ⓓ	ⓔ
①	High group	2	14	5	7	0
	Low group	6	12	2	2	0
②	High group	4	4	15	5	1
	Low group	5	2	9	1	4
③	High group	4	20	2	0	0
	Low group	7	10	5	0	2
④	High group	9	10	0	8	4
	Low group	5	4	0	10	0
⑤	High group	8	3	3	7	1
	Low group	2	7	7	6	6

기출문제답안 ④

42 Read the following and answer the question.

2005년 전국 10번

⟨A⟩

The following table of item analysis contains the most essential characteristics of a test item. The table can be interpreted as follows: the difficulty index is the proportion endorsing of the total test-taker group for the answer choice. The discriminability is represented by the point biserial correlation for the answer choice. The answer key is denoted by "*" in the "key" column.

⟨B⟩

Item Analysis Statistics

Choice	Proportion Endorsing			Biserial Correlation	Key
	Total Group	Low Ability Group	High Ability Group		
a	.18	.20	.10	−.11	
b	.22	.29	.11	−.20	
c	.09	.18	.01	−.22	
d	.48	.26	.78	.45	*
Other	.03	.07	.00	−.22	

Calculate the figure of following:

(1) Difficulty: _____
(2) Discriminability: _____

모범답안 (1) Difficulty: 0.48
(2) Discriminability: 0.45

43 Read the text and follow the direction.

2010년 16번

The following is a conversation between two students about a first draft S2 produced in a writing class.

S1: I have never heard of pluralism. Pluralism in your writing is not clear to me. <u>What is "pluralism"?</u>
S2: Don't know the word?
S1: <u>No, I really didn't understand.</u> I think maybe you define pluralism a little bit.
S2: Uh… in the Cold War, there is only one superpower and is the United States. But after that time, Europe became another superpower and the power of the United States is declined….
S1: Began to decline?
S2: Yes. The power of the United States began to decline. So this situation is pluralism.
S1: OK. Now I understand that. <u>But here I think you should state reasons in the introductory part why pluralism started.</u>
S2: Hmm. Right, I'll revise it and we'll talk about it again.

Identify the type of conversation and explain the features of the interaction between S1 and S2 in an English writing class citing the underlined sentences.

Choose all and only the correct statements about the interaction.
ⓐ Meaning negotiation occurs in this conversation.
ⓑ S1 requests clarification of the concept of "pluralism" through display questions.
ⓒ S1 gives comments on both meaning and organization in S2's draft.
ⓓ S1's negative feedback on the form leads to an unsuccessful uptake by S2.
ⓔ The conversation demonstrates a process-oriented approach to writing through peer review.

문제분석	구분	교과 교육
난이도 ★☆☆	평가목표	conferencing 활동을 통해서 습득될 수 있는 교실의 활동내용을 서술하는가?
	채점기준	1점: 과정 중심 쓰기에서 conferencing 이다. 1점: referential질문으로 의미에 대해 질문한다. 1점: 서론에 집중하며 전체 구성을 언급한다. 1점: 초안과정에서 내용과 구성에 집중하여 토론한다.

모범답안 The conversation is conferencing in a process-oriented writing. S1 asks referential questions to clarify and negotiate the meaning of 'pluralism'. S1 gives comments on the organization of the first draft by suggesting changing the introductory part to focus on content and organization in the conference. (45 words)

기출문제답안 ⓐ, ⓒ, ⓔ

CHAPTER 04 영어교수법

01 Read the teacher log and follow the directions. 【2 points】

2023년 B1번

Teacher Log

　Skill-integration is considered more and more important in modern language learning, but I found that at any one time I was almost always teaching just one skill in isolation. As part of my development as a teacher, I wanted to integrate multiple language skills and pursue a more real-life style of communication. To do this, I first investigated my own class practices. I video-recorded eight lessons. After reviewing the video files, I found that in six lessons I taught only one skill. In the other two, I was only able to integrate listening and speaking but never reading or writing. I drew up a plan to integrate language skills more often. What I did was implement the project-based learning approach so that students could collaborate in groups to advance their projects. I conducted the experiments over the second half of the semester and gathered the data. Then, I video-recorded another eight lessons toward the end of the semester to test the effectiveness of the measure I had implemented. After I analyzed the videos and the data, the results were as follows: two of the lessons showed the integration of speaking and reading skills, two other lessons integrated reading and writing skills, and one lesson integrated all four skills! Based on these results, I feel the approach really improved my teaching practice and my ability to teach students with the four skills in an integrated fashion.

Fill in the blank with the TWO most appropriate words.

　The log above describes how the teacher addresses a problem in the classroom and resolves it through a systematic process of inquiry. Sometimes referred to as teacher research or classroom research, _____ is considered an important part of self-reflective teacher development. It usually involves four steps: planning, acting, observing, and reflecting. Its major goal is to improve both student learning and teaching effectiveness.

모범답안　action research

02 Read the passages and follow the directions. 【4 points】

⟨A⟩

Project-based learning (PBL) is a teaching method that facilitates students to use an inquiry process with an integrated goal and interrelated subsidiary tasks. One possible procedure for implementing PBL is provided below.

Students collaboratively set the goal and scope of the project. This makes students feel in control of their own projects from the beginning. Once the goal is set, students as a group actively discuss and decide upon what to include in their project. When collecting information for the project, students develop integrated language skills in meaningful ways. Students then create their projects collaboratively with their group members. Finally, students present their projects in class. When assessing student projects, the teacher evaluates students' learning progress, focusing on the process as well as the product.

⟨B⟩

Referring to the procedure as described in ⟨A⟩, Ms. Park, a middle school English teacher, implemented PBL into her class over six weeks. Each week, one class session was allocated for the PBL project. When each session was over, Ms. Park briefly wrote a teacher's log to record events and observations. Some entries of her logs are provided below.

Week 1

| I decided on a specific goal for the project and announced it to students. The goal was to make tourist brochures and distribute them to the local communities. I assigned students to groups of four. I also provided guidelines on the project. | 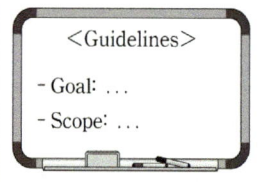 |

Week 2

| The groups explored possible destinations to include in their brochures. Students also searched the Internet for various brochures and analyzed the sections within. They found details including attractions, activities, and food. |  |

Week 3

| The groups conducted a survey on their classmates' recommendations for the destination their group decided upon. They did so by asking and responding to each other. Then they summarized the survey results. | 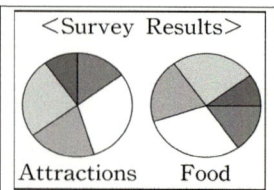 |

Week 4

The students worked closely in a group to make their brochures. Upon completion, they prepared for a group presentation.

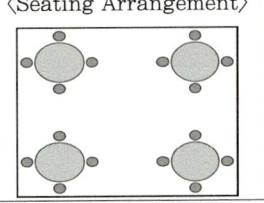
〈Seating Arrangement〉

Week 5

Each group gave a ten-minute presentation. Students also prepared for distributing the brochures to the local communities.

Week 6

As the final step, I evaluated students' brochures based on a rubric, which consisted of vocabulary, grammar, and layout.

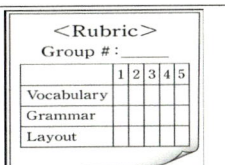

Identify the TWO weeks in 〈B〉 that do NOT follow the procedure provided in 〈A〉. Then, explain how the identified weeks deviate from the procedure in 〈A〉.

문제분석	구분	교과 교육
난이도 ★★☆	평가목표	PBL수업과정을 시행하지 않은 주를 구체적으로 서술하는가?
	채점기준	1점: Week 1 1점: 학습자들은 project의 목표와 범위를 협동하여 설정한다. 1점: Week 6 1점: 학습평가는 과정과 결과물 모두를 평가한다.
모범답안		Week 1 and week 6 are not followed. In week 1, teacher set the goal and guidelines for the project rather than the students collaboratively decided for their project. In week 6, the evaluation was based on the language product such as vocabulary, grammar, layout, not considering the students' learning progress. (51 words)

03 Read the passages and follow the directions. 【4 points】

2024년 B7번

⟨A⟩

Mr. Kim, a middle school English teacher, attended a materials development workshop last week. There he learned that a variety of factors impact a learner's task performance which he could manipulate to adjust the level of task difficulty. One is language of input that learners have to process, such as the range and complexity of vocabulary and grammar. Another factor has to do with the processing demands of a task, which refer to the amount of mental effort required in working out answers. Besides these two factors, the conditions under which a task is performed also play an important role. Below are the notes he took during the workshop.

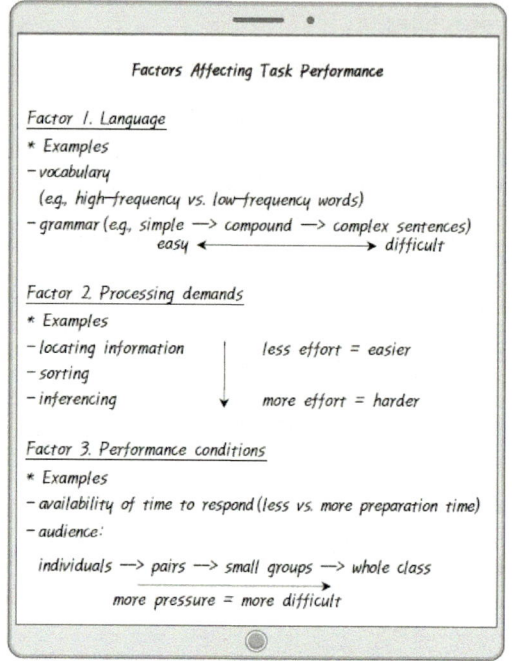

⟨B⟩

Based on what he learned at the workshop, Mr. Kim adapted one of the tasks from the textbook as shown below.

The original task

1. Read the following passage and answer the questions.

   Now we're going to see the most famous church in Britain, Westminster Abbey. Westminster Abbey is where the kings and queens have been crowned. We'll have about half an hour to look around the Abbey. We'll all meet again at the west door of the Abbey at four o'clock. If you get lost, then just call me. Remember it's a holy place, so behave yourselves.

   1) What is the name of the building that the people are going to see?
   2) Why are the people advised to behave themselves?

2. Choose a famous building or place in your neighborhood. Introduce it in front of the whole class.

The adapted task

1. Read the following passage and answer the questions.

> Now we're going to see the most famous church in Britain, Westminster Abbey. In Westminster Abbey, the kings and queens have been crowned. We'll have about half an hour to look around the Abbey. We'll all meet again at the west door of the Abbey at four o'clock. You may get lost. Then just call me. Remember it's a holy place, so behave yourselves.

1) What is the name of the building that the people are going to see?

2) Why are the people advised to behave themselves?

2. Choose a famous building or place in your neighborhood. Introduce it to your partner.

Identify the TWO factors in 〈A〉 that Mr. Kim addressed to adjust the difficulty of the original task in 〈B〉. Then explain how each factor was addressed in the adapted task, respectively, with evidence from 〈A〉 and 〈B〉.

문제분석	구분	교과 교육
난이도 ★★★	평가목표	과업 수행의 수준을 위해 활동의 난이도를 구체적으로 서술하는가?
	채점기준	1점: Factor 1을 적용한다. 1점: 관계절이나 복합절을 없애고 문장을 간단하게 하여 쉽게 만들었다. 1점: Factor 3을 적용한다. 1점: 전체교실수업을 짝수업으로 하여 압박을 낮추었다.
모범답안		Factors 1 and 3 are adopted to adjust the task. For Grammar, more simple or compound sentences were used to make the content easier rather than complex clauses with 'if clause' or relative clause, 'where'. For Performance conditions, whole class task was changed to pair work to lessen pressure. (51 words)

04. Read the conversation and follow the directions. [2 points]

2022년 A2번

> T1: Hello, Ms. Kim. You seem to be in deep thought. Anything bothering you?
> T2: Good morning, Mr. Lee. I'm thinking of how to make my English class more effective.
> T1: Yeah, I've been thinking about that, too.
> T2: You know, our textbook is organized by separate language skills. But the four skills are rarely separable from each other, I think.
> T1: True. Speaking almost always implies a listener, and writing and reading share obvious links.
> T2: That's exactly what I mean.
> T1: Actually, I've been adapting the textbook since last semester so that my students can be exposed to the language they will encounter in the real world.
> T2: Sounds great. How have you been doing it?
> T1: For example, I usually have pre-reading discussion time to activate schemata. It helps to make links between speaking, listening, and reading. My students actively engage in those kinds of tasks.
> T2: That can be a good way. Or I could create a listening task accompanied by note-taking or followed by a group discussion.
> T1: Great idea. I think just a slight change can make a big difference.
> T2: Right. I'll try to make some changes and let you know how it goes. Thanks for sharing your experience!
>
> *Note:* T = teacher

Fill in the blank with the ONE most appropriate word.

> In the above conversation, the two teachers are talking about the _____ approach, which is now typical within a communicative, interactive framework. The approach can give students greater motivation and make them engage more actively, which can convert to better learning outcomes.

모범답안   integrated (integrative)

05 Read the passage and answer the question.

2003년 전국 10번

Background Information: ESL Intermediate Textbook: Geography 1	

Procedures:
• Talk about 'the globe'
• Practice words related to the globe
• Watch a video titled 'Understanding Globes'
• Read a chapter in the textbook
   – discuss the content of the chapter
   – answer problem-solving questions
• Describe latitude and longitude co-ordinates
   – find the cities on the globe
• Assignments: reading about 'Earth'
	Notes:
	whole class
	
	pair work
	
	group work
	with handout

It is one of the integrated approaches which encourage the teaching of all four skills. It integrates the learning of some specific subject-matter content with the learning of a second or foreign language. When language becomes the _____, learners are pointed towards matters of intrinsic concerns. Students learn better when instruction addresses students' needs. The information that students acquire is perceived as interesting, useful, and leading to a desired goal.

Complete the passage with FIVE appropriate words in the word list.

⟨Word list⟩

| informational | to | communicative | awareness | content |
| process | integration | medium | convey | method |

모범답안   medium to convey informational content

06 Read the passage and answer the question.

> Gestalt means a sense of wholeness, an integration of the various parts of self. According to this theory, people become fragmented in contemporary life, pulled in so many different directions that they lose their sense of being grounded. Similar to the existential approach, Gestaltists are concerned with issues related to freedom and responsibility, especially in the present moment. Yet, Gestaltists are intensely action-oriented. Gestalt therapy emphasizes human perfectibility; the Gestaltists place a great emphasis on nonverbal experience. In fact, Gestalt therapy places the body on the same level as the mind. The basic idea of Gestalt therapy is that any organism seeks to maintain its internal organization through exchanges with its environment. It does this through the process of awareness: first, an awareness of an imbalance in its internal organization; second, an awareness of something in the environment that can restore balance. The organism recognizes the relationship between itself and its environment as an integrated unit, an organized, meaningful whole. Human life is an unending series of incomplete gestalts. When we are living well, we are aware of our needs. As these needs express themselves through our thoughts, feelings, and actions, we become aware of what it is in the environment that will satisfy them, and we move to close the gestalt. When we are not living well, we are unaware of our needs. Consequently, we are unaware of what will satisfy our needs, and we do not move to close the gestalt. Failure to close the gestalt leads to psychological fragmentation, which, in turn, leads to anxiety, frustration, and conflict which we experience as we blindly grope to put the pieces together again.

Write down ONE teaching method and TWO supporting words respectively from the text above.

모범답안

Teaching Approach	Supporting words
(A) Whole Language Approach	wholeness, integration
(B) Total Physical Response	action-oriented, nonverbal experience

07 Read the passage and identify the three numbers from ⟨B⟩ to match with ⟨A⟩.

2010년 18번

⟨A⟩

1. The teacher gives students an excerpt from a newspaper advice column.

   > Dear Tom,
   > My boss keeps inviting me to play golf every Sunday. But I want to spend more time with my wife. Should I refuse my boss and risk my promotion, or should I risk my marriage?
   > Confused Man

2. Students are divided into small groups to discuss the letter. Each group is asked to choose a position on how to solve the problem.

⟨B⟩

Task Evaluation Sheet

An interactant relationship concerns who holds the information to be exchanged to achieve the task goals.	shared	a
	split	b
Goal orientation concerns whether the task requires students within each group to agree on a single outcome or allows them to disagree.	convergent	c
	divergent	d
Outcome options: Closed tasks are those where there is a predetermined solution, while open tasks are those where there is no predetermined one.	open	e
	closed	f

구분	교과 교육
평가목표	과업의 유형을 이해하고 분석하는가?
채점기준	ⓐ shared: 활동 참가자들이 같은 정보를 나눈다. ⓒ convergent: 목표는 하나의 결과가 있는 과업으로 일치를 이루는 것이다. ⓔ open: 결과물은 정해져 있지 않다.

모범답안 a, c, e

08 Read the following and answer the question.

Fighting Jet Lag

Pre-task
- The teacher shows visual materials related to jet lag and elicits experiences from students.

Task Cycle 1
- The teacher asks students to brainstorm, in pairs, ways to overcome jet lag.
- Pairs select three items from what they have brainstormed.
- Pairs rehearse how to explain their choices and then present their list to the class with justifications.

Task Cycle 2
- The teacher distributes copies of a magazine article about overcoming jet lag and has students write down the three ways mentioned in the text.
- Pairs compare their list to that of the article.
- Students decide which pair has the most similar ways.

Post-task
- Students circle adverbial phrases expressing time and place in the magazine article.
- Students complete a grammar worksheet.

Identify the FOUR pedagogical features of the task activity mentioning each task procedure and explain them with supporting evidence.

Which of the following is NOT a correct statement about the activity?

① It winds down with work on specific language features.
② It restricts language use to predetermined language items.
③ It helps learners engage in completing tasks collaboratively.
④ It includes opportunities for planned production.
⑤ It integrates language skills across the two task cycles.

구분	교과 교육
평가목표	대화에 나타난 상호작용을 최근 영어교수법에서 논의되고 있는 관점으로 이해한다.
채점기준	1점: 통합수업으로 말하기, 읽기, 쓰기가 이루어진다. 1점: 협동학습이다. 1점: 짝활동에서 연습을 통해 전체에게 준비된 내용을 발표한다. 1점: 학습자의 언어 연습으로 활동이 정리된다.

문제분석
난이도 ★★☆

모범답안
The activity integrates language skills of speaking, reading a magazine and writing down the list across the task cycles. The activity includes opportunities for planned production while students complete tasks collaboratively in a group. Students practiced with specific language features they previously performed at post-task stage. (47 words)

 ②

09 Read the passage and follow the directions.

2009년 16번

Ms. Yoon introduces the lesson content about favorite school subjects by asking students what subjects they studied at school and makes a list on the board. Students are then asked to classify the subjects into group categories. The teacher then tells the class about subjects she liked and hated, and explains why. The teacher then reads the instructions for a speaking activity: "Tell your partner about the school subjects you like best and least and explain your reasons." Before beginning, students are given three minutes to write down what they will say in the speaking activity.

The students begin the speaking activity and talk about their school subjects. In the process of completing the activity, the students occasionally stop to think about and discuss language-related problems, i.e. gaps in their interlanguage knowledge, to resolve their misunderstandings in communication. After finishing the activity, each student prepares a brief oral presentation about their partner's favorite subjects. The teacher selects a few students to present their partner's answers to the whole class.

After presentations, the teacher gives the students a brief written transcript of two native speakers of English doing the same speaking activity they just completed. Individually, the students read the transcript and underline all the phrases that are used by the native speakers to express 'likes' and 'dislikes' of school subjects. The teacher then reviews these with the students. Following this, the teacher has the students find all the examples of comparatives and superlatives in the transcript and figure out how they differ in usage.

Based on task-based approach, explain the features of each activity for three phases, pretask, task cycle, and language focus with evidence.

Choose all and only the correct statements about the approach.
ⓐ The teacher uses a consciousness-raising approach to teach linguistic items.
ⓑ During the speaking activity, there is a greater focus on accuracy than fluency.
ⓒ During the speaking activity, focus on form occurs within a context of focusing on meaning.
ⓓ Specified grammar structures are presented before the speaking activity.
ⓔ The lesson is an example of a constructivist approach to learning.

문제분석	구분	교과 교육
난이도 ★★★	평가목표	4 skills을 통합하기 위한 수업을 통해 과업 교수 방법을 서술하는가?
	채점기준	1점: (pretask) 좋아하는 과목을 이야기하며 schema를 활성화한다. 1.5점: (task cycle) 의미에 집중하면서 오류에 CR을 한다. 1.5점: (language focus)

모범답안 For pretask, a warmup activity, students activate their schema by discussing favorite subjects. During task cycle, students discuss their favorite subjects and the reasons within a context of focusing on meaning with consciousness raising on their errors. For language focus, students review and analyze the usage of target forms. (45 words)

기출문제답안 ⓐ, ⓒ, ⓔ

10 Read the passage in ⟨A⟩ and the two teachers' reflections in ⟨B⟩, and follow the directions. 【10 points】

⟨A⟩

Mr. Kim and Ms. Jo, English teachers, attended a workshop for language teachers where they both gained a lot of useful information to promote student learning. Below is part of the information from the workshop.

Teachers need to…
(1) keep in mind that their course goals and/or procedures can be modified.
(2) offer students a variety of learning strategies to develop learner autonomy.
(3) involve students in self-/peer-evaluation instead of evaluating them alone.
(4) assess students frequently throughout the semester.

⟨B⟩

Mr. Kim's reflection
To develop English writing abilities, my students engaged in writing activities. I simply assumed that paragraph writing would be enough for my students. However, I realized that I should change the initial course goal after assessing my students' first classroom writings. Their writing abilities were well above my expectations so I changed the goal set earlier and included essays. Since I believe that one-shot assessment at the end of the course is not effective for enhancing student learning, I carried out assessment periodically over the whole course period. I also believe assessment should be objective and that students' self-assessments are rather subjective in some ways. So, I did all the periodic assessments by myself, not asking students to evaluate their own work.

Ms. Jo's reflection
In my class, students were expected to develop debating skills in English. I organized my lesson in this way: brief mini-lectures, short video presentations to provide content for debating practice, followed by small group debating practice. I taught a range of learning strategies so that my students could become independent language learners utilizing those strategies whenever needed. For improving students' oral skills, I thought that arranging assessments multiple times, not just once, would be better. So I carried out assessments every two weeks during my instructional period. Based on the results of the assessments, I noticed that strictly following the lesson procedure was rather challenging to my students. However, I kept the same procedure over the course period since I believe maintaining consistency is crucial in order not to confuse students.

(1) Based on ⟨A⟩, identify TWO elements that Mr. Kim employed in his course and ONE element that he did not employ, and provide evidence from ⟨B⟩.
(2) Based on ⟨A⟩, identify TWO elements that Ms. Jo employed in her course and ONE element that she did not employ, and provide evidence from ⟨B⟩.

문제분석	구분	교과 교육
난이도 ★★☆	평가목표	각 교사의 수업을 workshop에 근거하여 설명할 수 있는가?
	채점기준	(1) 김교사 1점: (1) 학습자의 수준에 따라 목표가 조정된다. 1.5점: (4) 정기적인 형성평가가 실시된다. 1.5점: (3) 객관적이지 않아서 자기/ 동료평가를 사용하지 않는다. (2) 조교사 1점: (2) 전략을 배워서 자율적 학습자가 된다. 1점: (4) 정기적인 형성평가로 말하기 능력을 평가한다. 1점: (1) 수업과정은 일관성을 가져서 학생들이 혼동되지 않도록 한다.

모범답안

(1) Mr. Kim employs (1), (4) but does not employ (3). Based on the students' proficiency level, the course goal is modified. After he diagnoses his students level, he includes essay writing. He implements regular, frequent, formative assessment during the semester. He does not use students' self/ peer evaluation since it does not give objective assessment. (54 words)

(2) Ms. Jo employs (2), (4) but does not employ (1). Students can be autonomous by using a range of strategies in and outside classroom. She also employs regular formative assessment every two weeks to improve students' oral skills. However, the lesson procedure is kept consistent to keep the students from being confused with changing processes. (53 words)

11. Read the passage in ⟨A⟩ and the teacher talk in ⟨B⟩, and follow the directions. [10 points]

⟨A⟩

(Below are notes that Ms. Shin, a new teacher, took of her senior teacher's advice on how to make her class communicatively oriented.)

Senior teacher's suggestions

- Objective: Get class centered on language functions rather than grammatical structures.
- Error targeted: Focus only on global errors impeding communication of meaning.
- Strategy: Encourage the use of communication strategies.
- Feedback: Provide correction implicitly.

⟨B⟩

(Below is Ms. Shin's talk at the beginning and closure of her single-activity class.)

Today, you are going to practice how to make requests using the question forms you learned from the last class. To do this, you will be doing an activity in pairs where you need to fill in a book order form by asking your partner for the necessary information. While doing this, you will get a chance to use the question forms to make requests. If you can't come up with the exact words to express the meaning you intend during the activity, you can try using similar words you know or even gestures, instead. Now, I will hand out the copies of the order form. Then, you can begin the activity with the student next to you. You'll work in pairs. OK, here are your copies.

⋮

All right, now it's time to wrap up. I think you all did a great job on the form-filling activity exactly as I told you when the class started. But there is one and only one language element I want to briefly point out today. I noticed some of you missed 's' in some verbs like "He come" while talking. It should be "comes" not "come" though meaning is still clear without 's.' Apart from this, you seem to be fairly familiar with making requests now. Next time, we will focus on how to ask for permission.

(1) Based on ⟨A⟩, identify TWO suggestions that Ms. Shin's class conforms to and provide evidence for each identified suggestion from ⟨B⟩.
(2) Identify TWO suggestions that Ms. Shin's class does NOT conform to and explain with evidence from ⟨B⟩.

문제분석	구분	교과 교육
난이도 ★★☆	평가목표	수업의 개선영역과 부족한 영역을 구체적으로 잘 서술할 수 있는가?
	채점기준	(1) 실시한 제안 2점: (objective) 책 주문을 완성하기 위하여 요청사항을 연습한다. 2점: (communication strategies) 유사어나 제스쳐로 의사소통전략을 사용한다. (2) 실시하지 않은 제안 2점: (global error correction) 동사에 -s가 나와야 하는 local 오류를 수정한다. 2점: (implicit feedback) explicit 피드백으로 형태에 집중한다.

모범답안

(1) Ms. Shin's class conforms to objective and communication strategies. The students practice making a request using the question forms to complete the task of collecting the information for the book order form. They use communication strategies, similar words or gestures, for the communication difficulty. (46 words)

(2) Ms. Shin's class does not follow global error correction and implicit feedback. She just corrects a local language error, 'He come' after the third person singular. She gives explicit negative feedback, or explicit correction with metalinguistic terms, 'missed 's' in some verbs'. (41 words)

12. Read the two lesson procedures for teaching comparatives in ⟨A⟩ and ⟨B⟩, and follow the directions. 【10 points】

2017년 논술 B8번

⟨A⟩

Class A

Lesson objectives: Ss will be able to discuss and present their travel experiences using comparatives.

1. T tells a story about travel experiences.

   > Let me tell you about two trips I took, one to Singapore and the other to Bangkok. I really enjoyed my trip to Bangkok. It was more interesting than my trip to Singapore. Singapore was a little more boring than Bangkok. Although Singapore was cleaner and nicer, I thought Bangkok was a more fun city to travel in.

2. T articulates the lesson objectives and asks Ss to form groups of six.

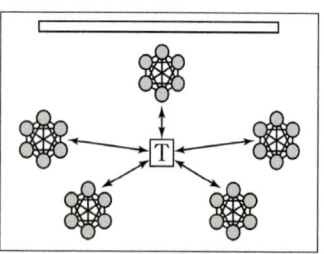

   T : Teacher
   O : Student

3. Ss begin a consensus building activity. During this activity, Ss compare locations according to a list of given adjectives (e.g., safe, beautiful, historic) on a worksheet. (T helps Ss as needed.)

	Your chosen place	Your group's agreed-upon place
safe	Busan	Daegu
beautiful	Jeju	Jeju
historic		
...		
_____ (your idea)		

   Ss compare and discuss their ideas using comparatives. (T gives feedback. Ss correct ill-formed utterances.)

   S : Busan is beautifuler.
   T : Beautifuler?
   S : Beautiful, more beautiful.
   T : More beautiful?
   S : Busan is more beautiful.
   T : More beautiful. OK.

4. In groups, Ss discuss where the better and worse places to visit are. (T walks around the classroom to see if all the Ss are participating in the discussion. If Ss are reluctant to join in group work, T encourages them to participate.)

5. Ss work on a summary together within their group. T allows Ss to choose a role within their group (e.g., leader, timekeeper, note-taker, reporter). (T monitors their work and helps out as needed.)

6. Each group presents their summary to the class.

⋮

Note: T = teacher, S = student

⟨B⟩

Class B

Lesson objectives:
(1) Ss will learn comparative forms;
(2) Ss will be able to make sentences using comparatives.

1. T explains the grammatical form of comparatives and writes the following chart on the board:

safe	safer
beautiful	more beautiful
cheap	cheaper
expensive	more expensive
...	...

   (T stays at the front of the class the entire time, and Ss sit in orderly rows in silence.)

2. T instructs Ss to pay attention to the lesson.

   T : Teacher
   O : Student

3. T plays a recording line-by-line, and Ss listen and repeat. (T instructs them to repeat in unison.)

4. T checks if Ss understand the comparative forms. (T asks questions, Ss answer individually, and T gives feedback.)

   T: What is the comparative form of 'safe'?
   S: Safer.
   T: Good. What about 'beautiful'?
   S: More beautiful.
   T: Very good. Then what about 'cheap'?
   S: More cheaper.
   T: No, not 'more cheaper'. It's 'cheaper'.

5. Ss do more choral repetition. (T plays the recording again, pausing it after key phrases, and Ss repeat them immediately.)

Recording	Students
A: What is cheaper, taking trains or taking buses?	What is cheaper, taking trains or taking buses?
B: Taking buses is cheaper than taking trains.	Taking buses is cheaper than taking trains.
A: Which one is safer?	Which one is safer?
B: Taking trains is safer than taking buses.	Taking trains is safer than taking buses.
....	....

6. T asks Ss to repeat key phrases individually. (T corrects Ss' errors explicitly.)

   ⋮

Note: T = teacher, S = student

(1) Identify and compare the roles of the teacher in each class, and explain them with evidence from the text.

(2) Explain and compare how the teacher in each class manages the classroom with evidence.

문제분석	구분	교과 교육
난이도 ★★★	평가목표	교사의 역할과 교실운영에 대하여 구체적으로 서술하는가?
	채점기준	(1) 교사 역할 1점: (A교사) facilitator/ resource 1점: 입력을 통해 배우고 스스로 오류 수정한다. 1점: (B교사) controller 1점: 교사가 규칙을 제시하고 명시적으로 오류 수정한다. (2) 교실운영 1점: (교실A) 학습자 중심 1점: 협동학습안에서 의견합치 활동을 한다. 1점: (교실B) 교사 중심 1점: 개별과 합동 반복으로 연습한다.

모범답안

(1) Teacher in class A acts as a facilitator and resource. Teacher provides comprehensible input with comparative form while telling her story about travel experiences. Teacher guides students to self-repair their own errors with repetition feedback. Teacher in B is a controller. Teacher presents and explains the target form, comparatives and provides explicit correction. (55 words)

(2) Class A indicates learner-centered activity with groups of six. Students are seated in a group to discuss and complete the consensus building activity under collaborative interaction. Class B is teacher-centered activity with whole class seating arrangement. Students practice with the target structure as an individual or choral drills. (50 words)

13 Read the passage and follow the directions. 【2 points】

Learning a second language (L2) may be viewed as the gradual transformation of performance from controlled to less controlled. This transformation has been called proceduralization or automatization and entails the conversion of declarative knowledge into procedural knowledge. According to this argument, the learning of skills is assumed to start with the explicit provision of relevant declarative knowledge and, through practice, this knowledge can hopefully convert into ability for use. At the same time, it is important to understand that learning an L2 may proceed in a different way. For example, some have wondered if incidental L2 learning is possible as a consequence of doing something else in the L2. Simply put, the question is about the possibility of learning without intention. The answer is still open, but, at present, it appears that people learn faster, more and better when they deliberately apply themselves to learning.

Read Mr. Lee's teaching log below and fill in the blank with the ONE most appropriate word from the passage above.

Through my teaching experience, I've learned that different students learn in different ways. Considering the current trend in teaching and learning, I believe that students should be provided with more opportunities to be exposed to the learning condition. Minsu's case may illustrate that point. At the beginning of the semester, Minsu introduced himself as a book lover. He wanted to read novels in English but was not sure if he could. I suggested that he didn't have to try to comprehend all the details. Indeed, Minsu has benefitted a lot from reading novels. He said he learned many words and expressions even though he did not make attempts to memorize them. I will continue observing his progress as his way of _____ learning is of great interest.

모범답안   incidental

14. Examine the consulting report and follow the directions. 【10 points】

Teacher: Ms. Song	Consultant: Mr. Cho Date: Dec. 2nd

Before consul-tation	In my class, I taught grammatical structures as follows: I expected my students to learn practiced structures, but they still had difficulty in using them in real context. T: She will go swimming. (showing a picture of 'John riding a bike') "Ride a bike." S1: John will ride a bike. T: Good. (showing a picture of 'Mary playing the piano') "Play the piano." S2: Mary will play the piano. T: Very good. (showing a picture of 'Tom visiting a museum') "Visit a museum." S3: Tom visit a museum. T: No, you should say, "Tom will visit a museum." .... T: (showing a picture of 'people going to a movie') What will they do? S4: They will go to a movie. T: Very good. (turning to S5, showing a picture of 'students singing a song') What will they do?
Mr. Cho's advice	The following are pieces of Mr. Cho's advice: • Utilize an e-portfolio. • Use other types of questions. • Employ various authentic materials. • Provide other types of feedback. • Assign specific roles to students in group work.
After consul-tation	After the consultation, I made changes in teaching grammar as follows: T: Good morning, class. Winter vacation is coming soon. I will go to Jeju Island and travel around. Minji, what will you do this vacation? S1: I go to Grandma's house in Busan. T: Minji, I go to Grandma's house? S1: Oh… eh… I will go to Grandma's house. T: Perfect! What about Bora? Do you have any plans? S2: Um… I… I take guitar lessons. T: I take guitar lessons? S3: Uh… I will take guitar lessons. T: Good! What a great plan! Why do you want to do that?

(1) Identify the type of teaching technique which Ms. Song used before the consultation and explain the technique with evidence.
(2) Identify TWO changes that Ms. Song made based on Mr. Cho's advice, and then explain those two changes by comparing the classes before and after consultation with evidence.

문제분석

난이도 ★★★

구분	교과 교육	
평가목표	활동에서 나타난 drill 종류를 이해하고 개선된 수업활동을 서술하는가?	
채점기준	(1) 송교사의 수업활동	(2) 수업활동의 변화
	1점: mechanical/ meaningful drills	1점: (질문유형)
	1점: 미래시제 연습	1점: display에서 referential 변화
	1점: 구 대체연습의 반복활동	1점: (피드백)
	1점: 형태와 의미 연결	1점: 명시적에서 암시적 피드백 변화

모범답안

(1) Ms. Song used mechanical and meaningful drills to let her students practice the target structure of future tense. She provides the cue phrases with the pictures and students repeat the same structures, substituting with the given phrases. Students connect form and meaning to make phrases for the pictures using the target structure. (52 words)

(2) There are two changes, question types and feedback. Ms. Song used different question types, from display questions to ask for the predetermined correct answers, to referential questions to elicit students' own language to facilitate communicative competence. She used different feedback on the students' answers. She gave some implicit feedback on meaning to expand students' communicative ability compared to the explicit feedback. (55 words)

15 Read two middle school students' opinions about an English lesson posted on the online bulletin board and their teacher's teaching log, and follow the directions. 【10 points】

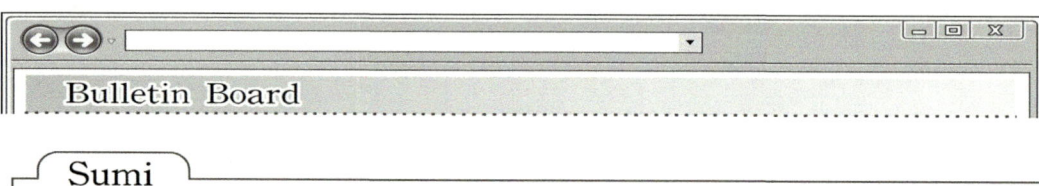

Bulletin Board

Sumi

I loved today's lesson! When the teacher asked questions about the words and expressions related to cooking using the recipe from a cooking magazine, I was able to clearly figure out the meaning of what we were supposed to learn. It was really motivating to use the recipe for learning about the words and expressions used practically for cooking. But I made a few errors, such as telling the difference between "slice" and "chop," that I think I will repeat again despite the teacher's correction. When I make errors, I want him to give me some time to think about why I make them and how I can correct them myself.

Inho

When the teacher asked us to bring a recipe from a cooking magazine yesterday for today's lesson, I wondered why. But when he asked questions about some words and expressions related to cooking using the recipes we brought, I realized why. When asking and answering about them using the cooking material with the teacher and then with my partner, I came to clearly understand the meaning of the words and expressions. Plus, it was very fun and exciting. But I didn't like that he corrected my errors when I misused the word "pan" in "boiling water in the pan": I prefer getting correction from my friends because it makes me feel more comfortable.

My Teaching Log

What I put emphasis on in today's class

I always want my students to have a clear understanding of what I teach, so today I tried to teach the points using materials used in real life rather than the ones in the textbook. To my surprise, they really loved the way I taught today. They participated in the lesson with a lot of enthusiasm.

The things I have to improve in the next class

While leading the activity, for convenience' sake, I corrected the errors that students made. Considering their opinions, however, I have to use alternate ways to give them a chance to correct their errors individually or in pairs.

(1) Based only on the bulletin board and the teaching log, identify ONE feature of the teacher's lesson that the students liked, and explain TWO reasons why they liked it.
(2) Address ONE problem with the lesson, and suggest TWO solutions from the teacher's standpoint by supporting them with rationale.

문제분석	구분	교과 교육	
난이도 ★★☆	평가목표	수업에서의 장점과 단점을 근거로 하여 개선점을 구체적으로 설명하는가?	
	채점기준	(1) 수업의 장점	(2) 문제와 해결책
		1점: 실제자료인 요리잡지 이용한다.	1점: 피드백에 문제가 있다.
		1점: 내적동기가 된다.	1점: 오류에 대해 생각할 시간이 없다.
		1점: 표현이 쉽고 명확하다.	1점: 동료오류로 편하게 해준다.
		1점: 실제생활과 연관이 있다.	1점: 스스로 오류를 할 수 있다.

모범답안

(1) The students liked the idea of using authentic material, cooking magazine. The material has interests to get them intrinsically motivated and more involved in the activity. With the interaction of teacher and other peers, the words and expressions could be clearer and easier to understand since it is related to their real lives. (52 words)

(2) The lesson has some problems with corrective feedback. Teacher's feedback is not effective since it is explicitly presented to students. Teacher needs to give students some preparation time to think about their errors, which can lead to self-repair. Teacher should ask students to do peer-feedback on their errors to make them more comfortable than teacher's explicit correction. (58 words)

16 Examine the class observation checklist and notes after observing a colleague's class, and follow the directions. 【10 points】

2014년 논술 B2번

Observation Checklist

Instructor: Sumi Kim Unit: 4. Personal Health
Topic: How to treat acne Function: Giving advice
Period: 2/8 Date: Nov. 11

Areas	Criteria	Scale*		
Lesson Preparation	• have a clearly developed lesson plan	1	②	3
	• prepare interesting multimedia materials	1	2	③
Instructional Strategies	• give clear directions	1	②	3
	• use an appropriate grouping strategy for group activities	①	2	3
	• provide level-appropriate activities	1	②	3
Affective Aspects	• create a warm and accepting atmosphere	1	2	③

* 1=poor, 2=average, 3=good

Notes

- A fun video clip on acne. Ss loved it.
- T was kind and patient.
- Group activity (same-ability grouping)
  ‣ Higher-level students did well. Had no problems.
  ‣ Lower-level students had a hard time completing the task. Seemed like they needed some help.

(1) Identify one strong point and one weak point of the lesson based on the data above. Support each of your choices with details from both the checklist and the notes.
(2) Address the problems the lower-level students are experiencing by suggesting two possible solutions and supporting them with your rationales.

문제분석	구분	교과 교육	
난이도 ★★★	평가목표	수업과정에서 나타나는 장점과 단점을 파악하고 low-level 학생들을 위한 해결책을 제시하는가?	
	채점기준	(1) 수업의 장단점 1점: (multimedia)를 사용한다. 1점: 실제자료로 쉽게 이해한다. 1점: (grouping)에 문제가 있다. 1점: 낮은레벨은 과업완성이 어렵다.	(2) 문제와 해결책 2점: (scaffolding)을 통해 높은레벨의 학생이 도움을 준다. 2점: (directions)를 명확히 하여 쉽게 이해할 수 있도록 한다.

모범답안

(1) One strong point of this lesson is the multimedia use of a fun video clip. The use of authentic material helps them understand the content easier. In contrast, the weak point is shown to be a grouping, same-ability grouping. The lower-level students had a hard time completing the task without appropriate guidance. (52 words)

(2) There are some solutions for the lower-level group students. First, scaffolding by the teacher or more advanced peers should be provided. They complete the task with level-appropriate help and guidance. Second, clearer directions make them easier and more comprehensible to complete the task. (43 words)

17 Read the parts of Mr. Kang's lesson plans for his level-differentiated classes, and follow the directions. 【25 points】

2011년 논술 1번

Advanced Level	Intermediate-Low Level
T : Last class, we learned how to make passive forms. Today, we'll learn when it's better to use the passive form instead of the active one. Suppose that someone broke into your apartment and you found your laptop was missing. What would you say about your laptop? S1: I would say, "My laptop was stolen." T : That's right. Do you know who stole it? S2: No, I don't. T : Correct. Let's do another example. People constructed the Pyramids in ancient times, but you don't know exactly who constructed them. What would you say about the Pyramids? S3: The Pyramids were constructed in ancient times. T : Great. Can anyone tell us when passive sentences are preferred to their corresponding active sentences? Ss: When we don't know who did something. T : Good. Let's go through a passage together. Try to understand the passage, while also paying attention to the passive forms used in the passage.	T : Last class, we talked about the way to say that something was done. Today, we'll see why people say, "Something was done," rather than say, "Someone did something." Imagine this. Someone broke into your apartment. You couldn't find your computer. It was gone! What would you say about your computer? S1: I would say, "My computer was stolen." T : That's right. Do you know who stole it? S2: No, I don't. T : Correct. Let's do another example. People built the Pyramids long ago. But you do not know exactly who built them. What would you say about the Pyramids? S3: The Pyramids were built long ago. T : Great. So we can say the same idea two ways. We can say, "People built the Pyramids long ago." Or, "The Pyramids were built long ago." Now, when is it better to say, "The Pyramids were built long ago"? Ss: When we don't know who built them. T : Good. Let's go through a passage together. Try to understand the passage. Let's see if you can find any sentences like "The Pyramids were built long ago."
TASK **Step 1** T : I'm going to read you the passage twice. First, I'll read it at normal speed and then I'll read it again as slowly as possible. As you listen, write down as many words and phrases as possible. Have you ever seen the Pyramids of Egypt? Have you ever wondered why they were built and how they were built? The Pyramids were built because the kings wanted to live after they died. They thought that they would live after they died. The Pyramids were constructed on the west side of the Nile River. They were built there because the sun rises in the east and sets in the west. They believed that the king and the sun god would be born and born again, just like the sun. The Pyramids were very difficult to build, but the whole world can enjoy them.	**TASK** **Step 1** T : I am going to read you the passage twice. Both times, I will read it very slowly and clearly. As you listen, write down any words you hear. [the same passage as the one for the advanced level]
Step 2 T : Now, in groups of three, share your notes and see whether your group can come up with its own version of the text. Once your group has reconstructed the text, check it to make sure the meaning is similar to the text you heard. Also check it carefully for grammatical mistakes.	**Step 2** T : Now, let's rewrite the text. First, in groups of three, put together all the words that each member heard. Then, working in your group, try to make sentences with those words. And then compare your group's sentences with other groups' sentences. Using all the sentences available, rewrite the text. And check it to make sure the meaning is similar to the text I read.
Step 3 T : Now, I'll pass out the original text that I read to you. Compare your group's text with the original one. How is the original different from yours? Look at both content and passive forms. And then make a presentation about the differences you've found between the two texts.	**Step 3** T : Now, I will give you the original text. On the text, I've already underlined some parts. [Only the passive forms in the text are underlined.] Mark the parts in your group's text that you think match those underlined parts. Make your group's text as similar as possible to the original text.

(1) Based on the first part of lesson, identify THREE ways how Mr. Kang makes his talk more comprehensible for the Intermediate-Low level and explain them with evidence from the underlined parts, comparing two classes.
(2) Based on the Tasks in the lesson, explain TWO ways in Step 1 and Step 2 to make easier for Intermediate-Low level.
(3) In relation to traditional ways of teaching grammar, describe TWO characteristics of the task given in the lesson plans.

모범답안

(1) On the syntactic level, teacher breaks one meaningful unit into four sentences to introduce a context more easily, instead of one whole sentence. As for lexical simplicity, he uses the simplified words, 'built', 'long ago', instead of 'constructed' and 'ancient times'. He provides uses actual example sentences, instead of metalanguage, passive and active. (53 words)

(2) In step 1, teacher reads the text for better comprehension in a slow and clear manner, rather than normal listening speed for natural listening practice. In step 2, students rewrite to focus on meaning to make it similar to the original, without considering grammatical mistakes. (45 words)

(3) In the task, the students rewrite in their own language and compare with the original text to learn the use of passive forms in student-centered activity. The language form is implicitly taught in context with completing the task, rather than just teacher's explicit explanation on forms. (46 words)

18 Read the English test task specifications in ⟨A⟩ and the teacher's reflective journal in ⟨B⟩, and follow the directions. 【4 points】

2019년 A12번

⟨A⟩

	Test Task Specifications
Category	Description
Purpose	To determine students' current levels and place them into the most appropriate speaking courses
Time allocation	2 minutes (1 minute for preparation and 1 minute for speaking)
Task type	Picture-cued tasks
Scoring method	Analytic a. Criteria: Content, Fluency, Accuracy, Pronunciation b. Each criterion is worth 5 points and the score for this task is added up to 20.
Scoring procedure	a. Two examiners: a primary examiner who conducts the test and a secondary examiner who observes the test b. If there is a difference of more than 2 points in total, the examiners discuss rating disagreements based on the recorded test to arrive at a rating that they agree upon.

⟨B⟩

I understand that some students have potential strengths in learning languages, and in order to check my students' aptitude in English, I conducted a speaking test with picture-cued tasks. For each task, students looked at pictures and prepared for 1 minute and then described them for 1 minute. I found that 1 minute was not enough for my students to prepare their answers, so I felt that I needed to change the time allocation for the task. In addition, although my rating and the other examiner's rating seemed consistent, I realized that my approach, providing a global rating with overall impressions using a single general scale, was not very effective because the scores didn't give much helpful information to students. … There was one student's test yielding very different scores, so we (primary and secondary examiners) had a discussion about the recorded test and found that I gave the wrong score by mistake. It was good that we recorded the test even though both of us were present during the test.

Identify TWO categories that the teacher did NOT follow in the test task specifications from ⟨A⟩. Then, support your answers with evidence from ⟨B⟩.

문제분석	구분	교과 교육
난이도 ★★☆	평가목표	시험의 과업을 위한 조건과 평가의 관계성을 상세히 설명하는가?
	채점기준	1점: (purpose) 1점: 현재레벨을 평가하는 것은 적성평가가 아니다. 1점: (scoring method) 1점: 분석적평가는 하나의 점수로 평가되지 않는다.

모범답안   Two categories that teacher didn't follow were purpose and scoring method. The purpose was to check students' current level, but students' aptitude was assessed for potential strengths. Teacher didn't follow analytic scoring but used holistic scoring in one single score. It was not effective to provide helpful information to students. (50 words)

19 Read the dialogue and follow the directions. 【2 points】

2018년 A3번

> T1: There's no doubt that young children beginning school need the basics of reading, writing, and math.
> T2: I agree, but the big problem is determining the best way for them to get it. I think the classic mode of a teacher at the chalkboard, and books and homework is outdated.
> T1: True. That's why I have been looking at some teaching literature based on the ideas Jonathan Bergman and Aaron Sams came up with.
> T2: What do they suggest?
> T1: Well, they have reconsidered the role of the traditional classroom and home. So home becomes a classroom, and vice versa in this way of learning. Students view lecture materials, usually in the form of videos, as homework before class.
> T2: That's interesting. What's the focus in class?
> T1: That's the best part. Class time is reserved for activities such as interactive discussions or collaborative work supervised by the teacher.
> T2: I like it. But how does it benefit the students?
> T1: They can study the lectures at home at their own pace, or re-watch the videos, if needed, or even skip parts they already understand.
> T2: Right. And then, in class the teacher is present when they apply new knowledge. What about traditional homework?
> T1: That can be done in class, too. So, the teacher can gain insights into whatever concepts, if any, their students are struggling with and adjust the class accordingly.
> T2: What does the literature say about its effectiveness?
> T1: Amazingly, according to one study, 71% of teachers who have tried this approach in their classes noticed improved grades, and 80% reported improved student attitudes, as well.
> T2: That's fantastic. Let me read that when you're done. I want to look further into this.

Fill in the blank with the ONE most appropriate word.

> The teaching approach discussed by the two teachers is known technically as _____ learning in educational settings.

모범답안　flipped

20 Read the text and answer the question.

2009년 22번

> T: Do you like to see movies, Gilsu? What's your favorite movie?
> S: BIG.
> T: BIG! That was a good movie. That was about a little boy inside a big man, wasn't it?
> S: Yeah. Boy get surprise all the time.
> T: He was surprised. Usually little boys don't do the things that men do, right?
> S: No, little boy no drink.
> T: That's right. Little boys don't drink.
>
> *Note:* T=teacher, S=student

Identify which developmental stage for 'negation' that the student is. Explain the function of corrective feedback from the teacher's viewpoint and uptake from the students' viewpoint with evidence.

 **Which of the following is correct based on the dialogue?**
① The teacher gives implicit negative feedback on the student's errors.
② The student immediately responds to the teacher's corrective feedback.
③ The dialogue consists of a single Initiation-Response-Evaluation (IRE) exchange.
④ The student's last turn indicates that she is in the final stage in the acquisition of negation.
⑤ The tag question in the teacher's second turn functions as a referential question.

모범답안 The student's last turn, 'no drink' indicates that he is at the beginning developmental stage for negation. The teacher gives implicit negative feedback, recast, on the student's error focusing on meaning. The student does not notice the teacher's corrective feedback and produce successful uptake with repair but responds with the errors. (51 words)

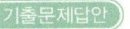 ①

21 Read the following and answer the question.

⟨Activity A⟩

Change the sentences as in the example, and check your answers with your partner. Then explain to your partner the grammatical rule(s) you applied.

[1] I have been to New York several times.

⇒ **I went to New York last month.**

[2] She has read the book before.

⇒ _____ a month ago.

[3] We have known about the problem for ages.

⇒ _____ yesterday.

⟨Activity B⟩

In pairs, read the following conversation extracts, focusing on the parts in italics. What is the difference between what Person A and Person B say? When would you use one form or the other? Share your thoughts with your partner.

[1] A: I*'ve won* a prize in the English-speaking competition.

  B: Yeah? I *won* a prize in the poetry competition last year.

[2] A: I*'ve seen* Romeo and Juliet twice.

  B: Me, too. I *saw* it last Tuesday and again on the weekend.

[3] A: A strange thing *happened* to me yesterday. I couldn't remember my cell phone number.

  B: Really? That *has happened* to me several times, too.

Which of the following is a correct statement about the activities?

① Both activities combine formal instruction on the target forms and their communicative use.

② Activity ⟨A⟩ is centered on promoting immediate gains in implicit knowledge of the grammar features.

③ Activity ⟨A⟩ requires discourse-level analyses of the target structures for their use in context.

④ Activity ⟨B⟩ encourages students to approach the target grammar points deductively.

⑤ Activity ⟨B⟩ helps raise students' awareness of the target forms through meaning-focused input.

문제분석 난이도 ★★★	구분	교과 교육
	평가목표	두 가지 다른 종류의 문법수업을 통해 수업목표와 활동의 특징을 서술하는가?
	채점기준	1점: 〈A〉 form-focused production 1점: 문장수준에서 분석한다. 1점: 〈B〉 inductive 수업 1점: 의미중심의 입력을 통해 목표문법을 분석한다.

모범답안 Activity 〈A〉 is form-focused production to promote explicit knowledge of the grammar features. It requires sentence-level analyses of the target structures for their grammatical knowledge. Activity 〈B〉 encourages students to approach the target grammar points inductively. It helps raise students' awareness of the target forms with their communicative use through meaning-focused input. (52 words)

기출문제답안 ⑤

22 Read the dialogue and follow the directions.

2009년 21번

S: My mom holded the baby rabbits and we patted them.
T: Did you say your mom held the baby rabbits?
S: Yes.
T: What did you say she did?
S: She holded the baby rabbits and we patted them.
T: Did you say she held them tightly?
S: Yes, she holded them tightly.

Describe all the pedagogical implications found in the dialogue between teacher and students.

기출문제

Choose all and only the correct statements about the class.
ⓐ Teachers need to speak more clearly and slowly.
ⓑ Students need to receive immediate feedback from their teachers.
ⓒ Students cannot acquire a language form until they are developmentally ready.
ⓓ Teachers should give more wait time for the students to answer questions.
ⓔ Students' attention to meaning can block their recognition of form.

모범답안 Students cannot acquire a language form until they are developmentally ready, even though they receive immediate feedback from their teachers. Teachers need to give some explicit explanation on grammatical error students make. When their attention focuses on meaning, 'hold tightly', it can block their recognition of form of past verb. (50 words)

기출문제답안 ⓒ, ⓔ

23 Read the following and answer the question.

2011년 20번

The comprehensible output hypothesis states that we acquire language when we attempt to transmit a message but fail and have to try again. Eventually, we arrive at the correct form of our utterance, our conversational partner finally understands, and we acquire the new form we have produced. In the process of modifying their interlanguage utterances for greater message comprehensibility, L2 learners undertake some restructuring that affects their access to their knowledge base.

(Before Mr. Park starts his lesson in a middle school English class, he asks students questions to warm up, starting with Mina.)

T: What did you do last weekend, Mina?
S: I visit my uncle in the hospital.
T: You visited your uncle in the hospital?
S: Yes, I visit him.
T: I see. Did you do anything else?
S: Yeah. Um, I see a movie.
T: You saw a movie?
S: Yes.
T: Great. What movie did you see?
S: I see the movie Avatar.

Choose all and only the correct statements about the student.

ⓐ From the perspective of the output hypothesis, the student's output reflects her acquisition of past-tense rules through pushed output.

ⓑ From the behaviorist point of view, the student needs more repetition and drill of past-tense forms.

ⓒ From the viewpoint of the focus-on-form approach, more focused intervention is needed to draw the student's attention to proper use of function words.

ⓓ According to the input hypothesis, the student needs more comprehensible input containing past-tense forms while her affective filter is kept low.

기출문제답안 ⓑ, ⓓ

24. Read the following and answer the question.

> **A Teacher's Lesson Note for an EOP (English for Occupational Purposes) Class**
>
> <u>Describe</u> the project
> - Have students engage in a SWOT (Strengths, Weaknesses, Opportunities, & Threats) analysis.
> - Simulate a SWOT presentation in front of the company's CEO.
>
> <u>Meet</u> the new language
> - Pool what students need to know. Provide key words & phrases through the analysis of a case study.
> - Draw students' attention to formal & informal styles of presentations.
>
> <u>Do</u> a SWOT project
> - Start a SWOT analysis using a case study.
> - Develop a SWOT analysis format for students.
> - Help students with preparing their group presentation.
>
> <u>Use and refine</u> it
> - Have students in each group present their parts of the SWOT analysis.
> - Prepare a peer assessment guideline of the presentation.

Identify one teaching approach of the lesson and explain it with THREE communicative features how students learn the language compared to traditional language teaching.

Which of the following is NOT correct about the class above?

① Target language input is presented in a decontextualized manner.
② Cooperative learning skills are necessary to complete the project.
③ Key vocabulary and language patterns are selected based on students' needs.
④ The activity has direct relevance to what students should be able to perform in the real world.
⑤ The teacher exposes students to different degrees of formality in using discipline-specific language.

문제분석	구분	교과 교육
난이도 ★★☆	평가목표	내용중심교수법의 EOP의 특성을 이해하여 구체적으로 서술하는가?
	채점기준	1점: 내용중심교수법이다. 1점: 학생들은 자신의 요구에 따라 어휘와 언어를 배운다. 1점: 학생들은 영역에 특화된 언어를 배운다. 1점: 협동학습으로 발표하고 평가한다.

모범답안 The lesson is content based approach. The students learn key vocabulary and language patterns based on their needs. They acquire different degrees of formality using discipline-specific language to perform in the real world. In cooperative learning, they work in a group to make a presentation and evaluate to each other. (50 words)

기출문제답안 ①

25. Read the following and answer the question.

2007년 전국 15번

(1) Learners read authentic texts from various genres and deal with real texts and functions of literacy. It is a philosophy of learning. Proponents of this approach believe that they are not just teaching reading; rather, they are guiding and assisting learners to develop as independent readers, writers, and learners. They believe that children become literate as they grapple with the meaning and uses of print in their environments.

(2) This generally emphasizes teaching children to match individual letters of the alphabet with their specific English pronunciations, with the idea that if children can "sound out" or "decode" new words, they will be able to read independently. In this approach, children are explicitly taught sound-symbol patterns, and often the conscious learning of rules.

(3) It teaches children to recognize whole words, commonly using flash cards or other techniques to help children quickly identify such common words as *of*, *and*, and *the*. It is based upon the notion that if children can recognize about 100 of the most frequently occurring words, they will be able to read about half of the words they encounter in most texts.

(4) This is based upon the notion that children should be taught to read through careful control and sequencing of the language and the sounds that they are exposed to.

Identify the reading teaching method for each activity with ONE or TWO words. Write them in order.

모범답안   (1) whole language   (2) phonics   (3) sight-word   (4) basal reader

26 Read the following class to find the advantages and drawbacks.

2006년 서울 7번

⟨Class⟩

- Age: 15 to 28
- Proficiency: from low-intermediated and advanced learners
- Mother tongue: Korean, Japanese, Spanish & German
- Gender: men and women
- Learning styles: auditory, visual, and kinesthetic individual or group predispositions etc.

Describe the THREE advantages and drawbacks that this heterogeneous class can provide.

모범답안

(1) • The classes are interesting because of the sheer richness of their human resources.
 • The classes are often bursting with energy precisely because of all the differences.
 • The students give scope for peer teaching.

(2) • The classes are difficult to meet the individual student's needs.
 • It is difficult to make sure that everyone in the classroom learns.
 • The teacher should make effort to find materials, activities, topics and a pace to suit most participants.

27. This passage is about the characteristics and types of task.

In some books, the word 'task' has been used as a label for various activities including grammar exercises, practice activities and role plays. However, these are not tasks in the sense the word is used here. All tasks should be 'goal-oriented'. In other words, the emphasis is on understanding and conveying meanings in order to complete the tasks successfully. Furthermore, all tasks should have a specific outcome, where the emphasis is on exchanging meanings not producing specific language forms. Here are several types of tasks:

- Listing

The outcome of listing would be the completed list by *brainstorming*, in which learners draw on their own knowledge and experience together, or *fact-finding*, in which learners find things out by asking people and referring to books, etc.

- Ordering and sorting

Sequencing items, actions, or events in a logical or chronological order, *ranking* items according to personal values or specified criteria, and *categorizing* items in given or created groups are included in this type.

- Comparing

This involves *comparing* information of a similar/different nature from multiple sources, as well as *matching* to identify specific points and then relate them to each other.

- Problem solving

This category includes *logic problems* like short puzzles, and *real-life problems* such as evaluating, suggesting, or agreeing on a solution.

Class Activity	Task (O/X)	Task Type
Discuss in pairs and write in your notebook as many things as possible that you can find in a kitchen.	O	(1)
Read the advice column in a small group and decide on what advice your group members will give in response to a reader's letter.	O	(2)
Write four sentences describing a picture individually first, and then read them to your partner.	X	X
Listen to accounts of a car accident and discuss which of four relatable pictures most accurately portrays what happened.	O	(3)
Ask/answer questions in a clerk/customer role using the following dialogue: 　A: How much is (this postcard)? 　B: It is (two) dollars. 　A: OK, I will take it.	X	X

Identify an appropriate task type for each number.

문제분석

난이도 ★☆☆

구분	교과 교육
평가목표	과업의 유형을 이해하고 표현하는가?
채점기준	(1) (listing) 가장 단순한 과업유형으로 항목을 나열한다. (2) (problem solving) 편지에 나타난 문제점을 읽고 조언을 결정한다. (3) (comparing) 사건과 관련된 그림을 연결한다.

모범답안　(1) listing　(2) problem-solving　(3) comparing

28 Read the teaching material and the "Teaching Procedure" and follow the directions.

- Teaching Procedure

	Activities	Principles
Step 1:	Presentation of the dialogue, and a discussion of the function and situation – people's roles, setting and topic	Teacher motivates students by talking with them about meeting friends on weekends.
Step 2:	Question-answer activities preceded by the teacher's modelling	Teacher helps students understand the meanings of the utterances in the dialogue.
Step 3:	Oral practice of key utterances of the dialogue segment, such as What do you do on Sundays/ Saturdays/ weekends....	Teacher refers to form implicitly, and provides comprehensible input.
Step 4:	Question-answer activities based on the dialogue segment, presenting some verb-noun chunks such as have lunch/ play soccer.... (The list is presented on the board.)	Students notice specific linguistic features in input.
Step 5:	Question-answer activities based on the dialogue, presenting some frequency adverbs: always/ usually/ often.	Students pay attention to specific linguistic features in input.
Step 6:	Question-answer activities related to the students' personal experiences, giving more examples of the communicative use and language forms	Students discover and generalize rules underlying the functional expressions or structures.
Step 7:	Interview activities through oral and written forms, using interview cards	Activities help students raise consciousness of grammar and incorporate forms into communicative tasks.

- Teaching Material (a recorded dialogue)

Joe   : What do you do on weekends?
David: Well, that depends. During the school year, I usually have to study on Saturdays.
Joe   : And how about on Sundays?
David: Well, we always have lunch together, you know, the whole family. Then after lunch, I sometimes go to the park and meet my friends.
Joe   : That sounds nice.

In the following passage, the teacher describes his/her rationale for using the Teaching Procedure. In the passage below, fill in each blank with ONE or TWO words.

I have chosen an instructional material which can promote the students' communicative language use through ①_____ instruction. Steps 1 through 3 are the introducing and checking stage, where I have guided the students to a clear understanding of the meaning of the utterances and provided implicit references to form through a carefully staged series of activities. From step 4 onward, I have drawn students' attention to the target language forms through controlling the content and pace of the lesson. This will help students notice the new linguistic features and targeted forms of the language. The progression is from a function to a form-focus.

In steps 6 and 7, I have helped students find out the specific features of the grammatical system and communicate with other students, which is a grammar ②_____ techniques. It may not lead directly and instantly to the acquisition of the grammatical item in question. But it may nevertheless trigger a train of mental processes that in time will result in accurate and appropriate production.

모범답안 ① task-based
② consciousness-raising

29. Read the dialogue in a classroom situation and suggest ONE sentence.

2004년 서울 6번

Teacher:	Why do you think the creature (an ammonite) used to live inside a shell like that?
Carl:	For protection.
Teacher:	What does protection mean? Any idea, Carl?
Carl:	It stop other things hurting it.
Teacher:	Right, it stops other things hurting it. Now if it came out of its shell, and waggled along the seabed, what would happen to it?
Carl:	It might get ate.
Teacher:	Yes. You can say it might get eaten by something else, yeah?

As you see in their talks, control is exerted and facilitated by the presequences which the teacher often employs to indicate that a question is coming, and to provide clues as to what an appropriate answer might be. It is also evident in the frequency with which the teacher interrupts pupil-turns so as to challenge, modify or supplement what is being said, or to reallocate the turn altogether. _____. In ordinary conversation, it is rare for errors to be identified interpretively, and very rare for the correction to be supplied by a listener. There is a marked preference for self-initiated self-correction. But in an instructional setting, there is likely to be a correct version which is not open to negotiation and many errors which cannot be allowed to stand. There may well be an organizational preference both for inviting self-correction and for using intonational and other devices for not marking the error too obtrusively. But if more subtle indications of inadequacy do not work, then the teacher has to supply the ommission.

Suggest ONE sentence to make it appropriate to the text above using ALL the words from the word list.

⟨Word list⟩

teacher's	such	are	the	of
interruptions	dominance	expressions	clear	

모범답안 Such interruptions are clear expressions of the teacher's dominance.

30 Read the extract from a lesson and answer the question.

2002년 서울 10번

(1) 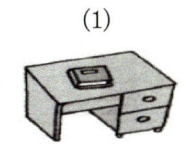 Teacher says: Pick up the book and put it in the drawer.

(2) 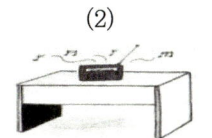 Teacher says: Turn off the tape recorder and give it to me.

Teachers believe in the importance of having their students enjoy their experience in learning to communicate in a foreign language. The way to do this is to base foreign language learning upon the way _____. This method is directed to right-brain learning, whereas most foreign language teaching methods are directed to left-brain learning. Right-hemisphere activities must occur before left hemisphere can process language for production. An adult should proceed towards language mastery through right-hemisphere motor activities, while the left hemisphere watches and learns.

Complete the passage with all the words in the word list.

〈Word list〉

| own | native | children | language | learn | their |

모범답안   children learn their own native language

31. Read the passage and follow the directions.

2012년 28번

Two middle school English teachers instruct their classes.

Teacher A: "Today I'm going to show you how to set a table. Before I do, I'll pass out spoons, forks, plates, and knives... Now watch what I do and follow along. I'm putting a plate on the table... Now put a plate on the table. On the table. OK?... Good job! Now I'm putting the fork on the left side of the plate. [*Teacher continues with other utensils.*] Well done! Now, what I'd like you to do is practice setting a table in pairs. One partner tells the other what to do and that partner follow the commands..."

Teacher B: "Everybody, today we have a mystery to solve. I have six picture clues. You will each be given just one picture. Then find a partner and exchange information in your own words. After that, find another partner and do the same until you have sufficient clues or the alloted time runs out. After gathering information, you will form groups of four and come up with a solution to the mystery. There are many possible solutions. You'll have 15 minutes. Finally, one member from your group will report your group's solution back to the class."

Identify a teaching methodology/ technique of each class and explain it with TWO features how language is acquired.

Which of the following lists all and only correct statements about the classes described?

ⓐ Teacher A models preposition use.
ⓑ Teacher A speaks and students respond verbally.
ⓒ The language practiced in both classes is predetermined by the teachers.
ⓓ Teacher B employs accuracy-based activities.
ⓔ In Teacher B's class, students are encouraged to communicate actively to exchange information.

문제분석	구분	교과 교육
난이도 ★★☆	평가목표	두 가지 다른 교수법을 활용한 교실 활동을 이해한다.
	채점기준	1점: (A) TPR 1점: 전치사를 가르치기 위한 교수법으로 학습자는 신체적으로 반응한다. 1점: (B) 문제해결법 1점: 문제를 해결하기 위하여 의사소통을 한다.

모범답안 Teacher A adopts total physical response to teach simple commands for setting a table. He focuses on modelling preposition uses by repetition and students respond physically. Teacher B employs a problem solving technique in a group. Students communicate to exchange information to conclude with one solution, as a fluency-based activity. (52 words)

기출문제답안 ,

32 Identify the teaching approach.

㉠ The main function of the classroom may be to provide comprehensible input in an environment conducive to a low affective filter.
㉡ The classroom is most useful for beginners, who cannot easily utilize the informal environment for input.
㉢ Students should never be required to speak unless they are ready to do so.
㉣ Error correction should be minimal in the class.

모범답안 Total Physical Response

33 Identify the teaching approach.

The teacher asks students to be silent, listen to commands in English, and then do exactly what s/he does. The students are encouraged "to respond rapidly without hesitation and to make a distinct, robust response with their bodies." For example, when the teacher commands students to run, students are to run with joy. Commands such as "Stand up! Walk! Stop! Turn! Sit down!" are then executed in succession. Next, commands are expanded to full sentences.

모범답안 Total Physical Response

34 Write down the teaching approach for the following.

- ㉠ It is important that students feel successful. Feelings of success and low anxiety facilitate learning.
- ㉡ Students should not be made to memorize fixed routines, and correction should be carried out in an unobtrusive manner.
- ㉢ Students must develop flexibility in understanding novel combinations of target language chunks. Novelty is also motivating.
- ㉣ Spoken language is emphasized and students will begin to speak when they are ready.
- ㉤ Students are expected to make errors when they first begin speaking, and work on the fine details of the language should be postponed until students have become somewhat proficient.

모범답안 Total Physical Response

35 Identify a teaching approach of the following.

Q: What is the role of the teacher?
A: Initially, the teacher is the director of all student behavior.
Q: What are some characteristics of the teaching/ learning process?
A: The first phase of a lesson is one of modeling. The instructor issues commands to a few students, then performs the action with them. In the second phase, these same students demonstrate that they can understand the commands by performing them along.

모범답안 Total Physical Response Method

36 Fill in the blanks with appropriate words.

Listening as a major component in language learning and teaching first hit the spotlight in the late 1970s with James Asher's (1977) work on Total Physical Response, in which the role of comprehension was given prominence as learners were given great quantities of language to listen to before they were encouraged to respond orally. Similarly, the Natural Approach recommended a significant "silent period" during which learners were allowed the security of listening without being forced to go through the anxiety of speaking before they were "ready" to do so. Such approaches were an outgrowth of a variety of research studies that showed evidence of the importance of input in second language acquisition. Stephen Krashen (1982), for example, borrowing insights from first language acquisition, stressed the significance of (㉠) or the aural reception of language that is just a little beyond the learner's (㉡).

모범답안 ㉠ input ㉡ current level

37 Fill in the blanks with one appropriate word each.

(㉠) refers to an unconscious process that involves the naturalistic development of language proficiency through understanding language and through using language for meaningful communication. (㉡), by contrast, refers to a process in which conscious rules about a language are developed.

모범답안   ㉠ acquisition   ㉡ learning

38 Read the following 'Teacher Talk' from 'Audio-Motor Unit' and 'Draw the Picture' techniques.

2002년 전국 11번

Audio-Motor Unit	Draw the Picture
Suppose you are at a restaurant. Join me in acting out the appropriate response. • Pick up your napkin. • Unfold it. • Pick up your fork in your left hand. • Pick up your knife in your right hand. • Cut a piece of meat. • Chew it.	Do exactly what I say. • Take out a sheet of paper. • Draw a circle in the middle of the paper. • Draw a square next to the circle. • Divide the square by half. • Color the right side of the square red. • Draw another square underneath the circle.

Describe the four similarities applied in both techniques.

모범답안   ① comprehension-based technique
　　　　　② commands by the teacher
　　　　　③ right-brain lateralization
　　　　　④ the same way as learning L1

39 Read the following and follow the directions.

Lesson Procedure

(1) Start by showing pictures of common shopping items (e.g., apples, milk, bread). Point to each item and ask, "What is this?" If students know, they answer, and if not, the teacher says the word and asks them to repeat it.

(2) Introduce common phrases used in shopping situations. Write them on the board and explain their meaning:
- "I would like to buy..."
- "How much is this?"
- "Can I have...?"

(3) The teacher uses gestures and visuals to aid understanding. For example, hold up an apple and say, "I would like to buy an apple."

(4) Have students repeat the phrases after the teacher. Then, hold up different items and ask individual students, "What would you like to buy?" The student responds using, "I would like to buy (item)."

(5) Ask the students to sit in a circle and go over the key phrases and vocabulary they learned during the lesson. Point to the objects and ask students:
- "What is this?"
- "How much is it?"
- "What would you like to buy?"

(6) Each student must complete one mini dialogue with the teacher, using the target language. For example:
- Teacher: "What would you like to buy?"
- Student: "I would like to buy a banana."

Complete the summary the TWO most appropriate words.

> This Natural Method is aimed at the goal of basic interpersonal communication skills. Everyday language instructions, conversations, shopping, listening to the radio are emphasized. The teacher was the source of the learners' input and the creator of an interesting and stimulating variety of classroom activities. The initial task of the teacher is to provide just a little beyond the learner's level, widely known as _____.

모범답안   comprehensible input

40 Read the following and follow the directions.

2009년 17번

In this teaching method, the learners repeat aloud the teacher's utterances of the examples below as they have heard them. They do this without looking at a printed text. The utterances must be brief enough to be retained by the ear. Sound is as important as form and order.

Example:
I borrowed *a* book. I borrowed *books*.
He plays the piano. *She* plays the piano.
I *like* apples. I *don't like* apples.

Choose all and only the correct statements about the class.

ⓐ Dialogues center on communicative functions and are not normally memorized.
ⓑ The target linguistic system is learned through the practice of language patterns.
ⓒ Sequencing is determined by the consideration of content or meaning which will maintain interest.
ⓓ 'Language is viewed as a set of habits,' so errors must be prevented at all costs.
ⓔ Explicit grammatical explanation is generally kept to a minimum.

문제분석	구분	교과 교육
난이도 ★☆☆	평가목표	ALM교수법에서 drill을 중시하여 문법은 최소화하는 활동을 이해하는가?
	채점기준	1점: 목표언어는 끝없는 반복 연습을 통해서 학습된다. 1점: 언어는 습관에 의해 만들어지므로 오류는 허용되지 않는다. 1점: 명시적으로 규칙을 가르치는 것은 최소화한다.

기출문제답안 ⓑ, ⓓ, ⓔ

41 What is the teaching approach with these features?

① It aims at teaching the language skills in order of listening, speaking, reading, and writing.
② The dialogues are learned by a process of mimicry-memorization.
③ Students learn dialogue sentences by heart, one by one.

모범답안 Audiolingual Method

42 Identify the teaching approach to explain the description of ㉠~㉣.

㉠ Language is primarily an oral phenomenon and written language is a secondary representation of speech.
㉡ The major focus of study is phonology and morphology.
㉢ Language is acquired through the over-learning of its patterns.
㉣ In learning languages, a student should begin with, the patterns of the language rather than deductive learning of grammatical rules.

모범답안 Audiolingual Method

43 What is the teaching method of the following description ㉠~㉣?

㉠ Linguistic competence is the desired goal.
㉡ The teaching of grammar is essentially inductive.
㉢ Accuracy, in terms of formal correctness, is a primary goal.
㉣ Errors are to be avoided at all costs.

모범답안   Audiolingual Method

44 Identify a type of drill.

The cue triggers a morphological or syntactic change in the pattern. The drills are excellent for testing the students' ability to encode grammatical relationships such as subject-verb agreement, indefinite article choice, count mass nouns, pronoun forms.

모범답안   substitution drill

45 Fill in the blanks with one appropriate word each.

Behavioral Psychology	Cognitive Psychology
Repetition and ① r_____	Analysis and insight
② S_____ – Descriptive	Generative – Transformational
③ S_____ method	Mentalism & intuition
Description – "what"	Explanation – "why"

모범답안   ① reinforcement   ② Structural   ③ Scientific

46 Identify the teaching approach of the following.

㉠ "Language is habit" so errors must be prevented at all costs.
㉡ Accuracy, in terms of formal correctness, is a primary goal.
㉢ Communicative activities come after a long process of rigid drills and exercises.

모범답안   Audiolingual Method

47 Identify the teaching approach to be developed from the description below.

Language learning is primarily a matter of transforming perceptions into conceptions. Language is a means of thinking, of representing the world to oneself, and children use language to represent their conceptions. According to these insights after observing children, a teaching method was formulated. This method teaches learners directly (without translation) and conceptually (without grammatical rules and explanations) a set of long connected sentences that are easy to perceive from the very beginning. The method emphasizes verbs and teacher's actions associating with the verbs.

모범답안   Direct Method

48 What is the teaching approach with these features?

- client-counselor relationship
- inductive strategy of learning
- no set syllabus
- interests in the affective nature of learning

모범답안   Community Language Learning

49 Describe the THREE demerits of Community Language Learning.

모범답안
① The counselor-teacher can become too nondirective.
② The inductive strategy of Community Language Learning is not so useful at the first stage of learning.
③ If the teacher is not a translation expert, there could be misunderstanding of the target language.

50 Identify the teaching approach.

Q: What is the role of the teacher?
A: The teacher's initial role is that of a counselor.
Q: What language skills are emphasized?
A: The most important skills are understanding and speaking the language. Reading and writing are also worked on, however, based upon what the students have already understood.

모범답안 Community Language Learning

51 Identify the teaching approach to describe the following.

Ⓐ Learning is facilitated if the learner discovers or creates rather than remembers and repeats what is to be learned.
Ⓑ Learning is facilitated by accompanying (mediating) physical objects.
Ⓒ Learning is facilitated by problem solving involving the material to be learned.

모범답안　Silent Way

52 Match the teaching approach with the teacher's roles.

〈Teaching approach〉
㉠ Total Physical Response　　㉡ Silent way
㉢ Community Language Learning　　㉣ The Natural Approach
㉤ Suggestopedia

〈Teacher's roles〉
ⓐ Active and direct role, 'the director of a stage play' with students as actors.
ⓑ Counselling parental analogy, providing a safe environment in which students can learn and grow.
ⓒ Teaching, testing, and getting out of the way, remaining impassive, resisting temptation to model, remodel, assist, direct, and exhort.
ⓓ Creating situations in which the learner is most suggestible and presenting material in a way most likely to encourage positive reception and retention, exuding authority and confidence.
ⓔ Being the primary source of comprehensible input, creating positive low-anxiety climate, choosing and orchestrating a rich mixture of classroom activities.

모범답안　㉠-ⓐ　㉡-ⓒ　㉢-ⓑ　㉣-ⓔ　㉤-ⓓ

53 Match a teaching approach with the each following feature.

① Silent Way   a. Students' silent period
② Natural Approach   b. Relaxed concentration
③ TPR   c. Teacher's color chart
④ Suggestopedia   d. Physical activity

모범답안   ① c ② a ③ d ④ b

54 Identify the teaching approach to explain the description of ㉠~㉤.

㉠ Effective communication is the desired goal.
㉡ Drill may occur, but peripherally.
㉢ Dialogs center around communicative functions and are not normally memorized.
㉣ Attempts to communicate are encouraged from the beginning.
㉤ Translation may be used where students need or benefit from it.

모범답안   Communicative Language Teaching

55 Identify a number of wrong description and change it to make appropriate.

"The notional syllabus," Wilkins says, "is in contrast with the grammatical and ① **situational** syllabuses because it takes the desired communicative capacity as the starting point. In drawing up a notional syllabus, instead of asking how speakers express themselves or when or where they use the language, we ask ② **what** it is they communicate through language. We are then able to organize language teaching in terms of the ③ **context** rather than the form of the language… A general language course will concern itself with those concepts and functions that are likely to be of widest value." Wilkins analyzes language needs within three categories: the conceptual or semantic-grammatical; the ④ **modal** which the speaker's attitude is conveyed; and the functional, which derives from the speaker's purpose in communication.

모범답안   ③ function

56 Identify the teaching approach of the following, ㉠~㉡.

㉠ Cooperative student-centered learning
㉡ Focus on the community of learners.
㉢ Focus on the social nature of language.
㉣ Use of authentic, natural language.
㉤ Holistic assessment techniques in testing.
㉥ Integration of the four skills.

모범답안   Communicative language teaching

57 Fill in each blank with TWO most appropriate words about Communicative Language Teaching.

Classroom goals are focused on all of the components of communicative competence and not restricted to grammatical or linguistic competence. Language techniques are designed to engage learners in the pragmatic, authentic, functional use of language for (1)_____. Fluency and accuracy are seen as complementary principles underlying communicative techniques. In the communicative classroom, students ultimately have to use the language, productively and receptively, in (2)_____.

모범답안   (1) meaningful purposes   (2) unrehearsed contexts

58 Identify the teaching approach of the following.

The learner is directly in touch with the realities being studied. It is contrasted with learning in which the learner only reads about, hears about, talks about, or writes about these realities but never comes in contact with them as part of the learning process. It involves direct encounter with the phenomenon being studied rather than merely thinking about the encounter or only considering the possibility of doing something with it.

모범답안   Experiential learning

59 Identify the syllabus of the following.

㉠ Language is a system for the expression of meaning.
㉡ The primary function of language is for interaction and communication.
㉢ The structure of language reflects its functional and communicative uses.

모범답안   functional syllabus

---

60 Fill out with one appropriate word to be common in the blank.

The role played by background knowledge in language comprehension is explained and formalized in a theoretical model known as _____ Theory. One of the basic tenets of this theory is that any given text does not carry meaning in and of itself. Rather, it provides direction for listeners or readers so that they can construct meaning from their own cognitive structure (previously acquired or background knowledge). The previously acquired knowledge structures accessed in the comprehension process are called _____.

모범답안   schema

memo

CHAPTER 05 문화 지도

01 Read the passages and follow the directions. 【4 points】

2022년 A10번

⟨A⟩

In most intercultural conflict situations, interactants are expected to defend or save their faces when they are threatened. Here, face refers to a person's sense of favorable self-worth or self-image experienced in communication. The various ways to deal with conflict and face are called facework or facework strategies. There are three general types of facework strategies used in intercultural conflict. Below are the three types and the specific behaviors displayed when employing a strategy.

Facework Strategies	Facework Behaviors
A. Dominating: an effort to control the conflict situation	A1. Assault the other verbally
	A2. Be firm in one's demands and do not give in
B. Avoiding: an attempt to save the other person's face	B1. Dismiss the conflict that threatens the other's face
	B2. Rely on a third party to manage the conflict
C. Integrating: an endeavor for closure of the conflict	C1. Offer an apology for the conflict
	C2. Mutually acknowledge each other's good points

⟨B⟩

Scenario 1
Michael and Ken are students from different countries taking the same class at an Australian university. They are partners for an assignment to meet twice a week. However, Michael is always late for the meetings. Ken feels frustrated because in his culture, punctuality is highly important and making others wait is regarded inconsiderate. Ken finally tells Michael how he feels. Hearing Ken's complaints, Michael is upset at first. He thinks Ken is fussing over nothing because in Michael's culture, people are more flexible with time. After consideration, he comes to understand Ken's position and admits his fault. Then, expressing his regret, he promises to be on time.

Scenario 2
Maria and Sue are students rooming together at a US university. They are from different countries. Maria loves hanging out with her friends and invites them to the room to talk and eat. They almost always leave after midnight. However, Sue is irritated because in her culture, staying late at someone's place is not normally acceptable. In contrast, Maria doesn't mind her friends staying late since in her culture, getting along well with other people is a high priority. Sue

considers directly telling Maria that her friends should not outstay their welcome. Not wanting to create an unpleasant situation, however, she instead decides to go to the library when her roommate's friends visit.

Based on ⟨A⟩, identify ONE facework behavior that Michael and Sue each display to deal with their intercultural conflicts in ⟨B⟩, respectively. Then, explain your answers with evidence from ⟨B⟩.

문제분석	구분	교과 교육
난이도 ★☆☆	평가목표	학습자 언어의 pragmatic 요소를 구체적으로 서술하는가?
	채점기준	1점: (Michael) C1 1점: 갈등을 일으킨 잘못을 인정하고 사과한다. 1점: (Sue) B1 1점: 잘못을 직접적으로 말하지 않고 회피한다.
모범답안		Michael displays C1 to make an apology for his lateness after admitting his fault that causes a conflict and promises not to be late. Sue displays B1 not to directly tell her roommate's faults but instead avoid the conflict situation and go to the library. (45 words)

02
Read the teacher's note in ⟨A⟩ and the lesson plan in ⟨B⟩, and follow the directions. 【4 points】

2021년 B8번

⟨A⟩

Teacher's Note

Last week, I attended a teacher training workshop on intercultural education. In the workshop, the trainer defined culture as the beliefs, way of life, art, and customs that are shared and accepted by people in a particular society. She also explained that understanding another culture involves constructing a new frame of reference in terms of the people who created it. I totally agree with her. I believe that in order to help my students develop intercultural competence, I need to have them understand their own frame of reference as well as the target culture's. I also think that it is necessary to utilize various materials to arouse students' interests. Below is the list of instructional techniques that the trainer taught us in the workshop.

- Artifact study: It is designed to help students discern the cultural significance of certain unfamiliar objects from the target culture. The activity involves students in giving descriptions and forming hypotheses about the function of the unknown object.
- Culture capsule: It is a brief description, usually one or two paragraphs, of some aspect of the target culture, followed by or incorporated with contrasting information about the students' native culture. Culture capsules can be written by teachers or students.
- Culture island: A culture island is an area in the classroom where posters, maps, objects, and pictures of people, lifestyles, or customs of other cultures are displayed to attract learners' attention, evoke comments, and help students develop a mental image.
- Native informant: Native informants can be valuable resources to the classroom teacher, both as sources of current information about the target culture and as linguistic models for students. Students can develop a set of questions they would like to ask before native speakers come to the class.

⟨B⟩

Lesson Plan

Unit 7. Hello From Around The World

Period	10th out of 12 sessions
Topic	Greeting customs in the UK
Goal	To teach about the ways in which people greet each other in the UK and how they are different from those in Korea

Preparation

Decorate the culture board in the English classroom with pictures and posters which illustrate the greeting customs of the UK.

Lesson Steps

1. Have the students check out the culture board and tell what they think about the pictures and posters.
2. Read aloud a short passage about greeting customs in the UK, which is prepared in advance, and have the students take notes.
3. Divide the students into small groups to compare their notes. Then, have them discuss and write the similarities and differences between Korea and the UK regarding the greeting customs.
4. Have the students imagine situations in which people from the two cultures meet. Ask them to write a conversation script based on the situation and to perform role-plays.

Based on ⟨A⟩, identify TWO instructional techniques that the teacher implements in the lesson plan, with corresponding evidence from ⟨B⟩.

문제분석	구분	교과 교육
난이도 ★★☆	평가목표	언어와 문화의 상관관계를 이해하고 교수 활동을 서술하는가?
	평가기준	1점: Culture capsule 1점: 두 나라의 차이점과 유사점을 서술한다. 1점: Culture island 1점: 교실안의 그림, 포스터를 이용하여 다른 문화에 대해 토론한다.

모범답안 Culture capsule and culture island are used. For culture capsule, differences and similarities between two cultures of Korea and UK are compared, discussed, and written. For culture island, students discuss their thoughts about different cultures in culture board using pictures and posters in classroom. (44 words)

03 Read the lesson procedure and write the TWO lesson objectives. Do NOT copy more than FIVE consecutive words. 【4 points】

2015년 A1번

The following is a sample lesson plan of culture-integrated language learning for 2nd year middle school students.

Lesson Procedure

(1) Students watch a video clip that shows an experiment, which is summarized below.

> The experiment shows that American mothers used twice as many object labels as Japanese mothers ("piggie," "doggie") and Japanese mothers engaged in twice as many social routines of teaching politeness norms (empathy and greetings). An American mother's pattern might go like this: "That's a car. See the car? You like it? It's got nice wheels." A Japanese mother might say: "Here! It's a vroom vroom. I give it to you. Now give this to me. Yes! Thank you." American children are learning that the world is mostly a place with objects, Japanese children that the world is mostly about relationships. Relationships usually involve a verb. Verbs are more important in Asian languages than in English. Asians tend to use an expression like "Drink more?" rather than "More tea?" when they perceive there is a need. Americans are noun-oriented, pointing objects out to their children, naming them, and telling them about their attributes. Nouns denote categories.

(2) Students share their own experiences about noun-oriented expressions as opposed to verb-oriented ones, and discuss different ways of thinking for those expressions.

(3) Students do Activity 1 in order to learn a variety of noun-oriented English expressions.

⟨Activity 1⟩ Fill in the blanks with appropriate words.

Verb-Oriented Expressions	Noun-Oriented Expressions
He works hard.	He is a hard worker.
My head aches.	I _____.
He is very humorous.	He has a good _____.
.....	.....

(4) Students discuss why noun-oriented expressions are more frequently used in English than verb-oriented ones.

(5) Students engage in the following activity to reinforce their awareness of the cultural difference between the West and the East.

Q : If you have a bad cold, which of the following wouldn't you say?
A : ① I've got a stuffy nose.
　　② I have a runny nose.
　　③ My nose is sick.

문제분석	구분	교과 교육
난이도 ★☆☆	평가목표	culture-integrated lesson에 따른 수업 목표를 구체적으로 서술하는가?
	채점기준	2점: 다른 문화에 대한 차이를 구별할 수 있다. 2점: 동사와 명사표현의 표현을 바꿀 수 있다.

모범답안	Students will be able to compare the different expressions according to the different cultures. Students will be able to convert the different language expressions from verb-oriented expressions into the noun-oriented expressions. (35 words)

04 Read the passages and follow the directions. 【4 points】

2024년 B10번

⟨A⟩

This semester, Ms. Kang, a high school English teacher, has been assigned to teach a new elective course called the 'Culture of English Speaking Countries.' The goal of the course is to help students develop intercultural competence. She consulted multiple resources including the national curriculum, books, and her colleagues from other schools who have taught similar courses in order to achieve the course goal. Based on her research, she has come up with the teaching plan presented below.

A Teaching Plan for 'Culture of English Speaking Countries'

1. Teaching Contents

Cultural Products
tangible and intangible creations produced or adopted by the members of the culture (e.g., tools, clothing, music, spoken language, etc.)

Cultural Practices
actions and interactions carried out by the members of the culture (e.g., greetings, being punctual, ways of interacting with elders, etc.)

Cultural Perspectives
perceptions, values, beliefs, and attitudes held by the members of the culture (e.g., religious beliefs, attitudes towards authority figures, etc.)

→ Intercultural Competence

2. Teaching Principles
   1) Integrate language skills and culture.
   2) Utilize different types of audiovisual aids.
   3) Avoid reinforcing associations between nationalities (countries) and cultures.
   4) Involve students in discovering English culture, instead of transmitting information.
   5) Assess students' achievements based on their performances at the end of the lesson.

⟨B⟩

Lesson Sequence

1. Preparation: Assemble a selection of pictures illustrating a variety of British and American dwellings.

2. In Class: 1) Write the word 'Houses' on the board, and ask students about the common housing styles in their local community.

   2) Show pictures of houses on the screen with their names one by one (e.g., ranch houses, cottages, brownstones, semi-detached houses, terraced houses, bungalows, duplexes, townhouses, etc.) and read the names with students.

   3) Play a video of two people talking in English about typical British and American housing styles and then check students' comprehension.

   4) Hand out a worksheet with the pictures and the names of houses. Have students classify the houses into two groups and write their names in the correct column. Check the answers together.

Houses in the UK	Houses in the US
e.g., semi-detached houses	e.g., ranch houses

   5) Divide students into groups of three. Have each group choose one house type and research online the types of materials used in the house, its layout, the characteristics of the rooms, walls, gardens, etc.

   6) Have each group give a short presentation in English about the house type they researched. Assess them using a scoring rubric.

Based on ⟨A⟩, identify the ONE teaching content that Ms. Kang incorporates and the ONE teaching principle that she does NOT conform to in her lesson sequence in ⟨B⟩. Then explain your answers with evidence from ⟨A⟩ and ⟨B⟩.

문제분석	구분	교과 교육
난이도 ★★☆	평가목표	intercultural competence를 높이기 위해 사용한 문화를 구체적으로 서술하는가?
	채점기준	2점: (Cultural product) 두 다른 나라의 주거형태라는 문화적 산물을 통합한다. 1점: 3)은 따르지 않는다. 1점: 각 나라와 문화의 연관성을 이해하고 분류하는 학습원리를 적용한다.

모범답안	Cultural product is incorporated. The teacher prepares 'dwellings' of two different cultures with using pictures, video and online materials. 3) is not conformed. The students compare typical British and American housing styles to classify the cultural differences in each country rather than avoiding association. (46 words)

05 Read the passage in ⟨A⟩ and the conversation in ⟨B⟩, and follow the directions. 【4 points】

2025년 B10번

⟨A⟩

Intercultural language learning in the classroom can be conceptualized as a series of four interrelated processes: *noticing, comparing, reflecting,* and *interacting*. First, noticing is for learners to experience new input about culture and attempt to understand it. Teachers may use various exemplifications of the target culture as input, such as videos, written texts, and cartoons. Second, comparing occurs when learners are engaged in identifying similarities and differences between learners' culture and the target culture. Third, reflecting implies that learners make personal interpretations of experiences and react to linguistic and cultural diversity. Finally, interacting involves learners communicating personal meanings about their experiences, exploring those meanings, and reshaping them in response to others. The two excerpts below are parts of students' speeches in class.

Excerpt from Seoyeon's Speech

"I imagined what I would and wouldn't like about attending a U.S. high school. I'd be excited about having many options for extracurricular activities, but I wouldn't want to join any sport teams because I don't like playing sports."

Excerpt from Taesoo's Speech

"I think the level of engagement in extracurricular activities seems different between Korean and U.S. high school students. For example, many U.S. high school students tend to spend much more time doing community service than Korean students."

As seen above, Seoyeon is most likely involved in the process of ①_____, and Taesoo is most likely involved in the process of ②_____.

⟨B⟩

(*Seoyeon and Taesoo are talking about their speeches.*)

Seoyeon: I really liked your speech. There are a lot of things we can do for the community when it comes to extracurricular activities.

Taesoo : Thank you. That was the exact point I wanted to make.

Seoyeon: I'd like to hear more about the ways in which we can serve our communities.

Fill in the blanks ① and ② each with the ONE most appropriate word from ⟨A⟩, in the correct order. Then, explain one of the four processes in ⟨A⟩ that Seoyeon in ⟨B⟩ is most likely involved in with evidence from ⟨B⟩.

문제분석	구분	교과 교육
난이도 ★★★	평가목표	2언어학습자의 새로운 문화학습의 과정을 구체적으로 서술하는가?
	채점기준	1점: reflecting 1점: comparing 1점: Seoyeon is in an interacting process. 1점: 자신의 경험을 이야기하고 태수에게 응답하여 추가정보를 더한다.
모범답안		① reflecting, ② comparing. Seoyeon is in an interacting process. She talks about her personal experiences about extracurricular activities. Responding to Taesoo's comment, she wants to extend to hear more about how to serve her communities. (35 words)

06 Read the following and answer the question.

2009년 30번

Lesson Procedure

(1) The teacher shows the students postcards from many different countries and introduces the activity by talking about the postcards that people send to their friends when they are on vacation.

(2) The teacher asks the students about the postcards they have sent home since arriving in the US: Who they have sent these to, what kinds of messages they have written on them, and what cultural aspects they have noticed on the postcards.

(3) The teacher has students form pairs. The teacher gives a prepared postcard to one student in each pair. Student A, who receives a postcard, describes it to Student B, who cannot see the postcard. Student B then attempts to discover the identity of the country on the postcard.

(4) Once all the students have completed the task, they share their postcards try to identify the culture-related aspects depicted on the postcards with the rest of the class.

(5) The teacher focuses on some aspects related to American culture and organizes these on the blackboard. The students discuss and compare them with their own cultures.

(6) As a follow-up assignment, the students are asked to bring in postcards from their countries. They are asked to write a brief paragraph about their own cultures.

Identify the TWO lesson objectives with the integration of culture and language skills in the speaking lesson above.

Which of the following is NOT correct about the lesson?

① The main teaching objective is to introduce and reinforce the skill of writing.
② During the lesson, learners are invited to share personal experiences.
③ The participants in this lesson are international learners who arrived in the US.
④ The primary skills dealt with in this lesson are speaking, cultural awareness and writing.
⑤ This lesson involves an information-gap activity and a follow-up writing assignment.

문제분석	구분	교과 교육
난이도 ★☆☆	평가목표	수업과정에 나타난 문화중심활동의 목표를 구체적으로 서술하는가?
	채점기준	2점: 학습자들은 통합수업안에서 다른 문화를 비교할 수 있다. 2점: 학습자들은 말하기와 쓰기 기술을 통합할 수 있다. (2점): 학습자들은 다른 정보를 가지고 의미협상을 할 수 있다. (2점): 학습자들은 자신의 문화를 정리하는 개별 쓰기를 할 수 있다.

모범답안
- Students will be able to compare the different cultures in a skill integration approach.
- Students will be able to integrate speaking and writing skills with cultural awareness.
- (Students will be able to negotiate meaning in information-gap activity to fill the gap.)
- (Students will be able to produce their personalized writing through briefing their culture in the follow-up writing assignment.)

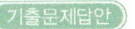

07 Read the passage in ⟨A⟩ and the conversation between two teachers in ⟨B⟩, and follow the directions. 【2 points】

⟨A⟩

The way you speak is affected in many ways. For example, how much attention you are paying to your speech may be one factor. When you are not paying much attention to the way you are speaking, your speech may be more casual. By contrast, if you are conscious about the way you are speaking, your output will be less casual. The social position of the person with whom you are engaging in conversation may also affect your language output. It is natural to use more formal language when you speak to someone whose social position is above yours. The sociolinguistic concept of solidarity should also be considered. If your interlocutor comes from the same speech community or shares a similar social or cultural identity with you, you will feel connected to him or her, and this will affect the way you deliver your message. In addition, where you are affects the formality of your output. When you are in a formal situation, a business meeting, you naturally use more formal language, and the opposite is true as well. Lastly, the channel or medium of language, that is, whether you deliver your message through speech or writing, can be another critical factor that affects your speech. All of these things need to be considered carefully, because they constitute what is called pragmatic competence which relies very heavily on conventional, culturally appropriate, and socially acceptable ways of interacting.

⟨B⟩

T1: I'm writing a recommendation letter for Miri. She is a good student, but she doesn't know how to adapt her conversational style when making a request. When Miri approached me, she said, "Hi, teacher, can you write me a recommendation letter?"

T2: Haha… I understand what you mean. Some of my students seem to have trouble making their speech style appropriate to the situation. Miri is just one example.

T1: Exactly! Still, I feel it's my responsibility to show them how speech styles differ across various situations. Hey, why don't we offer a special lecture on this topic?

T2: We can invite a guest speaker who can show the importance of selecting the appropriate conversational style to match the _____ of the situation.

Fill in the blank in ⟨B⟩ with the ONE most appropriate word from ⟨A⟩.

모범답안   formality

08 Read the conversation between a teacher and a student and follow the directions. 【2 points】

2016년 A8번

(Sujin, who is in an exchange programme in England, is having a conversation with her teacher, Ms. Connor.)

Sujin: Hi, how're you doing?
Connor: I'm doing well. Are you alright?
Sujin: Yes. Um… I have fun… but still intimidated by talking to people in English.
Connor: What's the problem?
Sujin: I have my British friend Kate in my class. Yesterday, she told me, "I like your jacket! Really unusual. Great on you." So I said, "Really? I don't think so." I felt she was rather embarrassed and something was wrong.
Connor: Oh, you should just say, "thank you" in that situation. Remember, cultural norms involving language use differ from country to country. Don't worry, you're on the right track. It's a normal process of learning in a new culture.
Sujin: Oh, I see. I should have understood her and said, "thanks." OK, thank you very much.

Complete the comments by filling in ① with TWO words and by filling in ② with ONE word. Write your answers in the correct order.

> Sujin experienced misunderstanding as she performed a ①_____ of compliment response in an interaction with her British friend. Since cultures differ from one another and language is inextricably interwoven with culture, cultural knowledge of language use in context plays a crucial role in cross-cultural communication. This entails the concept of ②_____ competence, one of the core components of communicative competence, which enables learners to use the L2 in socioculturally appropriate ways.

모범답안   ① speech act   ② sociolinguistic

09 Find the closest match for each pre-reading activity in ⟨A⟩ with its type in ⟨B⟩.

2004년 전국 15번

⟨A⟩

(1) What do you think?
   Think about your best friend. Where did you meet? What is it that you like about him or her? The following headings might help you:
   — how he or she looks
   — how he or she behaves to others
   — what he or she likes or dislikes

(2) These words from the story are related to trees.
   Look them up in the dictionary and write the meaning on a piece of paper.
   root   trunk   branch
   twig   sapling   undergrowth

(3) Look at the following sentences from the text. Are they by the pro-monarchist or the anti-monarchist? In which case is this clear and in which case is it less clear?
   a) For the Queen, if for nobody and nothing else, masses of ordinary people are anxious and willing to put out flags and throw a national party.
   b) It's all for the tourists really.
   c) There is a natural longing in human beings for legitimacy in government, for an ultimate concept of authority which exists by some kind of legitimate right.

⟨B⟩

a. Linguistic knowledge in a text
b. Cultural or conceptual awareness
c. Schema knowledge

모범답안   (1) c (2) a (3) b

10 The following passage is the teacher's written feedback.

2005년 서울 19번

⟨Version 1⟩	⟨Version 2⟩
I love movies. First, movies take us all over the world. We can see beautiful sights. We can learn about interesting cultures. You don't have to leave home. I love movies. Movies are just plain fun. You may have a hard day at work.	There are TWO main reasons why I love movies. The first reason is that movies take us all over the world. We can see beautiful sights and learn interesting cultures despite ever leaving home. After a hard day at work, it feels good to sit down with a good movie.

Complete the teacher's comments/ rationales why ⟨version 2⟩ has better organization discourse than ⟨version 1⟩.

모범답안 First, the paragraph is more coherent. In order to help the reader follow your ideas, you should bring some logical sequence for your ideas. Second, the relationship between sentences is explicitly signalled. Cohesive devices are helped to show how the sentences are related to connect meaning. (48 words)

11. Read the passage and follow the directions.

2013년 논술 4번

A second-year high school teacher wanted to diagnose the strengths and weaknesses of his students' writing ability. He asked the students to write a well-formed paragraph about Ho Chi Minh City, which they had visited on a school trip. The following are two writing samples that particularly attracted his attention.

[Writing Sample 1]

Last year I went to Ho Chi Minh City. It's a fascinating place. It is in Vietnam. It is located on a river. They say it was once an important trading center for the French. French effect was everywhere. You should visit there. I saw many building there. Many of them are built in French style. The famous French architect Gustave Eiffel designed a building there. Some cafe serve French-style bread. Many people, especially the older generations, learned French in school. Rich Vietnamese people still speak French today. Hotels and restaurants also have French food. Typically, Vietnamese people have a baguette, yogurt and orange juice for breakfast. All of those are French. The Vietnamese and the French fought, too. Then French left the country. You can see many museums and monuments. They show the country's long war history. So I think Ho Chi Minh City is a fascinating place to visit.

[Writing Sample 2]

For travelers to Southeast Asia, there is no more fascinating place to visit than Ho Chi Minh City. Due to historical importance as French trading center in Southeast Asia, French culture's influences remain pervasive in this city. For example, many inhabitant, especially older generation, learned French in school and can still speak it very well. Vietnamese elite also continue to speak French today. In addition, many cafe, hotel and restaurant serve French-style pastries, along with French item like asparagus and white potato. Typical Vietnamese breakfast would consist baguette, yogurt and orange juice, which are all French item. French influence's another sign is that many building in the city were built in French style. This can be seen, for example, in Saigon Central Post Office. It has French Gothic style since it was designed and constructed by famous French architect Gustave Eiffel. Numerous museum and monument also document country's long — and often bloody — history of conflict between Vietnamese and French. Although French eventually left country, cultural influences continue. If you are looking for unique city to visit in Southeast Asia, Ho Chi Minh City is excellent choice.

Write three well-formed paragraphs that compare and contrast the two writing samples in terms of content, organization, and language use. First, in one paragraph, discuss the content. Second, in another paragraph, discuss organization (cohesion and coherence). Third, in the last paragraph, discuss language use (i.e., grammar, vocabulary, etc.). Include the following in each paragraph.

- A topic sentence
- Two key points (similarities and/or differences)
- A supporting example for each key point

문제분석	구분	교과 교육
난이도 ★★☆	평가목표	학생의 글을 content, organization, language use에 따라 비교분석할 수 있는가?
	채점기준	(content) 역사적 내용을 쓴 점은 유사하다. (organization) 논리적 지속성이 있는 글과 명확치 않은 글의 차이가 있다. (language use) 어휘와 문법의 다양한 사용이 있는 글과 제한되어 있는 글 사이에 차이가 있다.

모범답안

  As for content, writing Samples 1 and 2 share similarity of writing about the historical influences of French culture on Vietnamese architecture.
  For organization, Sample 1 shows inconsistency in cohesion devices and references are not clear to make the text difficult to understand. In contrast, Sample 2 has consistency from the third person viewpoint and uses appropriate cohesion devices to follow logical flow in the text.
  As for language use, Sample 1 shows a low proficiency level of vocabulary and grammar structure. The same word is repeated and most of sentences are simply structured with just one subject and verb. In Sample 2, more phrasal expressions and complex sentences are used. (110 words)

12. Read the text and follow the directions.

2011년 27번

Happy Thanksgiving!

Teaching Procedure

1) In a computer lab, the teacher places students in groups of three and asks them to search the Internet for information about how Americans celebrate Thanksgiving. The teacher recommends TWO or three pre-researched sites.
2) Students read the information on the sites, find three ways Thanksgiving differs from Chuseok, and then write a paragraph describing them in English.
3) Students then find TWO or three images on the Internet that support the differences they will show.
4) Students post their paragraphs and images on the class webpage bulletin board.
5) Once students have posted, they must then comment on other groups' posts.
6) As the students post, the teacher monitors the posts and gives feedback on each.

Identify the web teaching activity of teaching and explain the THREE advantages of the procedure related to the language and culture connection with evidence.

Choose all and only the correct statements about the activity.

ⓐ The procedure allows students to make choices about what they wish to write about the given topic.
ⓑ The procedure integrates language skills and involves computer-mediated communication.
ⓒ The procedure provides students with plenty of drill, practice, and tutorial explanation.
ⓓ The procedure promotes inquiry-based learning to foster understanding of the target culture.

문제분석	구분	교과 교육
난이도 ★★☆	평가목표	webquest 활동을 통하여 문화와 통합기술을 위한 탐구학습을 구체적으로 서술하는가?
	채점기준	1점: (webquest) 활동이다. 1점: 4기능의 통합과 문화를 함께 탐구한다. 1점: CMC활동이다. 1점: 스스로 연구, 토론활동, 피드백이 제공된다.

모범답안 This activity is webquest activity. It promotes inquiry-based learning to foster understanding of the target culture while they integrate language skills of reading, speaking and writing. The procedure involves computer-mediated communication of research and posting. It also provides students with self-study of research, discussion, feedback on others on the Internet. (50 words)

기출문제답안 ⓐ, ⓑ, ⓓ

13 Read the passage in ⟨A⟩ and the lesson plan in ⟨B⟩, and follow the directions.

⟨A⟩

In designing activities for cultural instruction, it is important to consider the purpose of the activity, as well as its usefulness for teaching language and culture in an integrative fashion. The most basic issue in cross-cultural education is increasing the degree to which language and culture are integrated. Several suggestions for dealing with this issue are as follows:

1. Use cultural information when teaching vocabulary. Teach students about the cultural connotations of new words.
2. Present cultural topics in conjunction with closely related grammatical features whenever possible. Use cultural contexts for language-practice activities, including those that focus on particular grammatical forms.
3. Make good use of textbook illustrations or photos. Use probing questions to help students describe the cultural features of the illustrations or photos.
4. In group activities, use communication techniques for cultural instruction, such as discussions and role-plays.
5. Teach culture while involving the integration of the four language skills. Do not limit cultural instruction to lecture or anecdotal formats.

⟨B⟩

Lesson 4. World-famous Holidays

Objec-tives	Students will be able to 1. introduce world-famous holidays using *-er than*, and 2. perform activities related to the holidays to deepen their understanding of diverse cultures.
Step 1	• T asks Ss to speak out about anything related to the pictures in the textbook on p. 78. • T asks Ss some questions to elicit their ideas about what cultural features they see in the pictures of world-famous holidays. • Ss tell each other about the cultural differences among the holidays based on the pictures.
Step 2	• T tells Ss about the origins of the world-famous holidays in detail. • T explains the cultural characteristics of those holidays. • T shares his experiences of holidays, and Ss listen to T's stories.
Step 3	• T has Ss listen to a story about the world-famous holidays, and underline the expressions of comparative forms in the story on p. 79. • T talks with Ss about the meanings and functions of the expressions based on the cultural characteristics of the holidays.

		• T asks Ss, in pairs, to search the Internet for more information about cultural differences among the holidays and to describe the differences using comparative forms.
Step 4		• T introduces new words in the story on the screen. • T explains the meanings of the words (*traditional, adapting, polite*, etc.), comparing them with their synonyms and/or antonyms. • Ss note the words and memorize them using mnemonic devices.
Step 5		• T has Ss sit in groups of four, and choose one distinct aspect of the world-famous holidays, such as costume, food, and festivals. • Ss write a culture capsule in groups about the differences. • T gives preparation time, and each group performs a role-play based on the culture capsule in front of their classmates.

Identify the TWO steps from ⟨B⟩ that do NOT correspond to the suggestions in ⟨A⟩. Then, support your answers, respectively, with evidence from ⟨A⟩ and ⟨B⟩.

문제분석

난이도 ★★★

구분	교과 교육
평가목표	문화와 어휘 수업에서 다루지 못한 내용을 찾아 구체적으로 서술하는가?
채점기준	1점: (Step 2) 1점: 통합수업이 아니라 교사의 이야기 형식을 듣게 된다. 1점: (Step 4) 1점: 문화적 함축된 의미 학습 없이 유사어와 반대어로 어휘를 학습한다.

모범답안 In Step 2, teacher just tells and explains and students listen to the teacher's stories in anecdotal formats rather than developing integrated language skills. In Step 4, teacher explains the meanings of new words with synonyms and antonyms without cultural connotations of new words. (43 words)

14 Read the passage and answer the question.

Listen to the two dialogues on the audio-tape and compare the differences between them.

Dialogue (1)	Dialogue (2)
W: I'm home.	W: Excuse me. I have a prescription for my daughter's knee problem.
M: Got the medicine for Sarah?	M: OK. It would also help if you gave her an extra calcium tablet everyday.
W: Here it is. And give her an extra calcium tablet.	W: Do you think it is really necessary?
M: Must we?	M: Yes, I am afraid that is.
W: Fraid so.	

Choose all and only the correct statements about the dialogues.
ⓐ Students will develop formality-awareness.
ⓑ Students will become aware of cross-cultural differences.
ⓒ Students will become familiar with the use of gestures in communication.
ⓓ Students will distinguish the differences in register between the two dialogues.
ⓔ Students will understand the interpersonal relationships of the speakers in each dialogue.

기출문제답안 ⓐ, ⓓ, ⓔ

memo

CHAPTER 06 이해 능력 지도

01 Read the passages and follow the directions. 【4 points】

2025년 B7번

─────────── ⟨A⟩ ───────────

(*Mr. Choi, a supervising teacher, is talking with his student teacher, Ms. Han, about her lesson plan.*)

SupT: Ms. Han, I checked your lesson plan and found a couple of things that may help improve it.

ST : Oh, did I miss anything?

SupT: As you know, before you get to the main listening stage, we want students to recognize the purpose of listening, right?

ST : Yeah, and it sounds quite challenging. How can I do that?

SupT: You can try activating schemata. Making connections between personal experiences and learning can facilitate students' comprehension.

ST : Oh, I see.

SupT: And I recommend intensive listening. You know, authentic conversations have a lot of contractions. So, how about playing parts of a radio show focusing on particular language features?

ST : Good idea. Thank you. Is there anything else I missed?

SupT: Hmm, why don't you also try making some creative activities? Students can sing a song or chant, or they can record their own voice.

ST : Got it. I'll try to find some that are exciting.

SupT: Great. That's all I wanted to point out.

ST : Your suggestions are extremely helpful. I'll make some changes following your advice.

SupT: If you have any questions, don't hesitate to ask.

ST : I really appreciate your advice.

Note: SupT = supervising teacher, ST = student teacher

─────────── ⟨B⟩ ───────────

After the conversation, Ms. Han revised her lesson plan based on Mr. Choi's suggestions. Below are the original and modified lesson plans.

Original Lesson Plan

Stage	Teaching & Learning Activities
Pre-listening	T shows the aim of the listening activity. T asks about what will happen to a person in a picture. T engages Ss in small talk.
While-listening	T asks Ss to listen to a story. T asks Ss to make inferences about the main topic of the story. T asks Ss to retell the story.
Post-listening	T asks Ss to write a summary on the story. T asks Ss to present on their summaries. T provides comments on Ss' presentations.

Modified Lesson Plan

Stage	Teaching & Learning Activities
Pre-listening	T presents the purpose of the listening activity. T asks Ss to predict what will happen to a person in a picture. T engages Ss in small talk.
While-listening	T asks Ss to listen to a story. T asks Ss to guess what the main topic of the story is. T asks Ss to do a gap-filling activity.
Post-listening	T asks Ss to summarize the story. T asks Ss to act out assigned scenes from the story. T provides feedback on Ss' performances.

Note: T = teacher, Ss = students

Identify the supervising teacher's TWO suggestions from ⟨A⟩ that are reflected in the modified lesson plan in ⟨B⟩. Then, explain your answers with evidence from ⟨B⟩.

문제분석	구분	교과 교육
난이도 ★★☆	평가목표	개정교수법에서 추천하는 내용을 구체적으로 서술하는가?
	채점기준	1점: intensive listening 1점: gap-filling 활동을 통해 상세 듣기 활동을 강화한다. 1점: creative activities 1점: 이야기의 한 부분을 연기한다.
모범답안		Intensive listening and creative activities are two suggestions. During while-listening, the teacher can make the students intensively listen to the particular language information with gap-filling activity. For post-listening, the teacher can make some creative activity to ask the students to act out assigned scenes from the story. (47 words)

02 Read the passages and follow the directions. 【4 points】

2025년 A11번

⟨A⟩

Ms. Kim, an English teacher, is selecting lesson objectives to implement into a new lesson. The following are the lesson objectives for reception and production.

Lesson Objectives

Reception
R1. Students can recognize reduced sounds of words.
R2. Students can identify specific details from a text or discourse.
R3. Students can distinguish between literal and implied meanings.

Production
P1. Students can explain the sequence of an event in the right order.
P2. Students can write a simple journal, letter, or email.
P3. Students can argue for and against a topic in a respectful manner.

⟨B⟩

Step	Teaching Procedure
Step 1	In groups, students brainstorm the pros and cons of using AI in education and create a mind map. Pros (AI): convenient, immediate feedback, no constraints (place, time) Cons (AI): distracting, cheating, less human interaction

Step 2	Students listen to an audio clip on AI and digital tools in class and complete a worksheet.
	
	▶ Listen to the conversation carefully and follow the directions below.
	
	A. Mark the sentences True or False.
	1. Sora says that the use of AI should be prohibited in the classroom. [T/F]
	2. Inho asks an AI chatbot to do his assignment. [T/F]
	3. Minji compares the outputs on a topic from three different AI chatbots. [T/F]
	
	B. Match the person with his or her concern.
	  Inho • • Excessive screen time
	  Minji • • False information
	  Sora • • Theft of personal data

Step 3	Students work together and write rules for the use of digital tools in class. ┌───┐ │ Class Rules for the Use of Digital Tools │ │ 1. *e.g., Never download software to a school device without permission.* │ │ 2. _____. │ │ 3. _____. │ │ │ │ ◆ Useful expressions for polite agreement or disagreement │ │ – I agree. That's a good idea. That's right. │ │ – I don't think/believe so. I don't agree/ disagree (with you). │ │ – What do you think? Would you agree with me? Don't you agree? │ └───┘

Identify ONE lesson objective for reception and ONE lesson objective for production from ⟨A⟩ that the teaching procedure in ⟨B⟩ targets. Then, explain your answers, respectively, with evidence from ⟨B⟩.

문제분석

난이도 ★★☆

구분	교과 교육
평가목표	이해력과 표현력의 목표를 실현한 단계를 구체적으로 서술하는가?
채점기준	1점: R2 1점: 대화를 듣고 T/F를 표시하고 각 우려점을 연결한다. 1점: P3 1점: 공손한 동의와 비동의 표현을 인식한다.

모범답안 R2 is applied to Step 2. For reception, students listen to the conversation to mark true or false and match with each concern. P3 is applied to Step 3. For production, students identify useful expressions for polite agreement or disagreement about the use of digital tools. (46 words)

03 Read the passages and follow the directions. 【4 points】

2024년 A8번

⟨A⟩

Research suggests that L2 learners employ various listening strategies to increase comprehension of what they listen to. These strategies can be classified into two types: local or micro-strategies (Type 1) and global or macro-strategies (Type 2). Below are some specific strategies from each type.

Type 1
1) Identifying cognates
2) Using context to infer the meaning of words
3) Determining to skip unknown words or phrases

Type 2
1) Making predictions about the content based on titles or phrasal cues
2) Informing oneself about the context of the input (e.g., speakers, situations)
3) Recognizing the type of a listening text (e.g., news broadcasts, lectures, business presentations, job interviews)

⟨B⟩

In an attempt to improve his students' listening comprehension, Mr. Jung, a middle school English teacher, wanted to identify the strategies that his students apply to their listening process. In order to do so, he played a monologue to his students in class and paused the audio after each segment. He asked the students to think aloud while they were listening. Below are two of the audio segments Mr. Jung used and what Minji and Dongho, two of his students, were thinking as the audio was being played.

Audio Segment 1
I think social media is a waste of time. I'm totally addicted, I have to say. But there really isn't much going on.

Hmm, a waste of time? Maybe he's going to say something negative about using social media.
Minji

Audio Segment 2
I just spend hours just, sort of, checking other people's profiles, looking at their pictures. I don't know, it's a bit sneaky.

Sneaky? It's a new word. I don't think I need to know its meaning at the moment.
Dongho

Identify the ONE specific listening strategy from each type in ⟨A⟩ that Minji and Dongho applied to their listening process in ⟨B⟩, respectively. Then explain your answers with evidence from ⟨A⟩ and ⟨B⟩.

문제분석	구분	교과 교육
난이도 ★★☆	평가목표	두 학생의 듣기 활동에서 사용된 듣기 전략을 찾아 구체적으로 서술하는가?
	채점기준	1점: Minji – Type (2:1) 1점: 구를 이용하여 전체 내용을 미리 예상한다. 1점: Dongho – Type (1: 3) 1점: 내용에 영향을 미치지 않는 새로운 단어는 신경쓰지 않는다.

모범답안 Minji applied Type (2, 1) making predictions and Dongho applied Type (1, 3) skipping unknown words. Minji predicted in advance the whole audio clip with using the phrasal cues 'a waste of time'. Dongho determined to skip a new word 'sneaky,' that did not affect to understand the meaning. (47 words)

04. Read the passage in ⟨A⟩ and the master plan in ⟨B⟩, and follow the directions. 【4 points】

2022년 A8번

⟨A⟩

Ms. Yoon is an English teacher at a local middle school. According to her school curriculum, students should be able to use a combination of top-down and bottom-up processing when they practice the receptive skills of English, that is, listening and reading. Bottom-up processing is the processing of individual elements of the target language for the decoding of language input, while top-down processing refers to the use of background knowledge in understanding the meaning of a message. Now, she is developing a master plan for one of the units she will teach next semester. To help her students achieve this curriculum goal, she makes efforts to ensure that both bottom-up and top-down processing are practiced during each lesson period.

⟨B⟩

Ms. Yoon's Unit 1 Master Plan

1. Lesson: Challenge & Courage
2. Objectives

   Students will be able to:
   - listen to a dialogue and explain the content
   - ask for reasons and make decisions
   - read a text and retell the story
3. Study points
   - Functions: asking for and giving reasons
   - Forms: passive, subject-verb agreement
4. Time allotment: 8 periods, 45 minutes each

Period	Section	Learning Activities
1st	Listen 1	• Listen to a series of phrases for consonant/vowel linking between words • Listen to short sentences to discriminate between rising and falling intonation
2nd	Listen 2	• Listen to a dialogue and find the main idea • Do a sentence dictation activity with the active and passive voice

5th	Read 1	• Read the introductory paragraph and predict what will come next • Distinguish sentences containing subject-verb agreement errors
6th	Read 2	• Recognize whether a sentence is in the active or passive voice • Change base forms of verbs into the past participle by adding '-ed / -en'

Based on ⟨A⟩, identify TWO periods in ⟨B⟩ in which the teacher focuses on both types of processing. Then, explain your answers with evidence from ⟨B⟩.

문제분석	구분	교과 교육
난이도 ★★☆	평가목표	comprehension-based 학습을 위한 processing 방법을 서술하는가?
	채점기준	1점: 2nd period 1점: 주제를 찾고 두 개의 다른 수동/능동태를 연습한다. 1점: 5th period 1점: 예상전략을 사용하고 주어동사 오류를 구별한다.
모범답안		In 2nd and 5th periods, the teacher focuses on both topdown and bottomup processing. The teacher focuses on the listening data to get students to understand main ideas and reproduce two different voices. The teacher lets students use the prediction strategy and distinguish the language errors of subject-verb. (49 words)

05 Read the following and answer the question.

2012년 20번

⟨A⟩

(*A high school English teacher's beliefs on how listening should be taught are described as follows;*)

When I teach listening, I want my students to focus more on trying to infer meaning from contextual clues rather than the recognition of sounds, words, or sentences. I believe that the process of listening is more heavily influenced by world knowledge that a listener brings to a text, called schematic knowledge, as opposed to the language items that are available within the text itself. I advise students to rely on content and formal schemata when unsure about the speaker's message. For more effective listening, I often encourage my students to use strategies such as predicting and inferencing to get the meaning.

Which stages of the procedure in ⟨B⟩ are not in accordance with the teacher's beliefs described in ⟨A⟩?

⟨B⟩

The following is the procedure of a lesson that she has tried to design based on her beliefs for listening in ⟨A⟩.

ⓐ Before listening, Ms. Lee shows students the title 'Kyle's Shopping Trip' of a DVD clip to be viewed.
ⓑ The teacher plays the clip once without the sound, and asks students to guess what the purpose of the conversation is, what the relationship between the speakers is and so on.
ⓒ The teacher illustrates how certain words may be linked in natural speech. Then the teacher plays the clip with the sound on and asks students to find words that are linked in the speech stream.
ⓓ The teacher replays the clip and asks students to confirm or reject the prediction that they have made.
ⓔ The teacher plays the clip again and students listen attentively for some phrasal verbs to identify specific details of the conversation.
ⓕ The teacher summarizes what happened in the conversation.

모범답안   ⓒ, ⓔ

06 Read the following and follow the directions. Complete the objectives with ONE appropriate word for each blank.

2006년 전국 17번

Objectives: Students will be able to a. listen selectively for (1)_____. b. apply bottomup processing. The teacher says to students, "Okay, listen, everybody. I'm going to read five sentences. Show me the 'Yes' sign if the verb has an -ed ending, and show me the 'No' sign if it doesn't. Okay? Does everybody understand what to do? Okay, I'm going to read the first sentence." The teacher reads five sentences. All sentences have the structure of 'subject + verb'. Students show their signs after listening to each sentence.	Objectives: Students will be able to a. make (2)_____. b. apply topdown and bottomup processing. The teacher distributes handouts to students. In the handout is a telephone message with some missing words. The teacher tells the students to read the message and decide what kinds of information are missing. Then he has the students listen to the recorded message and fill in the blanks.

모범답안   (1) morphemes   (2) inferences

07 Read the following passage and answer the questions.

2003년 서울 3번

  The features of real-world listening input include the use of time-creating, facilitation, and compensation devices. To ease the production of speech, the speaker normally uses time-creating devices. These are used to gain time for the speaker so that he can formulate what to say next in spontaneous speech. One typical example is the use of pause fillers. Despite the lack of syntactic or lexical functions that pause fillers serve, they help the speaker to solicit more time to plan and in turn to furnish the listener with more processing time. The pressure of time in real-life communication also renders it necessary for the speaker to use facilitation devices to ease speech production. Effective listeners need to identify and be familiar with these devices in free speech. The use of less complex structures is one of these devices. Formulaic language use is another device to facilitate speech production. These devices will normally give the impression of fluency; they serve the function of filling unwanted pauses. As effective listeners, students need to understand their function. Due to the speed of natural speech, listening input has to be processed very quickly. Fortunately, redundancy in natural speech does allow some processing time. The three typical ways to build in redundancy are repetition, reformation, and rephrasing. Speakers always find themselves correcting or improving what they have already said. They may repeat part of the speech or express their ideas in a different way. This kind of redundancy is necessary to help understanding on the part of the listener. Effective listeners therefore identify these elements of redundancy and are able to guess meanings with the help of compensation devices.

(1) Fill in the blanks in the following table, using the words from the passage.

Devices	Examples
① _____ devices	Me too, So am I, I see what you mean, I'm sure you're right but … etc.
② _____ devices	um, urh, eh, etc.
compensation devices	Well, you're not gonna believe this, but my girlfriend and I—you know Lisa? I think you met her at my party—anyway, she and I drove up to Point Heve, you know, up in Marin County, etc.

(2) Based on information from the passage, complete the following sentence, using ALL the words in the box. The word can be used more than once.

The learner needs to understand that these three devices are there to _____, and not to distract the listener's attention or to impede understanding.

⟨Box⟩

| listener's | speaker's | production | speech |
| facilitate | processing | and | of |

모범답안   (1) ① facilitation   ② time-creating
(2) facilitate listener's processing and speaker's production of speech

08 A novice high school teacher uses dictogloss as a classroom task for the first time. Follow the directions. 【15 points】

2013년 논술 1번

Task Description
- Inform students that the class will work on the dictogloss task with a specific focus on passive voice.
- Have students write down key words while they are watching the 7-minute-long news clip once.
- Ask students to work in groups of 8 for 20 minutes to reconstruct the story.
- Have students watch the clip one more time.
- Distribute the transcript and ask them to review it at home.

After the class, Ms. Kim wants to find out what students think about the dictogloss task. She asks the leader of each group to give comments. Their written comments are presented below.

- 1st group leader: The story seemed interesting, but it went on and on. After watching it, we could barely remember anything we heard, except a few words like boy, locked, shivering, and scared. The teacher asked us to listen carefully for examples of passive voice, but we couldn't notice many. There were too many new and confusing expressions.
- 2nd group leader: It was our first time to do this activity, so it was very, very difficult. Also, we didn't know anything about the story before watching the clip, so we were lost.
- 3rd group leader: When we worked in groups, some students hardly had any chance to talk. So we could not share our ideas well.

(1) Based on the students' comments on the task, explain the three most notable problems in the way the task was done.
(2) Propose an instructional suggestion for each problem to make this dictogloss task more effective and engaging.

문제분석	구분	교과 교육	
난이도 ★★☆	평가목표	교실수업에 나타난 dictogloss task의 문제점 세 가지를 파악하고 교육적 제안점을 제시할 수 있는가?	
	채점기준	(1) 문제점 • 어려운 어휘가 있는 언어적 문제 • 내용이 새로워서 이해의 어려움 • 학생들의 참여가 공평하지 않음	(2) 제안점 • 과업전 활동으로 쉽게 한다. • schema활동으로 내용을 쉽게 한다. • 인원수를 줄여 참여하게 한다.

모범답안

(1) There are some problems in the dictogloss activity. First of all, the students have difficulty understanding the text due to some language problems such as unfamiliar and difficult words and expressions. Second, the content of task was new to students to make it difficult to understand. Third, students have no equal opportunities to participate in the group work. (53 words)

(2) For some suggestions, pre-task activity for key vocabulary is needed. Students discuss unknown words and expressions to understand the text better. Second, when students are not familiar with the content, schema activation can be used to draw out background knowledge. Finally, the number of group members needs reducing for more participation to share information. (53 words)

09 Read the passage and follow the directions.

2011년 22번

In Subin's class, the teacher plays a dialogue in four segments. After each segment, she stops the recording and asks students to complete a meaning-construction map as in the example below. They work individually and write, on their map, what they think the topic is and what clues lead them to think so.

Listening Script
A: What do you think?
B: Not bad. I like the menu. It's quite attractive.
A: You should get quite a few visitors once it's up and running.
B: I hope so. I've spent a lot of time on the graphics.
A: I've also set up the payment system, as you requested.
B: Good. Make sure it works on different browsers.
A: I'll work on the server today, and we should be able to get everything online in a day or two.
B: Excellent. I'm looking forward to getting a lot of hits.

Subin's Map

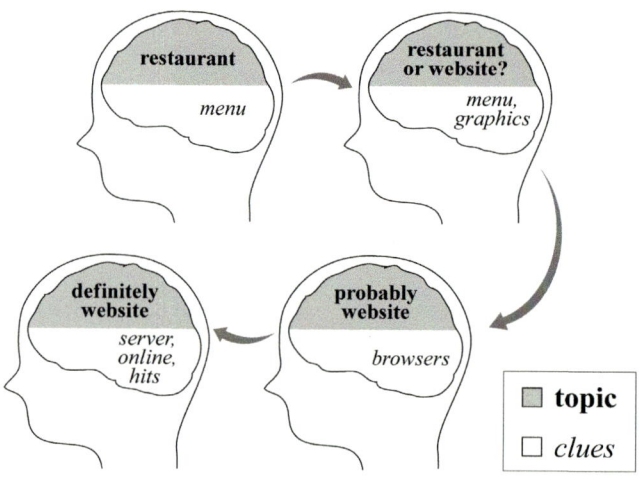

Identify a listening approach and explain it with THREE features about the listening activity related to the Subin's map with evidence.

Choose all and only the correct statements about the activity.

ⓐ The activity is usually used in a product-oriented approach to teaching listening.
ⓑ Some clues activate competing content schemata.
ⓒ The activity requires exclusive use of memory and social strategies.
ⓓ Subin goes through changes in her understanding.

문제분석	구분	교과 교육
난이도 ★★☆	평가목표	듣기학습이 진행되는 수업의 방법으로 4개의 단위로 나누어서 진행하는 과정중심 교수법을 이해하고 구체적으로 서술하는가?
	채점기준	1점: process-oriented수업이다. 1점: 학습자의 인지적 내용이 변화되어 간다. 1점: 인지전략인 추론을 사용하여 내용을 이해한다. 1점: menu나 graphics 같은 단서는 내용 스키마를 활성화시킨다.
모범답안		The activity is a process-oriented approach. It is a process to change the cognitive messages several times in the listener's mind. Subin uses cognitive strategy, inferencing to understanding the content. Some clues like menu, graphics, and server activate her content schema to make a conclusion of the text. (48 words)

기출문제답안

10. Read the following and answer the question.

2013년 19번

Lesson Procedure

Pre-listening Activity
1. Have Ss think about the following questions:
    - Do you like plants? Why or why not?
    - Have you ever grown a plant?
2. Introduce the talk and its topics.
    - Amazing qualities of plants
    - The benefits of growing plants
3. Have Ss guess about the content of the talk.

While-listening Activity
1. Have Ss listen to the talk and check whether their predictions are correct.
2. Have Ss listen again to find out key information, jotting down important words.

Post-listening Activity
1. Have Ss read the listening script where several words and phrases are blanked out, and then reconstruct it in pairs.
2. Have Ss discuss in groups whether they agree or disagree with the speaker of the talk and why.

Note: Ss = students

Complete the summary to describe the lesson procedure with ONE appropriate word.

⟨Summary⟩

The listening text is from a talk given by a famous plant expert. During pre-listening, the teacher activates students' ①_____ related to the talk. The teacher integrates reading, listening, speaking, and writing. During while-listening, the teacher encourages students to use listening strategies such as ②_____. The students promote ③_____ learning by working to discuss to each other during post-listening activity.

Which of the following is NOT a correct statement about the lesson procedure described above?

① The teacher provides multiple opportunities to listen for analysis of genre and language.
② The teacher promotes cooperative learning during the post-listening activity.
③ The teacher encourages students to use listening strategies such as note-taking.
④ The teacher activates students' schematic knowledge relating to the talk.
⑤ The teacher integrates reading, listening, speaking, and writing.

문제분석	구분	교과 교육
난이도 ★★☆	평가목표	듣기활동에서의 topdown 방식의 기본원리를 실제 교실방법으로 서술하는가?
	채점기준	1점: 듣기전 활동에서 스키마를 활성화시킨다. 1점: 듣기 활동을 하는 동안에는 note taking같은 전략을 사용한다. 1점: 듣기 후 활동에서는 함께 협동하면서 토론한다.

모범답안   (1) schema   (2) note-taking   (3) cooperative

기출문제답안 ①

11. Read the passage and follow the directions.

2002년 서울 13번

In pedagogical terms, it is possible to draw a distinction between bottom-up and top-down approaches to listening comprehension. Bottom-up listening activities focus learners on the individual elements and building blocks of the language. Decoding oral utterances, discriminating between individual sounds, in particular those with minimal contrasts, and identifying different stress, rhythm and intonation patterns feature prominently in the early stages of learning, and the student is only gradually moved _____. In a listening comprehension course, the assumption that learning is a gradual, linear and additive process is evident in the way the input is staged. While bottom-up processing is evoked from sounds, top-down processing is evoked from schema activation that the listener brings to the text. In this sense, with low-level learners who would clearly be challenged by such input, the difficulty can be minimized by letting them hear the text as often as necessary and providing a range of activities of increasing complexity. In the listening classroom for experiment group, besides the tasks in the course book, the author designed other text-related tasks for most of lessons. In these tasks, not only listening skill but also speaking, reading and writing skills are involved. Integrated skills are brought into the regular coursework rather than as a separate component and usually underlined in listening tasks. Learners should understand and apply strategy use. For instance, the first time they hear the text, they might be asked to identify how many speakers they hear. The second time they hear the text, they can be given a list of key words and asked to enumerate how often they hear the words. Lastly, they can identify the number of questions they hear.

(1) Complete the passage, with EIGHT words in the word list. You can use the same word more than once.

| from | to | text | word | sound | sentence |

(2) Write down THREE types of top-down listening activities from the passage.

모범답안 (1) from sound to word, to sentence, to text
(2) schema activation, integrated skills, strategy use

12 Read the following and answer the question.

2008년 18번

Activity Procedure

a. The students in a 2nd year of Korean middle school begin by listening to a text that contains examples of correct usage of present progressive tense with stative verbs.
b. They first process the text for meaning.
c. Then they listen again, this time focusing their attention on the target grammatical feature.
d. Next, they use the data to try to arrive at an explicit understanding of the rule.
e. Finally, there is an opportunity for the learners to try to use the correct grammatical structure in their own sentences.

Describe how the target form is integrated with listening for language acquisition in the classroom activity above.

Which of the following does NOT correspond to the activity above?
① It employs a deductive way of teaching grammar.
② It develops both listening ability and language acquisition.
③ It aims to teach grammar by helping learners attend to form.
④ It helps students produce language by understanding the rules.
⑤ It guides students to discover grammar through mapping form and meaning.

모범답안 Through the whole activity, it develops both listening ability and the acquisition of target form. It aims to teach grammar by helping learners attend to form through form-meaning mapping. It employs an inductive way of teaching grammar and guides students to discover rules. Eventually, it helps students produce language by understanding the rules. (53 words)

13 Read the following passage and answer the question.

2002년 전국 8번

> When I say empathic listening, I am not referring to the techniques of "active" listening or "reflective" listening, which basically involve mimicking what another person says. By empathic listening, I mean listening with intent to understand. I mean seeking first to understand, to really understand. It's an entirely different paradigm. Empathic listening gets inside another person's frame of reference. You look out through it. You see the world the way they see the world. You understand their paradigm. You understand how they feel. Empathy is not sympathy. Sympathy is a form of agreement, a form of judgement, and it is sometimes the more appropriate emotion and response. But people often feed on sympathy. It makes them dependent. The essence of empathic listening is not that you agree with someone; it's that you fully, deeply understand that person, emotionally as well as intellectually.

Identify the FOUR benefits of the empathic listening from the passage.

모범답안
① It builds trust and respect.
② It enables the speakers to release their emotions.
③ It encourages you to deeply understand the situation of others.
④ It creates a safe environment for collaborative problem solving.

14 Read the passage and answer the questions.

2002년 서울 11번

> Multimedia applications are helping teachers to teach foreign languages regardless of (①). CD ROM titles are being used to present information in multiple forms that can be personalized far more easily than paper methods. In teaching listening comprehension to students in class, for instance, many schools previously relied on videotapes of movies and a large stack of printed materials. Some students did well with these resources; others, less motivated, got bogged down in the dense texts.
>
> With web technology, the school now restructures a series of teaching tasks according to (②). Students are required to complete a certain amount of work to ensure that they understand the concept. The listening comprehension task incorporates multimedia animation of moving objects to help every student understand both the meaning of them and their related language expressions. The most advanced task involves a web search where students are asked to fill in a worksheet, while they are surfing the web. Students often explore the web sites further in order to find out information which the teacher asks them to search.
>
> Multimedia applications can help teachers change the teaching style from the traditional approach—a teacher talking at the front of the classroom, coupled with listening comprehension assignments—to a more (③) approach that takes advantage of the natural curiosity of students of all ages. Multimedia applications enable students to explore information through the web sites, to model experiments, and to collaborate with one another.

Fill in each blank with the most appropriate word(s) from the list.

| technology | teaching style | learning style | complexity |
| problem solving | hands-on | task-based | whole-language |

모범답안 ① learning style ② complexity ③ hands-on

15. Read the passages and follow the directions. 【4 points】

2025년 A12번

⟨A⟩

　Metacognitive awareness of reading strategies is considered a conscious procedure utilized by readers to enhance text comprehension and encourage active reading. Understanding its importance, Ms. Yu, a high school English teacher, used the Metacognitive Awareness of Reading Strategy Questionnaire to measure students' awareness on three categories of reading strategies. These include Global Reading Strategies (GLOB), Support Reading Strategies (SUP), and Problem-Solving Strategies (PROB). She also interviewed her students after the survey.

The Metacognitive Awareness of Reading Strategy Questionnaire

Category	Item	1	2	3	4	5
GLOB	G1. I have a purpose in mind when I read.					
	G2. I think about what I know to help me understand what I read.					
	G3. While reading, I decide what to read and what to ignore.					
	G4. I take an overall view of the text to see what it is about before reading it.					
	...			...		
SUP	S1. I paraphrase what I read to better understand it.					
	S2. I take notes while reading to help me understand what I read.					
	S3. While reading, I translate from English into my native language.					
	S4. I use reference materials (e.g., a dictionary) to help me understand what I read.					
	...			...		
PROB	P1. When the text is unclear, I re-read it to increase my understanding.					
	P2. I try to guess the meaning of unknown words or phrases.					
	P3. I adjust my reading speed according to what I am reading.					
	P4. I try to visualize information to help understand what I read.					
	...			...		

Note: 1 = never, 2 = occasionally, 3 = sometimes, 4 = usually, 5 = always

─── ⟨B⟩ ───

Based on the survey results, Ms. Yu conducted interviews with the students who reported low ratings in the survey. Parts of the interview excerpts are below. One of the interview questions was "Do you feel challenged while reading?" After the interview, Ms. Yu identified reading strategies that students need to promote their active reading skills.

Interview Excerpts

S1: "I thought reading was just about understanding the words. When I don't understand something, I tend to skip over it. I think if I try to draw a picture in my mind when I'm not sure, I'll understand texts much better."

S2: "I usually analyze texts sentence-by-sentence until I fully understand them. After checking my low ratings on the questionnaire, I found that reading selectively may help me become a more efficient reader."

Note: S = student

Identify the TWO items of reading strategies in ⟨A⟩ that Ms. Yu may apply to her reading instruction in relation to ⟨B⟩. Then, explain your answers, respectively, with evidence from ⟨B⟩.

문제분석	구분	교과 교육
난이도 ★★☆	평가목표	읽기를 위해 사용한 전략방법을 구체적으로 서술하는가?
	채점기준	1점: G3 1점: 선택적 읽기를 통해 문장별 분석없이 효율적인 읽기를 실시한다. 1점: P4 1점: 마음속에 그림을 그려 내용 이해를 잘 할 수 있도록 한다.

모범답안: G3 and P4 may be applied. S2 needs to read selectively to become a more efficient reader by avoiding sentence-by-sentence analysis of the text. S1 needs to draw a picture in her mind to understand the text better rather than skipping over something that she is not sure. (49 words)

16 Read the worksheet in ⟨A⟩ and the class observation note in ⟨B⟩, and follow the directions. 【4 points】

2023년 A9번

― ⟨A⟩ ―

(Worksheet)　　　　　　　　　Family History

　　　　　　　　　　　　　　　　　　　　Group Name: _____
　　　　　　　　　　　　　　　　　　　　Student Number & Name: _____

Role	Assignment	Student Assigned
Discussion Leader	Keeping the conversation going if it falters	
Passage Chooser	Choosing three passages that are important to the story to discuss	
Word Master	Showing the meanings of new words	
Grammar Checker	Using syntactic clues to interpret the meanings of sentences	
Story Summarizer	Summing up the story briefly	
Online Manager	Posting the activity outcome to the web or social network service	

■ Before Reading

Can you guess who will mention the following statements? Match the pictures of the characters in the story with their corresponding statements.

■ While Reading

Based on the text about the Brown and the Garcia families, complete the following figure.

■ After Reading

What do you think about the characters in the story? Complete the sentences.

1. I feel sorry for _____ because _____.
2. I think _____ is a nice person, but _____.

⟨B⟩

Mr. Han's Class Observation Note

2. How did the teacher use teaching aids?	I set up a Reader's Club using a metaverse platform. While doing the reading activity in an online environment, each student took a specific role. I checked students' comprehension of the passage using the worksheet.
3. Did all the students participate actively?	The students looked absorbed in reading the three paragraphs of the text. After the reading activity, they actively participated in the discussion, carrying out their assigned roles. S1 managed the discussion and controlled each student's speaking time. S2 used an online dictionary when one student asked the meaning of a word, 'crane', and shared a picture of a crane with its meaning. S3 selected one linguistically complex sentence and explained its structure to the other students. S4 uploaded the summary that S5 wrote to the cloud and posted it on the class blog. Lastly, S6 selected another three paragraphs that they would read in the next class.
4. Did the students use suitable reading strategies?	During the discussion, students used various reading strategies such as activating schema, allocating attention, previewing, skimming, scanning, and criticizing. My students were pretty good at making guesses based on the pictures. I also noticed that using a graphic organizer helped students comprehend the story. By comparing and contrasting the two families, they extracted information from the text. My students understood the text very well based on the figure.

Identify the role that S2 performed in the group activity with the TWO most appropriate words from ⟨A⟩, and identify the tool that Mr. Han used at the 'While Reading' stage in ⟨A⟩ with the TWO most appropriate words from ⟨B⟩. Then, explain your answers, respectively, with evidence from ⟨A⟩ and ⟨B⟩. Do NOT copy more than FOUR consecutive words from ⟨A⟩ and ⟨B⟩.

모범답안 S2 performed word master using online dictionary. S2 shared the meaning of new word, 'crane' with picture with other students. Teacher used the tool, graphic organizer. He helped students understand the text by comparing and contrasting between two families with completion of the figure. (43 words)

17 Read the passage in ⟨A⟩ and the lesson plan in ⟨B⟩, and follow the directions. 【4 points】

⟨A⟩

Teachers can employ a variety of techniques when teaching reading that will help enhance students' reading comprehension. For instance, at the preparation stage, the prediction technique can be used: Pictures or photos and titles can be viewed quickly to give the students an idea of the overall content of the text. While reading, if students find some words difficult, the teacher may help them to guess their meanings by looking at the surrounding words. Also, as for the reading content, the teacher can employ the outlining technique, which can help the students see the overall organization of the text by reconstructing the ideas or events. After reading, diverse techniques can be used in order to check the students' level of comprehension: scrambled stories, finding the author's purpose, and examining grammatical structures.

⟨B⟩

(*Below is part of Mr. Kim's lesson plan. He is preparing a handout for his students.*)

Objectives		• Students will read the text about modern tourists and find the main idea. • Students will identify the topic and the details of the text based on the handout. • Students will write a summary about the text based on information given in the handout.
Teaching-Learning Activities		
Introduc-duction	Greeting & Roll-call	• T and Ss exchange greetings. • T checks if all the Ss are present.
Develop-ment	Activity 1	• T hands out a reading text, "Tourists Today." • T asks Ss to skim through the text. • T asks if Ss understand the gist of the text. • T asks Ss to read the text again. • T distributes the handout about the reading text.

Tourists Today

Many contemporary tourists avoid encountering reality directly but thrive on psuedo-events in their tourism experiences thus affecting tourism entrepreneurs and indigenous populations. For one, many tourists prefer to stay in comfortable accomodations, thereby separating themselves from the local people and environment. For instance, sleeping in a hotel filled with the comforts of home may insulate them from the fact that they are in a foreign land. In addition, much of the tourism industry is bolstered by the use of tourist-focused institutions such as museums and shopping centers. The needs of the contemporary tourists have induced entrepreneurs to build tourist attractions for the sole purpose of entertaining visitors. This detracts from the colorful local culture and presents a false view of the indigenous cultures. The other group affected by modern tourism is the local population. These people find themselves learning languages in a contrived way based on the changing tides of tourist groups solely for marketing purposes.

Furthermore, when curious visitors do venture outside their cultural bubbles, they enjoy, albeit intrusively, watching locals doing their daily tasks, thereby making them the subject of the tourist gaze. In sum, while tourism is on the rise, the trend is to maintain a distance from the real environment rather than to see the locations for their own values, and this negatively affects tourism entrepreneurs and local people.

Handout

Topic sentence: Modern tourists' demands _____.

A. Effects on tourism entrepreneurs	B. Effects on local populations
• Provide comfortable accommodations	• Learn tourists' languages
• Create tourist-focused entertainment attractions	• Become the objects of the tourist gaze

Based on 〈A〉, identify the technique that the teacher employed in the handout in 〈B〉. Then, complete the topic sentence in the handout.

모범답안 Outlining technique is used. Modern tourists' demands create the separation from real values of the local people and cultures, which brings negative effects on tourism development in general. (28 words)

18 Read the following and complete the passage with ONE word each.

2013년 22번

Below is an excerpt of a reading lesson. The teacher selected two different reading texts from a magazine. The texts shared a common topic on nature conservation. Each text had 10 sentences and was about 100 words long. She combined the two original texts and scrambled the sentences to get students to be aware of how __(1)__ texts are constructed. The students are led to use the __(2)__ strategy for general ideas.

Lesson Procedure

Step 1
- Show Ss several pictures about environmental pollution, and then have them talk about why it happens and what they can do to prevent it.
- Have Ss read the newly-formed text quickly, for about 30 seconds, to find out what the text is about, without focusing on every word.

Step 2
- Have Ss read the text individually, but now more carefully.
- Explain that the text is a combination of two shorter ones.
- In groups of three, have Ss divide the text into two separate ones that make sense.
- Have a member of each group give a presentation about how and why they divided the text the way they did.

Step 3
- Show Ss the original versions of the two texts, and have Ss compare them with their own.
- Have Ss vote for the most accurately restored versions.

Note: Ss = students

Which of the following is a correct statement about the lesson procedure above?

① The students are led to use the scanning strategy for details.
② It involves a one-way information-gap task to promote meaning negotiation.
③ It helps students to be aware of how coherent texts are constructed.
④ It serves to increase students' passive vocabulary through extensive reading.
⑤ The teacher uses simplified reading materials to provide comprehensible input.

문제분석	구분	교과 교육
난이도 ★★☆	평가목표	읽기수업에서 각 전략의 역할과 기능을 이해하는가?
	채점기준	두 개의 분리된 글을 하나의 글로 만들 때 coherent한 글을 작성한다. 전체적인 내용을 이해하기 위하여 빠르게 읽는 skimming전략을 쓴다.

모범답안 (1) coherent (2) skimming

 ③

19 Read the passage and follow the directions. 【2 points】

2017년 A6번

The following is part of a lesson procedure that aims to facilitate students' comprehension of a text concerning global warming.

1. Before reading the text, T activates Ss' background knowledge concerning global warming and provides other relevant information to help Ss to have a better comprehension of the text.
2. T instructs Ss to read the text quickly in order to grasp the main ideas. In doing so, T tells them not to read every word.
3. T asks Ss to reread it quickly for specific information, such as the type of disasters caused by global warming.
4. T instructs Ss to read the text again at their own pace.
5. T checks Ss' overall comprehension by having them write a brief summary of the text.
6. T then checks Ss' understanding of the details by using a cloze activity.

Identify the two kinds of expeditious reading that the teacher instructs students to use in steps 2 and 3 with ONE word, respectively. Write them in the order that they appear.

모범답안 skimming, scanning

20. Read the passage and complete the summary with ONE word each.

2011년 17번

Below is an excerpt of a reading lesson based on a three-part framework. The reading passage, about 300 words long, is about a boy's adventure. The ending of the story is intentionally omitted by the teacher so that students can learn how to construct a cohesive and coherent text.

Lesson Procedure

Pre-reading Activity
- Have Ss watch a 2-minute English video clip related to the reading passage and then answer questions about the clip.
- Give Ss half a minute to find previously learned discourse markers (e.g. however, therefore, as a result, etc.) in the passage while reading quickly through it.

Reading Activity
- Have Ss first read the story by themselves, complete the story in pairs by predicting the ending based on the storyline, and then write it down in about 50 words. While they carry out the task on their own, T circulates, offering feedback, suggestions, or language help Ss may need to accomplish the task.

Post-reading Activity
- Have each pair make a presentation about their version of the ending of the story in English.
- Have Ss vote for the most interesting ending.

Note: T = teacher, Ss = students

This lesson procedure above helps the students develop cooperative learning skills to work out on the probable ending to complete the story in pairs. While the pairs are working, the teacher assumes the role of facilitator and resource to circulate for some assistance to facilitate the task. For warmup activities, the students' (1)_____ is activated by letting them watch the video clip related to the topic of reading. The students are also led to use the (2)_____ strategy to quickly find some discourse markers. At the post-reading stage, they are asked to present their own conclusion to be evaluated for its interesting element.

Which of the following is NOT a correct statement about the lesson procedure?

① It helps the students develop cooperative learning skills.
② The teacher assumes the role of facilitator and resource.
③ It activates the students' background knowledge.
④ The students are asked to determine the accuracy of their predictions.
⑤ The students are led to use the scanning strategy.

문제분석

구분	교과 교육
평가목표	읽기활동의 단계에 나타난 교수원리를 이해한다.
채점기준	1점: 읽기 전 활동으로 이전의 지식인, schema를 불러일으킨다. 1점: 읽는 과정에서 discourse markers를 빠르게 찾는 scanning을 한다.

난이도 ★☆☆

모범답안 (1) schema (2) scanning

21 Read the following and answer the question.

> The following text is superficially ___(1)___ but makes no sense and is therefore not ___(2)___:
>
> *A puppy is sitting on a stool. A stool is often made of wood. Carpenters work with wood. A piece of wood can be bought from a lumber store.*
>
> In this text, the relationships between propositions are overtly signalled by means of lexical repetition, yet the propositions are not logically connected in terms of how we perceive the world. On the other hand, we can provide a good example of a short text that seemingly has no overt ___(3)___ devices yet makes perfect sense:
>
> *The picnic was ruined. No one remembered to bring corkscrew.*
>
> The text is not ___(4)___, but it is ___(5)___. Coherence is created due to the fact that the writer and the reader share the knowledge. The extra-textual knowledge is imperative for the perception of coherence in the text.

Fill in the blanks with the word of either *coherent* or *cohesive*.

모범답안 (1) cohesive (2) coherent (3) cohesive (4) cohesive (5) coherent

22 Based on the think-aloud data, identify the reading strategy that the student is using. Use ONE word. 【2 points】

2014년 A10번

> Computers have the potential to accomplish great things. With the right software, they could help make science tangible or teach neglected topics like art and music. They could help students form a concrete idea of society by displaying on screen a version of the city in which they live.
> In practice, <u>computers make our worst educational nightmares come true</u>. While we bemoan the decline of literacy, computers discount words in favor of pictures or video. While we fret about the decreasing cogency of public debate, computers dismiss linear argument and promote fast, shallow romps across the information landscape. <u>While we worry about basic skills, we allow into the classroom software that will do a student's arithmetic or correct his spelling.</u>

— Well, nightmares? The author thinks computers do harm to education.

— Hmm . . . the author is blaming computer software for a decline in basic skills.

모범답안　inferencing

23 Read the following and answer the question.

2007년 전국 11번

> Gregory is about forty-five and his hair is starting to go grey. Everybody knows Gregory because he is a television news anchor. He has done this very well for ten years and enjoys it quite a lot. Yesterday, his boss suggested Gregory change his job. Gregory knows his boss wants a younger man to take his place and doesn't care what happens to Gregory. The new job could never be as good as his old one. He has no one to discuss the problem with at home and this makes it worse.
>
> (1) Why does everybody know Gregory?
> (2) Gregory will probably not accept a new job and decide to resign instead. Agree or disagree with this statement in about thirty words.
> (3) In the very competitive world of television broadcasting, a youthful and attractive appearance is often more important than age and experience.
>
> True ☐ / False ☐

Comprehension step	Explanation
(a) Literal	Literal comprehension focuses on information explicitly stated in the text.
(b) Reorganization	Students have to organize for themselves some of the information explicitly expressed. They have to summarize information or handle it in a different sequence.
(c) Inferential	Students are required to go beyond the immediate text. They have to make use of their own experience and intuition, and possibly predict outcomes.
(d) Evaluative	Students are required to make judgments. They have to make use of their own knowledge of a particular subject.
(e) Appreciative	At this advanced level of response to a text students have to be emotionally and aesthetically sensitive to what they are reading.

Match the test items above (1)–(3) with its appropriate comprehension step (a)–(e).

모범답안 (1) a (2) c (3) d

24. Suppose that an English teacher makes worksheet ⟨B⟩ after reading ⟨A⟩.

2002년 서울 14번

⟨A⟩

Several recent studies on reading have emphasized the importance of providing explicit training in when, where, and how to use various reading strategies. Given the importance of using strategies, teachers need to be able to introduce them into the classroom while students are reading.

⟨B⟩

Choose the most appropriate sentence after each given text.

Last week, Tom's wife had an accident. Tom's youngest child, David, was at home when it happened. He was playing with his new toy car. Tom had given it to him the week before, for his third birthday. Suddenly, David heard his mother calling 'Help! Help!'

√ a. He ran to the kitchen.
  b. He went on playing with his car.
  c. He started to cry.

His mother had burned herself with some hot cooking oil.

  a. She was very foolish and Tom was angry with her.
√ b. She was crying with pain and the pan was on fire.
  c. He ran back to fetch his car.

Choose ONE reading strategy that the teacher intends to teach though the worksheet ⟨B⟩.
- guess the meaning of a word
- guess a grammatical relationship
- guess a discourse relationship
- guess about a cultural reference
- guess what is going to come next

모범답안 guess what is going to come next

25 Read the passage and follow the directions. 【4 points】

2017년 A13번

It was once assumed that reading comprehension could be understood as a kind of serial processing – that is, reading comprehension entails processing discrete units of words and sentences sequentially. This was one of the main assumptions behind the phonics approach. However, F. Smith explained that the serial processing operations underlying the phonics approach are contradicted by the fact that it is often impossible to make decisions about the sound of upcoming letters and words until the context (e.g., such as a word context or a sentence context) surrounding the item has been understood. When decoding an isolated word starting with 'ho–' for example, it would be impossible to assign a(n) _____ value to 'o' until one knew whether the whole word was 'house' 'horse' 'hot' or 'hoot.' In the same way, when decoding the word 'read' at the sentence level, it is impossible to assign a(n) _____ value to the vowel sequence 'ea' until it is known whether the sentence containing the word 'read' refers to the past or the present.

Fill in both blanks with the ONE most appropriate word from the passage. (Use the SAME word.) Then write the main idea of the passage. Do NOT copy more than FOUR consecutive words from the passage.

문제분석	구분	교과 교육
난이도 ★★☆	평가목표	읽기 교수법의 다른 두 종류를 이해하고 구체적으로 서술하는가?
	채점기준	1점: sound가치는 문장을 이해하지 않고는 오류가 나타날 수 있다. 1.5점: 읽기는 전체 어휘의 의미를 이해하는 것이다. 1.5점: 어휘는 분리된 특성이 아니라 하나의 전체로 학습된다.
모범답안		The blank is sound. The phonics approach of reading is limited because it does not account for the importance of context for correct pronunciation and meaning of words. Readers need to understand the surrounding context to properly decode and interpret certain words or letter sequences. (45 words)

26 Read the conversation and identify the type of reading that Ms. Kim recommends to Mr. Hong. Use TWO words. 【2 points】

2015년 A5번

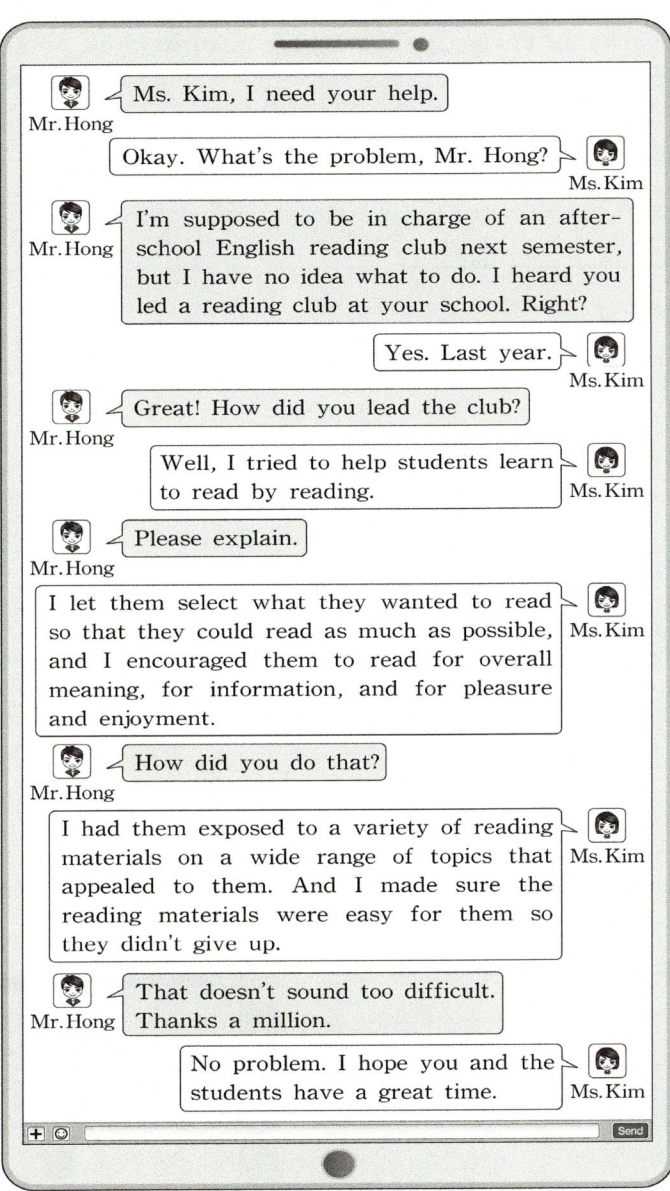

모범답안　extensive reading

27 Fill out the blank with one appropriate word.

The major objective of _____ reading is developing the ability to decode messages by drawing on syntactic and lexical clues, and the emphasis as in all reading is on skills for recognition rather than for production of language features.

모범답안   intensive

28 Read the passage and follow the directions.

2009년 15번

After reading a story, the students build a mind map of the story in a post-reading group activity. Students discuss the content of the story first and then go on-line to create mind maps using a computer program. This program provides templates to help build thoughts and information using pictures, images, words and multimedia.

Here is an example of the template: How to use this template:

1. Type the title of the story in the symbol labeled 'STORY TITLE'.
2. Type appropriate information about characterization, themes and so forth into the subsymbols.
3. Add symbols to further explain your ideas using the Create tool box.

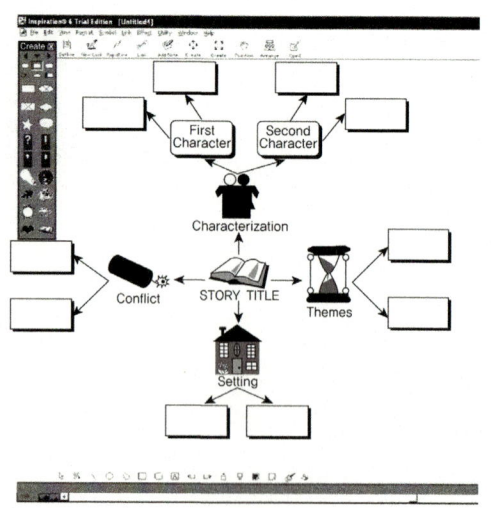

Describe the THREE features of teaching reading in hypertext in order to help students understand the text with their rationales and supporting evidence.

Choose all and only the correct statements about the activity.

ⓐ This activity requires a bottom-up processing of input for reading.
ⓑ This activity is based on the assumption that reading involves a passive and linear processing of information.
ⓒ This activity uses the organization of hypertext that mirrors different aspects of schema.
ⓓ This activity allows users to visualize and organize the story they have read.
ⓔ This activity promotes the mastery learning of each sublevel before learning the whole concept.
ⓕ This activity helps to show how characters, setting, themes and conflicts are connected in a story.

문제분석	구분	교과 교육
난이도 ★★★	평가목표	읽기지도를 위한 hypertext 사용법을 이해하고 서술하는가?
	채점기준	1점: 하이퍼텍스트 활동으로 전체개념을 이해해야 한다. 1점: 읽는 방법은 다양하게 열린 읽기이다. 1점: 글의 인물, 세팅, 주제등이 상호연결된다. 1점: 학생들은 글을 시각화하고 구성하며 다양한 스키마를 활용한다.

모범답안 The hypertext activity aims to learn the whole concept before learning of each sublevel. The reading is multi-linearity and open-endedness. Students show how characters, setting, themes and conflicts are interconnected in a story. Students visualize and organize the story they have read to activate different aspects of schema. (48 words)

기출문제답안 ⓒ, ⓓ, ⓕ

29. Complete the passage with ONE same word in the blanks.

An interactive-compensatory model has renewed interest in researching lower order skills. Language processing is organized into levels ranging from graphic recognition to high-level schemata representing world knowledge. The interactive-compensatory model of reading suggests that processing at one level can compensate for deficiencies at another level. According to this model, a reader who lacks fast _____ word recognition skills would try to compensate by using more controlled activation of processes at higher levels, for example, contextual information and top-level schemata. However, increased dependencies on higher-level processing do not necessarily mean more effective use of it; deficiencies in _____ word recognition may seriously hamper the reader's use of higher-level processing. Indeed, some scholars argue that, for second language readers, word recognition skills are essential to rapid comprehension.

모범답안 automatic

30. Fill in the blanks with TWO appropriate words. The same words are used.

Readers can easily be overwhelmed by a long string of ideas or events. The strategy of _____ or grouping ideas into meaningful cluster helps the reader to provide some order to the chaos. Making such _____ can be done individually, but they make for a productive group work technique as students collectively induce order and hierarchy to a passage. Early drafts of these maps can be quite messy—which is perfectly acceptable.

모범답안   semantic mapping

31. Fill in the blank with the ONE most appropriate word.

How do readers construct these meanings? How do they decide what to hold on to, and having made that decision, how do they infer a writer's message? These are the sorts of questions addressed by what has come to be known as (   ), the hallmark of which is that a text does not by itself carry meaning. The reader brings information, knowledge, emotion, experience, and culture to the printed word. The theory emphasizes this other side of the reading process, the conceptually driven, or top-down processing that brings a whole host of into the arena of making decisions about what something "means".

모범답안   schema

32 Read ⟨A⟩ and ⟨B⟩ and follow the directions.

2008년 전국 12번

⟨A⟩

One study was carried out with three groups of seven-year-olds who heard a story about a hunter from the (fictitious) Targa people. A week before being told the story, one group of children had heard a passage that described the Targa as Eskimos living in a cold climate; the second group had heard that the Targa were American Indians living in the desert; and the third group had heard information about people living in Spain which was irrelevant to the hunting text. After listening to the story, the first two groups were asked questions about climate and living conditions, although the story contained no information about either; but interestingly, the listeners claimed that it was in the story they had just been told. This indicates that the children were using prior knowledge to interpret what they heard and seemed unaware of the extent to which they were drawing on such knowledge. Moreover, the third group remembered the story less well than the other two groups, which suggests that a text on a familiar topic is easier to understand, even if the information it contains is novel. It should be remembered that inappropriately applied background knowledge may distort, rather than support, comprehension if it causes the listeners to force the content of a text into an existing schematic script.

⟨B⟩

You are teaching English oral skills to an intermediate-level group of Korean high school students, who are preparing for their first tour of New York. The following are some class activities available for the students:

a. A ten-minute role-play involving asking directions on the street in an American city.
b. A ten-minute discussion on the effects of global warming in the U.S.
c. A ten-minute talk by the teacher about the travel arrangements, using the information pack on the city of New York.
d. A ten-minute talk by the teacher on the Korean parliamentary system.

Based on ⟨A⟩, fill in the blanks with TWO items for ① and ② each from ⟨B⟩ and describe the reason for ③.

	items	Reasons
appropriate	①	familiar topic or prior knowledge
inappropriate	②	③

모범답안

	items	Reasons
appropriate	① a, c	familiar topic or prior knowledge
inappropriate	② b, d	③ unrelated topic to students' needs

33. Read the passage and follow the direction.

2006년 서울 15번

Presenting pictures, asking questions about the text to be read, and offering vocabulary warm-up are some of the activity types teachers can use at the pre-reading / pre-listening stage in a language classroom. Sometimes they may wonder: Do these activities actually enhance students' comprehension of texts in the second language? Do they have the same effects for students at all proficiency levels? Research shows that visual materials such as pictures or drawings presented before a listening or reading task generally enhance comprehension, particularly when learners are at a fairly low level of proficiency. On the other hand, they do not significantly enhance comprehension for more proficient readers or listeners. In general, non-pictorial pre-reading/ pre-listening activities such as studying vocabulary or answering pre-questions have been found more effective for learners at higher levels.

⟨Summary⟩

There are many possible (1) _____ of pre-reading/ pre-listening activities teachers can employ in the classroom. However, the effects of such activities on comprehension could vary in accordance with students' (2) _____.

Complete the summary by filling with TWO consecutive words for each blank from the passage.

모범답안 (1) visual materials (2) proficiency levels

CHAPTER 07 표현 능력 지도

01 Read the teacher's journal and follow the directions. 【2 points】

2024년 B1번

Teacher's Journal

Speech acts are a minimum unit of communication, which I believe are an important aspect of the pragmatic knowledge L2 learners need to learn to avoid unsuccessful communication. My students, for instance, have shown quite a few communication failures over time. When I tried to find out what their failures have in common, I realized they did not recognize the fact that an utterance may have some hidden intended effects on the hearer. Indeed, our communication is _____ in nature in that when we are saying something, we can mean something else.

I recall a couple of examples in particular. One day, in class, I said to my student, "What a wonderful picture you have drawn! I really like it." The student responded, "Oh, you like it? You can have it." In this case, since I made a compliment, I expected a simple thank-you from the student. Beyond my expectation, he seemed to believe that I wanted to own his picture. In a poetry class, I once said to another student of mine, "Would you like to read the poem?" The student replied, "No, I wouldn't." In the second case, I made a request, but the student seemed to think I was asking her to tell me if she was willing or unwilling to read the poem. In both cases, it is apparent that my students misunderstood the _____ acts my utterances performed.

Fill in the blanks with the ONE most appropriate word. Use the SAME word in both blanks.

문제분석	구분	교과 교육
난이도 ★☆☆	평가목표	의사소통을 하는데 말 속에 숨겨진 의도된 표현을 말하는 것은 무엇인가?
	채점기준	illocutionary는 학습자가 특정 상황이나 의도에 따라 언어를 사용하여 특정 행위를 수행하는 것을 의미한다.
모범답안	illocutionary	

02 Read the passages and follow the directions. 【4 points】

⟨A⟩

Ms. Min, a novice middle school English teacher, conducted a survey on the teaching practices of English teachers. She asked 47 local English teachers to vote for one principle they use most often for designing communicative activities. Her purpose was to find out design principles other teachers favored and then apply them to her own teaching. She analyzed the survey responses, and the results are shown below.

No	Design Principles	Vote Counts
1	Utilize consensus-building activities in which students work together to come to an agreement on given topics.	3
2	Make activities personalized where students talk about their own thoughts, opinions, feelings, and experiences.	16
3	Allow students to choose from a list of topics to talk about so that activities are communicative and manageable.	8
4	Use tasks that require students to produce concrete and tangible outcomes, such as an itinerary or map, as a result of communication.	13
5	Employ fun and playful activities, such as games, that have a competitive element.	7
	Total Counts	47

⟨B⟩

After the survey, Ms. Min developed communicative activities by applying some of the principles.

[Activity 1]

Work in groups. Think about your life at the age of ten. Answer the questions below. Then talk to your group members and find out if you have any similar experiences.

- Do you remember your teacher? What was s/he like?
- Were there any places you particularly liked or disliked? Why?
- Who were your friends? What were they like?
- What did you use to do before/after school or during the breaks?
- What was your favorite game?

[Activity 2]

Work in pairs. Each student receives a different card. Ask questions to each other in turn about the things on your card.

Card A	Card B
Ask your partner questions about Australia: - about big cities and their locations - about native people	Ask your partner questions about Australia: - about its flag - about wildlife
Here are the answers to your partner's questions: - Flag:  - Wildlife: kangaroos, koalas, emus, a lot of animals not found elsewhere	Here are the answers to your partner's questions: - Big cities and their locations:  - Native people: Aboriginals, arrived 65,000 years ago, many tribes, have lived in harmony with the land

[Activity 3]

Work in pairs. Each student receives either Worksheet A or Worksheet B. Talk with your partner to complete Daniel's class schedule using the example dialogue below.

S1: Which class does Daniel have on Mondays at 9:00?
S2: He has English.

Worksheet A

Daniel's Class Schedule

Time	Monday	Tuesday	Wednesday	Thursday	Friday
9:00-9:50		Korean			
10:00-10:50	Math		Physics	Biology	English
11:00-11:50		English			Spanish
11:50-13:00	Break				
13:00-13:50	Sports		Music	Sports	

Worksheet B

Daniel's Class Schedule

Time	Monday	Tuesday	Wednesday	Thursday	Friday
9:00-9:50	English		Spanish	Korean	Arts
10:00-10:50		Physics			
11:00-11:50	Biology		History	Math	
11:50-13:00	Break				
13:00-13:50		Music			History

Based on 〈A〉, for each of the two most popular design principles, identify the ONE activity in 〈B〉 that the principle has been applied to, respectively. Then explain your answers with evidence from 〈A〉 and 〈B〉.

문제분석 난이도 ★★★	구분	교과 교육
	평가목표	의사소통활동을 위한 원리에 따른 각 활동을 찾아 구체적으로 서술하는가?
	채점기준	1점: (Principle 2) Activity 1 1점: 개인적 경험에 대한 자신의 생각을 말한다. 1점: (Principle 4) Activity 3 1점: 실제적인 출력인 교실계획서를 완성한다.

모범답안 Principle 2 is applied to Activity 1. Students talk about their thoughts and feelings towards their personal experiences about teachers, places and etc. Principle 4 is applied to Activity 3. Students need to talk to each other to complete the tangible outcome or class schedule using the two different worksheets. (47 words)

03 Read the passage in ⟨A⟩ and conversation in ⟨B⟩, and follow the directions. 【4 points】

2023년 A10번

⟨A⟩

Second language learners pass through a predictable sequence of development. Since the early 1990's, some research has investigated the acquisition of pragmatic abilities in the L2. 'Requesting' is one of the pragmatic features that has received attention. In a review of studies on the acquisition of requests in English, six stages of development were suggested.

	Characteristics	Example
1	Using body language or gestures	*Sir (pointing to the pencil).* *Teacher (holding the paper).*
2	Using verbless expressions	*A paper. / More time.*
3	Using imperative verbs	*Give me. / Give me a paper.*
4	Using 'Can I have _____?' as a formulaic expression	*Can I have some candy?*
5	Using 'can' with a range of verbs, not just with 'have'	*Can you pass me the book?*
6	Using indirect requests	*I want more cookies.*

─────────────── ⟨B⟩ ───────────────

(*Students are doing a problem-solving task in groups. S1 plays the role of moderator in the activity.*)

S1: We have to find some ways to make the environment more sustainable. Suhee, what's your opinion?
S2: I'm sorry, but nothing comes to mind now. I need more time to think.
S1: Okay. Minho, how about you? Can you share your ideas with us?
S3: We should use one-time products as less as possible.
S1: Hold on, Minho. What does 'one-time products' mean? Can I have some examples?
S3: Well, paper cups, plastic bags…
S2: Ah, I see. You mean 'disposable products', right?
S1: Minho, I like your idea.
S2: Driving electronic cars reduces air pollution.
S3: Sounds great.

Based on ⟨A⟩, identify the developmental stages where S1 and S2 are, respectively. Then, explain your answers with evidence from ⟨B⟩.

문제분석	구분	교과 교육
난이도 ★★☆	평가목표	요청하기 위한 언어 기능을 언어발달 단계를 통해 구체적으로 서술하는가?
	채점기준	1점: S1 (단계 4 & 5) 1점: can 조동사를 다양한 동사와 함께 사용할 수 있다. 1점: S2 (단계 6) 1점: 간접적 요청의 표현이 가능하다.
모범답안		S1 is in the stages 4 and 5. S1 extends the use of 'can' with other various verbs and different subjects to make request, like 'can you share..' and 'can I have...'. S2 is in the stage 6 with using indirect request, 'I need more time to think'. (48 words)

04
Read the passage in ⟨A⟩ and the email in ⟨B⟩, and follow the directions. 【4 points】

2023년 B6번

⟨A⟩

  Ms. Hong, a new English teacher, had a hard time getting her students to talk in her English speaking class. She investigated the issue and found a checklist related to the problems that hinder the students' active engagement in speaking. The checklist consisted of seven categories with descriptions: no preparation time, uneven participation, poor listening ability, lack of speaking strategy use, mother-tongue use, nothing to say, and inhibition. Based on her observations, she evaluated how often her students struggled with the problems in the checklist during her English speaking class.

Class Observation Checklist

Descriptions	Scale 1	2	3
1. Students need some quiet time before they are engaged in a speaking activity.		✓	
2. In group activities, some of the students free-ride without contributing to the discussion.		✓	
3. Students have listening difficulties when engaged in speaking activities.	✓		
4. Students are not aware of speaking strategies and need to develop their own.			✓
5. When students speak the same mother tongue, they tend to use it in group work, especially when the teacher is far away.			✓
6. Students complain that they cannot think of anything to say.		✓	
7. Students are often inhibited from trying to say things in English in the speaking class.			✓

Note: 1 = seldom, 2 = sometimes, 3 = often

  Ms. Hong gave careful thought to six, out of the seven problems, that she checked as "sometimes" or "often" in the checklist. She came up with satisfactory solutions to four of the problems; but for the other two, she decided to ask for help. She sent an email about the two problems to Mr. Park, a head teacher, in order to seek some advice. He replied as in ⟨B⟩.

	⟨B⟩	
Send	FROM	parkminsu5827@school.korea
	TO	Ms. Hong (Teacher)
	SUBJECT	Re: Asking for advice

Dear Ms. Hong,

I am sorry to reply to your email so late. I have thought about the two problems you mentioned in your email, and my suggestions for the problems are, in brief, as follows:

The first problem arises quite often in speaking classes. If the task you want to do in class is based on group work, I think you need to choose a task such as jigsaw that we talked about the other day. When I included that activity in my English speaking class, the students' participation increased significantly overall while they were pooling all their information in groups. The second problem is another one that happens frequently in English speaking classes. Why don't you appoint one of the group members as monitor? I think the very awareness that someone is monitoring helps the students put more effort into using the target language.

Based on ⟨A⟩ and ⟨B⟩, identify the TWO problems Ms. Hong asked for Mr. Park's advice about. Then, explain why he made the suggestions for her two problems, respectively. Do NOT copy more than FOUR consecutive words from ⟨A⟩ and ⟨B⟩.

문제분석	구분	교과 교육
난이도 ★★☆	평가목표	말하기 활동에서의 문제점을 제시하고 해결책을 구체적으로 서술하는가?
	채점기준	1점: (uneven participation) 1점: jigsaw활동으로 무임승차하는 사람없이 모두 참여할 수 있다. 1점: (mother-tongue use) 1점: 모니터학생을 이용하여 교사가 없을 때 영어를 사용할 수 있도록 한다.
모범답안		The problems are uneven participation and mother-tongue use. Jigsaw can increase the students' overall participation since they have to pool all their information to complete their group task without free riders. Having a monitor student in a group makes students put more effort to use English while teacher is not present. (51 words)

05. Read the passage in ⟨A⟩ and the teacher's log in ⟨B⟩, and follow the directions. [4 points]

2021년 A8번

⟨A⟩

In an attempt to better understand language development, a three-tiered approach has been proposed, encompassing the following components for investigating production changes: complexity, accuracy, and fluency. Complexity generally refers to the lexical variety and syntactic elaborateness of the learner's linguistic system. Accuracy involves the correct use of the target language, while fluency concerns a focus on meaning, automatization, and real-time processing. These three constructs can be applied to appraise written or spoken language skill (i.e., performance) as well as to assess the state of the linguistic knowledge that supports this performance (i.e., proficiency).

⟨B⟩

Teacher's Log

In order to evaluate the progress of their speaking ability, I usually have my students read a story and then tell about it in their own words. It's not easy to measure all aspects of their speech at once. On the part of the students, it's also not easy to focus on more than one aspect simultaneously. So, I usually give my students two presentation opportunities and ask them to pay more attention to one aspect over the others in each presentation session. In the first presentation session, I focus on how naturally and clearly the content is delivered. To that end, I evaluate students' presentations based on the speed of their talk and the number of pauses and false starts. For the second presentation session, I record and transcribe the students' oral performance for a closer look. At this point, the presentation is evaluated especially by calculating the ratio of independent and dependent clauses and tallying the number of different verbs used.

Based on ⟨A⟩, identify the component that the teacher focuses on in each presentation session mentioned in ⟨B⟩, respectively. Then, support your answer with evidence from ⟨B⟩. Do NOT copy more than FOUR consecutive words from ⟨A⟩ and ⟨B⟩.

문제분석	구분	교과 교육
난이도 ★★☆	평가목표	말하기 과업에서 필수 요소인 fluency, accuracy, complexity의 용도를 이해하고 구체적으로 서술하는가?
	채점기준	2점: (Fluency) 내용에 대한 자연스럽고 명확한 전달과 말의 속도에 집중한다. 2점: (Complexity) 종속절, 독립절과 다양한 동사의 사용이 평가된다.

모범답안 For 1st session, fluency is focused. Teacher focuses on the students' natural and clear delivery of the content, and the speed of the talk with less pauses and false starts. For 2nd session, complexity is focused. The uses of dependent and independent clauses and the uses of different verbs can be evaluated. (50 words)

06 Read the following and answer the question.

2010년 20번

You Are a Witness!

(1) The teacher prepares a set of four picture cards showing the story of a minor car accident. She divides the class into four groups, with four students in each group. She tells the class that they are going to witness a car accident, but that they can see only one card.

(2) The teacher flashes one picture card to each group for a few seconds only. Then she asks the members of each group to discuss and agree on what they have just seen.

(3) The teacher assigns each member of each group a number: 1, 2, 3, and 4. Then she re-groups students as follows: 1234 1234 1234 1234 → 1111 2222 3333 4444

(4) The teacher asks the members of the new groups to describe what each person saw and to decide on the sequence of the accident.

Which of the following is correct about the activity above?

① Students are encouraged to produce different sequences of the story through interaction.
② The activity requires students to exchange information to perform the task.
③ The story is jointly constructed through an imitative speaking activity.
④ The activity focuses on improving language accuracy through the repeated speaking task.
⑤ One member in each group must have most of the information and transfer it to the rest of the members.

07 Read the passage in ⟨A⟩ and the part of the individual conference in ⟨B⟩, and follow the directions. 【4 points】

2020년 B10번

⟨A⟩

In an oral presentation. Mr. Lee gave his students the following rubric in advance and let them know that their performance would be evaluated across four categories: (a)content & preparation, (b)organization, (c)language, and (d)delivery. After the students' presentations were over, Mr. Lee had a conference session with each student to discuss his or her strengths and weaknesses. The students in Mr. Lee's class did an oral presentation. Mr. Lee gave his students the following rubric in advance and let them know that their performance would be evaluated across four categories. After the students' presentations were over, Mr. Lee had a conference session with each student to discuss his or her strengths and weaknesses.

PRESENTATION ASSESSMENT FORM

Evaluation Categories	Scale
	1 poor — 2 — 3 — 4 — 5 excellent
I. Content & Preparation	
1. Interest & Value of topic	1 2 3 4 5
2. Informativeness of content	1 2 3 4 5
3. Preparedness	1 2 3 4 5
II. Organization	
1. Introduction (giving an overview)	1 2 3 4 5
2. Main body (supporting details & examples)	1 2 3 4 5
3. Conclusion (summarizing the presentation)	1 2 3 4 5
III. Language	
1. Accuracy (accurate use of grammar)	1 2 3 4 5
2. Appropriateness	1 2 3 4 5
3. Fluency	1 2 3 4 5
4. Pronunciation	1 2 3 4 5
IV. Delivery	
1. Confidence (not overly dependent on notes)	1 2 3 4 5
2. Gestures & Facial expressions	1 2 3 4 5

― ⟨B⟩ ―

(*The following is part of the individual conference that Mr. Lee had with one of his students, Yuna.*)

L: Your presentation was pretty good.

Y: Thank you, Mr. Lee.

L: Yeah, you were really prepared. And so you got a perfect score on that area.

Y: I tried my best to make my PPT slides as informative as possible.

L: I know! They were really impressive. And your topic was really good.

Y: Thank you! How was my pronunciation?

L: Overall, I think your language was easy for the other students to follow. But you may want to try to use your language more appropriately. For example, some expressions you used like you guys and you know, may not be appropriate in this kind of presentation.

Y: I see. Thank you for your feedback.

L: I also noticed that you referred to your cue cards too frequently without looking at the audience.

Y: I did?

L: Yes, you did. Your presentation would have been much better if you had shown more confidence in your presentation task.

Y: I agree.

L: Other than that, everything looked fine.

Note: L = Mr. Lee, Y = Yuna

Identify TWO of the four evaluation categories that Mr. Lee thinks reflect Yuna's weak points. Then, provide evidence for each identified category from ⟨B⟩.

모범답안 Categories of (III) language and (IV) delivery are weak points. Students could not use appropriate language for the formal presentation situation. Her presentation showed the lack of confidence with looking at cue cards too much instead of looking at the audience. (40 words)

08 Read the passage in ⟨A⟩ and the conversation in ⟨B⟩, and follow the directions. 【4 points】

2022년 B6번

⟨A⟩

Conversation is co-constructed by two or more people, unfolding dynamically in real time. For conversational discourse to be successful, the participants have to know how to organize the events in it; that is, they need to achieve cohesion. A cohesive relation is one in which the interpretation of one element in the discourse presupposes, and is dependent upon, another. In English, along with the grammatical cohesive devices such as reference, substitution, ellipsis, and conjunction, cohesion in conversation can also be achieved using lexical cohesive devices.

Lexical cohesive devices by which links are made across a conversation include the use of synonyms, antonyms, repetition of the same content words, words exhibiting general-specific relations, and words displaying part-whole relations. The use of lexical cohesion is an indicator of topic consistency, and hence contributes significantly to the sense that speakers are talking to topic, and the talk, therefore, becomes more coherent.

⟨B⟩

(*Two friends are having a conversation in the wallpaper aisle at a hardware store.*)

S1: Isn't it funny that wallpaper is in fashion again?
S2: Yeah, I thought it was gone forever.
S1: Me, too. So, you are redoing your kitchen?
S2: Yup. And I want to use one of these.
S1: Good idea. (pointing to a roll of wallpaper) How about that?
S2: You mean the one on the top shelf?
S1: Yeah, do you like it?
S2: Uh-huh. It will go with my dining table.
S1: Have you been to Lesley's new office?
S2: I have, actually. It was huge and everything was so well organized.
S1: Yeah. And she had the same wallpaper.
S2: Oh, that's right. I remember that.

Note: S = speaker

Based on ⟨A⟩, identify TWO lexical cohesive devices used in the conversation in ⟨B⟩. Then, provide evidence from ⟨B⟩ for each identified lexical cohesive device.

문제분석	구분	교과 교육
난이도 ★★☆	평가목표	lexical cohesive devices의 쓰임과 내용을 구체적으로 서술하는가?
	채점기준	1점: (repetition) 1점: 같은 내용단어인 'wallpaper'를 반복 사용한다. 1점: (part-whole) 1점: 부엌이라는 전체 개념에 대하여 ' 'top shelf'나 'dining table'이 포함된다.

모범답안 Lexical cohesive devices, repetition and part-whole relations were used. As for repetition, the same content word, 'wallpaper' was repeated to continue the same topic. As for part-whole relations, the whole word 'kitchen' was connected with the part words, 'top shelf' and 'dining table'. (43 words)

09 Read the passage in ⟨A⟩ and the interaction in ⟨B⟩, and follow the directions. 【4 points】

2020년 A5번

⟨A⟩

　Different words and phrases can be used to organize the structure and manage the flow of ongoing conversations. Language elements of this function include different types such as conjunctions, cataphoric words, hedges, and back channel cues. Conjunctions join words, phrases, or clauses together. Cataphoric words refer forward to other words which will be used later in the conversation. Hedges are words or phrases employed not to express the truth of a statement categorically, and back channel cues indicate that one is paying attention to his or her interlocutor's speech. As using these types of language is associated with discourse and strategic competence, the ability to use them in an effective way constitutes part of communicative competence.

⟨B⟩

(Two students are doing a task on finding differences between each other's pictures without showing them to each other.)

S1:　Do you see any people in your picture?
S2:　I have a man. He is tall.
S1:　Is he the only person?
S2:　I also have a woman in my picture.
S1:　There are two in mine, too. What are they doing?
S2:　They are sitting together.
S1:　That's one difference. They are standing in mine.
S2:　What is the woman wearing?
S1:　She is wearing a jacket.
S2:　What color is it?
S1:　It's black.
S2:　That is the same in my picture.
S1:　Oh, wait, on her jacket, I found this. There is a letter P on it.
S2:　I also see a P on her jacket in my picture.
S1:　What about the man? What is he wearing?
S2:　He is in a blue coat. It is sort of neat.
S1:　The man's coat is brown in mine. That's another difference.

Note: S = student

Identify TWO types among those mentioned in ⟨A⟩ that are used in ⟨B⟩. Then, provide evidence for each identified type from ⟨B⟩.

문제분석	구분	교과 교육
난이도 ★★☆	평가목표	대화체에서 활용되는 다양한 전략적 도구의 종류를 서술하는가?
	채점기준	1점: (Cataphoric words) 1점: 나중에 올 내용을 미리 가리킨다. 1점: (Hedges) 1점: 직접적으로 말하기 보다 부드럽게 표현한다.

모범답안 Cataphoric words and hedges are used in ⟨B⟩. Cataphoric word, 'this' in 'I found this' refers to a 'letter P' in the later statement. Hedge, 'sort of' is used for less direct expression to make the statement softer rather than explicitly expressing the word. (45 words)

10 Read the activity procedure and identify the type of learning activity with ONE word. 【2 points】

2016년 A3번

⟨Activity Procedure⟩

Step 1	• T places various information on a different job in each of the four corners in the classroom. (Each corner is labelled with a different letter, A, B, C, or D.) • T assigns individual Ss a letter (A, B, C, or D) in order to create four groups of four Ss, each of which is a base group composed of A to D.
Step 2	• T provides Ss in each base group with handouts. (Each handout has a set of questions about four different jobs.) • T helps Ss understand that they should be interdependent upon one another not only for their own learning but also for the learning of others throughout the activity. • T informs Ss which corner to go to based on their letter in order to form four different expert groups.
Step 3	• Ss move to their expert groups and find out information about different jobs through discussions and answer the questions on the handouts. • T circulates within the groups and makes sure each of the Ss has all the answers.
Step 4	• Ss return to their initial base groups and exchange the information through discussing what they learned in the expert groups. • All the base groups present their findings to the whole class and decide which job they would like most.

Note: T = teacher, S = student

모범답안 jigsaw

11 Read the passage and answer the question.

2007년 서울 15번

⟨Classroom Activity⟩

- Each group member receives a different piece of information.
- Students regroup in topic groups composed of people with the same piece to master the material and prepare to teach it.
- They return to home groups to share their information with each other.
- They synthesize the information through discussion.
- Each student produces an assignment of part of a group project to demonstrate ① _____ of all the information presented by all group members.

Language acquisition is facilitated by students interacting in the target language. Teachers not only teach language, but also they teach cooperation as well. The efforts of an individual help not only the individual to be rewarded, but also others in the class. Although they work together, each student is individually accountable. ② _____ is distributed. Social skills such as acknowledging another's contribution, and keeping the conversation calm need to be explicitly taught.

Fill in the blanks with appropriate words in the word list.

⟨Word list⟩

| leadership | facilitation | proficiency | attention |
| synthesis | implication | | |

모범답안   ① synthesis   ② leadership

12 Read the passage and follow the directions.

2005년 서울 16번

N : Excuse me, can I use this phone to make a call?
NN: No, sorry. This is the house phone. Where do you want to call? (*The tourist is somewhat taken aback by the direct question.*)
N : I need to call a friend in town. (*spoken somewhat reluctantly*)
NN: In the city you can use the phone on that desk. Dial zero first and the operator will pass you onto the outside line.
N : Thank you.
Note: N=native English-speaking tourist, NN=non-native English-speaking hotel receptionist

The receptionist in the dialogue is in control of the information and has the language ability to impart this information, although there is a problem with sociolinguistic norms and linguistic delivery. In this type of exchange, native English speakers would probably not say "Where do you want to call?" because it can be perceived as an invasion of one's privacy. Instead, the receptionist would probably ask ①_____? Initially, the receptionist's direct question might have created ②_____ failure — the tourist could have felt insulted and gotten angry. Soon, however, the tourist understood that the receptionist was simply asking for information in order to give the answer.

(1) Fill in blank ① using ALL and ONLY the words in the box below.

| long-distance | call | inside | the | a | or |
| calling | city | it | are | is | you |

(2) Fill in the blank ② with ONE word from the passage.

모범답안 (1) Are you calling inside the city or is it a long-distance call?
(2) sociolinguistic

13 Read the conversation and follow the directions. 【2 points】

2015년 A4번

> T: The other day we were talking about the Battle of Waterloo. And we've already talked about the two main generals in that war. Does anybody remember who they are?
> S: Napoleon and Wellington.
> T: Correct, but don't forget that Wellington is a title which he received for his military successes. Born Arthur Wesley, he became the Duke of Wellington in 1814. He received that title for ending the Peninsular War by storming what city?
> S: Toulouse.
> T: That's right. Shortly after, Napoleon abdicated and was imprisoned on Elba. And when did the Battle of Waterloo take place?
> S: 1815.
> T: Very good. Napoleon escaped Elba and was attempting to restore his rule. It wasn't until his defeat at Waterloo by Wellington that Napoleon's reign finally came to an end. Now we're going to see …
>
> *Note:* T = teacher, S = student

Complete the comments on the conversation above by filling in the blank with ONE word.

> The conversation above is part of a teacher-student talk in the classroom in which a teacher and students mainly give and receive specific information. Among types of speaking functions, the type shown in the conversation refers to situations where the focus is on information rather than on the participants. The conversation above serves a(n) _____ function in that its priority is not the interpersonal function of speaking but information exchange.

모범답안   transactional

14 Read the following to describe the class.

2004년 전국 13번

⟨Activity⟩

The class has 30 EFL students at an intermediate level of proficiency. They meet four times a week for 50 minutes each class.

- Step 1: The teacher has the students divide into groups of five. Since there are thirty students, that creates six groups of five students.
- Step 2: One member of each group is given a picture strip story. There are six pictures in a row on a piece of paper, but no words. The pictures tell a story.
- Step 3: The student with the story shows the first picture to the other members of his or her group, while covering the remaining five pictures. The other students try to _____ what they think will happen in the second picture. The first student tells them whether they are correct or not. He or she then shows the second picture and asks them to _____ what the third picture will look like.
- Step 4: After the entire series of pictures has been shown, the group gets a new strip story and they change roles.

⟨Principles⟩

Natural language learning takes place as students use pictures to freely express themselves through guided practice. Students, working in groups, can interact with each other in a cooperative learning environment. The learning experience is interesting as it does not focus on language form but on communicating meaning. With the emphasis on meaning and interaction the learning process makes it less likely for students to use their native language.

Complete the activity by filling in the blanks with the SAME word.

모범답안   predict

15 Read the passage in ⟨A⟩ and the conversation in ⟨B⟩, and follow the directions. 【4 points】

2014년 A2번

⟨A⟩

A typical conversation organized around making requests has a common overarching sequence of interactional moves:
- A greeting exchange
- Preliminary moves toward a forthcoming request
- Making the request
- Short negotiation about the request
- Acceptance/Rejection of the request
- Closing/Thanking

⟨B⟩

(A low-proficiency English learner asks her roommate, a native speaker of English, to go buy some bread for her.)

Jisu: Hi, Kelly.
Kelly: Hi, Jisu.
Jisu: Buy me bread, OK?
Kelly: Do you want bread?
Jisu: Yeah.
Kelly: So, there's no bread in the fridge?
Jisu: Sorry?
Kelly: You don't have bread?
Jisu: No.
Kelly: So, do you want me to go to the supermarket and get some bread for you?
Jisu: What was that?
Kelly: Do you want me to get bread for you?
Jisu: Yeah.
Kelly: Do you want it right now?
Jisu: Tomorrow morning.
Kelly: OK. I'll get it for you later tonight.
Jisu: OK. Thank you.

* *Note:* Jisu = low-proficiency learner, Kelly = native speaker of English

Based on ⟨A⟩, identify one sequence that deviates from the sequence of interactional moves in ⟨B⟩ and explain your answer with example utterance from ⟨B⟩. Identify the negotiation strategy that Jisu uses when she does not understand Kelly and explain your answer with example utterance from ⟨B⟩.

문제분석	구분	교과 교육
난이도 ★★☆	평가목표	discourse를 위하여 대화체에서 문제가 되는 요소와 함께 전략을 서술하는가?
	채점기준	1점: (preliminary move)를 따르지 않는다. 1.5점: 요청을 하기 전에 직접적으로 요청한다. 1.5점: (clarification request)인 sorry를 사용하여 의사협상 전략을 쓴다.
모범답안		The conversation deviates a sequence of preliminary move. Jisu doesn't make an utterance of explanations or accounts before request but directly asks request, "Buy me bread". She uses a negotiation strategy of clarification request, 'sorry?' when she doesn't understand Kelly's previous statement. (42 words)

16 Read the following and answer the question.

2012년 24번

An English teacher developed the following procedure for teaching pronunciation. (Prominent syllables are marked by large-capital letters.)

Step 1

a. The teacher writes the following three versions of the sentence I'm listening on the board: —I'm LIStening. —I'M listening. —I AM listening.

b. Students practice producing all three versions.

Teacher asks:	Student should respond:
What are you doing?	I'm LIStening.
Who's listening?	I'M listening.
Why aren't you listening?	I AM listening.

Step 2

With an explanation on how to chunk, the teacher asks students to listen and circle the prominent words.

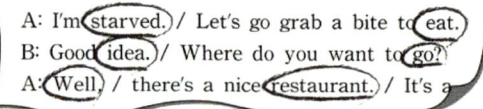

Step 3

a. Students write down words for the items that they want to bring for a picnic.

apple, pasta, napkin, pear, pepper, popcorn, pizza, spoon, soup...

b. The teacher asks students to play a game called 'The perfect picnic' with the whole class, using the words that they chose.

Example: Student A says, "We're having a picnic, and I'm bringing pears." Student B says, "We're having a picnic. A is bringing pears, and I'm bringing popcorn." Student C says...

Describe each pedagogical purpose of teaching pronunciation to explain how students acquire the target pronunciation, citing each step 1, 2, and 3 with supporting evidence.

Which of the following is correct about the teaching procedure above?

① Students learn chunking implicitly in Step 2.
② The activities focus on minimal pairs of segments.
③ The activities encourage students to focus on stress at the word level.
④ The activity in Step 3 is constructed to be a mechanical pronunciation drill.
⑤ The procedure facilitates students' movement from controlled to automatic processing or production of L2 phonology.

문제분석	구분	교과 교육
난이도 ★★☆	평가목표	suprasegmental 레벨의 의미를 두는 강세 발음지도방법을 단계별로 구체적으로 서술하는가?
	채점기준	2점: (step 1) 최소단위의 suprasegmental로 대화형식으로 prominence를 연습한다. 1점: (step 2) 어휘의 모음으로 명시적으로 연습한다. 1점: (step 3) 의미있는 의사소통적 드릴로 연습한다.
모범답안		Step 1 focuses on minimal pairs of suprasegmentals in controlled practice and students focus on prominence at the discourse-level. In step 2, students learn chunking of words explicitly to practice prominence. Step 3, students practice in a meaningful and communicative drills. (47 words)

 ⑤

17 Read the passage and follow the directions.

2011년 29번

Student A's Worksheet

Directions: Read sentences 1-4 to your partner, and then circle the words you hear in sentences 5-8 as they are read by your partner.

1. He gave me a hug.
2. Hand me the pin.
3. This room is full of cats.
4. The men will come soon.

5. I'd like to see the **chimp/champ**.
6. That's my **luck/lock**.
7. They **spun/spin** around.
8. I fell over a **rock/rack**.

Student B's Worksheet

Directions: Circle the words in sentences 1-4 as they are read by your partner, and then read sentences 5-8 to your partner.

1. He gave me a **hug/hog**.
2. Hand me the **pen/pin**.
3. This room is full of **cots/cats**.
4. The **man/men** will come soon.

5. I'd like to see the champ.
6. That's my lock.
7. They spun around.
8. I fell over a rock.

Identify whether the focus of activity is segmental or suprasegmental and explain with THREE pedagogical focuses of the activity with supporting evidences.

 Choose all and only the correct statements about the activity.
ⓐ The activity focuses on phonemic differences of vowel sounds.
ⓑ The activity requires students to distinguish suprasegmental features.
ⓒ The activity places greater importance on accuracy than on fluency.
ⓓ The activity forces students to practice different registers.

문제분석	구분	교과 교육
난이도 ★☆☆	평가목표	segmental을 가르치는 발음학습의 특성을 구체적으로 서술하는가?
	채점기준	1점: segmental연습을 하는 수업이다. 1점: 모음발음 연습을 한다. 1점: 발음을 이해하고 표현한다. 1점: 언어의 정확도에 집중한다.

모범답안 The activity is to practice segmental features of pronunciation. It places greater importance on the vowel sounds, 'chimp' or 'champ' and etc. The activity helps students comprehend and produce the vowel sounds through pair work. The activity requires students to practice language accuracy than fluency. (45 words)

기출문제답안 ⓐ, ⓒ

18 Read the following and answer the direction.

2006년 서울 8번

Teacher A	Teacher B
T: So, now we're going to do some practice. Listen to me and repeat. "Bob is tall." "Bob is tall." Ss: Bob is tall. T: Good! Sue. Ss: Sue is tall. T: Good! Earrings. Minsu? Ss: Sue is earrings. T: Is? Sue HAS earrings. Everyone? Ss: Sue HAS earrings. T: Mary. Ss: Mary HAS earrings.	T: OK. I'm going to point to someone and you make a statement about that person. Ready? Eric. Minsu? S: Eric is handsome. T: Is he? Yes, right. Susan. Mijin? S: Susan has short hair. T: She does? (shakes head) S: Oh… Um… TOM has short hair. T: Good. Repeat! Tom has short hair. Ss: Tom has short hair. T: Good. Tom's almost bald! (laughs)

Note: T = teacher, S = student

Compare and contrast the two teachers' drills A and B in terms of instructional focus.

모범답안 Both drills focus on language accuracy. The drills in ⟨B⟩ use more meaningful drills than do the drills in ⟨A⟩. The drills in ⟨A⟩ use a single-slot substitution drill. Both drills do not require communicative function in order to produce a correct response as in the Audiolingual Method. (48 words)

19 Read the passage and follow the directions.

2010년 27번

⟨Complaint and Apology⟩

1. Ms. Yang, an English teacher at a middle school, has students look at a picture showing some wet towels on the floor. She asks them to make and act out a conversation in pairs with Student A complaining and Student B apologizing.

2. After the role-play, Ms. Yang asks students to write their scripts. Then she shows a script of similar conversation done by native speakers and asks students in pairs to compare their own with the following:

> NS 1: Why are these wet towels on the floor? Please pick them up and hang them up to dry.
> NS 2: Gosh! I'm really sorry. I forgot all about them.
>
> * NS : Native Speaker

3. Students in pairs are asked to revise their scripts and practice the dialogue. Ms. Yang gives feedback.

Identify the instructional approach of teaching the language skills in the lesson. Explain it with the stages 1 and 3 in terms of language skills.

Choose all and only the correct statements about the activity.

ⓐ The first stage focuses on function rather than on form.
ⓑ The teacher presents authentic language input at the beginning stage.
ⓒ The lesson is designed to reinforce speaking skills through writing.
ⓓ The lesson is sequenced from a controlled speaking activity to a free speaking activity.
ⓔ Students are given opportunities to develop language accuracy.

문제분석	구분	교과 교육
난이도 ★☆☆	평가목표	말하기 수업의 통합적 과업을 이해하고 구체적으로 언어기능을 서술하는가?
	채점기준	1점: 통합 교수법이다. 1점: 형태보다는 기능에 중심을 두고 과업을 수행한다. 1점: (Stage 1) 말하기로 시작하여 쓰기활동이 통합된다. 1점: (Stage 3) 언어를 수정하고 연습하는 정확도에 집중한다.

모범답안 The lesson is an integrated approach to teach speaking skills through writing activity. At at stage 1, Students perform the task based on the situation to focus on function of complaining rather than on form. At at stage 3, students develop language accuracy through revising and practicing the dialogue. (50 words)

기출문제답안 ⓐ, ⓒ, ⓔ

20 Fill in the blank of teaching activity with the ONE most appropriate word from the passage.

Learner A has a train timetable showing the times of trains from Newtown to Shrewsbury. Learner B has a timetable of trains from Shrewsbury to Swansea.

⟨Learner A⟩	⟨Learner B⟩
Newtown departure 11:34 13:31 15:18 16:45 Shrewsbury arrival 12:22 14:18 16:08 18:25	Shrewsbury departure 13:02 15:41 16:39 18:46 Swansea arrival 17:02 19:19 20:37 22:32

Together, the learners must work out the quickest possible journey from Newtown to Swansea. Again, of course, it is important that they should not be able to see each other's information. So, learners have to pool _____ to solve a problem.

모범답안 information

21. Read teaching activities ⟨A⟩ and ⟨B⟩ and answer the question.

⟨A⟩

Asking for Help

One student looks at card A. The other student looks at card B. Students practice the conversation in pairs.

Card A: You want your friend to help you with some homework.
A: (Check if B is busy.)
B: _____
A: (Ask him/her to help you.)
B: _____

Card B: Your friend wants you to help him/her with some homework.
A: _____
B: (Tell him/her you are not busy.)
A: _____
B: (Refuse. Give a reason.)

⟨B⟩

Asking for Help

Student A: Have you ever been in a situation where you needed help? Describe the situation to your partner.
Student B: Listen to your partner. Draw a picture to show the situation. Talk about the picture with your partner.

Compare and contrast the two activities ⟨A⟩ and ⟨B⟩ in terms of activity type and purpose of learning.

Which of the following is NOT correct?
① ⟨A⟩ is a more controlled activity than ⟨B⟩.
② ⟨A⟩ is for less proficient learners than ⟨B⟩.
③ ⟨B⟩ is a more divergent activity than ⟨A⟩.
④ ⟨B⟩ is less cognitively demanding than ⟨A⟩.
⑤ ⟨B⟩ is a more meaning-oriented activity than ⟨A⟩.

문제분석	구분	교과 교육
난이도 ★☆☆	평가목표	communicative와 non-communicative 교실 활동의 특성을 구체적으로 비교하는가?
	채점기준	1점: 〈A〉는 제한된 의사소통 기술 연습을 한다. 1점: 〈A〉 통제되고 구조화된 반응을 한다. 1점: 〈B〉 다양하고 열린 반응을 한다. 1점: 〈B〉 의미중심으로 자신의 생각을 말한다.

모범답안 〈A〉 is a more controlled activity with limited communication skills to complete the dialogues. It is suitable for less proficient learners to elicit more controlled and structured responses. 〈B〉 is a more divergent and cognitively demanding activity. 〈B〉 needs to produce students' own ideas to solve the task in a context in a meaning-oriented activity. (55 words)

기출문제답안 ④

22 ⟨A⟩ represents two kinds of drills. Read the following and answer the direction.

2006년 전국 18번

⟨A⟩

(1)
- T: What did you do this weekend?
- S: I went fishing.
- T: That sounds fun. Did you go fishing too, Mina?
- S: No.
- T: What did you do then?
- S: I went swimming with my sister.

(2)
- T: I ate an apple. What did I eat?
- S: You ate an apple.
- T: Alright. I bought a book. What did I buy?
- S: You bought a book.
- T: Now, I wrote a letter. What did I write?
- S: You wrote a letter.

Note: T = teacher, S = student

⟨List⟩

a. It requires conveying meaning in the real world.
b. It aims at recognizing and memorizing the structural pattern.
c. It provides no link between form and meaning.
d. It lets the students give an open response.

Identify the type of drill and the TWO features from the ⟨list⟩.

Type of drill	Features
(1) _____ drill	___, ___
(2) _____ drill	___, ___

모범답안

Type of drill	Features
(1) communicative drill	a, d
(2) mechanical drill	b, c

23 Read the passage and follow the directions. Choose all the numbers among ①~④ in ⟨B⟩ for 'absence' in ⟨A⟩.

2006년 전국 5번

⟨A⟩

An organizational pattern recurrent in conversation is that of two adjacent utterances, which are produced by different speakers, and are related to each other in such a way that they form a pair type. They are called an adjacency pair. Question-answer, greeting-greeting, and offer-acceptance/ refusal are some examples of adjacency pairs. In adjacency pairs, utterances are related so that a particular *first pair part* sets up the expectation of a particular *second pair part*. For example, a question expects a reply and they form a pair type; an offer expects an accept or a decline, and each of the latter forms a pair type with the former. So strong is this expectation that if the second pair part does not occur, its 'absence' will be noticed by participants.

⟨B⟩

(1) Woman: Hi, Annie.
　　Mother: Annie, ① <u>didn't you hear someone say hello to you</u>?
　　Woman: Oh, that's okay, she smiled hello.
　　Mother: You know you're supposed to greet someone, don't you, Annie?
　　Annie: (hangs head) Hello.

(2) Jack: Well, I really must go now.
　　Amy: Where are you going?
　　Jack: Oh, I have to check out a book from the library.
　　Amy: ② <u>That's nice</u>. I'll come with you.
　　Jack: (looks a bit uncomfortable) ③ <u>Oh, er… well, actually, I have to go to the post office, first</u>.

(3) Wife: My mother wants us to visit her this weekend.
　　Husband: (reading the newspaper) England is going to the World Cup!
　　Wife: ④ <u>Did you hear me</u>?
　　Husband: Sorry, dear. What was that?
　　Wife: You never listen to me!

모범답안　①, ④

24 Read the conversation in ⟨A⟩ and the two writing drafts in ⟨B⟩, and follow the directions. 【4 points】

2023년 B7번

─────── ⟨A⟩ ───────

(Mr. Min, a middle school English teacher, is talking with his student, Jinhee, about her writing.)

T: Jinhee, I think you put a lot of effort into this first draft.

S: Yeah. But I think I made many mistakes.

T: Don't worry. I'll give you some comments on the categories you need to improve so that you can revise your draft. Can you do that?

S: Yes.

T: Great. Let's begin with content. I like your story, but it'll be better if you add more details here. Do you remember that we discussed how to use supporting details last week?

S: Yes, I do.

T: Good. I also saw that you had problems with organization.

S: You're right. Many events are popping up in my mind, but I can't put them logically.

T: One way to solve the problem is to use linking words such as *and, so, but, however, then, thus*, and so on, in order to show a logical sequence of events.

S: I see.

T: Two more categories are vocabulary and grammar. These two expressions here need to be changed. Look up the appropriate expressions in a dictionary. In addition, *swimed* here and *very not much* here are not correct. Think about how you can correct them.

S: Okay.

T: If you have any questions, just let me know. I'm looking forward to reading your second draft.

S: Thank you.

Note: T = teacher, S = student

─────── ⟨B⟩ ───────

⟨First draft⟩

I went to a game park with my family last weekend. When we arrived, we ate delicious snacks. I swimed in the pool. My father did not swim. My mother did it very not much. We went on the rides. It was very funny and smily. We were very tired. We took a taxi to come home.

⟨Second draft⟩

> I went to a game park with my family last weekend. When we arrived, we ate delicious snacks. Both my brother and I love sweets. My brother got three cups of ice cream and I got strawberry cake. I swimed in the pool, but my father did not swim. My mother did it very not much. Then, we went on the rides. It was very funny and smily. We were very tired, so we took a taxi to come home.

Identify the TWO categories Jinhee revised in the second draft based on Mr. Min's comments in ⟨A⟩. Then, explain how she revised the categories, respectively, with evidence from ⟨B⟩.

문제분석	구분	교과 교육
난이도 ★☆☆	평가목표	학습자의 writing draft에 대하여 교사의 조언으로 개선된 사항 두가지를 구체적으로 서술하는가?
	채점기준	1점: (content) 1점: 맛있는 스낵에 대하여 상세내용을 더한다. 1점: (organization) 1점: 사건의 논리적 구성을 위해 연결어를 사용한다.
모범답안		Content and organization were two categories. Jinhee added more details of the story to support the fact that her family ate delicious snacks such as her brother got three cups of ice cream and she got strawberry cake. She used linking words for a logical sequence of events such as 'but', 'then', and 'so'. (54 words)

25. Read this high school student's writing below and follow the directions.

2010년 논술 1번

My Favorite Season

Summer is my favorite season. The temperature is good for me. I like the summer clothing and the outdoor activities. I am never bored during **a** summer. Sometimes I don't like the hot wether because it **make** me uncomfortable. I can go outside anytime without **puting** on much clothing. A light shirt and shorts with sandals for my feet are always enough, while jeans and a light jacket is usually enough for cool evenings. On special events I can dress **me** up without making everything wrinkled by wearing a heavy coat. Actually, I **have bought** a heavy coat on sale from the department store yesterday. What I like most about this season are participating **at** outdoor activities. I really like swimming when the air is warm and the sun is shining. I also like a winter sports. Basketball is fun too. Our friends like to go to the court in the afternoon for an exciting game. Both basketball and the bike riding to the court are pleasant ways to start a summer morning. They made me excited. These are my reasons of liking summer. It is really my favorite season.

(1) Write one summative feedback to indicate the strong and weak points of the content and organization of this student's writing. And, there are a total of TWELVE errors in the student's writing that are categorized into six different error types. Find all the errors (including the six underlined ones) and draw a table on your answer sheet which lists errors found and correction symbols and their meanings. The first row has been completed for you.

error(s) found*	correction symbol and its meaning
puting on	"S" for incorrect spelling

(2) Write another paragraph which states TWO advantages and TWO disadvantages of using correction symbols when giving feedback.

문제분석	구분	교과 교육
난이도 ★★☆	평가목표	학습자의 글을 읽고 각 내용을 구체적으로 분석하는가?
	채점기준	〈Content & Organization〉 2점: (장점) 두개의 명확한 주제와 상세 예시로 구성되어 있다. 2점: (단점) 어떤 문장들은 coherence를 따르지 않아 연관성이 없다. 〈Correction Symbols〉 2점: (장점) 학습자 스스로 오류수정을 할 수 있다. 2점: (단점) 내용은 무시하고 문법에만 집중할 수 있다.

모범답안

(1) This writing is well organized with two clear major ideas supported by detailed examples. In the topic sentence, summer clothing and outdoor activities are suggested as the reason the student likes the summer. Some supporting ideas are provided with examples to help comprehension. However, some sentences do not follow coherence, being irrelevant to the main idea. (52 words)

error(s) found	correction symbol and its meaning
puting on/ wether	"S" for incorrect spelling
a winter/ a summer	"AR" for incorrect article usage
are participating/ is usually	"NA" for incorrect number agreement
Our friends/ me up	"PN" for incorrect pronoun forms
made me/ have bought a	"T" for incorrect tense expression
of liking/ at outdoor	"P" for incorrect preposition

(2) As for advantages, students can self-correct their errors to become autonomous learners. They can notice the language problem according to their language level. As for disadvantages, students should study what each symbol means, which can be a stressful and time-consuming activity. They can overlook the content and organization since they just focus on the grammar errors. (55 words)

26 Read the following and answer the question.

2008년 19번

초대   파일   화상   전화   도움

대화창

Teacher : Hi, students! This synchronous conferencing will allow you to post your opinions to the conference at any time, to be read and responded to at any time. Your opinions and responses will help each other develop ideas while writing.

Indigo3 : The conferencing system becomes a bit like a rough sketch book, with responses from other students about our own ideas.

Monkey : That's true. But I also realized I was improving my language while writing. Now I can write "It seems to me that everyone studies English well at middle schools," instead of writing "Everyone studies English well at middle schools."

Rose99 : With this sentence you can start another paragraph because you see ... this is something else you are going to talk about.

Indigo3 : OK. Let me check.

Identify in which writing approach the dialogue is used. Explain the purposes of this dialogue during the process of writing in terms of the teaching focus and each student's roles with evidence.

Which of the following does NOT describe the written dialogue above?

① This conferencing allows students to scaffold their peers.
② Some students have a chance to review their own writing.
③ This conferencing provides summative feedback on students' writing.
④ One student gives feedback on coherence through interaction.
⑤ The teacher encourages students to brainstorm their ideas.

문제분석	구분	교과 교육
난이도 ★★☆	평가목표	쓰기의 feedback의 유형으로서 개인별 conferencing의 특징을 이해한다.
	채점기준	1점: conferencing은 과정중심쓰기에서 나타난다. 1.5점: 학생들의 생각과 글의 구성에 대해 피드백을 제공한다. 1.5점: 언어사용에 대한 피드백으로 언어사용이 개선된다.
모범답안		The dialogue is used in process-oriented writing. The dialogue provides formative feedback on the students' ideas and organization of 'another paragraph...' in the process of writing. The dialogue helps to scaffold their peers through commenting on language uses,'it seems to me ....' Students have a chance to revise and improve their language for their own writing. (56 words)

기출문제답안 ③

27 Read the teacher's reflection and follow the directions. 【4 points】

Teacher's Reflection

This semester I have been using a checklist in my English writing class to help my students revise their drafts by themselves. The checklist I provide for my students covers the following areas: content, organization, grammar, vocabulary, and mechanics. Below is a part of the checklist.

Areas	Indicators	Yes	No
(1) _____	I use correct subject and verb agreement.		
	I use verb tense correctly.		
(2) _____	I put a period at the end of every sentence.		
	I use capital letters correctly.		
	I spell the words correctly.		

At first, the checklist didn't seem feasible because there was little improvement, especially in organization in writing. To find the reason, I held group conferences with the students and discovered that the indicators for organization were too complicated for them to understand. Some of them included more than one aspect to check simultaneously. So, I divided those indicators into two or three separate sentences so that one indicator assesses only one aspect. Since the revision of the indicators, the students' organization has gotten much better.

However, some students still had problems using the checklist appropriately. So, I ran a couple of training sessions to teach the students what the indicators meant and how they should be utilized. First, we read the indicators and I asked if they made sense. Then, I had them practice checking particular errors with a sample paragraph I had prepared. Since the training sessions, the students have been making significantly fewer errors. Overall, the use of the checklist has worked well in the revision process.

Fill in the blanks (1) and (2) with the ONE most appropriate word from the teacher's reflection, respectively. Then, explain how the teacher solved the problems encountered while using the checklist. Do NOT copy more than FIVE consecutive words from the passage.

문제분석	구분	교과 교육
난이도 ★★☆	평가목표	쓰기지도에서 효과적이고 구체적인 평가방법에 대하여 서술하는가?
	채점기준	1점: (1) grammar 1점: (2) mechanics 1점: 체크리스트에서는 한 영역에 대해서만 평가해야 한다. 1점: 훈련을 통해 학생들이 오류를 줄일 수 있다.

모범답안 (1) grammar, (2) mechanics, Through group conferences, the checklist clearly showed that one indicator assessed one aspect of the organization. Training sessions helped students understand the meaning of each indicator. Students practice c particular errors using a sample paragraph. (42 words)

28 Read the passage in ⟨A⟩ and the activities in ⟨B⟩, and follow the directions. 【4 points】

⟨A⟩

One of the reasons we can communicate successfully, especially in writing, is because we have some understanding of genre, socially recognized ways of using language for particular purposes. Genre represents the norms of different kinds of writing shared among people within a particular community. The emphasis on the social dimension of genre is a major characteristic of genre-based approaches to teaching writing.

A genre-based writing instruction involves students in an in-depth analysis of texts in the genre in which they are going to be writing. In particular, students are asked to analyze three essential features of the genre using example texts: 1) the *context*, which includes the situation and audience, 2) the *content*, which indicates the information and message conveyed, and 3) the *construction*, that is, how the texts of the genre are typically constructed in terms of the layout and language. When students are done with this task, they are in a position to create their own writing within the genre.

⟨B⟩

Activity 1

(*After conducting a reading lesson about volunteering, a middle school English teacher prepares a poster-making activity for recruiting volunteers. He plans to have his students analyze the features of the poster genre before they make their own posters.*)

■ Ask the students to share their volunteering experiences.
■ Have the students examine the poster and answer the questions in the worksheet.

Worksheet

1. Why are some words capitalized?
2. Does the poster use full sentences? If not, why?

Activity 2

(*Believing writing reviews is an important skill that her students should be equipped with, a high school English teacher prepares a genre-analyzing kit with which the students figure out the characteristics of the book review genre.*)

■ Tell the students they are going to read a book review.
■ Have the students use the genre-analyzing kit while reading the book review.

Book Review

"I Really Want the Cup Cake"
Written by Philip Kent
Illustrated by Terra Wang
Ages 3–5 | 20 Pages
Publisher: Green Books | ISBN: 978-1-338-95941-2
What to expect: Rhyme, Dessert, Self Control
(or lack thereof)

Honestly, who of us hasn't wanted to dive in, just a teeny, tiny bit, to that delicious-looking cup cake left on the table? Just a bite couldn't hurt, could it? In this hilarious story about a little boy and his dog, that's exactly what they are trying *not* to do.

Reviewers' Genre-Analyzing Kit

1. Who do you think the review is aimed at?
2. When would people write this kind of text?

Based on ⟨A⟩, identify ONE essential feature of the target genre that each activity in ⟨B⟩ focuses on, respectively. Then, explain your answers with evidence from ⟨B⟩.

문제분석	구분	교과 교육
난이도 ★★☆	평가목표	장르중심 쓰기에서 핵심사항을 선택하여 구체적으로 서술하는가?
	채점기준	1점: 활동 1 (Construction) 1점: 글이 어떻게 구성되었는지를 분석한다. 1점: 활동 2 (Content) 1점: kit를 통해 독자를 분석하고 상황을 이해한다.

모범답안 Construction is for Activity 1. The poster-making activity helps students analyze how the poster was constructed through finding out the capitalization and sentence features. Context is for Activity 2, A genre-analyzing kit gets students to analyze the readers and understand the situation of reading the review. (46 words)

29 Read the text and follow the directions.

2010년 25번

The table below lists the self-assessment results of 19 students in a writing class. The teacher has decided to give them a follow-up lesson on writing skills about which more than half of them show dissatisfaction.

(unit : number of the respondents)

Self-assessment Items	SD	D	A	SA
1. I'm getting better at generating interesting and original ideas.	8	7	4	0
2. I'm gaining skill at organizing my ideas and putting them together logically.	4	10	3	2
3. My final drafts have fewer grammatical errors than they did before this course.	4	2	7	6
4. My use of vocabulary has expanded in my writing over the course of this semester.	0	4	9	6
5. My papers now contain fewer errors in spelling and punctuation than they did previously.	7	8	2	2

SD : strongly disagree, D : disagree, A : agree, SA : strongly agree

Identify the THREE items which shows the students' dissatisfaction and suggest the activities for follow-up lessons with supporting evidences.

Choose all the activities the teacher will use in the follow-up lesson from the list.
ⓐ peer-reviewing centering on mechanics
ⓑ filling in the blanks with appropriate words to describe a picture
ⓒ re-sequencing the sentences of a fractured paragraph back into their original order
ⓓ brainstorming and sharing ideas in a small group
ⓔ transformation activity using grammatical forms

문제분석

구분	교과 교육
평가목표	self assessment를 통해 얻은 부족한 skill을 위한 보충활동을 서술하는가?
채점기준	(1) brainstorming (2) re-sequencing the sentences (5) peer-reviewing on mechanics

모범답안 For item 1, brainstorming and sharing ideas in a small group is recommended to generate ideas. For item 2, re-sequencing the sentences of a fractured paragraph would develop organization and coherence. For item 5, peer-reviewing on mechanics can be used as students have difficulty writing spelling and punctuation. (48 words)

기출문제답안 ⓐ, ⓒ, ⓓ

30. Read the following and put the activity in order matched with process writing.

2008년 서울 16번

(1)

1. Have students work with a partner, and get each to read what the other has drafted so far. They should make notes of things in their partner's draft.
2. They now return their papers to each other and discuss the summary and the points that they have noted, beginning with the good points and going on to the things that need clarifying or improving. In the process, they should try to jointly improve what they have written.

(2)

1. Talk about various elements which might be included in an account of a personal experience. Note down the results of your discussion in a mind map.
2. Select a personal experience that you would like to write about. Use your mind map to decide which elements will be the most interesting or significant for the particular experience you plan to describe.

(3)

Help students produce ideas which can eventually be incorporated into composition by using the following mnemonic (A DAD CAN).

A Associate the theme with something else.
D Define it.
A Apply the idea.
D Describe it.
C Compare it with something else.
A Argue for or against the subject.
N Narrate the development or history of it.

모범답안   (2) – (3) – (1)

31 Read the following and answer the question.

2013년 23번

A high school English teacher conducted a survey with 50 high school English teachers in her school district as part of action research. The teachers were asked to indicate how well the statements in the survey described their teaching practice. Below are the results.

How Do You Teach English Writing?

Statements	No. of respondents per category*			
	1	2	3	4
1. I emphasize students' final writing products.	30	10	8	2
2. I involve students in the process of planning, drafting, revising, and editing.	1	4	35	10
3. I focus mostly on grammar and mechanics when giving feedback.	22	14	9	5
4. I focus mostly on content and organization when giving feedback.	5	8	25	12
5. I involve students in group writing tasks more than individual writing tasks.	34	3	6	7
6. I have students keep a journal and write as often as possible in English at home.	32	5	7	6
7. I meet with individual students to help with work in progress.	5	6	18	21

*1=not at all; 2=not really; 3=well; 4=very well

Complete the survey results with ONE appropriate word for each blank.

⟨Result⟩

More teachers tend to use a process-based approach rather than a product-based one. The teachers as a whole focus on content and organization more than language ①_____ when giving feedback. Individual writing tasks are widely utilized in the classroom. Small number of teachers foster writing habits through home assignments. More than half of the teachers use ②_____ by giving one-to-one feedback on their content and organization to support the revision process.

Which of the following is a correct statement according to the survey results above?

① More teachers tend to use a product-based approach rather than a process-based one.
② The teachers as a whole focus on accuracy more than content and organization when giving feedback.
③ Collaborative writing tasks are widely utilized in the classroom.
④ The majority of the teachers foster writing habits through home assignments.
⑤ More than half of the teachers use conferencing to support the revision process.

문제분석	구분	교과 교육
난이도 ★★☆	평가목표	교사의 쓰기지도에서의 특성을 이해하는가?
	채점기준	1점: 피드백을 줄 때 언어의 정확성보다는 내용이나 전체구성에 초점을 둔다. 1점: 교사가 내용에 초점을 두는 피드백인 conferencing을 이용한다.

모범답안	(1) accuracy	(2) conferencing

기출문제답안 ⑤

32. Read the passage in ⟨A⟩ and part of a lesson procedure in ⟨B⟩, and follow the directions. 【4 points】

2019년 A14번

⟨A⟩

(Below are suggestions from a conference for teaching L2 writing.)

To help students to write effectively…

(a) Start with pre-writing activities with little emphasis on ungrammaticalities and incorrect spelling.
(b) Have drafting and revising stages in a recursive way.
(c) Provide meaning-focused feedback.
(d) Offer students opportunities to think about their own writing.

⟨B⟩

(*The following is part of Ms. Song's lesson procedure for teaching how to write an argumentative essay.*)

Steps:
1. T provides background information about artificial intelligence and Ss watch videos related to the topic.
2. Ss discuss the topic in groups and brainstorm.
3. Ss sketch their ideas and write the first drafts, focusing on content.
4. T reviews Ss' drafts and provides corrective feedback that reformulates ill-formed expressions.
5. Ss revise their drafts once, based on the feedback, and then hand in their final drafts to T.
6. T asks Ss to write reflective journals about their writing.

Note: T= teacher, Ss=students

Identify TWO suggestions from ⟨A⟩ that Ms. Song does NOT implement in ⟨B⟩. Then, support your answers with evidence from ⟨B⟩.

문제분석	구분	교과 교육
난이도 ★☆☆	평가목표	process-writing지도에서 따르지 않는 원리에 대하여 구체적으로 서술하는가?
	채점기준	1점: (b) 1점: 초고를 한번 쓰고 제출하는 직선형방법을 사용한다. 1점: (c) 1점: 의미보다는 형태중심의 피드백을 제공한다.

모범답안 Ms. Song does not follow the two suggestions, (b) and (c). Students write and revise their draft once and then move on to final draft in a linear way rather than recursive way in a process-based writing. The teacher provides form-focused feedback with language correction of providing correct form rather than meaning-focused feedback. (52 words)

33 Read the passage and complete it with ONE same word.

2004년 전국 17번

Teacher response to student writing needs to cover all facets of students' texts, including issues of content, organization, style, grammar, and mechanics. However, for a variety of reasons, it is neither necessary nor desirable for a teacher to respond to every problem on every draft of a student essay. On early drafts, students most likely will be generating, focusing, and organizing their _____. A teacher's responses should help them do this by giving them feedback that will lead them to develop their _____ fully and present them effectively. Responses should assist the writer in revising the content of his paper. On later drafts, student writers must be encouraged to proofread, edit, and correct their papers.

모범답안 ideas

34. Read the following and answer the question.

Teaching Procedure

- The teacher sets up guidelines on how to write essays.
- The teacher explains to the students how to use multimedia during the writing process.
- The teacher collects the first drafts of the students' essays via e-mail.
- The teacher opens up an online blog for the class to post the first drafts of their essays.
- Each student reads one of his/her peers' essays and posts three well-thought-out feedback statements on the blog.
- The teacher asks the students to read the feedback received from their peers and to revise their first drafts. When they have questions about the feedback, they should e-mail them to their feedback providers.
- The teacher gives his/her own feedback to each student via e-mail.
- The teacher asks the students to post their revised essays on the blog.

Identify the type of writing approach and explain the features of communication type when giving students feedback.

Which of the following is NOT correct according to the passage?

① This procedure enhances students' participation in giving feedback on their peers' essays.
② Students can give and receive feedback through asynchronous communication.
③ This procedure is based on a process-oriented approach to writing.
④ Students compose messages in unplanned ways through real-time communication.
⑤ This procedure includes both one-to-one and one-to-many communication.

문제분석	구분	교과 교육
난이도 ★★☆	평가목표	이메일을 통한 쓰기활동의 특성을 구체적으로 서술하는가?
	채점기준	1점: process-oriented approach이다. 1점: 학생들이 서로 피드백을 제공한다. 1점: 비실시간 의사소통으로 생각이 정리된 피드백을 제공한다. 1점: 일대일과 일대 다수의 의사소통이 포함된다.

모범답안 This procedure is based on a process-oriented approach to writing. This procedure enhances students' participation to give peer-feedback on their peers' essays. Students can give and receive well-thought-out feedback through asynchronous communication. This procedure includes both one-to-one and one-to-many communication. (41 words)

 ④

35 Read the passage and answer the question.

2012년 25번

This is a procedure for teaching writing used by a middle school English teacher.

1) The teacher shows pictures of pets to students and asks what kinds of pets they like.
2) The teacher gives each of students a short story of a dog and a set of four sequential pictures showing its storyline, telling them that they are going to read and write the story as accurately as possible. The story contains a number of regular past tense verbs.
3) Students read the story silently for 3 minutes and return the story to the teacher but keep the pictures.
4) After putting some key words from the story on the board, the teacher reads the whole story aloud.
5) With the aid of the pictures and key words, students write the story as closely as they can remember.
6) The teacher collects students' writings and later corrects them by crossing out incorrect regular past tense forms, providing corresponding correct forms above them.
7) In the next class, students receive their writings and look over their errors and the teacher's correction.

Identify the approach of teaching writing in the lesson. Explain the approach with the features of the procedure with supporting evidence.

Choose all and only the correct statements about the activity.

ⓐ The procedure reflects the process-oriented approach to writing instruction rather than the product-oriented approach.
ⓑ The procedure is designed in a way to lessen students' cognitive processing load placed on retelling the story in writing.
ⓒ The teacher's correction is focused on grammatical accuracy of students' writings.
ⓓ Students choose the topic for their writing taking their interests into consideration.

문제분석	구분	교과 교육
난이도 ★★★	평가목표	쓰기 작품을 읽고 분석하는 product-oriented writing의 한 유형을 구체적으로 서술하는가?
	채점기준	1점: product-oriented approach이다. 1점: 교사가 주제를 선택하여 도델글을 제시한다. 1점: 학생들은 '재진술'활동을 통해 인지적 어려움을 낮춘다. 1점: 교사의 오류수정은 문법적 정확성에 초점을 둔다.

모범답안 The procedure reflects the product-oriented approach to writing. Teacher chooses the topic, pets, for the writing lesson to provide the model writing. The writing is designed to lessen students' cognitive processing load through retelling the story. The teacher's correction is focused on grammatical accuracy of their writing. (47 words)

기출문제답안 ⓑ, ⓒ

36 Read part of an online forum discussion between two Korean high school English teachers and follow the directions.

Ms. Lee: I always tell students to examine the model composition closely and copy it once word for word. Just before they start their own compositions, they're told they won't have a chance to revise their work. I grade students' work using the model composition as a yardstick. After grading, I always correct linguistic errors and return papers to the students. I believe that my students will learn from these corrections and use more accurate language in future compositions. Interestingly, though, my students still repeat the same errors. Am I taking the right approach?

Mr. Kim: Well, there're two approaches to teaching writing: a process-oriented approach and a product-oriented approach. I'd recommend that you try the alternative approach to the one you're currently using.

(1) Identify the approach Ms. Lee is using and describe the characteristics of the approach Mr. Kim recommends.
(2) Drawing on the natural order hypothesis, explain why Ms. Lee's error correction may not be working.
(3) Suggest a writing task for Ms. Lee which incorporates the principles of social constructivism and explain its rationale.

문제분석	구분	교과 교육
난이도 ★★★	평가목표	쓰기지도상의 방법과 학습이론을 쓰기지도방법에 적용하여 서술하는가?
	채점기준	(1) 쓰기 교수법 1점: product-oriented쓰기이다. 1점: 모델글을 통해 학생들은 정확하게 쓰는데 초점을 둔다. 1점: 김교사는 process-oriented를 추천한다. 1점: 학생들이 자신의 생각을 계획하고, 여러번 쓰고, 수정할 수 있다. (2) Natural order hypothesis 2점: 자연순서가설에 따르면 언어형태는 일정한 순서로 습득된다. 1점: 준비가 되지 않은 언어는 학습되기 어렵다. 1점: 학습자의 언어수준을 고려해야 한다. (3) Social Constructivist 1점: Collaborative writing과제를 제시한다. 1점: 글쓰기를 위하여 한 학생이 한 문장을 쓰고 다른 학생이 연결한다. 1점: 서로 도와 이야기를 구성한다. 1점: 비슷한 발달영역안에서 서로 돕는다.

모범답안

(1) Ms. Lee used product-oriented writing. This writing approach encourages students to imitate or write the correct language from the model composition as closely as they can. Mr. Kim recommends a process-oriented approach. Students are able to improve language skills by writing with their own ideas through the stages of planning, drafting and revising. (54 words)

(2) According to the natural order hypothesis, a language form and structure will be acquired in a certain order. Learners cannot be successfully taught until they are developmentally ready to acquire the form. Therefore, Ms. Lee has to consider the learners' proficiency levels and needs to match her teaching procedure. (50 words)

(3) Collaborative writing task can be effective to bring students together to write in class. A group of students are given a sentence to start the story. They, then, interact to co-construct a story. During the process, they scaffold with each other within their zone of proximal development while teacher provides feedback or answers questions. (54 words)

37. Read part of a lesson plan and follow the directions. 【4 points】

2016년 전공B3번 서술형

Lesson Procedure

Stage 1
- T shows video clips on environmental campaigns.
- T encourages Ss to brainstorm.
- T asks Ss to discuss their previous experiences in pairs.

<Purposes>
- ✓ To arouse Ss' interests and motivation
- ✓ To activate Ss' _____

Stage 2
- T shows new words and structures, and then explains how to use them within a sentence.

New Words	Grammatical Structures
transportation, recycle, mayor,	to leave ~, leaving ~, to protect ~, protecting ~,

- Please circle the right form in the sentences.
  1. We require you (to leave/leaving) your cars.
  2. ...

- T has Ss read an article related to environmental problems with the following questions in mind:
  - What are the problems?
  - What are the causes of the problems?
  - How can you solve the problems?

Stage 2
- T asks Ss to write down key words related to the topic.

<Trash Problems in Our City>
- Problems: dirty roads, _____, _____
- Causes: no trash cans, _____, _____
- Solutions: recycling bins, _____, _____

- T instructs Ss to combine the key words into a phrase or a sentence.
- T demonstrates how to connect sentences by using the markers in the box and asks Ss to write their sentences coherently.

  Markers: Now, Firstly, Secondly, So, Thus, As a result, Therefore, . . .

Stage 3
- T has Ss write a suggestion letter to their mayor based on what Ss wrote.

  Dear Mayor,
  _____
  _____

- T distributes rubrics for peer-evaluation to Ss.
- T asks Ss to exchange their drafts.

Note: T = teacher, S = student

Fill in the blank in the <Purposes> box in Stage 1 with ONE word. Then identify ONE way the teacher directly prepares students to write a well-organized suggestion letter in Stage 2, and explain it with evidence. Do NOT copy more than FIVE consecutive words from the passage.

문제분석	구분	교과 교육
난이도 ★★★	평가목표	쓰기활동의 종류인 guided writing 활동을 위한 특징을 구체적으로 서술하는가?
	채점기준	1점: (schema)를 활성화한다. 1점: guided 쓰기지도를 실시한다. 1점: 편지쓰기에 필요한 어휘, 구조, 배경지식을 제공한다. 1점: 구, 문장을 순차적으로 연습할 수 있다.

모범답안 schema, The teacher provides a guided writing to give students related material for the composition. First, teacher provides the words and structures and background information that would be needed to write the letter. The key words, phrases and sentences can be practiced in order through exercises. (45 words)

38 Read the lesson procedure and complete the objectives by filling in each blank with TWO words. 【2 points】

2014년 전공A9번

Students: 2nd year middle school students
Approximate time: 45 minutes
Lesson objectives:
Students will be able:
- to describe a daily routine using correct verb forms and ①_____ from a sample paragraph
- to revise writing through ②_____ on first drafts

Lesson Procedure
1. The teacher asks students what they do when they get home every day.
2. Students take turns asking and answering questions about their daily routine in pairs. Students take notes on each other's answers.
3. The teacher provides a sample paragraph, and students choose the correct expressions.

> (As soon as/ Since) Taebin finishes school, he goes to taekwondo. When he arrives, he puts on his workout clothes, and (first/ then) he practices. (After/ Before) he finishes, he rides his bike home. (As soon as/ After that), he takes a shower. (After/ Next), he eats his dinner. (Before/ When) he finishes dinner, he does his homework. (Before/ While) he goes to bed, he brushes his teeth.

4. Students use their notes to write a short paragraph about their partner's daily routine.
5. Students exchange writings and underline their partner's mistakes using the checklist.
   - Are the present forms of verbs used correctly?
   - Are the events described in time order?
   - Is time order indicated using the expressions focused upon in the sample paragraph?
   - Is punctuation used correctly?
6. Students rewrite their paragraph based on Step 5.

모범답안   ① time expressions
           ② peer-feedback/ editing

39 The followings are extracts from a composition written by a learner of English and tips for writings.

2003년 서울 6번

⟨A learner's Work⟩

 My landlady is called Mrs. Jones. My landlady lives on a ground floor of house. It is a very old house. Sometimes it rains. Water comes through a roof. My room is not at top of a house. My room is dry.

⟨Tips for Writing⟩

___①___ refers to the explicit linguistic signalling of relationships within a text.

- Use ___②___ to combine more than two sentences:
- Use ___③___ to avoid a lot of unnecessary repetition:
- Use ___④___ to mark new information or something already stated in the text:

⟨Word list⟩

| modals | articles | pronouns | cohesion | conjunctions |
| coherence | logics | implicitly | rationale | |

모범답안 ① cohesion ② conjunctions ③ pronouns ④ articles

40 This is an advanced student's writing. Read the following and answer the question.

2003년 전국 13번

Taste and smell are affected by aging, but their changes are less understood and appreciated. People who are in contact with the elderly will tell you they have TWO major complaints—food and their children. The complaint about food is easily explained when one considers how the taste buds work. Distributed over the tongue, they last no longer than a few days each and then are replaced. In keeping with the general slowing-down process, they are renewed more slowly than they are used up. This means that the total number of effective taste buds declines, and therefore, food tastes less savory. Extensive dentures that cover a large portion of the oral cavity diminish the perception of taste even further. In addition, there is a close interrelationship between smell and taste. Anyone who has ever had a cold can testify to the fact that while the cold lasts, not only is the sense of smell reduced, but food loses its taste as well. There is a similar deterioration in the sense of smell as a result of the process of aging.

Identify TWO types of cohesive devices that are used in the passage.

모범답안   reference, conjunction

41. Read the following and answer the question.

[The teacher speaks in front of the class in the classroom.]

T: OK, today we've learned how to construct a topic sentence. You did a good job. Here's your homework. First, write a paragraph about your weekend plans and post it on our class blog. Second, you should respond to at least two persons' writings.

When you give comments, please focus on content as well as on grammar. If you need to, you can visit some grammar websites that are linked to the class blog. I have already posted the evaluation criteria on the blog. If you have any questions, log into the chat room from 8 to 9 pm on Thursday, and I'll answer them. See you then.

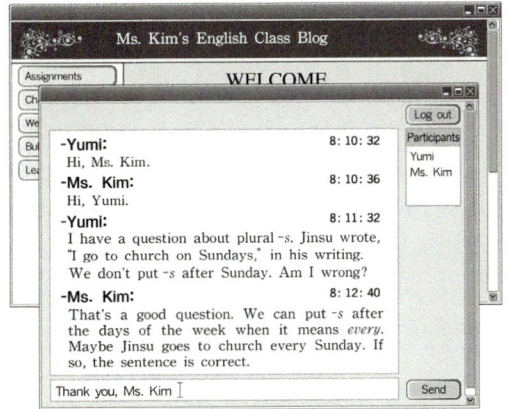

Which of the following is NOT a correct statement about the assignment above?

① It can be done with the help of online resources.
② It allows students to utilize synchronous communication.
③ It compels students to exchange feedback with each other.
④ It creates a computer-mediated communication environment.
⑤ It requires students to post their scoring rubric on the blog.

42. Read the following and fill in each blank with the ONE most appropriate word about the lesson procedure.

2013년 28번

Below is an excerpt of an English lesson procedure developed by a high school teacher.

Step 1. Ask questions relating to the topic.
- Do you talk to your parents a lot? Why or why not?
- Who do you talk to when you have a problem?

Step 2. Provide a reading text and have Ss read it individually.

> Dear Dr. Teen,
> Recently, our family moved to a new city. My husband and I knew this would not be easy for our teenage daughter, but we thought she would adjust in time. It has now been two months, and we are really starting to worry about her. She used to be very outgoing and talkative. But, now she spends a lot of time in her room and will not talk to us. She seems uninterested in school, and her grades are slipping. Why won't she communicate with us? What can we do? Please help!
>
> Worried Mother

Step 3. Ask comprehension-checking questions.
Step 4. In groups of four, have Ss discuss and come up with the best advice for the worried mother.
Step 5. Have each group write a letter to the worried mother, using the advice they chose. Each group exchanges their letter with another group and offers comments.
Step 6. Have each group revise their own letter, taking into account the feedback from another group.
Step 7. Explain the errors that Ss made frequently during discussion. Have them engage in pattern practice.

Note: Ss = students

The lesson procedure uses the mother's letter as ①_____ to make learner's ②_____, since it encourages students to understand the letter before producing problem solution. It helps students in developing oral skills by moving from free to controlled activities.

Which of the following is NOT a correct statement about the lesson?

① It uses the mother's letter as input to encourage learner output.
② It engages students in a problem-solving activity to offer advice on a given problem.
③ It encourages students to work cooperatively through group work and feedback.
④ It utilizes different types of meaning-focused activities such as discussion.
⑤ It assists students in developing oral skills by moving from controlled to free activities.

문제분석	구분	교과 교육
난이도 ★☆☆	평가목표	Process-writing의 진행 단계와 문제 해결을 위한 협력과업에 대해 이해하는가?
	채점기준	1점: 활동의 시작이 편지를 이해해야 하는 input에서 시작된다. 1점: 학생들의 output은 문제해결을 만들어 내는 것으로 연결된다.
모범답안	① input ② output	

43 Read the following and answer the question.

The following excerpts are two students' writing samples with feedback from their teachers:

Sample [1]

> Do you remember your middle school's life? Well, compared to high schools, middle schools end up more earlier. Also, middle school students don't worry about their future as much as high schoolers. However, there is a big similarity between middle school and high school, which is both students have to study a lot, and the fact that most of them go to academy.

Teacher comments:
Nice work! You started with an attractive question, which is a good organizational skill for the introduction of an essay. When you rewrite, please try to add your own story about your school life to make the essay more appealing.

Sample [2]

> All Koreans **enters** school, and **learns** many things. They **entered** elementary
>   Agr   Agr   Tns
> school, Middle school, High school. Total, there **is** twelve **grade**. In elementary
>   Agr   Agr
> school, Koreans **learned** six **year**. In middle school, they **learned** three **year**
>   Tns   Agr   Tns   Agr
> and same in high school.

Agr = Agreement; *Tns* = Verb tense

Compare and contrast the TWO characteristics of teacher's feedback in Sample [1] and [2] through the stages of process writing.

Choose all and only the correct statements about the teacher's feedback.

ⓐ In Sample [1], the teacher provides feedback on organization and content.
ⓑ In Sample [2], the teacher gives feedback selectively focusing on specific types of errors.
ⓒ In Sample [2], the teacher uses error codes as a means of corrective feedback.
ⓓ Both teachers provide reformulations of students' language to assist their revision process.

문제분석	구분	교과 교육
난이도 ★☆☆	평가목표	쓰기지도를 위한 feedback의 유형을 구체적으로 서술하는가?
	채점기준	2점: (1) 초고단계에서 내용과 구성에 대한 피드백을 한다. 2점: (2) 오류코드를 이용하여 문법오류에 대하여 간접적인 피드백을 한다.
모범답안		In Sample [1], teacher provides feedback on organization and content, focusing more on introductory part at the drafting stage. In Sample [2], teacher gives feedback focusing on specific types of grammatical errors. He uses error codes as a means of corrective feedback to indicate the incorrect language. (45 words)

기출문제답안 ⓐ, ⓑ, ⓒ

44 Read the text and follow the directions.

2010년 22번

Activity Procedure

(1) Ask students to listen to a five-minute lecture while jotting down the main points. Then, give students four minutes to summarize the lecture using their notes

(2) Ask students to listen to the lecture again while they write down as many additional main points of the lecture as possible. Then, give students three minutes to revise their summary using all of their notes.

(3) Ask students to listen to the lecture one last time while they write down as many other main points of the lecture as possible. Then, give students two minutes to make a final revision of their summary.

(4) Ask students to check their grammar before submitting their summary.

Identify TWO types of listening skills. Explain how the other language skills are utilized in the activity with evidence.

Choose all and only the correct statements about the activity.
ⓐ Opportunities for self-correction are provided.
ⓑ The activity helps improve students' note-taking skills.
ⓒ Intensive listening is required for the activity.
ⓓ The activity helps students develop both receptive and productive skills.
ⓔ The teacher's explicit feedback is provided in order to assist students' revision.

문제분석	구분	교과 교육
난이도 ★★☆	평가목표	Dictogloss 활동을 통해 학생들이 배우는 내용을 구체적으로 서술하는가?
	채점기준	1점: extensive와 intensive듣기활동을 한다. 1.5점: 듣기와 쓰기의 통합기술을 연습한다. 1.5점: 문법수정을 통해 언어를 발달시킨다.
모범답안		Extensive and intensive listening are used to write down main idea and additional points. The activity helps students develop both receptive skill of listening and productive skill of summarizing. Opportunities for self-correction to check grammar are provided to develop accurate language skills. (45 words)

기출문제답안 ⓐ, ⓑ, ⓒ, ⓓ

45 Choose one correct activity type for each writing.

2006년 전국 20번

(1) The teacher asked students to write a weekly diary by using blogs and gave individual feedback for their online entries over one semester.
   self-writing: _____

(2) The teacher wrote the sentence, "Once upon a time, there was a beautiful princess." and asked each student in an online chat group to add a sentence in turn until the story was completed.
   collaborative writing: _____

(3) The teacher played a short news clip from the website, "BBC English Online" three times successively and then asked students in a group to rewrite the news story in their own words.
   controlled writing: _____

―――――――― 〈Word list〉 ――――――――
imitative writing   dictogloss   chain writing   dialogue journal
academic writing   project writing   genre writing

모범답안 (1) dialogue journal
         (2) chain writing
         (3) dictogloss

46 Read ⟨A⟩ and ⟨B⟩ and answer the question.

2009년 14번

⟨A⟩

The following sample writing in ⟨B⟩ was done by Mira in a classroom writing session after a lecture on the narrative structure of 'orientation − complication − resolution'. She was provided with the lead sentence on the board: 'When I walked out of school, a dog limped up to me.'

⟨B⟩

Title: The Dog

It was crying
so I took it home.
As soon as my mother came home from work.
she gave it a name.
We named it 'Spot'.
I bandaged its leg.
I had great fun with 'Spot'.

Write the comments in order to improve Mira's writing in ⟨B⟩ based on ⟨A⟩ in FOUR ways with the concrete examples.

Which of the following is the LEAST appropriate feedback to the writing in <B>?

① To improve the coherence of your writing, I recommend that you explain the reason why you named the dog 'Spot'.
② You need an orientation that is similar to the lead sentence at the beginning.
③ You need to change the period to a comma after 'came home from work'.
④ Your resolution 'I bandaged its leg' is dislocated (unconnected resolution).
⑤ Your last sentence is a complication without leading to a resolution.

문제분석	구분	교과 교육
난이도 ★★★	평가목표	narrative structure 안에서 교사의 feedback 방법을 구체적으로 서술하는가?
	채점기준	1.5점: 시작문장이 필요하다. 1.5점: 강아지의 이름을 'spot'이라고 붙인 이유를 글의 논리성을 위해 설명한다. 1점: 문장이 끝나지 않은데에는 쉼표가 필요하다.

모범답안	Mira needs an orientation that is similar to the lead sentence at the beginning to make meaning clear. She should explain the reason why she named the dog 'Spot' to improve coherence of the story. She needs to change the period to a comma after '~ came home from work' as the sentence is not completed. (55 words)

기출문제답안 ⑤

47 Read the following passage and answer the question.

2003년 서울 12번

- Purpose: To provide students with an opportunity to share privately in writing their reaction, questions, and concerns about school experiences with the teacher without any threat of reprisal or evaluation.
- Intended Audience: Students of 9th grade and over in Korea.

⟨Journal entry by Miyoung⟩

Yesterday at about eight o'clock I was sitting in front of my table holding a fork and eating tasteless noodles which I usually really like to eat but I lost my taste yesterday because I didn't feel well. My head seemed to be broken. I had to cook by myself even though I was sick. The noodles were cold, but I was still sitting there and thinking about my mother. finally I threw out the noodles and went to bed.

⟨Teacher's response⟩

I was quite surprised when I heard that you were not well yesterday. I hope you are fine now. But at the same time, I'm glad you really communicate what you were feeling. When you eat cold noodles next time, you'd better be careful. Now you would learn that if you eat a wrong food, your head can be broken.

If you want to do another entry related to this one, you could have a dialogue with your "sick" self. What would your "healthy" self say to the "sick" self? Start the dialogue with your "sick" self speaking first.

Identify the teaching technique and explain it with the THREE pedagogical features of using this technique to teach writing.

모범답안 This activity is a dialogue journal. The principal objective is for the student to carry on a meaningful conversation with the teacher. Teachers can become familiar with students' learning progress and affective states. Teachers do not evaluate the students' language use but give feedback on meaning. (49 words)

48 ⟨A⟩ is the example for grammar instruction and ⟨B⟩ is the picture on the features of the activity. Fill in each blank.

2007년 전국 5번

⟨A⟩

(a) Write or say statements about John, modelled on the following example: *John drinks tea, but he doesn't drink coffee.*
   ① like : ice cream / cake
   ② speak : English / Italian
   ③ enjoy : playing football / playing chess

(b) The class is given a dilemma situation ('You have seen a good friend cheating in an important test') and asked to recommend a solution.

(c) Choose someone you know very well, and write down their name. Now compose true statements about them according to the following model:
   He/She likes ice cream; or He/She doesn't like ice cream.
   ① enjoy : playing tennis
   ② drink : wine
   ③ speak : Polish

(d) Practising conditional clauses, learners are given the cue *If I had a million dollars*, and are asked to suggest, in speech or writing, what they *would do*.

⟨B⟩

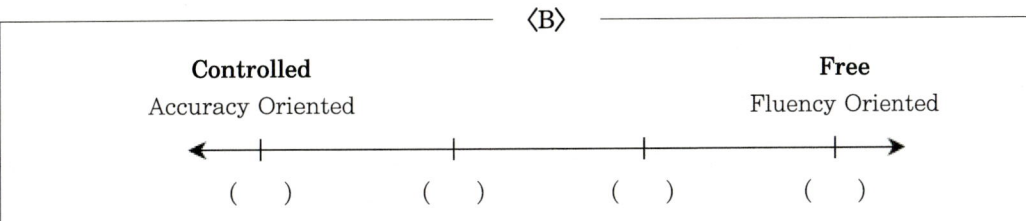

Controlled — Accuracy Oriented   Free — Fluency Oriented

( )   ( )   ( )   ( )

모범답안   (a) – (c) – (d) – (b)

CHAPTER 08 문법 지도

01
Read the teacher's beliefs in ⟨A⟩ and the part of the lesson plan in ⟨B⟩, and follow the directions. 【4 points】

2024년 B11번

⟨A⟩

I believe that lesson goals should be framed from the students' perspective, focusing on what they can achieve through the lesson. Furthermore, I usually ask my students to vocalize these goals together. I also place importance on teachers trying to motivate their students. So, I seek out some interesting video clips online that can keep my students engaged. Crucially, I prefer inductive activities and try to provide learning targets within context. Lastly, I believe it's essential to conclude the lesson by summarizing the main points, and especially at the final stage, I like to ask referential questions that are more related to the students' life.

⟨B⟩

Stages	Teaching & Learning Activities
Introduction	• T and Ss exchange greetings. • T presents today's lesson objective on screen and reads it together with Ss: "We will be able to describe the meanings of words that express feelings."
Development #1	• T plays a video clip that shows different cartoon characters with a variety of emotional expressions. • T checks Ss' understanding of the video clip. • T provides reading passages that include the following words. *like, excite, love, bore, dislike, bother, worry, fear, annoy, confuse, believe, suggest, demonstrate, infer* • T asks Ss to underline the words that they do not know and infer the meanings from the context. • T asks Ss to circle the words related to feelings or emotions. • T asks Ss to look up the meanings of the unknown verbs in the dictionary.
Development #2	• T presents the target rules: "In English, it is more typical, more frequent, so unmarked, for the person who experiences emotional feelings to appear in the subject position of the sentence."

	• T tells Ss about the meanings of the two sentences: *Sue likes the dogs.* vs. *The dogs please Sue.* • T distributes the following handout. In the following sentences, the arrows indicate who experiences the feelings described by the verbs 'bothers' and 'loves.' (1) Julia loves her sister. ↙ (unmarked, more typical) (2) Julia bothers her sister. ↗ (marked, less typical) Sentence (1) is more typical, so unmarked, because the subject, Julia, experiences the feeling of love. Sentence (2) is marked because the object, her sister, experiences the feeling of being bothered. Now, let's work on the following sentences and determine whether they are unmarked or marked: a. Julia worried her sister. (ⓐ) b. Julia feared her sister. (ⓑ)
Consolidation	• Using the PPT slides, T recaps the main points of the lesson. • T asks questions: "In the sentence 'Julia confuses her sister,' who is being confused?" "If we say 'Julia upset her father,' who was upset, Julia or her father?" • T bids farewell to Ss.

Note: T = teacher, Ss = students

Fill in the blanks (ⓐ) and (ⓑ) with "unmarked" or "marked." Then choose the TWO stages in ⟨B⟩ that do NOT correspond to the teacher's beliefs in ⟨A⟩, and explain your answers with evidence from ⟨A⟩ and ⟨B⟩.

모범답안 (a) marked, (b) unmarked. Stages of Development 2 and Consolidation do not correspond. In the Development, teacher first presents the target rules with each sentence and lets students determine the types of verbs in a deductive activity. For Consolidation, teacher uses display questions to have correct language answers. (48 words)

02
Read the passage in 〈A〉 and the examples in 〈B〉, and follow the directions. 【4 points】

2022년 B11번

─── 〈A〉 ───

Focus on form is one of the approaches to L2 instruction that has been proposed to develop learners' fluency and accuracy. It occurs when learners briefly pay attention to linguistic items within a larger meaning-focused context. Focus on form can be accomplished in various ways. A basic distinction is drawn between 'reactive focus on form' (where attention to form arises out of some problem in a participant's production as in A1 and A2) and 'pre-emptive focus on form' (where the participants make a particular form the topic of the conversation even though no actual problem has arisen as in B1 and B2).

	Options	Description
Reactive	A1. Implicit feedback	The teacher or another student responds to a student's error without directly indicating an error has been made, e.g., by means of a recast or a clarification request.
Reactive	A2. Explicit feedback	The teacher or another student responds to a student's error by directly indicating that an error has been made, e.g., by formally correcting the error or by using metalanguage.
Pre-emptive	B1. Student-initiated focus on form	A student asks a question about a linguistic form.
Pre-emptive	B2. Teacher-initiated focus on form	The teacher gives advice about a linguistic form he/she thinks might be problematic or asks the students a question about the form.

─── 〈B〉 ───

Example 1 (*It is Monday morning and a group of students have just arrived for their English class. The teacher starts the class by asking the students about their weekend.*)

T : So what did you do this weekend?
S1: I ran my first marathon!
T : Wow! Did you finish?
S1: Yes, eventually…. It was actually a half-course marathon, but really challenging.
T : Way to go! (turning to S2) How about you?
S2: I had gone to the park…
T : You need to use the past simple when you say the things you did over the weekend.
S2: I has b…, I had?
T : Past simple. For example, I saw, I did, or I played …

S2: Ah! I went to the park with my family last weekend.
T : Great! How was it? Did you and your family enjoy it?
S2: Very much.

Example 2 (*Students are doing a communicative task with their conversation partner in their English class. The students are asked to set a date when they can do a project together. While students are checking the date, the teacher shuttles back and forth among the groups.*)

S1: Teacher, is it okay to just say December eighteen?
T : December eighteen?
S1: Yeah, like December eighteen or January seventeen.
S2: You know, we need to fix the date we meet together, and we want to make sure the right way of saying dates.
T : Mmm. It's okay but it sounds a little casual. Usually December THE eighteenth or THE eighteenth of December.
S1: Aha! December THE eighteenth.
T : Yeah, good.

Note: T=teacher, S=student

Among the options A1, A2, B1, and B2 in ⟨A⟩, identify the option of focus on form used in each example in ⟨B⟩, respectively. Then, support your answers with evidence from ⟨B⟩.

문제분석	구분	교과 교육
난이도 ★★☆	평가목표	두가지 다른 피드백의 종류를 구체적으로 서술하는가?
	채점기준	1점: (Example 1) A2 1점: 학습자의 동사오류가 나타난 후에 명시적 피드백으로 문법용어를 이용한다. 1점: (Example 2) B1 1점: 학습자의 질문으로 교사가 정확한 형태를 설명한다.
모범답안		Example 1 is A2. Explicit feedback was used with the metalanguage, 'past simple' after the student made an error in the verb form. Example 2 is B1. Student-initiated focus on form occurred based on the student's question, "is it okay to say December eighteen?" and teacher explained the correct form. (52 words)

03 Read the passages and the teaching journals, and follow the directions.

2017년 B1번

〈A〉

Form-focused instruction (FFI) can be split into TWO types: focus on formS and focus on form. According to R. Ellis (2001), FFI includes both traditional approaches to teaching forms based on structural syllabi and more communicative approaches, where attention to form arises out of activities that are primarily meaning-focused (p. 2).

〈B〉

Mr. Song

My students often tell me that they feel overwhelmed by the number of grammatical structures they have to learn. While thinking about ways to help students develop grammatical competence, I decided to teach grammar explicitly in class. Today I spent most of the class time on explaining grammatical rules using meta-linguistic terms. Although some of the students initially showed some interest in learning about the rules, many of them got bored, with some dozing off after ten minutes or so.

Miss Oh

Most of my students find grammatical rules difficult and boring. So I decided to implement a new approach. For this approach, I typed up the reading passage in the textbook and deliberately italicized the target structures, hoping that this would help my students notice how the target structures function. After I passed out the reconstructed reading passage, I had my students read it by themselves and then work together in groups, cross-checking their understanding.

Referring to the terms in 〈A〉, identify the type of form-focused instruction exemplified in each of the teachers' teaching journals, and explain with supporting evidence from 〈B〉. Do NOT copy more than FOUR consecutive words from the passage.

문제분석	구분	교과 교육
난이도 ★★★	평가목표	form-focused 수업에서 formS와 form의 차이를 구체적으로 서술하는가?
	채점기준	1점: (송교사) focus on formS approach 1점: 교사는 명시적으로 규칙을 설명하고 학생들은 문장에 적용한다. 1점: (오교사) focus on form approach 1점: input enhancement를 이용하여 글에서 목표형태를 집중하게 한다.

모범답안   Mr. Song implements focus on formS approach to teach the grammatical structures without contexts. He explicitly presents the rules with metalinguistic terms to let students apply them in the structure. In contrast, Ms. Oh implements focus on form approach using input enhancement in contexts. Students implicitly notice the target structure in the reading passage. (53 words)

04 Read Ms. Lee's opinions about the grammar lesson in ⟨A⟩ and the sample lesson plan in ⟨B⟩, and follow the directions. 【4 points】

2018년 B5번

⟨A⟩

I think teachers should keep in mind that the ultimate goal of any grammar lesson is to build up communicative ability. In order to achieve this goal, I believe that classroom activities should not focus on practicing structures and patterns in a meaningless way. Instead, they should be designed to involve students in real communication. By doing so, grammar lessons will be able to encourage the students' interest in learning and elicit more active and meaningful interaction with others in the classroom.

⟨B⟩

Subject	High School English	Students	1st-year students
Title	Lesson 9 My Dream	Date	Nov. 24th
Objectives	• Students will familiarize themselves with the expression "If I were … ." • Students will be able to communicate using the expression "If I were … ."		

		Teaching-Learning Activities
Intro-duction	Greeting & Roll-call	• T and Ss exchange greetings. • T checks if all the Ss are present.
	Review	• T reviews materials from the previous lesson.
	Stating Objectives	• T introduces the objective of the lesson.
Develop-ment	Activity 1	• T hands out a text that contains several instances of "If I were …" • Ss scan the text and highlight all the sentences including "If I were …." • Ss check the ones they highlighted with T. • T tells Ss to pay attention to the verb form "were."
	Activity 2	• T tells Ss that she is going to read a passage on "My Dream." • T explains difficult words in the passage. • T reads the passage at a normal pace. • Ss jot down the key words in the passage as T reads. • Ss reconstruct the passage individually. • T hands out the original text to Ss.

	Activity 3	• T has Ss form groups of three. • T asks Ss to think of a job that they would like to have in the future. • Ss use "If I were … " to share their opinions about their future dream jobs. • Assuming that their dreams come true, TWO Ss take a reporter's role and interview the other S asking how he or she feels about his or her job. • Ss take turns and continue the activity.
	Activity 4	• T hands out a worksheet. • Ss put together sentence fragments to form complete sentences. • T reads out complete sentences and each S checks their own answers. • T writes 3 more sentences using "If I were…" on the board. • T asks Ss to read the sentences.
Consolidation	Review	• T reviews what Ss learned.
	Closure	• T hands out homework and announces the next lesson. • T says goodbye to Ss.

Note: T = teacher, S = student

Based on ⟨A⟩, choose the ONE most appropriate activity in the development stage that reflects Ms. Lee's opinions. Then, support your choice with evidence from ⟨B⟩. Do NOT copy more than FOUR consecutive words from the passage.

모범답안 Activity 3 provides the students with communicative activity using the target expression, 'if I were ….' Students begin with thinking of their own ideas related to their future jobs, use the target structure to share their ideas, and role play to each other in an interview situation. (47 words)

05 Read the passage and answer the directions. 【4 points】

⟨A⟩

Language learning can be classified into different types in various ways in terms of how learners process linguistic form to acquire rules that govern its use. One way is to distinguish inductive learning from deductive learning. This distinction is made by taking into account how a rule is learned in relation with its specific instances.

⟨B⟩

(Below are parts of TWO teachers' instruction procedures for teaching past tense verb forms in hypothetical conditionals.)

Teacher A's Class

- T explains to Ss that past tense verb forms should be used in sentences with *if* clauses to describe hypothetical situations.
- T asks Ss to complete sentences with appropriate verb forms to show hypothetical situations

> 1. I _____(can) fly to you, if I _____(be) a superhero.
> 2. If he _____(have) a time machine, he _____(will) go back in time.

- T asks Ss to read a short text with sentences describing hypothetical situations.

> If I had a spaceship, I would fly to Mars. I would also build my own house there and live forever, if there were both oxygen and water. Unfortunately, I don't have lots of money to buy a spaceship. . . .

- T asks Ss to write a paragraph starting with the given expression.

> If I lived on Mars, . . .

Teacher B's Class

- T gives back the written texts about hypothetical situations Ss produced in the previous class and provides their reformulated texts T has produced at the same time. Only incorrect verb forms in Ss' writings are changed in T's reformulation as in the examples.

> ⟨A student's original writing⟩
> If I have last year to live over again, I will exercise more and eat less junk food because I can be healthier. I will spend more time with my friends and have better grades, if I am more active and watch less TV. . . .

> ⟨The teacher's reformulated text⟩
> If I had last year to live over again, I would exercise more and eat less junk food because I could be healthier. I would spend more time with my friends and have better grades, if I were more active and watched less TV. . . .

- T asks Ss to compare T's reformulated sample with their writings and to underline all the words in the sample that are different from those in their writings.
- T asks Ss to find what the underlined words have in common and in what way they differ from the ones used in their original writings in terms of language form.
- T asks Ss to work out the rule that applies to all their underlined words based on their findings in the previous step.

Identify the type of learning applied to each class in ⟨B⟩ based on ⟨A⟩. Then explain how each class orients students toward its identified type of learning with supporting evidence.

문제분석

난이도 ★★★

구분	교과 교육
평가목표	문법지도의 deductive와 inductive 학습의 특징을 서술하는가?
채점기준	1점: (Class A) 연역법 1점: 교사는 명시적으로 문법규칙을 설명하고 학생은 쓰기에 적용한다. 1점: (Class B) 귀납법 1점: 학생은 자신이 쓴 글에 대해 비교하고 규칙을 발견한다.

모범답안 Deductive learning is applied for Class A. Teacher explicitly explains the rules of target form, and students apply the rule into writing through some practices. Inductive learning is applied for Class B. Students write their own text and compare with the teacher's sample text to find out the gaps in language form. They discover the rule for themselves. (57 words)

06 Fill out the blanks ㉠, ㉡ with appropriate words.

Formalists have relied mostly on a (㉠) form of teaching – moving from the statement of the rule to its application in the example. Activists have advocated the apprehension by the students themselves of the way the language is working. They prefer students to develop a rule or generalization themselves after they have heard (or seen) certain forms and used them in a number of ways; this is a process of (㉡) learning (moving examples to a rule).

모범답안   ㉠ deductive   ㉡ inductive

07 Read the passage and fill out the blank.

2007년 전국 7번

> The value of meaning-focused communicative activities that provide learners with comprehensible input and opportunities to improve and correct their own output through interaction with others has been demonstrated repeatedly.
>
> S1: I had a frightening dream last night.
> S2: Last night...
> S3: And I know the beginning of the story.
> S2: Wait. Wait. Wait. There is something wrong with this sentence. Is it a dream or dreams?
> S1: A dream, dreams, a dream?
> S2: I think it's a dream.
> S1: I had a dream. OK? It was so scary and I couldn't sleep at all.
> S2: Oh my!
>
> However, form-focused activities as in the dialogue above emphasizing the features of particular grammar points are also necessary in order for learners to develop accuracy. Such activities range from indirect approaches to grammar instruction, such as the focus-on-form activities, to traditional formal instruction where students are presented with grammar rules, examples, and practice exercises. These form-focused approaches have been found to be effective in developing the learner's ability to use _____ if instruction is followed by opportunities to encounter the instructed grammar point in communicative usage.

Fill out the blank using THREE words in the word list.

⟨Word list⟩

| grammatical | practice | meaning |
| control | forms | communicatively |

문제분석

난이도 ★☆☆

구분	교과 교육
평가목표	form-focused 수업의 목표를 이해하고 서술하는가?
채점기준	문법수업에서 form-focused 수업은 과거의 수업방식과는 다르게 학습자가 먼저 수행하고 이해한 내용에 대하여 언어적 문제점을 분석하는 방식으로 이루어진다.

모범답안   grammatical forms communicatively

08 Read the following and answer the question.

2012년 23번

Teaching Procedure

Step 1: Ms. Park asks students where they went last summer and what they took on their journey. Then she writes down the following sentences on the board and explains the difference in form and meaning between the TWO sentences using the terms 'past tense' and 'past participle(pp)'.

I <u>took</u> a light jacket.

I <u>should have taken</u> a warm jacket.

Step 2: Ms. Park hands out a story from a magazine that includes the target structure 'should+have+pp'. She asks students to read the story carefully and look for the examples of 'should+have+pp' in the given text.

> Kate travelled across the Australian desert. She made no preparations. She didn't take a map, and she didn't take a cell phone. Soon after she set off, she got lost and got trapped in a flash flood. Later, looking back on it, she said, "I should have taken a map. I should have taken a cell phone..."

Step 3: Ms. Park asks students to think about their own previous journey and complete the worksheet below.

Worksheet

I _____ on my journey.	I should have _____ on my journey.
I took a light jacket on my journey.	I should have taken a warm jacket on my journey.

Step 4: Ms. Park asks students to write a story using the sentences they have produced in the worksheet above, and to share their writings with the partners.

Among the steps, identify TWO steps based on meaning and explain them with evidence in the teaching procedure.

Which of the following is NOT correct about the teaching procedures above?

① Metalinguistic terms are used to help students understand the target structure in Step 1.
② Students are encouraged to find the target structure in the text in Step 2.
③ Students connect the target structure to their personal experiences in Step 3.
④ Students are asked to proceduralize the target structure with a focus on meaning in Step 4.
⑤ The procedure promotes rule discovery to improve implicit knowledge of target structure.

문제분석	구분	교과 교육
난이도 ★★☆	평가목표	deductive 학습에서 의미를 중심으로 하는 문법수업 단계를 찾아 구체적으로 서술하는가?
	채점기준	1점: (step 3) 1점: 목표구문과 자신의 경험을 연결한다. 1점: (step 4) 1점: 목표구문을 이용하여 자신의 이야기를 만든다.
모범답안		The steps 3 and 4 are meaning-based. In step 3, students connect the target structure to their personal experiences on journey complete the task. In step 4, students proceduralize the target structure to make their own story with a focus on meaning. (42 words)

 ⑤

09 Read the following and answer the question.

2010년 24번

⟨A⟩

Activity A

The basic meaning of *down* has to do with movement from a higher position or level to a lower one. Based on the description, match the items in [1] with those in [2].

[1]   a. movement and position
   b. decreasing, lowering, and reducing
   c. collapsing and attacking

[2]   1. Go and lie down on your bed. ____
   2. The water breaks down the walls. ____
   3. It's a bit hot here. Turn the thermostat down. ____

⟨B⟩

Activity B

1. Read the following about your country.

   > In this country, you **have to** start school at the age of 7. You **can** drive when you are 17, but you **can't** buy alcohol until you are 18. You also **have to** wait until you turn 18 before you **can** vote. Men **have to** serve in the military, but women **don't have to**.

2. Listen to a similar conversation about England.
3. Mark the differences between your country and England on the worksheet.

Fill in the blank with the ONE most appropriate word.

> While activity ⟨A⟩ presents the phrasal verbs in each sentence, activity ⟨B⟩ requires students to use grammatical points at the _____ level. It emphasizes receptive language skills by raising awareness on the target form to help students notice the target structure through input enhancement.

Which of the following is correct?

① Both activities present the grammar points based on the rule-driven approach.
② Activity 〈A〉 requires students to use phrasal verbs at the discourse level.
③ Activity 〈A〉 focuses on students' use of metalanguage.
④ Activity 〈B〉 emphasizes productive language skills by using the target form.
⑤ Activity 〈B〉 helps students notice the target structure through input enhancement.

문제분석	구분	교과 교육
난이도 ★★★	평가목표	input enhancement을 활용하여 문법수업을 하는 방법을 구체적으로 서술하는가?
	채점기준	• discourse의 입력을 통해 목표어에 집중할 수 있게 한다. • input enhancement는 문법수업을 위한 의사소통식 방법이다. • 목표어가 되는 부분에 볼드체를 이용하여 noticing할 수 있게 한다. • 입력을 중심으로 목표어를 배울 수 있게 한다.
모범답안	discourse	

기출문제답안 ⑤

10. Read the passage in ⟨A⟩ and examine the teaching procedure in ⟨B⟩. 【3 points】

⟨A⟩

Processing instruction, a type of focus-on-form instruction, is based on the assumption that when processing input, L2 learners have difficulty in attending to form and meaning at the same time due to working memory limitations. Not surprisingly, they tend to give priority to meaning and tend not to notice details of form. Processing instruction uses several principles to explain what learners attend to in the input and why. Below are some of these principles.

The Lexical Preference Principle: In (1), both -es and boy convey the same information, 'the third person singular.' Yet, learners prefer to focus on the lexical item, boy, to arrive at meaning, and often ignore the grammatical item, -es, while processing the sentence. (1) The boy studies in the library, not at home.

The First Noun Principle: Learners tend to process the first noun or pronoun they encounter in a sentence as the agent of action. For example, they may misinterpret (2) as "Jack collected the data for the project." (2) Jack let Joe collect the data for the project.

The Event Possibilities Principle: Event possibilities refer to the likelihood of one noun being the agent of action as opposed to another. Since it is more likely in the real world that a dog would bite a man than the other way around, learners would likely misinterpret (3) as "the dog bit the farmer." (3) The dog was bitten by the farmer.

In processing instruction, teachers provide students with structured input activities, taking into consideration the principles above. In a structured input activity, students are forced to attend to form in order to comprehend a sentence.

⟨B⟩

Teaching Procedure

1. Explicit Explanation: Explain how a past tense sentence is constructed in English. Then inform students of why they tend not to notice the past tense marker -ed and thus misinterpret past tense sentences.

2. Structured Input Activity: Have students read six sentences and decide whether they describe an activity that was done in the past or usually happens in the present. Then, check the answers together.

Sentences	Present	Past
(1) They watched television at night.	☐	☐
(2) They watch television at night.	☐	☐
(3) I walk to school on Mondays.	☐	☐
(4) I walked to school on Mondays.	☐	☐
(5) We played soccer on weekends.	☐	☐
(6) We play soccer on weekends.	☐	☐

Identify the principle in <A> that the teaching procedure in <B> focuses on. Then explain how the structured input activity in <B> helps students correctly process the target form for meaning.

문제분석	구분	교과 교육
난이도 ★★★	평가목표	문법지도인 input processing의 이론에서 실제 교실활동의 적용방법을 구체적으로 서술하는가?
	채점기준	1점: (Lexical Preference Principle)에 적용된다. 1점: 구조화된 입력안에서 의미에, 그 다음에 형태를 배울 수 있게 한다. 1점: 형태와 의미를 연결하여 언어적 정확성을 발달시킨다.
모범답안		The teaching procedure <B> focuses on Lexical Preference Principle in <A>. In structured input activity, students can first process meaning and then notice the tense form by comparing the difference between present and past verbs. In this way, language accuracy is developed based on form-meaning mapping. (47 words)

11. Read the worksheet and follow the direction.

⟨Worksheet⟩

Choose the sentence that goes with the picture.

| a) The man *bit* a snake.
b) The man *was bitten by* a snake. | a) The elephant *frightened* the mouse.
b) The elephant *was frightened by* the mouse. | a) The mother *fed* the child.
b) The mother *was fed by* the child. |

The goal of input-processing instruction is to encourage learners to make better form-meaning connections than they would if left to their own devices. There are three key components. As in the worksheet above, for example, they are encouraged to match pictures with bold-typed forms which carry the active and passive voice. In other words, a form-meaning relationship in the picture explains the use of the passive to ① _____ the patient of a sentence by placing it in subject position. Secondly, the picture leads them to attend to the form of the verb to determine whether the subject is the agent of the verb, as is most generally the case, or the patient, as is the case with passive verbs. Finally, the worksheet represents a structured-input activity where learners have the chance to process the targeted feature in a controlled manner. Unlike the traditional grammar instruction, this activity is designed to help learners naturally process ② _____ in accordance with their interlanguage.

⟨Word list⟩

recover   input   topicalize   output   ignore   feedback

모범답안 (1) topicalize (2) input

12 Read the following and answer the question.

2010년 19번

> T: Here is a sentence using the words think and problem : *I thought about the problem.* Now you make one using the words talk and problem.
> S: We talked about the problem.
> T: Good. Argue and result.
> S: We argued about the result.
> T: Good. Discuss and advantages.
> S: We discussed about the advantages.
> T: No. With discuss, we do not use about.
> S: Really? OK. We discussed the advantages.
> Note: T = Teacher, S = Student

Which of the following is correct about the conversation?

① The activity is designed to map form onto function.
② The teacher intentionally leads the student to commit an error.
③ The meanings of the words are taught explicitly to the student.
④ The student has to attend to meaning in order to perform the activity.
⑤ The purpose of the lesson is to help develop language use through meaningful conversation.

문제분석	구분	교과 교육
난이도 ★★☆	평가목표	garden path 전략의 문법수업원리를 이해하는가?
	채점기준	• 교사는 부분적인 규칙을 제시한다. • 교사는 의도적으로 학생들이 오류를 만들도록 유도한다. • 교사는 예외가 되는 규칙을 제시한다.

기출문제답안 ②

13 Read the passage and answer the question.

2013년 26번

For his 1st-year middle school students, Mr. Lee developed the following lesson procedure for teaching how to express actions that happened in the past:

Step 1. Listen carefully and decide whether Minsu did these things yesterday. Check the correct boxes as you listen.

	The action happened yesterday.	The action did not happen yesterday.
1	✓	
2		
3		
4		

Instructor's script:
1. Minsu watched a baseball game on TV.
2. Minsu walked his dog in the park.
3. Minsu will listen to classical music.
4. Minsu played computer games at home.

Step 2. What did you do yesterday? Raise your hand if you did each activity yesterday.
1. Who watched a baseball game on TV?
2. Who walked their dog in the park?
3. Who listened to classical music?
4. Who played computer games at home?

Describe one each characteristics of lesson Steps (1) and (2) of grammar instruction from the students-centered perspective.

Choose all the correct statements about the lesson procedure.
ⓐ Learners must pay attention to verb forms in order to determine the temporal reference of each sentence.
ⓑ The instructor offers metalinguistic information to teach the concept of pastness that has low communicative value.
ⓒ Students are encouraged to make form-meaning connections appropriately in Step 1.
ⓓ The instructor mostly provides display questions to his students in Step 2.

문제분석	구분	교과 교육
난이도 ★★☆	평가목표	과거시제를 익히기 위한 form-focused 수업을 서술하는가?
	채점기준	2점: (step 1) 학습자들이 형태-의미를 연결하여 동사형태에 주의를 기울일 수 있도록 한다. 2점: (step 2) 교사의 referential질문을 통해 자신의 상황에 대해 목표어를 이용해 서술한다.

모범답안 In Step 1, learners are encouraged to make form-meaning connections appropriately as they must pay attention to verb forms in order to determine the temporal reference of each sentence. In step 2, learners have a chance to notice the form for their own situation following the teacher's referential questions. (49 words)

기출문제답안 ⓐ, ⓒ

14 Read the following and answer the question.

2013년 15번

⟨Activity A⟩

1. Complete the table below with the things you have to do this week, using "be going to." Leave two spaces empty.

	Mon.	Tues.	Wed.
Afternoon			
Evening			

2. Talk to several other students and arrange a time to see a movie with them. You might need to change your schedule.

⟨Activity B⟩

In pairs, do the following tasks in English:

1. Talk about the differences between adjectives ending in —ed and —ing.

> We felt moved by his story.
> *We felt moving by his story.
> It was a really exhausting day.
> *It was a really exhausted day.

2. Indicate whether the sentences below are grammatical(G) or ungrammatical(U) focusing on the underlined words.

> 1. They seemed pleasing with the outcome. (G/U)
> 2. I saw the most amazed film yesterday. (G/U)
> 3. He felt disappointed about the test results. (G/U)
> 4. The most annoyed thing was her rude attitude. (G/U)
> 5. The incident could be embarrassing for him. (G/U)

3. Write a rule that can explain the differences between the two types of adjectives.

Among two activities, identify one more explicit activity and explain how the activity helps students acquire new language form with supporting evidence.

Which of the following is a correct statement about the above activities?

① Activity A has students explain the target form in a decontextualized setting.
② Activity B is aimed at encouraging students to automatize the target structure through communication.
③ Activity B fosters students to learn the language points through a discovery activity.
④ Both activities have students analyze the data containing exemplars of the targeted features.
⑤ Both activities require students to use metalinguistic terms.

구분	교과 교육
평가목표	학습자 중심의 문법 교수법을 구체적으로 서술하는가?
채점기준	1점: (Activity B) 명시적 문법활동이다. 1점: 의식올리기를 통해 목표문법을 배우도록 한다. 1점: 예시가 포함된 자료를 분석한다. 1점: 규칙을 스스로 찾아낸다.

모범답안 Activity B is an explicit activity. It fosters students to learn the target language form through consciousness-raising instruction. The students acquire the new language by analyzing the data containing exemplars of the targeted features. They could discover a rule by themselves. (41 words)

기출문제답안 ③

15 Read the following context and answer the questions.

2012년 논술 3번

⟨Context⟩

Ms. Park recognized Jitae's problem regarding the third-person singular subject-verb agreement after reviewing his speech sample from the performance assessment. Then Ms. Park had a conference with Jitae. She found that, in the first grade of middle school, Jitae was explicitly taught how to put -s at the end of verb stems and then practiced the subject-verb agreement through transformation exercises (e.g., run → runs). Since then, Jitae has been exposed to the grammatical morpheme through reading materials but has not been given chances to use the form in conversation. After checking up on Jitae's knowledge, Ms. Park was convinced that he still retained the grammatical knowledge about the rule. In the classroom, however, Ms. Park has observed Jitae making the same errors frequently in conversation.

(1) Based on both the cognitive and the sociocultural approach of second language learning, describe ONE problem associated with the teaching method through which Jitae learned the third-person singular subject-verb agreement.
(2) Discuss how to apply ONE technique/task for the cognitive approach and ONE for the sociocultural approach in the classroom and explain why the technique/task would help Jitae correctly use the target grammatical morpheme in conversation.

문제분석	구분	교과 교육
난이도 ★★★	평가목표	수업방법의 문제점과 해결 technique/task을 각 approach로 설명할 수 있는가?
	채점기준	(1) 인지적과 사회문화적 관점에서 문제점 2점: (cognitive) 목표어를 declarative에서 procedural지식으로 활용하지 못한다. 2점: (sociocultural) 목표어를 실제 상황에 사용하지 못한다. (2) 인지적과 사회문화적 관점에서 해결책 1점: (cognitive) consciousness-raising task 1점: 예시문장을 문제 비교하고 문법 규칙을 발견한다. 1점: (sociocultural) jigsaw task 1점: 문제해결을 위해 의미협상을 한다.

모범답안

(1) As for cognitive problem, the teacher has not given Jitae an opportunity to convert declarative knowledge to procedural one, which makes him difficult to use the target rule in context. As for sociocultural problem, he has not had a chance to use the form in social interaction to apply it, but does mechanical drill practices as rote-learning. (57 words)

(2) As for cognitive task, output task can let Jitae use the grammatical rule in their own context. The focus on meaning and context makes the grammar practice more engaging and relevant. As for sociocultural task, jigsaw task helps Jitae interact with the target form in a group to use the target form to negotiate meaning while solving the problem. (58 words)

CHAPTER 09 어휘 지도

01 Read the passage in ⟨A⟩ and the lesson plan in ⟨B⟩, and follow the directions.

2025년 A12번

─── ⟨A⟩ ───

Ms. Kim, a high school English teacher, attended an ICT workshop for English teachers. There she learned how to select digital tools that best fit her students' needs and use them appropriately. Below is the list of principles she took note of during the workshop.

<Guiding principles for using digital tools>
① Encourage students to independently explore and discover language rules.
② Support learners with diverse learning styles (e.g., auditory styles, visual styles).
③ Teach digital ethics (e.g., citing properly).
④ Assess student achievement and provide individualized feedback.

─── ⟨B⟩ ───

Draft of the Master Plan

Unit	Save the Earth
Objectives	Students will be able to: • identify the main idea and details of a text or discourse • write an opinion using textual and non-textual elements • use digital tools responsibly and ethically

Period	Contents	Technology
1st	• Introduce the topic, 'Save the Earth.' • Watch a video on environmental problems. • Teach how to use the Internet properly (e.g., locating information, sourcing, netiquette).	– Online videos – Internet search engines

2nd	• Make predictions about a text using titles and pictures. • Read the passage, 'Plastic Pollution.' • Identify key words and main ideas.	– Word cloud generator to visualize key concepts
3rd	• Provide definitions of new words. • Teach grammar points explicitly using drills.	– PPT slides
…	…	…
7th	• Brainstorm ideas to solve environmental problems and share in groups. • In groups, create a 'Save the Earth' poster.	– Online collaborative writing platform
8th	• Exhibit groups' posters on the walls. • Conduct a team-based quiz and provide comments to groups.	– Online quiz platform

Based on ⟨A⟩, identify the TWO guiding principles that Ms. Kim does NOT conform to in her lessons in ⟨B⟩. Then, explain your answers, respectively, with evidence from ⟨B⟩.

문제분석	구분	교과 교육
난이도 ★★☆	평가목표	디지털 도구를 사용하는 원리에 어긋나는 내용을 구체적으로 서술하는가?
	채점기준	1점: Principle 1 1점: 교사가 어휘의 정의를 제공하고 문법규칙을 명시적으로 가르친다. 1점: Principle 4 1점: 팀에 근거한 퀴즈를 수행하고 그룹에 대한 평가를 제공한다.
모범답안		Principles 1 and 4 are not conformed. In 3rd period, the teacher provides definitions and teaches grammar points explicitly using drills rather than discovery learning. In 8th period, the teacher conducts a team-based quiz and provides comments to groups rather than individual feedback. (45 words)

02 Read the passage in ⟨A⟩ and the teaching procedures in ⟨B⟩, and follow the directions.

2023년 B10번

⟨A⟩

The basic aspects the students need to know about a lexical item are its written and spoken forms, and its denotational meaning. However, there are additional aspects which also need to be learned, as are described in the following table.

Aspects	Descriptions
Grammar	A grammatical structure may be lexically bound, and lexical items also have grammatical features.
Collocation	Collocation refers to the way words tend to co-occur with other words or expressions.
Connotation	The connotations of a word are the emotional or positive-negative associations that it implies.
Appropriateness	Students need to know if a particular lexical item is usually used in writing or in speech; or in formal or informal discourse.
Word formation	Words can be broken down into morphemes. Exactly how these components are put together is another piece of useful information.

⟨B⟩

Teaching Procedure 1

1. Present the following expressions in the table. Ask students to choose which expressions are possible.

do my homework	(O/X)	make my homework	(O/X)
do some coffee	(O/X)	make some coffee	(O/X)
do the laundry	(O/X)	make the laundry	(O/X)

2. Ask students to find more examples using *do* and *make*, referencing an online concordancer.

Teaching Procedure 2

1. Ask students to identify countable and uncountable nouns.

advice	employee	equipment	facility
information	money	proposal	result

2. Tell students to choose the expression of quantity that does NOT fit with the noun in each sentence.

> (a) The researchers found [*a significant proportion of / some of / most of*] the results were not corroborated by other sources.

Identify ONE aspect in ⟨A⟩ that each teaching procedure in ⟨B⟩ focuses on, respectively. Then, explain your answers with evidence from ⟨B⟩.

문제분석	구분	교과 교육
난이도 ★★☆	평가목표	어휘 수업에서 주요하게 다루어지는 핵심 활동을 찾아 구체적으로 서술하는가?
	채점기준	1점: (Teaching procedure 1) Collocation 1점: 온라인 concordancer를 통해 많은 예시로 함께 쓰이는 동사유형을 학습한다. 1점: (Teaching procedure 2) Grammar 1점: 양을 표현하는 가산/불가산 명사를 확인한다.

모범답안   Teaching procedure 1 focuses on Collocation. Students choose the words which co-occur with the verbs 'do' and 'make' and find more examples in the online concordancer. Teaching procedure 2 focuses on Grammar. Students identify countable and uncountable words and choose appropriate quantifiable expressions for each noun. (46 words)

03 Read the passage in ⟨A⟩ and the word entries in ⟨B⟩, and follow the directions.

2021년 A12번

⟨A⟩

A corpus is a collection of texts of written or spoken language from various sources presented in electronic form. It provides evidence of how language is used in real situations, from which lexicographers can analyze millions of examples of each word to see how real language behaves. Many contemporary dictionaries, therefore, incorporate the features derived from the analyses of corpus data, some of which are shown below.

(1) Frequency: statistical data on how often words are used in the language
(2) Collocation: information on what other words commonly occur with the word in focus
(3) Context: information on which particular field (e.g., law, engineering, medicine) or social situation (e.g., formal vs. informal) a word is used in
(4) Authentic example sentences: sentences from what users of the language actually write or say in books, newspapers, speeches, or recorded conversations, etc.

⟨B⟩

Both Dictionary X and Dictionary Y are developed in part by incorporating data from corpora.

Dictionary X

shed [ʃed] UK🔊 US🔊
verb (*past tense* and *past participle* **shed**, *present participle* **shedding**)
[transitive]

1. GET RID OF   to get rid of something that you no longer need or want
2. DROP/FALL   to drop something or allow it to fall

> **Word Partners**
> ♦ shed *jobs/workers/staff*
> ♦ shed *weight/pounds/kilos*
> ♦ shed *an image*
> ♦ shed *your inhibitions*
> ♦ shed *a load*
> ♦ shed *tears*

Dictionary Y

shed UK🔊 US🔊 [ʃed]
verb [shedding], [shed], [shed]

1. ⟨transitive⟩ to get rid of something you do not need or want

> **USAGE BOX**
> **Shed** is mainly used in journalism. In everyday English, people usually say that one **gets rid of** something.

2. ⟨transitive⟩ to lose a covering, such as leaves, hair, or skin, because it falls off naturally, or to drop something in a natural way or by accident

---

With regard to the word 'shed,' identify ONE corpus-based feature described in ⟨A⟩ for each dictionary in ⟨B⟩, respectively. Then, provide evidence from ⟨B⟩ for each feature that you choose.

문제분석	구분	교과 교육
난이도 ★★☆	평가목표	어휘를 개별 요소로서가 아니라 함께 사용되는 어휘군과 용도를 이해하기 위한 사전의 개념을 구체적으로 서술하는가?
	채점기준	1점: (Dictionary X) collocation 1점: 목표단어와 함께 쓰이는 단어들을 습득한다. 1점: (Dictionary Y) context 1점: 어떤 상황에서 목표 단어가 쓰이는지 이해한다.

모범답안 In Dictionary X, collocation or word partners are described. Students acquire what words can occur with the target word, 'shed' together. In Dictionary Y, context is provided in the usage box. Students understand the situation where the target words can be used, such as in journalism and formal language. (47 words)

04 This is the data of the analysis on "extent" through concordance program.

2006년 전국 13번

selves to it, but the actual	extent	of the immunity is
international practice". To an	extent	the anger is to be
he possessor. The nature and	extent	of the control and
that there was an enormous	extent	of subterranean wro
leaders well before the full	extent	of the damage was
probably to an even greater	extent	_ Hitler's image was
he case before, to a growing	extent	of the person of th
arbance so as to clarify its	extent	and its limitations

The teacher can use a concordancer to find examples of authentic _____ to demonstrate features of vocabulary, typical collocations, a point of grammar or even the structure of a text. The teacher can generate exercises based on examples drawn from a variety of corpora, for example gap-filling exercises and tests. Students can work out rules of grammar or _____ and lexical features for themselves by searching for key words in context. Depending on their level, they can be invited to question some of the rules, based on their observation of patterns in authentic language. Students can be more active in their vocabulary learning: depending on their level, they can be invited to discover new meanings, to observe habitual collocations, to relate words to syntax, or to be critical of dictionary entries. Students can be invited to reflect on language use in general, based on their own explorations of a corpus of data, thus turning themselves into budding researchers.

(1) Complete the passage with the ONE most appropriate word. Use the SAME word.
(2) Choose the THREE activities for the vocabulary teaching from ⟨activity list⟩.

⟨activity⟩

(a) inference clues (b) phoneme discrimination
(c) bilingual dictionary (d) internalization of vocabulary
(e) explicit focus on forms

모범답안 (1) usage (2) (a), (d), (e)

05 Read the passage and complete it with ONE word each from the ⟨list⟩.

2005년 전국 9번

⟨A⟩

Concordancing

Computers are expert at storing and sorting large amounts of information. Concordancing programs are increasingly being used in the language classroom. A concordance is a type of index that searches for occurrences of a word or combinations of words, affixes, phrases, or structures within a corpus, and can show the immediate ① _____. The output from a concordance search can be used in the preparation of teaching materials, such as ② _____ and vocabulary activities.

Context…	Word	…Context	Reference
That my own	heart	drifts and cries, having no…	Deep Analysis
By the shout of the	heart	continually at work	And the wave
Nothing to adapt the skill of the	heart	to, skill	And the wave
The tread, the beat of it, it is my own	heart	,	Träumerei
Because I follow it to my own	heart		Many famous
My	heart	is ticking like the sun:	I am washed u
The vague	heart	sharpened to a candid co…	The March Pa
Contract my	heart	by looking out of date.	Lines on a Yo
Having no	heart	to put aside the theft	Home is so Sa

⟨B⟩

Voice Recognition & Production

Voice recognition refers to the capability of an automatic-speech recognition (ASR) software to accept spoken dictation. The current state-of-the-art ASR technology sheds light on the possibility of incorporating CALL for the ③ _____ communication in class. In addition, the current text-to-speech (TTS) technology has made it possible to develop speech production programs that read text aloud. ASR and TTS have great potential for English teaching and ④ _____ testing.

⟨Word list⟩

grammar   pseudo-oral   performance   context

모범답안 ① context ② grammar ③ pseudo-oral ④ performance

06 Read the passage in ⟨A⟩ and the teacher's journal in ⟨B⟩, and follow the directions.

2020년 A1번

⟨A⟩

  Vocabulary is a core component of language knowledge and provides much of the basis for how well learners listen, speak, read, and write. Without extensive knowledge of vocabulary or diverse strategies for acquiring new words, learners are often unable to produce as much language as they would like. Knowing a word does not simply mean knowing its surface meaning. Rather, it involves knowing diverse aspects of lexical knowledge in depth including phonological and morphological forms and syntactic and semantic structures. Therefore, activities that integrate lexical knowledge of form, meaning, and use should be included in class.

⟨B⟩

Teacher's Journal

Ms. Kang and I read an article on teaching vocabulary and discussed how we can improve the way we teach vocabulary. We realized that we have been heavily focused on expanding the size of our students' vocabulary. As a result, they seem to know a lot of words but do not understand or use them properly in context. So, we came up with the following activities that we believe help our students develop _____ of vocabulary knowledge across form, meaning, and use. Vocabulary activities to be implemented:

• Trying to pronounce the target words by listening to a recorded text
• Analyzing parts of the target words (e.g., prefixes and suffixes)
• Guessing the meanings of the target words using contextual cues
• Studying concordance examples to see various contexts and collocation patterns
• Writing a short story using the target words

모범답안   depth

07 Read the dialogue and fill in both blanks with the ONE most appropriate word. (Use the SAME word in both blanks.)

2018년 A8번

S: Ms. Lee, can I ask you a question?
T: Sure, go ahead.
S: I went over your feedback on my essay, and I really appreciate it. You pointed out the expression "die" could be revised to "pass away."
T: Yes, I did.
S: I don't understand the difference between the TWO expressions. As far as I understand, they have the same meaning.
T: Oh, I see. That's actually an example of a(n) _____.
S: Hmm … .
T: Let me make it clearer with another example. How do you think someone would feel if they were called "poor"?
S: Well, they may feel bad.
T: Okay, what about "less privileged"?
S: Oh, I understand your point. TWO words or expressions may mean the same thing, but we may have different feelings and attitudes about them.
T: That's the point. A(n) _____ is a polite word or expression that you use instead of a more direct one, to avoid shocking or upsetting someone.
S: Interesting!
T: Good.
S: Thank you, Ms. Lee. Your feedback is always helpful.

Note: T= teacher, S= student

모범답안   euphemism

08 Read the following and complete the summary with ONE word for each blank.

2013년 16번

A middle school teacher implements the vocabulary work as below.

(1) Work in pairs and choose one of the three verbs that most likely appears before each phrase.

do	make	take	
	√		a lot of noise
			family photographs
			a lot of mistakes
			the housework

(2) Check your answers with another student.
(3) Using a concordancing program on the Internet, find other phrases that can be used with the three verbs.
(4) Make your own conversation about a familiar topic (e.g., family life) using the phrases you have found on the Internet, and practice it in pairs.

〈Summary〉

The activity integrates a speaking activity into vocabulary work. It gives students a chance to use lexical phrases at the ①_____ level, talking about their family. It focuses on teaching how some verbs ②_____ with various noun phrases as a set. It asks students to use multimedia to understand how words group together.

Which of the following is NOT a correct statement about the procedure?

① It integrates a speaking activity into vocabulary work.
② It gives students a chance to use lexical phrases at the discourse level.
③ It focuses on teaching how some verbs collocate with various noun phrases.
④ It involves practicing lexical phrases using cue-response drills.
⑤ It asks students to use multimedia to understand how words group together.

문제분석	구분	교과 교육
난이도 ★★☆	평가목표	어휘의 collocation을 가르치는 수업절차를 이해하는가?
	채점기준	1점: collocation이 되는 어휘구를 자신의 가족에 대해 이야기하면서 discourse 수준에서 연습을 한다. 1점: 각 동사가 다른 명사구와 collocate되는 것에 초점을 둔다.

모범답안 ① discourse ② collocate

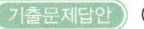 ④

09 Read the following and complete the summary with ONE word for each blank.

―― ⟨A⟩ ――

Below is a sample interaction from an activity used in a middle school English classroom.

S1: I have to do a diet. [T indicates an error by facial expression.]
S1: I have to do a diet.
T: [Writes 'diet' on the board.] What verb do we usually use when we start a diet?
S2: 'Go on'
T: Yes, that's right. [Writes 'go on' on the board.] How about if you've already started a diet?
S2: 'Be on'
T: Yes, if you are trying to lose weight by eating less food, then you are on a diet. [Pause] What did you eat for breakfast?
S1: Rice, eggs and vegetables.
T: Sounds like you ate a balanced diet.
S1: Balanced?
T: Yes. [Writes 'balanced' on the board.] If you eat all of the things you need to eat, we say you eat a balanced diet. What adjectives can we use with 'diet'?
S2: 'Healthy'
T: And?
S2: 'Unhealthy'
T: Yes. You can also use 'poor'. [Writes 'healthy', 'unhealthy' and 'poor']

Note: T = teacher, S = student

―― ⟨Summary⟩ ――

The activity emphasizes multi-word units. A focus is on ①_____ relations of words as students learn new words by using collocation rules. The activity develops students' knowledge of ②_____ relations of a word by suggesting several similar words to the target word.

기출문제

Choose all the correct statements about the activity.

ⓐ The activity emphasized multi-word units.
ⓑ The teacher makes students aware of collocations.
ⓒ Students learn new words by using morphological rules.
ⓓ Little focus is on paradigmatic relations of words.
ⓔ The activity develops students' knowledge of polysemous use of a word.

문제분석	구분	교과 교육
난이도 ★★★	평가목표	어휘지도에서 syntagmatic과 paradigmatic relation에 대하여 이해하는가?
	채점기준	1점: (syntagmatic) collocation의 사용으로 언어의 횡적인 관계를 의미한다. 1점: (paradigmatic)목표어와 유사어로 대체어로 쓰이는 단어의 관계를 의미한다.

모범답안 ① syntagmatic ② paradigmatic

기출문제답안 ⓐ, ⓑ, ⓔ

10 Read the following and answer the question.

Activity Procedure

(1) Work in groups of three and choose one topic from the list below: computer, country, family, food, hobby, holiday, library, movie, school, sport

(2) Brainstorm with your group members, and make a word web like the example shown below for the topic of your choice. For the boxes, come up with words (i.e., subtopics) that are related to the topic.

(3) Choose two subtopics and write, in the ovals, words that are related to them.

(4) Make sure to leave the pentagon and two boxes blank so that the topic and subtopics may be guessed by other groups.

(5) Show your web to other groups, and ask them to guess the topic and subtopics that should be in the pentagon and boxes, respectively, of your web.

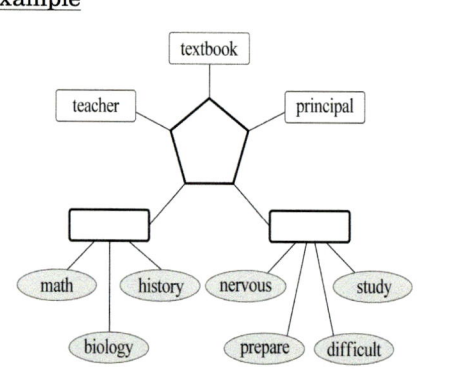

Example

Describe THREE advantages of the vocabulary activity to help students acquire the target words.

Which of the following is the LEAST appropriate description of the activity above?

① It provokes students to retrieve the words they already know.
② It helps students learn vocabulary from each other through interaction.
③ It allows students to work with words from different parts of speech.
④ It focuses on patterns of lexical repetition and chunking in connected discourse.
⑤ It helps students to visualize associative networks of thematically related words.

문제분석

난이도 ★★☆

구분	교과 교육
평가목표	word web 어휘 활동의 특징을 구체적으로 서술하는가?
채점기준	1점: 의미적으로 서로 연관되는 단어를 끌어낼 수 있다. 1점: 다양한 문법형태를 배울 수 있다. 1점: 영상화하여 연관된 의미를 볼 수 있다.

모범답안 The activity provokes students to retrieve the words they already know by associating each word in meaning. It allows students to work with words from different parts of speech by categorizing nouns of subject matters, verbs, or adjectives. It helps students to visualize associative networks of thematically related words in the figure of word web. (55 words)

기출문제답안 ④

11 Read the following and answer the question.

2008년 11번

The teacher is giving a lesson using *A Structured Word Net*.

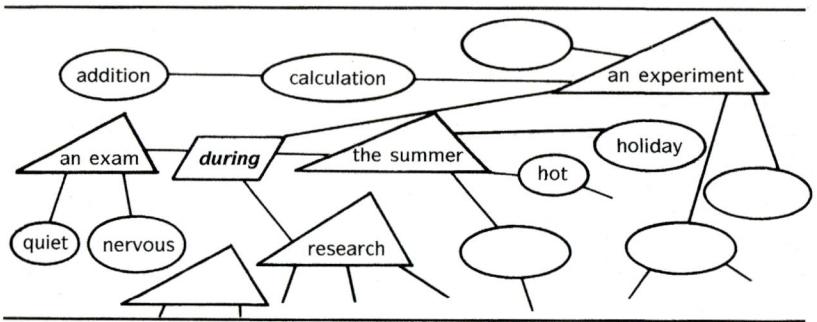

Teacher: Try to add as many words to the net as possible.
Teacher: (looking at the word net) Now, you can say like this using the words in the net. During an exam the room is very quiet and I feel nervous.
Teacher: Try to use the words you have added to the net in your sentence. Write some examples here.

In the classroom task above, the teacher tries to make the structural principles underlying the organization of the net more ①_____ by adding symbols in 'A Structured Word Net'. The teacher can then elicit and demonstrate relations of dependency between the words. These dependencies are either of a structural semantic nature, or grammatical nature, involving developing awareness of parts of speech. This is one way of learning grammar through the procedure of asking questions about words. Therefore, this classroom task can be shown to lead to the learner's ②_____ acquisition of grammatical information via ③_____.

⟨Word list⟩

lexis   information   intentional   overt   covert   acquisition

모범답안   ① overt   ② covert   ③ lexis

12 Read the following excerpts and answer the question.

2008년 29번

(1) Teaching a Low Frequency Word
   S: What does regurgitate mean?
   T: It means 'repeat ideas from the book.' The re- at the beginning means 'again,' so that is where the 'repeat' part of the meaning comes from. From this, can you guess the meaning of reconsider?

(2) Teaching a High Frequency Word
   S: What does punish mean?
   T: That's a useful word, although I hope it is not needed in this class. It means 'make someone suffer because they have done something wrong.' Let's look at some examples:
   • She was punished for coming home late.
   • He was severely punished for telling a lie.
   • What is the punishment that you hate the most?
   • Tell me some things that you get punished for.

Which of the following is correct?

① In (1), the teacher leads the student to learn the word by memorizing its first language translation.
② In (1), the teacher directs the student's attention to the use of the word in various contexts.
③ In (2), the teacher switches the student's attention from the word to the use of word parts knowledge.
④ In (2), the teacher leads the student to incidental learning of the word.
⑤ In (2), the teacher provides the student with word family and collocation information of the word.

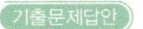 ⑤

13. Read the passage and follow the directions.

2005년 서울 4번

> With rank beginners, it is probably necessary to explicitly teach all words until students have enough vocabulary to start making use of the unknown words they meet in context. But beyond this most basic level, incidental learning should be structured into the program in a principled way. Taking an incremental view of vocabulary acquisition, such elaboration and consolidation are both crucial. Explicit approaches to vocabulary learning, whether teacher-led in a classroom or through self-study, can only provide some elements of lexical knowledge. Even lexical information amenable to conscious study, such as meaning, cannot be totally mastered by explicit study, because it is impossible to present and practice all of the creative uses of a word such as collocation and register constraints that a student might come across.

Identify an approach of vocabulary teaching according to learners' different proficiency levels and explain the rationales why the approach is more appropriate for the level with evidence.

모범답안 Beginner students need to learn vocabulary in explicit approach. But, as they become more proficient in language, incidental learning should be implemented. First, the words learned in different contexts leads to long-term memory. Second, some word knowledge such as collocation and register constraints can only be fully comprehended through sufficient exposure. (51 words)

14 Read the following passage and follow the directions.

2002년 서울 9번

⟨A⟩

(1) For many of us, our perspective on teaching vocabulary was greatly influenced by the top-down, naturalistic, and communicative approaches of the 1970s and 1980s. The emphasis was implicit, incidental learning of vocabulary. We were taught the importance of directing L2 students to recognize clues in context, to use monolingual dictionaries, and to avoid defining words or glossing text with their bilingual equivalents.

(2) Some research points to the ineffectiveness of using implicit vocabulary instruction and the need for a much stronger word level or bottom-up approach than had been previously advocated. It argues that explicit vocabulary instruction has an effect on students' overall interest and motivation in learning words, which may in turn explain how students receiving explicit instruction have improved comprehension of texts.

⟨B⟩

a. dictionary work
b. word unit analysis
c. listen and read the story
d. semantic mapping
e. find clues in the context

Choose any or all the activities in ⟨B⟩ for each vocabulary learning in ⟨A⟩.

모범답안 　(1) c, e　(2) a, b, d

15 Read the texts and follow the directions.

2008년 전국 13번

The classroom conversation below is an example of procedural vocabulary at work. The declarative knowledge or meaning being asserted is 'anesthetic'. The procedural words used to break this down include 'put', 'someone', 'make', 'them', and so on.

Teacher: And some drugs can also be used as anesthetics, like…
Student: What is anesthetic?
Teacher: Oh er… when you put someone to sleep, you make them go to sleep before an operation.
Student: Sleep?
Teacher: Yes, you anesthetize them… you give them a drug or anesthetic that makes them sleep… so they have no pain… you make them sleepy.

This classroom exchange illustrates the process whereby the student begins to develop or confirm hypotheses about the verb valency or the grammatical dependencies between the verb and its frame, animate subject and object NPs, as well as about the derivational link between the noun-form and the verb-form of anesthetize. In addition, the acquisition of the meaning of the word anesthetic is negotiated through the use of ①_____ vocabulary. Therefore, students need to be taught how to use ②_____ vocabulary in order to effectively learn the ③_____ vocabulary. Communicative competence includes not only the idealized ④_____ knowledge we have of word meaning, but the ⑤_____ knowledge we draw on in converting that knowledge to performance.

Complete the passage by writing down with either *procedural* or *declarative* for each blank.

모범답안   ① procedural ② procedural ③ declarative ④ declarative ⑤ procedural

16 Read the below and follow the directions.

2004년 서울 2번

Multimedia software is the term used for computer programs that combine multiple types of media. Multimedia refers to the integration of text, graphics, animation, sound, video, and music, all under the computer's control. Multimedia software is a relatively new concept that can be integrated into the language curriculum. It demands active participation and provides the opportunity for users to manipulate media, expressing themselves through graphics, animation, sound, video, and music. There is lots of multimedia software available as CD-ROM titles that teachers can use in the foreign language classroom. Besides this, some teachers download authentic language materials available free of charge from web sites. Others use computer-mediated communication tools to enhance students' listening and speaking skills. Because students in grade school are so familiar with multimedia, multimedia programs are believed to inspire motivation and access creative thoughts that paper and pencil can not. This is one of the reasons why teachers need to be well informed about the use of multimedia in the classroom as a learning tool. They need to be prepared to make educated decisions about the learning tools that new technologies provide.

Explain how you would use each of the THREE multimedia tools mentioned in the passage to motivate students.

모범답안   ① CD-ROM: It provides the opportunity to use the various media to make class learning more active.
② Web sites: Authentic materials are available to get information regardless of time and place.
③ Computer-mediated communication tools: Students are familiar with the tools and easy to access.

17 The following is a teacher's lesson plan based on CALL (Computer Assisted Language Learning).

2002년 전국 13번

Kids Make the News

Goal: Writing and publishing for an audience
Time: 1 hour (15 minutes on the Net)
Site: http://www.kidnews.com/news.html
Notes: This site publishes writing by kids from around the world. Note that not everything sent to Kid News will be published, so it's important to point this out and make alternative arrangements for a display of the work done—perhaps as a poster in the classroom.

Preparation:
- Find five or six easy stories from the Kid News site.
- Organize a walk-around comprehension activity with questions stuck on the walls and articles spread around the class.
- Students have to find the questions on the walls and then walk around trying to find which article they refer to, and then answer them.

Online:
- Give students a chance to look around the site and see for themselves what kind of stories are there and how they are presented.

Offline:
- Brainstorm some interesting events that have happened locally, then divide the class into groups and assign one event to each group.
- Give plenty of time for students to prepare their stories before sending them off to the website.

When the class is being implemented as above, describe the positive effects of CALL in terms of the following FOUR aspects, *materials*, *approach*, *learners*, and *writing*.

모범답안

① Materials: CALL materials provide various authentic contexts.
② Approach: Project work in task-based instruction stimulates students' active interaction and integrated teaching.
③ Learners: Learners are intrinsically motivated to become self-determined and autonomous to complete the project.
④ Writing: Process-writing within real contexts occurs in the classroom.

PART 02

해설편

CHAPTER 01   2언어습득 및 학습이론
CHAPTER 02   영어교재론 및 교육과정
CHAPTER 03   영어평가
CHAPTER 04   영어교수법
CHAPTER 05   문화 지도
CHAPTER 06   이해 능력 지도
CHAPTER 07   표현 능력 지도
CHAPTER 08   문법 지도
CHAPTER 09   어휘 지도

CHAPTER 01 2언어습득 및 학습이론

01

핵심 개념정리

Salience in Language Learning

Salience, in the context of language learning, refers to the prominence or noticeable aspects of language features. When it comes to vocabulary in EFL (English as a Foreign Language) contexts, salience plays a significant role in learning. Here are some effects:

(1) **Retention and Recall**: Salient vocabulary tends to be more memorable. Words that stand out due to their frequency, relevance, or connection to personal experiences are easier to remember and recall. Learners are more likely to retain salient vocabulary over time.

(2) **Motivation and Engagement**: Salient vocabulary items can enhance motivation and engagement in learning. When learners encounter words that are relevant to their interests, needs, or immediate use, it can stimulate their interest in the language, making learning more engaging.

(3) **Contextual Learning**: Salient vocabulary often emerges in meaningful contexts, aiding comprehension and understanding. When words are presented in context, especially in situations that are relevant or intriguing to learners, it helps them understand the usage and meaning more effectively.

(4) **Prioritization in Learning**: Salient words are often prioritized in language teaching materials or lessons. Teachers tend to highlight and emphasize words that are crucial for communication or frequently used in various contexts, ensuring learners focus on important vocabulary.

(5) **Natural Acquisition**: Salient vocabulary may align with what learners are naturally exposed to in authentic language use. Words that appear frequently in texts, media, or daily conversations become salient due to their regular occurrence, aiding in natural language acquisition.

In essence, salience in vocabulary learning can positively impact learners by improving retention, motivation, comprehension, and overall engagement with the language.

02

> 핵심 ELT 읽기

학습자 언어 발달 단계

(1) **Presystematic stage**

- The stage of random errors : when the learner is unaware of the existence of a particular rule in the target language. These are random.

- "The different city is another one in the another two." Inconsistencies like "John cans sing," "John can to sing," and "John can singing," all said by the same learner within a short period of time, might indicate a stage of experimentation and inaccurate guessing.

(2) **The emergent stage of learner language**

- Backsliding (U-shaped learning): This phenomenon of moving from a correct form to an incorrect form and then back to correctness: The learner seems to have grasped a rule or principle and then regresses to some previous stage.

- The learner is still unable to correct errors when they are pointed out by someone else. Avoidance of structures and topics is typical.

- The learner has begun to discern a system and to internalize certain rules. These rules are legitimate in the mind of the learner, although they may not be correct by target language standards.

(3) **The systematic stage**

- The learner is now able to manifest more consistency in producing the second language.

- The most salient difference between the second and third stage is the ability of leaners to correct their errors when they are pointed out - even very subtly to them.

(4) **The stabilization (postsystematic) stage**

- The learner has relatively few errors and has mastered the system to the point that fluency and intended meanings are not problematic.

- Fossilization: At this point learners can stabilize too fast, allowing minor errors to slip by undetected, and thus manifest fossilization of their language.

- Self-correct: The system is complete enough that attention can be paid to those few errors that occur and corrections be made without waiting for feedback from someone else.

03-06

오류의 원인과 유형

1. Sources of Error

1) **Overgeneralization** is a process common in both first and second language learning, in which a learner **extends the use of a grammatical rule** of linguistic item beyond its accepted uses, generally by making words or structures follow a more regular pattern. For example, a child may use 'ball' to refer to all round objects, or use 'mans' instead of 'men' for the plural of man.

2) Language **interference** is most often discussed as a source of errors known as negative transfer. Negative transfer occurs when speakers and writers transfer items and structures that are not the same in both languages. Within the theory of contrastive analysis (the systematic study of a pair of languages with a view to identifying their structural differences and similarities), the greater the differences between the two languages, the more negative transfer can be expected. The results of positive transfer go largely unnoticed, and thus are less often discussed. Nonetheless, such results can have a large effect. Generally speaking, the more similar the two languages, are the more the learner is aware of the relation between them, the more positive transfer will occur.

2. Types of Errors

1) **Global error** is an error in the use of a major element of sentence structure, which makes a sentence or utterance difficult or impossible to understand. For example, *I like take taxi but my friend said so not that we should be late for school. This may be contrasted with a local error, which is an error in the use of an element of sentence structure, but which does not cause problems of comprehension. For example, * If I heard from him I will let you to know.

2) Attitudes to error correction vary not only among teachers but also among students. A teacher may be influenced by:
  - The fact that English is their second language and great emphasis was placed on correctness at their teacher training college.
  - The fact that as a native speaker they have never had to worry about their English.
  - A particular approach. In the 1960s a teacher using Audiolingualism would have adopted a behaviorist approach to error. More recently a teacher following the Natural Approach (influenced by second language acquisition theory) would have adopted a wholly different approach. Other approaches, such as Suggestopedia and Total Physical Response, highlight the psychological effects of error correction on students.

As for students, we not only have to consider their age but also their approach to learning. Some students are risk-takers, while others will only say something if they are sure it is correct. While being a risk-taker is generally positive as it leads to greater fluency, some students only seem to be concerned with fluency at the expense of accuracy. The same can be true when it comes to writing. Some students take an eternity to produce a piece of writing as they are constantly rubbing out what they have written while at the opposite extreme the writing is done as fast as possible without any planning or editing.

07

핵심 개념정리

Learners' Interlanguage

Early L2 learners often produce utterances that deviate from the norms of the target language:

1. Mismatched Lexical Class	• This deviation occurs when a learner uses a word from the wrong lexical class (e.g., using a noun instead of a verb, or an adjective instead of an adverb). • (WHY) Learners may confuse word forms or not fully understand how different lexical classes function. Learners directly translate from their native language, where the lexical class might differ.	• "She is very talent." (Instead of the adjective "talented") • "He is a bored person." (Instead of the adjective "boring")
2. Semantic Deviation	• Semantic deviation happens when the meaning of the utterance is ill-formed or does not make sense within the context. • (WHY) Learners might misinterpret word meanings or confuse similar-sounding words. They might lack contextual knowledge or collocational awareness.	• "The cat baked the cake." (Semantically odd because cats don't bake) • "I need to eat medicine." (Illogical use of "eat" with "medicine")
3. Number of Arguments	• This deviation occurs when the number of arguments (subjects, objects, complements) required by the verb is incorrect—either too many or too few. • (WHY) Learners may overgeneralize patterns or misunderstand verb valency (how many arguments a verb takes). Cross-linguistic interference may also cause argument mismatch.	• "She gave to me." (Missing the direct object.) • "He explained me the problem." ("Explain" does not take an indirect object.)

4. Word Order	• This deviation occurs when learners violate the typical word order of the target language (e.g., subject-verb-object in English). • (WHY) Learners might transfer word order rules from their native language (e.g., SOV structure from Korean to English).	• "Beautiful is the sky." (Instead of "The sky is beautiful.") • "I to the store went." (Instead of "I went to the store.")

08

핵심 개념정리

의미형상 과정(Trigger - Signal - Response - Reaction)

According to Doughty, the essential feature of the **negotiation sequence** is the opportunity that is provided to the learner to process utterances in the L2 which become more comprehensible. Her negotiation model incorporates a **trigger, a signal, a response, and a reaction**. A **trigger** is an utterance or part of an utterance that is not understood. A **signal** is used by the interlocutor to express a lack of comprehension. A **response** then comes from the first speaker trying to repair the problem. A **reaction** is an extension or a response to the repair. This model is similar to the one employed by Gass and Varonis (1985), although they use the term **"indicator"** instead of **"signal."** Gass and Varonis also included two types of responses: direct (often wh-questions) and indirect (repetition, use of intonation). Direct and indirect responses are considered without further differentiation since both are part of the **negotiation process**.

(1) 협상 절차

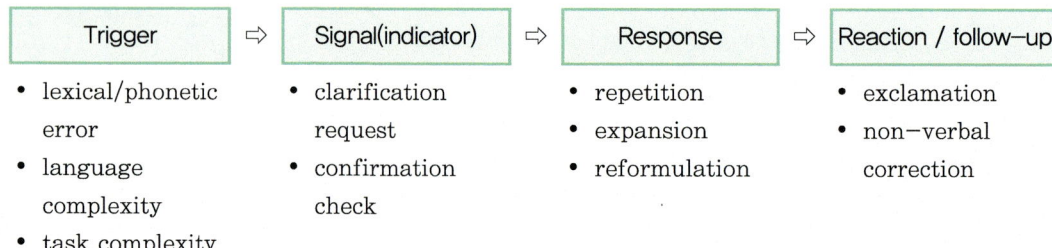

- Trigger
  - lexical/phonetic error
  - language complexity
  - task complexity
- Signal(indicator)
  - clarification request
  - confirmation check
- Response
  - repetition
  - expansion
  - reformulation
- Reaction / follow-up
  - exclamation
  - non-verbal correction

(2) 협상을 통한 교수-학습원리

① Use of L2 in interaction: L2 acquisition
② Negotiation of meaning: vocabulary acquisition
③ Negotiation of vocabulary meaning: **deeper understanding** of meaning & use of new vocabulary in new contexts
④ Meaningful output: necessary to language learning as **meaningful input**

09

문항 해설

제시된 대화문을 보면 의사소통과정에 있어서 상호작용의 중요성이 의미협상(meaning negotiation) 개념으로 설명될 수 있다. 'high marks'라는 학습자에게 익숙하지 않은 표현을 알아듣지 못하여 발생하는 의사소통 문제가 발생의 유발자(trigger)가 된다. "High marks?"라고 질문함으로써 자신이 의사소통에 있어서 어려움을 겪고 있다는 신호(signal)를 보낸다. 해결책으로 문제가 되는 표현에 대해 상대방이 설명해 주면서 응답(response)를 하고, 이해 가능한 입력으로 수정된 상호작용구조는 외국어 학습자에게 새로운 표현을 이해하여 다음 대화로 나아갈 수 있도록 도와주고 있다.

10

문항 해설

교사와 학생의 대화를 통해 어떠한 형식의 피드백과 상호작용이 일어나고 있는가를 파악해야 한다. 첫 부분의 대화에서 교사는 학생에게 명시적 오류수정을 주는 대신에 의미적으로 계속적인 의사소통을 시행하고 있다. 학생의 오류 'it rain~'이나 '~I wet'에 대해 문법적 피드백을 주지 않고 내용의 확장을 통한 대화를 계속 이어나간다. 하지만 중간부분에서 학생이 'mosquitoes …eat me'라고 했을 때 'bite me'라고 두 번 반복하면서 오류수정을 시도하고 학생은 그를 받아들여 수정된 출력(modified output)을 하고 있다. 교사는 학생들과 의미있는 대화를 위해 답이 정해져있지 않은 referential 질문을 실시하고 있다. 학생이 교사의 오류수정에 'bite me'라고 응답하는 uptake가 일어나고 있다. 이러한 학생들의 완성되지 않은 발화들인 중간언어(interlanguage)는 교실에 있는 모든 다른 학생들에게 노출된다고 말할 수 있다.

11-12

문항 해설

2언어를 배우는 중간언어(interlanguage) 체계 안에서 나타나는 언어의 오류를 설명하고 있다. 이 단계들이 체계적으로 일어나고 있으며 내적으로 문법이 발달되는 과정을 외부적으로 보이는 것을 설명해주고 있다. 이러한 습득단계는 모국어 어린이 학습자에게도 공통적으로 나타난다는 데 의의가 있다.

핵심 개념정리

부정어(negation) 습득 단계

- Stage 1: The negative element is typically placed before the verb or the element being negated: *No bicycle. *No have any sand. *I not like it.

- Stage 2: At this stage, 'no' and 'not' are alternated with 'don't'. however, 'don't' is not marked for person, number, or tense and it may even be used before modals like 'can' and 'should': *He don't like it. *I don't can sing.

- Stage 3: Learners begin to place the negative element after auxiliary verbs like 'are', 'is', and 'can'. But at this stage, the 'don't' form is still not fully analysed: You can't go there. *He can't eat nothing. *She don't like rice.

- Stage 4: 'Do' performs its full function as a marker of tense and person: It doesn't work. We didn't have supper. For some time, however, learners may continue to mark tense on both the auxiliary and the verb: *I didn't went there. *She doesn't wants to go.Stage 1: The negative element is typically placed before the verb or the element being negated: *No bicycle. *No have any sand. *I not like it.

13-14

핵심 ELT 읽기

의미 협상을 위한 전략

1. Negotiation of Meaning strategies training

In the study, participants were divided into three groups of English proficiency levels; high, mid, and low. They received an explicit training of negotiation of meaning strategies at the pre-teaching and while-teaching stages. At the initial period, they were introduced about the strategies, and at the beginning of each two-way communication task, they were reminded of the strategies uses. The five types of negotiation of meaning strategies as described by Long (1980, 1983a) and Pica and Doughty (1985a) were the basis of the study; they were **comprehension check, confirmation check, clarification requests**, appealing for help, and repetition.

(1) **Comprehension check**: These are made by the speaker to check if the preceding utterance has been correctly understood by the listener. They usually consist of questions, either tag questions, repetition with rising intonation, or questions or any expression established whether the message is understood by the addressee: (eg) Do you understand?/ You know what I mean?/ Do you get it?

(2) **Confirmation checks**: These are made by the listener to establish that the preceding utterance has been heard and understood correctly. They include repetition accompanied by rising intonation any expression that the speaker would like to make sure that it is understood: (eg) A: I was chuffled./ B: You were pleased? A: Yes.

(3) **Clarification requests**: These are made by the listener to clarify what the speaker has said and include statements: (eg) "I don't understand," wh-questions, yes/ no questions, and tag questions or any expressions that elicits clarification of the utterance (eg) What?/ Huh?/ Uh?

(4) **Appealing for help**: Any expression that shows that the speaker has trouble: (eg) Could you say it again?/ Pardon me?

(5) **Repetition**: These include the speaker's partial, exact, or expanded repetitions of lexical items from his or her own preceding utterances.

2. Two-way Communication Tasks

Brumfit (Hedge 1993) defines the aim of communication in the classroom as to develop a pattern of language interaction within the classroom which is as close as possible to that used by competent performers in the mother tongue in normal life. In his discussion, Brumfit (Ellis 1997) claimed that communication tasks will help develop learners' communication skills and they will contribute **incidentally** to their linguistic development. Communication tasks aid **fluency** by enabling learners to activate their linguistic knowledge for use in natural and spontaneous language use, such as when taking part in conversation. Therefore, communication tasks in the classroom can create opportunities for the language learners to use target language and develop their linguistic competence, especially two-way **communication tasks**.

Two-way tasks were claimed to be facilitative in triggering the production of strategies for **meaning negotiation**. According to Doughty and Pica (1986), a two-way task, a task in which both participants have shared information in order to complete a task, encourages the speakers to produce more **negotiation of meaning**. Additionally, two-way tasks provide an opportunity not only to produce the target language, but also through conversational adjustments, to manipulate and modify it (Gass & Varonis 1985). The two-way communication tasks in this study comprised of **problem-solving tasks**, **information gap task** and **storytelling task**.

M1: Ok, Fon. What's the matter on you?

H2: I really want to study abroad, but my parents they don't support me.

M1: **Really? Why?** → Confirmation check strategy

H2: Umm..my parents don't want me to stay far from home. They would like me to study here, but I don't like it. I want to be independent.
Do you understand me? → Comprehension check strategy

M2: Yes, I understand. I ever been through this problem before. **Did you try to tell your parents what is the best?** → Modification of the use of past simple tense

(1) Problem-solving task

Problem-solving task is considered as a **two-way** task in the study. As defined by Willis (1996), problem-solving tasks involve a more intellectual and analytical skill from learners. In addition, a two-way problem-solving task is designed to encourage co-operation and **conversational negotiation**. In this study, there were three problem-solving tasks where participants were presented with real-life problems and have to discuss to agree to a solution. For example, participants discussed their personal problems to find solutions, or giving them a situation in which they exchanged their opinions or make a decision. As in the interaction between **low-proficiency** level student and **high-proficiency** level student in a problem-solving task showed the awareness of the mismatch between incorrect and correct tense of the low-proficiency level student.

(2) Information gap task

Information gap is a task that involves **conveying or requesting information** from the pair or group members. There are two important characteristics in information gap task. One is that the focus is on the **information** and not on language forms. Two is that it requires communicative interaction to reach the goal. The information gap task was widely used among researchers in interaction and claimed to contribute to interaction research methodology. This task has been found to generate more opportunities for the interactants to negotiate than do tasks that do not require a **convergent outcome**, such as opinion exchange and free conversation. In this study, there were three information gap tasks in which the participants were required to restore portions of incomplete passages, or they were given a person's picture and they had to describe the person as well as asking for information of their friend's picture.

(3) Story-telling Task

The story-telling task is considered as **two-way task** which provides rich possibilities for students to learn from one another and share **experiences** while receiving important practice in using their English skills (Ko et al., 2003). During the task, the students were required to tell a 4-5 minute personal narrative about an embarrassing, exciting, sad or funny event that had ever happened to them, then the students told their stories to their peers.

15

문항 해설

학습자의 오류가 있는 발화에 대해 교사는 다른 종류의 피드백으로 응답하고 있다. [1] 박교사는 학생의 오류발화에 대하여 '~ for your brother'로 수정하여 긍정적 증거(positive evidence)를 주는 암시적 피드백인 recast방법을 이용하고 있다. 의사소통을 위한 대화가 단절되지 않으므로 교사는 언어적 부분을 해결하려고 하기 보다는 의미적으로 대화를 계속 유지하고 있다. 하지만 학생은 recast를 받고도 수정을 하지 못하므로 수정이 필요한 이해(uptake with needs repair)가 일어났다고 할 수 있다. [2] 이교사는 'Pardon... whose book?'이라는 명확도를 위한 요청(clarification request) 피드백을 이용하여 학생의 출력을 시도하고 있다. 교사는 학생의 현재 발화에서 한 단계 발전할 수 있도록 학생의 ZPD안에서 도움을 주고 있다. 학생은 교사의 피드백을 받고 스스로 수정(self-repair)을 하여 'He lost my book'이라고 말하므로 수정을 한 이해(uptake with repair)를 보여준다.

16

문항 해설

〈대화 1〉은 교사가 학생의 잘못된 발화에 대하여 'I'm not sure what you're saying there.'라고 응답하는 상위언어(metalinguistic) 피드백으로 학생과의 의미협상을 시도한다. 그 후에 학생이 교사와의 의미협상을 통해 자신의 발화를 목표 발화의 형태로 수정하고 조정할 수 있도록 하는데 초점을 두고 있다. 〈대화 2〉에서는 교사가 먼저 학생에게 이해 가능한 발화인 긍정적 증거(positive evidence)를 제공하면서 학생이 새로운 입력을 받아들일 수 있도록 하고, 학생과 교사의 상호작용적인 대화를 통해 학생의 이해도를 최대화하도록 한다.

핵심 개념정리

의미 협상

(1) Negotiation: What speakers do in order to achieve **successful communication** in conversational analysis: For conversation to progress naturally and for speakers to be able to understand each other it may be necessary for them to:
   - indicate that they understand or that they want the conversation to continue
   - help each other to express **ideas**
   - make corrections when necessary to what is said or how it is said

(2) Interaction Hypothesis: The hypothesis that language acquisition requires or greatly benefits from interaction, communication and especially negotiation of meaning: When interlocutors attempt to overcome problems in **conveying their meaning**, it results in both additional input and useful **feedback** on the learner's own production.

(3) Modified speech: A term used by linguists to describe speech which is deliberately changed in an attempt to make it sound more educated or refined: The change is usually temporary and the speaker lapses back to his or her normal speech pattern.

(4) Comprehensible input: The idea that exposure to comprehensible input which contains structures that are slightly in **advance of a learner's current level** of competence is the necessary and sufficient cause of second language acquisition.

17 – 18

문항 해설

학습자의 언어발달, 곧 내재화(internalization)를 위한 최상의 상태는 근접발달영역(zone of proximal development)으로서 학습의 필수 성분이다; 학습은 자신의 환경에 속해 있는 사람들이나 또래들과 협력하여 상호작용할 때에만 나타날 수 있는 다양한 내적발달과정(internal developmental processes)들을 일으킨다. 이 단계들이 내면화 되면 발달적 성과의 일부가 된다. ZPD 영역 내에서 개념화시키는 한 방법으로 규칙 단계, 즉 지적 행동에 대한 통제가 있다. 상호 심리적 활동에서 내부 심리적 활동으로 넘어가면서 학습자는 타인규제(other-regulation)로부터 자기규제(self-regulation)로 이동된다고 알려져 있다. 타인 규제를 받을 때 학습자는 타인의 도움을 받으며 학업 수행을 할 수 있다. ZPD는 상호작용절차 과정에서 학습자가 외부 영향들을 조절할 수 있고 자주적 문제 해결 능력을 갖추었을 때, 자기규제에 도달하게 된다. 타인규제가 없거나 그것에 반응하지 않을 때 학습자는 타인규제단계에 있을 것이며, 이 단계에서 학습자는 주위 환경에 있는 사물들에 의해 쉽게 규제 받는다. ZPD 영역 내의 도움은 타인 규제가 지속되는 한 계속 제공되지만 학습자가 자주적 기능이 가능할 때에야 비로소 없어진다는 이유에서 scaffolding의 형태로 비유 표현되어 왔다. 전통적으로, scaffolding의 개념은 전문인이 초보 학습자가 더 높은 규제 단계에 도달할 수 있게 도와주는 지지 행동을 뜻해 왔다.

> **핵심 ELT 읽기**

언어 지도에서의 근접발달지대(Zone of Proximal Development & Scaffolding)

An important aspect of sociocultural theory is the notion of mediated learning. Essentially this suggests that learning relies on the transmitted experiences of others. Initially, learners depend on others with more experience than themselves and gradually take on more responsibility for their own learning in joint activity. This is sometimes described as a process of guided participation as learning is mediated through the guidance of a more knowledgeable other. Through repeated participation in a variety of joint activities the novice gradually develops new knowledge and skills. The process involved is often referred to as scaffolding.

Scaffolding refers to learning that results from two or more people interacting during the process of completing a classroom activity or during any setting where language is being used, and where one person (e.g. the teacher or another learner) has more advanced knowledge than the other (the learner). During the process, **discourse** is jointly created through assisted or mediated performance. For example in a classroom setting the teacher assists the learners in completing learning activities by observing what they are capable of, providing a series of guided stages through the task, and through **collaborative dialogue**, scaffolding the learning process by initially providing support (the "scaffold") and gradually removing support as learning develops. Learning is initially mediated and directed by the teacher or other more advanced learners and is gradually **appropriated** by the individual learner. Throughout, the teacher provides opportunities for **noticing** how language is used, **experimenting** with language use, practicing new modes of discourse and **restructuring** existing language knowledge – essential aspects of teaching.

Central to learning from this perspective is the **zone of proximal development**, which focuses on the **gap** between what the learner can currently do and the next stage in learning – the level of **potential development** – and how learning occurs through negotiation between the learner and a more advanced language user during which a process of scaffolding occurs. To take part in these processes the learner must develop **interactional competence**, the ability to manage exchanges despite limited language development. Personality, motivation, cognitive style may all play a role in influencing the learners willingness to take risks, his or her openness to social interaction and attitudes towards the target language and users of the target language.

Language learning is facilitated by interactions like the ones above in which the interaction proceeds as a kind of **joint problem-solving** between teacher and student.

During the process the teacher assists the learner in using more complex language through a type of assisted performance, and this is central to how many aspects of language use can be learned. The kind of discourse or talk that occurs in language classrooms also reflects both the pedagogical strategies the teacher employs (e.g. in trying to facilitate negotiation of meaning, interaction and feedback, or to provide scaffolding for activities) as well as the kind of learning community that develops in the classroom.

19

> 핵심 개념정리

언어학습에서 MBTI의 중요성

The Myers-Briggs Type Indicator (MBTI) is a popular personality assessment tool used to categorize individuals into one of 16 personality types based on their preferences in four dichotomous dimensions: **extraversion/ introversion, sensing/ intuition, thinking/ feeling, and judging/ perceiving**. While MBTI is not specifically designed for language learning, understanding one's personality type can have some relevance in second language learning contexts for the following reasons:

① Learning Style Awareness: MBTI can provide insights into individuals' preferred learning styles, such as whether they prefer structured or flexible learning environments, group collaboration or independent study, and hands-on experiences or theoretical explanations. By understanding their own learning preferences, language learners can tailor their learning strategies to better suit their needs, making the language learning process more effective and enjoyable.

② Communication and Interaction: MBTI can help language learners understand their communication preferences and tendencies. For example, extraverted learners may prefer interactive language learning activities that involve social interaction and group discussions, while introverted learners may feel more comfortable with solitary activities such as reading or writing. By recognizing these preferences, language learners can choose communication strategies and language learning activities that align with their personality type, leading to more productive and satisfying language learning experiences.

③ Interpersonal Dynamics: In language learning contexts that involve group work or collaborative activities, understanding the MBTI preferences of fellow learners can facilitate better interpersonal communication and collaboration. Learners with different personality types may have varying communication styles, decision-making approaches, and conflict resolution strategies. By recognizing and respecting these differences, language learners can navigate interpersonal dynamics effectively and foster positive relationships with language partners.

④ Self-awareness and Growth: Engaging with MBTI can promote self-awareness and personal growth, which are essential components of successful language learning. By reflecting on their personality type and associated strengths, weaknesses, preferences, and tendencies, language learners can identify areas for improvement and develop strategies to overcome challenges. Additionally, understanding how their personality type influences their language learning process can empower learners to take ownership of their learning journey and make informed decisions about their language learning goals, priorities, and strategies.

While MBTI can offer valuable insights into individuals' personality preferences and learning styles, it's important to recognize that personality is complex and multifaceted, and individuals may exhibit a range of behaviors and preferences that extend beyond their MBTI type. Therefore, while MBTI can be a useful tool for self-reflection and self-awareness in language learning, it should be used in conjunction with other factors and considerations to create a holistic and personalized approach to language learning.

20

핵심 개념정리

7가지 학습 스타일: ESL 지도 전략

When we think about lesson planning, the saying, "It's not what you do, it's how you do it" rings especially true. I like to tell teachers and educators, "It's not the lessons you planned, it's how you planned your lessons." You may have created a brilliant lesson plan on paper, but if you don't have a strategy to actually carry it out in the classroom, you are heading for some bumpy rides and unpleasant surprises! Thankfully, a solid ESL teaching strategy remedies all that by giving you a map and a compass to navigate your ESL classroom.

The students you interact with have **different personalities, learning styles** and **preferences**. A great ESL teaching strategy is one that integrates a variety of methods and techniques — appealing to this diversity of students — while allowing you to maintain relative flexibility to adapt to various classroom situations. Students are humans, too. They differ from each other in their preferences. When it comes to learning a new language, each student receives, processes and stores information differently. Some students may thrive using traditional papers and pencils, while others prefer collaboration and even hands-on activities. If their ideal learning styles are not recognized in the classroom, studying becomes drudgery — and students who have a hard time tend to lose their motivation.

Luckily, reaching out to different students isn't guesswork for ESL teachers anymore. Differences in student preferences have been loosely categorized into 7 major **learning styles**. The categories are defined broadly, and it's not uncommon to find students that fit into more than one. Sure, you may have an oddball who doesn't seem to fit into any group — but by appealing to these major learning styles and shaking up your classroom routine, you will be well on your way to reaching more students than ever before. We have included a comprehensive description of the seven learning styles below. Recommended classroom activities and teaching strategies are also included as a bonus to help you to be a better, strategic ESL teacher!

1. Visual (spatial)

Pictures, images and spatial understanding are the preferred learning media of **visual** learners. These learners love to see lessons come to life, and often sit at the front of the class to not only get a full view of their teacher's body language and facial expressions, but also to avoid potential visual obstructions and distractions. Visual learners are your detailed note takers. They think in **pictures** and learn best from visual displays, slide shows, posters, clips and other visual tools. Sometimes, simple things like writing an **outline** of your grammar lesson on the board will also satisfy your visual learners' desire to take notes and capture everything in their own creative and vivid manners.

2. Aural (auditory-musical)

Auditory learners rely primarily on **music and sound** for their learning. Information is often best acquired through verbal lectures, discussions and mini-presentations. Auditory learners interpret the underlying meanings of words through listening to the **tone, pitch, speed and other phonological nuances** of your speech. Because written information may have little meaning to these students, auditory learners **enjoy reading text aloud** and may even bring a tape recorder to record your lecture. While your auditory learners are perfectly content with you giving a 60-minute lecture, strategically integrating audio books, songs and movies into your lesson will stimulate their brain and wake up your non-auditory learners.

3. Verbal (linguistic)

These are students who learn best **through words** regardless of whether they are communicated in speech or writing. When learning something new, students who belong to this category prefer **hearing a detailed explanation** over viewing a physical, visual demonstration. Like the auditory learners, verbal learners thrive in a traditional classroom lecture. However, they are also very interpersonal and welcome opportunities to interact with words and sounds through **discussions, asking questions** and teaching others. In general, verbal learners make great teacher's helpers and thrive in group activities that involve lots of **interactions and words**.

4. Physical (kinesthetic)

Your hyperactive students may simply be your curious **kinesthetic** learners who prefer using their body, hands and sense of touch to **explore the world**. These students tend to have trouble sitting for long periods of time, but with the right strategy you may be able to enthrall these energizer bunnies. **Kinesthetic** students are easily distracted and are often the classroom culprit for distracting others. Instead of countering them with commands or harsh words, striking a healthy balance between quiet and **hands-on** activities will allow these active learners to touch, feel and experience the fullness of lessons. ESL games such as pantomime and charades are not only great for giving your **kinesthetic** learners an opportunity to redirect their energy, but also for re-invigorating your half-awake class.

5. Logical (mathematical)

These students prefer using **logic, reasoning** and **systems**. You may find them to have a keen sense for numbers, sequence association and problem solving. As a teacher, you can feed your logical students by including classroom activities that involve multi-step processes, data collection, and mysteries. You could break things like gender and verb conjugations into tables and charts. When relevant, create worksheets that incorporate geometry and money so your logical students can have a practical ESL experience.

6. Social (interpersonal)

Group learning streamlines the learning experience of **social/interpersonal** learners. They are quite verbal and are always anxious to apply what they have learned in interactive settings. Teacher gives social butterfly a chance to spread their wings and fly with meaningful activities and teach a lesson on **social** awareness, etiquette or cultural differences. Incorporating **peer editing, peer teaching** and **group discussions** into the curriculum will dramatically enrich the learning experience of these happy talkers.

7. Solitary (intrapersonal)

As the name suggests, these kind of students are your **quiet** angels who can work alone with minimal directions from the teacher. Oftentimes mistaken as the shy ones of the classroom, solitary learners can be quite extroverted when given the opportunity. The desire for **self-study** keep solitary learners away from active, voluntary classroom participation. In a group setting, your solitary learner may seem reserved, inactive or even indifferent. To engage your solitary learners and keep them from finishing an entire group project on his/her own, teachers are encouraged to have a more structured group activity that assigns distinctive tasks and roles to every individual of the group.

The **Myers-Briggs** Type indicator contributes four more dimensions to learning style: **extraversion vs. introversion, sensing vs. intuition, thinking vs. feeling,** and **judging vs. perceiving**. Several of these dimensions appear to significantly influence how students choose to learn languages, according to recent research. Other important style aspects that may relate to language learning performance are leveling-sharpening of detail, **reflectivity-impulsivity,** and **constricted-flexible** thinking. Additional research needs to be conducted on all style dimensions in order for teachers to understand more about the basic stylistic preferences of their students.

21-27

핵심 개념정리

(1) 의사소통 전략

전략 유형	설명
Circumlocution	Using different words or phrases to express their intended meaning: If learners do not know the word 'grandfather' they may paraphrase it by saying 'my father's father'.
Approximation	Using of a target language vocabulary item or structure, which the learner knows is not correct, but which shares semantic features with the desired item to satisfy the speaker: 'friends' for 'acquaintances'
Literal translation	Translating word for word from the native language: 'pig meat' for 'pork.'
Word coinage	Creating new words or phrases for words that they do not know; For example, 'picture place' for 'art gallery'
Language switch	Inserting a word from their L1 into a sentence, and hope that their interlocutor will understand
Appeal to authority	Asking an interlocutor for the correct word or looking up on the dictionary is a communication strategy.
Non-verbal strategies	Using gesture and mime to augment or replace verbal communication.
Avoidance	Avoidance, which takes multiple forms, has been identified as a communication strategy. Learners may learn to avoid talking about topics for which they lack the necessary vocabulary or other language skills in the second language. Learners sometimes start to try to talk about a topic, but abandon the effort in mid-utterance after discovering that they lack the language resources needed to complete their message.
(Semantic avoidance)	Learners may avoid a problematic word by using a different one, for example substituting the irregular verb make with the regular verb ask. The regularity of "ask" makes it easier to use correctly.

(2) 학습 전략 유형

1. Direct Strategies

1) Memory strategies
- Creating mental linkage: grouping, associating, elaborating
- Applying images and sounds: using imagery, semantic mapping
- Reviewing well: structured viewing
- Employing action: using mechanical techniques

2) **Cognitive strategies**
- Practicing: repeating, recombining, practicing naturalistically
- Receiving and sending messages
- Analyzing and reasoning
- Creating structure for input and output

3) **Compensatory strategies**
- Guessing intelligently
- Overcoming limitations in speaking and writing

2. Indirect strategies

1) **Meta-cognitive strategies**
- Centering your learning
- Arranging and planning your learning
- Evaluating your learning

2) **Affective strategies**
- Lowing your anxiety
- Encouraging yourself
- Taking your emotional temperature

3) **Social strategies**
- Asking questions
- Cooperating with others
- Empathizing with others

Three categories of learning strategies are **metacognitive** strategies, or the executive strategies that individuals use to plan for, monitor, or evaluate learning; **cognitive** strategies, or the manipulation of learning materials by reorganization, grouping, and elaboration of new ideas, or the relating of new ideas to prior knowledge; and **social-affective** strategies, by which the learner calls upon another person for assistance or works cooperatively with others on a common task. Selected learning strategies from Chamot and O'Malley (1992) are:

- Advance Preparation: Rehearsing the language needed for an oral or written task

- Organizational Planning: Planning the parts, sequence, and main ideas to be expressed orally or in writing

- Selective Attention: Attending to or scanning key words, phrases, linguistic markers, sentences, or types of information

- Resourcing: Using reference materials such as dictionaries, encyclopedias, or textbooks

- Deduction: Applying rules to understand or produce language or solve problems

- Elaboration: Relating new information to prior knowledge, relating different parts of new information to each other, or making meaningful personal associations to the new information

- Inferencing: Using information in the text to guess meanings of new items, predict outcomes, or complete missing parts

- Questioning for Clarification: Eliciting from a teacher or peer additional explanation, rephrasing, examples, or verification

- Cooperation: Working with peers to solve a problem, pool information, check a learning task, or get feedback on oral or written performance

28-31

핵심 ELT 읽기

2언어습득에서의 오류수정 피드백

1. Types of Corrective Feedback

(1) **Explicit correction:** Clearly indicating that the student's utterance was incorrect, the teacher provides the correct form.
S: (phonological error) … and the cr…crane
T: And the crane. We say crane.

(2) **Recasts:** Without directly indicating that the student's utterance was incorrect, the teacher implicitly reformulates the student's error, or provides the correction.
S: (grammatical error) Maple saps?
T: Yeah… we collect maple sap. Good.

(3) **Clarification requests:** By using phrases like "Excuse me?" or "I don't understand," the teacher indicates that the message has not been understood or that the student's utterance contained some kind of mistake and that a repetition or a reformulation is required.
S: Can, can I made a card? (multiple errors)
T: Pardon?
S: Can, can I made a card on the … for my little brother on the computer?

(4) **Metalinguistic clues:** Without providing the correct form, the teacher poses questions or provides comments or information related to the formation of the student's utterance (for example, "Do we say it like that?" "That's not how you say it in Korean.")
S: (multiple errors) Uhm, a, a elephant growls."
T: Do we say with an article?

(5) **Elicitation:** The teacher directly elicits the correct form from the student by asking questions (e.g., "How do we say that in Korean?"), by pausing to allow the student to complete the teacher's utterance (e.g., "It's a….") or by asking students to reformulate the utterance (e.g., "Say that again."). Elicitation questions differ from questions that are defined as metalinguistic clues in that they require more than a yes/no response.

(6) **Repetition:** The teacher repeats the student's error and adjusts intonation to draw

student's attention to it.

2. Terms of Corrective Feedback

There are various terms used in identifying errors and providing corrective feedback in the SLA literature, the most common being **corrective feedback, negative evidence,** and **negative feedback**. Because of possible confusion arising from the use of this terminology, a brief review of the definitions of terms and of the different types of feedback is presented below. Chaudron (1988) has pointed out the fact that the term corrective feedback incorporates different layers of meaning. In Chaudron's view, the term 'treatment of error' may simply refer to 'any teacher behavior following an error that minimally attempts to inform the learner of the fact of error' (p. 150). The treatment may not be evident to the student in terms of the response it elicits, or it may make a significant effort to elicit a revised student response. Finally, there is the true correction which succeeds in **modifying the learner's interlanguage** rule so that the error is eliminated from further production. Lightbown and Spada (1999) define corrective feedback as: Any indication to the learners that their use of the target language is incorrect. This includes various responses that the learners receive. When a language learner says, 'He go to school everyday', corrective feedback can be **explicit**, for example, 'no, you should say goes, not go' or **implicit** 'yes he goes to school every day', and may or may not include **metalinguistic information**, for example, 'Don't forget to make the verb agree with the subject'. (p. 171-172)

According to Schachter (1991), **corrective feedback, negative evidence,** and **negative feedback** are three terms used respectively in the fields of language teaching, language acquisition, and cognitive psychology. Different researchers often use these terms interchangeably. The feedback can be explicit (e.g., grammatical explanation or overt error correction) or implicit. Implicit correction includes, but is not limited to, **confirmation checks, repetitions, recasts, clarification requests, silence,** and even **facial expressions** that express confusion. Long (1996) offers a more comprehensive view of feedback in general. He suggests that environmental input can be thought of in terms of two categories that are provided to the learners about the target language (TL): positive evidence and negative evidence. Long defines positive evidence as providing the learners with models of what is grammatical and acceptable in the TL; and negative evidence as providing the learners with direct or indirect information about what is unacceptable. This information may be: Explicit (e.g., grammatical explanation or overt error correction) or implicit (e.g., failure to understand, incidental error correction in a response, such as a confirmation check, which reformulates the learners' utterance without interrupting the flow of the conversation, in which case, the negative feedback simultaneously provides additional positive evidence and perhaps also the absence of the items in the input. (p. 413)

Long (2001) more recently has offered the following framework incorporating the different types of positive and negative evidence in relation to the linguistic environment, i.e., input. According to the above classification, negative evidence and positive evidence constitute the only two types of evidence available to the language learner. Each type is further divided into subtypes. The frequency of occurrence in different second language

(L2) learning contexts as well as the differential effects of different types of negative evidence on interlanguage (IL) development will be discussed in the following sections of this literature review.

3. Theoretical Stances On The Role Of Corrective Feedback In SLA

The theoretical pendulum has swung back and forth regarding the role assigned to negative evidence in the process of SLA. There is a debate on the nature of the driving force behind SLA, i.e., whether it is **positive evidence** or **negative evidence** that has the greater impact. According to **nativist theory**, advocated by Chomsky (1975), negative evidence hardly plays any role at all. This is due to the fact that, for the nativists, what makes language acquisition possible is Universal Grammar (UG), the system of principles, conditions, and rules that are elements of properties of all human languages (p. 29). That is to say, in this view of language learning, what makes the acquisition of language possible is UG, and the innate linguistic mechanism that is available to all humans. UG advocates have argued that instruction, including negative evidence, has little impact on forms within UG anyway, since it will temporarily change only language behavior and not IL grammars (Carroll, 1996; Cook, 1991; Schwartz, 1993). In this view, changes in the IL grammar are the result of positive linguistic evidence. In addition, Krashen (1982, 1985) believes that SLA is the result of **implicit processes** operating together with the reception of **comprehensible input**. Conscious learning can only act as a monitor that edits the output, after it has been initiated by the acquired system. From this, then, it follows that explicit data, whether in the form of negative evidence or in the form of explicit instruction, can only affect the learning rather than the acquisition of the target language.

Krashen's input hypothesis posits that it is subconscious acquisition that gains dominance, and that learning cannot be converted into acquisition, even though adults can both subconsciously acquire languages and consciously learn about languages. In short, for Krashen, as for the nativists, negative evidence has a barely discernable effect on SLA. Krashen's views and theories of language learning have been challenged on the grounds that while comprehension is essential for language acquisition, such acquisition does not entail unconscious or implicit learning processes; and that noticing is indispensable for the acquisition process.

According to the **noticing** hypothesis, in order for input to become **intake** for L2 learning, some degree of noticing must occur, and that it is corrective feedback that triggers that learners' **noticing of gaps** between the target norms and their IL, and thus leads to subsequent grammatical restructuring. According to Schmidt (1990), subliminal language learning is impossible, and that **intake** is what learners consciously notice. This requirement of **noticing** is meant to apply equally to all aspects of language (p. 149). Language learners, however, are limited in what they are able to notice. The main determining factor is that of **attention**. As Schmidt (1994) points out, while the intention to learn is not always crucial to learning, **attention** to the material to be learned is (p. 176). **Attention**, in addition, also controls access to conscious experience (p. 176), thus allowing the acquisition of new items to take place. Gass (1988, 1990, 1991), moreover, has argued against the notion that learners, with the mere presentation of comprehensible input, would convert it to intake and subsequently to output. According to her, for learners to be able to **internalize input** in order to affect the acquisition process, they must not only comprehend this input, but also must notice the mismatch between the input and their own IL system. She points out that 'nothing in the target language is available for **intake** into a language learner's existing system unless it is consciously noticed' (1991, p. 136).

Corrective feedback, for Gass, functions as an **attention getting device**. She further argues that without direct or frequent corrective feedback in the input, which would permit learners to detect discrepancies between their learner language and the target language, fossilization might occur. Gass and Varonis (1994), moreover, point out that "the awareness of the mismatch serves the function of triggering a **modification** of existing L2 knowledge, the results of which may show up at a later point in time" (p. 299). Similarly, Ellis (1991) shares the view that the acquisition process includes the steps of noticing, comparing, and integrating. There is further evidence of the role of corrective feedback in the hypothesis testing models of acquisition. In these models, the learner is assumed to formulate hypotheses about the TL, and to test these hypotheses against the target norm. In this model of learning, corrective feedback, or negative data, plays a crucial role (Bley-Vroman, 1986, 1989).

Ohta (2001) takes corrective feedback a step further by showing that if the correct form is provided, learners may have the chance to compare their own production with that of another. In this way, corrective feedback may stimulate hypothesis testing, giving the learner the opportunity to grapple with form-meaning relationships. Corrective feedback that does not provide the correct form, on the other hand, may force the learners to utilize their own resources in constructing a reformulation. In either case, corrective feedback may facilitate L2 development. According to Chaudron (1988), the information available in feedback allows the learners to confirm, disconfirm, and possibly modify the hypothetical, transitional rules of their developing grammars. These effects, however, "depend on the learners' readiness for and attention to the information available in feedback. That is, learners must still make a comparison between their internal representation of a rule and the information about the rule in the input they encounter" (p. 134). Finally, Schachter (1991), with reference to the above views, points out that it is due to the **corrective feedback** the learners receive that they abandon their wrong hypotheses and immediately switch to formulating new ones. On the question of what kind of evidence can disconfirm incorrect hypotheses about the L2, White (1988) states that positive evidence alone is insufficient. Concerning whether or not L2 acquisition can progress on the basis of positive evidence alone, she further suggests that it cannot, and that "there will be cases where change from X to Y will require negative evidence" (p. 148). There are certain situations, she argues, which entail negative evidence, i.e., drawing learners' attention to the fact that certain forms are not allowed in the target language.

According to White (1988), **negative evidence** is particularly required when learners adopt grammars that generate a superset of the grammars actually allowed in the target language. In other words, negative evidence is necessary when the learners need to go from a broader grammar (superset) to a narrower grammar (subset). A case in point is that there is no positive evidence that highlights that English does not allow null subjects. Corrective feedback, in cases like the **ungrammaticality** of null subjects in English, she argues, will help put L2 learners on the right track. This brings us to the view of SLA as cognitive skill acquisition. In this view of learning, language acquisition includes interaction between input, the cognitive system, and the learner's perceptual motor system. According to this model of language learning, feedback is essential (Johnson, 1988, 1996). This is due to the fact that "it has the properties of informing, regulating, strengthening, sustaining, and error eliminating".

Given the considerable research on the role of corrective feedback in SLA from the various models of acquisition discussed in this review, it seems that there is a growing belief that interaction between innate and environmental factors is necessary for language acquisition. In this model, Long (1996) proposes that: Environmental contributions to acquisition are mediated by selective attention and the learner's developing L2 processing capacity, and that the resources are brought together most usefully, although not exclusively, during negotiation for meaning. Negative feedback obtained during negotiation work or elsewhere may be facilitated of SL development, at least for vocabulary, morphology, and language specific syntax and essential for learning certain specifiable L1-L2 contrasts. According to this model of acquisition, interaction that includes implicit corrective feedback is facilitative of L2 development. Interest in the impact that corrective feedback has on IL development, and in the roles of both teachers and students in corrective feedback episodes, has spawned a number of recent studies on the topic.

32

문항 해설

교사가 실시하고자 하는 교수법과 학생의 기대치와 학습스타일이 맞지 않아 생기는 어려움을 설명하고 있다. 교사는 입력을 극대화하고 또한 출력을 할 수 있는 장을 마련해 주면 상호작용적 활동이 높아지고 그에 따라 언어습득이 효과적으로 이루어질 것이므로 상호작용(interaction)이 2언어습득에 필수적이라고 믿고 있다. 반면에 학생은 교사의 너무나 강력한 English only정책에 있는 교실환경으로 인하여 긴장하고 걱정이 높아지므로 정의적 필터(affective filter)가 과도하게 높아짐을 알 수 있다. 그래서 학생의 정의적 필터가 높기 때문에 이해가능한 입력(comprehensible input)을 다 받아들이지 못할 수 있게 된다는 것이다. 학생은 활동을 하기 전에 언어적 지식을 활용할 준비시간을 필요로 한다. 교사가 도움(scaffolding)이나 피드백을 제공하지 않고 학생들이 스스로 문제해결을 하고 자기수정을 하도록 하고 있다. 교사가 언어형태(language form)를 가르치지 않는 것이 문제이므로 형태중심(form-focused) 교수법이 해결책이 될 수 있다.

33

문항 해설

　　진수는 외적보상(extrinsic reward)에 대한 기대없이 영어를 배우고, 영어를 사용하는 외국인들과 의사소통하고 함께 하고 싶어 하므로 내적이고 통합적 동기(intrinsically and integratively motivated)가 되어 있다고 할 수 있다.

　　헤리는 캐나다 교수의 문학 수업을 들으면서 때로는 모든 것을 다 이해하는 것은 아니지만 그것이 그녀를 괴롭히진 않는다고 하였으므로 애매모호함(ambiguity)에 대하여 높은 관용성(high tolerance)을 가지고 있다고 할 수 있다. 그러나, 그룹스터디모임을 할 때, 약간의 긴장감을 느끼지만 위험감수를 하려고 하기 때문에 이 걱정은 학습을 방해하는 부정적인 영향을 주는 걱정(debilitative anxiety)이 아니라 긍정적 걱정(facilitative anxiety)으로 작용했음을 알 수 있다.

　　미진은 사회적 지위에 도움을 줄 것이므로 영어를 학습한다고 하였으므로 외적으로 동기가 되어있다. 작은 그룹의 말하기 활동에 참여하는 것을 좋아한다고 하였으므로 높은 의사소통 참여성(willingness to communicate)을 가지고 있다고 볼 수 있다. 높은 수준의 과업들이 미진을 불안하게 하지만 이 긴장이 그것들을 잘 할 수 있도록 그녀를 격려한다고 하였으므로 이 걱정은 촉진제(facilitative)로 작용하였다. 영어로 된 무언가를 읽을 때 모르는 단어가 나오면 늘 사전을 찾아본다고 하였기 때문에 애매모호함에 대한 낮은 관용성(low tolerance of ambiguity)을 가졌다고 할 수 있다.

34-35

문항 해설

　　피드백의 형태를 묻는 질문이다. 위 교사의 피드백 형태를 보면 (a) 'Excuse me?'는 명확성요청 피드백으로서 앞의 화자의 말을 잘 못 알아들었거나 문제가 있을 때 쓸 수 있는 방법이 된다. (b) 'You saw a movie?'는 recast로서 의미에 집중하는 것처럼 보이나 학생의 잘못된 동사를 교사가 고쳐서 다시 말하는 형태가 된다. 이 피드백에서 주의할 점은 위 지문에서 보이는 것처럼 학생이 그 규칙을 아직 받아들일 준비가 안 되었을 때는 그냥 지나쳐 버릴 수 있는 피드백이 된다. (c) 'But you saw a movie LAST Sunday, and last Sunday is in the past, right?'는 상위언어피드백으로서 교사가 명확하게 답을 수정해 주지는 않으나 그 문법성을 설명해 준다. (d) 'So, the correct verb is SAW, not SEE.'는 명시적 수정의 형태로서 학습자의 잘못된 부분을 지적하고 수정해주는 피드백이다.

36

문항 해설

　　지문에 나타난 2언어습득과 학습에 관한 저자의 견해는 언어가 우리들이 알고 있는 지식을 반영하고, 우리의 경험을 나타낸다는 것이다. 실제적인 언어사용을 통한 언어 학습을 중시하고, 주의집중(attention)을 언어학습의 중요한 요소라고 주장한다. 실제자료의 사용을 중요하게 여기며 입력을 주목할 수(noticeable) 있도록 해야 하는 교사의 역할을 강조한다. 충분한 양의 용례(usage)를 통하여 입력의 빈도수를 높이는 것이 언어 습득에 영향을 미친다고 믿고 있다. 실제 내용, 즉 맥락(context)안에서 다양한 형태와 의미 연결(form-meaning mapping) 연습이 언어습득에 중요한 역할을 하고 있다.

> 핵심 ELT 읽기

2언어 구성하기

Language has come to represent the world as we know it; it is grounded in our perceptual experience. Language is used to organize, process, and convey information from one person to another, from one embodied mind to another. Language is also used to establish and maintain social relationships and to enact functions. Language and its use are mutually inextricable; they determine each other.

Learning language involves determining structure from **usage** and this, like learning about all other aspects of the world, involves the full scope of cognition: the remembering of utterances and episodes, the categorization of experience, the determination of patterns among and between stimuli, the generalization of conceptual schema and prototypes from exemplars, and the use of cognitive models, metaphors, analogies, and images in thinking. At the same time, there is an all-important **social dimension** to the process. There is nothing that so well characterizes human social action as language. It is in the coadaptation in the micro-discursive encounters between conversation partners that learners experience relevant and accessible exemplars from which they will learn.

Cognition, consciousness, experience, embodiment, brain, self, human interaction, society, culture, and history—in other words, phenomena at different levels of scale and time (Larsen-Freeman & Cameron, 2008)—are all inextricably intertwined in rich, complex, and dynamic ways in language, its use, and its learning. So we require perspectives on dynamic interactions at all levels, perspectives provided by general approaches such as Emergentism, Chaos/Complexity Theory, and Dynamic Systems Theory as they apply to usage based theories of language and first language acquisition and second language acquisition. This article applies these approaches to investigate linguistic constructions, their cognition, and their development. We focus on the second language development of English verb-argument constructions (VACs: VL verb locative; VOL, verb object locative; VOO, ditransitive) with particular reference to the following:

- construction learning as concept learning following the general cognitive and associative processes of the induction of categories from experience of exemplars in conversational interaction;

- the empirical analysis of usage by means of corpus linguistic descriptions of English native-speaker and nonnative speaker speech over time;

- the islands (Tomasello, 1992) comprising each construction and the effects of frequency and type/token frequency distribution of their constituent exemplars, their prototypicality, and their contingency of **form-meaning use mapping**;

- computational (connectionist) models of these various factors as they play out in the emergence of constructions as generalized linguistic schema.

In addition to the general approaches we have just enumerated, our theoretical framework is also informed by cognitive linguistics, particularly constructionist perspectives, **corpus linguistics**, and psychological theories of cognitive and associative learning as they relate to the induction of psycholinguistic categories from social interaction. The basic tenets are as follows: Language is intrinsically symbolic. It is constituted by a structured network of constructions as conventionalized **form-meaning-use** combinations used for communicative purposes. As speakers communicate, they coadapt their language use on a particular occasion. From such repeated encounters, stable language-using patterns (Larsen-Freeman & Cameron, 2008) emerge. The patterns are eventually broken down and their **form-meaning-use** is extended in novel ways. Usage leads to these becoming entrenched in the speaker's mind and for them to be taken up by members of the speech community.

Constructions are of different levels of complexity and abstraction; they can comprise concrete and particular items (as in words and idioms), more abstract classes of items (as in word classes and abstract grammatical constructions), or complex combinations of concrete and abstract items (as mixed constructions). The acquisition of constructions is **input-driven** and depends on the learner's experience of these **form-meaning-use** combinations in interactions with others. They develop following the same cognitive principles as the learning of other categories, schemata, and prototypes (Cohen & Lefebvre, 2005; Murphy, 2003). Creative linguistic usage emerges from the collaboration of the memories of all of the utterances in a learner's entire history of language use.

37

문항 해설

이메일 내용에서 민희는 키홀더를 수집하는 것이 취미임을 알 수 있다. 4명의 학생들이 각기 대답하는데 S1은 주어가 생략되며, 동사와 목적어의 위치가 한국어 어순과 동일하게 하는 오류를 범했다. 그에 해당하는 피드백으로는 (b)의 어순을 바로 잡고 누가 수집하고 있는지를 물으면서 주어에 대해 인지하도록 유도하고 있다. S2는 의미적 내용에 대한 오류이다. 사진 수집이 아닌 키홀더임을 상기시키며 발화 수정을 유도하고 있는 (a)와 연계되고 있다. S3은 동사의 오류(collecting)에 관한 것으로 동사의 적절한 사용을 제시하는 (c)의 피드백이 유용하며, S4는 질문의 의도와 다른 대답을 한 것을 상기시키면서 의도한 질문에 대한 답을 할 수 있도록 유도하는 (d)의 피드백이 적절하다.

38

문항 해설

보기의 대화문을 보면 NNS가 'I go cinema'라고 잘못된 발화를 하자 NS는 'Uh?'라고 하면서 피드백 clarification request를 주었다. 하지만 NNS는 NS의 의도를 파악하지 못하고 그 전 발화에 last night 라는 부사어만 추가하여 발화한다. 그러자 NS는 동사형태(현재형 go가 아닌 과거형 went로 써야 함), 동사형태를 수정해 주기 보다는 의미에 초점을 맞춰 'Oh, last night'이라고 발화하며 NNS의 의도를 이해한다. 이것은 상호작용가설(interaction hypothesis)의 관점으로 볼때 NS와 NNS의 의사소통에 문제가 생겼을 때 의미협상(meaning negotiation)이 일어나고 이런 과정을 통해 의사소통이 이뤄지는 것을 보여준다. 여기서 주목할 점은 비록 상호작용이 성공적으로 이루어진다 하더라도 발화의 문법상의 오류가 수정(modify)되거나 습득된다든지 NNS가 말한 밀어낸 출력(pushed output)이 항상 modified 되는 것은 아니라는 것이다.

> **핵심 개념정리**

상호 작용

Long's Interaction hypothesis proposes that language acquisition is strongly facilitated by the use of the target language in interaction. In particular, the negotiation of meaning has been shown to contribute greatly to the acquisition of vocabulary (Long, 1990). In a review of the substantial literature on this topic, Nation (2000) relates the value of negotiation to the generative use of words: the use of words in new contexts which stimulate a deeper understanding of their meaning. In the 1980s, Canadian SLA researcher Merrill Swain advanced the output hypothesis, that meaningful output is as necessary to language learning as meaningful input. However, most studies have shown little if any correlation between learning and quantity of output. Today, most scholars contend that small amounts of meaningful output are important to language learning, but primarily because the experience of producing language leads to more effective processing of input. Modified interaction may include elaboration, slower speech rate, gesture, or the provision of additional contextual cues.

- *comprehension checks* (efforts by the native speaker to ensure that the learner has understood)
- *clarification requests* (efforts by the learner to get the native speaker to clarify something which has not been understood),
- *self-repetition or paraphrase* (the native speaker repeats his or her sentence either partially or in its entirety).

39

> **문항 해설**

상호작용가설(interaction hypothesis)은 이전의 Krashen의 입력가설(input hypothesis)을 반박하면서, 단순히 충분한 입력이 들어온다고 해서 습득이 이루어지지는 않는다고 주장한다. 입력을 습득으로 하기 위해서는 계속되는 수정(modification)과 상호작용(interaction)이 뒤따라야 된다고 주장하고 있다. 그리고 이는 교사나 상급 수준의 학생의 도움(scaffolding)으로 입력된 내용이 자신의 것으로 발전되어 갈 수 있음을 의미하고 있다. 입력이 학습자의 지식체계의 이해(intake)가 되기 위해서는 단순히 입력으로 끝나는 것이 아니라 인지적 처리과정을 거쳐야만 한다는 것을 설명하고 있다. 상호작용가설에서는 습득이 일어나기 위해서는 단순한 입력의 습득만이 아니라 학습자의 의미협상(negotiation), 조정(adjustment), 선택적 주의집중(selective attention), 출력(output)의 과정이 필요하다.

40-42

문항 해설

외국인을 위한 발화(foreigner talk)와 엄마가 쓰는 발화(motherese)의 차이점을 설명하고 있다. 두 가지의 발화는 비슷한 특징을 가지고 있으면서 동시에 차이점을 보여주고 있다. 두 발화는 모두 상대방의 이해를 돕기 위하여 발화를 조정할 수 있으나 foreigner talk는 정보를 교환하기 위하여 하는 반면에 motherese는 기본적으로 어머니가 자녀에게 사용하는 전형적인 발화형태로서 발화를 단순화하여 아이들이 이해하기 쉽게 함으로써 의사소통능력을 가능한 한 북돋워 주려고 한다. 또한, foreigner talk의 여러 가지 유형에 관한 문제로, 일반적으로 말하는 속도보다 천천히 얘기하며, 관계대명사를 이용하지 않은 단순한 문장 구조를 이용하면서 첫 번째 언급했던 것보다 명확한 발화를 시도하고, 이해를 돕기 위해서 단순한 구문, 'five blocks'를 반복하여 말하고 있다. foreigner talk에서는 일반적 발화에 비하여 맥락이 제거되고 온전히 내용어만을 위주로 말하고 있음을 알 수 있다.

핵심 개념정리

외국인을 위한 발화(Foreigner talk)

- It is slower and louder than normal speech, often with exaggerated pronunciation.
- It uses simpler vocabulary and grammar. For example, articles, function words, and inflections may be omitted, and complex verb forms are replaced by simper ones.
- Topics are sometimes repeated or moved to the front of sentences.
- This speech contains ungrammatical adjustments and has a higher proportion of statements than instructions and questions.
- It promotes communication, establishes a special kind of affective bond between the speakers and serves as an implicit teaching mode.
- This speech is likely to be significantly more oriented to the 'here and now' than the normal conversation.
- Simple vocabulary, using high-frequency words and phrases
- Long pauses, loud volume
- Careful articulation, slow rate of speech, stress on key words
- Topicalization (topic at the beginning, then a comment about it)
- More syntactic regularity, simplified grammatical structures
- Retention of full forms (eg. less contraction, fewer pronouns)

(examples)

Mom look at your homework?   *You have Indians in Korea?*

Would you give us pencil?   *See, Semi's made mouth real scary.*

43

문항 해설

외국인교사와 2언어 학생의 대화 구조에서 서로를 이해하기 위해서 의미협상을 하고 있다. 교사가 'advantages'라는 어휘 대신에 'good points'라는 좀 더 단순한 어휘의 사용과 if-절의 위치를 바꿔주거나, 명료화, 확인 혹은 반복, 이해 가능한 입력을 통해 상호작용의 구조를 수정함으로 언어의 의미를 활성화하여 학습자의 이해도에 맞추어 이해가능한 입력(comprehensible input)을 이용하고 있다.

44

문항 해설

본문은 2언어 학습자가 함축된 의미(implied meaning)를 잘 이해하지 못한다는 의미에서 자주 인용되고 있다. 위의 Tony는 영화 티켓이 있다는 말을 하면서 Susan을 초대하고 있으나 Susan은 의도적이든 아니든 '단지 티켓이 있다'라는 발화(locutionary)의 수준의 해석에서 머물러 연극을 재밌게 보라고 인사를 하게 된다. 내포된 의미를 이해하기 위해서는 발어내 행위(illocutionary force)에서 이해되어야 하는 행간의 의미를 읽어야 한다는 것이다. 또한 이런 실수가 일어나는 것은 단어나 문법적인 것을 몰라서 생기는 실수가 아니라 맥락안에서, 즉 담화(discourse) 차원에서 생기는 실수라고 봐야 한다.

핵심 개념정리

발화 행위(Speech Acts)

The philosopher J.L. Austin (1911-1960) claims that many utterances are equivalent to actions. When someone says: "I name this ship" or "I now pronounce you man and wife", the utterance creates a new social or psychological reality. Such utterances can be analysed using a threefold distinction: locutionary, illocutionary and perlocutionary acts.

- Locutionary acts: these are simply the speech acts which have taken place.

- Illocutionary acts: these refer to the **real actions** which are performed by the utterance, where saying equals doing, as in betting, plighting one's troth, welcoming and warning.

- Perlocutionary acts: these refer to the **effect of the utterance** on the listener, who accepts the bet or pledge of marriage, is welcomed or warned.

Some linguists have attempted to classify illocutionary acts into a number of categories or types. David Crystal, quoting J.R. Searle, gives five such categories:

- Representatives: the speaker is committed to the truth of a proposition: affirm, believe, conclude, deny, report

- Directives: the speaker tries to get the hearer to do something: ask, challenge, command, dare, insist, request

- Commissives: the speaker is committed to a (future) course of action: guarantee, pledge, promise, swear, vow

- Expressives: the speaker expresses an attitude about a state of affairs: apologize, deplore, congratulate, regret, thank, welcome
- Declarations: the speaker alters the external status or condition of an object or situation, solely by making the utterance: I baptize you, I resign, I sentence you to be hanged by the neck until you be dead, I name this ship...

45

문항 해설

동기는 학습 성공, 실패를 결정짓는 중요한 요소 중의 하나이다. a는 회사에서 승진을 위한 내적 동기의 도구적 지향(instrumental orientation)이고, b는 부모의 외부적인 동기로 자녀를 통합적 지향(integrative orientation)을 하게하고, c는 회사라는 외부적인 동기의 힘으로 도구적 지향을 하고 있으며, d는 내적 동기로 그 문화에 통합하고자 하는 유형이다.

핵심 개념정리

동기의 종류

A distinction has been made between integrative and instrumental orientations. An integrative orientation (desire to learn a language from a positive affect toward a community of its speaker) was more strongly linked to success in learning a second language than an instrumental orientation (desire to learn a language to attain certain career, educational, or financial goals), later studies showed that both orientations could be associated with success.

Intrinsically motivated activities are ones for which there is no apparent reward except the activity itself and behaviors are aimed at bringing about certain internally rewarding consequences, namely, feeling of **competence** and **self-determination**. **Extrinsically** motivated behaviors are carried out in anticipation of a reward from outside and beyond the self. Typical extrinsic rewards are money, prizes, grades, and even certain types of positive feedback.

A convincing stockpile of research on motivation strongly favors intrinsic drives, especially for long-term retention. However, intrinsic motivation is of course not the only determiner of success for language learner. No matter how you want to accomplish something or how hard you try, you may not succeed for a host of other reasons. But if the learners in your classroom are given an opportunity to do language for their own personal reasons of achieving competence and **autonomy**, those learners will have a better chance of success than if they become dependent on external rewards for their motivation.

	Intrinsic	Extrinsic
Integrative	L2 learner wishes to integrate with the L2 culture (eg. for immigration or marriage)	Someone else wishes the L2 learner to know the L2 for integrative reasons (eg. Japanese parents send kids to Japanese language school)
Instrumental	L2 learner wishes to achieve goals utilizing L2 (eg. for a career)	External power wants L2 learner to learn L2 (eg. corporation sends Japanese businessman to US for language training)

46

핵심 개념정리

학습 유형

처음에 든 5가지 유형은 행동주의 이론에 적합하며, 나머지 3가지 유형은 Ausubel이나 Rogers의 학습 이론으로 잘 설명된다. 모든 8가지 학습유형은 외국어 학습과 관련이 있기 때문에, 제2언어 학습의 '낮은' 단계는 행동주의적 접근방법이나 교수법으로 보다 잘 이루어지고 있는 반면, '높은' 단계는 인지적 접근방법에 의한 교수법으로 보다 효과적으로 교수된다는 시사점을 얻을 수 있다. Gagne의 8가지 학습유형은 다음과 같다.

Signal Learning	This generally occurs in the total language process: human beings make a general response of some kind (emotional, cognitive, verbal, or nonverbal) to language.
Stimulus-response learning	Simple lexical items are, in one sense, acquired by stimulus-response connections; in another sense they are related to higher-order types of learning.
Chaining	This is evident in the acquisition of phonological sequences and syntactic patterns—the stringing together of several responses—though we should not be misled into believing that verbal chains are necessarily linear; generative linguists have wisely shown that sentence structure is hierarchical.
Verbal association	The fourth type of learning involves Gagne's distinction between verbal and nonverbal chains, and is not really therefore a separate type of language learning.
Multiple discriminations	These are necessary particularly in second language learning where, for example, a word has to take on several meanings, or a rule in the native language is reshaped to fit a second language context.
Concept learning	This includes the notion that language and cognition are inextricably interrelated, also that rules themselves—rules of syntax, rules of conversation—are linguistic concepts that have to be acquired.

Principle learning	This is the extension of concept learning to the formation of a linguistic system, in which rules are not isolated in rote memory but conjoined and subsumed in a total system.
Problem solving	This is clearly evident in second language learning as the learner is continually faced with sets of events that are truly problems to be solved—problems every bit as difficult as algebra problems of other "intellectual" problems. Solutions to the problems involve the creative interaction of all eight types of learning as the learner sifts and weighs previous information and knowledge.

47

핵심 개념정리

임여성(Redundancy)

Redundancy is considered a vital feature of language. It shields a message from possible flaws in transmission (unclarity, noise). In this way, it increases the odds of predictability of a message's meaning. On ambiguity, the phonological level, the **redundancy of phonological rules** may clarify some vagueness in spoken speech; a speaker may know that 'thisrip' must be 'this rip' and not 'this srip' because the English consonant cluster 'sr' is illegal (Pinker, 1994). It is this feature of redundancy that has been said to be important in allowing humans to acquire a complex grammar system. A child acquiring language must abstract away grammatical rules based on the input which he hears. Redundancy in language allows the child's **inductions** to be more stable by presenting more salient evidence upon which these inductions are based. Redundancy therefore provides the sufficient stimulus needed to acquire a complex grammar system. A common concept in linguistics is economy of storage; only unpredictable information is said to be stored in one's "mental grammar". Redundancy aids this process, increasing the odds of predictability by acting as a noise filter. Language **fluency** is proficiency in a language, most typically foreign language or another learned language. In this sense, fluency actually encompasses a number of related but separable skills:

- Reading : the ability to easily read and understand texts written in the language
- Writing : the ability to formulate written texts in the language
- Comprehension : the ability to follow and understand speech in the language
- Speaking : the ability to speak in the language and be understood by its speakers.

To some extent, these skills can be separately acquired. Generally, the later in life a learner approaches the study of a foreign language, the harder it is to acquire auditory comprehension and fluent speaking skills. Reading and writing a foreign language are skills that can be acquired more easily after the primary language acquisition period of youth is over, however.

48-50

핵심 개념정리

긍정적 & 부정적 전이

When the relevant unit or structure of both languages is the same, **linguistic interference** can result in correct language production called positive transfer—correct meaning in line with most native speakers' notions of acceptability. An example is the use of cognates. Note, however, that language interference is most often discussed as a source of errors known as **negative transfer**. Negative transfer occurs when speakers and writers transfer items and structures that are not the same in both languages. Within the theory of contrastive analysis (the systematic study of a pair of languages with a view to identifying their structural differences and similarities), the greater the **differences between the two languages**, the more negative transfer can be expected. The results of positive transfer go largely unnoticed, and thus are less often discussed. Nonetheless, such results can have a large effect. Generally speaking, the more similar the two languages, are the more the learner is aware of the relation between them, the more positive transfer will occur. For example, an Anglophone learner of German may correctly guess an item of German vocabulary from its English counterpart, but word order and **collocation** are more likely to differ, as will **connotations**. Such an approach has the disadvantage of making the learner more subject to the influence of 'false friends' (**false cognates**).

51

핵심 개념정리

화석화(Fossilization)

Interlanguage fossilization is a stage during second language acquisition. When mastering a target language (TL), second language (L2) learners develop a linguistic system that is self-contained and different from both the learner's first language (L1) and the TL (Nemser, 1971). This linguistic system has been variously called **interlanguage** (IL) (Selinker, 1972), **approximative system, idiosyncratic dialects** or **transitional dialects** (Corder, 1971), etc.

According to Corder (1981), this temporary and changing grammatical system, IL, which is constructed by the learner, approximates the grammatical system of the TL. In the process of L2 acquisition, IL continually evolves into an ever-closer approximation of the TL, and ideally should advance gradually until it becomes equivalent, or nearly equivalent, to the TL. However, during the L2 learning process, an IL may reach one or more temporary restricting phases when its development appears to be detained. A permanent cessation of progress toward the TL has been referred to as fossilization (Selinker, 1972). This linguistic phenomenon, IL fossilization, can occur despite all reasonable attempts at learning (Selinker, 1972). Fossilization includes those items, rules, and sub-systems that L2 learners tend to retain in their IL, that is, all those aspects of IL that become entrenched and permanent, and that the majority of L2 learners can only eliminate with considerable effort (Omaggio, 2001). Moreover, it has also been noticed that this occurs particularly in adult L2 learners' IL systems (Nemser, 1971; Selinker, 1972, Selinker & Lamendella, 1980.).

Selinker (1972) suggests that the most important distinguishing factor related to L2 acquisition is the phenomenon of fossilization. However, both his explanation that "fossilizable linguistic phenomena are linguistic items, rules, and subsystems which speakers of a particular native language will tend to keep in their interlanguage relative to a particular target language, no matter what the age of the learner or amount of explanation or instruction he receives in the target language" (Selinker, 1972) and his hypotheses on IL fossilization are fascinating in that they contradict our basic understanding of the human capacity to learn. How is it that some learners can overcome IL fossilization, even if they only constitute, according to Selinker, "a mere 5%" (1972), while the majority of L2 learners cannot, 'no matter what the age or amount of explanation or instruction'? Or is it perhaps not that they cannot overcome fossilization, but that they will not? Does complacency set in after L2 learners begin to communicate, as far as they are concerned, effectively enough, in the TL, and as a result does motivation to achieve native-like competence diminish?

The concept of fossilization in SLA research is so intrinsically related to IL that Selinker (1972) considers it to be a fundamental phenomenon of all SLA and not just to adult learners. Fossilization has received such wide recognition that it has been entered in the Random House Dictionary of the English Language (1987). Selinker's concept of fossilization is similar to that of Tarone (1976), Nemser (1971), and Sridhar (1980), all of whom attempted to explore the causes of fossilization in L2 learners' IL. Fossilization has attracted considerable interest among researchers and has engendered significant differences of opinion. The term, borrowed from the field of paleontology, conjures up an image of dinosaurs being enclosed in residue and becoming a set of hardened remains encased in sediment. The metaphor, as used in SLA literature, is appropriate because it refers to earlier language forms that become encased in a learner's IL and that, theoretically, cannot be changed by special attention or practice of the TL. Despite debate over the degree of permanence, fossilization is generally accepted as a fact of life in the process of SLA.

52-53

핵심 개념정리

2언어 습득 원리

1) The **Acquisition-Learning distinction** is the most fundamental of all the hypotheses in Krashen's theory. The 'acquired system' or 'acquisition' is the product of a subconscious process very similar to the process children undergo when they acquire their first language. It requires meaningful interaction in the target language – natural communication – in which speakers are concentrated not in the form of their utterances, but in the communicative act. The 'learned system' or 'learning' is the product of formal instruction and it comprises a conscious process which results in conscious knowledge 'about' the language, for example knowledge of grammar rules.

2) The **Monitor hypothesis** explains the relationship between acquisition and learning and defines the influence of the latter on the former. The monitoring function is the practical result of the learned grammar. According to Krashen, the acquisition system is the utterance initiator, while the learning system performs the role of the 'monitor' or the 'editor'. The 'monitor' acts in a planning, editing and correcting function when three specific conditions are met: that is, the second language learner has sufficient time at his/her disposal, he/she focuses on form or thinks about correctness, and he/she knows the rule. It appears that the role of conscious learning is somewhat limited in second language performance. According to Krashen, the role of the monitor is – or should be – minor, being used only to correct deviations from 'normal' speech and to give speech a more 'polished' appearance.

3) The **Natural Order hypothesis** is based on research findings (Dulay & Burt, 1974; Fathman, 1975; Makino, 1980 cited in Krashen, 1987) which suggested that the acquisition of grammatical structures follows a 'natural order' which is predictable. For a given language, some grammatical structures tend to be acquired early while others late. This order seemed to be independent of the learners' age, L1 background, conditions of exposure, and although the agreement between individual acquirers was not always 100% in the studies, there were statistically significant similarities that reinforced the existence of a Natural Order of language acquisition. Krashen however points out that the implication of the natural order hypothesis is not that a language program syllabus should be based on the order found in the studies. In fact, he rejects grammatical sequencing when the goal is language acquisition.

4) The **Input hypothesis** is Krashen's attempt to explain how the learner acquires a second language. According to this hypothesis, the learner improves and progresses along the 'natural order' when he/she receives second language 'input' that is one step beyond his/her current stage of linguistic competence. For example, if a learner is at a stage 'i', then acquisition takes place when he/she is exposed to 'Comprehensible Input' that belongs to level 'i+1'. Since not all of the learners can be at the same level of linguistic

competence at the same time, Krashen suggests that natural communicative input is the key to designing a syllabus, ensuring in this way that each learner will receive some 'i + 1' input that is appropriate for his/her current stage of linguistic competence

5) Finally, the fifth hypothesis, the **Affective Filter** hypothesis, embodies Krashen's view that a number of 'affective variables' play a facilitative role in second language acquisition. These variables include: motivation, self-confidence and anxiety. Krashen claims that learners with high motivation, self-confidence, a good self-image, and a low level of anxiety are better equipped for success in second language acquisition. Low motivation, low self-esteem, and debilitating anxiety can combine to 'raise' the affective filter and form a 'mental block' that prevents comprehensible input from being used for acquisition. In other words, when the filter is 'up' it impedes language acquisition. On the other hand, positive affect is necessary, but not sufficient on its own, for acquisition to take place.

54-55

문항 해설

학습유형중 하나로서 장의존(field dependence)과 독립(independence)이 학습에 크게 영향을 미치고 있다. 장독립성은 교실 수업등의 시험, 연습 등에서 성공할 확률이 높고 장의존성은 교실상황을 벗어나서도 넓게 생각할 수 있어 의사소통 상황이나 전체적 언어학습에서의 성공률이 높다고 볼 수 있다. 전략에는 학습(learning strategies)과 의사소통전략(communication strategies)으로 나뉘어질 수 있다. 학습전략에는 metacognitive, cognitive, socio-affective가 있으며 의사소통전략에는 circumlocution, code switching, prefabricated patterns등으로 학습자가 언어사용에 어려움을 겪을 때 사용할 수 있는 방법들이다.

CHAPTER 02 영어교재론 및 교육과정

01

핵심 개념정리

Digital Technology

(1) Cloud-based quiz platform

- Interactive Quizzes: The platform can offer interactive quizzes in various formats such as multiple-choice, fill-in-the-blanks, matching, or even speaking and listening exercises. These quizzes can cover vocabulary, grammar, comprehension, and other language learning.
- Instant Feedback: Learners can receive instant feedback on their quiz performance, helping them understand their strengths and weaknesses in the language. This immediate feedback fosters active learning and enables learners to correct mistakes in real-time.
- Adaptive Learning: The platform can utilize adaptive learning algorithms to tailor quiz content to each learner's proficiency level and learning goals. This ensures that learners are challenged appropriately and can progress at their own pace.

(2) Virtual reality (VR) simulation Apps

- Immersive Language Environment: VR simulation apps can recreate realistic language environments, such as a marketplace, restaurant, airport, or city street, where learners can interact with virtual characters and objects in the target language.
- Authentic Interactions: Learners can engage in authentic interactions with virtual characters, responding to questions, making requests, and participating in conversations.
- Real-time Feedback: VR apps can provide real-time feedback on language use, pronunciation, and comprehension, helping learners identify and correct errors.
- Multi-sensory Learning: VR technology enables multi-sensory learning experiences, allowing learners to hear, see, and interact with language in a dynamic virtual environment.

(3) Online platform

- Interactive Lessons: These lessons can include multimedia elements such as videos, audio recordings, interactive exercises, and quizzes to engage learners actively.
- Structured Curriculum: It can guide learners through progressively more complex language skills and concepts, ensuring a systematic approach to language acquisition.
- Personalized Learning Paths: The platform can provide personalized learning paths based on learners' proficiency levels, learning goals, and areas of interest.

02-06

> 핵심 개념정리

자료 개정

Materials adaptation means matching materials with the learner's needs, the teacher's demands and administration's purpose. To adapt materials we have to consider five major factors:

(1) Addition: Addition is an adaptation procedure which involves supplementation of extra linguistic items and activities to make up for the inadequacy/ insufficiency of materials. Addition of extra materials is necessary/ applicable/ appropriate when the following situations are faced:
- Areas are not covered sufficiently.
- Texts/ pictures/ tasks are not provided.
- Texts/ pictures/ tasks are fewer than needed.
- Tasks are limited in scope.
- Tasks are of limited range.

(2) Deletion/omission: Deletion is an adaptation procedure which involves removal of some of the linguistic items and activities which are found to be extra and unnecessary. So, deletion is a process in which materials are taken out rather than added. Materials should be reduced through omission when the following situations are faced:
- Learners are clear about a language point.
- Learners are competent in a skill.
- There are too many tasks on a particular area/ point.
- The item/ area concerned is not a priority.
- The item/ task is not well designed.
- The item/ task is not well-suited to its aim(s).
- The topic is not appropriate for learners.

(3) Modification/changing: Modification means changes in different aspects of materials, such as linguistic level, exercises, assessment system and so on. Modification of materials is applicable/ appropriate in the following situations:
- Texts are of inappropriate length.
- Materials are inappropriate to the aim.
- Materials are inappropriate to the learners' age/ experience.
- Materials are unclear, confusing or misleading.
- Tasks are badly designed.

(4) Simplification: This procedure is employed to make materials less complicated or easier to understand. If the language teaching material is found to be difficult or mechanical for the target learner, it (material) can be made suitable for the learner through the process of simplification.

(5) Rearrangement/ re-ordering: Rearrangement is a procedure of materials adaptation through which different parts of a course book are arranged in a different order or sequence. Rearrangement of materials helps to make them comparatively more interesting and appropriate for the learner as well as the teacher. Learners may reorder materials by:
- Matching their aims.
- Using a practice task for lead-in and elicitation.
- Revising an area earlier than the course book does.
- Comparing and contrast areas.
- Providing thematic unity.
- Providing an appropriate follow-up.

07-09

문항 해설

교육과정(curriculum)을 계획할 때 우선적으로 고려해야 하는 것은 요구분석(needs analysis)를 해야 하는데 이러한 요구분석은 목표를 설계하기 전 단계로, 이 분석을 통해서 전반적인 목표, 그 수업의 필요 및 교사와 학습자의 의견을 파악할 수 있다. 한 학습자 또는 학습 집단이 1) 어떤 언어를 학습하고 이를 구사하는 데 요구되는 필요를 파악하고 2) 그와 같은 필요의 우선순위를 조정하는 과정을 말한다. 필요 사항을 분석, 평가, 확인하기 위한 방법에는 주관적 또는 객관적 정보를 이용하게 된다. 예를 들면, 그 자료들은 설문조사, 테스트, 면접, 토의, 관찰, 내용 분석, 결과 해석 등 다양한 방법과 기법을 이용하게 된다. 이와 함께 장소, 청중, 교사의 수급상황과 같은 상황분석(situation analysis)을 하게 되고 그 다음 단계로 수업을 위한 교수요목(syllabus) 개발과 교재 개발이 이어진다.

핵심 ELT 읽기

교육과정의 방법

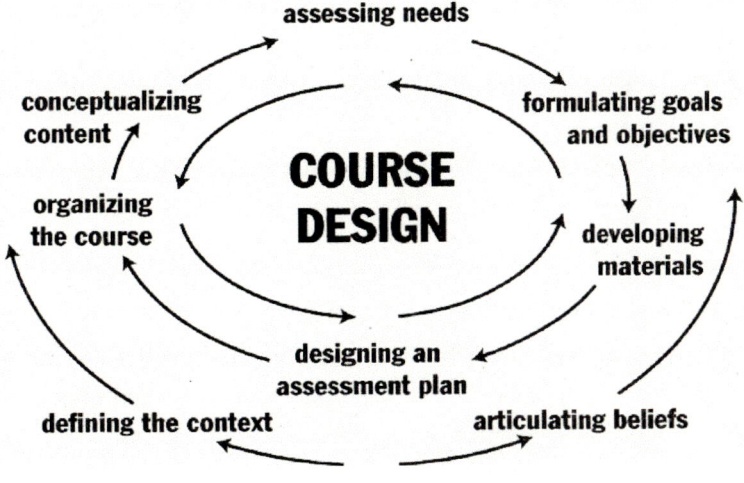

① **Needs Analysis**

언어교육을 위한 커리큘럼 계획단계에서 요구되는 기초 조사 영역으로 코스를 계획하거나 이해하는 첫번째 단계로 needs에 초점을 맞춘다. needs를 세 가지 구성형태로 세분화하면 a) necessities b) lacks c) wants로 나눌 수 있다.

② **Situation Analysis (environment analysis)**

코스를 계획하고 이해하는 데 두 번째 단계는 환경을 분석하는 situation analysis가 이루어지는 것이다. 효과적인 코스를 위해서는 다음과 같은 요소가 밑받침되어야 한다.

- Educational Setting
- Class characteristics
- Faculty characteristics
- Governance of course content

③ **Specifying Goals (코스의 내용과 수업의 목표를 결정하는 지침서)**

By the end of the speaking course, students will be able to:

- Participate in social conversations in English
- Speak with few hesitations and with only minor errors
- Successfully apply some form-focused instruction to their speech
- Self-monitor their speech for potential errors
- Participate in pair, group and whole-class discussions
- Give a simple oral presentation on a familiar topic

④ **Conceptualizing a Course Syllabus**

이 단계와 다음의 교과서 선택의 단계는 동시에 혹은 상호보완적으로 고려된다. 코스를 계획 할 때 교과서나 다른 자료에 대한 고려 없이 이루어질 수는 없다.

⑤ **Selecting Textbooks, Materials, and Resources**

- They should correspond to learners' needs. They should match the aims and objectives of the language program
- They should reflect the uses that learners will make of the language. Textbooks should be chosen that will help equip students to use language effectively for their own purposes.
- They should take account of students' needs as learners and should facilitate their learning processes.
- They should have a clear role as a support for learning. Like teachers, they should mediate between the target language and the learner.

⑥ **Assessment**

수업과 단원의 목표와 커리큘럼의 목표가 성취되었는가를 평가하기 위해서 다양한 형식이 제공된다.

- 전통식 평가법: quizzes, multiple-choice tests, fill-in-the-blank tests
- 중간/기말고사: short essays, oral production, open-ended questions
- 대체평가안: journals, portfolios, conferences, observations, interviews, self/peer-evaluation

⑦ Program Evaluation

효과적인 프로그램평가는 적절한 revision을 결정하기 위해 세 가지 구성요소인 교사, 학생, 프로그램을 고려해야 한다. 프로그램의 성공을 결정짓는 요소들에는;

- Methodology : 제반 교육적 활동(pedagogical practices)에 관한 연구; 이론적 토대 및 관련연구를 포함; 어떻게 가르칠 것인가?에 관련된 고려 사항은 모두 methodology이다.
- Approach : 언어 및 언어학습의 본질과 교육 현장으로의 적용가능성에 대한 이론적 입장
- Method : 언어적 목표를 달성하기 위해 일반화된 구체적 수업절차; 교사 및 학습자의 역할과 행동에 주된 관심이 있고, 언어적이고 내용적 목표, 교재, 수업의 계열성에는 부차적 관심이 있다; 다양한 교수-학습 상황에 널리 적용될 수 있다고 여겨진다.
- Curriculum/ Syllabus : 특정 언어학습 프로그램을 수행하기 위한 상세 내용; 특정 교수와 학습 상황. 특정 학습자집단의 욕구를 충족 시켜주기 위한 언어나 내용적 목표의 구체화와 교재 및 수업의 계열성에 주된 관심을 기울인다.
- Technique : 학습목표를 달성하기 위해 사용되는 모든 수업과정, 교수-학습 활동, 교수 기법들; task, procedure, activity, exercise 등도 같은 의미로 사용

English is used for communicating with foreigners at the workplace because English is accepted as the **medium** of international communications in four skills; speaking, listening, reading and writing. At the workplace, the act of communication can take place in various situations. The problems of communication in English can occur. The miscommunication between native and non-native speakers may be caused by a different interpretation of the sentence caused by the way of thinking and expressing ideas. The employees of private sectors are facing lot of problems in communicating with their superiors/ customers. This paper stresses the importance of English language and identifying the needs of the employers in acquiring English language communication.

1. What is Needs?

Needs refers to the students themselves would like to gain from the language course. This implies that students may have **personal aims** in addition to or even in opposition to the requirements of their jobs. (Robinson, 1991) Nadler (1989) stated that a need for training is usually defined as the difference between a goal or what is expected and what actually exists. There is no need unless somebody feels a lack of some kind. He classified needs into three types.

2. What is Needs Analysis?

According to White (1988), **needs analysis** procedure in the field of language teaching was first used by Michael West in a survey report published in 1926. Nunan (1988) describes that during the 1970s, needs analysis procedures were first used in language planning. While such procedures had a long tradition in other areas of adult learning, their use in language teaching became widespread with their adoption and espousal by The Council of Europe's modern language project. In the Council of Europe's documents, **needs analysis** was used as the initial process for the specification of **behavioral objectives**. It was from these objectives that more detailed aspects of the syllabus, such as functions, notions, topics, lexis and structural exponents were derived.

- Needs Analysis is concerned with identifying **general and specific language needs** that can be addressed in developing goals, objectives and content in a language program. It may focus either on the general parameters of a language program as well as societal expectations or on specific needs. (Richard & Rogers, 1986)

- Needs Analysis is the use of **surveys** to identify both general and specific problems experienced by a target group, usually by comparing what exists with what would be preferred, and potential solutions to those problems. (Lawrence et al, 1991)

- Needs analysis is an investigation, in light of specification of the **tasks**. A learner or group of learners will be required to perform in the target language needed to be learnt in order to bring about proficiency in these particular tasks. The results of **needs analysis** can be used to determine suitable teaching techniques (Brumfit & Roberts, 1987)

3. Studies on Needs Analysis

Saravadee Sangsook (2007) studied the needs of employees for English communication in their careers at Bangkok Produce Merchandising Public Company Limited. The study focused on English skills that the employees would like to improve in order to create a definite plan for their English communication development in the future. The results showed that most respondents need English communication in their careers. Speaking was the most necessary skill in their careers. Most respondents would like to improve speaking skill at the higher degree. Panrattana Chenaksara (2005) conducted a research on "**Needs Analysis** for English Communication Skills of Thai Airways International Cabin Crew." The study explored the English communication skills problems of Thai Airways international cabin crew and analyzed the English training needs for English communication skills improvement. The results showed that listening and speaking skills were perceived as their problems. The major course of the listening problem was accent, especially Australian and Indian accents. English being a second language of the cabin crew was the main cause of the speaking problem.

10

문항 해설

교사의 교재평가에서 부족함(poor) 부분에 대해 개선해야 할 활동을 추가한다.

(1) 어휘활동에 연어(collocation)가 활용되지 않는 문제가 있다. 해결책으로 맥락안에서 연어를 통해 적절한 어휘를 사용하도록 하는 활동을 포함시킨다.

(2) 새로운 문법항목을 맥락에서 제시하지 못한다고 평가하고 있다. 해결책으로는 문법항목이 포함된 이야기 학습을 통해 맥락을 제공할 수 있다.

(5) 언어 형식(styles)이 사회적 상황과 맞지 않는다는 평가를 내리고 있다. 해결책으로는 적절한 언어사용을 나타내는 친구사이의 대화체를 제공할 수 있다.

수업자료와 교수방법을 결정하기 위해서 교육과정과 수업계획의 큰 틀 안에서 시작해야 한다. 교육과정을 작성하는 기본은 학습자의 요구, 즉 요구분석과 교육적 환경인 상황분석이 기본이 되어야 한다. 그 후에 전체적인 프로그램의 틀을 정할 수 있는 목표진술이 나옴으로써 어떤 수업을 할 수 있을 지 결정짓게 된다. 그후에 교수요목을 작성하여 자료와 수업절차, 수업의 목표 등이 정해지게 된다. 수업을 하고 난 후에는 수업에 대한 평가가 이루어질 것이고 모든 프로그램이 종료된 후에는 프로그램과, 교사, 학생에 대한 평가를 통하여 새로운 교육과정으로 개선될 수 있다.

11-12

핵심 개념정리

컴퓨터 매개 의사소통(Computer-mediated Communication)

Computer-mediated communication (CMC) is defined as any human communication that occurs through the use of two or more electronic devices. While the term has traditionally referred to those communications that occur via computer-mediated formats (e.g., instant messaging, email, chat rooms, online forums, social network services), it has also been applied to other forms of text-based interaction such as text messaging. Research on CMC focuses largely on the social effects of different computer-supported communication technologies. Many recent studies involve Internet-based social networking supported by social software. CMC can be broken down into two forms: synchronous and asynchronous.

(1) **Synchronous** computer-mediated communication refers to communication which occurs in real time. All parties are engaged in the communication **simultaneously**; however, they are not necessarily all in the same location. Examples of synchronous communication are video chats and FaceTime audio calls.

(2) **Asynchronous** computer-mediated communication refers to communication which takes place when the parties engaged are not communicating in unison. In other words, the sender does not receive an immediate response from the receiver. Most forms of computer mediated technology are asynchronous. Examples of asynchronous communication are text messages and emails.

(3) **Archive**: The archive of computer-mediated communication (CMC) process contains knowledge shared and information about participants' behavior patterns. Through CMC, group of students can engage in help consultation; assess learning; share the solution with the group; archive for **future reference**.

13

> 핵심 ELT 읽기

역할극

It is not enough merely to provide students with opportunities to speak in English, as teachers we need to encourage students to speak in a variety of different situations, and hence help them to learn to speak with confidence. The ideal would be to travel to different locations and carry out different tasks, the next best thing however is to enact those situations in a classroom. However, many teachers and students in an ESL class dread the words "role-play". Even though there is little consensus on the terms used in role-playing literature. Just a few of the terms which are used, often interchangeably, are "simulation," "game," "role-play," "simulation-game," "role-play simulation," and "role-playing game" (Crookall and Oxford, 1990a). The effective use of role-plays can add variety to the kinds of activities students are asked to perform. It encourages **thinking** and **creativity**; lets students develop and practice new language and behavioural skills in a relatively safe setting, and can create the **motivation** and **involvement** necessary for real learning to occur.

Unlike skits, role plays shouldn't be scripted out in detail, instead you should give the student a general scenario with different elements and suggested ideas for complications to occur. Role play cards can be a very useful tool here. For example:

Student A	Student B

• You are booking into a hotel.
• Elements: Book in to the hotel — you have a reservation.
• Complications:
  — You are on your own.
  — You want a shower.
  — You want breakfast in the morning.
  — You have an early meeting and must not be late.
	• You are a hotel receptionist.
	• Elements:
	  — Welcome the guest.
	  — Find them a room.
	• Complications:
	  — You can't find their reservation.
	  — You only have a double room with bath available.

Before asking them to perform a role play you should prepare the students by reviewing key vocabulary and asking questions. The questions should incorporate the major parts of the role play and the vocabulary/ idioms involved. After the question answer session the students should be comfortable with what they need to do;

- Allow them a few minutes to study the role cards and work out some key sentences. Give help where needed.

- Each role play should be performed at least twice with the students changing roles.

- In group situations have the stronger students act out the role play to the whole class.

- You as the teacher can take one of the roles if you need to.

- Avoid making corrections until the role play is finished.

- Don't let things get out of hand. If the role play decends into a slanging match, it might be entertaining, but you really should intervene.
- Recording or videoing role plays can be a very useful tool for giving feedback, but only if the students are comfortable with this.

14

문항 해설

교재 평가에 있어서 교재 A와 B 모두 사전 조건을 충족한 'Yes'판정을 받았다. 그 다음 평가로, 디자인과 설계(design and layout), 발음활동에서는 교재 A가 더 높은 점수를 받았으며 영역에 대한 비중(criteria weight)에 있어서는 학습자들의 주제 관심사의 비중이 기술 통합적인 분야보다는 더 높게 평가되었음을 알 수 있다. 그래서 결과적으로 교재B가 선택된다.

15

문항 해설

위 표는 교재에 대한 평가표로서 교재 선정을 할 때 기준으로 사용할 수 있다. C1과 C3은 교재의 겉표지의 디자인과 설계(design and layout)에 대해 검사하는 것으로 Y/N로 체크하는 것으로 되어있으며, C2와 C4는 C1과 C3보다 발화, 문법, 기능, 과업과 같이 좀 더 자세한 항목에 대한 점검 항목으로 점수를 주는 것으로 항목의 중요성의 정도를 표현하는 체크리스트이다. C2에서는 어떤 요소가 다른 요소와 비교하여 더 중요성이 있다는 기준이 존재하고, C2와 C4는 점수를 줌으로서 다른 두 요소보다 좀 더 심도있게 점검할 수 있는 항목들을 가지고 있다. C3는 겉모습으로 판단할 수 있는 외적 요소를 평가할 수 있는 평가기준이 된다.

16

핵심 개념정리

다층적 교수요목(Multi-layered Syllabus)

A multi-layered syllabus refers to a curriculum design approach that incorporates multiple layers of instruction, each addressing different aspects of language learning. This approach recognizes that language acquisition involves various interconnected components, such as vocabulary, grammar, pronunciation, cultural competence, and communicative skills:

- Foundational Skills: This layer focuses on building essential language skills, including vocabulary acquisition, basic grammar structures, and pronunciation fundamentals.

- Learners develop a solid foundation in the language's core components, enabling them to understand and produce simple sentences and engage in basic communication.
- Functional Language Use: This layer emphasizes the development of practical language skills for real-life communication. Learners learn how to use language in everyday situations, such as greetings, introductions, making requests, giving directions, and expressing opinions.
- Grammar and Syntax: This layer delves deeper into the study of grammar and syntax, exploring more complex grammatical structures, sentence patterns, and language rules. Learners gain a deeper understanding of the language's grammatical framework and learn how to apply these rules in different contexts.
- Vocabulary Expansion: This layer focuses on expanding learners' vocabulary repertoire, introducing new words, phrases, and idiomatic expressions related to specific topics, themes, or contexts.
- Cultural Competence: Learners gain insights into the target culture(s) associated with the language they are learning, developing intercultural competence and awareness.
- Language Skills Integration: This layer integrates various language skills, such as speaking, listening, reading, and writing, in authentic and meaningful contexts.
- Task-Based Learning: This layer emphasizes task-based learning approaches, where learners work on meaningful tasks and projects that simulate real-life communication situations.

By incorporating multiple layers of instruction, a multi-layered syllabus provides a comprehensive and holistic approach to second language learning, addressing the diverse needs and goals of learners while fostering proficiency across all language domains. This approach acknowledges the complexity of language acquisition and aims to support learners in developing well-rounded language skills and competence.

17

문항 해설

과업중심교수법(TBLT)의 기본개념을 지키지 못한 것이 step 4 이다. TBLT를 교수요목차원에서 보았을 때 문제점을 나타내고 있으므로 종합적/분석적(synthetic/analytic) 교수요목의 요소에 대한 비교로 문제점을 서술한다. 또한 분석적 교수요목의 특징으로서 언어를 따로 가르치지 않고 맥락안에서 전체로 가르쳐야 한다는 내용을 서술한다.

	Focus on Forms	Focus on Meaning	Focus on Form
Grammar Teaching	explicit grammar rules	implicit & incidental grammar rules	grammar rules in contexts
Syllabus	synthetic syllabus	analytic syllabus	analytic syllabus
Focus	grammar rules	learner & learning process	form in meaningful contexts
Lesson Procedure	mastering linguistic items: declines in motivation, attention	similar to L1 acquisition (interesting, relevant, communicative)	occasional attention on linguistic features in meaning-focused classroom
Demerits	• no needs analysis: no learning styles & preferences • linguistic grading: only pedagogic materials (basal reader, classroom language use)	• productive skills: far from native-like with grammatical competence after many years of classroom immersion: not sufficient approach	• study of the form is based on; meaningful contexts, not a predetermined and decontextualized linguistic form

18

> 핵심 개념정리

실물교재(Realia)

　Many proponents of communicative language teaching have advocated the use of authentic, real-life materials in the classroom. Realia are objects from real life used in classroom instruction by educators to improve students' understanding of other cultures and real-life situations. A teacher of a foreign language often employs realia to strengthen students' associations between words for common objects and the objects themselves. In many cases, these objects are part of an instructional kit that includes a manual and is thus considered as being part of a documentary whole by librarians. Realia are also used to connect learners with the key focal point of a lesson by allowing tactile and multidimensional connection between learned material and the object of the lesson. They are best represented by simple objects lending themselves to classroom settings and ease of control with minimum risk of accident throughout the student-object interaction. Technology has begun to impact the use of realia by adding the virtual realia option, whereby three-dimensional models can be displayed through projection or on computer screens, allowing the learner to see detail otherwise difficult to acquire and to manipulate the object within the medium on which it is displayed.

19

문항 해설

이 문제는 교수요목내용을 이해하고 해결할 수 있어야 한다. 교수요목을 종합적(synthetic)과 분석적(analytic)으로 분류하고 있다. 문법중심 교수요목은 종합적 교수법(synthetic approach)으로 그와 대조될 수 있는 개념적 교수요목(notional syllabus)을 분석적 교수법(analytic approach)로 크게 나누어서 보고 있다. 종합적 교수법에 비해서 분석적 교수법에는 학습 환경에서 언어적인 통제를 하려는 의도가 없다는데 그 차이를 두고 있다. 즉, 언어의 요소는 체계적으로 쌓아올려지는 개념이 아니라는 것이다. 대신에 다양한 형태의 언어적 구조가 초기부터 허용되고 학습자들의 과제는 전체 언어적인 차원에서 표현되어야 한다. 그런 의미에서 개념적 교수요목이 분석적 교수법의 원리에 부합된다는 것이다. 위의 설명으로 (1)이 문법을 중시한 종합적 교수법으로서 교사가 미리 준비된 언어적 항목을 가르치는 c와 연결되는 것을 알 수 있다. (2)와 (3)은 분석적 교수법으로서 의미를 중시하는 접근법임을 알 수 있다. (2)에서는 목표언어로 의사소통하는 것, 의미전달을 중시하고 학습자의 의사소통능력(communicative competence)에 중점을 두고 있는 것을 알 수 있으며 (3)에서는 최신 경향의 영어교육으로서 의미만이 아닌 의미와 형태(form) 모두에 그 중요성을 두고 있음을 알 수 있다. 형태중심 수업에서 보이는 것처럼 언어학습은 그 어느 쪽에도 치우치지 않고 양 쪽 모두에 그 중요성을 실어야 한다고 주장하고 있다.

20

문항 해설

교수요목 A는 상황중심 교수요목으로서 주어진 구조를 만드는 데 중점을 두는 결과중심 교수요목이다. 미리 정해진 언어항목(be동사+~ing)에 초점을 맞추는 활동이다. 교수요목 B는 서베이나 프로젝트 등의 과업중심 교수요목으로서 과업을 수행하는 것으로 경험을 토대로 한 학습이 된다. 또한 언어가 학습되는 방법, 전략을 활용하여 학습이 이루어진다.

21

문항 해설

두 종류의 다른 교수요목을 비교한다. 교수요목 A는 there is (not) ... 구문을 가르치려고 하는 structural 교수요목이고 교수요목 B는 인사, 질문...등의 기능적인 표현을 가르치는 functional 교수요목이다. 교수요목 A에서는 문법이 일정한 순서에 의해 구조적으로 가르쳐지며, 문법과 어휘의 명시적인 설명이 수업시간에 이루어진다. 교수요목 B에서는 실제로 사용되는 기능을 중심으로 수업이 이루어지며 어휘와 문법은 묵시적으로 교수된다.

22

문항 해설

교수요목 [A] 기능적 교수요목(functional syllabus)으로 주제에 따라 기능을 표현하는 연습을 하게 되고, 그에 맞는 기능과 활동을 하도록 학생들을 가르친다. 여러 다양한 활동을 통해 기능에 맞는 언어기능을 익힐 수 있도록 도와준다. 교수요목 [B] 상황적 교수요목은 상황을 바탕으로 문법과 어휘를 가르친다. 문법에 초점을 맞추고 있기에 과정보다는 결과적으로 분법을 정확하게 습득했는지를 중시한다.

핵심 개념정리

교수요목 유형

(1) Structural (formal) syllabus. The content of language teaching is a collection of the **forms and structures,** usually grammatical, of the language being taught. Examples include nouns, verbs, adjectives, statements, questions, subordinate clauses, and so on.

(2) Notional/ functional syllabus. The content of the language teaching is a collection of the **functions** that are performed when language is used, or of the notions that language is used to express. Examples of functions include: informing, agreeing, apologizing, requesting; examples of notions include size, age, color, comparison, time, and so on.

(3) Situational syllabus. The content of language teaching is a collection of real or imaginary situations in which language occurs or is used. A situation usually involves several participants who are engaged in some activity in a specific setting. The language occurring in the situation involves a number of functions, combined into a plausible segment of discourse. The primary purpose of a situational language teaching syllabus is to teach the **language** that occurs in the **situations**. Examples of situations include: seeing the dentist, complaining to the landlord, buying a book at the book store, meeting a new student, and so on.

(4) Skill-based syllabus. The content of the language teaching is a collection of specific abilities that may play a part in using language. Skills are things that people must be able to do to be **competent in a language**, relatively independently of the situation or setting in which the language use can occur. While situational syllabi group functions together into specific settings of language use, skill-based syllabi group linguistic competencies (pronunciation, vocabulary, grammar, and discourse) together into generalized types of behavior, such as listening to spoken language for the main idea, writing well-formed paragraphs, giving effective oral presentations, and so on. The primary purpose of skill-based instruction is to learn the specific language skill. A possible secondary purpose is to develop more general competence in the language, learning only incidentally any information that may be available while applying the language skills.

(5) Communicative Syllabus

① Task-based syllabus. The content of the teaching is a series of complex and purposeful **tasks** that the students want or need to perform with the language they are learning. The tasks are defined as activities with a purpose other than language learning, but, as in a content-based syllabus, the performance of the tasks is approached in a way that is intended to develop second language ability. Language learning is subordinate to **task performance**, and language teaching occurs only as the need arises during the performance of a given task. Tasks integrate language skills in specific settings of language use. Task-based teaching differs from situation-based teaching in that while situational teaching has the goal of teaching the specific language content that occurs in the situation (a **predefined product**), task-based teaching has the **goal** of teaching students to draw on resources to complete some piece of work (a **process**). The students draw on a variety of language forms, functions, and skills, often in an individual and unpredictable way, in completing the tasks. Tasks that can be used for language learning are, generally, tasks that the learners actually have to perform in any case.

② Content-based-syllabus. The primary purpose of instruction is to teach some content or information using the language. The students are simultaneously language students and students of whatever content is being taught. The subject matter is primary, and language learning occurs incidentally to the content learning. The content teaching is not organized around the language teaching, but vice-versa. Content-based language teaching is concerned with information, while task-based language teaching is concerned with **communicative and cognitive processes**. A science class taught in the language the students need to learn, possibly with linguistic adjustment to make the science more comprehensible.

23

핵심 개념정리

능력중심 교수요목(Competency-based Syllabus)

(1) Practical Benefits of Competency-Based Learning

- Efficient and potentially lower-cost degree/credential options for students
- Greater understanding of learning outcomes throughout the academic institution
- Courses, learning resources, and assessments aligned to well-defined goals
- Motivated and engaged students
- Increased student retention and completion rates, particularly when prior learning can be applied to degree progress
- Learners' improved ability to recognize, manage, and continuously build upon their own competencies and evidence of learning
- Employers' improved ability to understand graduates' competencies and learning achievements

- Outcomes-based frameworks for continuous improvement at course, program, and institutional levels

We found that competency-based education practices do not need to be dramatic or disruptive. Many effective approaches incorporate competency-based learning processes into existing course and curriculum structures. In fact, one of the reasons why there are so many different approaches is because educational institutions adapt competency-based learning to achieve their own goals. Competency-based learning does not happen in a vacuum. Nor does it need to be viewed as something outside or counter to our educational traditions and values.

Competency-based learning can be valuable for all of the stakeholders in our learning communities: learners have more opportunities to take ownership of their learning and expand their lifelong learning pathways; faculty grow professionally as they articulate the learning outcomes in their areas of expertise and embed them in rich learning experiences; academic leaders provide engaging curricula that advance knowledge and produce graduates who can demonstrate what they've learned; and institutional leaders focus on new ways of identifying barriers to success and achieving improved outcomes. The key characteristics of learner-centric, outcomes-based, and differentiated help us visualize what competency-based learning means to these stakeholders.

(2) Key Characteristics

① Learner-Centered: First and foremost, competency-based learning focuses on the learner as an individual. It provides opportunities for each individual to develop skills at their own pace, collaborate with others, collect evidence of learning, and become successful lifelong learners. Competency-based learning empowers learners to:
- Understand the competencies they need to master to achieve their goals
- Progress through learning processes without time constraints
- Explore diverse learning opportunities
- Collaborate in learning activities with communities of peers and mentors
- Create learning artifacts that represent their competencies
- Reflect on their own learning achievements
- See what they've mastered, what they still need to accomplish, and where to improve
- Develop an online academic identity, including the ability to manage competencies and portable evidence of learning from multiple sources

② Outcomes-Based

Competency-based learning starts with well-defined learning outcomes. The structure for competency-based learning comes from creating, managing, and aligning sets of competencies to learning resources, assessments, and rubrics, with analytics to track performance. Focusing on outcomes empowers faculty and academic leaders to:
- Develop robust sets of learning outcomes and competencies
- Reorient curricular design to start with learning outcomes rather than starting with time/term structures

- Build high-quality sharable resources, assessments, and rubrics designed to support learning outcomes
- Foster authentic assessment that includes demonstrated mastery of competencies
- Effectively identify risk in students' progress toward learning achievements and provide appropriate interventions
- Support transparent analysis of learning outcomes at every level of the institution
- Achieve short-term and long-term academic performance improvements focused on outcomes rather than inputs

③ Differentiated

Differentiation refers to competency-based learning practices that recognize and adjust to meet the needs of individual learners. Differentiation is multi-faceted and applies to learner support, communications and interventions, as well as learning processes.

- Prescriptive/ Diagnostic: providing different learning materials or assessments to learners based on what they've already mastered.
- Affiliation: learners receive different materials or delivery based on their relationship to the curriculum or program in cohorts or groups.
- Adaptive: content that is designed with learning alternatives and branching closely tied to the learner's specific interactions with the content.
- Choice: learners select from among different learning resources and pathways based on their own choices and preferences.
- Personalized messages &notifications: relevant, timely communications tailored to learners' individual activities and needs.
- Appropriate interventions: feedback, guidance, activities, or tasks designed to help individuals progress along their learning paths.

24

문항 해설

(1) 구조적 교수요목(structural syllabus)은 언어를 음소, 형태, 단어, 구조, 문장형태의 모음으로 보고 있다. 과업의 중심은 의미가 아니라 언어의 형태로 보는 교수법이다

(2) 어휘적 교수요목(lexical syllabus)으로서 언어를 문법이나 기능적인 측면보다는 어휘, 특히 다중어휘의 구성으로 보고 있다. 학습자의 언어학습이 다양한 미리 만들어진 구를 배움으로서 발전될 수 있다고 믿는다.

(3) 과업중심 교수요목(task-based syllabus)에서 언어는 다른 사람과의 의미협상을 통하여 자연스럽게 습득되어야 한다. 과업중심 교수법은 학습자들이 과업완수를 위해서 언어를 사용하는 것이며 그룹활동을 중시하는 협동교수법이다.

25

문항 해설

교수요목은 '무엇을 학습하는가'(what is to be learned)에서 '어떻게 학습하는가'(how the learning is done)로 변화되었다. 즉 형식(formal) → 기능(functional) → 과업중심(task) & 어휘(lexical) → 다층적 교수요목(multi-syllabus)의 순서로 방향성이 변화되었다. 본문에서 구조적 교수요목이 실패한 후 대안으로 제시되는 교수요목을 묻고 있으므로, 기능에 대한 내용인, giving advice나 making requests을 서술한다.

핵심 개념정리

기능 교수요목(Functional Syllabus)

Methods and approaches such as **Grammar Translation, Audiolingualism and Situational** Language teaching are based on the presentation and practice of grammatical structures and, essentially, a **grammar-based** syllabus. In 1972, the British linguist D.A. Wilkins published a document that proposed a radical shift away from using the traditional concepts of grammar and vocabulary to describe language to an analysis of the communicative meanings that learners would need in order to express themselves and to understand effectively. This initial document was followed by his 1976 work Notional Syllabuses, which showed how language could be categorized on the basis of notions such as quantity, location and time, and functions such as making requests, making offers and apologizing.

Wilkins' work was used by the Council of Europe in drawing up a communicative language syllabus, which specified the **communicative functions** a learner would **need** in order to communicate effectively at a given level of competence. At the end of the 1970s, the first course-books to be based on functional syllabuses began to appear. Typically, they would be organized on the basis of individual functions and the exponents needed to express these functions. For example, many course-books would begin with the function of 'introducing oneself', perhaps followed by the function of 'making requests', with typical exponents being 'Can I ….?', "Could you ….?", "Is it alright if I ….?' and so on. These would often be practised in the form of communicative exercises involving pair work, group work and role plays. It is interesting to compare this approach with a grammatical syllabus. In a typical grammatical syllabus, structures using the word 'would' tend to appear in later stages of the syllabus, as they are held to be relatively complex (e.g. "If I knew the answer, I would tell you"), whereas in a functional syllabus 'would' often appears at a very early stage due to its communicative significance in exponents such as 'Would you like ….?', which is extremely common and of great communicative value even to beginners. The need to apply a grammatical name or category to the structure is not considered important within the framework of a purely functional syllabus.

Criticisms of functional approaches include the difficulty in deciding the order in which different functions should be presented. Is it more important to be able to complain or to apologize, for example? Another problem lies in the wide range of grammatical structures needed to manipulate basic functions at different levels of **formality** (for example, 'Can I …..?'

as opposed to "Would you mind if I ….?"). In addition, although it is possible to identify hundreds of functions and micro-functions, there are probably no more than ten fundamental communicative functions that are expressed by a range of widely used exponents. There is also the apparently random nature of the language used, which may frustrate learners used to the more analytical and "building-block" approach that a grammatical syllabus can offer. Another apparent weakness is the question of what to do at higher levels. Is it simply a case of learning more complex exponents for basic functions or is one required to seek out ever more obscure functions (complaining sarcastically, for example)?

On the positive side, however, there is little doubt that **functional approaches** have contributed a great deal to the overall store of language teaching methodology. Most new course-books contain some kind of **functional syllabus** alongside a focus on grammar and vocabulary, thus providing learners with communicatively useful expressions in tandem with a **structural syllabus** with a clear sense of progression. In addition, the focus on communication inherent in the practice of functional exponents has contributed greatly to **communicative language teaching** in general. Finally, the idea that even beginners can be presented with exponents of high communicative value from the very start represents a radical shift from the kind of approach that began with the present simple of the verb 'to be' in all its forms and focused almost entirely on structure with little regard for actual communication in the target language.

26

핵심 ELT 읽기

실제성(Authenticity)

In education, authentic learning is an instructional approach that allows students to explore, discuss, and meaningfully construct concepts and relationships in contexts that involve **real-world problems** and projects that are **relevant to the learner**. It refers to a "wide variety of educational and instructional techniques focused on connecting what students are taught in school to real-world issues, problems, and applications. The basic idea is that students are more likely to be interested in what they are learning, more **motivated** to learn new concepts and skills, and better prepared to succeed in college, careers, and adulthood if what they are learning mirrors real-life contexts, equips them with practical and useful skills, and addresses topics that are relevant and applicable to their lives **outside** of school."

Authentic instruction will take on a much different form than traditional teaching methods. In the traditional classroom, students take a passive role in the learning process. Knowledge is considered to be a collection of facts and procedures that are transmitted from the teacher to the student. In this view, the goal of education is to possess a large collection of these facts and procedures. Authentic learning, on the other hand, takes a constructivist approach, in which learning is an active process. Teachers provide opportunities for students to construct their own knowledge through engaging in self-directed inquiry, problem solving, critical thinking, and reflections in real-world contexts. This knowledge construction is heavily influenced by the student's prior knowledge and experiences, as well as by the characteristics that shape the learning environment, such as values, expectations, rewards, and sanctions. Education is more **student-centered**. Students no longer simply memorize facts in abstract and artificial situations, but they experience and apply information in ways that are grounded in reality.

(1) Characteristics

The characteristics of authentic learning include the following:

- Authentic learning is centered on authentic, relevant, real-world tasks that are of interest to the learners.

- Students are actively engaged in exploration and inquiry.

- Learning, most often, is interdisciplinary. It requires integration of content from several disciplines and leads to outcomes beyond the domain-specific learning outcomes.

- Learning is closely connected to the world beyond the walls of the classroom.

- Students become engaged in complex tasks and higher-order thinking skills, such as analyzing, synthesizing, designing, manipulating, and evaluating information.

- Learning begins with a question or problem, which cannot be constricting in that it allows the student to construct their own response and inquiry. The outcome of the learning experience cannot be predetermined.

- Students produce a product that can be shared with an audience outside the classroom. These products have value in their own right, rather than simply for earning a grade.

- The resulting products are concrete allowing them to be shared and critiqued; this feedback allows the learner to be reflective and deepen their learning.

- Learning is student driven, with tutors, peers, teachers, parents, and outside experts all assisting and coaching in the learning process.

- Learners employ instructional scaffolding techniques at critical times.

- Students have opportunities for social discourse, collaboration, and reflection.

- Ample resources are available.

- Assessment of authentic learning is integrated seamlessly within the learning task in order to reflect similar, real world assessments. This is known as authentic assessment and is in contrast to traditional learning assessments in which an exam is given after the knowledge or skills have hopefully been acquired.

- Authentic learning provides students with the opportunity to examine the problem from different perspectives, which allows for competing solutions and a diversity of outcomes instead of one single correct answer.

- Students are provided the opportunity for articulation of their learning process and/or final learning product.

(2) Five standards

In order to address this challenge, a framework consisting of five standards of **authentic instruction** has been developed by Wisconsin's Center on Organization and Restructuring of Schools. This framework can be a valuable tool for both researchers and teachers. It provides "a set of standards through which to view assignments, instructional activities, and the dialogue between teacher and students and students with one another." Teachers can use the framework to generate questions, clarify goals, and critique their teaching. Each standard can be assessed on a scale of one to five rather than a categorical yes or no variable. "The five standards are **higher-order thinking, depth** of knowledge, **connectedness** to the world **beyond the classroom, substantive conversation,** and **social support** for student achievement."

① Higher-Order Thinking: This scale measures the degree to which students use higher-order thinking skills. Higher-order thinking requires students to move beyond simple recall of facts to the more complex task of manipulating information and ideas in ways that transform their meaning and implications, such as when students synthesize, generalize, explain, hypothesize, or arrive at some conclusion or interpretation.

② **Depth** of Knowledge: This scale assesses students' **depth** of knowledge and understanding. Knowledge is considered deep when students are able to "make clear distinctions, develop arguments, solve problems, construct explanations, and otherwise work with relatively complex understandings." Rather than emphasizing large quantities of fragmented information, instruction covers fewer topics in systematic and connected ways which leads to deeper understanding.

③ Connectedness to the World: This scale measures the extent to which the instruction has value and meaning beyond the instructional context. Instruction can exhibit connectedness when students address real-world public problems or when they use personal experiences as a context for applying knowledge.

④ Substantive Conversation: This scale assesses the extent of communication to learn and understand the substance of a subject. High levels of substantive conversation are indicated by three features: considerable interaction about the subject matter which includes evidence of higher-order thinking, sharing of ideas that are not scripted or controlled, and dialogue that builds on participants' **ideas** to promote improved collective understanding of a theme or topic.

⑤ **Social Support** for Student Achievement: The social support scale measures the culture of the learning community. Social support is high in classes where there are high expectations for all students, a climate of mutual respect, and inclusion of all students in the learning process. Contributions from all students are welcomed and valued.

(3) Examples

- ✓ **Simulation-Based Learning**: Students engage in simulations and role-playing in order to be put in situations where the student has to actively participate in the decision making of a project. This helps in "developing valuable communication, collaboration, and leadership skills that would help the student succeed as a professional in the field he/she is studying." Learning through simulation and role-playing has been used to train flight attendants, fire fighters, and medical personnel to name a few.
- ✓ **Student-Created Media**: Student-created media focuses on using various technologies to "create videos, design websites, produce animations, virtual reconstructions, and create photographs." In addition to gaining valuable experience in working with a range of technologies, "students have also improved their reading comprehension, writing skills, and their abilities to plan, analyze, and interpret results as they progress through the media project."
- ✓ **Inquiry-Based Learning**: Inquiry-based learning starts by posing questions, problems or scenarios rather than simply presenting material to students. Students identify and research issues and questions to develop their knowledge or solutions. Inquiry-based learning is generally used in field-work, case studies, investigations, individual and group projects, and research projects.
- ✓ **Peer-Based Evaluation**: In peer based evaluation students are given the opportunity to analyze, critique, and provide constructive feedback on the assignments of their peers. Through this process, they are exposed to different perspectives on the topic being studied, giving them a deeper understanding.
- ✓ **Project-Based Learning**: Begins with a problem or question that is the starting point for inquiry and which all products are created as a result of. Results in a single or series of products or artifacts that are created as a result or solution to the inquiry.

(4) Benefits

Educational research shows that authentic learning is an effective learning approach to preparing students for work in the 21st century. By situating knowledge within relevant contexts, learning is enhanced in all four domains of learning: cognitive (knowledge), affective (attitudes), psychomotor (skills), and psychosocial (social skills). Some of the benefits of authentic learning include the following:

- Students are more **motivated** and more likely to be **interested** in what they are learning when it is relevant and applicable to their lives **outside** of school.
- Students are better prepared to succeed in college, careers, and adulthood.
- Students learn to assimilate and connect knowledge that is unfamiliar.
- Students are exposed to different settings, activities, and perspectives.
- Transfer and application of theoretical knowledge to the world **outside** of the classroom is enhanced.
- Students have opportunities to collaborate, produce products, and to practice **problem**

solving and professional skills.

- Students have opportunities to exercise professional judgments in a safe environment.
- Students practice **higher-order thinking skills**.
- Students develop patience to follow longer arguments.
- Students develop flexibility to work across disciplinary and cultural boundaries.

27

핵심 개념정리

세계 영어(World Englishes)

World Englishes was proposed by Kachru to refer to the fact that there are **multiple and varied models of English** across cultures and that English is not limited to countries where it has traditionally been regarded as a mother tongue. World Englishes thus includes British, American, Australian as well as other mother tongue Englishes but also newer varieties of English that have emerged in countries that were once colonies and dependencies of the United Kingdom or the USA. These new Englishes are seen to take their place as legitimate varieties of English fulfilling distinctive functions in pluralistic societies such as Singapore, India, Pakistan, the Philippines, Nigeria and Fiji.

The **outer circle** is made up of post-colonial countries in which English, though not the mother tongue, has for a significant period of time played an important role in education, governance, and popular culture. The outer circle is one of the three concentric circles of World English described by linguist Braj Kachru in "Standards, Codification and Sociolinguistic Realism: The English Language in the Outer Circle" (1985).

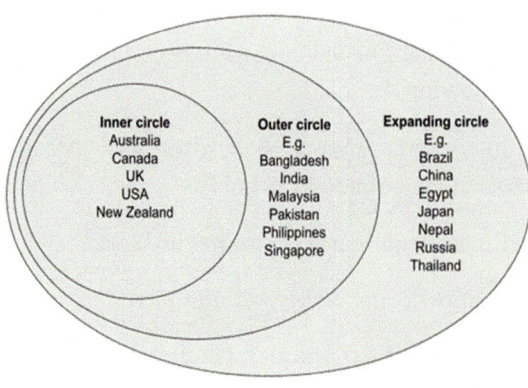

Low Ee Ling and Adam Brown describe the outer circle as "those countries in the earlier phases of the spread of English in non-native settings. ... where English has become institutionalised or has become part of the country's chief institutions" (English in Singapore, 2005). The labels **inner, outer, and expanding circles** represent the type of spread, the patterns of acquisition, and the functional allocation of the English language in diverse cultural contexts.

28

> **문항 해설**

교사가 학교 교복에 대한 사진이나 학교신문기사를 나누어주면서 실제자료를 이용하고 있다. 학생들은 통합된 기술(integrated skills)을 사용하도록 하고 있는데 글을 읽고, 노트하고 서로 알아낸 것을 토론하고, 쓰기를 하는 통합교육이 이루어진다. 학생의 이전의 지식(previous knowledge)을 활성화하는 것은 학생들이 이미 경험했던 내용에 대해 이야기해보도록 하는 것이다. 학생들이 장단점을 이야기하고 토론를 하면서 논쟁적 담화(argumentative discourse)를 내재적으로(implicitly) 배운다고 할 수 있다. 개별화 쓰기(personalized writing)는 자신의 의견을 한 단락 쓰는 것으로 이제까지 배운 것을 정리하는 수업의 마지막 단계인 통합(consolidation) 단계에 이루어진다.

29

> **문항 해설**

〈news script B〉에서 실제자료(authentic material)의 특징을 찾아 서술한다. 첫째, 어휘적 측면(lexical level)에서 구어체언어와 관용구(colloquial language and idioms), 'joshing around'와, 둘째, 통사적측면(syntactic level)에서 생략(ellipsis)으로 'ran so much'의 예시를 들 수 있다. 실제자료 선정기준으로 내용의 적합성(content suitability)와 코스의 목표(course objective)를 들 수 있다.

〈실제 읽기 자료를 선택하는 중요한 요소〉

Suitability of Content	• Does the text interest the student? • Is it relevant to the student's needs? • Does it represent the type of material that the student will use outside of the classroom?
Exploitability	• Can the text be exploited for teaching purposes? • For what purpose should the text be exploited? • What skills/strategies can be developed by exploiting the text?
Readability	• Is the text too easy/difficult for the student? • Is it structurally too demanding/complex? • How much new vocabulary does it contain? Is it relevant?
Presentation	• Does it look authentic? • Is it attractive? • Does it grab the student's attention? • Does it make him want to read more?~

30

> 핵심 ELT 읽기

통사적 & 어휘적 단순화(Syntactic and Lexical Simplification)

Different kinds of listening can be discerned, which are classified on the basis of a number of variables, involving purpose for listening, and type of text being listened to. These variables are mixed in different shapes, and each of them needs a special strategy (Vanpatten & Williams, 2007). Listening is a dynamic interaction of guessing approximation, expectation and idealization that naturally uses all the redundancies found in a representative discourse situation (Wang, 2010). The specific aims of the research are as follows:

- To find out whether **syntactic** and **lexical simplification** affects listening **comprehension**.
- To examine and measure the EFL students' perceived comprehension of listening texts by lexical and syntactic simplification.

The learners' success or failure in listening comprehension can be affected by many interfering factors. Among these factors, grammatical complexity of sentences and unfamiliarity of words should be taken into consideration. This research focuses on teaching listening at high school level.

(1) Simplification as a Learning Strategy

While listening is an undeniably complex process, it requires lexicon and syntax recognition and comprehension at its most fundamental level (Koda, 2005). Lexicon forms the foundation from which a learner builds meaning at a (a) sentence, (b) paragraph, and (c) discourse level. If the listener cannot access the meaning of a critical amount of vocabulary in a text, the listening process will break down. Grabe (2002) points out that both "a large recognition vocabulary and automaticity of word recognition for most of the words in the text" are central to an EFL learner's ability to comprehend a text under normal conditions.

While the importance of vocabulary in EFL listening is well established, the methods for accommodating EFL listeners with insufficient vocabularies vary widely and many are still in formative stages. Many approaches exist that claim to facilitate the EFL listening process. Some view authentic, or unmodified texts as the best medium for EFL learners; other use discourse levels. Still others create entirely new texts that are carefully composed using a limited lexical, syntactic, or discourse levels. Overall vocabulary knowledge is not only important in listening, but research also indicates that if a listener cannot readily access meaning for 95-98% of the specific vocabulary contained in a particular text, comprehension will be frustrated (Nation, 2001).

Young (1999) maintains that simplification will not necessarily aid comprehension of a text, rather the number of individual words that a learner will understand would increase.

This raises again the question of measuring the relationship between number of understood words and overall comprehension of a text (Hsuch-Chao, & Nation, 2000). Young (1999) concludes as well that simplification may overemphasize the importance of every individual word in a text, which could frustrate EFL learners, a concern that is echoed in other studies of simplification (Block, 1992).

(2) Syntactic Simplification

Blau (1990) studied the effect of sentence structure on the EFL listening comprehension of university students. It is suggested that sentence structure which made difference in the reading comprehension study (Blau, 1982) seems to be a less dominant modification when the input is aural rather than written. Cervantes and Gainer (1992) also conducted a study to explore the effect of syntactic simplification on EFL listening comprehension. The subjects were English major freshmen and seniors in a Japanese university. They proposed that syntactic simplification is an aid to EFL listening comprehension.

Besides, two studies investigate another kind of **paraphrase**. No absolute effectiveness of paraphrase was found in the studies. One study of Kelch (1985) tested the effects of syntactic modification which consists of (a) paraphrase, (b) synonym, and (c) parallel syntactic structures. It was found that there was an effect only for those passages with both modifications and a slower speech rate. The other study by Pica, Young, and Doughty (1987) investigated the listening comprehension of low intermediate adult EFL learners on directions to a task presented by a native speaker. Results show that subjects' listening comprehension was facilitated when the content of the directions was **repeated and rephrased in interaction**. However, reduction in linguistic complexity in the premodified input was not a significant factor.

(3) Simplified Listening Texts

One explanation for the conflicting findings in research involving modified and unmodified texts could be an interaction with the nature of the texts and the listener's proficiency levels. Following the results of other researchers, Oh (2001) questions the effect of proficiency might have on the effects of different modification. Boyle (1984) also conclude that lower proficiency levels appear to benefit more from certain type of modification has less positive effect on comprehension.

Petersen (2007) addresses the task of text simplification in the context of second language learning. A **data-driven approach** to simplification is proposed using a corpus of paired articles in which each original sentence does not necessarily have a corresponding simplified sentence, making it possible to learn where writers have dropped or simplified sentences. A classifier is used to select the sentences to simplify, and Siddharthan's syntactic simplification system (Siddharthan, 2006) is used to split the selected sentences.

Siddharthan proposes a syntactic simplification architecture that relies on shallow text analysis and favors time performance. The general goal of the architecture is to make text more accessible to a broader audience; it has not targeted any particular application. The system treats (a) apposition, (b) relative clauses, (c) coordination, and (d) subordination. Max (2005) applies text simplification in the writing process by embedding an interactive text simplification system into a word processor. At the user's request, an automatic parser analyzes an individual sentence and the system applies handcrafted rewriting rules. The resulting suggested simplifications are ranked by a score of syntactic complexity and potential change of meaning. The writer then chooses his or her preferred simplification. This system ensures accurate output, but requires human intervention at every step.

31

> 문항 해설

황교사의 수업일기에서는 교실에서 스스로가 더 많은 영어를 사용하기 위하여 자신의 말을 녹음하고 모니터해보고 있다. 교사의 전문성 발전을 위한 자기 평가이며, 자기성찰의 교수원리에 입각하여 교사중심의 수업을 진행하는 것임을 알 수 있다. 황교사는 학생 발화의 양에 관계없이 교사 발화에 중점을 두고 있으므로 교사중심의 수업을 하고 있음을 알 수 있다.

32-33

> 핵심 ELT 읽기

의사소통 교수법(Communicative Language Teaching)

(1) Academic influences

The development of communicative language teaching was also helped by new academic ideas. In Britain, applied linguists began to doubt the efficacy of **situational language** teaching, the dominant method in that country at the time. This was partly in response to Chomsky's insights into the nature of language. Chomsky had shown that the structural theories of language prevalent at the time could not explain the creativity and variety evident in real communication. In addition, British applied linguists such as Christopher Candlin and Henry Widdowson began to see that a focus on structure was also not helping language students. They saw a need for students to develop communicative skill and functional competence in addition to mastering language structures.

In the United States, the linguist and anthropologist Dell Hymes developed the concept of communicative competence. This was a reaction to Chomsky's concept of the linguistic competence of an ideal native speaker. **Communicative competence** redefined what it meant to "know" a language; in addition to speakers having mastery over the structural elements of language, according to communicative competence they must also be able to use those structural elements **appropriately** in different social situations. This is neatly summed up by Hymes's statement, "There are rules of use without which the rules of grammar would be useless." Hymes did not make a concrete formulation of communicative competence, but subsequent authors have tied the concept to language teaching, notably Michael Canale.

(2) Communicative syllabuses

An influential development in the history of communicative language teaching was the work of the Council of Europe in creating new language syllabuses. Education was a high priority for the Council of Europe, and they set out to provide syllabuses that would meet the **needs** of European immigrants. Among the studies used by the council when designing the course was one by the British linguist, D. A. Wilkins, that defined language using "notions" and "functions", rather than more traditional categories of grammar and vocabulary. Notional categories include concepts such as time, location, frequency, and quantity, and functional categories include communicative acts such as offers, complaints, denials, and requests. These syllabuses were widely used.

Communicative language-learning materials were also developed in Germany. There was a new emphasis on personal freedom German education at the time, an attitude exemplified in the philosophy of Jürgen Habermas. To fulfill this goal, educators developed materials that allowed learners to choose what they wanted to communicate freely. These materials concentrated on the various different social meanings a given item of grammar could have, and were structured in such a way that learners could choose how to progress through the course themselves. The materials were used in teacher training courses and workshops to encourage teachers to change to using a communicative syllabus. Two similar projects were also undertaken by Candlin at Lancaster University, and by Holec at the University of Nancy.

Meanwhile, at the University of Illinois, there was a study that investigated the effects of the explicit teaching of learning strategies to language learners. The study encouraged learners to **take risks while communicating**, and to use constructs other than rote memorized patterns. At the study's conclusion, students who were taught communicatively fared no worse on grammatical tests than students that had been taught with traditional methods, but they performed significantly better in tests of communicative ability. This was the case even for beginners.

CLT is usually characterized as a broad approach to teaching, rather than as a teaching method with a clearly defined set of classroom practices. As such, it is most often defined as a list of general principles or features. One of the most recognized of these lists is David Nunan's (1991) **five features of CLT**: An emphasis on learning to communicate through interaction in the target language.

- The introduction of **authentic texts** into the learning situation.

- The provision of opportunities for learners to focus, not only on language but also on the **learning process** itself.

- An enhancement of the learner's own personal **experiences** as important contributing elements to classroom learning.

- An attempt to link classroom language learning with language activities **outside the classroom.**

These five features are claimed by practitioners of CLT to show that they are very interested in the needs and desires of their learners as well as the connection between the language as it is taught in their class and as it used outside the classroom. Under this broad umbrella definition, any teaching practice that helps students develop their communicative competence in an authentic context is deemed an acceptable and beneficial form of instruction. Thus, in the classroom CLT often takes the form of pair and group work requiring negotiation and cooperation between learners, fluency-based activities that encourage learners to develop their confidence, role-plays in which students practise and develop language functions, as well as judicious use of grammar and pronunciation focused activities.

(3) Classroom activities

- Role-play
- Information gap
- Language exchanges
- Learning by teaching

- Interviews
- Games
- Pair-work
- Surveys

However, not all courses that utilize the Communicative Language approach will restrict their activities solely to these. Some courses will have the students take occasional grammar quizzes, or prepare at home using non-communicative drills, for instance. William Glasser's "control theory" exemplifies his attempts to **empower** students and give them voice by focusing on their basic, human **needs**: Unless students are given power, they may exert what little power they have to thwart learning and achievement through inappropriate behavior and mediocrity. Thus, it is important for teachers to give students voice, especially in the current educational climate, which is dominated by standardization and testing .

CHAPTER 03 영어평가

01-03

채점자 신뢰도 (Rater reliability)

- **Inter-rater reliability** has to do with the **consistency** between two or more raters who evaluate the same test performance (Jones, 1979). For **inter-rater reliability**, it is of primary interest to examine if the observations over raters are consistent or not, which may be estimated through the application of generalizability (Crocker & Algina, 1986).

- **Intra-rater reliability** concerns the consistency of one rater for the same test performance at different times (Jones, 1979). Both inter- and intra-rater reliability deserve close attention in that test scores are likely to vary from rater to rater or even from the same rater (Clark, 1979). For instance, the halo effect has been recognized as a serious problem when raters are required to score all test sections of a given tape and continually shift their scoring criteria (Starr, 1962). More studies on the issues of the **scoring reliability** in second language performance assessment seem very much in order.

04

핵심 개념정리

말하기 평가의 핵심 요소

In speaking assessment, the following four key principles are essential to ensure a fair, accurate, and meaningful evaluation of learners' speaking abilities:

1. Clarity: Clarity in speaking assessment means that the criteria, instructions, and expectations are clearly defined and communicated to both teachers and students. Clear criteria help learners understand what is being assessed, and clear instructions make the assessment process smoother and more consistent.
    - Providing a rubric with specific descriptors (e.g., pronunciation, fluency, coherence).
    - Giving explicit instructions on how to complete speaking tasks.
    - Offering sample responses to illustrate expected performance levels.

2. Authenticity: Authenticity refers to how realistic and relevant the speaking tasks are to real-world communication. The goal is to evaluate language use in contexts that learners are likely to encounter outside the classroom. Authentic tasks make the assessment more meaningful and motivating, as students see the practical value of their speaking skills.

- Role-plays simulating real-life situations (e.g., job interviews, ordering food).
- Problem-solving discussions related to daily life or professional scenarios.
- Using authentic prompts like news articles or videos to initiate conversations.

3. Integrated Skills Assessment: Integrated skills assessment involves combining speaking with other language skills, such as listening, reading, or writing. This approach reflects the reality of how language is used in communication. Speaking rarely occurs in isolation, so integrating skills offers a more comprehensive assessment of communicative competence.

   - Listening to a short audio clip and then discussing its content.
   - Reading an article and giving a spoken summary or opinion.
   - Engaging in group discussions that require both listening and responding.

4. Practicality: Practicality refers to the ease and efficiency of administering, scoring, and interpreting the speaking assessment. It considers the time, resources, and effort required. If an assessment is too complex or time-consuming, it becomes impractical for regular use.

   - Using simple, quick-to-administer tasks (like short interviews or paired conversations).
   - Employing scoring rubrics that are easy to understand and apply consistently.
   - Reducing the need for excessive preparation or technology.

When these principles are balanced, speaking assessments become valid, reliable, and relevant to learners' real-world communication needs.

05

핵심 개념정리

혼합형 학습(Blended Learning)

Blended learning, also known as hybrid learning, combines online digital media with traditional face-to-face classroom methods. It leverages the strengths of both approaches to create a more flexible and dynamic learning environment. Here are some of the key advantages:

- Flexibility and Convenience: Students can access online materials anytime, anywhere, making learning more adaptable to individual schedules. Ideal for learners with busy lifestyles or varying time commitments.

- Enhanced Engagement: Combines interactive online activities (like quizzes, videos, and forums) with hands-on classroom experiences; Keeps learners more motivated and engaged by varying the types of activities.

- Personalized Learning: Online components allow students to learn at their own pace,

- revisiting materials as needed. Teachers can tailor lessons to meet diverse learning needs by providing additional resources or challenges online.
- Improved Communication and Collaboration: Online platforms facilitate peer interaction through discussion boards, group projects, and collaborative tasks. Teachers can provide timely feedback through digital tools, enhancing support.
- Efficient Use of Classroom Time: Routine tasks (like quizzes or content delivery) are done online, freeing up classroom time for active learning and problem-solving activities. Flipped classrooms are a great example, where students study theory at home and practice in class.
- Access to Diverse Resources: Offers a rich variety of multimedia content, including videos, podcasts, interactive exercises, and simulations. Students can explore additional resources based on their interests or weaknesses.
- Data-Driven Insights: Learning management systems (LMS) track students' progress, providing valuable data on strengths and areas needing improvement. Teachers can analyze performance and adjust strategies accordingly.
- Adaptability to Modern Education Needs: Prepares learners for the digital world by incorporating technology into education. Supports lifelong learning habits by blending independent online study with guided classroom learning.

06-09

핵심 개념정리

다지선다형 질문을 작성하는 10가지 규칙

1. Use Plausible Distractors (wrong-response options)

- Only list plausible distractors, even if the number of options per question changes
- Write the options so they are homogeneous in content
- Use answers given in previous open-ended exams to provide realistic distractors

2. Use a Question Format

- Experts encourage multiple-choice items to be prepared as questions (rather than incomplete statements)

3. Emphasize Higher-Level Thinking

- Use memory-plus application questions. These questions require students to recall principles, rules or facts in a real life context.

- The key to preparing memory-plus application questions is to place the concept in a life situation or context that requires the student to first recall the facts and then apply or transfer the application of those facts into a situation.
- Seek support from others who have experience writing higher-level thinking multiple-choice questions.

4. Keep Option Lengths Similar

- Avoid making your correct answer the long or short answer

5. Balance the Placement of the Correct Answer

- Correct answers are usually the second and third option

6. Be Grammatically Correct

- Use simple, precise and unambiguous wording
- Students will be more likely to select the correct answer by finding the grammatically correct option

7. Avoid Clues to the Correct Answer

- Avoid answering one question in the test by giving the answer somewhere else in the test
- Have the test reviewed by someone who can find mistakes, clues, grammar and punctuation problems before you administer the exam to students
- Avoid extremes − never, always, only
- Avoid nonsense words and unreasonable statements

8. Avoid Negative Questions

- Students may be able to find an incorrect answer without knowing the correct answer

9. Use Only One Correct Option (Be sure the best option is clearly the best option)

- The item should include one and only one correct or clearly best answer
- With one correct answer, alternatives should be mutually exclusive and not overlapping
- Using MC with questions containing more than one right answer lowers discrimination between students

10. Use Only a Single, Clearly-Defined Problem and Include the Main Idea in the Question

- Students must know what the problem is without having to read the response options

10

> 핵심 개념정리

컴퓨터 조정 시험(Computer Adaptive Testing)

CAT successively selects questions so as to maximize the **precision** of the exam based on what is known about the examinee **from previous questions**. From the examinee's perspective, the difficulty of the exam seems to **tailor** itself to his or her level of ability. For example, if an examinee performs well on an item of intermediate difficulty, he will then be presented with a more difficult question. Or, if he performed poorly, he would be presented with a simpler question. Compared to static multiple choice tests that nearly everyone has experienced, with a fixed set of items administered to all examinees, computer-adaptive tests require fewer test items to arrive at equally **accurate scores**.

Adaptive tests can provide **uniformly precise scores** for most test-takers. In contrast, standard fixed tests almost always provide the best precision for test-takers of medium ability and increasingly poorer precision for test-takers with more extreme test scores. An adaptive test can typically be shortened by 50% and still maintain a higher level of precision than a fixed version. This translates into a time savings for the test-taker. Test-takers do not waste their time attempting items that are too hard or trivially easy. Additionally, the testing organization benefits from the time savings; the cost of examinee seat time is substantially reduced. However, because the development of a CAT involves much more expense than a standard fixed-form test, a large population is necessary for a CAT testing program to be financially fruitful. Like any computer-based test, adaptive tests may show **results immediately after** testing. Adaptive testing, depending on the item selection algorithm, may reduce exposure of some items because examinees typically receive different sets of items rather than the whole population being administered a single set. However, it may increase the exposure of others (namely the medium or medium/easy items presented to most examinees at the beginning of the test).

11-19

> 핵심 개념정리

언어평가의 원리

(1) Practicality

An effective test is practical; is not excessively expensive; stays within appropriate time constraints; is relatively easy to administer; has a scoring/ evaluation procedure that is specific and time-efficient. A test that takes a few minutes for a student to take and several hours for an examiner to evaluate is impractical for most classroom situations. A test that can be scored only by computer is impractical if the test takes place a thousand miles away from the nearest computer.

(2) Reliability

A reliable test is **consistent** and dependable. If you give the same test to the same students in two different occasions, the test should yield similar results. In order to allow better comparison, reliability coefficients for all the tests and subtests were estimated by the Kuder-Richardson Formula 21 (KR-21). The reliability estimate was also computed by the **Cronbach's alpha formula**. Both these formulas are measures of **internal consistency**. Raatz and Klein-Braley (1995) suggest that it is possible to perform an inner consistency analysis. The reliability of the whole test can be calculated using Cronbach's alpha.

- Student Related Reliability: The most common issue in student related reliability is caused by temporary illness, fatigue, a bad day, anxiety, and other physical and psychological factors which may make an observed score deviate from a true score.

- **Inter-rater reliability** has to do with the **consistency** between two or more raters who evaluate the same test performance (Jones, 1979). For **inter-rater reliability**, it is of primary interest to examine if the observations over raters are consistent or not, which may be estimated through the application of generalizability (Crocker & Algina, 1986).

- **Intra-rater reliability** concerns the consistency of one rater for the same test performance at different times (Jones, 1979). Both inter- and intra-rater reliability deserve close attention in that test scores are likely to vary from rater to rater or even from the same rater (Clark, 1979). For instance, the halo effect has been recognized as a serious problem when raters are required to score all test sections of a given tape and continually shift their scoring criteria (Starr, 1962). More studies on the issues of the **scoring reliability** in second language performance assessment seem very much in order.

- **Test administration** reliability deals with the conditions in which the test is administered. 예 Street noise outside the building, bad equipment, room temperature, the conditions of chairs and tables, photocopying variation

- Test Reliability: The test is too long, Poorly written or ambiguous test items

(3) Validity

① Content Validity

A test is valid if the teacher can clearly define the achievement that she is measuring. A test of tennis competency that asks someone to run a 100-yard dash lacks content validity. If a teacher uses the communicative approach to teach speaking and then uses the audiolingual method to design test items, it is going to lack content validity.

② Criterion-related Validity

(**Concurrent validity**) The test is administered **at the same time** as the criterion is collected. This is a common method of developing validity evidence for employment tests: A test is administered to incumbent employees, then a rating of those employees' job performance is, or has already been, obtained independently of the test. Note the possibility for restriction of range both in test scores and performance scores: The incumbent employees are likely to be a more homogeneous and higher performing group than the applicant pool at large.

(**Predictive validity**) The test scores are collected first; then at some later time the criterion measure is collected. For **predictive validity**, the example is slightly different: Tests are administered, perhaps to job applicants, and then after those individuals work in the job for a year, their test scores are correlated with their first year job performance scores. Another relevant example is SAT scores: These are validated by collecting the scores during the examinee's senior year and high school and then waiting a year (or more) to correlate the scores with their first year college grade point average. Thus predictive validity provides somewhat more useful data about test validity because it has greater fidelity to the real situation in which the test will be used. After all, most tests are administered to find out something about future behavior.

③ Construct Validity

A construct is an explanation or theory that attempts to explain observed phenomena. If you are testing vocabulary and the lexical objective is to use the lexical items for communication, writing the definitions of the test will not match with the construct of communicative language use.

④ Face Validity

Face validity refers to the degree to which a test looks right, and appears to measure the knowledge or ability it claims to measure: well-constructed, expected format with familiar tasks: test that is clearly doable within the allotted time limit: directions are crystal clear: tasks that relate to the course: a difficulty level that presents a reasonable challenge.

(4) Authenticity

The language in the test is as natural as possible. Items are contextualized rather than isolated. Topics are relevant and meaningful for learners. Some thematic organization to items is provided. Tasks represent, or closely approximate, real-world tasks. Characteristics are as follows:

- Resemble real-world tasks and activities.
- Can be structured as written or oral assessments completed individually, in pairs, or in groups.
- Often presented as ill-structured problems with no right answers.
- Ask students to communicate their knowledge orally or in writing to a specific audience and for specific purpose.

(5) Washback

Washback refers to the effects the tests have on instruction in terms of how students prepare for the test cram courses and "teaching to the test" are examples of such washback. In some cases the student may learn when working on a test or assessment. Washback can be positive or negative. Washback effect refers to the **impact of testing** on curriculum design, teaching practices, and learning behaviors. The influences of testing can be found in the choices of learners and teachers: teachers may teach directly for **specific test preparation**, or learners might focus on specific aspects of language learning found in assessments. Washback effect in testing is typically seen as either negative, or positive. Washback may be considered harmful to more fluid approaches in language education where definitions of language ability may be limited; however, it may be considered beneficial when good teaching practices result. Washback can also be positive or negative in that it either maintains or hinders the accomplishment of **educational goals**. In positive washback, teaching the curriculum becomes the same as teaching to a **specific test**. Negative washback occurs in situations where there may be a mismatch between the stated goals of instruction and the focus of assessment; it may lead to the abandonment of instructional goals in favor of test preparation.

20

문항 해설

(단락1) 타당도의 문제점은 구성 타당도로 설명될 수 있다. 〈Table 1〉의 평가표처럼 발음과 문법 요소만으로 전체적인 의사소통능력이나 실제 말하기수행을 평가할 수 없다. (단락 2) 점수표는 첫째, 유창성은 'excellent'라고 평가한다. 그 이유로 내용이 논리적이면서 그림에 대한 이야기를 전체적인 것에서 부분적인 것으로 연결을 한다. 자기수정을 통해 틀렸던 어휘를 본인 스스로 다시 수정할 수 있는 능력이 있다. (단락 3) 응집성(cohesion)점수는 'good to fair'로 평가할 수 있다. 응결장치(cohesion device)를 적절하게 활용하지 못하고 참조어(reference word)를 활용하지 못하여 잘못된 대명사를 사용하고 있다.

21

문항 해설

두 교사가 학습자들의 목표언어(비교급)를 이용한 쓰기 수행능력을 평가하기 위해서 평가하는 방법을 서술하는 문제이다. 두 교사의 평가노트에 나타난 내용을 토대로 하여 각 시험의 특성을 찾아 구체적으로 서술한다. 이교사는 연습활동을 통해 학생들이 비교급을 이용하여 개별 문장을 쓰는 연습을 하고 그 내용을 평가한다. 민교사는 각각의 문장들을 연결어(connectors)를 이용하여 이야기로 만들 수 있는 활동을 통해 평가한다.

22

핵심 개념정리

듣기 평가 유형

(1) Intensive Listening

Recognizing Phonological & Morphological Elements	Paraphrase recognition
• to ask test-takers to identify the stimulus from two or more choices • no context provided • Phonemic pair: consonants/ vowels, morphological pair, stress pattern in can't, one-word stimulus	• to ask test-takers to choose the correct paraphrase from a number of choices • sentence/ dialogue paraphrase

(2) Responsive Listening

- a question-and-answer format
- to provide some interactivity in lower-end listening tasks
- appropriate response to a question, open-ended response to a question

(3) Selective Listening

The purpose of such performance is not necessarily to look for global or general meanings, but to be able to comprehend designated information in a context of longer stretches of spoken language (classroom directions from a teacher, TV or radio news items, or stories). Assessment tasks in selective listening could ask students to listen for names, numbers, a grammatical category, directions (in a map exercise), or certain facts and events.

Listening Cloze	Information Transfer	Sentence Repetition
• cloze dictations, partial dictations • deletions are governed by the objective of the test • exact word method of scoring	• aurally processed information transferred to a visual representation • to force test-taker to select the correct bits and pieces to complete a task • picture-cued items, chartfilling,	• to repeat a sentence • to assess the ability to recognize and retain chunks of language and meaning

(4) Extensive Listening

Extensive performance ranges from listening to lengthy lectures to listening to a conversation and deriving a comprehensive message or purpose. Listening for the gist, for the main idea, and making inferences are all part of extensive listening.

23

> **문항 해설**

　(단락1) 말하기평가의 문제점을 각 학생별로 서술한다. 민수는 단순한 암기(mechanical memorization)와 낮은 동기(low motivation)의 문제점이 있다. 호민은 수정피드백(corrective feedback)을 받지 못하고, 전체적 오류(global errors)에 대한 수정을 원하고 있다. 수진은 수업내용과 수행시험에 연관성이 없어서 의사소통능력이 발전되지 못한다고 생각한다. (단락 2) 말하기 과업에서는 information gap활동이 추천될 수 있다. 의미있는 의사소통과 정확한 언어사용 모두를 발전시킬 수 있다. (단락 3) 문제해결을 역류효과(washback effect)의 측면에서 보면 수업목표에 의사소통의 개별 요소를 도입하고 수행평가(formative assessment)를 실시하여 학습효과를 높일 수 있다.

24

> **문항 해설**

　평가방법에 관한 문제이다. 평가 형식을 크게 분리(discrete-point)와 통합평가(integrative assessment)로 나누어서 볼 수 있는데 통합평가에는 dictation과 cloze test를 포함하고 있다. 그 중에서 cloze test에 대한 평가 일반에 대한 설명이다. cloze test는 그 안에서 무작위로 삭제된 빈칸(randomly deleted blank) 시험과 논리적으로 삭제된(rationally deleted) 시험으로 분류될 수 있다. 본 문제의 지문은 매 7번째로 빈칸을 만들어 놓은 전자의 경우를 가리키고 있다. 이는 명사나 동사 등 출제자가 어떤 특정한 목적을 가지고 빈칸을 만들어 놓은 논리적으로 삭제된 시험의 경우에 비해 피드백이 일관적이지 않다. 일관된 실수의 패턴을 보이기보다는 무작위의 오답이 나올 수 있으므로 체계적인 피드백을 기대하기는 어렵다고 봐야 하겠다.

25 – 28

> **핵심 개념정리**

Cloze와 C-Test

　Key words: proficiency, reliability, discriminatory/ discrimination power, construct validity, criterion-related validity, content validity, cloze test, C-Test

(1) Cloze Test

　Cloze test is now a well-known and widely-used **integrative** language test. Wilson Taylor(1953) first introduced the **cloze** procedure as a device for estimating the readability of a text. However, what brought the **cloze** procedure widespread popularity was the investigations with the **cloze** test as a measure of ESL proficiency (Jonz, 1976, 1990; Hinofotis, 1980; Bachman, 1982, 1985; Brown, 1983, 1993; Laesch & van Kleek 1987; Chapelle & Abraham 1990; see also Oller, 1979 for an overview). The results of the substantial volume of research on **cloze** test have been extremely varied. Furthermore, major technical defects have been found with the procedure. Alderson (1979, 1980, 1983), for instance, showed that changes in the starting point or **deletion rate** affect reliability and validity coefficients. Other researchers like Carroll (1980), Klein-Braley and Raatz (1984), Klein-Braley (1983, 1985), Farhady (1983b), and Brown (1993) have questioned the reliability and different aspects of validity of cloze tests. In view of all the criticisms made against the cloze procedure, Klein-Braley and Raatz proposed the C-Test as a modified form of the cloze test.

(2) C-Test

The C-Test consists of four or five short texts in each of which the **first sentence is left intact**, then the C-principle (or the rule of two) is applied: the second half of every second word is deleted, beginning with the second word of the second sentence. If a word has an odd number of letters, the 'larger' half is omitted. Numbers, proper names, abbreviations, and one-letter words such as 'I' are ignored in the counting. In the canonical C-Test each text will have either 20 or 25 blanks. The students' task is to restore the missing parts. Only entirely correct restorations are counted as correct (i.e., spelling problems are considered errors). The C-Test is believed to have a number of advantages over the cloze test. Some of the most important rewards of the C-Test are as follows:

- The use of a variety of passages allows for a better sampling and representation of the language and content. Also, a person with special knowledge in a certain field cannot have an unfair advantage all through the test.

- Since every second word is damaged, it is possible to obtain a better sampling of all the different language elements in a text.

- C-Tests are very easy for native speakers. But someone who doesn't know the language at all normally scores zero or close to zero.

- C-Tests are easy to construct, administer, and score. As there is only one acceptable solution in most cases, the scoring is more objective.

Ever since it was introduced, the C-Test has been the subject of many research studies and scholarly controversies. On one hand, some researchers have found the C-Test a highly **integrative**, **reliable** and **valid** measure of **overall language ability**. More specifically, Klein-Braley (1997) empirically compared the C-Test with a group of other reduced redundancy tests — classical cloze test, cloze elide test, multiple-choice cloze test, and standard dictation. She found that the best test to represent general language proficiency was the C-Test. Eckes and Grotjahn (2006) found clear evidence that the C-test is a highly reliable and unidimensional measure of general language proficiency. They found that "**lexis** and **grammar** are important components of general language proficiency as measured by C-tests."

However, research findings have not always been very consistent. Cohen et al. (1984), for instance, reported acceptable reliability and validity indices for their C-Test, but they could not find any clear pattern for macro-level processing in the C-Test, though they found indications of micro-level processing (i.e., language processing at or below sentence level). Dörnyei and Katona (1992) validated a C-Test against four different language tests including an oral interview, and a TOEIC. Their results confirmed that the C-Test is a reliable and valid instrument. Nevertheless, they noted that the C-Test was less efficient in testing grammar.

29-30

문항 해설

진단평가(diagnostic test)가 의미하는 바를 이해하고 서술할 수 있도록 한다. 첫째, 진단평가의 가장 큰 의미는 수업 전에 실시한다는 데 있다. 가르치는 내용을 얼마나 잘 배웠는지 평가하는 성취평가(achievement test)와 가장 큰 차이라고 할 수 있다. 그런 목적으로 학생들의 장점과 단점을 확인할 수 있으며 나아가 학습방향에 대한 가이드를 제시할 수도 있다.

핵심 개념정리

시험 유형

(1) A **diagnostic test** is a test that helps the teacher and learners identify **problems** that they have with the language. For example, at the start of the course, the teacher gives the learners a diagnostic test to see what areas of **language need** to be in the syllabus. In the classroom, progress tests given during the course can also act as diagnostic tests as they help the teacher and learners identify what areas will be looked at next on the course. The purpose of the test is to:
- diagnose students' strengths and weaknesses
- track and report on students' language gains
- be linked to curriculum/ teaching/ materials
- help students to plan their language learning
- inform curriculum development

It is common to assert that diagnostic tests are intended to probe the **strengths** and **weaknesses** of learners, but there is virtually no description, much less discussion of what the underlying constructs might be that should be operationalized in valid diagnostic tests.

(2) **Achievement Test** is designed to measure how much a language learners have successfully learned with specific reference to a **particular course, textbook, or program of instruction**, thus a type of criterion-referenced test. An achievement test is typically given at the end of a course, whereas when administered periodically throughout a course of instruction to measure language learning up to that point, it is alternatively called a progress test.

(3) **Proficiency Test** measures how much of a language someone has learned. The difference between a proficiency test and achievement test is that the latter is usually designed to measure how much a student has learned from a particular course or syllabus. A Proficiency test is **not linked** to a particular course of instruction, but

measures the learner's general level of language mastery.

(4) **Progress Test** may be regarded as similar to achievement tests but narrowed and much more specific in scope. This is an achievement test linked to a **particular set of teaching materials** or a **particular course** of instruction. The test is prepared by a teacher and given at the end of a chapter, course, or term are progress tests. The test helps the teacher to judge the degree of success of his or her teaching and to identify the weakness of the learners.

(5) **Aptitude Test** are designed to predict the ability of an individual to learn a foreign language given typical time of study and conditions for learning. Language aptitude refers to the **potential** that a person has for learning languages. This potential is often evaluated using formal aptitude tests, which predict the **degree of success** the candidate will have with a new language. Aptitude tests vary but many include evaluation of ability to manage sounds, grammatical structures, infer rules, and memory. Common uses:

- Selection and placement of language learners
- Understanding students cognitive strengths and weaknesses pertaining to language learning
- Placement of language learners in the most appropriate instructional settings in colleges/ universities or other formal classroom settings

31

> 핵심 개념정리

Portfolios

1. What are Language Portfolios?

They are a **collection of individual students' work** put together in a file or ring binder. They belong to the student and can be updated as language learning continues by adding to and taking away pieces of work. Language Portfolios are made up of three parts:

The Passport	This contains factual information about the language learner. It gives a history of the learners' language learning experiences which in this case refer to learning English. It may also contain any certificates or qualifications which show the learners' level in an internationally transparent manner. For our young learners this may mean a certificate they received from a summer camp they attended or a qualification they got from taking an English exam at school or in any other English language centre. It may also include a ticket to a theatre production in English, a film they saw or a trip abroad to an English-speaking country.

Language Biography	This is a personal history of the learners' language learning experience. For example it may include a short narrative about the summer camp which they went on and for which they have included the certificate in their passport section. It also includes self-assessment materials, such as the learner checklists and any aims that learners have for the future. These aims might be passing a specific exam, attending a course and feeling well prepared for it or being able to speak English to a visitor.

2. Advantages

- They enhance learners' **motivation** by providing something personal and tangible which they can build up and develop over the course.

- They help learners to **reflect** on their own learning and achievement by asking them to make choices, review, compare and organize their own work.

- They enable learners to look for new cultural experiences by opening their eyes to the possibilities available to them. Part of portfolio work involves 'show and tell' sessions where learners talk about their **experiences** and look at other portfolios.

- From a teacher's point of view, portfolios lead to greater learner **autonomy** since they involve self assessment, learner responsibility and parent involvement. Learners can work in their own time on different sections of the LP.

3. The problems with Language Portfolios

- First of all with large groups the storage of portfolios can be problematic. Of course, learners can look after them themselves but this always means there are lots of students who forget or lose their portfolio. I have found it is better to store them in class and only allow them home occasionally throughout the year. In this way it means they are readily at hand for parent interviews and of course class time.

- Secondly, as a teacher portfolios involve the provision of the folder and the organisation of the contents, which can be quite time consuming. However, once I had made templates for the three sections, found an attractive folder and decided on the topic to work on, learners could work at their own pace and the sessions ran themselves.

32

핵심 개념정리

규준참조평가와 준거참조평가

In terms of practicality, the tests can be divided into criterion-referenced and norm-referenced. The purpose of criterion-referenced tests is to classify people according to whether or not they are able to perform some task or set of tasks satisfactorily. Criterion-referenced tests have two positive virtues: they set meaningful standards in terms of what people can do, which do not change with different groups of candidates, and they motivate students to attain those standards. The criterion-referenced interpretation of a test score identifies the relationship to the subject matter. In the case of a mastery test, this does mean identifying whether the examinee has mastered a specified level of the subject matter by comparing their score to the cut score. The need for direct interpretation of performance means that the construction of a criterion-referenced test may be quite different from that of a norm-referenced test designed to serve the same purpose.

Scores from norm-referenced tests are used to compare students' progress to others in their peer group. Norm referenced tests may measure the acquisition of skills and knowledge from multiple sources such as notes, texts and syllabi, while criterion referenced tests measure performance on specific concepts and are often used in a pre-test/ post-test format.

33

핵심 개념정리

형성평가와 총괄평가

(1) Formative assessment

The goal of formative assessment is to monitor student learning to provide **ongoing feedback** that can be used by instructors to improve their teaching and by students to improve their learning. More specifically, formative assessments:

- help students identify their **strengths and weaknesses** and target areas that need work
- help faculty recognize where students are struggling and address problems immediately

Formative assessments are generally low stakes, which means that they have low or no point value. Examples of formative assessments include asking students to:

- draw a concept map in class to represent their understanding of a topic
- submit one or two sentences identifying the main point of a lecture

- turn in a research proposal for early feedback

(2) Summative assessment

The goal of summative assessment is to evaluate student learning **at the end of an instructional unit** by comparing it against some standard or benchmark. Summative assessments are often high stakes, which means that they have a high point value. Information from summative assessments can be used formatively when students or faculty use it to guide their efforts and activities in subsequent courses. Examples of summative assessments include:

- a midterm exam
- a final project
- a paper
- a senior recital

34

핵심 ELT 읽기

쓰기의 종합적 & 분석적 채점

This paper examines the strengths and weaknesses of holistic and analytic scoring methods, using the Bachman and Palmer's framework, which has six original categories of test usefulness, and explores how we can use holistic or analytic scales to better assess student compositions.

> Keywords: holistic scoring, analytic scoring, writing assessment, test usefulness

1. Theoretical background and rationale

In the assessment of writing, a major advantage of holistic over analytic scoring is that each writing sample can be evaluated quickly by more than one rater for the same cost that would be required for just one rater to do the scoring using several analytic criteria (cf. Davies et al, 1999). One possible disadvantage of **holistic** judgment is that different raters may choose to focus on different aspects of the written product. On the other hand, an advantage of **analytic scoring** is that raters are required to focus on each of various assigned aspects of a writing sample, so that they all evaluate the same features of a student's performance. But the practical disadvantage of analytic scoring, as indicated by Davies et al above, is that it is more time-consuming than holistic scoring. The choice of scoring method is not always easy.

The Bachman and Palmer (1996) framework of test usefulness can be relevant in helping teachers decide which type of test to use. This framework proposes six qualities of test usefulness: **Reliability, Construct Validity, Authenticity, Interactiveness, Impact,** and **Practicality**. Bachman and Palmer suggest that test developers develop an appropriate balance among these qualities by setting minimum acceptable standards. Weigle (2002), comments on the Bachman and Palmer (1996) framework by showing a comparison of holistic and analytic scales based on the same six qualities of test usefulness as follows:

Quality	Holistic Scales	Analytic Scales
Reliability	lower than analytic, but still acceptable	higher than holistic
Construct Validity	assume that all relevant aspects of writing ability develop at the same rate and can thus be captured in a single score; correlate with superficial aspects such as length and handwriting	more appropriate for L2 writers as different aspects of writing ability develop at different rates
Practicality	relatively fast and easy	time-consuming; expensive
Impact	single score may mask an uneven writing profile and may lead to misleading placements	more scales provide useful diagnostic information for placement and instruction; more useful for rater training
Authenticity	Reading holistically is a more natural process than reading analytically	Raters may read holistically and adjust analytic scores to match holistic impressions

1. Purpose of the research

Since not all teachers (native speakers and non-native speakers alike) are good at rating compositions, understanding the details of holistic and analytic evaluation systems can be beneficial for teachers, in their classroom assessment and in their training sessions. A clear-cut rating scale with detailed criterion can lead to positive **washback** in which students have clear **study goals**. The purpose of the present research is to serve as a starting point for rater training development and help students' set clearer study goals. This paper examines two scoring methods (holistic and analytic) by looking at their respective strengths and weaknesses using the Bachman and Palmer's framework and explores how holistic or analytic scales can better be used to assess student compositions.

2. Research design and method

Ninety students took a composition test in class (30 students per class), and their writing scripts were evaluated by three raters both holistically (using one evaluation item = overall) and analytically (using five rating items chosen by the author: grammar, vocabulary, organization, originality, cohesion). The author referred to Cohen (1994) in deciding the evaluation items and making criteria for the four labels (1,2,3,4).

The two types of scoring were conducted on two different days (with a three week interval) by the same raters. The scripts were evaluated by three raters using a four-point scale (1: "poor" to 4: "good"). The data analysis was conducted using a FACETS model so that three facets (students, raters, evaluation items) could be shown on the same continuum. The acceptable range for Infit and Outfit Statistics in the performance test was 0.6-1.4. (The items below 0.6 were included in a special category called overfitting, and the items above 1.4 were called underfitting in the Rasch model, and all items outside the general category were called misfitting.).

The students were all freshman students and their age range was between 18 and 20, and approximately half of them were male students. Their English proficiency level could be loosely described as intermediate and the test they took was part of their grade. The raters were trained using ten sample compositions that were collected from the same university students, so that the raters gained a rough idea of the students' proficiency level and sense of how the criterion should be used. The student composition topic was to discuss the proposal to have a five-day school week. Details concerning the rating procedure are summarized.

⟨holistic rating scale⟩

Raters: Three trained native speakers of English. Items: One evaluation item (Overall) Rating scale: A four-point scale (1, 2, 3, 4) was used with the criteria			
4 points	3 points	2 points	1 point

⟨analytic rating scale⟩

Raters: Three trained native speakers of English. Items: 5 criteria Rating scale: A four-point scale (1, 2, 3, 4) was used with the criteria				
Originality of Content	Organization	Vocabulary	Grammar	Cohesion & Logical Consistency

- For **practical and economical reasons, holistic** (one item evaluation) assessment can be used, but to avoid risky idiosyncratic ratings, **analytic assessment** (with several evaluation items) is strongly recommended.

- In terms of rating options, the best practice is to have multiple raters and multiple rating items. The next best practice is to have one overall evaluation item and multiple raters. In order of preference, the third choice would be to have one rater and multiple items. The least recommended solution would be to have one rater and one item. Even worse than this, however, would be to have one rater and an impressionistic scale.

- This study suggests that it is very risky for one classroom teacher to judge students using a holistic rating system.

- The more ratings a person receives, the higher the rating precision, though one obvious condition is that construct and content validity must come before statistical reliability. Otherwise, we do not know what the test is measuring.

35

문항 해설

본 지문의 교사의 주요목표는 상위 10%를 순위대로 매겨서 장학금을 수여하는 것이므로 상대평가(norm-referenced)의 표준화시험(standardized test)을 필요로 한다. 읽기 시험이 (1) 전통적 다지선다형 문제 (2) T/F 문제 (3) 답이 되는 단어나 구에 ✓ 표시해야 할 문제로 구성되어있다. 이러한 종류의 읽기 시험은 특정한 코스에 대한 것이 아니라 전체적인 읽기의 이해도를 측정하기 위한 평가이므로 대규모 능력시험(proficiency test)에 해당된다. 표준화시험의 목표중의 하나는 학생들에게 총괄적인(summative) 피드백을 주기 위한 것이다. 채점방식은 정확한 답이 있는 객관식형식이므로 전문가가 필요하지 않다. 이 평가는 상위 10%를 선택해야 하므로 등수를 매기는 상대평가이다. 이해도 측정하는 선택형(selected-response) 시험이기 때문에 직접 답을 써야하는 구성형(constructed-response)은 포함되지 않는다.

핵심 개념정리

상대평가와 절대 평가 비교

Dimension	Criterion-Referenced Tests	Norm-Referenced Tests
Purpose	• To determine whether each student has achieved specific skills or concepts. • To find out how much students know before instruction begins and after it has finished.	• To rank each student with respect to the achievement of others in broad areas of knowledge. • To discriminate between high and low achievers.
Content	• Measures specific skills which make up a designated curriculum. These skills are identified by teachers and curriculum experts. • Each skill is expressed as an instructional objective.	• Measures broad skill areas sampled from a variety of textbooks, syllabi, and the judgments of curriculum experts.
Item Characteristics	• Each skill is tested by at least four items in order to obtain an adequate sample of student performance and to minimize the effect of guessing. • The items which test any given skill are parallel in difficulty.	• Each skill is usually tested by less than four items. • Items vary in difficulty. • Items are selected that discriminate between high and low achievers.
Score Interpretation	• Each individual is compared with a preset standard for acceptable achievement. The performance of other examinees is irrelevant. • A student's score is usually expressed as a percentage. Student achievement is reported for individual skills.	• Each individual is compared with other examinees and assigned a score—usually expressed as a percentile, a grade equivalent score. • Student achievement is reported for broad skill areas, although some norm- referenced tests do report student achievement for individual skills.

(1) **Norm-referenced tests** (NRTs) compare a **person's score against the scores of a group** of people who have already taken the same exam, called the "norming group." When you see scores in the paper which report a school's scores as a **percentage** – "Our school ranked at the 49th percentile" – or when you see your child's score reported that way – "Jiyoung scored at the 63rd percentile" – the test is usually an NRT. Most achievement NRTs are multiple-choice tests. Some also include open-ended, short-answer questions. The questions on these tests mainly reflect the content of nationally-used textbooks, not the local curriculum. This means that students may be tested on things your local schools or state education department decided were not so important and therefore were not taught.

(2) **Criterion-referenced tests** (CRTs) are intended to measure **how well** a person has learned a specific body of knowledge and skills. Multiple-choice tests most people take to get a driver's license and on-the-road driving tests are both examples of criterion-referenced tests. As on most other CRTs, it is possible for everyone to earn a **passing score** if they know about driving rules and if they drive reasonably well. In education, CRTs usually are made to determine whether a student has learned the material taught in **a specific grade or course**. An algebra CRT would include questions based on what was supposed to be taught in algebra classes. It would not include geometry questions or more advanced algebra than was in the curriculum. Most all students who took algebra could pass this test if they were taught well and they studied enough and the test was well-made.

36

문항 해설

학습자의 oral report로 인하여 학습자의 학습 과정 또는 언어사용에 대한 다양한 통찰이 생겨났다. 이 구두 보고서는 학습자들이 언어 학습 또는 언어를 이용한 과제수행 전, 도중, 이후에 작성한 것이다. 구두 보고서는 (a) 자기보고(self-report) (b) 자기관찰(self-observation) (c) 자기실현(self-revelation)을 반영하는 자료이다. 자기 보고 자료는 대개의 경우 학습자들에게 자신이 언어를 배우거나 사용하는 방법을 묘사하도록 요구하는 질문지에 나타난다. 자기관찰은 언어학습 및 언어사용의 실제적인 예를 이야기하는 것을 의미한다. 예를 들어, 가정법과 관련된 언어학습 또는 언어사용과 관련된 사건을 회고적으로 묘사하는 일지 또는 일기쓰기는 회고적인 자기 관찰로 간주된다. 자기실현 및 소리 내어 생각하기(think-aloud) 자료는 언어 학습 및 사용이 일어날 때만 쓸 수 있다. 이 세 가지 측정법 중, 자기 보고 자료는 몇 가지 실용적인 이유로 널리 사용되어 왔다. 그러나 자기 보고가 인지적 사건들과 관련없이 제시되어 왔기 때문에, 이 접근으로는 신뢰성이 의심되는 자료가 나올 수 있다. 때때로 연구가들은 언어 학습 및 언어 사용이 일어나는 시점 또는 가까운 시간 내에 그것들을 묘사한 자료를 얻기 위해 응답자들이 더 많은 자기관찰과 자기실현의 자료들을 제공하도록 노력한다. 자기실현과 자기관찰은 자기보고의 자료를 보완하기 위해서 학습과정에 대한 일치되는 평가를 만들어 내기 위해 만들어진 것이다.

37 – 42

핵심 개념정리

다지선다형 평가 항목분석

(1) **Item facility** (IF) is defined here as the proportion of students who answered a particular item **correctly**. Thus, if 45 out of 50 students answered a particular item correctly, the proportion would be 45/50 = .90. An IF of .90 means that 90% of the students answered the item correctly, and by extension, that the item is very easy.

(2) **Item discrimination** (ID) can be calculated by first figuring out who the **upper and lower students** are on the test (using their total scores to sort them from the highest score to the lowest). The upper and lower groups should probably be made up of equal numbers of students who represent approximately one third of the total group each.

(3) **Distractor efficiency** is related to item discrimination, the extent to which the distractors lure a sufficient number of test-takers.

Ideal items in an Norm-referenced test should have an average IF of .50. Such items would thus be well centered, i.e., 50 percent of the students would have answered correctly, and by extension, 50 percent would have answered incorrectly. In reality however, items rarely have an IF of exactly .50, so those that fall in a range between **.30 and .70** are usually considered acceptable for **NRT purposes**. Once those items that fall within the .30 to .70 range of IFs are identified, the items among them that have the highest IDs should be further selected for inclusion in the revised test. This process would help the test designer to keep only those items that are well centered and discriminate well between the high and the low scoring students.

43

문항 해설

과정중심교수법(process-based approach)에서 S2의 첫 번째 초고에 대해 S1과 S2가 동료협의(peer-conferencing)를 하고 있는 대화이다. 우선 두 학생이 pluralism이란 단어를 놓고 의미협상을 하는 과정과 S2의 초안 구성에서 서론 부분의 문제점에 대해 토론한다. 이러한 협의는 결과중심쓰기에서 완성된 마지막 작문에 대한 평가를 하게 되는 것과는 반대로, 서로의 의미협상을 통해 작문을 수정하고, 의미와 구조에 대한 토론이 주요 안건이다. 협의는 교사와 학습자 간의 일대일 직접 피드백으로 교사는 촉진자(facilitator)로서, 학생은 자기 성찰에 대한 내적인 동기를 부여받고 협의는 다음과 같은 다양한 기능을 제공한다.

- commenting on drafts
- responding to journals
- giving feedback on the test
- setting learning goals
- reviewing portfolios
- exploring strategies for weakness
- advising on a presentation

쓰기과업에 대한 피드백

Written feedback is an essential aspect of any English language writing course. This is especially true now with the predominance of the **process approach to writing** that requires some kind of second party feedback, usually the instructor, on student **drafts**. So dependant is current writing instruction on instructor feedback that Kroll (2001) describes it as one of the two components most central to any writing course with the other being the assignments the students are given. The goal of feedback is to teach skills that help students improve their writing proficiency to the point where they are cognizant of what is expected of them as writers and are able to produce it with minimal errors and maximum clarity.

1. Types of Feedback

The most prominently used methods feedback fall into two common categories: feedback on **form** and feedback on **content**. The most common methods of feedback on form are outright teacher **correction** of **surface errors**, teacher markings that indicate the place and type of error but without correction, and underlining to indicate only the presence of errors. The first requires students to copy the corrections and the latter two require students to correct the errors on their own. Feedback on content consists mainly of comments written by teachers on drafts that usually point out problems and offer **suggestions for improvements on future rewrites**. Students are usually expected to incorporate information from the comments into other versions of their papers.

Despite these negative aspects, there are effective points to some of the common methods of teacher feedback. Fathman and Walley (1990) discovered that when students receive grammar feedback that indicated the place but not type of errors, the students significantly improved their grammar scores on subsequent rewrites of the papers. This idea is echoed by Frodesen (2001), who notes that indirect feedback is more useful than direct correction. Written feedback has also been found to be effective when it is coupled with **student-teacher conferencing** (Brender, 1998; Fregeau, 1999). As noted earlier, many students find understanding written feedback problematic. Conferencing allows both students and teachers a chance to trace the causes of the problems arising from student writing and feedback, and to develop strategies for improvement. During these sessions, teachers can ask direct questions to students in order to gain a deeper understanding of student writings. Students are able to express their ideas more clearly in writing and to get clarification on any comments that teachers have made. Teachers can use conferencing to assist students with any specific problems related to their writing.

One important aspect of feedback that is often overlooked is the desires of students as to the kinds of feedback they wish to receive. Fregeau (1999) notes that students want to participate in a process approach to writing that allows for multiple rewrites as well as conferencing of some sort. Brender (1998) asserts that students want to take part in conferencing and find it more effective than written comments. Leki (1990) points out that students prefer error correction methods that label mistakes and let them make corrections on their own. Finally, Cohen and Cavalcanti (1990) mention that students want to have some kind of feedback pertaining to the content of their writings.

2. Suggestions for Appropriate and Effective Feedback

Teachers have to come up with an effective method of feedback that takes into account the shortcomings of common methods of feedback, the positive aspects of them and the desires of students. The **goals** of a particular writing course are one of the main factors that need to be considered when determining how to provide feedback. Feedback that is a mismatch with assignment or course goals may be one of the factors contributing to students not knowing how to properly respond to it. Among these are consideration of course and assignment goals, the stage of the writing process and the form of the feedback.

Aside from the aforementioned effectiveness of marking errors for student **self-correction**, other methods of feedback on grammar can be productive in improving students' writing skills. To lessen student confusion, teachers should consistently use a standard set of symbols or markings to indicate place and type of error and train the students in what kinds of **corrections** to make based on each symbol. Lists of proofreading symbols can easily be found in most writing textbooks, or teachers can create their own. Furthermore, teachers should familiarize students with the system so they will not be surprised when new symbols occur.

Many of the same kinds of improvements that can be made for feedback on form can also be made for feedback on content. The failure of written comments dealing with content comes from a combination of using inconsistent, unclear comments along with not training students in how to properly use the feedback to improve. Teachers should consistently use a standard set of clear and direct comments and questions to indicate place and type of content feedback. These types of comments and questions should focus students' attention on the content of the composition and the process they followed instead of merely pointing out areas that the teacher found interesting or lacking. As Leki (1990) points out, these kinds of questions and comments can be used to create a dialog between the student and the teacher in order to give both a clearer understanding of how the assignment was and should be conceived and executed. Furthermore, teachers should, as with grammar, familarize students with the types of comments that will be used and train students in how to make use of the comments. Without training in how to use the comments to better their writing, students are likely to either ignore the comments, misunderstand them, or fail to use them constructively .

The comments that the teachers use and training that they give students can be further developed in individual conferences. Aside from using conferences to determine if students understand and are making use of feedback, teachers can also use them to explain their comments to the students. Conferences are an excellent time for teachers and students to ask direct questions to each other and uncover any misunderstandings by either party. One way to do this would be to present students with pre-conference sheets that allow them to prepare questions for the teacher beforehand. Likewise, the teacher should also prepare a list of comments and questions before the conference. I developed the following and found them to be very effective in providing feedback to my EFL students and fostering improvement in their writing skills.

CHAPTER 04 영어교수법

01

핵심 개념정리

실행연구(Action research)

Action research is widely used in the field of English teaching to improve the teaching and learning of the language. The cyclical process of **problem identification, data collection, analysis**, and **action** is particularly useful in English teaching because it allows teachers to tailor their teaching strategies to the specific needs and challenges of their students. Action research in English teaching can involve a wide range of activities, including:

① Identifying the **needs** of individual learners: Action research can help teachers identify the specific needs of their students in terms of their English language proficiency, learning styles, and cultural background. This information can then be used to develop teaching strategies that are more effective in meeting the needs of each individual student.

② Developing and testing **new teaching methods**: Action research can also be used to develop and test new teaching methods and materials. For example, a teacher might develop a new reading comprehension strategy and test it with a group of students. Based on the results, the teacher can refine the strategy and make it more effective.

③ Improving student **motivation**: Action research can also be used to improve student motivation in English language learning. For example, a teacher might explore ways to make English language learning more fun and engaging for students, such as through the use of games or multimedia resources.

④ Evaluating the **effectiveness of existing teaching methods**: Action research can be used to evaluate the effectiveness of existing teaching methods and materials. For example, a teacher might evaluate the effectiveness of a particular grammar teaching method by collecting data on student understanding and retention.

Overall, action research in English teaching can help teachers to develop more effective teaching strategies, improve student outcomes, and contribute to the ongoing development of the field.

02

핵심 개념정리

Project-based learning

Developing autonomy in project-based learning is an essential skill as it not only enhances their language proficiency but also fosters independent learning and critical thinking. Here are strategies to help students develop autonomy in project-based work:

(1) Clearly Define Project Goals and Expectations

- Set Clear Objectives: Ensure that students understand the goals and outcomes of the project. This helps them take ownership of their learning and stay focused on the task.

- Provide Rubrics: Use rubrics to outline the criteria for success. This gives students a clear understanding of what is expected, allowing them to self-assess their progress.

(2) Encourage Self-Directed Learning

- Research Skills: Teach students how to find and use resources independently, such as online articles, videos, or library materials. This encourages them to take control of their learning process.

- Time Management: Help students develop time management skills by setting milestones or deadlines within the project. This teaches them to plan and organize their work effectively.

(3) Foster Decision-Making and Choice

- Choice of Topics: Allow students to choose their own project topics or aspects of a larger project that interest them. This increases engagement and motivates them to take responsibility for their work.

- Decision-Making Opportunities: Encourage students to make decisions about how to approach the project, which tools to use, or how to present their findings. This builds confidence in their ability to make choices.

(4) Promote Collaborative Learning

- Group Work: Assign students to work in groups where they can share responsibilities, delegate tasks, and support each other. Collaboration helps students learn from peers and take responsibility for their contributions.

- Peer Feedback: Incorporate peer review sessions where students give and receive feedback. This encourages them to reflect on their work and make improvements independently.

(5) Provide Scaffolding and Support

- Guidance and Resources: Offer guidance and resources initially, but gradually reduce support as students become more confident and capable. This scaffolding approach helps students transition to independent work.

- Mini-Lessons: Conduct mini-lessons on specific skills or language points relevant to the project. This targeted instruction equips students with the tools they need to work autonomously.

(6) Integrate Technology

- Online Tools: Introduce students to online tools for project management, research, and presentation (e.g., Google Docs, Trello, Canva). These tools can facilitate independent work and collaboration.

- Digital Portfolios: Encourage students to create digital portfolios to document their learning process. This allows them to reflect on their work and showcase their achievements.

(7) Create a Supportive Environment

- Encouragement and Praise: Regularly encourage students and recognize their efforts. Positive reinforcement boosts their confidence and motivation to work independently.

- Safe Learning Environment: Create a classroom environment where students feel safe to take risks, make mistakes, and learn from them. This openness is crucial for developing autonomy.

(8) Real-World Connections

- Authentic Tasks: Design projects that have real-world relevance, such as creating a community survey or planning a school event. When students see the practical application of their work, they are more motivated to take ownership.

- By implementing these strategies, students can gradually develop the autonomy needed to successfully manage and complete project-based work, enhancing both their language skills and their ability to learn independently.

03 핵심 개념정리

과업의 난이도

When discussing factors that can affect task performance, particularly in language assessments, three key factors to consider are language demands, processing demands, and performance conditions:

1) **Language Demands**: Language demands refer to the **linguistic complexity** and requirements of the test content. This includes vocabulary difficulty, sentence structure complexity, language proficiency level required, and the clarity of instructions. Language demands can impact a test-taker's ability to understand the questions, comprehend the reading passages, and produce accurate responses. Factors such as the **familiarity** of the language used, the presence of **idiomatic** expressions or **cultural** references, and the **clarity** of language instructions can influence how well a test-taker performs.

2) **Processing Demands**: Processing demands involve the cognitive load and mental effort required to complete the test tasks. This includes factors such as the length and complexity of the test items, the speed at which responses must be generated, the amount of information that must be processed simultaneously, and the presence of distractors or irrelevant information. Processing demands can affect a test-taker's ability to allocate attention, maintain focus, manage time effectively, and apply problem-solving strategies. Test-takers with limited **cognitive resources or processing speed** may struggle to perform well under high processing demands.

3) **Performance Conditions**: Performance conditions encompass the testing environment and external factors that can influence test performance. This includes factors such as test anxiety, test format and administration mode (e.g., paper-based vs. computer-based), time constraints, test-taking strategies, access to accommodations or support resources, and the presence of distractions or disruptions during the test. Performance conditions can impact a test-taker's emotional state, motivation level, test-taking confidence, and overall task performance. Adequate preparation, familiarization with test formats, and effective stress management techniques can help mitigate the effects of performance conditions on test performance.

04

영어과 교육과정

통합 교수법

듣기, 말하기, 읽기, 쓰기의 언어기능을 점진적으로 함양하고, 네 기능을 **통합적**으로 사용할 수 있는 능력을 기르도록 한다.

언어 기능 \ 언어 구분	음성 언어	문자 언어
이해 기능	듣기	읽기
표현 기능	말하기	쓰기

교육과정의 언어 기능은 듣기, 말하기, 읽기, 쓰기의 네 가지 기능으로 구분되어 있다. 이런 구분은 네 기능이 서로 배타적인 영역임을 나타내거나 학습의 순서를 나타내기 위한 것이 아니다. 이는 가장 일반적인 언어 기능 분류에 따른 것으로 편의상 구분되어 제시된 것이라고 할 수 있다. 네 기능간의 관계는 **매개(medium)** 언어에 따라 음성 언어와 문자 언어로 또는 이해 기능과 표현 기능으로 분류될 수 있다. 또한 네 기능은 서로 연관이 있으며 한 기능의 향상은 나머지 세 기능의 촉진을 의미하고 한 기능은 다른 기능으로 전이되어 통합된다. 이해 기능과 표현 기능, 음성 언어와 문자 언어 간의 구분을 나타내는 점선은 이와 같은 기능 간의 상호 연관성을 나타내며 또한 기능 간의 **통합적 교수·학습 및 사용**을 의미한다.

The **integrated-skill** approach, as contrasted with the purely **segregated** approach, exposes English language learners to **authentic** language and challenges them to interact naturally in the language. Learners rapidly gain a true picture of the richness and complexity of the English language as employed for communication", says Rebecca Oxford, University of Maryland in her paper "Integrated Skills in the ESL/EFL Classroom." As observed by many experts – an integrated approach bridges the gap that often **separates** the language and the content classrooms. It provides a wholesome learning experience to the learner. It prepares him for the **real-world** challenges. Having said that, this paper aims at exploring the effects of applying **integrated approach** to the teaching of English reading and writing class within our college. It discusses the following dimensions, including (1) the conduct of current English reading and writing classes within our college (2) the factors that affect reading and writing classes (3) the attitude analysis of English language teachers in our college when teaching English reading and writing class (4) the needs analysis of teachers and students that are to improve the achievements on the curriculum (5) the advantages of applying the Integrated Skills Approach to the teaching in the above classes. Suggestions and recommendations of the research are to be offered to for advancements on the design of English reading and writing curriculum.

05

문항 해설

본문에서 지리과목의 교과서를 가지고 ESL 중급수준의 학습자가 언어를 습득하는 모형인 내용중심교수법(content-based instruction)에 대해 설명하고 있다. 이러한 통합수업(integrated lesson)에서 과목을 학습하다 보면 듣고, 말하고, 쓰고, 읽기의 네 가지 기능을 모두 활용하게 된다. 동시에 특정 분야의 내용으로 연계할 수 있어 학습자들의 요구(needs)를 만족시키면서 학습자들의 관심 분야의 내용을 배우기 때문에 흥미롭고, 유용할 수 있다. 학습자들의 외적지향(extrinsic concerns)보다는 내적지향(intrinsic concerns)을 중심으로 학습할 교과 내용 또는 그와 관련된 주제나 정보를 중심으로 영어를 교수하는 방법을 말한다. 수업의 내용은 의사를 전달하는 데 사용되는 언어 형태를 가르치는 것이 아니라 언어를 통하여 배우거나 의사소통하게 되는 교과목(subject matter)을 말한다. 이 교수법은 학습자들이 교실에서 수학, 사회, 과학 등 교과를 학습하면서 진정한 의사소통과 정보 교환에 초점을 두어 영어를 추가적으로 학습하게 되므로 교과를 중심으로 영어를 가르쳐야 한다는 관점에서 출발한다.

핵심 개념정리

내용중심 교수법

According to Brinton, Snow, and Wesche (1989), CBI refers to "the integration of particular content with language teaching aims.. the **concurrent** teaching of subject matter and second language skills." A strong form of CBI regards the "target language largely as the vehicle through which subject matter content is learned, rather than as the object of subject." In other words, content is the main focus of instruction, but the improvement of language skills is a concurrent goal. In the strong version of CBI, this is achieved by the intensive use of the language, not through its study.

The CBI approach is comparable to English for **Specific Purposes** (ESP), which usually is for vocational or occupational needs, or English for **Academic Purposes** (EAP). The goal of CBI is to prepare students to acquire the languages while using the context of any subject matter so that students learn the language by using it within the specific context. Rather than learning a language out of context, it is learned within the context of a specific academic subject.

Keeping students **motivated** and interested are two important factors underlying content-based instruction. Motivation and interest are crucial in supporting student success with challenging, informative activities that support success and which help the student learn complex skills (Grabe & Stoller, 1997). When a student is motivated and interested in the material he is learning, that student makes greater connections between topics, elaborations with learning material, and can recall information better (Alexander, Kulikowich, & Jetton, 1994: Krapp, Hidi, & Renninger, 1992).

- Language is text- and discourse-based.
- Language use draws on integrated skills.
- Language is purposeful.

06

문항 해설

'Gestalt means a sense of wholeness, and integration of the various parts of self.' 라는 문장에서 볼 수 있듯이 Gestalt이론은 완전성을 의미하는 것으로 총체적 언어교수법(whole language approach)과 연계되며, 비언어 경험, 즉 집약적인 활동과 연결시킨다. 마음(mind)과 같은 수준으로 신체의 움직임을 중시한다고 하여 TPR 교수법과 같은 시각으로 학습을 이해한다고 볼 수 있다.

핵심 개념정리

총체적 언어 교수법(Whole Language Approach)

언어는 별개의 부분으로 이루어진 집합체가 아닌 하나의 전체(whole)로 간주하는 총체적 교수법으로, 구어와 문자 언어의 듣기, 말하기, 읽기, 쓰기의 상호 연결성을 가지고 학습되어야 한다는 교수법이며 다음의 내용들을 중시한다.

- Cooperative learning
- Participatory learning
- Student-oriented learning
- Focus on the community of learners
- Focus on the social nature of language
- Use of authentic, natural language
- Meaning-centered language
- Holistic assessment techniques in testing
- Integration of the 'four skills'

07

The task types in language learning can be categorized based on three key dimensions: interactant relationship, goal orientation, and outcome options. Let's break them down with clear explanations and examples.

1. Interactant Relationship: Who Holds the Information?

This concerns how information is distributed among participants in a task.

- Shared Information: All participants have access to the same information and work together using common knowledge. (Example) A group reads the same article and discusses the main idea.

- Split Information: Each participant has different pieces of information, and they must exchange details to complete the task. (Example) A jigsaw reading activity where students have different parts of a story and must share information to reconstruct it.

2. Goal Orientation: Do Students Need to Agree?

This refers to whether students must reach a single shared conclusion or if multiple perspectives are acceptable.

- Convergent Tasks: Require learners to agree on one final outcome through discussion and negotiation. (Example) Deciding on the best solution to a problem (e.g., planning a school event with a limited budget).

- Divergent Tasks: Allow students to have different opinions or solutions, fostering creativity and multiple perspectives. (Example) Debating the pros and cons of online learning, where students can have differing viewpoints.

3. Outcome Options: Is there a fixed answer?

This determines whether the task has a predetermined correct answer or if multiple answers are possible.

- Closed Tasks: Have a single correct solution or a fixed answer. (Example) Solving a logic puzzle or answering comprehension questions with factual responses.

- Open Tasks: Have multiple possible answers and allow for creativity and interpretation. (Example) Writing a short story or discussing personal opinions on a topic.

Task Dimension	Type	Description	Example
Interactant Relationship	Shared	Everyone has the same information	Reading an article and summarizing together
	Split	Different students hold different information	Jigsaw reading activity
Goal Orientation	Convergent	One agreed-upon outcome	Deciding on the best travel destination as a group
	Divergent	Multiple valid answers	Sharing opinions on a controversial topic
Outcome Options	Closed	Fixed, correct answer	Solving a math problem
	Open	Multiple possible answers	Writing a personal reflection

08

문항 해설

교실활동에서 과업중심(task-based) 교수법의 예시를 보여주고 있다. 이 교수법은 학생의 동기부여와 흥미도를 이끄는 과업 전(pre-task) 단계에서 시작하여, 그룹활동과 발표로 이어지는 과업단계, 학생의 활동에서 문제로 보이는 언어형식을 중심으로 하여 수업이 이루어지는 과업 후단계로 이루어져 있다. 과업 활동단계에서는 학생들의 그룹활동으로 Cycle 1에서 연습(rehearse) 활동으로 실제의 과업활동을 준비할 시간이 주어지게 된다. 언어의 말하기와 읽기, 쓰기 등의 통합 기능(integrated skills)활동이 나타난다. 과업 후 단계에서는 학습자의 과업 수행의 자유로운 의사소통 후에 나타난 언어적 오류를 이용하여 연습하고 분석하는 언어 분석활동의 수업을 하게 된다.

09

문항 해설

본 지문에 나타난 수업은 통합수업(integrated lesson)을 하기 위해서 다양한 방법들을 시도하는 수업이다. 우선 교사는 최상급과 like나 dislike 동사가 같이 연결된 표현 등을 가르치는 언어 수업속에서 의사소통연습을 하는 것이 궁극적 목표라고 할 수 있다. 수업의 시작에서는 학생들이 best나 least 표현을 할 수 있도록 준비하는 시간을 주고, 그에 대한 자신의 언어와 실제언어 사이의 차이를 인식하게 하는 의식올리기(consciousness-raising) 방법을 이용하고 있다. 말하기 활동을 하는 과정에서 학생들이 언어형태를 토론하는 시간을 가지면서 의미속에서 형태(form)를 공부하는 focus on form이 이루어진다. 학습자들이 그룹 활동에 의해 수업이 이루어짐으로서 서로의 활동결과를 비교하고 토론함으로서 구성주의 방법을 수업에서 이용한 것임을 알 수 있다.

핵심 개념정리

통합 수업(Integrated Lesson)

- context : English Language school in Korea
- level : High Intermediate
- course focus : Multiple skills, emphasis on oral skills
- students : 12 young adults, wishing to improve English skills
- focus : [situational] occupations, work, employment opportunities
  [functional] expressing likes and dislikes
  [formal] ing gerunds; vocabulary for types of workers

Warm-up (L) - 5 min.
T : asks Ss to name careers, jobs, occupations and writes them on the board.
T : briefly tells about a job she had as a waitress in a restaurant - how she found the job, the interview, and what the job was like

A. Presentation (L, R, S) — 10 min.

T : directs Ss to the opening page of Lesson 2, a full-page advertisement for summer employment at a "water park" in Clear Lake, Texas.

T : tells Ss to skim the page individually and decide if they would like to work at Clear Lake Water Park.

T : asks Ss to pair up and tell what they like or don't like, and why they feel that way.

T : engages the whole class in a brief whole-class discussion of what Ss liked and didn't like, and puts a few key phrases on the board (good pay, benefits, discounts on rides in the park, flexible hours, etc).

B. Listening Focus (L, R, W, S) — 10 min.

T : directs Ss to the second page, and plays a CD recording of a conversation in which a man named Jacques describes why he doesn't like his job. T plays the conversation once for general listening...... and a second time for Ss to look at and complete the written exercise in the book that requires using the -ing form of verbs like work, write, apply, etc.

T : asks Ss to compare their responses with their partner and make any corrections.

C. Grammar Focus (L, R, W, S) — 15 min.

In the next exercise, Ss are asked to "make one list of job-related activities you like and another list of those you dislike."

T : then calls attention to the expressions in the book: I can't stand/ I don't mind/ I enjoy/ I hate/ I prefer + V-ing (-ing form of verb)

T : puts Ss into groups of four and directs them to share their likes and dislikes, using the expressions + gerund. T offers some suggestions as prompts.

D. Focus on types of workers (R, S, L, W) — 10 min.

On the next page, six types of workers are described and pictured: realistic, investigative, artistic, social, enterprising, and conventional.

T : directs Ss to the page and calls on six Ss to each read aloud one of the short descriptions; T makes a few pronunciation corrections.

T : then directs Ss to reread the descriptions and write a short paragraph describing themselves. Ss can use the gerunds used in the descriptions.

Wind down (L, S) — 5 min.

T : asks Ss to look over their paragraph descriptions, and to revise them if they want to for homework.

T : calls on selected Ss and asks them about what type of worker they are, and if they like or dislike a job they have had.

10

핵심 개념정리

형성 & 총괄 평가(Formative & Summative Assessment)

Formative assessment, including **diagnostic** testing, is a range of formal and informal assessment procedures conducted by teachers during the learning process in order to modify teaching and learning activities to improve student attainment. It typically involves qualitative feedback (rather than scores) for both student and teacher that focuses on the details of content and performance. It is commonly contrasted with **summative assessment**, which seeks to monitor educational outcomes, often for purposes of external accountability. The type of assessment that people may be more familiar with is summative assessment. The table shows some basic differences between the two types of assessment.

	Summative Assessment	Formative Assessment
When	At the end of a learning activity	During a learning activity
Goal	To make a decision	To improve learning
Feedback	Final judgement	Return to material
Frame of Reference	Sometimes normative (comparing each student against all others); sometimes criterion	Always criterion (evaluating students according to the same criteria)

11

핵심 개념정리

의사소통 전략

Faerch and Kasper (1983) defined communication strategies as "potentially conscious plans for solving what to an individual presents itself as a problem in reaching a particular communicative goal." While the research of the last decade does indeed focus largely on the compensatory nature of communication strategies, more recent approaches seem to take a more positive view of communication strategies as elements of an overall strategic competence.

1) Avoidance strategies

It is a common communication strategy that can be broken down into several subcategories. The most common type of avoidance strategy is syntactic or lexical avoidance within a semantic category, phonological avoidance, and topic avoidance.

2) Compensatory strategies

① Code switching: It is the use of a first or third language within a stream of speech in the second language. In a multilingual society, each language uniquely fulfills certain roles and represents distinct identities, and all of them complement one another to serve "the complex communicative demands of a pluralistic society". In order to meet "the complex communicative demands," speakers who live in a community and household where two or more languages coexist frequently switch from one language to another, either between or within utterances.

② Circumlocution: A circumlocution is a way of saying or writing something using more words than are necessary instead of being clear and direct. For instance, it is using many words such as "a tool used for cutting things such as paper and hair" to describe something simple "scissors".

③ Approximation: An approximation is an inexact representation of something that is still close enough to be useful.

④ Foreignizing: 외국어의 단어를 몰라 모국어의 단어를 그대로 사용하면서 외국어의 음운 규칙이나 음성체계를 적용하는 경우이다.

⑤ Word-coinage: 말하는 이가 의미가 통할 수 있는 새로운 단어를 만들어서 사용하는 것이다. 예를 들면, 'machine' 대신에 'mechanicist'을 사용하는 경우이다.

⑥ Stalling or time-gaining: 적절한 표현이 머리에 떠오르지 않아 시간이 필요한 경우 'uh, well, let's see, as a matter of fact'같은 표현을 사용하여 상대방으로 하여금 잠시 기다리게 한다.

strategy of avoidance	
syntactic avoidance	가정법을 몰라서 쓰지 않는다.
lexical avoidance	way라는 말을 표현할 수 없어서 road라는 어휘로 회피한다.
phonological avoidance	음운적 난점 때문에 rally란 단어 대신에 hit the ball이라고 말한다.
topic avoidance	골프에 대해서 잘 모르기 때문에 골프에 대한 화제를 꺼내려 하지 않는다.
compensatory strategies	
prefabricated patterns	어떤 내용의 구나 문장을 내재화하지 않고 외워서 사용하는 것
appeal to authority	2언어 화자에게 직접 물어 보는 것
code switching	2언어 화자의 이해와는 무관하게 모국어를 사용하는 것
approximation	학습자가 알고 있는 하나의 목표어 어휘항목이나 구조의 사용 eg) waterpipe를 pipe로
word coinage	요망되는 개념을 전달하기 위하여 신어를 만듬 eg) balloon 대신에 airball
circumlocution	학습자는 합당한 목표어 항목이나 구조를 사용하지 못하여 물건이나 행동의 특징 또는 요소를 묘사함
mime	학습자는 어휘항목이나 행동 대신 비언어적 전략을 사용함. 박수갈채를 나타내기 위하여 손뼉을 침

12

교사의 역할

(1) Traditional Role of English teachers

The traditional method is largely **teacher-centred**, with the teachers hogging the limelight always. They lecture at length on particular topics and students listen to them with rapt attention – this has been the methodology for teaching English for decades now. Using this methodology, teachers have been teaching **discrete points** of grammar or phonology in separate lessons, focusing mainly on the formal features of the language at the expense of encouraging students to use the language. Repetitive practice, mechanical drills and memorization of grammar rules are certain important aspects of this approach to language teaching. This approach could be regarded as what Wilkins (1976) calls a **"synthetic"** approach in which "different parts of the language are taught separately and **step by step** so that acquisition is a process of gradual accumulation of parts until the whole structure of language has been built up." This **linear** approach to language learning is explained well by Nunan (1996). Nunan likens it to the construction of a wall in the following manner: "The language wall is erected one linguistic brick at a time. The easy grammatical bricks are laid at the bottom of the wall, and they provide a foundation for the more difficult ones. The task for the learner is to get the linguistic bricks in the right order: first the word bricks, and then the sentence bricks. If the bricks are not in the correct order, the wall will collapse under its own ungrammaticality." Freire (1982) calls this the "banking" system of education in which the learners are considered to be similar to bank accounts into which regular deposits are made to be drawn later for specific purposes like examination. Obviously, the onus here lies on the individuals making the deposits for it is they who are responsible for earning the money and it is only they who can make the bank accounts swell. Using this analogy for the traditional language classroom would inevitably mean that the teacher is almost like the Titan, Atlas, of Greek mythology.

(2) Focus on the Learner

As we have already seen, the traditional method of teaching English makes the teacher the all-powerful authority in the classroom, almost obliterating the existence of the learner sometimes. Dewey (1938) objected to this kind of spoon-feeding of knowledge, and pointed out the importance of the role of the learner as an active agent in his or her learning. Dewey laid the foundation of what we now call **learner-centredness**, a term which has now gained tremendous currency in English language teaching. It reflects, as Tudor (1996) points out, a widespread desire in the language teaching community to develop means of allowing learners to play a fuller, more active and participatory role in their language study. However, learner-centredness in ELT is not a product of a single school of thought, but a result of the confluence of several innovative perspectives on language teaching. Among them, mention must be made of;

- **Humanistic approaches** to language teaching which developed during the later half of the twentieth century and which talked about giving equal attention to both the intellectual and the emotional development of the learner
- **Communicative language teaching**, which developed in the 1960s and 1970s and which was both a reaction against the prevalent structure-oriented drill methods of language teaching popular during the time and a result of the desire to make language teaching more flexible and more responsive to students, real world communicative needs.

(3) Innovative role of the teacher in task-based language teaching

① In the current paradigm of Task-based Language Teaching (TBLT), which is basically an offshoot of communicative language teaching, learner-centredness has found a new expression. The main conceptual basis for TBLT is, as Nunan (2004) points out, "**experiential learning**" or "learning by doing". In this way, TBLT goes a long way in breaking down the hierarchies of the traditional classroom because the very act of trying to complete a **communicative task** involves planning and using strategies on the part of the learner.

② A communicative task has been defined by Nunan (2004) as a piece of classroom work that involves learners in comprehending, manipulating, producing, or interacting in the target language while their attention is focused on mobilizing their grammatical knowledge in order to express meaning, and in which the intention is to convey meaning rather than to manipulate form.

③ We see how in a learner-centred approach to language teaching, like TBLT, for instance, the role of the learner is significantly altered, as the learner is in the thick of all classroom activities getting a **hands-on practical experience** of using the language for communicative purposes. But does it mean that the role of the teacher in such a case is diminished? The answer is a firm "NO" because though the teacher is not really the focus here, the teacher performs an important mediational role (Feuerstein, 1991) which encompasses a wide range of responsibilities, albeit qualitatively different from the traditional role of the teacher as the disseminator of information.

④ In teaching through **mediation**, the teacher becomes a true **facilitator** of learning for the language learners, guiding them through **dialogic communication** (Vygotsky, 1978) as they **co-construct** knowledge with the teacher. In this process, the teacher's role of the instructor who teaches new language to the learners is not shunned altogether, but it is restricted. The teacher is expected to be a guide by the side, an advisor who advises his learners after monitoring their strengths and weaknesses. S/he also plans the tasks for the future and stimulates the learners intellect by presenting new language and motivating them.

⑤ One important thing that needs to be understood is that however much teachers teach, they do not have any real control over a learner's **natural process** of acquiring a second or a foreign language and achieving communicative ability in it. Therefore, the teacher could at best create a classroom environment that is conducive to language learning. The communicative skills of the learners can be developed if they are **motivated**. Hence, teachers should facilitate this process by creating diverse communicative activities, especially intended for pair-work and group-work, that are interesting and challenging to the learners, as they progress in the path of acquiring and using the target language beyond the textbook and the classroom.

13

핵심 개념정리

우연적 학습(Incidental Learning)

In incidental teaching, learning is not planned by the instructor or the student, it occurs as a **byproduct** of another activity – an experience, observation, self-reflection, interaction, unique event, or common routine task. This learning happens in addition to or apart from the instructor's plans and the student's expectations. An example of incidental teaching is when the instructor places a train set on top of a cabinet. If the child points or walks towards the cabinet, the instructor prompts the student to say "train." Once the student says "train," he gets access to the train set. Here are some steps most commonly used in incidental teaching:

- An instructor will arrange the learning environment so that necessary materials are within the student's sight, but not within his reach, thus impacting his **motivation** to seek out those materials.
- An instructor waits for the student to **initiate** engagement.
- An instructor prompts the student to respond if **needed**.
- An instructor allows access to an item/activity contingent on a correct response from the student.
- The instructor fades out the prompting process over a period of time and subsequent trials.

Incidental learning is an occurrence that is not generally accounted for using the traditional methods of instructional objectives and outcomes assessment. This type of learning occurs in part as a product of **social interaction** and **active involvement** in both online and onsite courses. Research implies that some unassessed aspects of onsite and online learning challenge the equivalency of education between the two modalities. Both onsite and online learning have distinct advantages with traditional on-campus students experiencing higher degrees of incidental learning in three times as many as online students. Additional research is called for to investigate the implications of these findings both conceptually and pedagogically.

14

> 핵심 개념정리

Drills의 유형

It is defined as a technique that focuses on a minimal number (usually one or two) of language forms (grammatical or phonological structures) through some type of repetition. In a substitution drill, the teacher provides a sentence, students repeat; teacher cues students to change one word or structure in the sentence, students repeat.

1) Mechanical drills have only one correct response from a student, and have no implied connection with reality. **Repetition drills** require that the student repeat a word or phrase whether the student understands it or not. (repetition drill, substitution drill, transformation drill, response drill, choral drill)

> T: The cat is in the hat.
> Ss: The cat is in the hat.

2) Meaningful drills may have a predicted response or a limited set of possible responses, but it is connected to some form of reality. The process may continue on as the teacher reinforces certain grammatical or phonological elements.

> T: The woman is outside. [pointing out the window at a woman] Where is she, Hiro?
> S1: The woman is outside.
> T: Right, she's outside. Keiko, where is she?
> S2: She's outside.
> T: Good, Keiko, she's outside. Now, class, we are inside. Hiroko, where are we?
> S3: We are inside.

3) Communicative drills offer students the possibilities of an open response and negotiation of meaning, so it is called "**form-focused** communicative practice." This exercise is an attempt to force students to use the past tense, but allows them to choose **meaningful** replies.

> T: Good morning, class. Last weekend, I went to a restaurant and I ate salmon. Juan, what did you do last weekend?
> Juan: I went to park and I play soccer.
> T: Juan, "I play soccer" or "I played soccer"?
> Juan: Oh… eh… I played soccer.

15

실제 자료와 실제성

Authentic texts have been defined as real-life texts, not written for pedagogic purposes. (Wallace 1992:145) They are therefore written for native speakers and contain real language. They are materials that have been produced to fulfil some social purpose in the language community. (Peacock (1997), in contrast to non-authentic texts that are especially designed for language learning purposes. The language in non-authentic texts is **artificial** and **unvaried**, concentrating on something that has to be taught and often containing a series of false-text indicators that include:

- perfectly formed sentences (all the time)
- a question using a grammatical structure, gets a full answer
- repetition of structures
- very often does not read well

The artificial nature of the language and structures used, make them very unlike anything that the learner will encounter in the real world and very often they do not reflect how the language is really used. They are useful for teaching structures but are not very good for improving reading skills (for the simple fact that they read unnaturally). They can be useful for preparing the learner for the eventual reading of real texts. If authentic texts have been written not for language learning purposes but for completely different ones, where do they come from and how are they selected?

The sources of **authentic** materials that can be used in the classroom are infinite, but the most common are newspapers, magazines, TV programs, movies, songs and literature. One of the most useful is the Internet. Whereas newspapers and any other printed material date very quickly, the Internet is continuously updated, more **visually stimulating** as well as being interactive, therefore promoting a more active approach to reading rather than a passive one.

From a more **practical** point of view, the Internet is a modern day reality, most students use it and for teachers, there is easier access to endless amounts of many different types of material. Often by having unlimited access in the work place, looking for materials costs nothing, only time. Authentic materials should be the kind of material that students will need and want to be able to read when travelling, studying abroad, or using the language in other contexts outside the classroom. Authentic materials enable learners to interact with the real language and content rather than the form. Learners feel that they are learning a target language as it is used **outside the classroom**. When choosing materials from the various sources, it is therefore worth taking into consideration that the aim should be to understand meaning and not form, especially when using literary texts with the emphasis being on what is being said and not necessarily on the literary form or stylistics. Nuttall gives three main criteria when choosing texts to be used in the classroom **suitability of content, exploitability** and **readability**. Suitability of content can be considered to be the most important of the three, in that the reading material should interest the students as well as be relevant to their needs. The texts should motivate as well as. **Exploitability** refers to how the text can be used to develop the students' competence as readers. A text that can not be exploited for teaching purposes has no use in the classroom. Just because it is in English does not mean that it can be useful. **Readability** is used to describe the combination of structural and lexical difficulty of a text, as well as referring to the amount of new vocabulary and any new grammatical forms present. It is important to assess the right level for the right students.

⟨Important Factors in Choosing Authentic Reading Materials⟩

Suitability of Content	• Does the text interest the student? • Is it relevant to the student's needs? • Does it represent the type of material that the student will use outside of the classroom?
Exploitability	• Can the text be exploited for teaching purposes? • For what purpose should the text be exploited? • What skills/ strategies can be developed by exploiting the text?
Readability	• Is the text too easy/ difficult for the student? • Is it structurally too demanding/ complex? • How much new vocabulary does it contain? Is it relevant?
Presentation	• Does it look authentic? • Is it attractive? • Does it grab the student's attention? • Does it make him want to read more?

- **Authenticity** of the texts which we may use as input data for our students
- **Authenticity** of the learners' own interpretations of such texts
- **Authenticity** of tasks conducive to language learning
- **Authenticity** of the actual social situation of the classroom language

16

다양한 레벨의 ESL 수업 지도

In multilevel adult English as a second language (ESL) classes, teachers are challenged to use a variety of materials, activities, and techniques to engage the interest of the learners and assist them in their educational goals. This recommends ways to choose and organize content for multilevel classes; it explains **grouping strategies**; it discusses a self-access component, independent work for individual learners; and it offers suggestions for managing the classes.

(1) The Multilevel Class

Teachers use the term multilevel to identify any group of learners who differ from one another in one or more significant ways. Arguably, every class is multilevel because learners begin with varying degrees of competence and then progress at different rates in each of the language skills: listening, speaking, reading, and writing (Bell & Burnaby, 1984; Santopietro, 1991; Wrigley & Guth, 1992). However, in many adult ESL classes, there are even more variables that affect the levels within the class. Some programs place learners of all levels, from beginning to advanced, in a single class. Often such classes include speakers of many native languages, some that use the roman alphabet, some that do not. Learners may have varying degrees of literacy in their first language as well as in English (Bell, 1991; Santopietro, 1991; Wrigley & Guth, 1992). Other factors that add to diversity in the classroom and to rate of progress in learning English are the type and amount of a learner's previous education; the learning **style preference**; learner expectations of appropriate classroom activities; and the culture, religion, sex, and age of each learner (Guglielmino & Burrichter, 1987).

(2) Needs Assessment

To ensure some success for all learners in the multilevel classroom, teachers must determine what each **learner needs** and wants to learn. This is accomplished through ongoing **needs assessment** that includes both standardized tests and alternative assessment, one-on-one interviews with learners, group discussions, and learner observation (Alexander, 1993; Holt, 1995; Isserlis, 1992; Wrigley & Guth, 1992). Throughout the needs assessment process, it is important that adult learners are actively involved in choosing the direction and content of their learning (Auerbach, 1992; Wrigley & Guth, 1992). Techniques for selecting the content or themes of class activities might include whole or small group brainstorming and prioritizing activities, and documentation and prioritization of **individual learner goals** ("I need English for…"). (Auerbach, 1992 for additional suggestions on using learner themes.)

(3) Planning for the Multilevel Class

Planning for multilevel classes requires the ability to juggle many different elements as teachers must provide activities that address the learning styles, skill levels, and specific learning objectives of each individual (Bell & Burnaby, 1984; Wrigley & Guth, 1992). Teachers can use a variety of techniques and grouping strategies and a selection of self-access materials to help all learners be successful, comfortable, and productive for at least a portion of each class time. The planning is time-consuming and the classroom management is exhausting. However, the alternative to this effort planning and using activities that meet the needs of only those learners whose skills fall somewhere in the middle<will frustrate those with **lower skills**, and bore the more **advanced learners**.

When planning and teaching the multilevel ESL class, as with any adult ESL class, the teacher must remember that learner perceptions of what constitutes sound language learning may not match those of the teacher. The teacher's enthusiasm and goodwill can usually encourage learners who resist unfamiliar and non-traditional classroom activities to participate fully in the class. However, where there is a mismatch between learner and teacher perceptions of useful activities, teachers should be prepared to include activities that meet learner expectations (Wrigley & Guth, 1992). For example, a story developed from a **language experience approach (LEA)** activity could be a source for grammatical drills or for pronunciation exercises.

(4) Grouping Strategies

The use of grouping strategies can form the basis for the multilevel class as teachers mix and match groups, pair learners, and allow time for individual or solo activities during each class period (Bell, 1991; Berry & Williams, 1992). Certain factors should also be considered in setting up group and pair activities, including differences in age, social background, country of origin, and educational background, as well as English ability. Some learners might not be comfortable in groups with other learners they consider to be more prominent or of higher status. And some men may resist being in groups where women are the leaders. Although the teacher can often encourage reluctant learners to try new activities, sensitivity to potential difficulties arising from group and pair work is necessary. Class discussions of cultural and personal differences in learning styles and interaction patterns may help overcome initial resistance (Wrigley & Guth, 1992).

- Whole Group activities are appropriate initially for beginning a new class and regularly for daily **warm-up** time. They can focus the entire group on a theme that later involves various individual and small group tasks. The whole group can participate in a class project to create a finished product (such as a book, bulletin board, or video), where each learner completes a part of the task based on individual abilities and interests (Bell, 1991). Other initial whole group activities that lend themselves to follow-up activities at various difficulty levels include reading comic strips or photo stories; listening to audiotapes or viewing videotapes; taking field trips; learning songs; and brainstorming on topics of interest.

- Small Group work provides opportunities for learners to **use their language skills** and is often **less intimidating** than whole group work. Small groups can be set up according to interest or ability, and need not be equal in size or permanent (Bell & Burnaby, 1984).

  ① **Heterogeneous** groups are made up of learners who have disparate skills. Cross-ability grouping allows stronger learners to help others and maximizes complementary learner strengths (Bell, 1991). Activities suitable for **cross-ability** groups are jigsaw activities; board games; and creating posters, lists, art, and multimedia projects.

  ② **Homogeneous** groups are made up of learners who have roughly equal skills (for example, all are literate or are orally fluent). Activities often suitable for like-ability groups are problem-solving, sequencing, and process writing.

- Pairs of learners working together have the greatest opportunity to use communicative skills. Like-ability pairs succeed when partners' roles are interchangeable or equally difficult (Bell, 1991). Activities for homogeneous pairs include information gap (where the assignment can only be completed through sharing of the different information given each learner), dialogues, role plays, and pair interviews.

- Cross-ability pairs work best when partners are given different roles and heavier demands are placed on the more proficient learner (Bell, 1991). Some examples are LEA stories where one dictates and one transcribes, interviews where one questions and one answers, and role plays where one learner has a larger role than the other.

(5) Using Self-Access Materials

When learners are doing independent or solo activities in the multilevel classroom, using self-access materials can enable them to take **responsibility** for choosing work appropriate to their **individual levels** and interests (Bell, 1991; Berry & Williams, 1992). A self-access component includes activities from all skill areas as well as vocabulary, grammar, and pronunciation exercises. With self-access materials, each task is set up so that learners need minimal, if any, assistance from the teacher to accomplish the activity. Directions are clear and answers (when applicable) are provided on the back of the activity allowing learners to informally evaluate their own work without teacher intervention (Bell, 1991). When used regularly in the classroom, self-access time can foster a relaxed environment where learners decide how and when to interact with one another, with their teacher, and with English.

Teachers need not have their own rooms to set up self-access corners; a box of materials can travel with the teacher to workplace sites, community centers, or church basements. The following are some materials to include in the self-access collection: art supplies such as scissors, markers, crayons, pens, pencils, paints, paper in various sizes, types, and colors, glue, tape, stapler, stencils, stamps, and magazines for collages, and directions for projects (e.g., draw pictures of the native country, draw a calendar and put in holidays, draw the U.S. map); crossword puzzles; articles and books for a range of reading levels; partner dialogues, in envelopes, with directions; information gaps; scrambled sentences;

interview questions (with tape recorder and blank tape); writing tasks for individuals, pairs, or groups; board games and puzzles; review materials from topics, structures, and functions covered in class; contact assignments such as drawing a map of the neighborhood or telephoning for information; high interest videos and taped radio segments with teacher-made activities; and computer software programs to choose from.

17

채점기준표

(1)	언어 변용	구조적(structural) 수준	A: 전체의 한 문장으로 발화
			I: 여러개의 의미군으로 분리
		어휘적(lexical) 수준	A: constructed와 ancient times
			I: built나 long ago
		상위언어(metalanguage)	A: metalanguage 용어
			I: examples 이용
(2)	과업 복합성 차이점	듣기 속도	A: 일상의 자연스러운 속도 듣기
			I: 느리고 명확한 속도의 듣기
		밀어낸 출력(pushed output)	A: 가능한 많은 어휘와 phrase output
			I: 어떠한 어휘의 output 가능
		형태와 의미	A: 문법과 의미 mapping
			I: 의미 우선
		글(text) vs 문장(sentence)	A: text reconstruction
			I: sentence construction
		추후활동	A: 자신의 글과 원본 비교
			I: 원본과 유사한 재구성
(3)	과업중심 교수방법	전통적 교수법과의 차이점	학습자중심의 상호작용
			학습자의 출력
			내용에 대한 묵시적 문법 학습

Note: A=advanced, I=intermediate

18

핵심 개념정리

적성 시험(aptitude test)

Aptitude Tests is a vital part of the selection process for various companies. A tool to assess a candidate's general **logic, problem-solving** and **language abilities**, and aptitude tests generally forms the first step for **selection**. Language **aptitude** refers to the potential that a person has for learning languages. This potential is often evaluated using formal aptitude tests, which predict the degree of success the candidate will have with a new language. **Aptitude** tests vary but many include evaluation of ability to manage sounds, grammatical structures, infer rules, and memory. An **aptitude** test is a systematic means of testing candidate's abilities to perform specific tasks and react to a range of different situations. The tests each have a standardised method of administration and scoring, with the results quantified and compared with all other test takers. The Modern Language Aptitude Test (MLAT) evaluates language aptitude.

In the classroom, **aptitude** test is conceived as a prognostic measure that indicates whether a student is likely to learn a second language readily. It is generally given before the student begins language study, and may be used to **select** students for a language course or to **place** students in sections appropriate to their ability. Language **aptitude** may be fixed but there are many things teachers can do in the area of learner training to improve the learner's ability. These include helping learners identify their preferences for learning; thinking about learning styles, and then looking at how these can be developed; and developing learner autonomy by teaching learners how to study effectively.

19

핵심 개념정리

거꾸로 교실(Flipped classroom)

Flipped classroom is an instructional strategy and a type of **blended learning** that reverses the traditional learning environment by delivering instructional content, often **online, outside of the classroom**. It moves activities, including those that may have traditionally been considered homework, into the classroom. In a flipped classroom, students watch online lectures, collaborate in online discussions, or carry out research at home and engage in concepts in the classroom with the guidance of a mentor.

In the traditional model of classroom instruction, the teacher is typically the central focus of a lesson and the primary disseminator of information during the class period. The teacher responds to questions while students defer directly to the teacher for guidance and feedback. In a classroom with a traditional style of instruction, individual lessons may be focused on an explanation of content utilizing a lecture-style. Student engagement in the traditional model may be limited to activities in which students work independently or in small groups on an application task designed by the teacher. Class discussions are typically centered on the teacher, who controls the flow of the conversation. Typically, this pattern of teaching also involves giving students the task of reading from a textbook or practicing a concept by working on a problem set, for example, outside school.

The flipped classroom intentionally shifts instruction to a **learner-centered model** in which class time explores topics in **greater depth** and creates **meaningful learning** opportunities, while educational technologies such as online videos are used to 'deliver content' outside of the classroom. In a flipped classroom, 'content delivery' may take a variety of forms. Often, video lessons prepared by the teacher or third parties are used to deliver content, although online collaborative discussions, digital research, and text readings may be used.

Flipped classrooms also redefine in-class activities. In-class lessons accompanying flipped classroom may include activity learning or more traditional homework problems, among other practices, to engage students in the content. Class activities vary but may include: using math manipulatives and emerging mathematical technologies, in-depth laboratory experiments, original document analysis, debate or speech presentation, current event discussions, peer reviewing, project-based learning, and skill development or concept practice Because these types of active learning allow for highly differentiated instruction, more time can be spent in class on higher-order thinking skills such as problem-finding, collaboration, design and **problem solving** as students tackle difficult problems, work in groups, research, and construct knowledge with the help of their teacher and peers. Flipped classrooms have been implemented in both schools and colleges and been found to have varying differences in the method of implementation. A teacher's interaction with students in a flipped classroom can be more **personalized** and less didactic, and students are actively involved in knowledge acquisition and construction as they participate in and evaluate their learning.

20

문항 해설

제시된 대화문에서 교사와 학습자의 대화는 의미를 중심으로 진행되고 있다. 전체 대화문이 IRE (initiation, response, evaluation) 형식으로 이루어지고 있다. 학생의 오류에 대해 교사는 직접적으로 문법적인 오류를 수정하지 않고 의미적, 암시적으로 접근하는 피드백(recast)을 제공하고 있다. 학생이 교사의 묵시적인 오류수정에 반응하고 있지 않다. 학생의 마지막 응답에서 보면 정확한 부정어의 사용을 습득하지 못하는 초보단계에 머물러 있음을 알 수 있다. 교사의 두 번째 응대에서 나타나는 부가의문문은 질문자가 답을 알면서 상대의 동의를 구하고 있으므로 display question이다.

21

문항 해설

교실활동 〈A〉와 〈B〉에서 보여지는 문법 수업의 차이점을 논하고 있는 문제이다. 〈A〉는 제시된 문법연습 문제처럼 시제가 바뀌었을 때 동사유형을 바꾸는 통제된(controlled) 문법 문제로서 문법규칙의 명시적 지식(explicit knowledge)를 익히는 수업이다. 문장별 수준의 문법을 익히므로 문장단위(sentential-level)로 분석하고 있다. 수업 〈B〉는 대화형식을 통해 문법형식을 익히게 되는 귀납법(inductive) 방식의 문법수업을 채택하고 있다. 의미중심의 입력을 통해 목표문법을 학생들이 인식하도록 도와주는 의식올리기(consciousness-raising)방법을 채택하고 있으며 의사소통을 위한 언어사용이 포함되는 문법수업이 되고 있다는 것을 알 수 있다.

22

문항 해설

먼저 대화문을 분석할 때, 학습자가 hold의 과거형인 held를 *holded라고 잘못 사용하고 있는데, 교사가 암시적 피드백, recast 방법을 이용하여 학습자의 오류를 암시적으로 수정해 주려고 하고 있으나 학습자는 교사가 두 번째로 수정해주는 문장에서 tightly를 softly로 바꾸는 의미수정만 가능할 뿐 문법적인 오류인 *holded는 오류로 인식하지 못하고 있다. 이 부분은 학습자가 문법적 오류를 수정하는 단계에 이르지 못했음을 설명하고 있다. 다시 말하여, Krashen의 자연적 순서가설(natural order hypothesis)에 의하면 학습자가 아직 동사의 불규칙 과거형을 인식할 수 있는 단계에 이르지 못했다고 볼 수 있는 것이다. 학습자가 아직 문법적 형태를 습득할 수 있는 단계가 되지 않았기 때문에 교사의 반복되는 오류수정을 인식하지 못하고 있다. 즉, 교사는 문법적 오류를 인식시키기 위해 똑같은 문형을 반복하며, 새로운 의미를 추가하는 부사를 덧붙여 제시하고 있으나, 학습자는 오히려 첨가된 부사의 의미만 인식하여 교사의 문법적 오류에 대한 수정을 인식하지 못하고 있다. 학습자가 의미에 대하여만 집중을 한 결과, 문법에 대한 인식을 하지 못하고 같은 잘못이 반복되고 있으므로 맞는 설명이다.

23

문항 해설

학생들은 교사의 오류수정으로 이루어지는 수정피드백을 이해하지 못하고 의미적으로만 접근하므로 계속 잘못된 발화를 계속하고 있는 것을 볼 수 있다. 그래서 행동주의적 교수법으로 보았을 때 더 많은 반복과 과거형 동사 유형연습이 필요하다는 것을 알 수 있다. 동시에 입력가설법 측면에서, 교사는 학생이 동사 과거형에 대한 인지능력이 전혀 없으므로 과거형 동사가 들어간 많은 언어자료를 제공함으로써 자연스럽게 익히게 하는 것이 바람직하겠다고 볼 수 있다.

핵심 ELT 읽기

출력 가설(Output Hypothesis)

The comprehensible output (CO) hypothesis states that we acquire language when we attempt to transmit a message but fail and have to try again. Eventually, we arrive at the correct form of our utterance, our conversational partner finally understands, and we acquire the new form we have produced. The originator of the comprehensible output hypothesis, Merrill Swain (Swain, 1985), does not claim that CO is responsible for all or even most of our language competence. Rather, the claim is that "sometimes, under some conditions, output facilitates second language learning in ways that are different from, or enhance, those of input" (Swain and Lapkin, 1995, p. 371). A look at the data, however, shows that even this weak claim is hard to support.

(1) Learner Output

The aim of this article is to provide useful techniques for teaching in the language classroom and address three issues crucial in learner output: **negotiation of meaning, learner production,** and **repair work**. The first two sections explain the theoretical background based on research findings. The third section suggests ways in which some of these findings may be applied to classroom situations. The fourth section summarizes the main points of the article, in particular, their implications in classroom teaching.

(2) Learner production and Language learning

Recently, several second language acquisition (SLA) researchers have systematically argued that the function of L2 learners production is not only to enhance fluency and indirectly generate more comprehensible input, but also to facilitate second language learning by providing learners with opportunities to produce **comprehensible output** (Krashen 1985, 1989, 1994; Long 1983, 1990; Van Patten 1990). Learners achieve this by **modifying** and approximating their production toward successful use of the target language.

Swain and Lapkin (1995:373) maintain that in the process of modifying their **interlanguage** (IL) utterances for greater message comprehensibility, L2 learners undertake some restructuring that affects their access to their knowledge base. "the assumption is that this process of modification contributes to second language **acquisition**" (Swain and Lapkin 1995:373). Many scholars have concluded that opportunities for comprehensible input and output are equally important in language learning (Swain 1985, 1995; Swain and Lapkin 1995; Shehadeh 1991; Pica et al., 1989, 1993, 1996).

Similarly, many of these studies have shown that interactions, where the negotiation of meaning between native speakers/ nonnative speakers and nonnative speakers/ nonnative speakers is prevalent, are also important for the production of comprehensible output. It is through the negotiation of meaning that both learners and their interlocutors work together to provide comprehensible input and produce comprehensible output.

Pica, Holliday, et al., (1989:65) pointed out that "although... research has focused mainly on the ways in which **negotiated interaction** with an interlocutor helps the learner to understand unfamiliar L2 input, we believe that it is also through negotiation that learners gain opportunities to attempt production of new L2 words and grammatical structures as well." Negotiated interactions are important not only because they provide NNSs with an opportunity to receive input, which they have made comprehensible through negotiation, but also because these interactions provide NNSs with opportunities that enable them to **modify** their speech so that the output is more **comprehensible**.

(3) Repair work and Language learning

According to Schegloff et al., (1977) and Schegloff (1979), there is a cline in conversations. In normal conversation, the norm is **self-initiated and self-completed repair**. In non-normal conversation, the proportion of other-initiations and other-completions is higher than would be expected. In situations where there is a constant failure to repair, interlocutors will eventually cease to converse. It has also been observed that in NS/NS discourse (Schegloff et al., 1977) and NS/ advanced NNS discourse (Kasper 1985), the vast majority of repair is content and pragmatic repair rather than linguistic (phonological, lexical, morpho-syntactic) repair.

These observations suggest the thesis that success in L2 learning may be measured by the proportion of self-initiated, self-completed repair in relation to other-initiated, other-completed repair, and by the proportion of content and pragmatic repair in relation to linguistic repair. Thus, the more self-initiated, self-completed content and pragmatic repair, the more native-like the interaction will be. However, the more other-initiated, other-completed linguistic repair, the less native-like the interaction will be. Hence, the optimal L2 learning environment is one in which self-initiated, self-completed content and pragmatic repair dominates.

Research that investigated NS/NNS and NNS/NNS negotiated interaction has confirmed the importance of self-initiated, self-completed repair over other-initiated, other-completed repair (Kasper 1985, Shehadeh 1991). Shehadeh (1991) found that self-initiated clarification attempts occurred in significantly greater proportions than other-initiated clarification requests (70 percent versus 30 percent, respectively). Instances of self-initiated comprehensible output occurred in significantly greater proportions than instances of other-initiated comprehensible output (73 percent versus 27 percent, respectively). These findings confirmed that to have conversations that require the kind of performances associated with successful language learning, students need to focus on self-initiated, self-completed repair.

(4) Negotiation of meaning and Learner interaction

The results of these empirical studies and observations may provide some useful insights into classroom teaching. This section will suggest two different but closely related sets of pedagogical implications: those that relate to negotiating meaning and learner/ learner interaction, and those that relate to repair work.

One of the main underlying principles of the studies on negotiating meaning is that all data emphasize task-based instruction and learner/learner interaction. Thus, the first set of pedagogical implications for language learning relates to activities that involve the negotiation of meaning in dyadic and group interactions. In terms of classroom practice, this means that educators should introduce such activities as **problem solving, decision making, opinion exchange, picture dictation,** and **jigsaw tasks**. These types of activities provide an ideal atmosphere for negotiating meaning in appropriate contexts. Learners have opportunities to receive input that they have made comprehensible through negotiation and at the same time, to produce comprehensible output, an output which learners have made comprehensible to other learners through negotiations.

The implications of the studies on the **negotiation of meaning** match paradigms such as the communicative language approach, which centers on learner/learner interactions. Indeed, this teaching approach emphasizes interactions that involve problem solving, decision making, and opinion exchange, picture dictation, and jigsaw tasks—all standard communicative exercises for developing **fluency** in the target language (TL) (Brumfit 1984, Widdowson 1990).

Teachers who use the communicative approach can justify these types of activities because they encourage learners to produce comprehensible output in the direction of TL-like performances. The findings of interactional studies support the importance of interaction and the negotiation of meaning in developing proficiency in the target language, thus confirming the importance of negotiated interactions in the production of comprehensible output, one of the basic principles of the communicative language approach.

(5) Repair work

The second set of pedagogical implications relates to repair work in the language classroom. The main conclusion here is that if repair leading to comprehensible output is integral to successful language learning, then not only are clarification requests (other-initiations) important, but more importantly, the extent to which self-repair is used. Therefore, **self-initiated clarification** attempts and **self-initiated comprehensible output** should be encouraged as preferred classroom strategies, which are strategies in NS/NS interaction (Schegloff et al., 1977).

Since the main goal of learning an L2 is to approximate NS/NS interaction, creating situations that encourage the production of **self-initiated comprehensible output** is a motivating teaching strategy. In conversations, these situations give the learner more opportunities to use the TL and are significantly more frequent than other-initiated clarification requests and instances of other-initiated comprehensible output (Gaskill 1980, Kasper 1985, and Shehadeh 1991).

It must be cautioned that in the monolingual classroom, there is the possibility that students, in the process of their negotiated interactions and repair work, might resort to their shared mother tongue (MT) to complete the task or the activity required. Nonetheless, assuming that learners are motivated and desire to learn the TL, it is possible to argue that learner-use of the MT in performing the activities required is a more remote possibility than might be expected.

In Shehadeh's (1991) study, the two NNS subjects (ages 24 and 32) who shared one MT background (Arabic) interacted completely in English (the TL) rather than resorting to their shared MT to complete the tasks. This supports Long and Porter's (1985:224) conclusion that "the findings concerning mixed first language groups do not mean, of course, that group work will be unsuccessful in monolingual classrooms, which is the norm in many EFL situations... the research clearly shows that the kind of negotiation work of interest here is also very successfully obtained in the group of the same first language background."

24

문항 해설

직업적 목적을 위한 영어(EOP: English for occupational purpose)수업을 위해서 교사가 내용중심(content-based) 영어 교수법으로 수업 노트를 정리하고 있다. 이 수업은 학습자의 학습의 장이 직장이라는 구체적인 학습의 맥락안에서 이루어지므로 언어입력도 맥락화(contextualized) 되고 있다. 이러한 내용 학습이 그룹에서 행해지고 동료 평가의 지침을 따르게 한다. 그러므로 주요 언어는 학습자의 필요에 의해 구성되고, 활동도 학습자가 현장에서 필요한 내용에 부합되도록 하고 있다. 이러한 수업은 학습자에게 자신의 학습의 장, 즉 각각의 분야(discipline)에 맞는 특정한 언어를 배우도록 한다.

25

문항 해설

(1) 총체적 언어교수법(whole language approach)에서 실제자료를 활용하여 독립적 학습자가 되도록 하여 교실 상황과 개인·사회적 측면을 고려해서 제시하고 있다.
(2) 발음중심 교수법(phonics approach)으로서 새로운 단어의 "소리내어 읽기"나 "의미 해독"을 통해서 소리와 글자에 관한 접근을 하고 있다.
(3) 일견어휘 학습법(sight word method)은 플래시 카드를 이용하여 자주 활용되는 단어 위주로 학습한다.
(4) 초급읽기(basal reader approach)는 선택적 읽기를 통한 초보자를 위한 읽기 방법이다.

핵심 개념정리

읽기와 쓰기 지도

(1) Part-Centered Methods: code-emphasis & bottom-up (parts → whole)

① Phonics	• Match individual letters of the alphabet with their specific English pronunciations • Children can sound out or decode new words • Children are explicitly taught sound-symbol patterns, and the conscious learning of rules • First learn individual sounds, and later put them together into combinations, and then into words • Sound-letter relationships with the knowledge of phonemic awareness
② Linguistic Approaches	• With a scientific knowledge of language • It contains regular spelling patterns so that they can infer the letter-sound relationships in words • take-bake-lake-cake / went-cent-tent-bent
③ Sight word/ Look-say method	• Recognizing whole words, using flash cards or other techniques to help children quickly identify such common words as 'of', 'and', and 'the' • Knowing the most frequent words will help students learn to read more efficiently • Once children can recognize words, comprehension takes care of itself.
④ Basal reader	• Children should be taught to read through careful control and sequencing of the language and the sounds that they are exposed to. • Graded, sequenced, controlled

(2) Socio-Psycholinguistic Approaches: meaning-emphasis & top-down (whole → parts)

① Language Experience Approach	• If children are given material to read that they are already familiar with, it will help them learn to read. • If the actual language and content of the stories are familiar to readers, they should be able to learn to read it even more easily. • Having students generate their own stories. • Transcripts of the stories become reading material. • Allowing children to see a direct link between oral and written language.
② Literature-based Approach	• Using students' literature with the intention of focusing on meaning, interests, and enjoyment • Holding an individual conference about their reading • Individual skills should not be taught • Students' interests and individual needs are respected to facilitate their success and skill development.
③ Whole Language Approach	• Language serves personal, social, and academic aspects of children's lives. • Children become literate as they grapple with the meaning and uses of print in their environments. • Storybook reading, writing their own texts • LEA and Literature-based approach belong within Whole Language Approach. • It incorporates all of the language skills, not only one discrete skill. • Uses of authentic texts from various genres is vital

26

> **문항 해설**

이 학급은 같은 레벨의 교실(homogeneous class)이 아니라, 나이, 능숙도, 모국어, 성별 및 학급 스타일이 각각 다른 교실(heterogeneous class)이다. 학급 내에서의 다양성은 장점과 단점의 성격을 지니고 있다. 장점으로는 학급 내 서로 다른 성별, 능숙도, 모국어 등 다양한 학생이 존재하기 때문에 서로 돕는(collaboration/ scaffolding) 협동학습(cooperative learning)이 동료 간에 상호작용을 통해서 발생할 수 있으며, 서로 간의 문화적 배경의 다양성으로 인해 한 주제에 대해 다양한 의견 및 배경지식이 제시될 수 있어 흥미를 증가시켜 주면서 학습의 동기부여에도 기여해준다. 반면, 이러한 긍정적 측면이 부정적인 면들을 보여주기도 하는데, 학급 내 다양성으로 인해 교사는 교과 목적을 달성하기 위해 학습자의 수준별(proficiency level), 학습 유형(styles) 및 필요와 기대(needs & expectations)를 만족시켜주기 위해 활동 고안 및 자료수집에 있어서 까다로울 수 있으며, 각 학습자들이 학습하는 내용을 잘 이해하고 숙지하고 있는지에 대해서 확인하는데 어려움이 있을 수 있다. 교실 상황에서의 다양한 수준, 배경지식, 요구, 목적 등을 고려할 때, 같은 유형의 그룹보다는 다양한 그룹유형이 더 가깝다. 이러한 다양성을 고려하므로 다양한 활동, 그룹워크, 다양한 자료 제시 등을 고려해야 한다. 개인별 학습 차이는 학습자들이 2언어를 배울 때 어떤 방법으로 배우는지, 얼마나 빨리 배우는지, 얼마나 학습을 성공했는지에 대한 차이점을 지칭한다. 이러한 차이점들로는 언어 학습 적성과 학습 동기와 같은 일반적 요인들과 특수한 학습자 전략이 포함된다. 이들 차이점들은 본래 인지적(cognitive), 정의적(affective), 사회적(social)일 수 있다. 언어 학습에서 학습자 개별 차이들에 영향을 주는 요인들로는 age, sex, previous experience with language learning, proficiency in the native language, personality factor, attitudes, motivation, general intelligence (IQ), sociological preference (e.g. learning with peers vs. learning with teacher), cognitive styles, and learner strategies 등이 있다.

27

> **문항 해설**

과업유형 (1) brainstorming에 관련된 것으로 첫 번째 '나열하기(listing)'에 속하는 과업이며, (2) 독자의 편지에서 충고를 제시해주는 실제 문제에 관련된 것으로 '문제 해결' 관련 과업이다. (3) 교통사고에서 다양한 의견들이 있으면서 비교 및 대조하는 것으로 '비교(comparing)'에 해당하는 과업이다. 두 번째 활동은 한 그림을 묘사하는 문장들을 적어 놓기만 하고, 순서를 정하는 단계까지 가지 않았기 때문에 과업유형이라 보기 어려우며, 마지막 활동은 단순 대화 구문을 반복 훈련하는 것으로 과업이라고 볼 수 없다. 과업이 되기 위해서는 어떤 과업을 성공적으로 해결하기 위한 의미의 이해와 의사 전달의 활동이 포함되어야 한다.

핵심 ELT 읽기

과업의 유형

Listing and brainstorming	You can list people, places, things, actions, reasons, everyday problems, things to do in various circumstances etc. 예 In pairs, agree on a list of four or five people who were famous in the 20th century and give at least one reason for including each person; Can you remember your partner's busiest day?
Ordering and sorting (sequencing, ranking, or classifying)	예 In pairs, look at your list of famous people. Which people are most likely to remain popular and become 20th century icons? Rank them from most popular to least popular, and be prepared to justify your order to another pair.
Matching (captions/ texts/ extracts to pictures; headlines to texts)	예 Read the four headlines A to D. Match two pieces of information to each headline. Explain to your partner how you did this. What clues did you find? Did you both use the same clues?
Comparing (based on two similar texts or pictures: 'Spot the Differences')	Learners can compare their own work with that of another learner or another pair or group. 예 Compare your list of possible 20th century icons with your partner's list. Did you have any people in common? Tell each other why you chose them. How many reasons did you both think of? Finally, combine your two lists, but keep it to five people.
Problem-solving (based on common problems)	Problem-solving tasks are over too quickly — learners agree on the first solution that comes to mind, using minimal language. The instructions for the town centre traffic problem in the example below incorporate six or seven ways of generating richer interaction. 예 Think of a town centre where there is too much traffic. In twos, think of three alternative solutions to this problem. List the advantages and disadvantages of each alternative. Then decide which alternative would be the cheapest one, the most innovative one, the most environmentally friendly one.
Sharing personal experiences & story telling	Activities where learners are asked to recount their personal experiences and tell stories are valuable because they give learners a chance to speak for longer and in a more sustained way. And it is something we often do in real-life. The instructions for activities where learners are encouraged to relate things from their personal lives are often rather vague and open-ended. In order to encourage richer interaction, we usually need to add a clear goal, make instructions more precise, and give clear completion points.

28

문항 해설

이 문제는 대화문과 활동과 원리에 관한 내용을 통합하여 읽으면서 주어진 보기의 교수과정에 대한 이론적 설명을 비교하여 답을 찾을 수 있다. 이 수업은 학생들의 의사소통 언어사용을 발전시키기 위해 과업을 중심으로 전체 수업이 이루어지고 있는 과업중심 교수법이다. 2단계의 원리(Teacher helps students understand the meanings of the utterances in the dialogue.)에서 알 수 있듯이 교사는 의미(meaning)을 전달하기 위하여 명시적 지도(explicit references to form) 방법이 아닌 암시적으로 접근한다. 4단계의 질문과 대답활동은 학생들이 목표의 문법을 알아차릴 수(noticing) 있게 하고, 6~7단계를 통해서 학생들과 상호작용을 통해 목표 문법체계를 획득할 수 있다. 이런 형태중심 교수법(form-focused instruction)의 하나인 의식올리기 방법은 직접적으로 학습을 유도하지는 않는다.

핵심 개념정리

과업중심 교수법 모형

PRE-TASK PHASE
INTRODUCTION TO TOPIC AND TASK
Teacher explores the topic with the class, highlights useful words and phrases, and helps learners understand task instructions and prepare. The teacher introduces the topic and gives the students clear instructions on what they will have to do at the task stage and might help the students to recall some language that may be useful for the task. The pre-task stage can also often include playing a recording of people doing the task. This gives the students a clear model of what will be expected of them. The students can take notes and spend time preparing for the task.

TASK CYCLE		
TASK	PLANNING	REPORT
Students do the task, in pairs or small groups. Teacher monitors from a distance, encouraging all attempts at communication, not orrecting.	Students prepare to report to the whole class (orally or in writing) how they did the task, what they decided or discovered. Meanwhile the teacher is available for the students to ask for advice to clear up any language questions they may have.	Some groups present their reports to the class, or exchange written reports, and compare results. The teacher chooses the order of when students will present their reports and may give the students some quick feedback on the content.

LANGUAGE FOCUS	
ANALYSIS	PRACTICE
Students examine and then discuss specific features of the text or transcript of the recording. They can enter new words, phrases and patterns in vocabulary books.	Teacher conducts practice of new words, phrases, and patterns occurring in the data, either during or after the Analysis.

29

문항 해설

 교실 상황을 읽고 분석하여 이론적인 배경을 쌓아가는 문제는 교수법의 중요한 한 분야이다. 위의 교실 수업은 상호작용이 일어나는 것은 분명하나 교사의 질문과 피드백이 주도권을 잡고 있는 수업형태라고 할 수 있다. 교사는 학생의 발화를 끊임없이 반복하거나 수정함으로써 주도권을 잡고 있음을 명백히 보여주고 있다. 학생의 언어적 오류에도 즉각적으로 수정해줌으로써 학생에게 스스로 발견해낼 여지를 주지 않고 있다. 그런 측면에서 교사가 수정하는데 있어 좀 미루고 단지 억양을 바꾸거나 단서를 던져줌으로써 학생 스스로 수정할 수 있는 기회를 주는 것도 좋은 방법이 될 수 있겠다. 또 다른 측면으로 이 수업에서는 IRF (initiation-response-feedback)의 형태를 볼 수 있다. 교사가 질문의 형태로 수업의 내용을 시작하고 학생들의 응답을 이끌어 낸다. 그 학생의 응답에 대하여 교사의 피드백이 뒤따라온다. 이때 위의 본문에서 설명한 것처럼 교사가 바로 맞는 답의 피드백을 주기보다는 학생이 스스로 발견해 낼 수 있는 방법을 만들어준다면 교실상황이 더 학생중심으로 이루어질 수 있을 것이다. 그와 같은 방식으로 모든 내용을 교사가 시작하기보다는 학생이 먼저 시도할 수 있는 방법을 제시하는 것도 필요하다.

30-37

문항 해설

 행동과 연계해서 학습하는 Total Physical Response 교수법을 설명하고 있다. TPR은 우뇌학습(right-brain learning)을 강조하여, 학습이 먼저 우뇌에서 기능하면 자연스럽게 좌뇌로 연계되어서 자연스럽게 학습이 이루어진다는 개념이다. 어린이들이 모국어를 배우는 것과 같은 방법으로 새로운 언어를 습득한다고 본다.

핵심 개념정리

Total Physical Response

 The founder of the TPR method, James Asher (1977) noted that children, in learning their first language, appear to do a lot of **listening** before they speak, and that their listening is accompanied by **physical responses**. He also gave some attention to **right-brain learning**. According to Asher, motor activity is a right-brain function that should precede left-brain language processing. Asher was also convinced that language classes were often the locus of too much anxiety and wished to devise a method that was as stress-free as possible, where learners would not feel overly self-conscious and defensive. The TPR classroom, then, was one in which students did a great deal of listening and acting. The teacher was very directive in orchestrating a performance: "The instructor is the director of a stage play in which the students are the actors" (Ahser, 1977, p.43).

- Meaning in the target language can often be conveyed through actions.
- The students' understanding of the target language should be developed before speaking.
- Students can initially learn one part of the language rapidly by moving their bodies.

- The imperative is a powerful linguistic device through which the teacher can direct student behavior.
- It is very important that students feel successful. Feeling of success and low anxiety facilitate learning.
- Correction should be carried out in an unobtrusive manner.
- Spoken language should be emphasized over written language.

38

문항 해설

Audio-Motor unit과 Draw the picture (TPR) 학습법은 모두 이해중심 교수법으로서 교사의 명령을 학생들이 행동으로 옮기면서 하는 행동이다. 모국어 어린이들이 배우는 방법과 같으며 우뇌의 작용을 통하여 이루어진 학습방법을 강조한다. 두 학습법의 차이는 맥락화(contextualization)와 문화적 내용(cultural meaning)으로 볼 수 있다. TPR은 맥락이 제한된 명령형의 문장만을 이용하여 상급 학습자에게는 적합하지 않다는 단점이 있다. 그를 해결하기 위해서 Audio-Motor unit에서는 맥락화된 문장의 연계성을 통해서 문화적인 학습, 내용중심으로 학습이 이루어지면서 TPR 학습의 문제점을 보완하고 있다. Audio-Motor unit는 보다 실제 생활과 연관되게 학습할 수 있도록 맥락화하고 행동의 일련과정을 포함시킨 활동이다.

39

문항 해설

Natural approach는 학습자들이 충분히 입력을 받은 후에 그를 바탕으로 출력을 할 수 있다는 이해가 능한 입력(comprehensible input) 가설과 침묵기(silent period)의 개념을 기본으로 하고 있는 교수법이다. 현대적인 의미의 의사소통 교수법과 유사하고 대부분의 상황을 어린이들이 모국어를 배울 때의 상황과 유사하게 접근함을 강조하고 있다. 또한 유사한 교수법으로 구체적인 활동인 명령어 사용, 게임, 역할극과 소그룹 활동을 제시하는 Total Physical Response가 있다.

핵심 개념정리

이해중심 교수법

(1) Comprehensible input

According to Krashen, we acquire language only when we receive **comprehensible input** (CI). This hypothesis claims that we move from i to i+1 by understanding input that contains i+1. In this equation, i represents previously acquired linguistic competence and extra-linguistic knowledge. Extra-linguistic knowledge includes our knowledge of the world and of the situation— that is, the context. The +1 represents new knowledge or language structures that we should be ready to acquire.

(2) Silent period (pre-production)

According to Stephen Krashen, most new learners of English will go through a silent period which is an interval of time during which they are unable or unwilling to communicate orally in the new language. The **silent period** may last for a few days or a year depending on a variety of factors. It occurs before English Language Learners are ready to produce oral language and is generally referred to as the **pre-production stage** of language learning. ELLs should not be forced to speak before they are ready and we don't want to embarrass students by putting them on the spot.

ELLs need time to listen to others talk, to digest what they hear, to develop receptive vocabulary, and to observe their classmates interactions. When they do speak, we want the speech to be real and purposeful instead of contrived. This does not mean your students are not learning. They may understand what is being said, but they are not yet ready to talk about it.

Teacher instruction is an important factor in the length of the silent period. If the teacher provides "hands-on" activities and has students interact in small groups, ELLs will be able to participate in the life of the classroom a lot sooner. They will feel more confident in risking oral language. It should not be assumed that young learners of English do not feel embarrassment or shyness when attempting to speak in a second language.

40-46

핵심 개념정리

청화식 교수법(Audiolingual Method)

(1) Principles

ALM	CLT
Mastery or overlearning is sought.	Effective communication is sought.
Drilling is a central technique.	Drilling may occur, but peripherally.
Demands more memorization of structure-based dialogs	Dialogs, if used, center around communicative functions and are not normally memorized.
Communicative activities only come after a long process of rigid drills and exercises.	Attempts to communicate may be encouraged from the very beginning.
Translation is forbidden at early levels.	Translation may be used where students need or benefit from it.

This method is based on the principles of **behavior psychology**. It adapted many of the principles and procedures of the Direct Method, in part as a reaction to the lack of speaking skills of the Reading Approach. New material is presented in the form of a dialogue. Based on the principle that language learning is habit formation, the method fosters dependence on mimicry, memorization of set phrases and over-learning. Structures are **sequenced** and taught one at a time. Structural patterns are taught using **repetitive drills**. Little or no grammatical explanations are provided; grammar is taught inductively. Vocabulary is strictly limited and learned in context. Teaching points are determined by contrastive analysis between L1 and L2. There is abundant use of language laboratories, tapes and visual aids. There is an extended pre-reading period at the beginning of the course. Great importance is given to precise native-like pronunciation. Use of the mother tongue by the teacher is permitted, but discouraged among and by the students. Successful responses are reinforced; great care is taken to prevent learner errors. There is a tendency to focus on manipulation of the target language and to disregard content and meaning.

- The teacher must be careful to insure that all of the utterances which students will make are actually within the practiced pattern. For example, the use of the AUX verb have should not suddenly switch to have as a main verb.
- Drills should be conducted as rapidly as possibly so as to insure automaticity and to establish a system.
- Ignore all but gross errors of pronunciation when drilling for grammar practice.
- Use of shortcuts to keep the pace of drills at a maximum. Use hand motions, signal cards, notes, etc. to cue response. You are a choir director.
- Use normal English stress, intonation, and juncture patterns conscientiously.
- Drill material should always be meaningful. If the content words are not known, teach their meanings.
- Intersperse short periods of drill (about 10 minutes) with very brief alternative activities to avoid fatigue and boredom.
- Introduce the drill in this way: a. Focus (by writing on the board, for example) b. Exemplify (by speaking model sentences)

(2) Drills and Techniques

A technique commonly used in older methods of language teaching particularly the Audiolingual method and used for practicing sounds or sentence patterns in a language based on guided repetition or practice. A drill which practices some aspect of grammar or sentence formation is often known as pattern practice. There are usually two parts to a drill. (a) The teacher provides a word or sentence as a stimulus (the call-word or cue) (b) Students make various types of responses based on repetition, substitution or transformation.

① Repetition Drill: Students repeat teacher's model as quickly and accurately as possible.
② Chain Drill (open-ended drill): Students ask and answer each other one-by-one in a circular chain around the classroom.
③ Single Slot Substitution Drill: Teacher states a line from the dialog, then uses a word or a phrase as a "cue" that students, when repeating the line, must substitute into the sentence in the correct place (Multiple-slot Substitution Drill: Same as the single slot

drill, except that there are multiple cues to be substituted into the line)
④ Transformation Drill: Teacher provides a sentence that must be turned into something else, for example, a question to be turned into a statement, an active sentence to be turned into a negative statement, etc
⑤ Question-and-answer Drill: Students should answer or ask questions very quickly.
⑥ Moving Slot Substitution (Progressive Substitution): Students know that by substituting words in various slots, they would get a number of sentences, understand the order of their occurrence and the grammatical categories. This drill puts a double burden on the learners' memory. They must remember the preceding sentence in which they have substituted and they must make a new one according to the cue word given.

47

> 핵심 개념정리

전통적 교수법

(1) Grammar Translation Method

- Classes are taught in the mother tongue, with little active use of the target language.
- Much vocabulary is taught in the form of lists of isolated words.
- Long elaborate explanations of the intricacies of grammar are given.
- Grammar provides the rules for putting words together, and instruction often focuses on the form and inflection of words.
- Reading of difficult classical texts is begun early.
- Little attention is paid to the content of texts, which are treated as exercises in in grammatical analysis.
- Often the only drills are exercises in translating disconnected sentences from the target language into the mother tongue.
- Little or no attention is given to pronunciation.

(2) Direct Method

- Classroom instruction is conducted exclusively in the target language.
- Only everyday vocabulary and sentences are taught.
- Oral communication skills are built up in a carefully traded progression organized around question-and-answer exchanges between teachers and students in small, intensive classes.
- Grammar is taught inductively.
- New teaching points are taught through modeling and practice.
- Concrete vocabulary is taught through demonstration, objects, and pictures; abstract vocabulary is taught by association of ideas.

- Both speech and listening comprehension are taught.
- Correct pronunciation and grammar are emphasized.

48-50

문항 해설

CLL에서 가장 중시하는 점은 교사와 학생의 우호적인 관계로서 학습자가 가장 편안한 상태에서 수업이 잘 이루어 질 수 있다고 믿는다. 교사는 상담자(counselor)로서 학습자는 의뢰인(client)으로서 치유해주어야 할 관계로서 보고 있다. 학습자의 정의적 상태를 가장 중시하여 절대로 강압적이지 않고 학습자가 필요하다면 교사는 번역을 해주고 문법은 귀납적으로 수업된다.

핵심 개념정리

공동체 언어 학습(Community Language Learning)

- Students are to be considered as learner-clients and the teacher as a teacher-counselor.
- A relationship of **mutual trust and support** is considered essential to the learning process.
- Students are permitted to use their native language, and are provided with translations from the teacher which they then attempt to apply.
- Grammar and vocabulary are taught inductively.
- Chunks of target language by the students are recorded and later listened to – they are transcribed with native language equivalents to become texts the students work with.
- Students apply the target language independently and without translation when they feel inclined/ confident enough to do so.
- Students are encouraged to express not only how they feel about the language, but how they feel about the **learning process**, to which the teacher expresses empathy and understanding.
- A variety of activities can be included (for example, focusing on a particular grammar or pronunciation point, or creating new sentences based on the recordings/ transcripts.

51-53

문항 해설

Silent way의 가장 중요한 원리는 교사의 침묵으로 학생 스스로 개발해 나가는 것이므로 색깔도표 등의 도구를 활용한다. Natural Approach는 모국어를 습득하는 과정처럼 먼저 많은 입력을 받는 단계, 즉 침묵의 단계를 거쳐 발화를 하게 된다. Total Physical Response는 많이 듣고 그에 따라 신체적 행동을 하면서 서서히 발화단계로 나아가다. Suggestopedia는 환경의 중요성을 강조하여 편안한 환경과 바로크식 음악의 도움으로 학습자의 잠재능력을 끌어내어 언어학습발달에 도움을 준다.

핵심 개념정리

Designer Methods

(1) Silent Way encourages the teacher to assume a distance that prevents him/her from providing direct guidance when at times such guidance would be helpful. It is criticized as being too focused on building structure, and misses out on cultural input through the language, and the silence of the teacher can prevent students from hearing many active models of correct usage that they may find useful. In trying to create a less teacher-orientated classroom, many say that the Silent Way goes too far to the opposite extreme. Other problems are a little more practical in nature. Getting together the "classic SW" prerequisite materials can take a lot of time and money – there is the sound-color chart, 12 word charts each containing around 500 words, and 8 Fidel Charts for the English language alone. And don't forget the actual cuisenaire rods as well! In order to maximize the learning potential of students using the Silent Way, teachers would have to be prepared to invest quite heavily in materials.

(2) Krashen's theories and the Natural approach have received plenty of criticism, particularly orientated around the recommendation of a silent period that is terminated when students feel ready to emerge into oral production, and the idea of comprehensible input. Critics point out that students will **emerge** at different times (or perhaps not at all!) and it is hard to determine which forms of language input will be **comprehensible** to the students. These factors can create a classroom that is essentially very difficult to manage unless the teacher is highly skilled. Still, this was the first attempt at creating an expansive and overall approach rather than a specific method, and the Natural Approach led naturally into the generally accepted norm for effective language teaching.

(3) Total Physical Response owes a lot to some basic principles of language acquisition in young learners, most notably that the process involves a substantial amount of listening and comprehension in combination with various **physical responses** (smiling, reaching, grabbing, looking, etc) – well before learners begin to use the language orally. It also focused on the ideas that learning should be as fun and **stress-free** as possible, and that it should be dynamic through the use of accompanying physical activity. Asher (1977) also had a lot to say about **right-brained** learning (the part of the brain that deals with motor activity), believing it should precede the language processing element covered by the left-brain.

(4) Suggestopedia provides some valuable insights into the power of cognition and creating/ employing techniques that make students feel **comfortable and relaxed**, and suggestible to the material being learned. Unfortunately it does not provide for the majority of language teaching environments teachers typically encounter. The dim lighting, large comfortable chairs and music selections are not readily available to the majority of schools, and these environmental factors are certainly close to impossible for very large classes. As with other methods, it does not take account of the fact that many learners in many countries do not necessarily bring an intrinsic desire to learn the language into their English lessons, and its basic foundations in cognitive theory in some ways limit it as a method to the realm of adult learning.

54-59

문항 해설

　　의사소통능력(communicative competence)을 기르기 위해서는 무엇을 가르치고 배워야 하는가? Wilkins (1979)는 문법중심 교수요목이 학습자가 목표어를 어떻게 표현해야 하는가에 대한 '어떻게'에 대한 답변이라면 상황중심 교수요목은 학습자가 언제, 어디서 목표어를 사용해야 하는가에 '언제'와 '어디서'에 대한 답변이라고 했다. 그러나 언어교육에서 이보다 더 중요한 것은 학습자가 '무엇'을 표현해야 하는가에 대한 대답을 제시해야 한다는 것이다. 학습자가 2언어를 통해 표현할 수 있기를 기대하는 개념이 무엇이며 어떤 언어기능을 수행하는가? 학습자가 어떤 종류의 일에 대해 의사소통하기를 원하는가? NFS는 학습자가 목표언어로 표현하고자 하는 의미와 학습자가 그 언어로 사용하게 될 기능(function)에 따라 수업이 구성되고 있음을 설명해야 한다. 의사소통을 위한 내용과 기능을 결정하고 그에 따라 상황이나 문법형태가 따라야 된다는 것이다. 기능적 교수요목(functional syllabus)을 주장하는 학자들도 문법규칙과 상황을 중요시하지 않는 것이 아니라 의사소통적인 외국어 교육이 되기 위해서는 상대적인 중요성으로 보아 의미-기능(meaning-functions)이 일차적으로 고려되고 문법이나 상황이 차후에 고려될 수 있다는 것이다. 이와 같은 의미-기능중심의 교수요목은 의사소통력 향상에 초점을 주어 거기에 필요한 의미와 기능 등을 가르쳐야 한다고 하여 의사소통 교수요목이라고도 한다.

60

문항 해설

　　듣기와 읽기지도에서 이용되는 schema이론은 학습자가 지니고 있는 이전의 경험과 지식이 학습에 도움이 된다는 이론이다. schema를 이용하여 현재 학습의 장에서 많이 권장되는 하향식 처리과정(top-down processing)을 활용할 수 있게 된다. 새로운 정보를 기존의 정보나 경험과 통합해서 이해할 수 있기 때문에 전체적인 장을 이해하는 데 훨씬 도움이 될 수 있다.

Schema Theory

Schema theory that in comprehending language people activate relevant schemata allowing them to process and interpret new experiences quickly and efficiently. When encountering a topic in reading or listening, the reader activates the schema for that topic and makes use of it to anticipate, infer, and make different kinds of judgments and decisions about it. Schema theory plays an important role in theories of second language reading and listening comprehension.

- schema: the larger-order mental frameworks of knowledge (content/formal)
- script: (cognitive psychology) units of meaning consisting of sequences of events and actions that are related to particular situations. For example a "restaurant script" is our knowledge that a restaurant is a place where waitress, waiters, and cooks work, where food is served to customers, and where customers sit at tables, order food, eat, pay the bill, and depart. A person's knowledge of this "script" helps in understanding the following paragraph; Tom was hungry. He went into a restaurant. At 8pm, he paid the bill and left. Although all the facts are not mentioned in the paragraph, the readers' knowledge of a restaurant script, i.e. the usual sequence of events for this situation, provides this information.

01-02

핵심 ELT 읽기

상호 문화적 능력(intercultural competence) 지도

As Kramsch points out teaching culture in traditional foreign language education was limited to the transmission of information about the people of the target country and their general attitudes and worldview. The facts that language is a social practice and culture is a complex social construct have been ignored. According to Kramsch, intercultural communicative competence can be reached or at least approached by sensitizing the learners for realizing, acknowledging and tolerating difference, meeting a person with other cultural and social peculiarities and making them aware of the relativity of their judgment. Thus cultural content in language teaching has to be determined so as to present the difference in an appropriate way. Kramsch differentiates new lines of thought for culture teaching which seem to emerge today:

A. Establishing a sphere of interculturality: Since communication in a foreign language is also communication between cultures, an intercultural approach includes a reflection on both the target and native culture. In this sense an effective language teaching has to embrace both perspectives.

B. Teaching culture as an interpersonal process: If language is seen as a social action, then meaning is constructed through social interaction. As a consequence, we should not teach fixed, normative cultural facts but rather a process of communication and suggest strategies appropriate and helpful for understanding otherness.

- culture capsule: A culture capsule is a brief description of some aspect of the target language culture (e.g., what is customarily eaten for meals and when those meals are eaten, marriage customs, etc.) followed by, or incorporated with contrasting information from the students' native language culture.

- culture island: A culture island is an area in the classroom where posters, maps, objects, and pictures of people, lifestyles, or customs of other cultures are displayed to attract learners' attention, evoke comments, and help students develop a mental image.

- artifact study: It is designed to help students discern the cultural significance of certain unfamiliar objects from the target culture. The activity involves students in giving descriptions and forming hypotheses about the function of the unknown object.

- native informant: Native informants can be valuable resources to the classroom teacher, both as sources of current information about the target culture and as linguistic models for students. Students can develop a set of questions they would like to ask before native speakers come to the class.

C. Teaching culture as difference: Students must be made aware of the heterogeneity of cultures: due to the growth of multiculturality and multiethnicity of societies national cultural characteristics are losing even more of their overall validity. Cultural identities are made up of a range of aspects; one always has to consider further specifications as age, gender, religion, ethnic background, social class, education, etc.

D. Crossing disciplinary boundaries: Teachers are encouraged to broaden the range of their knowledge by reading literature, studies by social scientists, ethnographers, sociolinguists in order to present information beyond the field of linguistics and challenge, maybe even motivate their learners and provide them with an appealing presentation of the target society.

03

문항 해설

수업의 목표를 서술하기 위해서는 문화통합(culture-integrated) 언어사용에 대한 이해가 필요하다. 이 수업은 다른 문화에서 나타나는 언어의 특성을 이해하고 그에 따라 이해력과 표현력을 위한 언어(receptive and productive language)를 가르치고 있다. 수업의 목표를 서술할 때 meaning & form과 input & output을 문화와 관련하여 서술한다. (1) reception: 언어를 이해하고 연습하며, (2) production: 그에 맞는 상황에서 사용할 수 있도록 하는 것으로 분류하여 수업의 목표를 서술할 수 있다.

04

핵심 개념정리

상호문화에 대한 이해능력 (Intercultural Competence)

Intercultural competence refers to the ability to effectively navigate and communicate across cultural boundaries, understanding and respecting cultural products, practices, and perspectives. This concept is essential for learners to develop as they engage with a new language and culture:

(1) Cultural Products: Cultural products encompass various forms of expression, such as literature, art, music, film, cuisine, and other creative works produced by a particular culture. Intercultural competence involves understanding and appreciating these cultural products in their original context, as well as interpreting and analyzing them through the lens of the target language. Learners explore and engage with cultural products to deepen their understanding of the cultural values, beliefs, and traditions

embedded within them.

(2) **Cultural Practices**: Cultural practices refer to the behaviors, rituals, customs, and traditions that shape daily life within a particular culture. Intercultural competence involves recognizing and respecting these practices while also learning how to navigate and participate in them appropriately. Through language learning, learners gain insight into cultural norms, etiquette, and social conventions, enabling them to interact respectfully and effectively in diverse cultural settings.

(3) **Cultural Perspectives**: Cultural perspectives encompass the worldview, attitudes, beliefs, and values that influence how individuals perceive and interpret the world around them. Intercultural competence requires learners to develop an awareness of different cultural perspectives, recognizing that there are multiple ways of viewing and understanding the same phenomena. By engaging with authentic cultural materials and interacting with native speakers, learners gain exposure to diverse perspectives, challenging their own assumptions and broadening their cultural empathy and understanding.

Intercultural competence is not only about acquiring language proficiency but also about developing cultural awareness, sensitivity, and adaptability. Through exposure to cultural products, practices, and perspectives, learners become more adept at navigating intercultural interactions, bridging communication gaps, and building meaningful connections with speakers of the target language. Intercultural competence enhances learners' ability to communicate effectively in diverse contexts, fostering mutual respect, empathy, and intercultural understanding.

05

핵심 개념정리

상호문화를 위한 언어학습 과정 (Processes of Intercultural language learning)

Intercultural language learning can be enriched through the processes of noticing, comparing, reflecting, and interacting.

1. Noticing

① This step involves learners becoming aware of cultural aspects and linguistic features in the target culture. This is the stage of exposure and observation.

② Example Activity
- Task: Watch a video of a Japanese tea ceremony.
- Student Experience: Students observe the gestures, language, and rituals involved, such as bowing, the use of polite expressions, and specific movements for pouring tea.

- Outcome: A student might notice, "People bow several times and use honorific language during the ceremony. It seems very formal."

2. Comparing

① Learners compare the target culture to their own, identifying similarities and differences. This stage fosters critical thinking and cultural awareness.

② Example Activity

- Task: Compare birthday celebrations in Korea and the U.S. using videos and group discussions.
- Student Experience: Korean students might share their experience of "eating seaweed soup and having family gatherings" versus "cutting a birthday cake with friends at a party" in the U.S.
- Outcome: A student might reflect, "In Korea, birthdays often emphasize family, while in the U.S., friends play a bigger role. Both cultures value sharing food, though."

3. Reflecting

① Learners think deeply about their personal reactions to the observed cultural differences and similarities, considering how they relate to their own beliefs and values.

② Example Activity

- Task: Write a journal entry about how language reflects cultural values.
- Student Experience: After learning about the use of formal and informal pronouns in French (tu and vous), students reflect on the cultural significance of politeness and hierarchy.
- Outcome: A student might write, "I think it's fascinating how the French language has specific words to show respect. In Korean, we also use honorifics, but it's more about the age difference than formality."

4. Interacting

① Definition: Learners communicate their ideas and experiences, actively engaging with others to share and reshape their understanding of cultural diversity.

② Example Activity:

- Task: Participate in a classroom debate about cultural stereotypes and how they affect cross-cultural communication.
- Student Experience: One student shares, "I used to think Americans were too direct, but now I realize it's their way of being honest." Another responds, "That's interesting! In my culture, we avoid direct comments to keep harmony."
- Outcome: Through dialogue, students reshape their interpretations, realizing that cultural norms are situational rather than universally rigid.

06

문항 해설

　수업절차를 살펴보면 단계(1) 교사가 여러 나라에서 온 엽서를 보여주고 오늘 하게 될 활동에 대해서 설명을 한다. 단계(2) 학생들이 직접 보낸 엽서의 내용과 종류들에 대해 이야기해 보는 시간을 가진다. 단계(3) 학생들은 짝으로 구성되어 선생님이 미리 준비해둔 엽서를 한 명이 가지고 설명하고 다른 한 명은 그 엽서가 해당되는 나라를 알아 맞춘다. 단계(4) 서로 엽서를 보면서 문화 관련요소를 모든 학생과 나눈다. 단계(5) 교사는 미국의 문화요소에 대해 설명하고 학생들은 자신들의 문화와 비교해본다. 단계(6) 추후 활동으로 학생들은 자기나라의 엽서를 가져와서 각 문화에 대하여 한 문단을 작성해보게 한다. 위의 활동 절차에서 보이는 것처럼 이 수업은 학생들이 서로의 개인적 경험을 나누고, "… since arriving in the US" 어구를 통해서 미국에 온 국제 학습자(international learners)임을 알 수 있다. 주요 언어기술은 서로 의견을 말하는 말하기, 서로의 문화를 공유하는 문화적 의식(cultural awareness)과 엽서쓰기의 쓰기활동이 포함되어 있음을 알 수 있다. 학습자A는 엽서를 보고 설명하고 B는 보지 않고 그 나라를 맞추어야 하는 정보차이활동(information-gap activity)이 포함된다. 이 수업의 목표는 단순히 쓰기기술을 소개하고 강화하기 위한 것이 아니라 통합된 언어기술을 활용하여 다양한 문화를 인지하는 데 있다고 할 수 있다.

영어과 교육과정

문화 지도

　영어권 및 비영어권의 다양한 문화를 학습하여 타문화에 대한 이해를 높이고, 문화에 대한 올바른 판단력과 가치관을 기르도록 한다. 영어가 사용되는 사회의 문화를 이해하는 것은 영어로 그 사람들과 의사소통하는 능력을 기르는데 필수적이며, 현대사회에서는 다양한 문화에 속한 사람들과 영어로 의사소통할 기회가 늘어나기 때문에 다양한 문화를 이해하는 것이 폭넓은 의사소통능력을 기르는 데 도움이 될 것이다. 문화 지도에서는 설명 위주의 수업보다는 주어진 과제를 수행하거나 체험 학습 형태의 교수방법을 활용하여 효과적인 영어 수업을 하게 할 수 있다. 게임이나 놀이를 이용하여 학생들이 알아야 할 문화적 내용을 무의식적으로 학습하거나, 토론 또는 원어민과의 질의응답을 통해서 정보나 의견을 주고 받으면서 수업을 진행할 수도 있다. 특히, 문화 교육에서는 역할극(role play)이나 마임(mime) 등을 통해 해당 문화에서의 의사소통 방식을 실제로 해 봄으로써 습득할 수 있고 우리나라의 의사소통 방식과의 차이점을 알아볼 수도 있다. 예를 들면, 자기를 소개하는 방법에 대한 문화적 차이를 알아보고 실제로 수행해 보는 것이다. 이때, 수업 장면을 녹화하여 교사와 학생들이 함께 다시 점검하며 토론한다면 더욱 효과적인 수업이 이루어질 수 있다. 문화 교육의 소재로는 그림이나 사진을 이용하여 몸짓이나 표정들이 각각의 문화에서 다르게 이해되는 것 알아보기, 상황에 맞는 적절한 의사소통 방식의 차이 이해하기 등이 있다. 멀티미디어 기자재를 이용하여 동영상 자료를 함께 보면서 해당 차시와 연계될 수 있는 문화적 내용을 학습하는 것도 도움이 될 것이다. 이때, 가장 중요한 것은 특정 문화에 대한 정형화된 생각을 전달하기 보다는 균형 잡힌 가치관을 형성할 수 있도록 학습 자료 및 학습 활동을 계획하는 것이다.

07

핵심 개념정리

언어의 형식성 (Formality in language learning)

Formality in language learning refers to the appropriate use of language styles depending on the social context, relationship between speakers, and the purpose of communication. It's about selecting words, phrases, and structures that match the level of formality required in a given situation.

(1) Key Aspects of Formality

① Context Awareness: Formality changes based on setting (formal vs. informal) and audience (authority figures vs. peers).

- Formal: "Good morning, Professor Smith. I would like to inquire about the assignment deadline."
- Informal: "Hey, what's up? Do you know when the assignment's due?"

② Linguistic Features

- Vocabulary: Formal language uses more precise and complex words (e.g., request vs. ask for).
- Grammar: Formal contexts often require full sentences and proper syntax.
- Tone and Politeness: Formality often includes polite expressions (e.g., Would you mind…?).

③ Purpose and Relationship: Formality reflects the relationship between speakers (e.g., student to teacher vs. friends). It also aligns with the purpose of communication (e.g., giving a presentation vs. chatting casually).

(2) Why Is Formality Important in Language Learning?

- Pragmatic Competence: Learners develop the ability to choose the appropriate language style for different social contexts.
- Avoiding Miscommunication: Using an overly informal tone in a professional context can seem rude or unprofessional.
- Cultural Awareness: Understanding cultural expectations helps learners integrate more naturally into various social settings.

(3) Teaching Formality:

- Role-Playing: Simulate different scenarios (e.g., job interviews vs. friendly chats).
- Speech Style Comparison: Analyze dialogues to identify formal and informal elements.
- Contextual Practice: Encourage students to rewrite informal sentences in a formal style and vice versa.

> 핵심 ELT 읽기

영어학습자의 말하기 능력 개선 방법

(1) Speech Acts

In the philosophy of language and linguistics, **speech act** is something expressed by an individual that not only presents information but performs an action as well. For example, the phrase "I would like the kimchi; could you please pass it to me?" is considered a speech act as it expresses the speaker's desire to acquire the kimchi, as well as presenting a request that someone pass the kimchi to them. According to Kent Bach, "almost any speech act is really the performance of several acts at once, distinguished by different aspects of the speaker's intention: there is the act of saying something, what one does in saying it, such as requesting or promising, and how one is trying to affect one's audience". The contemporary use of the term goes back to J. L. Austin's development of performative utterances and his theory of locutionary, illocutionary, and perlocutionary acts. Speech acts serve their function once they are said or communicated. These are commonly taken to include acts such as apologizing, promising, ordering, answering, requesting, complaining, warning, inviting, refusing, and congratulating.

- A **locutionary act**: the performance of an utterance: the actual utterance and its apparent meaning, comprising any and all of its verbal, social, and rhetorical meanings, all of which correspond to the verbal, syntactic and semantic aspects of any meaningful utterance;

- an **illocutionary act**: the active result of the implied request or meaning presented by the locutionary act. For example, if the locutionary act in an interaction is the question "Is there any salt?" the implied illocutionary request is "Please pass the salt to me." or at least "I wish to add salt to my meal.";

- and under certain conditions a further **perlocutionary act**: the actual effect of the locutionary and illocutionary acts, such as persuading, convincing, scaring, enlightening, inspiring, or otherwise getting someone to do or realize something, whether intended or not.

(2) Instructional Approaches

Communicative and **whole language instructional approaches** promote **integration** of speaking, listening, reading, and writing in ways that reflect natural language use. But opportunities for speaking and listening require structure and planning if they are to support language development. **Outside the classroom**, listening is used twice as often as speaking, which in turn is used twice as much as reading and writing (Rivers, 1981). Inside the classroom, speaking and listening are the most often used skills (Brown, 1994). They are recognized as critical for functioning in an English language context, both by teachers and by learners. These skills are also logical instructional starting points when learners have low literacy levels (in English or their native language) or limited formal education, or when they come from language backgrounds with a non-Roman script or a predominantly oral tradition. Further, with the drive to incorporate workforce readiness skills into adult ESL instruction, practice time is being devoted to such speaking skills as reporting, negotiating, clarifying, and problem solving.

(3) What is speaking?

Speaking is an interactive process of constructing meaning that involves producing *and* receiving and processing information. Its form and meaning are dependent on the **context** in which it occurs, including the participants themselves, their collective **experiences**, the physical environment, and the purposes for speaking. It is often spontaneous, open-ended, and evolving. However, speech is not always **unpredictable**. Language functions (or patterns) that tend to recur in certain discourse situations (e.g., declining an invitation or requesting time off from work), can be identified and charted. For example, when a salesperson asks "May I help you?" the expected discourse sequence includes a statement of need, response to the need, offer of appreciation, acknowledgement of the appreciation, and a leave-taking exchange. Speaking requires that learners not only know how to produce specific points of language such as grammar, pronunciation, or vocabulary *(linguistic competence)*, but also that they understand when, why, and in what ways to produce language *(sociolinguistic competence)*. Finally, speech has its own skills, structures, and conventions different from written language. A good speaker synthesizes this array of skills and knowledge to succeed in a given speech act.

(4) What does a good speaker do?

A speaker's skills and speech habits have an impact on the success of any exchange. Speakers must be able to anticipate and then produce the expected patterns of specific discourse situations. They must also manage discrete elements such as turn-taking, rephrasing, providing feedback, or redirecting. For example, a learner involved in the exchange with the salesperson described previously must know the usual pattern that such an interaction follows and access that knowledge as the exchange progresses. The learner must also choose the correct vocabulary to describe the item sought, rephrase or emphasize words to clarify the description if the clerk does not understand, and use appropriate facial expressions to indicate satisfaction or dissatisfaction with the service. Other skills and knowledge that instruction might address include the following:

- producing the sounds, stress patterns, rhythmic structures, and intonations of the language
- using grammar structures accurately
- assessing characteristics of the target audience, including shared knowledge or shared points of reference, status and power relations of participants, interest levels, or differences in perspectives

- selecting vocabulary that is understandable and appropriate for the audience, the topic being discussed, and the setting in which the speech act occurs
- applying strategies to enhance comprehensibility, such as emphasizing key words, rephrasing, or checking for listener comprehension
- using gestures or body language
- paying attention to the success of the interaction and adjusting components of speech such as vocabulary, rate of speech, and complexity of grammar structures to maximize listener comprehension and involvement

09

문항 해설

읽기를 위한 주요 전략으로서 읽기 전 활동이 있다. 이는 학습자들이 글의 내용을 세부적으로 자세하게 읽기 전에 전체적인 내용을 파악함으로써 빨리 효과적으로 글을 이해하는 데 도움을 주고 있다. (1) 스키마는 읽어야 할 내용과 연관하여 학습자들이 가진 관련정보를 끌어내어 읽게 될 글의 내용을 이해하게 쉽게 해준다. (2) 언어적 지식(linguistic knowledge)은 글에 있는 단어를 미리 학습함으로써 언어적인 어려움을 덜어주는 데 목적을 두고 있다. (3) 문화적 인식(cultural awareness)은 왕국과 연관된 내용의 질문을 풀면서 문화에서 올 수 있는 어려움에 도움을 주는 것이다.

핵심 개념정리

읽기 전 활동(Pre-reading Activities)

(1) Students predict the story from the headline

The students may need dictionaries and you should be careful of puns and double meanings. Students should work in pairs, and feedback ideas to the board/teacher.

(2) Students predict the story from a picture

① Predict vocabulary

Once students know the topic of the article, they predict words that they think they will read. Again, feedback these predictions to the board. As students read, they should tick the words they find. Which pair predicted the most words?

② Vocabulary/Sentence selection

Students are given a group of words (sentences), some of which are from the article, others are not. Students decide which ones are from the article. Obviously, they need to know the topic of the article.

(3) Activating Prior Knowledge

One of the most important variables with learning is a student's prior knowledge. By tapping into what students already know, teachers help with the learning process. This is because learning is relating the new information, or concepts, to what we already know. Strategies to activate prior knowledge include: Brainstorming, Graphic Organiser, and Introduction of Key Words.

10

문항 해설

작문의 피드백을 교사가 어떻게 설명해 주느냐에 관한 문제이다. [1]에서 [2]의 글로 변환되었을 때의 가장 큰 차이점은 전체 글의 내용을 명확히 하기 위하여 연결어구(cohesive devices)가 적절히 사용되고 있다는 점이다. [1]에서는 문장들이 개별적으로 따로 떨어져 있어서 의미상의 연관을 보이지 않는 반면, [2]는 문장들 간에 ~why, the first~, also, because, and, after 등을 이용하여 논리성(coherence)과 응집성(cohesion)이 있는 논리적 연결을 해주고 있다.

11

문항 해설

두 학생의 글에 대하여 내용, 구성, 언어사용(content, organization, language use)을 비교 분석하여 서술한다. 교사로서 학생의 쓰기에 대한 평가를 내리는 것이므로 구체적이고 예시를 이용하여 명확하게 비교할 수 있도록 서술한다. 첫 단락에 content는 유사점으로 historical influences, daily lives, 'trading center', 'central post office' & 'food', 'language'가 있다. 두 번째 organization의 차이점으로 cohesion devices, viewpoint, 'first, second..' & 'in addition', 'although'등을 찾아볼 수 있다. 마지막으로 language use의 차이점으로 grammatical structure, vocabulary, 'since..' & 'history of conflict'등이 있다.

12

문항 해설

본 수업과정은 webquest라는 인터넷수업을 실시하는 과정을 설명하고 있다. 우선 학생들은 교사에 의해 주어진 추수감사절 이라는 주제아래 인터넷 조사를 하고, 그를 통해 미국의 추수감사절과 우리의 추석을 비교하여 자신들이 한 연구결과에 대해 기록한다. 본문 수업의 모든 과정이 학생들이 필요한 정보를 직접 인터넷에서 수집하고 작성하여 새로운 내용을 습득해 나가는 탐구중심(inquiry-based) 수업이 되고 있음을 알 수 있다. 교사에 의해서 주어진 주제안에서 학생들이 쓰고 싶은 것을 선택하도록 하는 webquest 활동이다. 이 수업은 대표적인 4기능 통합수업으로서 토론을 통한 듣기와 말하기, 인터넷을 통한 읽기와 스스로 작성해보는 쓰기가 포함되며 ICT를 이용하여 수업이므로 맞는 설명이다.

탐구 중심 학습법(Inquiry-based learning)

Inquiry-based learning is difficult to describe in a fixed and straightforward way. When viewed from a curricular perspective, it is often seen as a process that provides opportunities for learners to engage in the practices of life beyond the classroom — using the tools and methods of scientists, artists, problem solvers, or citizens in society — to gain a **deeper understanding** of themselves and the world around them. This process is **situated, personal, action-based, social,** and **reflective**. It is also a critical process, one that questions received knowledge and social structures, and even its own processes. Thus, it invites a continual questioning of what it means to teach and learn, what counts as knowledge, and what meaning or action follows from learning. The very notion of inquiry-based learning must itself be subject to this critical examination.

Most versions of inquiry learning see a **continuing cycle** or **spiral of inquiry** (Bruner), one version of which is shown here. This is a model for how people engage in inquiry, such as those proposed for the process of writing or Dewey's for thinking. Some such models emphasize immersion in phenomena prior to more focused investigation; this is what Hawkins calls "messing about". Others emphasize action growing out of the inquiry. For example, liberatory education (Freire, 1970) conceives two stages, one in which people become aware of their oppression and a second, which builds upon the first, in which they transform that state. There is usually a strong caution against interpreting steps in the cycle as all being necessary or in a rigid order. In fact, inquiry learning is less well characterized by a series of steps for learning than it is by situated learning. This is a phrase describing how learning happens as a function of the activity, context and culture in which it occurs, rather than through abstract and decontextualized presentations.

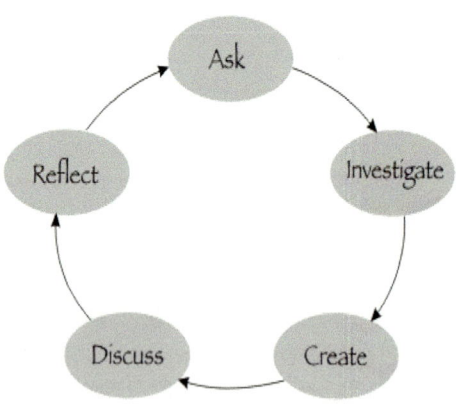

People thus learn through their participation in a community of practice. Learning is a process of moving from the periphery of a community to its center, that is, going from legitimate peripheral participation to full enculturatation. Most of this process is **incidental** rather than deliberate. Inquiry-based learning is manifested in a variety of curricular and instructional approaches, which can be roughly grouped according to the aspects of the inquiry cycle they emphasize.

For example, the open school movement of the 1960's invited students and teachers to look beyond the realm of textbooks to the larger community in the formulation of questions for study. **Problem-based learning** sets the formulation of questions as a task for the learner. An emphasis on rich, authentic materials for investigation can be seen in materials-based and research-based curricular approaches. **Project-based learning** emphasizes the creative aspects of learning through extended projects and performances. **Discussion and collaboration** are important in cooperative learning and in much of the writing process work. **Response-centered classrooms** highlight the reflective and constructive aspects of meaning-making.

13

문항 해설

어휘와 문법요소를 가르치면서 문화와 통합수업으로 실시한다.
1. 어휘를 가르칠때는 문화적 함축된 의미(cultural connotations)를 가르친다.
2. 관련된 문법적 요소와 연결하여 문화적 주제를 제시한다.
3. 교과서 그림이나 사진을 활용한다.
4. 그룹활동으로 토론과 역할극 같은 문화수업을 위한 의사소통 기술을 활용한다.
5. 강의나 일화형식(anecdotal format)이 아니라 4기능 통합으로 문화를 가르친다.

2단계의 교사가 자신의 이야기를 일화식으로 하고 학생은 듣는 수동적인 활동은 적절치 않다. 4단계에서 어휘수업을 동의어나 반의어등의 비교와 암기식 방법을 쓰는 것은 문화적 함축된 의미를 가르치는데 적절치 않다.

14

문항 해설

대화 (1)은 비형식적(informal) 화법으로 나누는 대화체이고, 대화 (2)는 형식적(formal) 화법을 이용하고 있는 것을 알 수 있다. 학생들이 두 대화체의 격식이 다른 특징들을 통해 형식성에 대한 의식(formality-awareness)을 향상시킬 수 있다. 대화의 문체(register), 즉 형식적인 언어인지 평상어인지 그 차이를 인식하게 하는 것이 이 두 대화를 가르치는 목표라고 할 수 있다. 학생들은 대화내용을 통해 화자의 관계를 추측할 수 있다. 즉 대화 (1)은 친한 사이인 가족관계로 볼 수 있고 대화 (2)는 약사와 손님의 형식적인 언어를 사용하는 관계임을 알 수 있다.

CHAPTER 06 이해 능력 지도

01

핵심 ELT 읽기

듣기 활동

1. Intensive Listening:

Intensive listening focuses on helping learners pay close attention to specific details and language features in an audio text. It's different from extensive listening, which focuses on general comprehension.

(1) Key Characteristics:

- Language Features: Focus on pronunciation, intonation, stress, or specific grammatical structures; Emphasize authentic speech patterns like contractions (e.g., "gonna," "wanna").
- Short, Authentic Texts: Uses radio shows, songs, podcasts, or short conversations that reflect natural language use; Typically, repeated listening is encouraged to notice language patterns.
- Focused Listening Tasks: Identifying contractions or reduced forms (e.g., "I'm gonna" instead of "I am going to"); Noticing intonation and stress patterns that indicate emotions or emphasi; Filling in blanks or transcribing short segments to reinforce detailed listening.

(2) Benefits: Helps learners improve accuracy and comprehension of spoken English; Builds phonological awareness and the ability to understand fast, connected speech.

2. Creative Activities:

Creative activities encourage learners to express themselves freely while using the language they are learning. They involve imaginative and engaging tasks that make learning fun and meaningful. Examples of Creative Activities:

- Singing Songs or Chants: Enhances pronunciation, rhythm, and intonation; Makes language practice enjoyable and memorable; Example: Singing a popular song and focusing on contractions like "don't," "can't," "I'll."
- Voice Recording Projects: Students record themselves telling a story or giving a presentation; Helps build confidence and fluency as they practice speaking naturally; Encourages self-assessment by listening to their recordings.
- Drama or Role-Play: Students act out scenarios or perform short skits; Develops communicative competence and fluency in a fun way.

- Creative Storytelling: Learners create their own stories or poems and share them with classmates; Builds narrative skills and vocabulary usage.

3. Why Are These Activities Useful?

- Authentic Use of Language: Students practice using language in ways they would in real life.
- Enhanced Motivation: Engaging tasks increase student involvement and enthusiasm.
- Confidence Building: Creative tasks reduce anxiety and make students feel more comfortable experimenting with language.

02

핵심 ELT 읽기

이해능력 vs 표현능력 (Reception vs Production)

(1) Reception vs. Production

Dimension	Reception (Input)	Production (Output)
Focus	Understanding and processing language	Creating and expressing language
Skills	Listening and Reading	Speaking and Writing
Examples	Recognizing sounds, identifying details, interpreting meaning	Explaining events, writing texts, debating respectfully

(2) Reception Objectives:

Reception involves listening and reading skills—the ability to comprehend and process incoming language. The objectives listed here focus on helping students recognize, identify, and understand information.

① R1: Students can recognize reduced sounds of words.

- This means students can identify connected speech and contractions (e.g., "gonna" instead of "going to").
- Helps in understanding natural, fluent speech and enhances listening skills.

② R2: Students can identify specific details from a text or discourse.

- This focuses on scanning and listening for precise information, such as dates, names, or key facts.
- Essential for tasks like comprehension questions or note-taking.

③ R3: Students can distinguish between literal and implied meanings.

- This involves recognizing both direct statements and underlying messages (e.g., sarcasm, irony, or figurative language).
- Supports critical listening and reading comprehension.

(3) Production Objectives:

Production involves speaking and writing skills—the ability to express thoughts, ideas, or arguments clearly and accurately. The objectives listed focus on articulating ideas in various formats.

① P1: Students can explain the sequence of an event in the right order.
- This means students can narrate or describe a process chronologically, such as telling a story or giving instructions.
- Develops skills in organizing thoughts logically.

② P2: Students can write a simple journal, letter, or email.
- Focuses on written communication for everyday contexts.
- Encourages practical writing skills with correct formatting and appropriate tone.

③ P3: Students can argue for and against a topic in a respectful manner.
- Promotes debating skills and the ability to articulate contrasting opinions.
- Fosters critical thinking and respectful dialogue.

03

> 핵심 ELT 읽기

듣기 전략

In the context of second language learning, listening strategies can be categorized into two main types: local or micro strategies and global or macro strategies. These strategies help learners effectively comprehend spoken language and improve their listening skills.

(1) Local or Micro Strategies: These strategies focus on the specific techniques and tactics that learners can employ during individual listening tasks or interactions. They involve processing smaller units of language and details within the listening input.

(2) Global or Macro Strategies: These strategies focus on overarching approaches and techniques that learners can apply across various listening tasks or contexts. They involve processing larger units of language and understanding the overall structure and organization of the listening input.

- Predicting: Anticipating the topic, main ideas, or specific information based on context clues or prior knowledge before listening to the audio.
- Identifying Keywords: Listening for and identifying key words or phrases that convey essential information or signal important points.
- Recognizing Signpost Words: Paying attention to cue words or phrases (e.g., "however," "on the other hand") that indicate shifts in topic, contrast, or sequence.
- Using Context Clues: Inferring meaning from surrounding words, phrases, or non-verbal

cues to aid comprehension.
- Note-taking: Taking brief notes or jotting down keywords, main ideas, or important details while listening to help retain information and organize thoughts.
- Clarifying Meaning: Asking for clarification, repetition, or confirmation of understanding when encountering unfamiliar or ambiguous language.
- Listening for Main Ideas: Identifying the main topic, theme, or purpose of the listening passage without getting bogged down in details.
- Recognizing Discourse Markers: Paying attention to discourse markers (e.g., "first," "next," "finally") that signal the structure and organization of the listening passage.
- Summarizing: Summarizing the main points, key ideas, or important details of the listening passage in one's own words after completing the task.
- Making Inferences: Drawing logical conclusions or making educated guesses about implied information or unstated meanings based on the context and clues provided.
- Monitoring Understanding: Monitoring comprehension throughout the listening process and adjusting strategies as needed to enhance understanding and resolve confusion.
- Evaluating: Reflecting on one's listening performance, identifying strengths and weaknesses, and setting goals for improvement.

04-06

핵심 ELT 읽기

듣기 지도: 상향식과 하향식

In 'real-life' listening, our students will have to use a combination of the two processes, with more emphasis on '**top-down**' or '**bottom-up**' listening depending on their reasons for listening. Imagine the following situations: Over lunch, your friend tells you a story about a recent holiday, which was a disaster. You listen with interest and interject at appropriate moments, maybe to express surprise or sympathy. That evening, another friend calls to invite you to a party at her house the following Saturday. As you've never been to her house before, she gives you directions. You listen carefully and make notes. How do you listen in each case? Are there any differences? With the holiday anecdote, your main concern was probably understanding the general idea and knowing when some response was expected. In contrast, when listening to the directions to a party, understanding the exact words is likely to be more important – if you want to get there without incident, that is!

The way you listened to the holiday anecdote could be characterised as top-down listening. This refers to the use of **background knowledge** in understanding the meaning of the message. Background knowledge consists of **context**, that is, the situation and topic, and co-text, in other words, what came before and after. The context of chatting to a friend in a casual environment itself narrows down the range of possible topics. Once the topic of a holiday has been established, our knowledge of the kind of things that can happen on holiday comes into play and helps us to 'match' the incoming sound signal against our expectations of what we might hear and to fill out specific details. In contrast, when listening to directions to a friend's house, comprehension is achieved by dividing and decoding the sound signal bit by bit. The ability to separate the stream of speech into individual words becomes more important here, if we are to recognise, for example, the name of a street or an instruction to take a particular bus.

In reality, **fluent listening** normally depends on the use of **both processes** operating simultaneously. Think about talking to your friends (in your first language) in a noisy bar. It is likely that you 'guess' the content of large sections of the conversation, based on your knowledge of the topic and what has already been said. In this way, you rely more on top-down processing to make up for unreliability in the sound signal, which forms an obstacle to bottom-up processing. Similarly, second-language listeners often revert to their knowledge of the topic and situation when faced with unfamiliar vocabulary or structures, so using top-down processing to compensate for difficulties in bottom-up processing. On the other hand, if a listener is unable to understand anything of what she hears, she will not even be able to establish the topic of conversation, so top-down processing will also be very limited. In the classroom, in real-life listening, our students will have to use a combination of the two processes, with more emphasis on top-down or bottom-up listening depending on their reasons for listening. However, the two types of listening can also be practised separately, as the skills involved are quite different.

(1) Top-down listening activities

Do you ever get your students to **predict** the content of a listening activity beforehand, maybe using information about the topic or situation, pictures, or key words? If so, you are already helping them to develop their top-down processing skills, by encouraging them to use their knowledge of the topic to help them understand the content. This is an essential skill given that, in a real-life listening situation, even advanced learners are likely to come across some unknown vocabulary. By using their knowledge of context and co-text, they should either be able to guess the meaning of the unknown word, or understand the general idea without getting distracted by it. Other examples of common top-down listening activities include putting a series of pictures or sequence of events in order, listening to conversations and identifying where they take place, reading information about a topic then listening to find whether or not the same points are mentioned, or inferring the relationships between the people involved.

(2) Bottom-up listening activities

The emphasis in EFL listening materials in recent years has been on developing top-down listening processes. There are good reasons for this given that learners need to be able to listen effectively even when faced with unfamiliar **vocabulary or structures**. However, if the learner understands very few words from the incoming signal, even knowledge about the context may not be sufficient for her to understand what is happening, and she can easily get lost. Of course, low-level learners may simply not have enough vocabulary or knowledge of the language yet, but most teachers will be familiar with the situation in which higher-level students fail to recognise known words in the stream of fast connected speech. Bottom-up listening activities can help learners to understand enough linguistic elements of what they hear to then be able to use their top-down skills to fill in the gaps.

The following procedure for developing bottom-up listening skills draws on dictogloss, and is designed to help learners recognise the divisions between words, an important bottom-up listening skill. The teacher reads out a number of sentences, and asks learners to write down how many words there would be in the written form. While the task might sound easy, for learners the weak forms in normal connected speech can make it problematic, so it is very important for the teacher to say the sentences in a very natural way, rather than dictating them word-by-word.

Learners can be asked to compare their answers in pairs, before listening again to check. While listening a third time, they could write what they hear, before reconstructing the complete sentences in pairs or groups. By comparing their version with the correct sentences, learners will become more aware of the sounds of normal spoken English, and how this is different from the written or carefully spoken form. This will help them to develop the skill of recognising known words and identifying word divisions in fast connected speech. Successful listening depends on the ability to combine these two types of processing. Activities which work on each strategy separately should help students to combine top-down and bottom-up processes to become more effective listeners in real-life situations or longer classroom listenings.

07

문항 해설

시간 생성 기제(time-creating device)는 지속적인 발화가 되도록 다음 발화를 준비하도록 시간을 마련하는 개념으로, 의미는 없지만 발화하는 동안 시간을 벌 수 있는 기제이다. 활성화(facilitation)는 발화를 촉진한다는 개념으로 미리 만들어진(formulaic) 언어를 사용함으로 유창성이 있다는 인상을 줄 수 있다. 보상기제(compensation devices)는 반복(repetition), 재구성(reformation)과 고쳐말하기(rephrasing)를 통해 의미를 명확히 해주고 있다. 예를 들어 사람을 설명하는데 그 사람에 관해서 추가적인 내용을 다시 설명해줌으로써 기억을 상기시켜 주고 있다.

08

문항 해설

dictogloss 과업의 문제점으로 첫째, 주요단어와 표현에 대하여 학생들의 이해가 부족하다. 둘째, 내용에 대한 이해가 부족하여 과업이 어렵다. 셋째, 그룹이 너무 커서 모든 학생이 고르게 참여하기가 어렵다. 해결책으로 과업 전 활동을 통해 학생들에게 주요단어와 표현을 학습할 수 있는 기회를 제공한다. 또한 학생들의 이전 지식을 활성화 하여 내용이해를 할 수 있도록 도움을 준다. 마지막으로, 그룹의 수를 3~4명으로 줄여서 각자에게 개별의 역할을 주어 협동학습이 일어날 수 있게 한다.

핵심 개념정리

2언어 언어습득을 위한 Dictogloss활동

Dictogloss represents a major shift from traditional dictation. When implemented conscientiously, dictogloss embodies sound principles of language teaching which include the following:

1) **Learner Autonomy**. Learner autonomy involves learners having some choice as to the what and how of the curriculum and, at the same time, feeling responsible for and understanding their own learning and for the learning of classmates (van Lier, 1996). In dictogloss, as opposed to traditional dictation, students reconstruct the text on their own after the teacher has read it aloud to them just twice at normal speed, rather than the teacher reading the text slowly and repeatedly. Also, students need to help each other to develop a joint reconstruction of the text, rather than depending on the teacher for all the information. Furthermore, last step provides students with opportunities to see where they have done well and where they may need to improve. Swain (1999) believes that, students gain insights into their own linguistic shortcomings and develop strategies for solving them by working through them with a partner.

2) **Cooperation** among Learners. Traditional dictation was done as an individual activity. Dictogloss retains an individual element in which students work alone to listen to and take notes on the text read by the teacher. In dictogloss, learners work together in groups of between two and four members. Additionally, they have the opportunity to discuss how well their group did and, perhaps, how they could function more effectively the next time.

3) **Curricular Integration**. From the perspective of language teachers, curricular integration involves combining the teaching of content, such as social studies or science, with the teaching of language, such as writing skills or grammar. As in traditional dictation, with dictogloss, curricular integration is easily achieved via the selection of texts. For instance, if the goal is to integrate language and mathematics in order to help students learn important mathematics vocabulary and grammar, language teachers (in consultation with mathematics teachers and, perhaps, students) can use a mathematics text for the dictogloss. The discussion prior to the readings of the text helps students recall and build their knowledge of the text's topic. As Brown points out, "Writing this information [what students know on the topic] on the chalk board allows

the students to notice the wealth of information they have as a collective." In addition to promoting integration between language education and other curricular areas, dictogloss, also promotes integration within the language curriculum, as all four language skills — listening, speaking, reading, and writing — are utilized.

4) **Focus on Meaning.** In literacy education, the focus used to lie mostly on matters of form, such as grammar and spelling. In the current paradigm, while form still matters, the view is that language learning takes place best when the focus is mainly on ideas (Littlewood, 1981). Dictogloss seeks to combine a focus on meaning with a focus on form (Brown, 2001). As Swain (1999) puts it, "When students focus on form, they must be engaged in the act of meaning-making."

5) Thinking Skills. The definition of **literacy** has been expanded beyond being able to read and write to also being able to think critically about what is read and about how to best frame what is written. The discussion that takes place of dictogloss provides learners with chances to use thinking skills as they challenge, defend, learn from, and elaborate on the ideas presented during collaboration on the reconstruction task. Thinking skills also come into play as students analyze their reconstructed text in relation to the original. We can challenge students' skill at identifying main ideas by asking them to write summaries rather than text reconstructions and to elaborate on the texts read.

6) Dictogloss offers a **context-rich method** of assessing how much students know about writing and about the topic of the text. The text reconstruction task provides learners with opportunities to display both their knowledge of the content of the text as well as of the organizational structure and language features of the text. As students discuss with each other, teachers can listen in and observe students' thinking as they about a task. This real-time observation of learners' thinking process offers greater insight than does looking at the product after they have finished.

09

> **문항 해설**

듣기수업의 과정을 보여주고 있다. 대화 자료를 4개의 파트로 나누어 학습자들의 인지적 발전을 그림을 통해 보여준다. 이 활동은 듣기의 과정을 인지변화과정으로 보여주고 있는 과정중심교수법(process-oriented approach)이다. graphics, browsers, server 등의 단서가 되는 어휘들은 학습자의 이전의 지식인 스키마를 활성화하도록 한다. 전략으로는 학습자가 개인적으로 시행하는 활동으로 인지적 전략에 중점을 두고 있다. 학습자의 인지지도(cognitive map)에서 보여주는 것처럼 계속되는 인지 변화를 나타내고 있으므로 이해도에 여러 변화를 거치고 있는 것을 보여준다.

10-11

문항 해설

듣기 전 질문을 통해 학생들의 스키마, 즉 이전 지식을 활성화 시키고, 흥미를 유도한다. 듣기 중 활동에서는 듣기 활동을 하면서 학습자 자신이 예상했던 것을 맞추어보고, 중요한 단어들을 적어보는 이해도 중심 활동을 한다. 듣기 후 활동에서는 듣기 스크립트를 읽고, 짝과 함께 재구성하는 활동을 한다. 마지막으로 그룹 활동을 통해 듣기 내용에 대한 의견을 주고 받는 추후 활동을 실시한다.

12

문항 해설

이 수업은 먼저 예문을 제시하고 그 안에서 학생들이 규칙을 발견해내는 귀납법(inductive) 활동이다. 수업 과정을 살펴보면 첫째, 학생들은 현재 진행형의 정확한 용례들이 포함된 글을 듣고 내용을 중심으로 글을 이해한다. 여러번 들으면서 문법적 특성에 초점을 맞춘다. 그 다음, 자료를 이용하여 규칙을 명시적으로 이해하고 마지막으로 학생들은 정확한 문법구조를 이용하여 자신의 문장을 만들어 본다. 내용 중심의 듣기와 언어 습득을 동시에 발달시킬 수 있는 활동이 되며 학생들이 문법 형태에 집중하게 함으로써 문법을 가르치는 동시에 의미와 형태를 연결하여 문법 규칙을 발견해 내게 하고 있다. 마지막으로 그 규칙을 이용해서 자신의 문장을 생산해내는 것을 목표로 하는 활동이다.

13

문항 해설

감정이입 듣기(empathic listening)는 원활한 의사소통이 이루어지기 위한 요소로서, 상대방의 입장을 정서적 뿐만 아니라, 인지적으로 이해함으로 상호간의 신뢰감을 형성한다. 그러므로 논쟁이 되는 요소들이 발생해도 정서적 안정감을 통해 해결할 수 있으며, 정보의 공유와 상호간의 협력하는 환경을 조성할 수 있다. 이때 공감(empathy)은 동정(sympathy)과 다른 요소로서 타인의 경험과 감정을 예민하고 정확하게 공감하고 이해하는 것을 말한다. 즉, 상대방을 깊게 주관적으로 이해하면서도 결코 자기 본연의 자세를 버리지 않는 것이다. 반면 동정은 타인의 감정에 대해 공감하는 감정의 정체성으로서 불행한 상황과 고난에 대해 감정을 공유할 때 이용되는 것이 많다.

핵심 개념정리

감정이입 듣기(Empathic Listening)

Empathic listening (also called active listening or reflective listening) is a way of listening and responding to another person that improves mutual understanding and trust. It is an essential skill for third parties and disputants alike, as it enables the listener to receive and accurately interpret the speaker's message, and then provide an appropriate response. The response is an integral part of the listening process and can be critical to the success of a negotiation or mediation.

Empathy is the ability to project oneself into the personality of another person in order to better understand that person's emotions or feelings. Through empathic listening the listener lets the speaker know, "I understand your problem and how you feel about it, I am interested in what you are saying and I am not judging you." The listener unmistakably conveys this message through words and non-verbal behaviors, including body language. In so doing, the listener encourages the speaker to fully express herself or himself free of interruption, criticism or being told what to do. It is neither advisable nor necessary for a mediator to agree with the speaker, even when asked to do so. It is usually sufficient to let the speaker know, "I understand you and I am interested in being a resource to help you resolve this problem."

14

문항 해설

멀티미디어 프로그램의 외국어 학습 적용에 있어 반복 연습, 시험 채점, 코퍼스를 활용한 어휘 및 문법 지도 활용 및 CMC (computer-mediated communication)를 이용한 대화 기회 제공들의 장점을 활용할 수 있는 반면에 여전히 멀티미디어로 해결되지 않는 영역도 있다. 특히, 에세이 피드백에서 문법적 체크는 어느 정도 가능하지만, 텍스트를 읽고 에세이 주제에 관련성 있는 내용적인 측면, 구조적인 측면에서의 전체적 오류에 대해서는 피드백을 제시할 수 있는 영역에는 부족한 면을 가지고 있다. CMC는 교실 밖에서도 학습자들의 상호작용을 활성화시켜 주는 역할을 한다. CALL (computer assisted language learning)의 활용을 통해서 실제적인 자료, 통합적이면서 상호작용적인 측면, 학습자들의 정의적인 요소, 흥미를 고려해서 접근할 수 있는 장점을 가지고 있다. 언어의 부분적인 측면보다는 통합적이면서 전체적인 요소를 측정하는 데 더욱 유용하다.

핵심 ELT 읽기

Multimedia

Language teachers have been avid users of technology for a very long time. Gramophone records were among the first technological aids to be used by language teachers in order to present students with recordings of native speakers' voices, and broadcasts from foreign radio stations were used to make recordings on reel-to-reel tape recorders. Other examples of technological aids that have been used in the foreign language classroom include slide projectors, film-strip projectors, film projectors, videocassette recorders and DVD players. In the early 1960s, integrated courses (often described as multimedia courses) began to appear.

During the 1970s and 1980s standard microcomputers were incapable of producing sound and they had poor graphics capability. This represented a step backwards for language teachers, who by this time had become accustomed to using a range of different media in the foreign language classroom. The arrival of the multimedia computer in the early 1990s was therefore a major breakthrough as it enabled text, images, sound and video to be combined in one device and the integration of the four basic skills of listening, speaking, reading and writing (Davies 2011: Section 1). Examples of CALL programs for multimedia computers that were published on CD-ROM and DVD from the mid-1990s onwards are described by Davies (2010: Section 3). CALL programs are still being published on CD-ROM and DVD, but Web-based multimedia CALL has now virtually supplanted these media.

Following the arrival of multimedia CALL, multimedia language centres began to appear in educational institutions. While multimedia facilities offer many opportunities for language learning with the integration of text, images, sound and video, these opportunities have often not been fully utilised. One of the main promises of CALL is the ability to **individualise learning** but, as with the language labs that were introduced into educational institutions in the 1960s and 1970s, the use of the facilities of multimedia centres has often devolved into rows of students all doing the same drills (Davies 2010: Section 3.1). There is therefore a danger that multimedia centres may go the same way as the language labs. Following a boom period in the 1970s, language labs went rapidly into decline. Davies (1997: p. 28) lays the blame mainly on the failure to train teachers to use language labs, both in terms of operation and in terms of developing new methodologies, but there were other factors such as poor reliability, lack of materials and a lack of good ideas.

Managing a multimedia language centre requires not only staff who have a knowledge of foreign languages and language teaching methodology but also staff with technical know-how and budget management ability, as well as the ability to combine all these into creative ways of taking advantage of what the technology can offer. A centre manager usually needs assistants for technical support, for managing resources and even the tutoring of students. Multimedia centres lend themselves to self-study and potentially self-directed learning, but this is often misunderstood. The simple existence of a multimedia centre does not automatically lead to students learning independently. Significant investment of time is essential for materials development and creating an atmosphere conducive to self-study. Unfortunately, administrators often have the mistaken belief that buying hardware by itself will meet the needs of the centre, allocating 90% of its budget to hardware and virtually ignoring software and staff training needs (Davies et al. 2011: Foreword). **Self-access language learning** centres or independent learning centres have emerged partially independently and partially in response to these issues. In self-access learning, the focus is on developing learner **autonomy** through varying degrees of **self-directed learning**, as opposed to classroom learning. In many centres learners access materials and manage their learning independently, but they also have access to staff for help. Many self-access centres are heavy users of technology and an increasing number of them are now offering online self-access learning opportunities. Some centres have developed novel ways of supporting language learning **outside the context of the language classroom** ('language support') by developing software to monitor students' self-directed learning and by offering online support from teachers.

15 핵심 ELT 읽기

읽기전략을 위한 메타 인지 (Metacognitive awareness of reading strategies)

Metacognitive awareness of reading strategies refers to a reader's ability to plan, monitor, and evaluate their reading process. The three main categories of strategies identified in Ms. Yu's questionnaire—Global Reading Strategies (GLOB), Support Reading Strategies (SUP), and Problem-Solving Strategies (PROB)—serve distinct functions in enhancing reading comprehension.

1. Global Reading Strategies (GLOB): These are high-level, generalized strategies that readers use to plan and manage their reading process. They help readers establish a purpose for reading, maintain focus, and understand the broader structure or intent of the text.

① Examples:
- Previewing the text: Looking at titles, headings, subheadings, or images to get an overview of the content.
- Setting a purpose: Deciding why the text is being read (e.g., for information, pleasure, or analysis).
- Using context clues: Trying to understand meaning through surrounding text.
- Skimming for the main idea: Quickly identifying the central theme before reading in detail.
- Relating prior knowledge: Connecting the text to what the reader already knows to enhance understanding.

② Teaching Tip: Encourage students to practice pre-reading activities, like generating predictions or brainstorming what they know about the topic.

2. Support Reading Strategies (SUP): These strategies involve using external aids or tools to facilitate understanding and retention of the text. They provide additional scaffolding to assist readers in comprehending complex or unfamiliar material.

① Examples:
- Highlighting or underlining important text: Marking key ideas or terms for better focus and review.
- Taking notes: Summarizing or jotting down important points while reading.
- Using dictionaries or glossaries: Checking the meaning of unknown words or terms.
- Rereading for clarification: Going over a passage multiple times to ensure comprehension.
- Reading aloud: Verbalizing the text to engage auditory processing and improve focus.

② Teaching Tip: Model effective use of these tools in class and provide opportunities for students to practice using note-taking templates, glossaries, or highlighting tools.

3. **Problem-Solving Strategies (PROB)**: These are reactive strategies used to overcome comprehension difficulties encountered while reading. They help readers address challenges such as confusing language, unclear meaning, or unfamiliar vocabulary.

① Examples:

- Guessing the meaning of unfamiliar words: Using contextual clues to infer the meaning without relying on a dictionary.
- Adjusting reading speed: Slowing down for difficult sections and speeding up for easier parts.
- Pausing and rereading: Taking a moment to reflect and revisit unclear parts of the text.
- Visualizing: Creating mental images to better understand descriptions or narratives.
- Breaking down sentences: Parsing complex sentences into smaller parts for clarity.

② Teaching Tip: Teach explicit strategies for tackling difficult text, such as chunking, visualizing, or underlining confusing parts for later discussion.

4. Integrating the Strategies in Classroom Practice

Ms. Yu can incorporate these strategies into her teaching by:

- Explicit Instruction: Teach each strategy explicitly, with examples and guided practice.
- Modeling: Demonstrate how to apply the strategies during reading. For example, think aloud while reading a challenging text to show how to use context clues or adjust reading speed.
- Practice and Feedback: Allow students to practice the strategies independently or in groups and provide constructive feedback on their use.
- Reflection: Encourage students to reflect on which strategies they found helpful and when they applied them effectively.

By combining GLOB, SUP, and PROB strategies, students develop a holistic approach to reading, equipping them with the tools to navigate texts effectively and independently.

16

핵심 개념정리

도식 조직자(graphic organizer)

A graphic organizer, also known as a knowledge map, concept map, story map, cognitive organizer, advance organizer, or concept diagram is a pedagogical tool that uses visual symbols to express knowledge and concepts through relationships between them. The main purpose of a graphic organizer is to provide a visual aid to facilitate learning and instruction. A graphic organizer visually represents ideas, concepts, and relationships between various components. Concept maps and knowledge maps all are types of graphic organizers. You can use any chart or diagram as a graphic organizer to compare facts and depict a story. Well-designed graphic organizers should guide students to categorize key concepts, surface the interconnection of ideas, or help students construct knowledge.

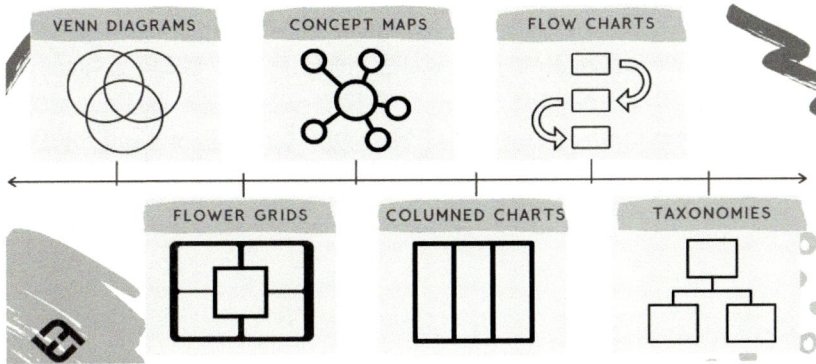

17

핵심 개념정리

읽기의 개요작성(outlining) 기술

Some students use only the outlining technique to get started in their writing. Formal outlining, which often results from **organized lists**, is a highly **analytical technique** that assumes the writer already knows the how, what, where, when, why, and who aspects of the topic. Writing without an outline turns into a chaotic process in which you can't cope with the thoughts rush. There are so many points you want to cover in your essay and express every idea that comes up to your mind. Furthermore, here also the opposite problem can appear: lack of information and futile attempts to start the paper inhibit the writing and you spend the threefold amount of time instead of doing the job quickly and qualitatively. But you shouldn't worry. The habit of writing the essay and ignoring the outline is inherent to many novice writers. We are going to show you some outlining techniques to transform your assignment into a quite simple and entertaining thing. The outline is actually a plan which contains the **main ideas** of the text and stands up for a starting point of the paper. It helps to gather all your thoughts and get a full picture of the future work but without many details.

18

문항 해설

제시된 읽기수업은 학생들의 협력과업을 통해 읽기능력을 향상시키는 데 중점을 두고 있다. 세부적인 특정정보를 파악하기보다는 전체적인 맥락을 파악해야 과업을 달성할 수 있다. 교과서 외의 실제자료를 핵심읽기로 활용했으므로 확장읽기(extensive reading)가 이루어지나 이 수업의 주목적은 각 어휘가 아니라 전체적인 의미 이해에 있음을 알 수 있다. 교사는 이해할 수 있는 정도의 입력(comprehensible input)을 제공하기 위해 단순화시킨 읽기자료가 아닌 실제자료를 있는 그대로 활용하고 있다. 학생들은 주어진 글을 흐름에 맞게 문단을 나누는 연습을 하면서 일관성있는 글(coherent text)이 어떻게 구성되는지 인식할 기회를 갖는다.

19-22

핵심 개념정리

읽기 전략

① Identify the **purpose** in reading.

Efficient reading consists of clearly identifying the purpose in reading something. By doing so, you know what you're looking for and can weed out potential distracting information.

② Use graphemic rules and patterns to aid in **bottom-up decoding**.

At the beginning levels of learning English, one of the difficulties students encounter in learning to read is making the correspondences between spoken and written English. These phonics approaches to reading can prove useful for learners at the beginning level and especially useful for teaching children and nonliterate adults.

- short vowel sound in VC patterns: *bat, him, leg, wish*
- long vowel sound in VCe (final silent e) patterns: *late, time, bite*
- long vowel sound in VV patterns: *seat, coat*
- distinguishing hard c and g from soft c and g: *cat vs. city, game vs gem*

③ Use efficient silent reading techniques for improving **fluency**.

Your intermediate-to-advanced level students need not be speed readers, but you can help them increase reading rate and comprehension efficiency by teaching a few silent reading rules.

④ **Skim** the text for main ideas.

Skimming consists of quickly running one's eyes across a whole text for its gist. Skimming gives readers the advantage of being able to predict the purpose of the passage, the main topic, or message, and possibly some of the developing or supporting ideas.

⑤ **Scan** the text for specific information.

The purpose of scanning is to extract specific information without reading through the whole text. For academic English, scanning is absolutely essential. In vocational or general English, scanning is important in dealing with genres like schedules, manuals, forms, etc.

⑥ Use semantic-mapping or clustering.
The strategy of semantic mapping, or grouping ideas into meaningful clusters, helps the reader to provide some order to the chaos. Making such semantic maps can be done individually, but they make for a productive group work technique as students collectively induce order and hierarchy to a passage.

⑦ Infer when you aren't certain.
Learners should utilize all their skills and put forth as much effort as possible to be on target with their hypotheses. The point here is that reading is, after all, a guessing game of sorts, and the sooner learners understand this game, the better off they are. The key to successful guessing is to make it reasonably accurate.

⑧ Analyze vocabulary.
- Look for prefixes (co-, inter-, un-, etc.) that may give clues.
- Look for suffixes (-tion, -tive, -ally, etc.) to indicate parts of speech
- Look for roots that are familiar
- Look for grammatical contexts that may signal information
- Look at the semantic context (topic) for clues.

⑨ Distinguish between literal and implied meanings.
This requires the application of sophisticated top-down processing skills. Implied meaning usually has to be derived from processing pragmatic information.

23

문항 해설

읽기를 하는 다양한 연습문제의 유형을 보여주고 있다. (a)-(e)는 단순한 형태에서 복잡하고 상급수준으로 올라가는 연속선상에서의 순서를 나타내고 있다. (1) 가장 기본적인 문자그대로의(literal) 읽기방법으로 Gregory를 사람들이 다 알고 있는 이유는 그의 직업에서 찾을 수 있다. (2) 글 안에서는 명시적으로 설명되지는 않으나 전체적인 내용으로 보아 TV방송국에서 나이나 경력보다 젊고 잘생긴 사람을 더 중요시할 때가 많이 있음을 추론(inferencing)할 수 있어야 한다. (3) 평가(evaluative)를 위한 연습 문제로서 글을 읽고 자기의 의견에 대한 판단을 내릴 수 있어야 한다.

핵심 개념정리

읽기 이해도의 5가지 수준

Different exercise types that can be used with a reading passage to focus on each of the 5 levels of comprehension are then examined, followed by practical experience in developing examples of exercise types for each level to accompany different kinds of texts.

Commercial ESL reading materials are also examined to determine the levels of reading comprehension they set out to teach and how they do so.

A. Literal comprehension (recognizing or recalling information stated explicitly in the text)
B. Reorganization (analyzing, synthesizing and organizing information that has been stated explicitly in the text)
C. Inferential comprehension (using information that has been explicitly stated along with one's own personal experience as a basis for conjecture and hypothesis)
D. Evaluation (making judgements and decisions concerning the value of worth of ideas in a text)
E. Appreciating (responding to the psychological, literary or aesthetic impact of the text on the reader)

24

문항 해설

언어를 학습하는 데 겪게 되는 여러 문제들을 해결할 수 있는 전략적 학습이 필요하다. 읽기에는 다양한 전략이 있는데, 학습자가 모르는 단어나, 문장의 흐름에 대해 추측(guessing)하는 전략의 유용한 측면에 대해서 설명하고 있다. [B]의 연습지를 보면 전반적으로 이야기의 흐름을 진행하다가, 그 이후의 이야기를 예측하는 활동으로 추측 중에서도 what is going to come next에 관한 미래에 대한 추측임을 알 수 있다.

- guess the meaning of a word
- guess a grammatical relationship
- guess a discourse relationship
- guess about a cultural reference
- guess what is going to come next

25

핵심 개념정리

전체단어학습법(Whole word method) vs 음운론 학습법(Phonics method)

(1) Whole Word method

The Whole Word method of literacy instruction instructs learners to recognize words as whole units without breaking them down into **sounds** or letter groupings. It focuses on the word as the minimum unit of meaning and therefore the essential base element of reading. Whole Word or whole language methods stand in direct contradiction to the **Phonics** method. While Phonics instruction emphasizes **sounds** as the smallest units of language to be learned and manipulated, whole language focuses on **comprehension** with words as the smallest units. This movement emerged from the philosophy of Holism (gestaltism), with is the theory that whole entities are more than the sum of their parts.

A purely Whole Word approach would not include any phonics instruction. Instead, the focus would be on helping kids to understand how to recognize words in relation to other words, in their context, and as a representation of what the word means. Whole Word approaches always emphasize learning to read through the act of reading. In practice, whole language instruction usually includes:

- sight-memorization techniques
- reading aloud
- prioritizing finding engaging reading material
- comprehension exercises

(2) Phonics method

Phonics is seen to be an improvement used method of learning the **approximate sounds** represented by letters (b=buh) first and then blending them with other sounds (*bl=bluh*) to decode and encode words in written form. This newer method attempts to eliminate the extraneous 'uh' sounds which were unavoidable in the older method. Children also learn strategies to figure out words they don't know. Phonics is considered an **analytical approach** where students analyze the letters, letter combinations and syllables in a word; in an effort to **decode** (1) the speech-sounds represented by the letters and (2) the meaning of the text. The advantage of phonics is that, especially for students who come to schools with large English vocabularies, it enables students to decode or sound-out a word they have in their speaking vocabulary.

A problem with teaching the reading of English with this analytical approach is that English words do not have a one-to-one speech-sound to symbol relationship. If they did have a one-to-one relationship, reading would be easier. In general, with a few common exceptions, the consonants do have a one-to-one speech-sound to symbol relationship but the vowels do not. For instance the letter 'a' represents one sound in the word 'say', a second sound in 'at', a third sound in 'any', a fourth sound in 'are', a fifth sound in 'all', a sixth sound in 'about', a seventh sound in 'father', an eighth sound in 'orange', and a ninth sound (silence) in 'bread'. The **speech-sounds** are sometimes influenced by (a) the letters surrounding the target vowel, (b) by the sentence containing the word and (c) the stress, or lack thereof, given to the syllable containing the letter.

Almost any combination of three letters with a central 'a' can reasonably be pronounced in a number of different ways. For instance the 'a' in 'pag' could be pronounced as in 'page' (long 'a'), 'pageant' (short 'a'), creepage (short 'i') or decoupage (short 'o' as in 'dot'). It therefore follows that beginning students will have a difficult time picking the appropriate sound when sounding-out words which are not in their speaking vocabularies. Fortunately, most readers quickly develop a subconscious word sense which helps them fluently pick the right sound based on the structure of the word and how that structure is related to other similar words they know. Some very common words do not fully follow common phonic patterns, so those words have to be memorized. Some books refer to these words as sight words, but it is probably better to refer to them as memory words because some books refer to sight words as those words which are so common they do not have to be analyzed or sounded-out. It does not seem like a good idea to have sight-words mean two different things when memory-words is available. The many **homonyms** in English such as *to, too,* and *two* create difficulties for students, even at the university level in regard to spelling. Drawbacks:

- For those who learn to speak by learning the whole **sound** of a word, phonics is not an ideal form of reading instruction, because these learners do not naturally break words into separate **sounds**.
- Some phonics programs use low-interest reading material and too many boring worksheets. Those drawbacks, of course, are not unique to a phonics program.

26-27

핵심 개념정리

읽기학습의 유형

(1) Extensive reading: reading for pleasure with emphasis on general understanding

- Students read as much as possible, perhaps in and definitely out of the classroom.

- A variety of materials on a wide range of topics is available so as to encourage reading for different reasons and in different ways.

- Students select what they want to read and have the freedom to stop reading material that fails to interest them.

- The purposes of reading are usually related to pleasure, information and general understanding. The purposes are determined by the nature of the material and the interests of the student.

- Reading is its own reward. There are few or no follow-up exercises after reading.

- Reading materials are well within the linguistic competence of the students in terms of vocabulary and grammar. Dictionaries are rarely used while reading because the constant stopping to look up words makes fluent reading difficult.

- Reading is individual and silent, at the student's own pace, and, outside class, done when and where the student chooses.

- Reading speed is usually faster rather than slower as students read books and other material they find easily understandable.

- Teachers orient students to the goals of the program, explain the methodology, keep track of what each student reads, and guide students in getting the most out of the program.

- The teacher is a role model of a reader for the students — an active member of the classroom reading community, demonstrating what it means to be a reader and the rewards of being a reader.

(2) Intensive reading: reading carefully for an exact understanding of text. Necessary for contracts, legal documentation, application forms, etc., to focus on the linguistic or semantic details of a passage, to require bottom up skills

(3) Critical reading commonly asks students to accomplish certain goals:
- to recognize an author's purposes
- to understand tone and persuasive elements
- to recognize bias

28

문항 해설

이 수업의 활동은 읽기 후 활동으로서 이야기에 대한 mind-map을 만드는 활동을 설명하고 있다. 학생들은 이야기를 읽고 이해하고 그 후에 mind-map을 작성함으로써 이야기의 전체적 흐름을 정리하는 것을 알 수 있다. 학생들은 이야기 내용을 전체적으로 토론한 후 컴퓨터 프로그램을 사용하여 mind-map을 만드는 과정을 보여준다. 위 수업과정은 읽기 후 활동으로서 글의 전체적인 내용이해에 따른 활동이므로 top-down processing을 근거로 하고 있다. 미리 만들어진 템플릿 도형안에 제목을 쓰고 제목을 중심으로 여러 다른 활동으로 연관되어 나아가고 있으므로 역동적이고 여러방향으로(multi-directional) 움직일 수 있다. 또한 학생들의 여러 다른 스키마, 즉 그림, 이미지, 단어와 다중매체를 반영하는 구성을 보여주고 있고 사용자들이 읽은 이야기를 hypertext를 이용하여 영상화하고 구성할 수 있게 한다. 읽기후 활동으로서 정리, 요약의 활동을 하며, 전체 개념을 학습한 후에 세부적인 요소들을 설명하고 있다.

핵심 개념정리

Hypertext

1. What is Hypertext

Hypertext is a **non-sequential (non-linear),** electronic, textual, hypermedia, and **interactive** environment. Hypertext creates an interactive environment where reading is contingent upon computers and possible by **multiple sources of information** linked together. Some researchers consider hypertext reading an invention as important as the printing press (i.e., Bolter, 1991). Having started as an idea in 1940s by Vannevar Bush's proposal, the development of hypertext and the emergence of hypertext environments have accelerated today. With the era of the Internet and multimedia technology, hypertext environments have moved from an imagery level to being a real part of our lives, especially of our education. As we become more able to digitize a wide variety of information and expose readers to more digitized media on computer screens, how a new technology such as hypertext can be interpreted and shaped by a community of L2 readers, as well as the way in which L2 readers understand, interpret, and value hypertext reading material as a new medium, is worth exploration. Thus, there is a need for research to discern the usefulness of hypertext technology in language classrooms. The findings from this study suggest the following issues need to be considered:

- Hypertext readers should be introduced to various formats of hypertext readings before they are exposed to this new medium. As discussed earlier in detail, **non-linear hypertext** sites confused all students regardless of their computer literacy levels. When considering the hypertext readings for classroom purposes. Educators need to include supportive instructions to establish schema for these types of readings.

- Readers in the hypertext environments should be exposed to **various types of media** during hypertext reading process (i.e., audio, video, text, and animation). The findings from this study showed that students displayed a tendency toward making use of any and all materials available to them. But when limitations were present in computer configurations, the situation caused students to experience problems in accessing audio and video sources over the Internet.

Hypertext technology presents a new environment for students, a new tool for educators, and a new area to explore for researchers. The findings of this study bring up an emerging concern of selecting and utilizing hypertext readings for classroom purposes. If students are not ready for this type of reading, educators are advised to either develop **schema-building** activities or avoid using this new genre. For researchers, the implications, better designs and implementation of hypertext environments deserve a thorough exploration. To conclude, this is still a road, which is less traveled.

2. Hypertext can help students read more effectively in several ways:

(1) Visual representation of information: Hypertext allows students to visualize the structure of a document, which can make it easier for them to understand and retain information. By using hyperlinks to connect related ideas or concepts, students can quickly move between different parts of a document and see how they are connected.

(2) Customized reading experiences: With hypertext, students can choose their own path through a document based on their interests and needs. This can help students stay engaged with the material and can make reading a more personalized and enjoyable experience.

(3) Access to additional resources: Hypertext allows students to access additional resources that are related to the material they are reading. For example, hyperlinks can provide definitions of key terms, visual aids, or links to related articles or videos. This can help students deepen their understanding of the material and can encourage them to explore related topics.

(4) Interactive learning: Hypertext can facilitate interactive learning by providing students with opportunities to engage with the material in different ways. For example,

hyperlinks can provide interactive quizzes or simulations that allow students to test their understanding of the material or apply it in a practical setting.

Overall, hypertext can help students read more effectively by providing a **visual representation of information**, allowing for customized reading experiences, providing access to additional resources, and facilitating interactive learning.

29

문항 해설

본문에서 낮은 레벨 처리과정(lower-level processes)과 높은 레벨 처리과정(higher-level processes)의 상호 보완적인 관계를 설명하고 있다. 낮은 레벨 처리과정은 "자동적 언어인식(automatic word recognition)"에 관한 것이며, 높은 레벨 처리과정은 내용이해(text comprehension)를 활성화시켜주는 요소로 작용하고 있음을 보여주고 있다. 모르는 단어가 나왔을 때 상위개념의 배경지식을 이용해서(추측) 해결할 수 있지만, 상위레벨의 사전지식(shemata)에 지나치게 의존할 경우, 의미적으로 왜곡시킬 수 있는 위험성을 제시해 줌으로써 무의식적으로 작업기억(working memory)에서 자동 처리되는 단어인식의 중요성을 설명하고 있다. 그렇다고 해서 높은 레벨 처리과정 요소들이 낮은 레벨 처리과정항목보다 어렵다거나 쉽다고 보기는 어렵다.

핵심 개념정리

상호작용적 보상체계(Interactive Compensatory Model)

Lower-level processes	Higher-level processes
• automatic linguistic processes • skill oriented • not easier than higher-level processes • lexical access, syntactic parsing, semantic proposition formation, and working memory activation	• comprehension processes • use of the background knowledge and inferencing skills • text model of comprehension, situation model of interpretation, background knowledge use and inferencing, and executive control processes

- A weakness in one area of knowledge or skills (e.g., lack of linguistic abilities for **automatic** word recognition) can be compensated for by strength in another area (e.g., using context clues and background knowledge).

- Difficulties lead to increased interaction and compensation (bottom-up processes & top-down processes), even among processes that would otherwise be more **automatic**.

30

핵심 개념정리

어휘 전략

Semantic mapping is a classroom technique in which a visual representation of ideas in a text or conceptual relationships within a text is used to assist with the reading of a text. The semantic maps may be teacher or student generated. Vocabulary Network is to help even beginning students learn to make semantic associations within particular superordinate headings. e.g. animal—puppy, kitten; color—red, blue, green. Semantic networks is the associations of related words that come to mind when a certain word is thought of. Bilingual speakers may have different semantic networks for words in their lexicons. For example, bilingual speakers of English and Spanish may associate 'house' with 'window' and 'boy' with 'girl', but in Spanish may associate 'house' with 'mother' and 'boy' with 'man'.

31-32

핵심 개념정리

schema

Imagine you are reading a story about a birthday party. Your content schema about birthday parties might include cake, candles, gifts, and singing "Happy Birthday." Even if the text doesn't mention some of these elements, you might infer their presence based on your existing schema. If the story mentions "blowing out the candles," you immediately connect that to a birthday party because your schema includes this concept.

Schema theory is a concept in cognitive psychology and language learning that explains how people use their background knowledge and experiences to understand and interpret new information. In reading, schemas (plural: schemata) act as mental frameworks that help readers organize and make sense of text. A schema is like a mental blueprint or organized knowledge structure stored in our memory. It includes everything we know about a topic—facts, experiences, cultural knowledge, and associations. When readers encounter a new text, they activate relevant schemata to help interpret and understand the information. This process is called top-down processing, where existing knowledge guides the interpretation of new input.

33

Multimedia 적용과 Web 기술

Technology has been used to both help and improve language learning. Technology enables teachers to adapt classroom activities, thus enhancing the language learning process. Technology continues to grow in importance as a tool to help teachers facilitate language learning for their learners. A Multimedia Application is an application which uses a collection of multiple media sources e.g. text, graphics, images, sound/audio, animation and/or video. Hypermedia can be considered as one of the multimedia applications. Examples of multimedia applications are World Wide Web, courseware, interactive TV, computer games, and virtual reality. Web technology refers to the means by which computers communicate with each other using markup languages and multimedia packages. It gives us a way to interact with hosted information, like websites. Web technology involves the use of hypertext markup language (HTML) and cascading style sheets. Web Technology is intrinsic to our lives and core to our students' future careers, and etc. This course supports exploration in careers related to the design, development, support, and management of hardware, software, multimedia, and systems integration services.

01

> 핵심 ELT 읽기

Illocutionary acts

Language learners often struggle with understanding implied meanings or hidden intentions behind utterances. In the teacher's journal example, the students focused on the literal meaning (locutionary act) rather than the intended social function (illocutionary act).

(1) Why do these misunderstandings happen?

- Lack of pragmatic knowledge: Learners may know vocabulary and grammar but fail to grasp pragmatic functions.
- Cultural differences: Different cultures use language acts differently, leading to misinterpretation.
- Literal vs. Implied meaning: Learners often focus on literal meanings without considering social context.

(2) Examples

① **Compliment misunderstanding:**

- Teacher's utterance: "What a wonderful picture you have drawn! I really like it."
- Illocutionary act: Making a compliment.
- Student's interpretation: Thought it was a hint of wanting the picture.

② **Request misunderstanding:**

- Teacher's utterance: "Would you like to read the poem?"
- Illocutionary act: Making a polite request to read aloud.
- Student's interpretation: Interpreted it as a question about willingness.

(3) Teaching Tips:

- Role-Playing activities: Practice illocutionary acts through scenarios, like giving compliments or making polite requests.
- Awareness exercises: Highlight how one utterance can have different illocutionary forces.

- Cultural context discussions: Help learners understand how different cultures interpret speech acts.

02

핵심 ELT 읽기

말하기 활동의 종류

(1) **Personalized activities** that encourage learners to express their thoughts, opinions, and experiences can be highly beneficial for language acquisition and communication skills development:

- **Discussion Circles**: Divide learners into small groups and assign them topics related to their personal experiences, interests, or opinions. Each learner takes turns sharing their thoughts or experiences on the topic while others listen attentively. After each participant has shared, group members can engage in discussions, ask questions, and express their opinions or reactions.

- **Journal Writing**: Encourage learners to keep a language learning journal where they can write about their daily experiences, reflections, and opinions in the target language. Provide prompts or topics related to personal interests, hobbies, travel experiences, cultural encounters, or current events to inspire writing. Learners can also share excerpts from their journals with classmates or discuss their entries in pairs or small groups.

- **Debates and Role-plays**: Organize debates or role-play activities on controversial or thought-provoking topics relevant to learners' lives or interests. Assign roles or positions for learners to argue for or against specific viewpoints, encouraging them to articulate their opinions, defend their arguments, and engage in persuasive communication. After the debate or role-play, learners can reflect on the experience and discuss their perspectives with classmates.

- **Personal Storytelling**: Invite learners to share personal anecdotes, memories, or stories from their lives in the target language. Encourage them to use descriptive language, vivid details, and expressive language to convey their experiences effectively. This activity not only provides opportunities for language practice but also fosters cultural exchange and interpersonal connections as learners share and listen to each other's stories.

(2) Tasks with **tangible outcomes** are activities that result in a concrete, visible product or achievement. These tasks provide learners with a clear goal to work towards and allow them to see the direct application of their language skills:

- **Creating Presentations**: Assign learners to create presentations on specific topics related to their language learning curriculum or personal interests. This could involve researching a topic, organizing information, and designing visual aids such as slideshows or posters. The tangible outcome is the completed presentation that learners can share with their classmates or present to the class, demonstrating their language proficiency and content knowledge.

- **Conducting Interviews**: Have learners conduct interviews with native speakers or other learners in the target language. This could involve preparing interview questions, conducting the interview, and transcribing or summarizing the responses. The tangible outcome is the interview recording or transcript, which allows learners to practice listening and speaking skills, gather information, and learn about different perspectives and experiences.

- **Organizing Events or Projects**: Assign learners to plan and organize language-related events or projects, such as language exchange sessions, cultural festivals, or community service projects. This could involve coordinating logistics, promoting the event, and collaborating with others. The tangible outcome is the successful execution of the event or project, which provides learners with practical experience using their language skills in real-life contexts and engaging with the community.

- **Designing Multimedia Presentations**: Have learners create multimedia presentations, such as digital stories, podcasts, or websites, in the target language. This could involve combining audio, video, images, and text to convey information or tell a story. The tangible outcome is the multimedia presentation that showcases learners' language skills, digital literacy, and creativity.

Tasks with tangible outcomes not only provide learners with opportunities to practice and apply their language skills in meaningful ways but also offer a sense of accomplishment and motivation as they see the results of their efforts. These tasks help make language learning more engaging, relevant, and rewarding for learners, ultimately contributing to their overall language proficiency and communicative competence.

03

문항 해설

요청하기(requesting)'라는 화용론적 능력 습득을 위한 발달 순서에 대한 문제이다. 각 단계의 동사 이용에 대한 특성을 파악하고 그 특성과 학생들의 발달단계를 연결하여 서술한다. 손동작이나 몸짓으로 의사표현을 시작하여, 동사없이 명사만 말하는 단계를 지나, 명령문을 이용하는 단계가 초보적 단계이다. 그 다음에는 미리 정해진 표현(formulaic expression)을 이용하고, 다른 동사에 응용하기도 하는 중급 단계로 나아간다. 마지막에는 간접적 요청(indirect requests)을 이용하여 완곡하게 요청하는 고급 단계로 발달해 가는 것을 이해할 수 있다.

04

문항 해설

홍교사가 영어시간에 말하기 지도를 하면서 생긴 문제점에 대하여 선임교사에게 이메일을 통해 조언을 구하고 있다. 이메일을 통해 교사가 해결점을 찾지 못하고 어려움을 겪는 두가지 영역은 학생들이 활동에 고르게 참여하지 않는 것과 모국어를 사용하지 않는 부분이라는 것을 찾아낸다. 선임교사가 제시한 해결책으로는 직소활동을 통해 무료승차하는 학생(free rider) 없이 모두 고루 참여할 수 있도록 하고, 모니터하는 학생을 임명해서 교사가 없는 상황에서도 모두 영어를 쓰는 노력을 할 수 있도록 제시하고 있다.

05 – 06

핵심 ELT 읽기

2언어 습득에서의 복합성, 정확성, 유창성

Many researchers and language practitioners believe that the constructs of L2 performance and L2 proficiency are multi-componential in nature, and that their principal dimensions can be adequately, and comprehensively, captured by the notions of **complexity, accuracy and fluency** (e.g. Skehan 1998; Ellis 2003, 2008; Ellis and Barkhuizen 2005). As such, complexity, accuracy and fluency have figured as major research variables in applied linguistic research. CAF have been used both as performance descriptors for the oral and written assessment of language learners as well as indicators of learners' proficiency underlying their performance; they have also been used for measuring progress in language learning.

A review of the literature suggests that the origins of this triad lie in research on L2 pedagogy where in the 1980s a distinction was made between **fluent versus accurate L2 usage** to investigate the development of **oral L2 proficiency** in classroom contexts. One of the first to use this dichotomy was Brumfit (1984), who distinguished between fluency-oriented activities, which foster spontaneous oral L2 production, and accuracy-oriented activities, which focus on linguistic form and on the controlled production of grammatically correct linguistic structures in the L2. The third component of the triad, **complexity**, was added in the 1990s, following Skehan (1989) who proposed an L2 model which for the first time included CAF as the three principal proficiency dimensions. In the 1990s the three dimensions were also given their traditional working definitions, which are still used today. Complexity has thus been commonly characterized as 'the extent to which the language produced in performing a task is elaborate and varied' (Ellis 2003: 340), accuracy as the ability to produce error-free speech, and fluency as the ability to process the L2 with **'native-like rapidity'** (Lennon 1990) or 'the extent to which the language produced in performing a task manifests pausing, hesitation, or reformulation' (Ellis 2003).

07

핵심 개념정리

Presentation에 필요한 요소

Oral presentations play a crucial role in developing communication skills, confidence, and proficiency in the target language. Effective oral presentations encompass several key elements, including content, organization, language use, and delivery:

① **Content**: The content of an oral presentation refers to the information, ideas, or messages that the speaker intends to convey to the audience. In second language learning, it's essential for presenters to select relevant and engaging topics that align with their language proficiency level and learning objectives. Presenters should conduct research, gather supporting evidence or examples, and organize their ideas coherently to ensure that the content is informative, well-developed, and logically structured.

② **Organization**: The organization of an oral presentation involves structuring the content in a clear and coherent manner to facilitate understanding and retention by the audience. Presenters should use a logical organizational framework, such as chronological order, spatial order, cause-effect relationships, or problem-solution format, to organize their ideas effectively. This helps presenters maintain the audience's attention, guide them through the presentation, and reinforce key points or arguments.

③ **Language Use**: Language use refers to the choice of vocabulary, grammar, and linguistic structures employed by the presenter during the oral presentation. In second language learning, presenters should strive for accuracy, clarity, and appropriateness in their language use, taking into account their language proficiency level and the expectations of the audience. Presenters should use varied vocabulary, sentence structures, and rhetorical devices to express their ideas effectively and engage the audience. Additionally, presenters should pay attention to pronunciation, intonation, and fluency to enhance comprehension and communication effectiveness.

④ **Delivery**: Delivery encompasses the manner in which the presenter delivers the oral presentation, including verbal and nonverbal aspects. Effective delivery involves using appropriate vocal expression, gestures, facial expressions, and body language to convey enthusiasm, confidence, and credibility. Presenters should maintain eye contact with the audience, speak clearly and audibly, and vary their intonation and pace to maintain audience engagement and emphasis key points. Additionally, presenters should project confidence, enthusiasm, and passion for the topic to captivate the audience's attention and leave a memorable impression.

By focusing on content, organization, language use, and delivery, presenters can deliver engaging and effective oral presentations that demonstrate their language proficiency and communication competence. Regular practice, constructive feedback, and reflection on presentation experiences can help learners improve their oral presentation skills and become more confident and proficient communicators in the target language.

08

> 핵심 개념정리

문법적과 어휘적인 결속성(Cohesion)

Cohesion is the grammatical and lexical linking within a text or sentence that holds a text together and gives it meaning. It is related to the broader concept of coherence. There are two main types of cohesion:

- grammatical cohesion: based on structural content
- lexical cohesion: based on lexical content and background knowledge.

① There are two **referential devices** that can create cohesion:
  - Anaphoric reference occurs when the writer refers back to someone or something that has been previously identified, to avoid repetition. Some examples: replacing "the taxi driver" with the pronoun "he" or "two girls" with "they". Another example can be found in formulaic sequences such as "as stated previously" or "the aforementioned".
  - Cataphoric reference is the opposite of anaphora: a reference forward as opposed to backward in the discourse. Something is introduced in the abstract before it is identified. For example: "Here he comes, our award-winning host… it's John Doe!" Cataphoric references can also be found in written text.

② **Ellipsis**: Ellipsis is another cohesive device. It happens when, after a more specific mention, words are omitted when the phrase must be repeated. A simple conversational example:
   A: Where are you going?
   B: To dance. (I am going to dance.)
  - A simple written example: The younger child was very outgoing, the older much more reserved. The omitted words from the second clause are "child" and "was".

③ **Substitution**: A word is not omitted, as in ellipsis, but is substituted for another, more general word. For example, "Which ice-cream would you like?" – "I would like the pink one," where "one" is used instead of repeating "ice-cream."

④ **Lexical cohesion** refers to the way related words are chosen to link elements of a text. There are two forms: **repetition** and **collocation**. Repetition uses the same word, or synonyms, antonyms, etc. For example, "Which dress are you going to wear?" – "I will wear my green frock," uses the synonyms "dress" and "frock" for lexical cohesion. Collocation uses related words that typically go together or tend to repeat the same meaning. An example is the phrase "once upon a time".

- **General-Specific Relations** refer to the hierarchical relationship between general terms (superordinate) and specific terms (subordinate) within a semantic field.

- Words displaying **part-whole relations** refer to terms that denote the relationship between a whole entity and its constituent parts.

09

핵심 개념정리

대화구성에 필요한 언어적 요소

(1) Cataphoric reference means that a word in a text **refers** to another **later** in the text and you need to look forward to understand. It can be compared with **anaphoric reference**, which means a word refers back to another word for its meaning. For example, 'When he arrived, John noticed that the door was open'. In the classroom, matching parts of sentences can help learners understand how cataphoric reference works, for example:

a) As she entered the building 1) Jim fell over

b) When he was running upstairs 2) the woman saw a huge crowd

(2) Anaphoric reference means that a word in a text **refers back** to other ideas in the text for its meaning. It can be compared with **cataphoric reference**, which means a word refers to ideas later in the text. For example, 'I went out with Jo on Sunday. She looked awful.' 'She' clearly refers to Jo, there is no need to repeat her name. In the classroom, asking learners to identify what or who the pronouns in a text refer to is one way to raise awareness. They can then practise this by using pronouns to replace words themselves. Comparing texts with well managed referencing to ones with poorly managed referencing can help students develop an idea of effective referencing even at low levels.

(3) We use **hedges** to **soften** what we say or write. Hedges are an important part of **polite conversation**. They make what we say less direct. The most common forms of hedging involve tense and aspect, **modal expressions** including modal verbs and adverbs, vague language such as 'sort of' and 'kind of', and some verbs. In academic writing, it is prudent to be cautious in one's statements so as to distinguish between facts and claims. This is commonly known as "hedging." Hedging is the use of linguistic devices to express hesitation or uncertainty as well as to demonstrate politeness and indirectness.

(4) Backchanneling is a strategy that provides students with the opportunity to converse about content informally, both during class and outside of the traditional class period.

- By leveraging student communication preferences for chatting and texting, as well as encouraging communication and **collaboration**, backchanneling keeps students **engaged** and involved.

- Every student has a voice: When using a backchannel, students don't have to wait for their turn to speak by raising their hands. In addition, a backchannel's nonthreatening environment allows both shy and more confident students to contribute to the conversation equally.

10-11

> 핵심 ELT 읽기

Jigsaw 활동

In education, **jigsaw** is a teaching technique invented by social psychologist Elliot Aronson in 1971. Students of an average sized class (26 to 33 students) are divided into competency groups of four to six students, each of which is given a list of subtopics to research. Individual members of each group then break off to work with the **"experts"** from other groups, researching a part of the material being studied, after which they return to their starting group in the role of instructor for their subcategory. The **jigsaw** strategy is a cooperative learning technique appropriate for students from 3rd to 12th grade. It is also used extensively in adult English Second Language (or ESL) classes. The strategy is an efficient teaching method that also encourages listening, engagement, interaction, peer teaching, and **cooperation** by giving each member of the group an essential part to play in the academic activity. Both individual and group accountability are built into the process. In ESL classrooms jigsaws are a four-skills approach **integrating** reading, speaking, listening and writing. Using the Jigsaw strategy as part of a classroom activity involves the following steps:

- Step 1: Identify a range of materials related to significant **topics** addressed in the lesson. Consider the students who will be involved in this exercise, and if necessary, try to identify selections of varying text difficulty and sophistication. For example, six different selections related to hurricanes can be collected for middle school students studying weather. A textbook excerpt might detail the atmospheric conditions that create hurricanes. An article might give an overview of some of the areas affected and economic consequences. An encyclopedia segment might provide a historical perspective of significant hurricanes. A short book chapter might describe precautionary measures that can be taken to prepare for hurricanes. A newspaper account could feature a personal narrative of experiences of a specific hurricane and the damages that resulted. And so on.

- Step 2: Organize the class into cooperative groups of 4 to 6 people, with the group size corresponding to the number of selections to be assigned. Each group member receives the task of reading one of the targeted selections. Depending on the nature of the group, the teacher may allocate the specific readings to each person, or the group itself may decide who will tackle which selection.

- Step 3: Next, students read their selections independently. If the materials are photocopied, encourage students to underline important information they will need to share with their group. "Sticky notes" are an option for materials that cannot be written upon. Students may also jot down notes, or follow a graphic **note-taking outline** provided by the teacher as a means for extracting important concepts from their passage.

- Step 4: All of the students who read the same selection now meet together as a new group to **compare** notes and discuss concepts and information they feel are most important. This second group also **creates a summary** of key points, a concept map, a graphic outline, or highlighted notes which will then be photocopied and handed to members of the original group when each person goes back to present what should be learned from this particular material.

- Step 5: The final piece to the Jigsaw activity involves a return meeting of the **original group**. During this time, individual group members share in turn the pertinent information related to each selection. The rest of the group is accountable for learning this new information, which will be assessed during the evaluation of this unit of study.

The Jigsaw strategy could be integrated into a number of classroom activities that are structured so that everyone does not have to read an entire work or even segments from the same work. The Jigsaw strategy is adaptable to a wide variety of curricular settings, and teachers will find it useful in a number of respects:

- Students can encounter a wider breadth of material than might be possible if every individual had to independently read all of the available sources.
- Students may elect to learn from materials more appropriate to their abilities and specific interests.
- Students receive support from class members in learning from their reading.
- Students gain practice in synthesizing what is important from what they read as they assume the role of "teacher" with their other group members.

There are several advantages of the jigsaw method. Teachers find it easy to learn, enjoy working with it, it can be used in conjunction with other teaching strategies and it can be effective even if it used for just an hour per day. There can be some obstacles when using the jigsaw method. One common problem is a **dominant student**. In order to reduce this problem, each jigsaw group has an appointed leader. The **leader** is responsible for being fair and spreading **participation** evenly. Students realize that the group is more effective if each student is allowed to present his or her own material before questions and comments are made. Dominance is eventually reduced because students realize it is not in the best interest of the group. Another problem is a slow student in the group. It is important that each group member present the best possible report to the group, as it is important that individuals with poor study skills do not present inferior reports to their jigsaw group. In order to reduce this problem, the jigsaw technique relies on **"expert"** groups. Students work with other individuals from other groups working on the same segment of the report. In this **"expert"** group they are given a chance to discuss their reports and gather suggestions from other students to modify their reports as needed. Another issue is that of bright students becoming bored. Research suggests that there is less boredom of bright students in the jigsaw classroom than in the traditional classroom. Bright students should be encouraged to develop the mind set of a teacher. By being a teacher a boring task can be changed into an exciting challenge.

Dealing with students that have been trained to compete can also cause difficulties. A goal of the jigsaw classroom is to **decrease competition** and **increase cooperation** and so competitive students can create difficulties. Research on the jigsaw classroom suggests that it is has its strongest effect when introduced in elementary school. If there is exposure to the jigsaw classroom at an early age, only an hour per a day is needed to maintain the impact of **cooperative learning** in later schooling. If Jigsaw is first introduced in the later years of school it can often be an uphill battle. Old habits can be hard to break but, over time, students participating in the jigsaw classroom in high school can benefit from the cooperative structure.

12

핵심 ELT 읽기

사회언어학적인 오류 (Sociolinguistic failure)

Sociolinguistic failure occurs when a language learner correctly uses vocabulary and grammar but fails to use language appropriately in a social or cultural context. In other words, the message may be linguistically accurate but pragmatically inappropriate or socially awkward. This failure often leads to misunderstandings or communication breakdowns. Below are some reasons sociolinguistic failure happen;

- Cultural differences: Different cultures have distinct ways of expressing politeness, making requests, or showing respect.

- Lack of pragmatic knowledge: Learners may not know the social norms and expectations tied to language use.

- Literal translation: Translating expressions directly from the native language can sound odd or inappropriate in the target language.

- Inadequate input: Classroom teaching often focuses on grammar and vocabulary rather than real-life language use.

13

핵심 개념정리

말하기 유형: 상업적(transactional)과 대인관계적(interpersonal) 기능

A distinction that is sometimes made between uses of language where the primary focus is on social interaction between the speakers and the need to communicate such things as rapport, empathy, interest and social harmony (**interactional function**), and those where the primary focus is on communicating information and completing different kinds of real world transactions (**transactional function**). Interactional communication is primarily person-orientated, whereas transactional communication is primarily message focused. Interactional and transactional language may differ in terms of such things as conventions for turn-taking, topics, and discourse management.

Text Type	Purpose	Planning
airport announcements	transactional	planned
job interview	transactional	(partly) planned
service encounter	transactional	unplanned
joke telling	interpersonal	(partly) planned
leaving a voice-mail message	transactional or interpersonal	unplanned
casual conversation	interpersonal	unplanned

14

핵심 개념정리

연속그림 이야기(Picture strip story) 활동

(1) Picture strip story has features such as (i) an information gap (ii) unpredictability (iii) feedback. Picture strip story is an example of problem-solving task. Problem-solving task is communicative since students share information, or work together or arrive at a solution. This gives students practice in negotiation of meaning.

(2) Strip Stories: This can be varied by asking the students to memorise the sentences on their strips and then telling their sentences to the rest of the group. The students must now re-arrange themselves, rather than the strips, to reassemble the story or account.
- Rewrite a known story or account.
- Place each sentence of the story on a strip of card or paper.
- Mix the strips and distribute them to the students.
- Each student reads out their strip and the whole class/group then discusses and works out how the strips should be assembled to form the correct sequence of the story.

- Explain to the students what is involved in sequencing a strip story.
- Elicit from the students the language they need to negotiate sequence.

15

문항 해설

대화가 자연스럽게 일어나는 과정을 통해 의미협상의 절차와 전략방법을 서술하는 문제이다. 빵을 사달라는 요청(request)을 하기 위해서 일어나는 대화상의 상호작용적 과정을 보여주고 있다. 실제적인 대화과정에서는 바로 요청을 하는 것이 아니라 인사를 먼저하고, 직접적인 요청의 말을 하기 전에 준비할 수 있는 예비적인 담화(preliminary moves)가 들어가야 하는데 그렇지 못한 것을 문제점으로 지적할 수 있다.

16

문항 해설

이 발음 활동은 초분절적(suprasegmental) 발음 강세연습이 통제된 연습(controlled practice)에서 자신의 이야기를 만들어내는 자동화된 연습(automatic practice)으로 발전해가는 과정을 설명하고 있다. Step 1에서 인접 쌍(adjacency pair)을 이용하여 강세가 어떻게 달라지는지를 학생들이 직접 연습하고 있다. Step 2에서는 교사가 모음(chunking)의 방법을 명시적으로 설명하고 학생들이 직접 글을 보며 연습해 보게 한다. 이 단계에서 초분절적(suprasegmental) 최소단위(minimal pair)에 초점을 맞추고 있다. 문장 전체의 의미를 이해해야만 명확한(prominent) 강세를 줄 수 있으므로 담화(discourse) 수준의 강세 활동이 된다. Step 3는 '완벽한 소풍' 활동으로 자신의 단어를 이용하여 활동을 만들어 가는 의사소통 연습(communicative drill)이라고 할 수 있다.

핵심 개념정리

EFL교실에서의 발음지도 특성

EFL pronunciation teaching should cover both the segmentals and the suprasegmentals as well as the training of the speech organs, such as lips, teeth, alveolar ridge, palate, tongue, vocal folds, ears, etc. The segmentals embody vowel and consonant sounds, preferably phonemes, as well as syllables. A phoneme is a set of similar sounds showing meaning differences or differentiating between words. And a syllable consists of a vowel as a compulsory element and one or more consonants at the onset and/or in the termination as optional elements, which is pronounced with a single contraction of the lungs. The English language has twenty vowel phonemes(twelve monophthongs and eight diphthongs) and twenty four consonant phonemes. The treatment of the segmentals basically includes sound contrast in words, pronunciation of vowel and consonant phonemes. The phonemes which are not available in the learner's mother tongue and problematic to him/her should receive special treatment in the teaching material and methodology and sufficient room in the learner's practice.

The suprasegmentals are comprised of stress in words and connected speech, rhythm, pitch, loudness, length, quality, tone and intonation that play an essential and natural role in English speech production and perception. As the Bengali speaking learner's mother tongue is syllable timed whereas English is stress timed, he/she inevitably finds mastering EFL pronunciation a very daunting task (Bell, 1996). Hence, the differences in suprasegmentals between the learner's mother tongue and the target language are momentous topics that he/she should not only be aware of but should make a conscious effort to study and focus on. The learner should be helped to retrain his/her speech organs which have so long been trained naturally and used to articulate the sounds in his/her L1. This tremendously helps him/her to comfortably and sufficiently use his/her articulators so as to produce the sounds of the target language in an intelligible manner.

17

문항 해설

학생 A와 B에게 각기 다른 연습지를 나누어주고 분절적(segmental) 레벨의 모음의 최소단위(minimal pair) 발음 연습을 실시한다. 다른 요소는 나타나지 않고 hug와 hog, man과 men 등의 분절적요소로서 모음(vowel)에서 나타나는 음소론 차이(phonemic difference)의 정확성(accuracy)에 초점을 두어 연습을 하고 있다.

18

핵심 개념정리

Drills 연습 유형

(1) **A mechanical drill** is one where there is complete control over the student's response, and where comprehension is not required in order to produce a correct response. 예

| T: book | S: Give me the book. |
| T: ladle | S: Give me the ladle. |

(2) **A meaningful drill** in language teaching and in particular Audiolingualism, a distinction between different types of Drills is sometimes made according to the degree of control the drill makes over the response produced by the student. It is one in which there is still control over the response, but understanding is required so that the student produces a correct response. 예

Teacher reads a sentence	Student chooses a response
I'm hot.	I'll get you something to eat.
I'm thirsty	I'll turn on the air conditioning.
I'm hungry	I'll get you something to drink.

(3) **A communicative drill** is one in which the type of response is controlled but the student provides his or her own content or information. It encourages students to connect form, meaning and use and to respond to a prompt using the grammar point but providing their own content. 예

> T: What time did you get up on Sunday?
> S: I got up _____.
> T: What did you do after breakfast?
> S: I _____.

19

문항 해설

본 지문의 교실 활동은 학생들이 '불평과 사과(complaint and apology)'라는 기능(function)을 위한 역할극(role-play)을 하는 활동이다. 수업 시작에 학생들이 역할극을 직접 실시하며 말하기 수행을 목표로 하는 자유활동(free activity)으로 시작한다. 그 후에 활동내용을 글로 기록함으로서 서로 비교하고 수정하여 정확성에 대한 연습으로 통제화된 활동(controlled activity)으로 수업과정이 정리한다. 즉, 이 수업은 학생들이 형태에 구애받지 않는 유창성 중심활동에서 시작하여 마지막 단계에서 언어를 수정하고 피드백을 받는 통제된 정확도(controlled accuracy) 활동으로 전개되어간다. 단계 1에서 불만을 말하고 사과하는 것에 대한 대화를 해봄으로써 자유롭게 기능에 대해 익히면서 학생들의 실제 수행이 실시된다. 단계 3의 스크립트를 수정해보는 단계를 거쳐 정확도가 강화됨을 알 수 있다.

20

핵심 개념정리

정보차 활동(Information gap activity)

Prabhu (1987) noted that there are three types of gaps; information gap, reasoning gap, and opinion gap. Information gaps suggest that any task should have a space or blank to be completed by the learner, through decoding or encoding information. For instance, a pair or a group of participants can be given a tabular representation to complete in the form of text. A reasoning-gap allows learners to infer, deduce, or identify the perception of relationship or patterns in a piece of information (Prabhu, 1987). The opinion gap establishes and articulates personal preferences, attitudes, or temperament to apply to a given experience. This may be attained through factual information or by stimulating an argument where an individual has to justify their opinion. In general, Prabhu (1987) feels that any task that meets this criterion is effective in learning the target language.

21

문항 해설

지문에 나타난 두 가지의 다른 말하기 활동을 비교한다. 〈A〉는 주어진 단서(cue)에 의하여 한정된 의사소통의 발화를 하는 초보단계의 통제된 활동이다. 그래서 통제된 활동으로 형태(forms)를 가르치기 위한 활동이며 화자의 언어적 능력이 낮을 때 적합한 활동이다. 〈B〉는 개방형(open-ended) 활동으로서 학습자의 다양한 의견을 요구한다. 인지적으로 더 많은 활동이 요구되고 의미에 중점을 두어야 한다. 〈A〉보다 인지적으로 더 많은 노력이 필요하고 학습자가 스스로 더 많은 생각과 의견을 만들어내어야 하는 활동이다.

핵심 개념정리

발산적과 수렴적(divergent and convergent) 사고 기술

Bringing facts and data together from various sources and then applying logic and knowledge to solve problems, achieve objectives or to make informed decisions is known as thinking **convergently**. The deductive logic that the fictional character Sherlock Homes used is a good example of convergent thinking. Gathering various tidbits of facts and data he was able to put the pieces of a puzzle together and come up with a logical answer to the question: Who done it?

(1) Divergent Thinking

Divergent Thinking is thinking outwards instead of inward. It is the ability to develop original and unique ideas and then come up with a problem solution or achieve an objective. Einstein was a strong **divergent thinker**. He asked simple questions and then did mental exercises to solve problems. For example, as a young man Einstein asked himself what it would be like to ride on a beam of light. It took him many years of thought experiments, however the answer helped him develop the special theory of relativity.

(2) Convergent Thinking

Standard IQ tests gauge **convergent** thinking. Pattern recognition, testing knowledge, **logic** thought flow and the ability to solve problems can all be tested and graded. However, there are no accurate tests able to measure divergent thinking skills. It's not surprising that creative skills can't be tested.

22

문항 해설

대화 (1) 지난주에 무엇을 했는지에 관해 과거시제의 동사를 연습하면서 의미를 이해하는 의사소통연습(communicative drill)이다. 실제 상황에서의 의미 전달을 하면서 학습자들로 하여금 닫힌 응답(closed-response)이 아니라 개방형 응답(open-response)을 통해 자신의 생각을 표현할 기회를 제시해주는 특성을 가지고 있다. 대화 (2) 교사가 대표 문장을 제시해주면, 학습자들은 주어를 변경하는 대체연습(substitution drill)을 하고 있다. 학습자가 의미를 이해하고 있는지 확인하기 어려우며 단순히 제한된 맥락에서 반복 훈련하는 기계적 연습이다. 이것은 구조유형(structural pattern)을 인지하고 암기하는 데 목적을 두고 있으며 형태와 의미 사이에 아무런 연계성을 제시하지 못하고 있는 특징을 가지고 있다.

핵심 개념정리

Drills 연습 유형

(1) **A mechanical drill** is one where there is complete control over the student's response, and where comprehension is not required in order to produce a correct response. 예

| T: book | S: Give me the book. |
| T: ladle | S: Give me the ladle. |

(2) **A meaningful drill** in language teaching and in particular Audiolingualism, a distinction between different types of Drills is sometimes made according to the degree of control the drill makes over the response produced by the student. It is one in which there is still control over the response, but understanding is required so that the student produces a correct response. 예

Teacher reads a sentence	Student chooses a response
I'm hot.	I'll get you something to eat.
I'm thirsty.	I'll turn on the air conditioning.
I'm hungry	I'll get you something to drink.

(3) **A communicative drill** is one in which the type of response is controlled but the student provides his or her own content or information. It encourages students to connect form, meaning and use and to respond to a prompt using the grammar point but providing their own content. 예

| T: What time did you get up on Sunday? |
| S: I got up _____. |
| T: What did you do after breakfast? |
| S: I _____. |

23

문항 해설

대화의 형태는 상호 주고 받는 대화의 인접쌍(adjacency pair)형태로 이루어지고 있다는 것을 알 수 있다. 상대방의 반응이 첫 번째 화자의 의도와 다른 내용의 답을 하거나 응답이 결여된 경우에는 무례하다고 보일 수도 있고 무시하는 것으로 보일 수도 있다. 〈B〉의 대화문에서 상대방의 대답 부분이 적절하지 못했을 경우에 그 결여가 상대방이나 제3자 혹은 발화자 자신에 의해 알아차려질 수 있다는 것을 의미하고 있다.

핵심 개념정리

인접쌍(Adjacency Pair)

An adjacency pair, used in **conversational analysis**, is a pair of conversational turns by two different speakers such that the production of the first turn (called a first-pair part) makes a response (a second-pair part) of a particular kind **relevant**. For example, a question, such as "what's your name?", requires the addressee to provide an answer in the next conversational turn. A failure to give an immediate response is noticeable and accountable. Many actions in conversation are accomplished through adjacency pair sequences, for example:

- offer – acceptance/ rejection
- greeting – greeting
- complaint – excuse/ remedy
- request – acceptance/ denial

24

문항 해설

두 종류의 초안을 비교하여 교사가 어디에 중점을 두고 피드백을 주었는지를 구체적으로 설명한다. 두 번째 초안에서는 내용에 상세내용을 더하여 주제내용을 보조해주는 역할을 더했고 글의 구성에서는 연결어를 더하여 논리적 연결성으로 이해가 잘 될 수 있도록 하였다.

영어과 교육과정

쓰기지도

쓰기는 목적에 맞는 다양한 형태의 글을 쓸 수 있도록 지도한다. 쓰기능력은 단순히 지식이나 원리를 배움으로써 향상되는 것이 아니며 글을 쓰는 과정에서 단어의 선택, 문장의 구조 및 연결관계, 글의 구성, 통일성과 명료성 등을 글의 목적과 독자의 반응을 예상하고 분석해야 하는 복합적인 능력이다. 따라서 쓰기 능력을 향상시키기 위해서는 과정중심의 쓰기지도 방법이나 전략중심의 지도방법이 활용되어야 할 것이다. 우리나라 학생들은 학년이 올라갈수록 읽기능력에 비해 쓰기능력이 떨어지는 현상이 나타난다. 이는 쓰기학습이 읽기에 비해 교육과정 운영시 소홀히 취급되기 때문이다. 따라서 쓰기학습 초기단계에는 통제된 학습활동을 마련하여 학생들의 동기를 유발해야 한다. 또 쓰기과정에서 학생들이 오류를 범하더라도 의미에 중점을 두면서 지속적으로 쓰기활동에 흥미를 가질 수 있도록 유도한다. 초기단계의 활동으로는 단일 주제나 이야기를 담은 그림, 지도, 도표 등을 시각자료로 이용하여 쓰기 활동에 적합한 상황을 제시하고 학습자의 동기를 유발할 수 있다. 교사는 학습자가 영어로 글을 쓰는 과정에서 생각을 이끌어내고 전개할 수 있도록 도와주고, 초안작성 및 수정작업에서는 학생들이 글을 쓰는 목적과 필자의 반응을 염두에 두고 자신의 흥미, 경험을 이끌어 내어 그것을 연계시킬 수 있도록 피드백을 제공하는 역할을 수행해야 한다. 이때, 교사들은 학생의 생각을 존중한다는 태도를 보이는 것이 중요하다. 또한, 해당 수업시간에 학습할 영어로 쓰인 글의 구조 및 형식을 분명하게 제시해야 한다. 이때, 읽기와 쓰기를 연계하여 지도하는 수업이 도움이 될 수 있다. 예를 들어, 주제를 명확히 제시하는 문장(thesis statement)과 핵심논제를 뒷받침하는 문장(supporting ideas)을 작성하는 방법을 알려주고 연습시킨다. 의사소통을 목적으로 하는 기능중심의 쓰기(writing on function) 활동에는 묘사, 사실이나 자료를 통한 증거제시, 비교 및 대조 등 다양한 방법을 활용하여 쓰기학습을 한다.

25

문항 해설

학습자 글에 대한 평가를 하는 문제이다. 단락 1은 학습자 글쓰기의 장단점을 서술한다. 장점으로(content)에 있어서 두 개의 명확한 주제와 상세 내용으로 잘 구성되어있으며 단점으로(organization)이 논리적으로 연관 없는 내용들이 문장에 포함되어 있어서 전체 흐름을 방해한다. 단락 2의 교정기호(correction symbol)표는 주어진 표에 문법적 오류의 예시와 기호를 작성한다. 단락 3에는 교정기호를 만드는 장단점을 서술한다. 장점으로 시간 절약이 되고 학습자가 스스로 오류를 수정할 수 있는 자율성이 발달될 수 있다. 단점으로는 교정기호의 의미를 이해해야 하는 수고가 필요하고 학습자가 문법요소에만 초점을 맞출 수 있다.

26

문항 해설

인터넷을 활용한 교사와 학생들의 쓰기에 대한 온라인 면담(online-conferencing)을 보여주고 있다. 학생들이 서로서로에게 쓰기에 대한 자신의 생각과 조언을 함으로써 도와주는 역할을 하는 비계(scaffolding)를 하고 그를 통해서 자신의 글을 검토해 볼 수 있는 기회를 가진다. conferencing의 주요 목적은 형성평가(formative feedback)로서 쓰기과정의 피드백을 통해 더 나은 글을 만들 수 있도록 도와주는 것이다. 일관성(coherence)은 학생들이 한 문장을 바탕으로 그 다음 문장을 만들어 보는 연습을 하면서 생겨날 수 있다. conferencing단계는 완전히 정리된 글을 가지고 논하는 것이 아니므로 학생들의 의견을 자유롭게 이야기하는 brainstorm의 역할을 한다.

27

핵심 개념정리

ESL 글쓰기의 채점 방법

The scoring guide contains 5 categories: **content, organization, vocabulary, grammar, and spelling and mechanics**. The categories in each essay may have different ratings, but the majority should be level 3 or above for a passing composition.

Content	The student addresses the questions in the prompt so that the writing is interesting and well-developed.
Organization	Clear paragraphing with ideas moving smoothly from general to specific or in another clear and logical order with specific details and examples clearly supporting the ideas presented.
Vocabulary	Words are specific, varied, and used correctly throughout.
Grammar	Verb tenses are used correctly. Overall, there are few grammar mistakes, and the meaning of sentences is clear.
Spelling & Mechanics	Most words are spelled correctly and most punctuation is used correctly.

When we talk about effective writing, we often think first about elements like **word choice**, **grammar** and **mechanics**, and **content** or evidence. But a really important part of effective writing—and effective thinking, too—is clear, **logical organization**. Maybe an analogy will help here. I know where every tool and ingredient is in my kitchen, and I can cook pretty efficiently. When I begin a recipe, I bring out all the ingredients, measure them, and line them up in the order in which I'll use them. Even complicated recipes seem fairly easy once I have everything laid out, and the organization gives me some sense of control.

In the chaos of my garage, on the other hand, I don't know where anything is, and I'll leave a faucet dripping for a week because I don't want to hunt down a screwdriver or a wrench. I find it hard even to imagine more complicated projects. My office looks like a shambles, too—and I've wasted a lot of time looking for a book or document that I know is here somewhere. Thinking and acting are both harder when things are disorganized.

The same principle affects you and me as writers and readers. When things are laid out in some sort of order, we can work with them more easily. If we can impose some kind of order on information, the **information is easier** to talk about, easier to **understand**, and easier to remember. If you choose a **clear, recognizable pattern** (for a single paragraph, and also for a whole essay), you find it easier to select details and choose transitions, and you also help your reader discover relationships that connect things, that make things seem more **coherent**.

28

핵심 개념정리

Genre 중심 교수법

A **genre approach** based on SFL can be implemented through the teaching- learning cycle recommended by Feez (1998). In this cycle, five stages are actualized by a teacher and students together: (1) building the *context*; (2) modeling and deconstructing the *text*; (3) joint *construction* of the text; (4) independent *construction* of the text; and (5) linking related *texts*. During the first stage, the teacher establishes the purpose and social contexts where the target text is used. During the second stage, the teacher presents exemplary target texts and analyzes the key structures and linguistic features of the genre by introducing activities to practice the language features. In the third stage, the students create a target text with the teacher or their peers together following the steps of the writing process. During the fourth stage, students create texts individually by themselves. In the final stage, the use of the target genre is compared to other situations or with other genres in the same situation.

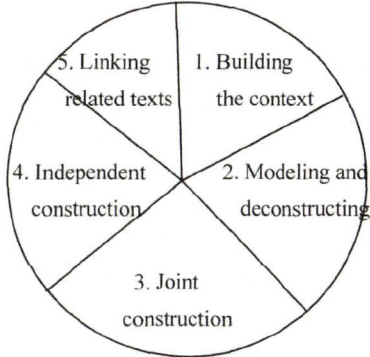

Stages of the Teaching-learning Cycle

Genre-based pedagogy is underpinned by the belief that explicit instruction enables learning to be best accomplished (Feez, 1995; Hyland, 2002b). Studies have shown that EFL writing should be explicitly taught in order for learners to be more proficient L2 users. Implementation of genre-based writing teaching in English classrooms could be effective in improving Korean learners' writing proficiency.

Systematic and explicit instruction on how students should construct texts to meet different purposes, audiences, and contexts is necessary. In particular, Korean EFL learners, who have little L2 writing experience may benefit from genre instruction. According to Hyland (2002b), genre-based teaching for novice writers is more appropriate than process-based approaches. Therefore, it can be concluded that explicit writing instruction should be incorporated into the middle school English curriculum. For example, Korean middle school students in the third grade have English class four times a week. Most current English textbooks consist of 12 units, and one unit is generally taught for eight hours. When each unit is finished, time for explicit writing instruction using the genre approach should be allotted once a month. Each teaching and learning cycle would follow the four stages suggested by Feez (1998): building the context; modeling and deconstructing; joint construction; and individual construction. The genre the students would learn could be chosen from among the topics of each unit, and one genre may be covered for four hours. If genre-based writing instruction is conducted in this way, students will be able to explore and write several different genres each year.

29

문항 해설

학생들의 자기 평가표를 읽고 잘 이루어지지 않은 부분을 찾아 알맞은 추후(followup) 활동을 결정하는 문제이다. 많은 수의 학생들이 재미있고 창조적 생각을 만들어내는 것에 약하고, 자신의 생각을 논리적으로 구성을 잘 하지 못하고, 정확한 spelling과 punctuation하는 기계적(mechanics)영역에 익숙하지 못하다고 평가를 내리고 있다. 그래서 교사는 학생들이 약한 부분 영역에 추후활동을 할 수 있다. 발음이나 스펠링 등의 기계적 내용에 대한 연습과 새로운 생각을 만들어 낼 수 있는 brainstorming등의 연습이 필요하게 될 것이다. 연결되지 않는 문장들을 다시 구성하여 제 위치로 놓는 연습이 논리적으로 구성하는 데 도움을 주게 될 것이다. 학생들은 문법이나 어휘에 어려움을 느끼지 않으므로 그 부분에 대해서는 교사가 추후활동을 실시하지 않아도 될 것이다.

30

문항 해설

과정중심쓰기(process writing)의 과정을 이용하여 그 안에 포함되어 있는 주요 내용을 찾아가는 문제이다. 과정중심쓰기는 여러 단계를 거치는데 크게 놓고 생각했을 때 처음에는 학습자들 스스로의 생각(ideas)을 만들어내기 위한 작업이 필요하고 후반부에는 언어적이고 문법적인 부분들을 체크하면서 글을 더욱 분명하고 정확도있게 만들어 주어야 한다. 만약, 전체적인 내용과 생각 발전되어야 하는 쓰기의 초기 단계에서 문법적인 세부내용(micro-level)을 확인하려고 하는 활동을 하게 된다면 생각을 발전시키는데 필요한 글의 흐름을 방해할 수 있다는 것을 명심해야 한다.

31

문항 해설

설문조사에 따르면 대부분의 쓰기수업은 완성된 결과물을 요구하는 결과중심교수법(product-based approach)보다는 계획, 초고, 수정, 정리(planning, drafting, revising, editing)로 이루어지는 과정중심교수법(process-based approach)에 기반을 두고 있다. 피드백의 경우 문법이나 구두점 및 부호에 관련된 언어적오류(linguistic errors)를 중점적으로 지적해주기보다는 내용이나 글의 구조에 초점을 두는 교사가 더 많으며 수업활동은 개별활동이 조별활동에 비해 많이 이루어졌다. 대부분의 교사가 학생들의 과업 중에 도와주면서 적절한 면담(conferencing)이 이루어지고 있다.

Process writing	
	• Stage 1: Generating ideas by brainstorming and discussion.
	• Stage 2: Students extend ideas into note form, and judge quality and usefulness of ideas and organise ideas into a mind map, spidergram, or linear form.
	• Stage 3: Students write the first draft in pairs or groups.
	• Stage 4: Drafts are exchanged, so that students become the readers of each others work and improvements are made based upon peer feedback.
	• Stage 5: A final draft is written.
	• Stage 6: Students once again, exchange and read each others' work and perhaps even write a response or reply.

Product writing	• Stage 1: Model texts are read, and then features of the genre are highlighted. • Stage 2: This consists of controlled practice of the highlighted features. • Stage 3: The organisation of ideas is as important as the control of language. • Stage 4: The end result of the learning process.

32-33

문항 해설

과정중심쓰기(process writing) 수업활동에 대한 내용을 묻는 문제이다. 우선 활동(1)은 학생들이 자신의 ideas를 중심으로 초고를 쓰고, 그 초고를 서로 동료 editing을 한 후, 그에 따른 피드백을 참고하여 다시 수정(revising)을 하는 마지막 단계의 활동이다. 활동(2)는 대화와 mind map을 사용하여 어떤 글을 쓸 것인지 결정하는 시작 단계로서 쓰기 전 활동에 해당된다. 활동(3)은 작문(composing)단계로 학생들이 결정한 주제와 개인경험을 어떻게 작문할 것인지를 안내하는 단계이다. 이 안내에 따라 학생들은 작문을 하게 된다.

핵심 개념정리

과정중심 쓰기(process writing) 단계

(1) Planning (Pre-Writing)

Pre-writing is any activity in the classroom that encourages students to write. It stimulates **thoughts** for getting started.

- Group Brainstorming: Group members spew out **ideas** about the topic. Spontaneity is important here. There are no right or wrong answers. Students may cover familiar ground first and then move off to more abstract or wild territories.
- Clustering: Students form words related to a stimulus supplied by the teacher. The words are circled and then linked by lines to show discernible clusters. Clustering is simple yet powerful strategy: 'Its visual character seems to stimulate the flow of association.'
- Rapid Free Writing: Within a limited time of 1 or 2 minutes, individual students freely and quickly write down single words and phrases about a topic. The time limit keeps the writers' minds ticking and thinking fast.
- WH-Questions: Students generate who, why, what, where, when and how questions about a topic. More such questions can be asked of answers to the first string of wh-questions, and so on. This can go on indefinitely.

(2) Drafting

At the drafting stage, the writers are focused on the **fluency** of writing and are not preoccupied with grammatical accuracy or the neatness of the draft. One dimension of good writing is the writer's ability to visualise an audience. A conscious sense of audience can dictate a certain style to be used. Depending on the genre of writing narrative, expository or argumentative), an introduction to the subject of writing may be a starting statement to arrest the reader's attention, a short summary of the rest of the writing, an apt quotation, a provocative question, a general statement, an analogy, a statement of purpose, and so on.

(3) Responding

Responding to student writing by the teacher (or by peers) has a central role to play in the successful implementation of process writing. Response can be oral or in writing, after the students have produced the first draft and just before they proceed to revise.

(4) Revising

When students revise, they review their texts on the basis of the **feedback** given in the responding stage. They reexamine what was written to see how effectively they have communicated their meanings to the reader. Revising is not merely checking for language errors (editing). It is done to improve **global content** and the **organization** of ideas so that the writer's intent is made clearer to the reader.

(5) Editing

At this stage, students are engaged in tidying up their texts as they prepare the final draft for evaluation by the teacher. They edit their won or their peer's work for **grammar, spelling, punctuation, diction, sentence structure** and **accuracy** of supportive textual material such as quotations, examples and the like. Formal editing is deferred till this phase in order that its application not disrupt the free flow of ideas during the drafting and revising stages.

(6) Evaluating

In evaluating student writing, the scoring may be **analytical** (based on specific aspects of writing ability) or **holistic** (based on a global interpretation of the effectiveness of that piece of writing). In order to be effective, the criteria for evaluation should be made known to students in advance.

(7) Post-Writing

This includes publishing, sharing, reading aloud, transforming, texts for stage performance, or merely displaying texts on notice-boards.

34

문항 해설

교사가 글을 쓰는 방법을 제시하고 멀티미디어를 사용하여 첫 번째 초고(draft)를 통해 피드백을 받고, 수정 및 보완하도록 한다. 쓰기를 모두 마친 후 최종쓰기인 글을 blog에 올리는 과정이다. 이것은 쓰기에서 과정중심(process-oriented) 과정에 해당되며, 동료들의 피드백을 통해서 학생들의 참여를 강화하고 이메일을 사용해서 상호작용함으로서 비동시적으로 대화가 이루어짐(asynchronous communication)을 알 수 있다. 그리고 일대일의 이메일 대화뿐만 아니라 블로그에서 여러 명과의 상호교류도 가능하게 된다.

35

문항 해설

이 수업은 중학교에서 결과중심(product-based) 쓰기지도의 과정을 설명하고 있다.

1) 준비(warmup) 단계로서 교사는 학생들에게 반려동물의 그림들을 보여주고 그들이 좋아하는 반려동물에 대해 이야기하게 한다.
2) 교사가 강아지에 대한 이야기와 4장의 그림을 주고 정확하게(accurately) 글을 쓸 것이라고 설명한다. 글에는 과거동사가 많이 포함되어 있다.
3) 학생들은 3분 동안 글을 읽고 교사에게 다시 돌려준다.
4) 교사는 핵심단어(keyword)를 칠판에 쓰고 소리내어 읽는다.
5) 학생들은 기억할 수 있는 만큼 원본과 가깝게 쓴다.
6) 교사는 학생들의 글에서 틀린 과거형동사에 대해 수정하고 맞는 유형으로 적어준다.
7) 다음수업에서 학생들은 교사가 오류수정을 해 준 자신들의 글을 돌려받게 된다.

이 교수방법은 형태(form)에 대한 정확도(accuracy)를 발달시키기 위한 결과중심교수법(product-based approach)이다. 교사가 이미 정해진 주제의 글을 보여 주고 학생들이 다시 써보게 하는 쓰기활동이다. 학습자에게 목표로 하는 글을 읽게 하고 그를 바탕으로 다시 써보게 하는 결과중심의 쓰기가 된다. 수업과정이 학생들의 인지적 처리(cognitive processing load)를 줄여주고 있다고 하는 것은 수업절차 5)를 보면 그림과 핵심단어의 도움으로 학생들이 새로운 것을 생각하는 인지적 어려움보다는 이미 주어진 글에 대하여 기억으로부터 회상하여 글을 써내려가도록 도와주고 있음을 알 수 있다. 즉, 학생들이 인지적으로 어려운 것을 새로 만들어내는 어려움보다는 이미 들었던, 혹은 보았던 내용을 기억해냄으로서 하는 활동이라 인지적으로 더 쉬울 수 있음을 의미한다. 교사의 수정이 문법적 정확성에 초점을 두고 있다고 하는데 수업절차 6)을 보면 교사는 학생의 글에서 과거동사형을 잘못 쓴 것을 정확한 유형으로 고쳐주는 오류수정을 하고 있음을 알 수 있다.

36

핵심 ELT 읽기

사회적 구성주의(Social Constructivism) 교실 적용

Learning theory of **social constructivism** incorporates a **learning process** wherein the student gains their own conclusions through the creative aid of the teacher as a facilitator. The best way to plan teacher worksheets, lesson plans, and study skills for the students, is to create a curriculum which allows each student to solve problems while the teacher monitors and flexibly guides the students to the correct answer, while encouraging critical thinking.

Instead of having the students relying on someone else's information and accepting it as truth, the students should be exposed to data, primary sources, and the ability to interact with other students so that they can learn from the incorporation of their experiences. The classroom experience should be an invitation for a myriad of different backgrounds and the learning experience which allows the different backgrounds to come together and observe and analyze information and ideas.

Hands-on activities are the best for the classroom applications of social constructivism, critical thinking and learning. Having **observations** take place with a daily journal helps the students to better understand how their own experiences contribute to the formation of their theories and observational notes, and then comparing them to another students' reiterates that different backgrounds and cultures create different outlooks, while neither is wrong, both should be respected. Some **strategies** for classroom applications of social constructivism for the teacher include having students working together and aiding to answer one another's questions. Another strategy includes designating one student as the "expert" on a subject and having them teach the class. Finally, allowing students to work in groups or pairs and research controversial topics which they must then present to the class.

Overall, the setting should include classroom applications of social constructivism within a few key concepts. The first is discovering and maintaining an individual's intellectual identity. This forces students to support their own theories, in essence taking responsibility for their words and respecting those of others. The next component is having the teacher ask **open-ended questions** and leaving time to allow the students to think and analyze a response, based on their experiences and personal inquiry. Open-ended questions and critical thinking encourage students to seek more than just a simple response or basic facts and incorporate the justification and defense of their organized thoughts.

The next step is allowing constant conversation between the students and teacher. This engagement creates a discourse of comfort wherein all ideas can be considered and understood and the students then feel safe about challenging other hypotheses, defending their own, and supporting **real-world situations** with abstract supporting data. These exercises and classroom applications of social constructivism will allow children to, at an early age or a late age, develop the skills and confidence to analyze the world around them, create solutions or support for developing issues, and then justify their words and actions, while encouraging those around them to do the same and respecting the differences in opinions for the contributions that they can make to the whole of the situation. Classroom applications of constructivism support the philosophy of learning which build a students' and teachers' understanding.

37

핵심 개념정리

Guided Writing

Writing is learned through apprenticeships, as teachers assist students during writing using **guided practice**. Many students need this expert guidance in a small-group context, particularly as they attempt to bridge the gap between the teacher's demonstration and **modeling** and their own independent writing. Young and poor writers have a limited control over strategies for writing. These writers do, however, learn strategic behavior for writing when these strategies are taught to them in clear and supportive ways. When **authentic and targeted modeling** of the ways in which writers work is presented by teachers and co-constructed with students during collaborative, rich discussion, learners develop understanding of the purposes, intrinsic motivation, and techniques of writing. Several excellent frameworks for writing instruction accomplish these goals, including modeled, shared, interactive, guided or independent writing. During guided writing instruction, in particular, students are provided with opportunities to experience successful and independent writing within the context of strong teacher support. Guided writing is taught to small groups in briskly paced, 20-minute lessons. These groupings should be flexible, based on observation of students' current needs, and might be implemented following a whole-class writing lesson.

① Engage students in a brief, shared experience. You might read a short but fascinating section of an informational text, for example, or conduct a brief experiment.

- Engage students in a rich conversation during this experience, expanding their linguistic ability for this topic.

- Have students explicitly rehearse the ways in which they may decide to write about this experience.

② Teach one or two specific strategies for writing.

- Remember to teach strategies for all levels of writing decisions, including composing, text and sentence structures, spelling, and punctuation.

- Provide brief examples or cue cards of strategies in order to support students' immediate use.

- Hold brief discussions with students about how they will integrate these strategies into their own writing during today's lesson.

③ Provide students with time (5-10 minutes) to write at the small-group table but individually and as independently as possible.

- Provide immediate individual guidance and feed forward while students write, assisting individual students in anticipation of needed reminders or assistance). Monitor students while they write and "lean in" in order to prompt and guide their thinking.

- Students should experience sustained attention to writing, producing a short but complete piece of writing.

④ Include a brief sharing activity in which each writer's immediate work is shared with an audience. This sharing will allow each writer to experience his/her newly written text as a whole.

38

핵심 개념정리

시간 표현(time expressions) 사용

Time expressions are often the key to understanding and planning written work. Students can improve their written and spoken accuracy by having a good grasp of the relationship between time expressions and tenses. This lesson includes an identification and matching exercise and is followed by a longer sentence construction exercise to give students practice in correct sentence structure.

39

문항 해설

텍스트 내에서 명시적인 언어학적 표시를 통해 문장 간의 구조적 연계를 강화시키는 개념으로 응집성(cohesion)에 관련된 내용이다. 응집성의 영역은 두 문장을 결합시키기 위해 종속절이나 연결어구 사용, 불필요한 반복을 피하기 위한 대명사 이용, 새로운 정보를 구분하기 위한 정관사, 부정관사의 활용의 영역에 해당된다. 위의 예문에서 볼 수 있듯이, 'my landlady'라는 명사가 반복되어 같은 단어로 언급됨으로서 응집성의 사용이 약하다는 것을 알 수 있다.

- (conjunctions) and, but, because, so, if, when, until, although, etc.
- (pronouns) he, she, it, this, that, etc.
- (articles) a, an, the

40

문항 해설

담화(discourse)는 문장과 문장이 연결되어서 글(text)을 형성하는 것으로 응집성(cohesion)과 논리성(coherence)을 고려해야 한다. 본문의 담화 내에서 사용하고 있는 'they (the taste buds)'라는 지시표현(reference)과 'therefore'라는 접속사(conjunction)를 사용함으로 응집성을 높여 주고 있다.

핵심 개념정리

연결어(cohesion devices)

Language comprehension involves finding **coherence** across utterances. The listener must be able to construct coherence by following the speaker's use of cohesion devices.

- Anaphora: reference back to an item previously mentioned in the text.
  e.g. My brother stayed at my apartment last week. He left his dog here.

- Exophora: reference to an item outside the text. e.g. (pointing) That's his dog.
- Lexical substitution: using a similar lexical item to substitute for a previous one.
  e.g. His dog ... that stupid animal ...
- Lexical chaining: using a related lexical item as a link to one already mentioned.
  e.g. The dog makes a mess ... it sheds everywhere, it tears up newspapers.
- Conjunction: using links between propositions, such as and, but, so.
  e.g. The dog is too much for me, but I promised I'd take care of it.
- Ellipsis: omission of lexical items that can be recovered by the listener through conventional grammatical knowledge. e.g. I promised to take care of it, so I will.

41

문항 해설

본 지문은 온라인 blog를 사용하여 학생들이 작문 과제를 하는 모습을 설명하고 있다. 교실 blog를 통해 학생들은 교사와 친구들 간의 피드백을 주고받을 수 있고 온라인 자료 또한 활용 가능하다. 이러한 대화양식은 실제시간(real-time)에 이루어지는 동시형 의사소통(synchronous communication)이라고 할 수 있다. 학생들이 자신의 채점 기준표(rubic scoring)를 blog에 올리는 것이 아니라 교사가 평가 기준(evaluation criteria)을 blog에 이미 올려놓은 상태에서 영어수업 blog를 실시한다.

42

문항 해설

그룹 토론을 통해 자유 활동(free activity)을 한 후 학생들의 오류를 수정하고 특정 패턴을 연습하는 통제 활동(controlled activity)으로 진행된다.

Step 1. 읽기전 질문으로 읽기 활동 전에 학생들이 내용을 예상할 수 있도록 한다.
Step 3. 이해도 확인질문을 주어서 학생들의 이해도를 확인한다.
Step 4. 그룹 활동을 통해 열린 과제인 문제해결활동을 완성한다.
Step 5-6. 다른 학생과의 피드백을 통해 말하기기술을 향상시킨다.
Step 7. 마지막 단계로서 부족한 형태(form)에 대한 연습(drill)이 이루어진다.

43

문항 해설

예시 [1]은 학생의 쓰기과업에 대해 전체적인 내용과 관련하여 피드백을 제시하고 있는 반면 예시 [2]에서는 오류 수정 기호(correction symbol: error codes)을 사용하여 학생이 문법적으로 틀린 부분을 표시하고 있다. 특히 [2]에서는 수 일치와 시제와 관련된 문법적 오류가 집중적으로 지적되고 있다. 하지만 두 예시 모두 수정되어야 할 부분을 교사가 직접적으로 고쳐주지 않으며 학생들이 다시 수정해볼 기회를 제공한다.

44

문항 해설

활동과정은 dicctogloss의 과정을 기술하고 있다. 이것은 dictation과 관련한 controlled writing의 한 형태로서 시험자는 지문의 내용을 이해해야 하고 phrases, 그 다음에는 주요 단어를 기억하고 그 후에 자신의 말로 이야기를 새로 작성해야만 한다. 듣기 형태로서는 phonemes, words, intonation, discourse marker등을 집중적으로 듣게 하는 intensive listening의 듣기 활동을 포함한다. 그래서 이해하고 글을 만들어내는 두 가지 활동이 모두 발달되는 수업활동이다.

45 & 47

핵심 개념정리

Types of writing

(1) Dictogloss

A paragraph is read at normal speed, usually two or three times: then the teacher asks students to **rewrite the paragraph** from the best of their recollections. A teacher, after reading the passage, distribute a handout with key words from the paragraph, in sequence, as cues for the students.

(2) Dialogue journal

Most classroom-oriented journals are what have now come to be known as dialogue journal. They imply an **interaction** between a reader and the student through dialogues or response. One of the principal objectives in a student's dialogue journal is to carry on a conversation with the teacher. Through dialogue journals, teachers can become better acquainted with their students, in terms of both their learning progress and their affective states, and thus become better equipped to meet students' **individual needs**.

(3) Chain writing

The teacher wrote the sentence, "once upon a time, there was a beautiful princess." and asked each student in an online chat group to add a sentence in turn until the story was completed.

(4) Imitative writing

To produce written language, the learner must attain skills in the fundamental, basic tasks of writing letters, words, punctuation, and very brief sentences. This category includes the ability to **spell correctly** and to perceive **phoneme-grapheme correspondences** in the English spelling system. It is a level at which learners are trying to master the mechanics of writing. At this stage, from is the primary if not exclusive focus, while context and meaning are of secondary concern.

46

> **문항 해설**

　　이야기 구조(narrative structure)를 쓰기 수업에서 소개하고 있다. '소개-사건전개-해결(orientation – complication – resolution)'로 연결되는 구조를 〈B〉에 비교하여 답하는 문제이다. 논리적 연결성(coherence)를 고려했을 때 왜 강아지의 이름을 Spot이라고 지었는지 서술해 준다면 훨씬 자연스러운 문장연결이 될 수 있으므로 그에 대한 피드백이 필요할 것이다. 교사가 학생들을 위해 칠판에 시작 문장을 제시했지만, 학생의 글 자체에도 소개부분이 필요하므로 시작문장을 써주는 것이 좋다. 앞부분이 절(clause)로 연결되어 있으므로 마침표가 아니라 쉼표로 바꿔줘야 하는 것이 적절하다. 갑자기 붕대를 감아 줬다는 내용이 나오므로 위 내용을 고려했을 때 어울리지 않는 결론이 될 수 있다. 이 글의 마지막 문장은 사건을 마무리 짓는 결론이 된다. 이야기 구조는 다음의 순서를 따른다.

- Beginning/ Orientation: This sets the scene, creating a visual picture of the setting, atmosphere and time of the story. Actors are introduced and clues are set in place for the coming complication.
- Problem/ Complication: This is where a problem or complication occurs that affects the setting, time or characters.
- Problem seems to be resolved/ Minor Resolution: seems to be resolved.
- New Problem/ Complication: The problem or complication is now often worse than before.
- Problem is solved/ Ending/ Resolution: The problem is solved and the story ends.
- Moral/ Coda/ Evaluative ending: There may be a moral or message at the end of the story.

48

문항 해설

통제된 글쓰기/ 말하기(Controlled writing/ speaking: accuracy)에서 자유글쓰기/ 말하기(free writing/ speaking: fluency) 정도에 따라 각 활동을 정확성과 유창성의 정도에 따라 구분하는 문제이다. (a)와 (c)는 형태를 제시하고, 그 형태에 맞게 동사와 명사를 활용하여 의미를 형성하는 활동으로, (a)는 John이라는 가상의 인물에 긍정/부정 패턴을 연습하는 것이고, (c)는 잘 알고 있는 사람에 관해 사실적 진술을 제시하는 것으로 상호작용을 통해 의미있는 문형을 만들 수 있으므로, (a)가 (c)보다 통제되어있다고 볼 수 있다. (b)와 (d)는 상황을 제시하면서 어떻게 대처할 것인가에 대해 쓰고 말하는 활동으로 (b)는 컨닝하는 친구에 관한 해결책으로 다양한 modalities를 사용할 수 있으며 (d)의 백만달러가 생긴다면 무엇을 할 것인지에 관해 조건절을 연습하는 활동이다. 이럴 때에 (b)가 더욱 다양한 의견이 제시될 수 있음으로, (b)가 (d)보다 말하거나 쓸 수 있는 영역이 더욱 크다고 할 수 있다.

핵심 개념정리

글쓰기 지도 유형

(1) Focus on accuracy

Accuracy-oriented approaches have stressed the importance of control in order to eliminate mistakes from written work. Students are taught how to write and combine various sentence types and manipulation exercises. → Controlled writing approach

(2) Focus on fluency

This approach encourages students to write as much as possible and as quickly as possible. The important thing is to get one's ideas down on paper. In this way, students feel that they are actually writing, not merely doing 'exercises' of some kind; they write what they want to write and consequently writing is an enjoyable experience. A fluency-approach, perhaps channelled into something like keeping a diary, can be a useful antidote (Free-writing approach).

(3) Focus on purpose

In real life, we normally have a reason for writing (purpose) and we write to or for somebody (audience). It is easy to devise situations which allow students to write purposefully: for example, they can write to one another in the classroom or use writing in role play situations (Communicative approach).

CHAPTER 08 문법 지도

01

핵심 개념정리

Display Questions vs Referential Questions

In second language learning, display and referential questions are two types of questions used by teachers to facilitate communication and promote language acquisition:

(1) Display Questions

- Purpose: Display questions are typically used to elicit known information or to check learners' comprehension of material that has already been presented. These questions often serve to review or reinforce previously taught content.

- Focus: Display questions focus on testing learners' ability to recall factual information, vocabulary, or grammatical structures.

- Question Structure: Display questions often have a closed format, meaning that there is typically only one correct answer or a limited set of possible answers. (eg) "What is the capital of France?" (This question tests the learner's knowledge of factual information.)

(2) Referential Questions:

- Purpose: Referential questions are designed to prompt learners to provide new information or express their opinions, thoughts, or ideas on a given topic. These questions encourage learners to use language creatively and communicatively.

- Focus: Referential questions focus on encouraging learners to engage in higher-order thinking skills, such as analysis, evaluation, inference, or problem-solving.

- Question Structure: Referential questions often have an open-ended format, allowing for a variety of possible responses. They may begin with question words such as "why," "how," or "what if." (eg) "Why do you think the character made that decision?" (This question prompts the learner to analyze and interpret the motivations behind a character's actions.)

Display questions are used to assess learners' understanding of previously taught material through recall or recognition to review and reinforce learning, while referential questions encourage learners to generate new language and engage in deeper levels of thinking and communication, promoting language production and critical thinking skills.

02

핵심 개념정리

Focus on Form

L2 learners in immersion classrooms can develop not only language proficiency but also content knowledge. Immersion classrooms have been found to yield learners who have high L2 proficiency with considerable comprehension competence and fluency; however, they still produce ungrammatical, ill-formed utterances. As a result, researchers have investigated different types of form-focused instruction as a way of promoting L2 accuracy along with the uninterrupted flow of communication. **Form focused instruction** is categorized into **a reactive approach and a proactive approach**, also being called preemptive. A reactive approach benefits immersion teachers in the way that it attracts learners' attention to form as teachers go through the content-based subject-matter or theme-based language arts classes maintaining the communicative flow.

Options	Description
Reactive focus-on-form	The teacher or another student responds to an error that a student makes in the context of a communicative activity.
1. Negotiation	
a. Conversational	The response to the error is triggered by a failure to understand what the student meant, it involves 'negotiation of meaning'.
b. Didactic	The response occurs even though no breakdown in communication has taken place; it constitutes a 'time-out' from communicating. It involves 'negotiation of form'.
2. Feedback	
a. Implicit	The teacher or another student responds to a student's error without directly indicating an error has been made, eg. by means of a recast.
b. Explicit	The teacher or another student responds to a student's error by directly indicating that an error has been made, eg. by formally correcting the error or by using metalanguage to draw attention to it.
Pre-emptive focus-on-form	The teacher or a student makes responds to an error that a student makes in the context of a communicative activity.
1. Student initiated	A student asks a question about a linguistic form.
2. Teacher initiated	The teacher gives advice about a linguistic form he thinks might be problematic or asks the students a question about the form.

03

핵심 개념정리

Focus on formS vs. Focus on form

Most researchers currently investigating the role of attention to form attribute the reawakening of interest in this issue to Michael Long. Long distinguished between a focus on forms, which characterized earlier, synthetic approaches to language teaching that have as their primary organizing principle for course design the accumulation of individual language elements form what he call focus on form. The crucial distinction is that focus on form entails a pre-requisite engagement in meaning before attention to linguistic features can be expected to be effective as follows:

Focus on FormS (accuracy)	Focus on Meaning (fluency)	Focus on Form (accuracy & fluency)
Grammar Translation Method & Audiolingual Method	Natural approach	Communicative Language Teaching

In short, focus on form instruction is a type of instruction that, on the one hand, holds up the importance of communicative language teaching principles such as **authentic communication** and **student-centeredness**, and, on the other hand, maintains the value of the occasional and overt study of problematic L2 grammatical formS, which is more reminiscent of **noncommunicative teaching**. Furthermore, Long and Robinson (1998) argue that the responsibility of helping learners attend to and understand problematic L2 grammatical formS falls not only on their teachers, but also on their peers. In other words, Long (1991) and Long and Robinson (1998) claim that formal L2 instruction should give most of its attention to exposing students to oral and written discourse that mirrors real-life, such as doing job interviews, writing letter to friends, and engaging in classroom debates; nonetheless, when it is observed that learners are experiencing difficulties in the comprehension and production of certain L2 grammatical formS, teachers and their peers are obligated to assist them **notice their erroneous use** and/or comprehension of these formS and supply them with the proper explanations and models of them. Moreover, teachers can help their students and learners can help their peers notice the formS that they currently lack, yet should know in order to further their overall L2 grammatical development.

Implicit	<------------------->				Explicit
Input Flood	Input enhancement	Recast	Dictogloss	Consciousness raising tasks	Garden path

Thus, Long and Robinson (1998) assert that teachers and curricula designers are not to focus instruction on the teaching/learning of specific L2 grammatical items. Instead, they should aim to help students learn how to use language in a way that emulates realistic communicative scenarios. For Long and Robinson (1998), focus on form instruction is different from modes of instruction that, in general, are aimed at teaching specific L2 grammatical formS, rather than presenting language as an mechanism for communication. This type of instruction, which Long and Robinson call focus on formS instruction, has been featured in the syllabi of methods such as the **Situational Language** Teaching and the **Audiolingual** Method. In these methods, instruction progresses as learners exhibit mastery of the sequentially-presented grammatical structures, and thus are generally **non-communicative** in the sense that they do not foster L2 development that enables learners to engage in real-life communication. In addition, such methods focus on the prescribed L2 grammatical formS that the teacher can transmit to his/her students; in this way, they are teacher-centered. Focus on form instruction, in contrast, is learner-centered due to its aim of responding to learners' **perceived needs** in a spontaneous manner.

Long and Robinson (1998) also argue that focus on form instruction is different from the purely communicative instruction, or what they call focus on meaning instruction. For them, focus on meaning instruction is paramount to spending little or no time on the discrete parts of language; instead, the interest is on the use of language in real-life situations. Such a mode of instruction is apparent in the **Natural Approach**, which, in theory, prohibits direct grammar teaching. In contrast, Long and Robinson (1998) assert that the occasional focus on the discrete-formS of the L2 via correction, negative feedback, direct explanations, recasts, etc., can help students become aware of, understand, and ultimately acquire difficult formS.

In sum, both focus on formS and focus on meaning instruction are valuable, according to Long and Robinson, and should complement rather than exclude each other. Focus on form instruction, in their view, maintains a balance between the two by calling on teachers and learners to **attend to form** when necessary, yet within a **communicative classroom environment**. However, Long and Robinso do not guarantee that focus on form instruction will lead to a specific level of L2 grammatical development within a certain time frame, presumably because of factors related to quality of instruction, intensity of instruction, and the stages of morphosyntactic development through which L2 learners must pass.

04

문항 해설

수업계획서를 통해 교사의 수업목표와 일치되는 형식(form)을 습득할 수 있는 의사소통 활동(communicative activity)을 찾는 문제이다. 활동3이 실제상황(authentic context)에서 학생들이 자신의 생각을 이용하여 목표형식(target form)을 사용하도록 하므로 형식과 의미(form-meaning)가 함께 이용되는 교육적 목적에 부합된다고 할 수 있다. 학습자들의 의미협상을 하는 상호작용을 통해 의사소통 활동이 될 수 있다. 다른 활동들은 통제된 활동이거나 교사의 설명을 통해 습득되는 형식으로 교사가 목표로 했던 의사소통식 문법수업의 취지와 맞지 않는다.

05-06

핵심 개념정리

귀납법과 연역법(Inductive and Deductive Approach)

(1) Inductive learning is the process of **discovering** general principles from facts. In a language classroom, an inductive approach involves getting learners to discover rules and how they are applied by looking at **examples**. The role of the teacher is to provide the language the learners need to discover the rules, to **guide** them in discovery if necessary, and then to provide more opportunities to practise. The inductive approach is often thought of as a more modern way of teaching: it involves discovery techniques; it seeks in some ways to duplicate the acquisition process; it often exploits authentic material; it has learners at the centre of the lesson; and the focus is on usage rather than rules. The teacher's aim in this lesson is that learners understand **meaning, form and use** of linking devices in formal writing.

   a. The teacher gives the learners a text to read and respond to.
   b. She then asks them to identify all the conjunctions in the text and then put them into 5 or 6 groups according to use, e.g. to add something, to make a contrast, to show a result.
   c. The learners themselves suggest headings for these categories.
   d. The teacher monitors and guides. Groups of learners then work with one category each to analyse structure, meaning and use, and finally present their findings to the class.

① Why use the inductive approach?

- It moves the focus away from the teacher as the giver of knowledge to the **learners** as **discoverers** of it. It moves the focus away from rules to **use**, our aim in teaching. It can be particularly effective with low levels and with certain types of young learners. It enables these students to focus on **use**, not complex rules and terminology.

- It encourages learner **autonomy**. If learners can find out rules for themselves then they are making significant steps towards being independent. We can take this further by letting learners decide what aspect of the language in a text they want to analyse. This kind of task – and the independence it fosters – is stimulating and motivating for many learners.

- If we use **authentic material** as our context, then learners are in contact with real language, not coursebook English. This approach naturally encourages more **communication**, as learners need to discuss language together.

- We are able to respond better to the **needs** of our learners. For example, we can clearly see and address problems with understanding of a certain rule or item of lexis as learners go through the process of identifying and analyzing it.

- We can support and encourage new learning **styles and strategies**. For example, this kind of approach is good to develop reflective learning and learning in groups, and encourages the strategy of using the English around us to find rules and examples.

(2) Deductive learning is the process of applying general principles to use. In a classroom, a deductive approach means teaching learners **rules** and then giving them opportunities to **apply** them through **practice**. The role of the teacher is to present the rules and organize the practice. The deductive approach is often thought of as a more traditional way of teaching: it is teacher-led and **teacher-centred**, at least at the presentation stage; it focuses initially on rules and then use; it often uses input language which is adjusted to the learners and not authentic. These do not in themselves have to be traditional ways of teaching, but they indicate a traditional approach. The teacher's aim is for learners to be able to use the present perfect continuous to describe a present result of a past action.

  a. The teacher shows the learners pictures of people who have been doing some kind of activity, for example somebody covered in paint, somebody who is very red and sweaty, somebody who is looking green and nauseous, and the learners match these pictures to others which show activities, e.g. a rollercoaster, a freshly painted room, a running track.

  b. The teacher then presents the new language by describing what these people have been doing.

  c. The learners listen and then repeat the language. The teacher then explains the structure, how it works, and how it is made.

  d. Learners then practise the language in another matching activity, where they have to report their findings in sentences, e.g. 'On card A, there is a man who has been eating chocolate cake, on card B there is a man who has been running for a bus'. Freer practice is a game where learners act and others guess what they have been doing.

① Why use the deductive approach?

- It can meet student expectations. For many learners the inductive approach is very new and somewhat radical, and it does not fit in with their previous learning experiences.
- It may be **easier**. A class using the deductive approach, if well planned, goes from easier to more difficult — which may be more appropriate for some learners. It can also be easier for less experienced teachers as there is more control of outcomes.
- We can **control** the level of input language more.
- We can control our learners' understanding of rules more — making sure that the ideas they form about language are the right ones. In this way we can try to avoid learners forming incorrect hypotheses.
- It may be a more **efficient** use of time; the inductive approach can take longer.
- It can be designed to meet the needs of more learning styles. The demands of the inductive approach make it more suitable for a specific kind of learner.
- It is used by many coursebooks and it fits in better with many syllabus structures.

07

문항 해설

이해할 수 있는 입력(comprehensible input)과 상호작용 (interaction)을 통해 의사소통 능력(communicative competence: fluency)을 강조하는 것이 의미중심 교수법이다. 하지만, 유창성만을 강조하다보면 정확성에 문제가 생겨서 보완하고자 형식중심교수법(form-focused approach)이 등장했다. 이것은 유창성을 우선 순위로 두면서 의사소통능력(communicative competence)에 필요한 형식을 동시에 학습할 수 있는 방법이다. 형식을 제시하는 활동으로는 명시적(explicit)으로 제시하는 것에서부터 우연한(incidental) 학습이 되도록 하는 묵시적(implicit) 방법까지 다양하다.

08

문항 해설

본 수업은 문법을 위한 연역법 수업을 의미중심으로 진행하고 있다. 단계1은 'past'와 'past participle'의 문법용어(metalinguistic terms)를 사용하여 학생들이 문법규칙을 이해하는 데 도움을 준다. 단계2에서는 글이 주어지고 그 안에서 배울 목표구조를 찾고 형식에 대해 주의기울임(noticing)을 할 수 있는 단계이다. 단계3에서 목표구조를 이용하여 자기의 문장을 만들어보면서 워크시트를 완성하는 활동을 한다. 단계4는 단계3에서 만들어낸 목표구문을 이용하여 이야기를 만들어내고 자신의 짝과 나누어 봄으로서 목표구조를 자동화(automatic: procedural)하여 적용하는 단계로 의미에 초점을 맞춘다.

09

핵심 ELT 읽기

입력 강화(Input Enhancement) 활동

Today, it is generally accepted that target grammatical form of L2 (second language) must be **noticed** to make **acquisition** happens and that SLA instruction must be integrated into language teaching by which the grammatical forms are presented to learners in meaningful context. IE (**Input Enhancement**), coined by Sharwood Smith (1991), is a deliberate manipulation to make specific grammatical features of L2 more salient. First of foremost, this technique underscores the fundamental role of input in language teaching. Likewise, the purpose of IE is to draw learners' attention to target linguistic form in L2 input.

According to Sharwood Smith (1991), learners could be led to noticing target form in two ways: **Input Flood (IF)** and **Textual Enhancement (TE).** Through IF, Sharwood Smith (1991) demonstrated the basic idea that the more frequent the exemplars of the target form appear in the input, the more likely the learners will notice the form. In other words, IF manipulates input by saturating L2 linguistic data with target form to draw learners' attention.

On the other hand, TE is a technique of manipulating the typographical features of a written text to increase the perceptual salience of target grammatical form. The typographical cues such as changing the font style, enlarging the character size, underlining, bolding, capitalizing, and highlighting with colours could be used. However, the question underpins the concept of IE is: Is it sufficient by exposing L2 manipulated input to learners? This question leads to further investigation as learners might not necessary parse the linguistic structure or make form-meaning connection. Therefore, a more specific question, 'How effective is IE?' emerges.

Wong (2005) defines of input as "samples of language that learners are exposed to in a communicative context or setting". At the same time, VanPatten (2003) describes input as "the language that a learner hears (or reads) that has some kind of communicative intent" (VanPatten, 2003: 25). It is clearly to note that both definitions emphasise the terms of "communicative". As claimed by VanPatten (2003), learners play communicative role to extract the meaning encoded in the meaning-bearing utterance or sentence. Through these interpretations, we could come to a understanding that L2 learning process engages learners as active participants in a communicative language classroom when they are exposed to L2 input.

Despite of communicative value of input, it is generally agreed that input is prerequisite for L2 acquisition. However, there is a need to explore whether manipulation is essential to mediate **input into intake**. Perceivably, the distinction between input and intake has been drawn in SLA literature. For example, Sharwood Smith (1993) defines input as "the potentially processable language data which are made available by chance or by design, to the language learner" whereas intake as "that part of input that has actually been processed …and turned to knowledge of some kind" (pp.167). This interpretation leads to ongoing debate about the role of consciousness and unconsciousness mechanism in learning process. Despite extensive research, it still remains controversial as to what type of cognitive mechanism is necessary for acquisition to occur (Svalberg, 2007: 289).

Firstly, Krashen (1982) draws a distinction between "learning" and "acquisition". Learning is the result of conscious process whereas acquisition is the product of subconscious process. According to Input Hypothesis, acquisition takes place when learners are exposed to comprehensible input which is a step more advanced than their current proficiency level. This perception not only implies that input is prerequisite for acquisition process, subconscious process also plays superior role compared to conscious process. In such a case, grammar instruction plays no role in L2 acquisition (Krashen, 1982).

Comprehensible Input Hypothesis has thus provokes considerable debate in SLA domain. Among the researchers, Schmidt (1990), contrary to Krashen's hypothesis, postulates that conscious awareness is crucial and necessary for L2 acquisition. According to Schmidt, only input **noticed** by learners will be mediated into **intake**. In contrast, disagree with Schmidt's (1990) strong Noticing Hypothesis, Tomlin & Villa (1994) posit that unconscious detection is the key process whereas conscious awareness only play facilitative role in L2 learning.

Schmidt (1990) outlines six factors influencing noticing when learners process the input, including perceptual saliency of input, frequency of input, instruction, task demands, readiness of learner and processing capacity of learner. During the ongoing debates between the two positions, Sharwood Smith (1993) proposes IE techniques which are linked to Schmidt's Noticing Hypothesis. IE techniques emphasise on the qualities of input, namely TE (related to input saliency) and IF (related to input frequency). Hereby, we could claim that the rationale for Sharwood Smith's (1993) IE is driven by Schmidt's (1990, 1995) Noticing Hypothesis. That is, Noticing Hypothesis is the theoretical basis for IE. From this point, the debate has indubitably shifted away from general question of "Is noticing necessary?" to more specific questions of "How noticing influence the learning outcome?" and "How intervention facilitate constrained grammar acquisition process?"

10-11

> 핵심 ELT 읽기

Processing Instruction: Theory, Research, and Commentary

In Part I, Foundations, VanPatten presents several publications authored by him and others that describe and discuss input processing and processing instruction (PI). Tracing the roots of the processing principles paradigm to work in child L1 acquisition, he also briefly touches on what he considers to be the greatest challenge to PI: how to apply L1 models of parsing to the L2 context. Whereas the L1 models are concerned with ambiguity resolution, he points out that it is not at all clear how the parsing mechanism can explicate acquisition processes for L2 context.

(1) In Input Processing in Second Language Acquisition, VanPatten sets out to define input processing as the conditions under which learners may attempt to make **connections** between **form** in the input and **meaning**. He also postulates that learners, because of working memory constraints and because they are paying attention to prosodic cues (that signal content or more meaningful words), are only able to process input for meaning before they can process it for form. This he calls the Primacy of Meaning Principle. This principle comprises five sub-principles: Learners process content before anything else (The Primacy of Content Words Principle),

- rely on lexical words to encode meaning as opposed to grammatical forms that indicate the same semantic information (The Lexical Preference Principle),
- are more likely to process non-redundant meaningful grammatical forms before processing redundant meaningful grammatical forms (The Preference for Nonredundancy Principle),
- are more likely to process meaningful grammatical forms before non-meaningful forms, irrespective of redundancy (The Meaning-before-Nonmeaning Principle),
- must not face a drain of attentional resources while processing sentential meaning before processing either redundant meaningful or nonmeaningful forms (The Availability of Resources Principle),
- and tend to process items in sentence initial position before those in medial and final

positions (The Sentence Location Principle).

Related to the principles above are learners' tendency to process the first noun or pronoun in a sentence as the subject/ agent (The First Noun Principle). This in turn comprises three sub-principles:

- learners' tendency to rely on lexical semantics rather than word order to process sentences (The Lexical Semantics Principle).
- relying on event probabilities rather than on word order (The Event Probabilities Principle)
- relying less on the first noun principle if preceding context constrains the possible interpretation of a clause or sentence (The Contextual Constraint Principle). However, VanPatten points out that none of these principles operates in isolation; sometimes several may act together or one may take precedence over another, and sometimes several "may collude" to delay acquisition.

(2) The Nature of Processing Instruction by Wynne Wong, sets out the three characteristics of Processing Instruction (PI), which she defines as "a type of focus on form instruction,":
- explicit information about the target structure
- explicit information about processing strategies
- structured input activities

Wong then goes on to describe how to develop Structured Input (SI) activities. She points out that without first identifying a processing problem (which will enable learners to drop their less than optimal strategies for efficient ones), it will not be possible to create SI activities that will help the learner reach the goal. The other guidelines for developing SI activities follow:

a. Present one thing at a time (which will not drain learners' resources)
b. Keep meaning in focus (which means that acquisition of grammatical items will only happen if learners are required to process propositional content)
c. Move from sentences to connected discourse
d. Use both oral and written input (so that more "visual" learners would benefit from seeing written input)
e. Have learners do something with the input (a reason for attending to the input)
f. Keep the learner's processing strategies in mind (For example, "if learners are relying on lexical items to interpret tense, then we may want to structure the activities so that learners are pushed to rely on grammatical morphemes instead of lexical adverbs to get tense").

She also describes the two types of SI activities used in PI: referential —those activities that require learners to pay attention to form in order to get meaning and which have a right or wrong answer —and affective activities— those activities that require learners to express an opinion or belief, but do not have right or wrong answers.

12

> **문항 해설**
>
> 본 지문의 활동은 문법지도에서 Garden Path 방법을 채택하고 있다. 즉, 학생들에게 기본적인 규칙을 가르쳐준 다음 학생들이 시도하게 한 후 예외가 되는 예문을 던져주고 그것이 틀렸을 때 그 예문에 대한 새로운 문법 규칙을 제시해준다. 즉, 교사가 학생에게 한 번에 모든 것을 가르쳐 주기보다는 부분적인 규칙을 가르쳐 준 후에 틀리기를 유도하고 틀렸을 때 새로운 규칙을 제시해 주는 방법이다.

> **핵심 ELT 읽기**

영어학습자를 위한 문법 지도

Many adult English language learners place a high value on learning grammar (Ikpia, 2003). Perceiving a link between grammatical accuracy and effective communication, they associate excellent grammar with opportunities for employment and promotion, the attainment of educational goals, and social acceptance by native speakers. Reflecting the disagreement that was once common in the second language acquisition research, teachers of adult English language learners vary in their views on how, to what extent, and even whether to teach grammar. Indeed, in popular communicative and task-based approaches to teaching, the second language is viewed primarily as "a tool for communicating rather than as an object to be analyzed". Nonetheless, most research now supports some attention to grammar within a meaningful, interactive instructional context.

(1) Focus on Form Instruction

Ellis (2001) defines focus on form as "any **planned or incidental instructional activity** that is intended to induce language learners to pay attention to linguistic form". This attention to form should take place within a **meaningful, communicative context**, making it an extension of communicative language teaching, not a departure from it. Instructors encourage learners to focus on form in several ways. Focus on form may be planned and focused on pre-selected structures, or it may be incidental, arising spontaneously at any point in a communicative activity. Teachers might design a task to encourage learners to notice forms in the input (e.g., prepositions of location such as *in, on, under*), or they might explicitly teach these forms and provide opportunities for **meaningful practice**. Focus on form may be **reactive**, including explicit corrections to student language; recasts; clarification requests; and other types of feedback. Focus on form is most frequently **teacher-initiated**, but it is also initiated by learners through questions and requests for explanation (Poole, 2005b).

Although second language acquisition research has not definitively answered many important questions regarding form-focused instruction, studies have provided promising evidence that focus on form is correlated with more acquisition of new grammar and vocabulary than non-form-focused approaches. Ellis (2001) found that learners who engaged in communicative, focus-on-form activities improved their grammatical accuracy and their use of new forms. Loewen (2002) found that short episodes of **corrective feedback** correlated with higher rates of correctness on subsequent tests. Some empirical studies have found that various focus-on-form techniques have led to more accurate use of target structures. A synthesis of the findings from a large review of research on the needs of English language learners suggested that they learn best with instruction that combines interactive approaches with explicit instruction.

Instructors should consider learners' **developmental readiness** when deciding whether a focus-on-form approach is appropriate in a given context. Since learners with low literacy often struggle to comprehend form in their first language, it is not advisable to teach them grammar in the second language until they have advanced into higher stages of literacy. It has also been suggested that focus on form should not be initiated with beginning learners (Ellis, 2006; Spada & Lightbown, 1999). Instead, learners should be encouraged to attend to form only after they have acquired basic structures and vocabulary and have developed a basic ability to communicate. Yet, Spada and Lightbown found that even in cases where learners are not developmentally ready to learn a form, intensive focus-on-form instruction can help them learn other structures that are associated with the target form. For example, learners who may not be ready to fully acquire the comparative structures in English could still begin to use and pronounce the comparative suffix *-er* and the comparative word *more* plus adjective. Conversely, advanced learners with academic goals may benefit from a more explicit approach, especially when learning complex structures and concepts (Andrews, 2007).

An instructor must also consider learners' **needs and interests** in identifying the best way to draw their **attention** to a form and practice using it in a meaningful context. For example, in an ESL class at an intermediate level of proficiency, an oral work report given at the end of a shift (e.g., "I mowed the lawn, then I weeded the flower beds") could be used to focus students' attention on the formation of the past tense. Finally, a focus-on-form approach may be more difficult to use in programs in which teachers are obligated to strictly follow mandated curricula or in which class sizes are too large to allow much individual feedback.

(2) Instructional Activities

Several strategies for integrating form and meaning in instruction have been presented in the literature. The implicit-explicit continuum persists within the body of techniques used to draw learners' attention to form. One of the more implicit techniques, the *input flood*, presents students with a text that contains many instances of the target form, with the expectation that students will notice it. In *input enhancement* technique, forms are highlighted with different colored inks, bold lettering, underlining, or other cues intended to raise students' awareness of a structure. Fotos (2002) describes an implicit *structure-based task* in which students compared two cities. Pairs of students told each other about features of familiar cities and recorded the information on task sheets. They were then instructed to write sentences comparing the cities according to the features they had described (e.g., "New York is bigger than Washington, DC"). Students were not explicitly taught comparative structures at any point during the task, but they had to use comparative forms to complete it. Afterwards, their instructor taught a lesson on comparatives, and students rewrote incorrect sentences, did more production exercises, and read stories that contained frequent instances of the comparative form.

Explicit techniques include *consciousness-raising tasks*, during which learners are encouraged to determine grammar rules from evidence presented, and the *focused communicative task*, which is designed to bring about the production of a target form in the context of performing a communicative task. The latter task is designed in such a way that the target feature is essential to the performance of the task. For example, a task might require one student to give another student detailed instructions for the creation of an origami bird. The first student will likely feel a need to use adverbs such as *first, now, then, and next* to talk the second student through the sequential steps of the task. *Error correction strategies* are another way to explicitly focus on form within a primarily meaning-focused activity, in that they help learners notice differences between their production and the target. Among these strategies, the *garden path technique* introduces a grammatical rule and then leads learners into situations in which they may **overgeneralize**, so they can consider the correct form. Nation & Newton (2008, p. 140) give the example of a typical garden path technique:

> T: Here is a sentence using these words: *think and problem. I thought about the problem.* Now you make one using these words: *talk and problem.*
> L: We talked about the problem.
> T: Good. *Argue and result.*
> L: We argued about the result.
> T: Good. *Discuss and advantages.*
> L: We discussed about the advantages.
> T: No. With *discuss* we do not use *about*.

In the example above, the student is corrected and thereby is made aware of the exception to the grammatical rule. Celce-Murcia (2007) suggests that, instead of creating grammar correction exercises using decontextualized sentences from learners' writing, teachers should create short texts that include common error types made by students in their writing. Students can work together to edit the more authentic texts, which helps them learn to correct their own work more successfully.

13

문항 해설

Step 1: 듣기과업을 통해 미래 시제와 비교하면서 과거 시제를 인식한다. 민수가 했던 일과 하지 않은 일을 구분해 들으면서 의미와 형식에 동시에 집중할 수 있다

Step 2: 교사는 학생들의 고유의 답이 나올 수 있는 referential questions을 이용하여 묻고 답하게 함으로써 과거시제의 사용에 대해 익힐 수 있는 시간을 제공한다.

14

문항 해설

본 지문의 활동은 목표형식인 '– be going to'를 가르치기 위한 수업으로 학생들이 문법적 요소들을 문맥 안에서 자동화하여 사용할 수 있도록 도와준다. 즉 의식올리기(consciousness raising) 활동을 이용하여 문법 활동을 묘사하고 있다. –ed와 –ing로 끝나는 형용사들이 사용되는 예시를 보여주고, 학생들이 그 규칙을 발견하도록 유도하는 수업이다. 이 문법 수업은 학생들이 문법 요소를 명시적으로 배우는 것이 아니라 문맥 안에서 스스로 그 규칙에 대해 생각해 볼 수 있도록 하는 학습자 중심 수업이다.

핵심 개념정리

의식 올리기(Consciousness-raising) 과업

(1) Consciousness-Raising task

Fotos and Ellis (1991) have introduced the use of a task type called a grammar CR task, which is a communicative task with a grammar problem to be solved interactively as the task content. The grammar CR task aims to raise learners' consciousness of particular grammatical features through the **development of explicit knowledge**. CR tasks demonstrated certain degrees of effectiveness in facilitating acquisition/learning of the target forms. Interaction in CR tasks plays the role of means for solving grammar problems that deal with target forms. Given that CR task gives opportunities to negotiate message and meaning.

(2) Interlanguage

The term interlanguage refers to the language produced by learners, both as a system which can be described at any one point in time as resulting from systematic rules, and as the series of interlocking systems that characterize learner progression. In other words, the interlanguage concept relies on two fundamental notions: the language produced by the learner is a system in its own right, obeying its own rules; and it is a dynamic system, evolving over time. Interlanguage studies thus moved one step Error Analysis, by focusing on the learner system as a whole, rather than only on its non-target-like features.

15

문항 해설

학습자의 문법적 오류에 대한 문제점과 해결할 수 있는 과업/방법(task/ technique)을 인지적 접근법(cognitive approach)와 사회문화적 접근법(sociocultural approach)으로 서술하는 논술 문제이다. 문제점으로 첫째, 인지적으로 학습자의 선언적(declarative) 지식이 절차적(procedural) 지식으로 전환되지 못하였고, 사회문화적으로 의사소통시 실제 대화에서 활용할 수 없었다. 해결책으로는 첫째, 인지적으로 의식올리기 과업을 통하여 문법규칙을 발견하고 적용할 수 있도록 한다. 사회문화적으로 jigsaw활동을 통해 학습자들이 상호작용하는 의사소통식 과업을 통하여 목표 형식을 사용할 수 있도록 한다.

핵심 개념정리

Cognitive approach vs Sociocultural approach

(1) Problem with the Teaching Method

① Cognitive Approach: The primary problem with the teaching method from a cognitive perspective is the lack of meaningful practice and contextualized use of the third-person singular subject-verb agreement. While Jitae was explicitly taught the rule and practiced it through transformation exercises, these activities were likely decontextualized and focused on form rather than meaning. The absence of communicative practice means that the knowledge remains inert, not easily retrievable or applicable in real-time conversation.

② Sociocultural Approach: From a sociocultural perspective, the problem lies in the lack of opportunities for social interaction and authentic use of the grammatical form. Language learning is seen as a socially mediated process, where interaction with more proficient speakers helps learners internalize linguistic forms. Jitae has not been given the chance to use the third-person singular forms in meaningful communication, limiting his ability to integrate this grammatical knowledge into his conversational language.

(2) Techniques/Tasks to Address the Problem

① Cognitive Approach: Output Task

- Task Description: Implement an output task where students must use the third-person singular forms in a simulated real-life scenario. For example, students can act out a scene where they talk about their daily routines or describe what their family members do on weekends.
- Rationale: This task encourages retrieval and application of grammatical knowledge in a meaningful context, enhancing proceduralization. By repeatedly using the target form in different contexts, students are more likely to internalize the structure and use it correctly in spontaneous conversation.

② Sociocultural Approach: Collaborative Dialogue (Peer Interaction)
- Task Description: Pair Jitae with a more proficient peer for a task that requires frequent use of the third-person singular forms. For example, they could work together to create a story about a third person (e.g., a superhero) and discuss what this character does every day.
- Rationale: This technique leverages the sociocultural principle of learning through social interaction. The more proficient peer can provide scaffolding, modeling the correct use of the form and offering corrective feedback in a supportive context. This interaction helps Jitae notice the correct form and practice it in a meaningful, communicative way, promoting internalization through social mediation.

CHAPTER 09 어휘 지도

01

핵심 개념정리

Guiding Principles for Using Digital Tools

In modern language education, digital tools offer enormous potential for enhancing learning experiences. However, their effectiveness largely depends on how they are used. Here are some guiding principles:

1. Encourage Learner Autonomy

- Use digital tools to promote independent exploration and self-directed learning: It helps learners take ownership of their learning and build critical thinking skills.

- Example: Allow students to use online grammar checkers or language apps to discover language rules on their own, rather than just giving them the answers.

2. Support Diverse Learning Styles

- Integrate tools that cater to various learning preferences, including visual, auditory, kinesthetic, and reading/writing learners: Tailoring to diverse learning styles boosts engagement and comprehension.

- Example: Use videos, podcasts, interactive quizzes, and collaborative writing apps to address different preferences.

3. Teach Digital Ethics and Safety

- Educate learners about responsible and ethical use of digital tools, including copyright, plagiarism, and digital privacy: Fosters digital citizenship and encourages responsible online behavior.

- Example: Teach students how to cite sources properly and how to evaluate the credibility of online resources.

4. Use Digital Tools for Formative Assessment

- Employ tools that assess students' progress and provide immediate feedback. Continuous assessment helps identify strengths and areas for improvement.

- Example: Use learning management systems (LMS) or quiz apps to track student achievement and give individualized feedback.

5. Foster Collaboration and Communication

- Use tools that enhance interaction and cooperation among students: Encourages social learning and peer-to-peer support.

- Example: Platforms like Google Workspace or collaborative whiteboards facilitate group projects and peer feedback.

6. Promote Critical Thinking and Creativity

- Incorporate tools that challenge students to think deeply and express their creativity: Supports higher-order thinking skills and active language use.

- Example: Let students create digital stories, blogs, or presentations that showcase their learning.

02

문항 해설

어휘학습을 위해서 기본적으로 의미(denotation)를 이해하는 것으로 시작된다. 그에 더하여 문법, 연어(collocation), 함축적 의미(connotation), 적절성(appropriateness), 단어형성(word formation)에 대한 지식이 필요하다. 그 중에서 본문은 연어와 문법을 지도하는 활동을 제시하고 있다. 연어수업은 온라인 concordancer 프로그램을 통해서 특정 동사와 함께 쓰이는 예시의 어휘를 선택하도록 하고 문법수업은 가산명사와 불가산명사에 대한 구별을 하는 활동을 실시한다.

03-05

문항 해설

concordance 프로그램을 통해서 어휘가 어떻게 사용되는지에 관한 용례(usage)와 맥락(context)사용을 보여주고 있다. 목표어휘와 함께 사용되는 맥락 및 다양한 문장의 활용을 통해 단어의 의미를 추론할 수 있으며, 다양한 의미적 활용을 제시함으로 일시적으로 의미를 암기하는 것이 아니라, 의미적 관계를 통해 여러 의미를 인지함으로 사용할 수 있도록 내재화할 수 있다.

핵심 개념정리

Concordance

(1) Concordance

Although corpora are now widely used in putting together ELT Dictionaries, and increasingly used in writing ELT materials, it is still rare, I think, for corpora, and especially for concordances to be used much in the ELT classroom. Firstly, I think many teachers are not quite sure what they are. To clarify, a corpus (plural corpora) is a collection of texts (for written corpora) or recordings of speech (for spoken corpora). A vast amount of language is gathered, and when sorted by a computer, this can provide a lot of data about how language is actually used, which words naturally collocate and so on. A concordance gives you all or some of the examples of how a particular word or phrase has been used in that corpora.

① **Pre-teaching vocabulary**

Before reading a text in class, you can select a small number of words to pre-teach and, rather than asking students to use dictionaries, give a concordance of each word to a different group, (or ask them to feed the word into an online concordancer). They should look at the examples and try to work out a definition— which they can then check in a dictionary. If students are likely to be put off my the more obscure examples, you can just pre-select some examples that are relatively straightforward. Groups can then feedback to each other, explaining the words. You may ask why not simply check in a dictionary in the first place— but there is evidence to suggest that students will gain a greater understanding of how to use a word, and be more likely to remember it, if they have seen it in several **contexts**.

② **Raising awareness of collocations**

A very simple activity is to produce a concordance with a word (such as waste), which has strong collocates, and then remove the keyword, asking students to guess what the missing word is. For example, can you do this one?

- Many of them were _____ workers, you know support staff, people who cleaned, cooked.
- Employment? – All _____ jobs, answered Claire. 'dishwasher, building janitor …'
- .. he does _____ tasks vaguely tied to insurance.
- If they do find a job, it's _____ labour.

③ **Clarifying easily confused words/ eliciting grammar rules**

Sometimes words have quite similar meanings, but are used slightly differently. For example, 'say' and 'tell'. Looking at two concordances, one for each word, can really help to clarify how these words are used differently. You can then ask students to try to explain the differences they have noticed. This can also work well for some grammar rules, such as the use of some and any, or too and enough.

④ **Error correction**

Once students are confident about using online concordancers, you can underline any **errors** in their written work; the kind where we just have to say 'We just don't say it like that in English.', and ask them to look up the keyword and see how it would be phrased in English, using the examples.

(2) Statistical nature of English vocabulary

Researchers into the **frequency** distribution of vocabulary have been aware that some words occur more frequently than others. The observations have direct implications for course design for the teaching and learning of vocabulary. There is a group of between

1,500 and 2,000 high **frequency words** that are the most important vocabulary learning goal. These words are so frequently and widely used that they need to be well learned as quickly as possible. Because of their usefulness, they deserve all kinds of attention from teachers and learners. The low frequency words, of which there are thousands, do not deserve teaching time, but gradually need to be learned. The most effective way of dealing with them is for the learners to work on strategies for learning and coping with them. These strategies can be the focus of the teacher's efforts.

(3) Uses of concordancing for language teachers

How can concordances help teachers of languages? We can summarise the uses of concordancers as follows:

- The teacher can use a concordancer to find examples of authentic usage to demonstrate features of vocabulary, typical collocations, a point of grammar or even the structure of a text.

- The teacher can generate exercises based on examples drawn from a variety of corpora, for example **gap-filling** exercises and tests.

- Students can work out rules of grammar or usage and lexical features for themselves by searching for key words in context. Depending on their level, they can be invited to question some of the rules, based on their observation of patterns in **authentic language**.

- Students can be more active in their vocabulary learning: depending on their level, they can be invited to discover new meanings, to observe **habitual collocations**, to relate words to syntax, or to be critical of dictionary entries.

- Students can be invited to reflect on language use in general, based on their own explorations of a corpus of data, thus turning themselves into budding researchers.

- If anyone tries to tell you that this sounds like the sort of work that goes on only at university level, don't believe them! Secondary school children are quite capable of making use of concordancers, providing you and they are well prepared for the task.

06

> 핵심 ELT 읽기

어휘지식에 대한 깊이와 범위

Vocabulary knowledge plays a very important role in reading tests and reading research has consistently found a word knowledge factor on which vocabulary tests load highly. Tests of vocabulary are highly predictive of performance on tests of **reading comprehension**. A lot of researches show that **depth of vocabulary knowledge, breadth of vocabulary knowledge** and reading comprehension are highly, and positively, correlated. Depth of vocabulary knowledge made a significant, and unique, contribution to the prediction of scores on reading comprehension beyond the prediction provided by the breadth of vocabulary knowledge. However, in Chinese situation, the correlation among the breadth and depth of vocabulary knowledge and reading comprehension ranges widely, which needs to be explored further with empirical evidences.

1. Four perspectives on the vocabulary-reading connection

The **relationship between vocabulary knowledge and reading comprehension** is complex and dynamic. Researchers have suggested several models to describe the relationship between vocabulary knowledge and reading comprehension. Anderson and Freebody (1981) offered three hypotheses labeled instrumentalist, aptitude and knowledge. The instrumentalist view sees vocabulary knowledge as being a major prerequisite and causative factor in comprehension. Good vocabulary knowledge enables good comprehension. The aptitude view sees vocabulary knowledge as one of many outcomes of having a good brain. Good reading comprehension is also one of these outcomes. Other outcomes might include skill at non-verbal puzzles and the ability to understand oral explanation. The knowledge view sees vocabulary as an indicator of good world knowledge. This world knowledge supports reading comprehension because the reader must bring as much information to the text as the reader expects to get from it. It is difficult to read about astrophysics if you know nothing about it. Mezynski (1983) suggested a fourth access hypothesis. The access view of the relationship between vocabulary knowledge and reading comprehension, like the instrumentalist view, sees vocabulary as having a causal relationship with comprehension provided that the vocabulary can be easily accessed. Access can be improved through practice. This access can involve several factors including **fluency** of lexical access, **speed** of coping with affixed forms, and speed of word recognition.

2. Research on breath of vocabulary knowledge and reading comprehension

Breath of vocabulary knowledge is defined as the number of words that a person knows. With native speakers, the objective of studies in this area has been to measure the number of words that they know in some absolute sense, whereas with second language learners the aim is often more narrowly defined in terms of their knowledge of items in a specified list of relatively high frequency words, such as the General Service List. Vocabulary size tests that are used for proficiency or placement purposes should include the broadest possible range of word families. An estimation of total vocabulary size can be attained in two ways. The first is based on sampling from a dictionary, and the second is based on corpus-derived lists of word families grouped by frequency. The dictionary sampling method involves selecting a dictionary that contains the number of word families that learners are expected to know, then testing a selection of those words. The problem with this method is that **higher frequency** words tend to have longer entries, and are thus more likely to end up on the test, which may skew the results.

The second method to estimate vocabulary size is to select word families according to their frequency in a **corpus**. Usually, these word families are grouped together into the first 1,000 most frequent words, the second 1,000 most frequent words, and so on. This kind of test has generally been used only with people with low English vocabularies, namely non-native speakers of English (Nation, 1990). There are currently two widely used vocabulary size tests available, the Eurocentres Vocabulary Size Test 10KA (EVST; Meara and Jones, 1990), the Vocabulary Levels Test (VLT; Nation, 1983, 1990). They are well documented in the literature. More specifically, there is research evidence available concerning their validity as assessment procedures for their intended purpose. They also represent innovations in vocabulary assessment and serve to highlight interesting issues in the test design.

3. Research on depth of vocabulary knowledge and reading comprehension

Depth of knowledge focuses on the idea that for useful higher-frequency words learners need to have more than just a superficial understanding of the meaning. According to Qian (1999), the depth dimension should cover such components as pronunciation, spelling, meaning, register, frequency, and morphological, syntactic, and collocational properties. There are two main approaches for measuring depth of vocabulary knowledge: a developmental approach and a dimensional approach (Read, 1997). The developmental approach uses scales to describe the stages of acquisition of a word. One scale that has received some attention is the Vocabulary Knowledge Scale, which has five levels.

Qian (1999, 2002, 2004) used the **depth-of-vocabulary-knowledge** (DVK) measure in his investigation of the relationship between L2 vocabulary knowledge and reading comprehension ability. DVK measure was intended to contribute to inferences about the test-taker's depth of receptive English vocabulary knowledge by measuring three vocabulary elements: synonymy, polysemy, and collocation. DVK measure accounted for a significant amount of the variance in the reading scores beyond what was predicted by a vocabulary breadth test.

However, he suggested caution should be exercised in generalizing the findings from the study because the concept of depth of vocabulary knowledge was only partially operationalized. However, In China LI (2003) showed in his study that the correlation between the depth of vocabulary (the preciseness of the word definition; the ability to choose the meaning of words according to the context; the syntactic characteristic of the vocabulary) and reading comprehension was lower than that of the breath of vocabulary and reading comprehension. He also made a tentative conclusion that polysemy might contribute little to reading comprehension.

07

핵심 개념정리

완곡어법(Euphemism)

Euphemism is mild or pleasant language used instead of language that is unpleasant or offensive, for example *pass away* instead of *die*. Sometimes we want to use language that is not direct. Perhaps we don't want to hurt somebody. Or, we are afraid they will be offended by language they see as "rude". Perhaps the subject matter is culturally taboo. For example, if we are talking to someone whose parent has just died, we could well use pass away instead of die: *I was sorry to hear that your mother passed away last week.* Here are some more examples of euphemistic language:

direct language	euphemistic language
I hear that you're pregnant.	I hear that you're expecting.
It's a UN programme for poor families.	It's a UN programme for underprivileged families.
She's just gone to the toilet.	She's just gone to wash her hands.
You're dismissed.	I'm afraid I'm going to have to let you go.

08

문항 해설

본 수업활동은 세 가지 동사 do, take, make가 함께 쓰이는 명사 구문에 대한 연어를 가르치고 있다. 이러한 어휘 지도를 통해 학생들은 어휘 사용에 대한 인식을 높일 수 있음과 동시에 말하기 활동에까지 참여하게 되어 어휘구(lexical phrase)를 담화 수준(discourse level)에서 사용할 수 있게 된다.

핵심 ELT 읽기

상급자를 위한 연어법(Collocation)

Many advanced students tend to have a number of distinguishing (negative) characteristics. First, they often lack motivation, especially if not working towards an external examination. This is compounded by the fact that they know, or feel they know, English grammar, having recycled the major structures countless times in previous years. In addition, they usually possess a good enough active vocabulary to get by in most everyday speaking situations, and so do not see the necessity for acquiring a lot of new items. Most, according to Lewis, will in fact remain stuck on the '**intermediate plateau**' (2000) and tend to continue producing both spoken and written language containing unnatural-sounding elements which grate on listener or reader, as words that do not usually co-occur together are thrown up unexpectedly. For example 'in the shell of a nut' (instead of in a nutshell) and 'I have overtaken the fear of driving' (instead of 'I have overcome the fear of driving') are recent examples from my students. If the reader (or listener) is confused, then the writer or speaker is likely to be at best frustrated or at worst completely misunderstood.

(1) Types of collocation

Learners need to be aware of the fact that words, in Thornbury's phrase, "hunt in packs." (1998:8) That is to say, all words have their own, unique collocational fields. Collocations can be defined in numerous ways, but for pedagogical purposes it is more **practical** to restrict the term to the following: two or three word clusters which occur with a more than chance regularity throughout spoken and written English. Below are the most easily distinguishable types:

- Verb + noun: throw a party / accept responsibility
- Adjective + noun: square meal / grim determination
- Verb + adjective + noun: take vigorous exercise / make steady progress
- Adverb + verb: strongly suggest / barely see
- Adverb + adjective: utterly amazed / completely useless
- Adverb + adjective + noun: totally unacceptable behaviour
- Adjective + preposition: guilty of / blamed for / happy about
- Noun + noun: *pay packet / window frame *compound nouns

(2) Why is collocation important for advanced learners?

"Students with good ideas often lose marks because they don't know the four or five most important collocations of a key word that is central to what they are writing about." (Hill 1999:5) As a result, they create longer, wordier ways of defining or discussing the issue, increasing the chance of further errors. He cites the example: "His disability will continue until he dies" rather than "He has a permanent disability." (2000:49-50)

There is no magic formula for correcting these mistakes. Collocations have to be acquired both through direct study and large amounts of quality input. The very concept of collocations is often not easy for learners. The essentially simple idea that word choice is seriously limited by what comes before and after "is perhaps the single most elusive aspect of the lexical system and the hardest, therefore, for learners to acquire" (Thornbury 2002:7) Once grasped, however, this new focus can re-awaken their interest and enthusiasm in the language. Teachers can highlight progress by periodically recording oral contributions and comparing written texts with earlier output and authentic material. Learning collocations, apart from increasing the mental lexicon, leads to an increase in written and spoken **fluency** (the brain has more time to focus on its message if many of the nuts and bolts are already in place in the form of collocations of varying length). As Lewis says, "**fluency** is based on the acquisition of a large store of **fixed or semi-fixed**

prefabricated items, which are available as the foundation for any linguistic novelty or creativity." (1997:15) Moreover, stress and intonation also improve if language is met, learnt and acquired in chunks. Quality input should lead to quality output. In seeing real advances in their spoken and written fluency highlighted, and understanding the importance of collocation in aiding these advances, students will, hopefully, be stimulated to increase their own, informed exposure to English. As a result, they will begin to lift clear of the intermediate plateau.

(3) Teacher's role

Hill argues that the problem for advanced learners is not so much with encountering vast numbers of new words (although extensive reading and listening which will contain new lexis is no doubt necessary) as with working with already half-known words and exploring their collocational fields. Ellis claims acquisition can be hastened "as a result of explicit instruction or **consciousness-raising**." (1997:133) The most useful role of the teacher, therefore, is in consciousness-raising, in encouraging noticing on the part of the learners. In other words, the teacher becomes more of a learning manager, giving students strategies to use outside the classroom while at the same time providing exposure to as much appropriate, quality language as possible.

(4) Teaching Implications

"No noticing, no acquisition." (Thornbury 1997) Teachers must raise learners' awareness of collocation as early as possible. Students who meet words initially with their common collocates use them far more **naturally**, pronounce them better and have a greater amount of ready-made language at their disposal to aid fluency, allowing more time to focus on the message. Learning **lexical strings** first seems to enable students to extract the grammar themselves as they begin analysing acquired language. For advanced learners, especially if new to the concept, teachers need to use activities highlighting collocation. They should also stress the importance of learners actively seeking an increasingly large amount of exposure to primarily written but also spoken language outside the classroom, and noticing collocations within that material.

09

문항 해설

어휘학습에서 본 지문의 내용과 같이 연어법(collocation)은 2언어 학습자에게 어려운 내용이 될 수 있다. 그 원리가 복잡하거나 어렵지는 않으나 어떤 논리에 따라 규칙을 배우는 것이 아니라 각각의 예를 암기해야 하기 때문이다. 본 지문의 수업에서 학생이 do a diet라고 잘못된 표현을 하는 경우에 교사는 go on, are on, balanced라는 다른 동사와 연계해서 가르치고 더 나아가 healthy나 unhealthy라는 형용사를 붙여 의미를 강화시킬 수 있음을 각각의 예를 통해 가르쳐야 하는 것이다. 이 수업은 명시적인 어휘 학습으로서 연어법을 배움으로서 어휘구(lexical phrase)의 다양한 유형을 배울 수 있다. 하나의 단어가 아니라 여러 단어를 함께 배우는 연어법 수업의 예이다. 위 활동은 healthy, unhealthy, balanced 등 한 부분에 들어갈 수 있는 전형적으로 쓰이는 다양한 어휘를 가르치는 것이므로 계열관계(paradigmatic relations)에 초점을 둔다고 할 수 있다. 교사는 학생들에게 diet와 같이 쓰이는 표현들인 연어법을 가르치고 학생들은 어휘의 다양한 의미적 사용측면에 대한 지식을 발달시키게 될 것이다.

핵심 개념정리

어휘의 계열관계와 통합관계(paradigmatic and syntagmatic relationship)

Every item of language has a *paradigmatic relationship* with every other item which can be substituted for it (such as *cat* with dog), and a *syntagmatic relationship* with items which occur within the same construction (for example, in *The cat sat on the mat*, *cat* with *the* and *sat on the mat*). The relationships are like axes, as shown in the accompanying diagram.

	Syntagmatic					
Paradigmatic	The	cat	sat	on	the	mat.
	His	dog	slept	under	that	table.
	Our	parrot	perched	in	its	cage.

Paradigmatic contrasts at the level of sounds allow one to identify the phonemes (minimal distinctive sound units) of a language: for example, *bat, fat, mat* contrast with one another on the basis of a single sound, as do *bat, bet, bit,* and *bat, bap, ban*. Stylistically, rhyme is due to the paradigmatic substitution of sounds at the beginning of syllables or words, as in: 'Tyger! Tyger! burning *bright* / In the forests of the *night*.'

On the lexical level, paradigmatic contrasts indicate which words are likely to belong to the same word class (part of speech): *cat, dog, parrot* in the diagram are all nouns, *sat, slept, perched* are all verbs. Syntagmatic relations between words enable one to build up a picture of co-occurrence restrictions within SYNTAX, for example, the verbs *hit, kick* have to be followed by a noun (*Paul hit the wall,* not **Paul hit*), but *sleep, doze* do not normally do so (*Peter slept,* not **Peter slept the bed*). On the semantic level, paradigmatic substitutions allow items from a semantic set to be grouped together, for example *Angela came on Tuesday* (Wednesday, Thursday, etc.), while syntagmatic associations indicate compatible combinations: *rotten apple, the duck quacked,* rather than **curdled apple *the duck squeaked*.

10

> **문항 해설**

본 수업 활동은 학생들이 선정한 주제를 가지고 어휘를 확장시켜나가는 word web 활동의 절차에 대해 설명하고 있다. 첫 단계에서 학생들이 web을 만들어 갈 때의 활동은 자신들이 알고 있는 어휘를 기억해내는 것으로 시작된다. 그룹활동으로 이루어지므로 상호작용으로 어휘를 배운다고 할 수 있다. 학생들의 word web은 명사, 동사, 형용사로 이루어져 여러 종류의 품사(parts of speech)의 어휘를 가지고 작업하는 것을 알 수 있다. web이 학생들이 주제 관련 어휘들의 관계(network)를 시각적으로 볼 수 있도록 도와주고 있다.

> **핵심 개념정리**

어휘 지도

1. What to Teach?

1) Meaning
- 학생에게 의미 전달은 가장 중요하다.
- connotation을 고려해야 한다. (bachelor는 비교적 중립적, 긍정적 의미를 함축하고 있으나, spinster는 부정적인 의미를 함축함)

2) Form, pronunciation and spelling
- 학생들은 단어의 품사를 알아야 한다.
- 영어는 문자와 발음, 철자가 모두 일치하지 않으므로, 어휘 발음 지도가 중요하다.(학생들이 어려운 발음은 drill을 통해 연습시키도록 해야 함)

3) Grammar
- 일반적 문법규칙에서 벗어나는 어휘 지도에 신중해야 한다: 단수와 복수(e.g. man-men), 불가산 명사(e.g. information), 특정한 전치사를 수반하는 동사(e.g. depend on)
- 동사와 형용사를 제시할 때 worry about, frightened of 같이 전치사를 같이 제시하는 것이 좋다.

4) Collocation
- Collocation이란 어떤 어휘와 특정한 어휘가 서로 긴밀하게 연결되는 관계를 의미한다 'in great detail' / 'in big detail'/ 'raise your hand' / 'lift your hand'.
- 영어와 한글의 일대일 대응 방식에서 벗어나 그 단어와 주로 어울리는 단어를 지도하도록 한다.

5) 기타
- 상황에 맞는 어휘: spectacles/ glasses/ specs 어느 상황에 어떤 단어를 사용하여 지도해야 하는지 판단해야 한다.
- 단어관계: 유의어, 반의어 등을 지도한다.
- 접사(접두사, 접미사)를 지도: higher level에 적합하다.

2. Denotative and connotative meaning

The denotative meaning of a word is its literal meaning — the definition you'd find in the dictionary. Take the word 'mother,' for example. The dictionary would define mother as a female parent. OK, but the word 'mother' probably creates emotions and feelings in you: it paints a picture in your mind. You may think of love and security or you may think of your own mother. The emotions and feelings that a word creates are called its connotative meaning.

Let us give you another example, the word 'cat'. The denotative meaning (how the dictionary defines 'cat') is: a carnivorous mammal, domesticated as a rat catcher or pet. But what is its connotative meaning? It depends. If you like cats, the word 'cat' may suggest graceful motion, affectionate playfulness, noble reserve and admirable self sufficiency. If you don't, the word might suggest stealthiness, spitefulness, coldness and haughty disdain.

This brings up an important point about connotation, because there are two different kinds of it — personal connotation and general connotation. Personal connotation is what we've just described with the word 'cat.' It's the emotions or feelings a word creates in you or in any one individual.

General connotation is different — it's what a word means to a large group of people; a mind picture that is shared. Take a man's beard, for example. In Victorian times, the image of a bearded man was that of a proper older gentleman — a grandfather, perhaps. But in the 1960's, a bearded man came to mean unshaven hippie. General connotation doesn't mean that everybody in the world thinks the same way about something, just that large groups of people do. When many words with strong connotations appear in the same news report, that news report is said to be 'slanted' or 'loaded.' This means that the words have been chosen to create either a favorable or unfavorable impression. Professor Vosovic of Stanford University has written two different accounts of the same event:

The same event, yes. But two very different accounts of it. How does each report make you feel? Since there are many words with negative connotations, people often use a form of speech called a euphemism to try and say the same thing in a more positive or pleasant way. Instead of saying 'you're fired,' they say 'we're downsizing.' Instead of talking about a corpse, they use the word 'remains.' Instead of calling somebody 'short', they say 'vertically challenged.' Since many people try not to offend, which of course is good, we end up with some pretty weird euphemisms — many coined in the name of Political Correctness and some made up just to be funny or have fun.

Translations from one language to another are often subject to great debate, since the connotative meaning of a word can be quite different from one language to another. The Bible was originally written in Hebrew. In English, the Sixth Commandment has been translated as 'Thou shalt not kill.' This Commandment has been invoked against everything from killing in self defense to bearing arms in time of war. Scholars believe that the original Hebrew term for 'to kill' actually meant 'murder.' So the proper translation of the Commandment should actually be: 'Thou shalt do no murder.' Misunderstandings occur between people of different cultures every day just because a word or group of words means different things to them. If we are all sensitive to this and try learn about these cultural differences, we may be able to figure out better ways to get along.

11

문항 해설

구조화된 어휘망(structured word net)이라는 단어 활동을 통하여 이미 알고 있는 단어에 의미의 연관성과 사용법을 더해가면서 익혀 나간다. 이 활동은 새로운 단어를 습득하는 명시적인 단어 수업활동이라기 보다는 기존에 가지고 있는 단어와의 연관성을 암시적(implicitly/ covertly)으로 이어 나가는 활동이다.

핵심 개념정리

Word Net

Word Net is a lexical database for the English language. It groups English words into sets of synonyms called synsets, provides short, general definitions, and records the various semantic relations between these synonym sets. The purpose is twofold: to produce a combination of dictionary and thesaurus that is more intuitively usable, and to support automatic text analysis and artificial intelligence applications. Word Net has been used for a number of different purposes in information systems, including word sense disambiguation, information retrieval, automatic text classification, automatic text summarization, and even automatic crossword puzzle generation.

12

문항 해설

본문의 두 활동은 모두 어휘를 가르치기 위한 의도적 학습(intentional learning)이라고 볼 수 있다. 활동 (1)은 단어분석을 통하여 빈도가 낮고 어려운 단어인 regurgitate를 가르치는 방법을 제시하고 있다. 교사는 re- 라는 접두어(prefix)의 언어분석을 통하여 새로운 어휘의 의미를 이해하게 하고 있다. 배운 단어의 사용을 맥락에서 추측해보도록 한다. 활동 (2)는 빈도수가 높은 어휘인 punish를 가르치는 방법으로 그 단어의 어족(word family)의 종류를 용례(usage)로 제시해 주고 의미를 설명해 준다. (2)의 방법은 어족과 연어를 이해하기 위한 활동으로 볼 수 있다. punish는 punished, punishment등으로 가르치고 연어로 쓰일 수 있는 punished for, severely punished, get punished for~에 대한 용례를 보여주고 있다.

핵심 ELT 읽기

2언어 지도를 위한 어휘중심교수법(Lexical Approach)

The lexical approach to second language teaching has received interest in recent years as an alternative to grammar-based approaches. The lexical approach concentrates on developing learners' proficiency with lexis, or words and word combinations. It is based on the idea that an important part of language acquisition is the ability to comprehend and produce lexical phrases as **unanalyzed wholes**, or "**chunks**," and that these chunks become the raw data by which learners perceive patterns of language traditionally thought of as grammar (Lewis, 1993). Instruction focuses on relatively fixed expressions that **occur**

frequently in spoken language, such as, "I'm sorry," "I didn't mean to make you jump," or "That will never happen to me," rather than on originally created sentences (Lewis, 1997a). This digest provides an overview of the methodological foundations underlying the lexical approach and the pedagogical implications suggested by them.

(1) A New Role For Lexis

- Lexis is the basis of language.
- Lexis is misunderstood in language teaching because of the assumption that grammar is the basis of language and that mastery of the grammatical system is a prerequisite for effective communication.
- The key principle of a lexical approach is that "language consists of **grammaticalized lexis**, not lexicalized grammar."
- One of the central organizing principles of any meaning-centered syllabus should be lexis.

(2) Types Of Lexical Units

The lexical approach makes a distinction between vocabulary—traditionally understood as a stock of individual words with fixed meanings—and lexis, which includes not only the single words but also the word combinations that we store in our mental lexicons. Lexical approach advocates argue that language consists of meaningful chunks that, when combined, produce continuous coherent text, and only a minority of spoken sentences are entirely novel creations.

The role of **formulaic, many-word lexical units** have been stressed in both first and second language acquisition research. (See Richards & Rodgers, 2001, for further discussion.) They have been referred to by many different labels, including "**gambits**" (Keller, 1979), "**speech formulae**" (Peters, 1983), "**lexicalized stems**" (Pawley & Syder, 1983), and "**lexical phrases**" (Nattinger & DeCarrico, 1992). The existence and importance of these lexical units has been discussed by a number of linguists. For example, Cowie (1988) argues that the existence of lexical units in a language such as English serves the needs of both native English speakers and English language learners, who are as predisposed to store and reuse them as they are to generate them from scratch. The widespread "fusion of such expressions, which appear to satisfy the individual's communicative needs at a given moment and are later reused, is one means by which the public stock of formulae and composites is continuously enriched" (p. 136). Lewis (1997b) suggests the following taxonomy of lexical items:

- words (e.g., book, pen)
- polywords (e.g., by the way, upside down)
- collocations, or word partnerships (e.g., community service, absolutely convinced)
- institutionalized utterances (e.g., I'll get it; We'll see; That'll do; If I were you …; Would you like a cup of coffee?)
- sentence frames and heads (e.g., That is not as…as you think; The fact/ suggestion/

problem/ danger was ...) and even text frames (e.g., In this paper we explore ...; Firstly ...; Secondly ...; Finally ...)

Within the **lexical approach**, special attention is directed to collocations and expressions that include institutionalized utterances and sentence frames and heads. As Lewis maintains, "instead of words, we consciously try to think of **collocations**, and to present these in expressions. Rather than trying to break things into ever smaller pieces, there is a conscious effort to see things in larger, more holistic, ways" (1997a, p. 204). **Collocation** is "the readily observable phenomenon whereby certain words **co-occur in natural text** with greater than random frequency" (Lewis, 1997a, p. 8). Furthermore, collocation is not determined by logic or frequency, but is **arbitrary**, decided only by linguistic convention. Some **collocations** are fully fixed, such as "to catch a cold," "rancid butter," and "drug addict," while others are more or less fixed and can be completed in a relatively small number of ways, as in the following examples:

- blood / close / distant / near(est) relative
- learn by doing / by heart / by observation / by rote / from experience
- badly / bitterly / deeply / seriously / severely hurt

(3) Lexis In Language Teaching And Learning

In the lexical approach, lexis in its various types is thought to play a central role in language teaching and learning. Nattinger (1980, p. 341) suggests that teaching should be based on the idea that language production is the piecing together of ready-made units appropriate for a particular situation. Comprehension of such units is dependent on knowing the patterns to predict in different situations. Instruction, therefore, should center on these patterns and the ways they can be pieced together, along with the ways they vary and the situations in which they occur. Activities used to develop learners' knowledge of **lexical chains** include the following:

- Intensive and extensive listening and reading in the target language.
- First and second language comparisons and translation–carried out **chunk-for-chunk**, rather than word-for-word–aimed at raising language awareness.
- Repetition and recycling of activities, such as summarizing a text orally one day and again a few days later to keep words and expressions that have been learned active.
- **Guessing** the meaning of vocabulary items **from context**.
- **Noticing** and recording language patterns and collocations.
- Working with dictionaries and other reference tools.
- Working with language corpuses created by the teacher for use in the classroom or accessible on the Internet such as the British National Corpus or COBUILD Bank of English to research word partnerships, preposition usage, style, and so on.

(4) The next step: putting theory into practice

Advances in computer-based studies of language, such as corpus linguistics, have provided huge databases of language corpora. In particular, the COBUILD project at

Birmingham University in England has examined patterns of phrase and clause sequences as they appear in various texts as well as in spoken language. It has aimed at producing an accurate description of the English language in order to form the basis for design of a **lexical syllabus** (Sinclair, 1987). Such a syllabus was perceived by COBUILD researchers as independent and unrelated to any existing language teaching methodology (Sinclair & Renouf, 1988). As a result, the Collins COBUILD English Course (Willis & Willis, 1989) was the most ambitious attempt to develop a syllabus based on lexical rather than grammatical principles.

Willis (1990) has attempted to provide a rationale and design for lexically based language teaching and suggests that a lexical syllabus should be matched with an instructional methodology that puts particular emphasis on language use. Such a syllabus specifies words, their meanings, and the common phrases in which they are used and identifies the most common words and patterns in their most natural environments. Thus, the lexical syllabus not only subsumes a structural syllabus, it also describes how the "structures" that make up the syllabus are used in natural language.

Despite references to the natural environments in which words occur, Sinclair's (1987) and Willis's (1990) lexical syllabi are word based. However, Lewis's (1993) lexical syllabus is specifically not word based, because it "explicitly recognizes word patterns for de-lexical words, collocation power for semantically powerful words, and longer multi-word items, particularly institutionalized sentences, as requiring different, and parallel pedagogical treatment" (Lewis, 1993). In his own teaching design, Lewis proposes a model that comprises the steps, **Observe-Hypothesize-Experiment**, as opposed to the traditional **Present- Practice-Produce** paradigm. Unfortunately, Lewis does not lay out any instructional sequences exemplifying how he thinks this procedure might operate in actual language classrooms.

(5) Lexical field

Dog and cat belong to the same lexical field, or set of words that somehow belong together. In fact, dog and cat belong potentially to several lexical field, together and individually. The relationship among items in a lexical field is conceptual and not referential.

① Hyponymy

- **Hyponymy** denotes a set of hierarchical semantic relationships.
  예 take dog as a superordinate, subordinate to it are all kind of dogs, pekingese, mutt terrier, dalmation, and labrador (these are the hyponyms)

- Lexical gap: The missing stage in the hierarchical tree is a lexical gap. : there's a thing or concept, but there's no lexical item to cover it.

② Meronymy

Another hierarchical semantic relationship is the meronym, which figure in the relation of whole part: 예 tail, whiskers, paw, ears, and snout all present parts of a dog.

③ Synonymy

Synonyms are words that supposedly mean the same thing, but that very explanation exposes the problem with synonymy. Synonym refer to the same thing, but much of their relative meaning isn't referential.
- **Denotative meaning**: a word's denotative meaning is referential.
- Connotative meaning: words connote according to associations that arise from their use. It is determined by speaker experience and intention, auditor reaction, context, and shared cultural understanding.
  예 dog/ dawg, dude, companion/ associate, and friend are all synonyms that denote the same thing but that carry with them quite different connotative.

④ Antonymy

Antonyms are words that mean the opposite of each other. Unlike synonymy and hyponymy, antonymy is a binary relationship — only two words at a time.
- Gradable: while conceptually opposite, they represent values near two end of a spectrum, with many values between them and sometimes even beyond them. 예 fat and thin (in between — pudgy, chunky, plump, healthy, slender, leam.) hot and cold, good and bad, slow and fast.
- Nongradable: called complementary antonyms. These are those that admit no more or less, just absolutes at opposite conceptual poles.
  예 single and married, male and female, and dead and alive are nongradable.

⑤ Homonymy

A word is polysemous when it carries more than one meaning. Hymonyms are words of radically different meaning that share a word form: either the same spelling, or the same pronunciation, or both.
  예 sink — a basin connected to plumbing, and to fall to a lower level. Sink the noun and sink the verb are homonyms, because they share a spelling and a pronunciation but have different meanings.

13

문항 해설

어휘 학습의 초기 단계에서는 명시적인 방법이 필요하지만, 어느 정도 수준이 될 경우에는 직접 교수보다는 다양한 문맥에서 자연스럽게 일어날 수 있게(incidentally) 어휘를 학습하게 되는 암시적(implicit)접근의 중요성을 언급하고 있다. 자연스러운 학습법을 통해 학습자가 예측하게 한다거나, 다양한 문맥에서 보게 되는 단어가 그 단어의 의미를 확장시켜 줄 수 있으며, 부가적인 노출은 기억을 강화시켜 주며, 연어, 언어사용역 제약, 빈도와 같은 것은 많은 노출에 의해서 완전히 습득될 수 있다. 하지만, 명시적 접근법은 비록 의미를 명시적으로 제시하고 연습함으로써 알 수 있지만, 여러 의미와 문법성을 가지고 있는 단어에 대해서 모두 제시하고 연습하게 하는 것에 한계가 있다는 것을 함께 언급하고 있다.

14

문항 해설

(1)는 암시적 어휘학습법(implicit vocabulary learning)에 해당하는 것이고, (2)는 명시적 어휘학습법(explicit vocabulary learning)에 해당한다. 암시적 어휘학습법에서는 직접 어휘의 의미를 제시하는 것보다 많은 노출을 통해서 그 의미를 파악하고, 맥락 안에서 그 단어가 가지는 의미를 유추함으로 어휘 학습하는 방법이다. 그러므로, ⓒ와 ⓔ의 활동, 즉 이야기를 듣거나 읽음으로써 어휘를 학습하거나, 맥락 안에서 그 의미를 파악하는 실마리를 찾는 활동이 암시적 어휘학습법에 해당한다고 할 수 있다. 반면 명시적 어휘학습법은 명시적으로 어휘의 의미를 제시하는 것으로, 사전 활용, 의미망 만들기, word unit를 분석함으로써 어휘 학습을 하는 활동이 이에 해당한다고 할 수 있다. 어휘 지도에서 고려할 사항은 많은 어휘 중에서 어느 것을 지도할 것인지를 결정하는 일이다. 지도할 어휘 선정 기준으로 Nation과 Newton(1997)에서는 사용 빈도와 범위, 다른 단어들과의 결합이 잘 되는지, 다른 단어의 정의를 잘 도와주는지, 다른 단어를 대치할 수 있는지 등을 고려해야 한다고 설명하면서 교사가 직접 지도하는 방법으로 word-building exercises, matching words with various types of definition, studying vocabulary in context, semantic mapping, split information activities focusing on vocabulary를 제시하였으며, 그 이외에도 시각자료 활용, 새로운 단어와 이미 알고 있는 단어의 연결, 동의어 활용, 추상적인 의미와 구체적인 의미를 연결하는 다양한 어휘 기법이 있다. 사용빈도가 낮은 어휘 수는 많기는 하지만, 자주 나타나지 않고 교재의 맥락에서 그 의미를 추측할 수 있으므로 교사가 직접 지도를 할 필요는 없다. 이러한 어휘는 이야기를 듣거나 읽기, 정보 교환 활동, 의사소통활동, 집단 활동 등을 통해 익히도록 간접 지도하는 것이 바람직하다.

15

문항 해설

> 아래 교실에서의 대화는 의사소통에 필요한 절차적 어휘(procedural vocabulary)가 사용되는 한 예시를 보여주고 있다. 'anesthetize'라는 어휘 분석에 사용되는 절차적 어휘 동사는 put, someone, make, them 등이 있다.
>
> 교사 : 그리고 어떤 약들은 또한 마취제로 쓰일 수 있는데, 예를 들면…
> 학생 : 마취제가 뭐예요?
> 교사 : 음… 누군가를 잠재워야 할 때, 수술 전 그 사람이 잠들도록 만드는 것이에요.
> 학생 : 잠들게 한다구요?
> 교사 : 네, 그 사람을 마취시키는 거죠… 약이나 마취제를 줌으로써 그를 잠들게 합니다… 그래야 고통이 없거든요… 그를 졸리게 만드는 것입니다.

이 교실에서 교사와 학생의 대화는 'anesthetize'라는 단어의 명사와 동사 형태 사이의 파생적 연관성뿐만 아니라, 동사와 동사 구조, 즉 유생 주어와 목적 명사구 사이의 보충어 수, 즉 문법적 의존성에 대한 가설을 학생이 전개 및 확증하기 시작하는 과정을 보여주고 있다. 게다가 'anesthetic'이라는 단어의 뜻은 상황적 어휘의 사용을 통해 교사와 협상을 하는 과정에서 익혀진다. 따라서 학생들은 효과적으로 선언적 지식(declarative knowledge)을 배우기 위해서는 절차적 어휘를 사용하는 방법을 배워야 한다. 의사소통능력(communicative competence)은 우리가 단어 의미에 대해 알고 있는 선언적 지식뿐만이 아닌, 우리가 그 지식을 수행(performance)으로 전환시키는 데 사용하는 절차적 지식이 포함한다.

16-17

> **문항 해설**

멀티미디어 프로그램의 외국어 학습 적용에 있어 반복 연습, 시험 채점, 코퍼스를 활용한 어휘 및 문법 지도 활용 및 CMC (computer-mediated communication)를 이용한 대화 기회 제공들의 장점을 활용할 수 있는 반면에 여전히 멀티미디어로 해결되지 않는 영역도 있다. 특히, 에세이 피드백에서 문법적 체크는 어느 정도 가능하지만, 텍스트를 읽고 에세이 주제에 관련성 있는 내용적인 측면, 구조적인 측면에서의 전체적 오류에 대해서는 피드백을 제시할 수 있는 영역에는 부족한 면을 가지고 있다. CMC는 교실 밖에서도 학습자들의 상호작용을 활성화시켜 주는 역할을 한다. CALL (computer assisted language learning)의 활용을 통해서 실제적인 자료, 통합적이면서 상호작용적인 측면, 학습자들의 정의적인 요소, 흥미를 고려해서 접근할 수 있는 장점을 가지고 있다. 언어의 부분적인 측면보다는 통합적이면서 전체적인 요소를 측정하는 데 더욱 유용하다.

> **핵심 ELT 읽기**

Multimedia

Language teachers have been avid users of technology for a very long time. Gramophone records were among the first technological aids to be used by language teachers in order to present students with recordings of native speakers' voices, and broadcasts from foreign radio stations were used to make recordings on reel-to-reel tape recorders. Other examples of technological aids that have been used in the foreign language classroom include slide projectors, film-strip projectors, film projectors, videocassette recorders and DVD players. In the early 1960s, integrated courses (often described as multimedia courses) began to appear.

During the 1970s and 1980s standard microcomputers were incapable of producing sound and they had poor graphics capability. This represented a step backwards for language teachers, who by this time had become accustomed to using a range of different media in the foreign language classroom. The arrival of the multimedia computer in the early 1990s was therefore a major breakthrough as it enabled text, images, sound and video to be combined in one device and the integration of the four basic skills of listening, speaking, reading and writing (Davies 2011: Section 1). Examples of CALL programs for multimedia computers that were published on CD-ROM and DVD from the mid-1990s onwards are described by Davies (2010: Section 3). CALL programs are still being published on CD-ROM and DVD, but Web-based multimedia CALL has now virtually supplanted these media.

Following the arrival of multimedia CALL, multimedia language centres began to appear in educational institutions. While multimedia facilities offer many opportunities for language learning with the integration of text, images, sound and video, these opportunities have often not been fully utilised. One of the main promises of CALL is the ability to **individualise learning** but, as with the language labs that were introduced into educational institutions in the 1960s and 1970s, the use of the facilities of multimedia centres has often devolved into rows of students all doing the same drills (Davies 2010: Section 3.1). There is therefore a danger that multimedia centres may go the same way as the language labs. Following a boom period in the 1970s, language labs went rapidly into decline. Davies (1997: p. 28) lays the blame mainly on the failure to train teachers to use language labs, both in terms of operation and in terms of developing new methodologies, but there were other factors such as poor reliability, lack of materials and a lack of good ideas.

Managing a multimedia language centre requires not only staff who have a knowledge of foreign languages and language teaching methodology but also staff with technical know-how and budget management ability, as well as the ability to combine all these into creative ways of taking advantage of what the technology can offer. A centre manager usually needs assistants for technical support, for managing resources and even the tutoring of students. Multimedia centres lend themselves to self-study and potentially self-directed learning, but this is often misunderstood. The simple existence of a multimedia centre does not automatically lead to students learning independently. Significant investment of time is essential for materials development and creating an atmosphere conducive to self-study. Unfortunately, administrators often have the mistaken belief that buying hardware by itself will meet the needs of the centre, allocating 90% of its budget to hardware and virtually ignoring software and staff training needs (Davies et al. 2011: Foreword). **Self-access language learning** centres or independent learning centres have emerged partially independently and partially in response to these issues. In self-access learning, the focus is on developing learner **autonomy** through varying degrees of **self-directed learning**, as opposed to classroom learning. In many centres learners access materials and manage their learning independently, but they also have access to staff for help. Many self-access centres are heavy users of technology and an increasing number of them are now offering online self-access learning opportunities. Some centres have developed novel ways of supporting language learning **outside the context of the language classroom** ('language support') by developing software to monitor students' self-directed learning and by offering online support from teachers.

Materials	- Mechanical Translation - Providing appropriate feedback to learners - Voice recognition - Grammar checking - Essay Marking
Activities	- Drills - Adaptive Testing - Corpora and Concordancing - Computer Mediated Communication - Multimedia Production

권영주 임용 전공
영어 교육론
임용 기출문제 해설서

초판 1쇄 발행 2023년 04월 05일
개정판 1쇄 발행 2024년 03월 15일
　　　2쇄 발행 2025년 04월 15일

편저 권영주
발행인 공태현　**발행처** (주)법률저널
등록일자 2008년 9월 26일　**등록번호** 제15-605호
주소 151-862 서울 관악구 복은4길 50 (서림동 120-32)
대표전화 02)874-1144　**팩스** 02)876-4312
홈페이지 www.lec.co.kr
ISBN 979-11-7384-019-7 (13740)
정가 35,000원